NON-PRICE DECISIONS
THE FIRM IN A MODERN CONTEXT

A. KOUTSOYIANNIS

Professor of Economics
University of Waterloo, Ontario, Canada

First published 1982 by
THE MACMILLAN PRESS LTD
London and Basingstoke
Companies and representatives
throughout the world

ISBN 0 333 26587 4 (hard cover)
ISBN 0 333 26588 2 (paper cover)

Typeset in 10/12pt Press Roman by
STYLESET LIMITED
Salisbury · Wiltshire

Printed in Hong Kong

To my father

Contents

PART TWO

THE GROWTH DECISION OF THE FIRM

PART FOUR

THE INVESTMENT DECISION UNDER
RISK AND UNCERTAINTY

Preface

This book is the sequel to *Modern Microeconomics*. It is designed for under-graduate microeconomic courses and theory of the firm courses, as *an extension* of the material covered in the traditional micro textbooks.

The last thirty years have seen major changes in the economic environment and the competitive behaviour of firms. (1) Oligopoly has become the main market structure in the industrialised Western countries. (2) Non-price compet-ition (product style, and advertising–selling strategy) has become more important than price competition. (3) Growth has become the main goal of large corpora-tions. Firms adopt complex growth strategies, including investment in the domestic market, conglomerate mergers and takeovers, and foreign direct invest-ment, which gives them the status of a multinational. (4) Fast technological progress, the rising power of labour unions, increasing government regulation and socio-political developments have all increased business risk and uncertainty. (5) Monetary and financial developments as well as tax regulations have induced firms to adopt complex financing strategies to implement their operating and investment-growth plans.

These developments have demonstrated the obsolescence of the traditional microeconomic textbooks, in which most of the exposition is devoted to price competition in largely irrelevant market structures, oligopoly is treated as an appendage, non-price competition is rarely mentioned, and growth strategy is completely ignored.

The developments in microeconomic theory over the last three decades have been impressive. Economic theorists have developed new models and techniques in their attempt to provide an adequate explanation of the new conditions and the changed pattern of competition. However, most of these developments have not found their way into textbooks, or have been compartmentalised in different areas of economics, marketing, business, management science and accounting, with the result that students do not have a chance to become aware of the interrelationships of the production, selling, investment-growth and financing activities of the firm.

The price strategy, the product strategy and the advertising strategy are the main means for implementing the growth strategy of the firm. In turn, the operating and growth activities of the firm require funds. The financing decisions affect the cost of capital to the firm, which is a widely used criterion in investment-growth decisions. Thus the operating decisions (price, product, selling strategy), the investment-growth decisions and the financing decisions of the firm are closely interrelated. Yet no attempt has been made to present the various decisions of the firm in an integrated framework simultaneously.

This intermediate textbook is the first to focus on non-price competition and on the growth-investment strategy of firms as core topics. Furthermore, it is the first textbook which adopts an 'interdisciplinary' approach which stresses the interdependence of the various decisions of the firm.

Decisions of firms are grouped in three categories:

(1)   *Operating decisions*: price—quantity; product style; advertising—selling tactics.
(2)   *Growth decisions*: expansion and diversification by investment in the domestic market; mergers and takeovers; investment in foreign markets.
(3)   *Financing decisions*: long-term financing with use of debt; retained earnings; issue of new stock.

Pricing decisions are analysed exhaustively in *Modern Microeconomics*. The other decisions are analysed in this volume. About half the book is devoted to the analysis of the growth-investment strategy of firms. A quarter is devoted to non-price competition (product style and advertising—selling strategy) and the remainder examines the financing decisions of the firm.

The book is divided into four parts. Part One includes an analysis of the non-price competition strategies of the firm. Part Two and Part Four examine in detail the investment-growth policy of the firm, while Part Three discusses the financing decisions of the firm.

In Part One (Chapters 1 and 2) we examine the two most important aspects of non-price competition. In Chapter 1 we analyse the product strategy of the firm. Several alternative hypotheses of 'optimal' product decision are presented in detail. Some applications of these models are also discussed. Finally, the effects of the product behaviour of firms are critically evaluated. In Chapter 2 we examine the selling strategy of the firm, with particular emphasis on the advertising decision. We begin with some models pertaining to explain the advertising decision of the firm. A large part of this chapter is devoted to the effects of advertising on the firm's profitability, on consumer demand and on resource allocation. A survey of the empirical work in this field shows that there is very little convincing evidence behind the impressive theoretical literature on the subject of advertising.

In Parts Two and Four we examine the investment-growth decision of the firm. These are probably the most important sections of the book, given the growth-seeking attitude of managers, the intense merger activity, the continuing takeover raids and the phenomenal expansion of multinationals over the last three decades.

In Part Two (Chapters 3–7) we discuss the various ways in which a firm can grow. In Chapter 3 we introduce some basic concepts of valuation theory which underlie the discussion of the remaining chapters. We also present (in an appendix) the elementary theory of portfolio selection under certainty. This explains the rationale of the substitution of the goal of owner-shareholder wealth maximisation for the traditional goal of profit maximisation in most of the literature on the investment decision. In Chapter 4 we examine the investment of firms under certainty. (The analysis of the investment decision under uncertainty is postponed until the last two chapters of the book, because it requires the knowledge of topics such as the optimal capital structure, the optimal dividend-retention policy and the cost of capital to the firm.) In Chapter 5 we develop alternative theories of mergers and takeovers. We also survey the extensive empirical work done on the causes and the effects of mergers and takeovers. In Chapter 6 we consider various issues arising from the decision of the firm to integrate vertically its operations. In this respect the most important decision relates to the determination of the transfer price: that is, the price that a producing division of the firm will charge to other (buying) divisions, so that the profit of the firm as a whole is maximised. Another crucial decision of a vertically integrated firm is the decision to close down a particular (producing or buying) division, if its operation does not contribute to the over-all profitability of the firm. This chapter concludes with a brief discussion of the effects of vertical integration on the degree of competition and on resource allocation. In Chapter 7 we examine the firm's decision to grow by investing directly in a foreign country, and what this means for competition. We first present several hypotheses about the motives of foreign direct investment. We next discuss the economic effects of foreign subsidiaries in host countries. A brief survey of the empirical work in this field reveals that more research is needed before a satisfactory theory of 'the decision to go abroad' is developed.

Part Three (Chapters 8–10) of the book includes an analysis of the financing policy of the firm. We concentrate on the issues of the long-term financing of the operations of the firm. These relate to the securing of money capital for the firm's investment projects. As we mentioned earlier, there are three long-term sources of funds: issues of stocks, issues of bonds, and retained profits. The firm has to decide in what proportions to use these sources, so as to minimise its cost of capital or attain other goals. In Chapter 8 we first present several theories relating to the optimal capital structure of the firm as measured by its debt–equity ratio. We then examine how a firm in practice can determine a capital structure suitable for its particular purposes. In Chapter 9 we examine alternative theories of the optimal dividend-retention policy of the firm, as well as how firms take dividend decisions in practice. Both chapters include a survey of the most important empirical studies in this area, so that the student gets some idea of what evidence we have about the competing hypotheses regarding the financing decisions. In Chapter 10 we discuss the cost of capital to the firm and we use it to derive the supply-of-funds schedule of the firm (which is essential in investment decisions). Numerical examples are used to illustrate the estimation of the cost of capital and the derivation of the supply-of-funds schedule in practice.

In Part Four (Chapters 11 and 12) we examine how decisions are taken under risk and uncertainty. Although we focus on the investment decision, the criteria and principles developed can be extended to other decisions of the firm under risk and uncertainty. This is probably the most challenging part of the book: the firm, in formulating (planning) its investment-growth strategy, must take into account uncertainty. The techniques that have been developed for dealing with uncertainty are often presented in mathematical form, which makes them appear more difficult than they really are. In order to keep the analysis at a level which is accessible to the non-mathematically inclined student, we have proceeded gradually. In Chapter 11 we use mainly a diagrammatic approach to present the most important traditional methods of evaluating investment proposals, such as the method of risk-adjusted discount rates, the 'certainty-equivalents' model, and the 'weighted average cost of capital' approach. The chapter concludes with a brief discussion of various criteria which are used commonly in various areas of economics (such as cost–benefit analysis, public finance and welfare economics) for the evaluation of investment projects under uncertainty. In Chapter 12 we present some modern sophisticated techniques which involve the analysis of the investment decision within a portfolio framework. Particular attention is given to the 'mean–variance' model and to the 'capital asset pricing model' (CAPM), which are considered as 'the theoretically most appropriate approaches' to the investment decision. These modern techniques are gaining wide support by theorists, and are increasingly being used in practice by the large corporations, which are aware that growth is the most important way for increasing their competitive power.

The book is written at an *intermediate level*. We have adopted the verbal method of presenting the material, with extensive use of diagrams to illustrate the verbal exposition. Mathematical proofs and derivations are presented in a smaller size of type so as not to interrupt the main theme.

One of the unique features of the book is that each theoretical topic is followed by a survey of the main empirical studies in the field. Thus the student is not simply exposed to alternative theoretical structures, but rather he is also given the opportunity to judge how far each of these structures (hypotheses) is substantiated by empirical evidence. The more technical discussion of these sections, however, can be skipped by the non-interested reader without loss of continuity.

The book is designed for undergraduate *general micro-theory courses*, as a *continuation* of the material covered in the traditional textbooks. The book can also be used as the basic text in undergraduate or postgraduate *specialised courses* dealing with the theory of the firm or the theory of managerial finance. In addition, the book can be particularly useful to students of Business Schools and Management Science Departments, because of its viewing of the firm in a wider context, and because of the empirical evidence included in most chapters which indicates 'empty boxes' and areas for further applied research.

The contents of this book provide the material for professional academics to expand and modernise the structure of courses on microeconomic theory and on the theory of the firm. This will spare students boring repetition of the same material in various years of their studies and equip them with better tools and models for analysing the real industrial world. The orientation of the book is towards understanding the behaviour of growth-seeking managers, and the intense merger activity, the aggressive takeover movement and the phenomenal expansion of multinationals in recent years.

It is hoped that the book will help the dissemination of the impressive developments of microeconomic theory over the last three decades, and enable students to analyse and understand better the changed pattern of competition and the new economic conditions of the modern industrial world.

I would like to express my thanks to Robert Kerton, who was very helpful and contributed many insights and ideas to various parts of the book. I am greatly indebted to Eric Kirzner, whose clear and incisive criticisms and suggestions have improved the presentation of Chapters 8—12 considerably. Lionel Needleman, Wayne Thirsk and Stanley Kardasz also made many helpful suggestions on particular sections of the book.

I am greatly indebted to Ann Wendt for skilful typing of a complex manuscript.

I dedicate this book to my father in grateful appreciation of his kindness, understanding and moral support when I most needed it.

Waterloo, Ontario   A. KOUTSOYIANNIS
October 1980

PART ONE

Product and Advertising Decisions

Introduction

The main means of competition and growth of firms are price, product and selling effort. Traditional economic theory has stressed price as the main policy variable of firms, despite the growing evidence to the contrary. In the late 1930s it became evident that oligopolistic markets were the main form of market structure in the manufacturing sector, and it was observed that in these markets price competition was avoided and that firms were increasingly using non-price weapons in their rivalry. Several studies found that prices had been fairly sticky for long periods of time despite changes in cost and demand conditions,[1] while product diversity and selling activities were intensified. Several reasons have been put forward for this widespread preference of oligopolistic firms for non-price competition.

(1) Price cuts can be matched immediately by rivals and may lead to ruinous price wars, while product imitations take time. Even when all rivals introduce product changes and/or advertise simultaneously, there is always the possibility of one being more successful than the others, while in a price war the elimination of weaker firms is certain. Of course, product wars and advertising wars can be as disastrous as price wars. Some striking examples are the 'speed wars' in the early years of development of railway transport in the USA which resulted in the bankruptcy of many railway companies,[2] and the 'style war' of the automobile industry which resulted in the elimination of the smaller car manufacturers in the USA.[3] Despite such experience, managers still consider price wars more dangerous than product rivalry or aggressive selling strategies.

(2) Technological progress has been spectacular over the last thirty years, and has resulted in greatly improved products, as well as completely new products,

---

[1] R. L. Hall and C. I. Hitch, 'Price Theory and Business Behaviour', *Oxford Economic Papers*, 1939; G. J. Stigler, 'The Kinky Oligopoly Demand Curve and Rigid Prices', *Journal of Political Economy*, 1947; A. Silberston, 'Price Behaviour of Firms', *Economic Journal*, 1970.

[2] See E. Chamberlin, 'The Product as a Variable', *Quarterly Journal of Economics*, 1953.

[3] J. A. Menge, 'Style Change Costs as a Market Weapon', *Quarterly Journal of Economics*, 1962, pp. 632–47.

materials and methods of production. Exploitation of such opportunities has led to an increase in product diversity.

(3) Tastes of consumers have been changing fast as a result of economic growth and increasing incomes. Greater purchasing power results inevitably in demands for improved standards of living, which can be attained only by improved varieties of existing products as well as new products.[4] Firms become aware of the changes in consumers' attitudes and respond to their demands by increasing the variety of available products.

(4) Firms have become increasingly aware of their power to influence the tastes and demands of buyers, by providing information about new product varieties through advertising and other selling activities. Product changes, combined with intensive selling effort, have become a more promising and more effective market weapon.

(5) Price reductions are disliked because they bring pressure for deterioration of the quality standards of the product. If price cuts are adopted repeatedly in the process of price competition, a point will be reached eventually, at which firms will have to lower the quality of their product, a fact that is resented by firms anxious to retain their standards and safeguard their goodwill.

(6) Firms have learned that a lag response to consumers' demands or to competitors' product and selling strategies may have serious effects on their market shares. This experience has led firms to frequent product changes so as not to be left behind the 'product race', as well as to routine 'defensive' advertising and other selling activities.

(7) While price changes are immediately obvious, product changes may not be easily detected by buyers. Even when detected, it is often difficult for buyers to judge whether the change is for the better or for the worse.

(8) In markets where buyers have developed the attitude of judging quality by price, firms avoid price cuts, even when cost considerations make such reductions possible. This is the case of the cigarette industry, where smokers seem to associate lower price with lower quality.[5]

(9) Similarly, in markets where 'customary' retail-price classes have developed, firms feel it necessary to preserve this price structure, adjusting their product to the 'price classes' when cost conditions change.

(10) Firms often use product changes as a way of absorbing increasing costs in order to avoid increases in price. Reduction in size or in the number of units included in traditional packages (cigarettes, matches, chocolate bars, weight of canned food or bottled commodities) has become a widespread practice in recent years. This policy is particularly attractive in conditions of price controls, customary price classes, and inflation.

(11) Firms have found that product changes are in many cases an effective

---

[4] J. M. Clark, *Competition as a Dynamic Process* (Brookings Institution, 1961).

[5] See W. H. Nicholls, *Price Policies in the Cigarette Industry* (Vanderbilt University Press, Tennessee, 1951).

method for raising prices. Price increases are more acceptable to buyers when associated with a product change.

(12) Firms have found that product differences make price discrimination more effective in the various segments of the market which have different elasticities.

Finally, firms have found out that their product strategy and selling activities are essential means for attaining growth.

Despite the increasing recognition of the importance of product changes and selling strategy as market weapons, economic theory has remained basically a theory of price, while non-price competition is brushed aside. Various aspects of product diversity and advertising have been discussed in economic literature, but there has been no successful effort to integrate product strategy, price strategy, selling strategy and other major decisions into a general-equilibrium approach of the firm. More deplorable is the fact that no effort has been made to introduce into economics textbooks the theoretical developments in the field of non-price competition. In this part of the book we attempt to fill this gap.

1. Product as a Market Weapon

I. DEFINITIONS AND HISTORICAL NOTES

A. Relationship of 'Product' to Other Policy Variables

Product variation, like price, advertising and any other policy variable, aims at the attainment of the goals of the firm. In this respect the use of product variations by firms is governed by similar considerations to the application of other competitive weapons. However, the importance attributed to these considerations is different for the various instruments of competition.

It is an observed fact that products change frequently in oligopolistic markets, while prices are less variable, and over long periods remain sticky (except for periods of inflationary cost increases), and advertising is often used in conjunction with product changes to make such changes more effective (see Chapter 2). Thus it seems that product variation and diversification (which is discussed in subsequent chapters) have become the major means of competitive behaviour.

Product changes require in most cases considerable funds, which must be committed for long periods of time. Thus product decisions cannot easily be retracted without substantial losses, while price and advertising decisions can be changed virtually overnight.[1]

All policy decisions involve both short-run and long-run considerations. However, product decisions have probably more serious long-run implications than other policy decisions, not only because of the long-run commitment of funds required, but also because of goodwill considerations. Economic theory seems to have stressed the damage to goodwill resulting from charging prices higher than rivals.[2] However, such damage can be offset by price concessions to customers. But the damage to goodwill from a lower standard product is much more difficult to undo.[3]

---

[1] See F. M. Scherer, *Industrial Market Structure and Economic Performance*, 2nd edn (Rand McNally, 1980), p. 375.

[2] See, for example, P. W. S. Andrews, *Manufacturing Business* (Macmillan, 1949). Also R. Barback, *The Pricing of Manufactures* (Macmillan, 1964).

[3] The damage to the goodwill of the Ford Company from the 'Pinto' model is a good example.

Time considerations enter product decisions in several additional respects. Product changes are the inevitable result of technological progress and of the desire of human beings for change. The firm has to choose a complex optimum product cycle: the product cycle must be long enough to allow the reaping of possible economies of scale. At the same time, firms have to consider the product policies of rivals, the threat from potential entrants, as well as the length of the product cycle which is optimal from the customers' point of view: customers desire change, but too frequent changes may be too costly for them both in money terms and in search activity.

Product strategy is closely related to research and development (R & D) activities. Such activities, when undertaken by firms, aim mostly at product research.

The effects of product changes are much more difficult to analyse than the effects of price changes, since product changes affect both the demand and the cost conditions of the firm. This is probably the reason why so little progress has been made in economic theory in the analysis of product strategies (see below).

'Product' is probably the most important policy variable in the modern oligopolistic world. It is an alternative competitive weapon to price, quantity and selling effort, but there is ample evidence that all four variables are most often simultaneously used by the firm in some mix that is considered optimal at any one time. The interrelationship of these policy variables may be presented in the form of a simultaneous-equation system. Denoting 'product' by V, price by P, quantity by Q, and selling activities by S, we may write (for the ith firm):

$$V_i = f_1(P_i, S_i, Q_i, W_1)$$

$$P_i = f_2(V_i, S_i, Q_i, W_2)$$

$$S_i = f_3(P_i, V_i, Q_i, W_3)$$

$$Q_i = f_4(P_i, V_i, S_i, W_4)$$

where W_1, W_2, W_3, W_4 are vectors (sets) of other determinants of the four major policy variables. For example W_1 would include such variables as the nature of the product (durable, non-durable), technological constraints, economies of scale, past changes of product (extent of change, frequency, success), competitors' product policies (past and anticipated for the future), and so on.

It should be clear that a 'general-equilibrium' approach is required for the simultaneous determination of the 'optimal mix' of the various policy variables.[4] However, we will adopt a partial-equilibrium analysis. This approach has merits not only as a method of analysis of complex behaviour but is also relevant to real-life situations in which firms attempt to reach the 'optimum policy-mix' gradually, by concentrating on one or a few aspects of policy at any one time.

[4] See D. Needham, *Economic Analysis and Industrial Structure* (Holt, Rinehart & Winston, 1969).

Sequential attention to the various problems and policies (goals) is the typical behaviour of firms in the modern industrial world.[5]

B.   'Product' as a Multidimensional Variable

To grasp the importance and analyse the implications of 'product' it is necessary to understand that 'product' has many aspects, and any one of them may be changed as a part of the product strategy of the firm. Product is a multidimensional variable. It includes:

  (i) Special technical characteristics (materials, mechanical construction, durability, taste, comfort, economy in use and maintenance, safety, dependability, ease of use, and so on).

 (ii) Quality standards.

(iii) Design, style, colour, packaging and other similar attributes.

(iv) Services rendered to customer (delivery and installation, servicing and maintenance, guarantees of performance, courtesy, attractiveness of premises, personality of sales staff, methods of doing business).

Given the above list of attributes, which is by no means exhaustive, it is obvious that product homogeneity is practically impossible. Products differ in one or more of these aspects, and such differences have a different appeal to different customers. Brand loyalty is explained partly by differences in some aspects of the product and partly by various types of selling effort of firms, which will be analysed in Chapter 2.

An interesting question is the degree of knowledge which customers have regarding the differences in the various attributes of the products of different firms in an industry, and the implications of this knowledge (for the policy of the firms as well as for government policy). To answer this question we must analyse the buyers in the industry into various groups. Buyers from an industrial firm may be:

  (i) Individual consumers.

 (ii) Other industrial firms which buy the product as an intermediate commodity for further processing.

(iii) Commercial dealers (retailers and wholesalers).

(iv) Service companies (transportation firms, hotels, laundries, recreational enterprises).

 (v) Institutional buyers (hospitals, prisons, universities, schools, international organisations).

(vi) Government authorities (government departments, local authorities).

---

[5] See M. Cyert and J. March, *A Behavioural Theory of the Firm* (Prentice-Hall, 1963).

Consumers usually buy from retailers, who stockpile the products of various firms (including sometimes their own brands). Although retailers (like wholesalers) are businesses seeking profits, it is legitimate to assume that their behaviour as buyers (from industrial firms) reflects the attitudes of their customers (the consumers in the case of retailers, or other firms in the case of wholesalers). It is true that commercial dealers (especially retailers) can to a certain extent influence the choice of their customers, but only in the short run, or under very special conditions.[6]

In general we may say that all types of industrial buyers have incomplete knowledge. However, the degree of knowledge differs considerably for the various groups. Consumers are the most ignorant of all groups, either due to their inertia and unwillingness to sacrifice time and effort for search of the 'best buy', or because the information available to them is incomplete, misleading or too complicated to process, and because they are the group most susceptible to advertising. Private enterprises may be expected to have the greatest possible degree of knowledge: in their efforts for cost minimisation they have acquired buying expertise and can effectively compare the various products offered to them. However, we must not forget that the buying divisions of such private enterprises are organised and run by managers who can only act with 'bounded rationality':[7] they have limited information, limited time, and limited ability for comparing alternative sources of supply. Furthermore, being human beings they can be influenced in different ways by the marketing strategies of selling firms. The same holds *a fortiori* for institutional buyers and government authorities, whose buying departments do not need to minimise purchase costs for their survival.

The degree of knowledge also depends on the concentration of buyers, on the media of communication and several other factors.

Given the limited knowledge of buyers, firms are encouraged frequently to change their products in one or more aspects. This policy renders the consumer's stock of knowledge rapidly obsolete as new products are offered in the market.[8] Consumers cannot acquire sufficient knowledge of continuously changing products. Influenced by other policies of firms (advertising, for example) they try the new varieties, and so the 'product race' is perpetuated.[9]

---

[6] See A. Koutsoyiannis, *Modern Microeconomics*, 2nd edn (Macmillan, 1979) ch. 2. For a different view see P. W. S. Andrews, *On Competition in Economic Theory* (Macmillan, 1964).

[7] H. A. Simon, 'A Behavioural Model of Rational Choice', *Quarterly Journal of Economics*, 1952, pp. 99–118.

[8] See P. Doyle, 'Economic Aspects of Advertising: A Survey', *Economic Journal*, 1968, p. 582.

[9] It should be noted that *product variation* is different from *product differentiation*. Product differentiation is attained not only by changes in the product but also by advertising (and other selling activities), brands and trade-marks, and convenience of location. This chapter deals with product changes only.

C. The Literature on Product Competition

The increasing importance of non-price competition has been stressed by many writers since the 1930s. Product changes and advertising have become the main competitive weapons. Despite this development economists have largely ignored product changes and have concentrated on models of *pure price equilibrium*, in which the product is given and price is adjusted by the firm in its attempt to maximise profit or attain other goals. Economic theory has predominantly been *price theory*. This is explained partly by historical reasons and partly by the complexity of the product, which does not lend itself to precise analytical treatment. Economists of the nineteenth century were unduly preoccupied with the problem of 'value', and thus concentrated on the study of determination of price. Twentieth-century economists seem to have followed the same line, with the result of a proliferation of models of price, in which quality is assumed fixed in order to obtain precise equilibria. In view of the developments over the last quarter of a century it is important that the analysis of pure price competition should be supplemented by an analysis of *pure quality competition*, as well as by an analysis of the other aspects of competition (advertising, innovation) and of the growth of firms. The different aspects of business behaviour should then be put together in a general-equilibrium approach to the study of the firm.

In this chapter we develop various models of *pure quality competition* in which price is held constant and firms adjust the quality of their product in order to attain profit maximisation or other goals.

Most of the existing studies of non-price competition concentrate on the effects of such competition on pricing behaviour and resource allocation. Thus they are in their essence price studies. They do not deal with the process of product adjustment by firms as a means of attaining specified goals. Chamberlin, in chapter 5 of *The Theory of Monopolistic Competition*, attempted to present a model of pure product equilibrium competition, in which price and advertising were kept constant; but his product model did not have the impact of his price model, partly because he and his contemporaries were still mainly preoccupied with price competition, and partly because his model was not fully developed, and hence was not particularly helpful in showing the process of adjustment of product to a given price (and advertising) structure. In his article 'Product as an Economic Variable' (*Quarterly Journal of Economics*, 1953) Chamberlin stressed the importance of product as a policy variable, but his attempt to build a model of product competition has added to the confusion surrounding product and its use as a competitive weapon.

Brems's analysis (in his *Product Equilibrium and Monopolistic Competition*, Columbia University Press, 1951), developed on lines similar to Chamberlin's, did not add anything substantial to earlier studies. A systematic analysis of pure product competition was attempted by Abbott (*Quality and Competition*, Columbia University Press, 1955). His models of vertical and horizontal quality competition are equilibrium models which suffer from most of the limitations of the neoclassical price theory of the firm. However, they are a useful point of departure.

In the 1960s Clark[10] and Heflebower[11] attempted to build 'realistic' theories of 'dynamic competition'. Both writers discuss the importance of product diversity in the modern oligopolistic world, without, however, presenting any precise model of business behaviour regarding product changes. In their work we can find some of the determinants of product change and its effects on the performance of the firm. We will draw on these writers' work in the last section of this chapter where we attempt a systematic presentation of the determinants of product changes.

In the 1960s many writers, associated mostly with business schools, have concentrated on the 'strategic behaviour' of large firms. These writers have produced some interesting work regarding the product decisions of firms. They have adopted a behavioural approach, based on observation of how firms actually behave.

Looking at the development of the literature on product as a policy variable we observe broadly the same pattern as in the development of the literature on pricing. The early models of product competition are profit-maximisation models, based on assumptions which bare little realism. Abbott has developed two managerialist models of product competition in which the goal of the firm is sales maximisation. These models, as we will see in a subsequent section, can to a certain extent explain the behaviour of the large oligopolistic firms. The most recent studies on product competition are behavioural in their nature, concentrating on a description of product decisions in large firms, and stressing the importance of organisational and informational variables on these decisions. In these models precision is sacrificed to realism.

In the subsequent sections we will present several product competition models. We begin with two models which are the diametric opposites of the traditional profit-maximisation price models: the assumptions of perfect knowledge and identical cost and demand conditions are retained, but price is taken as fixed and quality is allowed to vary until firms reach equilibrium. Subsequently we will present two models in which the goal of the firm is sales maximisation, attained with a fixed market price. Finally we will present a 'typical' behavioural model of product strategy, developed by Ansoff.[12]

D.   Types of Quality Variation or Product Competition

We may distinguish[13] three types of quality variation: vertical, horizontal and innovational.

[10] J. M. Clark, *Competition as a Dynamic Process* (Brookings Institution, 1961).

[11] R. B. Heflebower, 'Toward a Theory of Industrial Markets and Prices', *American Economic Review*, 1956.

[12] H. I. Ansoff, 'Toward a Strategic Theory of the Firm', *Economies et sociétés*, 1968, reprinted in H. I. Ansoff (ed.), *Business Strategy* (Penguin, 1969).

[13] See L. Abbott, *Quality and Competition* (Columbia University Press, 1955).

(i) *Vertical quality variation*

This refers to different grades of quality (properly described by 'lower' and 'higher', 'superior' or 'inferior' quality, and so on) which are associated with differences in costs: higher-quality grades cost more to produce. Clearly vertical quality differences consist of real differences in some material or technical attribute of the product: the octane content of petrol, thickness of steel, mileage available from a motor-car tire, hours of light of an electric bulb, natural or synthetic fibres in a material, and so on. The simplest kind of vertical variation is the difference in the size of the unit: canned foodstuffs in small and large cans, tomato sauce in small and large bottles, packets with fewer or more toffees. Abbott[14] implies that vertical quality variation can never be excessive for the consumer.

(ii) *Horizontal quality variation*

This refers to qualitative attributes (such as style, design, colour, texture, flavour) which do not give rise to major differences in costs. Such product differences are due to the fact that buyers differ in their social circumstances, values and tastes. Thus different attributes have different appeal to various groups of buyers: such qualities are neither 'better' nor 'worse' than others but merely better suited to some people's wants (and less suited to those of others), or more appealing to some people and less to others (a 'pure matter of taste'). Examples of horizontal quality variation are: neckties (of the same quality but with different colours), records (of the same quality but with different kinds of music), hairsprays or perfumes of the same quality but with different scent, shoes of the same quality but different height of heels, and so on.

(iii) *Innovational quality variation*

This refers to the introduction of new qualities which are considered superior (by all or the majority of buyers) to the existing ones *in all grades* of a commodity, for example the introduction of non-drip paints. Such innovational changes may or may not be associated with higher costs (and prices). If costs are higher, the prices of all grades will change. The characteristic of such quality changes is that they (eventually) render the existing range of grades obsolete: innovational grades gradually replace the existing grades. However, the differences between the various ('new') grades are in general maintained.

In the real world product changes may be a mixture of all three quality variations; horizontal-innovational changes in particular seem to have become increasingly important in recent years. For example, new styles of motor-cars have in general

[14] Ibid.

some technical feature that is new (although some 'deterioration' may also appear in some other features of the car, in which case all three types of quality changes occur simultaneously). Although such hybrid product changes are the rule rather than the exception, economists have tended to ignore them, on the grounds that they 'raise enormous analytical difficulties'.[15]

Separate models have been developed for vertical and for horizontal product competition. We shall examine some of them in the following section.

II.   MODELS OF PRODUCT COMPETITION IN THE 'NEOCLASSICAL' THEORY OF THE FIRM

A.   A Model of Vertical Quality Competition with Profit Maximisation

(i) *Assumptions of the model*

(1) The goal of the firm is profit maximisation.

(2) The price in the market is given.[16]

(3) Technology is given. The available technology allows the production of various *quality grades* (vertical differentiation) of the product in the market, each associated with different cost. The problem of the firm is to choose the quality grade which, given the market price, will lead to maximisation of its profit.

(4) Within each quality grade there are different varieties of the product (horizontal product differentiation). For example, take the necktie market. There are differences in quality grades: low-priced, medium-priced, high-priced neckties. This is vertical differentiation: the differences in price reflect differences in quality. Within the high-priced grade, neckties differ in style, colour, design and texture of material, and so on. This is horizontal differentiation: differences in attributes are not associated with differences in costs. Clearly firms can choose both horizontal and vertical quality differentiation, and in the real world they do compete with both types of product variation. However, in this model we assume, for analytical purposes, a given horizontal differentiation: each firm's product differs horizontally (in some attribute such as colour, style, design) from every other and attracts its own group of customers. It is also assumed that each firm produces a single variety and that within each quality grade the preferences of buyers are equally distributed. Given that costs within the same quality grade are the same, the above assumptions imply that firms (in the absence of quality differences) have identical market shares. Since the price is assumed fixed, in equili-

---

[15] Ibid.

[16] Price can be given either by custom, by government regulation, by a leader, by collusion, or it may have been established in the market without collusion as a result of the historical evolution of moves and counter-moves of rival firms; or price may have been set by a previous decision of the firm. This model is particularly relevant to the explanation of competition in markets where prices are rigid.

brium all firms in the industry will produce the same quality grade. The purpose of this model is to show how this equilibrium is reached. The assumption about given horizontal differentiation and evenly distributed preferences of buyers within each quality grade (but not between different quality grades) allows us to use a single diagram for showing the equilibrium of the firm *and* the industry. Furthermore, it allows the analysis of vertical quality adjustments (in a market with a fixed price) in isolation from horizontal adjustments. The latter will be analysed in a subsequent section with a separate model.

(5) Demand is assumed to be an increasing function of the height of the quality grade of the product (given the price, $\bar{P}$). Quality is also assumed continuously variable. Thus an improvement in quality shifts the firm's demand curve upwards and to the right.

(6) Consumers are assumed to have perfect knowledge and to act rationally, responding 'correctly' to changes in quality, buying more when quality improves.

(7) Firms have identical cost structures. Costs are assumed to have the traditional U-shape. It is further assumed that cost is an increasing function of the quality grade produced. That is, an improvement in quality shifts the cost curve upwards to the right.

(8) Firms have perfect knowledge of the quality grades of the product and the demand and cost curves associated with each grade.

(9) Firms adjust the quality grade of their product to the given price simultaneously, but without collusion. This behaviour results from the assumption of perfect knowledge and of identical cost and market shares of the firms.

(ii) *Short-run equilibrium*

In Figure 1.1 we depict a set of pairs of cost–demand curves each associated with a certain quality grade. Given that both cost and demand are increasing functions of quality, a pair higher up and to the right indicates a higher-quality grade.

Given the market price $\bar{P}$, the existing firms will choose the quality grade (cost–demand pair) that yields maximum profit. (It is assumed that entry does not take place in the short run.)

The equilibrium of the firm is shown in Figure 1.1. We draw a price line through $\bar{P}$ and we mark the output sold at each quality, defined by the intersection of the successive demand curves with the price line. Thus at price $\bar{P}$ the level of demand will change from X_1 (corresponding to quality grade one) successively to X_8 as the quality of the product improves. Note that the demand shifts with quality improvements, but at a decreasing rate, implying that consumers become 'saturated' as quality improves. (We do not want after all a garment that lasts for twenty or thirty years!)

We next find the unit costs that the firm will incur if it decides to attain increasing sales (levels of output) by improving the quality grade of its product. If the firm adopts quality one, its average cost will be a' (on AC_1), and it will

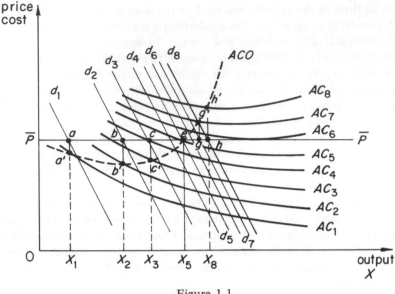

Figure 1.1

realise excess unit profit equal to aa', given $\bar{P}$. Similarly, if the firm improves its quality to grade two, its average cost will be b' (on AC_2) and it will be earning excess profits equal to bb' per unit of output. If the firm produces grade five, it will break even, since at point e the unit cost (on AC_5) is equal to price $\bar{P}$, and the firm will be earning just normal profit. Further improvements in quality will fail to bring in additional demand adequate to cover the higher cost involved (at the given price $\bar{P}$). To the right of e the unit cost is higher than $\bar{P}$ and the firm realises losses. If we join the points $a', b', \ldots, h'$ which represent the unit costs associated with each quality option (at the market price $\bar{P}$), we obtain the firm's *average cost option curve* (*ACO* in Figure 1.1). That is, the average cost option curve is a sort of supply curve: it shows the unit cost of supplying the different quantities demanded of different qualities at the given market price $\bar{P}$.[17]

The average-cost option curve would be a straight line with positive slope if unit costs were constant. With the assumed U-shaped costs, the option curve will also be U-shaped. (1) As quality improves we have a double effect on costs. First, the cost curve shifts upwards, indicating higher unit costs at all levels of output. In Figure 1.2 the average cost curve shifts to AC_2 as quality improves (on d_2), and the unit cost would be a'' if the output remained at X_1. (2) However, with the shift of the demand to the right (associated with the improvement in

[17] Abbott (*Quality and Competition*) says that the option curve is a 'sort of demand curve'. This is misleading, since the demand associated with the alternative quality options is shown on the price line. The option curve denotes costs of supply (for given $\bar{P}$) and hence it is a 'special type of supply curve'. Thus we have changed the notation used by Abbott.

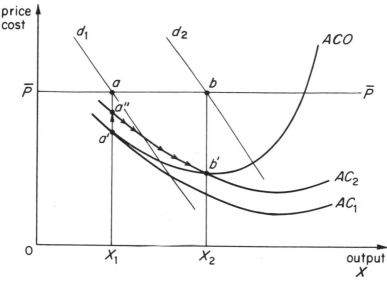

Figure 1.2

quality) production increases to X_2, and we have a sliding movement to the right along the (higher) cost curve AC_2, which will imply a lowering of unit cost (point b' in Figure 1.2). If the slope of the AC curve is steep, the second effect will more than offset the increase in cost caused by the upward shift of the cost curve, so that up to a certain level of quality improvement the unit cost will be declining. Eventually, however, the second effect will not be adequately strong to offset the first, thus leading to a definitely increasing cost of supply, and the ACO curve will turn upwards (Figure 1.3). The falling part of the ACO curve is irrelevant for the equilibrium of the firm, since it would always pay the firm to improve quality and realise increased unit profits. The relevant part for decision-making is the rising segment of the ACO curve.

It should be clear that the *shape* of the ACO curve depends on the shape and shifts of the average cost curves.[18]

The *position* of the option curve depends on the number of firms in the industry. As the number of firms increases (that is, with entry in the industry) the ACO curve shifts upwards to the left, because the share of the firm shrinks (at each quality grade) as entry occurs, while the cost curve associated with each quality grade is not affected by entry (Figure 1.4). Similarly, exit of firms shifts the ACO curve to the right, as the market share (at each quality grade) increases

---

[18] If the AC has a flat stretch (as in the modern theory of costs), then the ACO and the MCO curves will be straight lines with positive slopes, with the MCO curve lying above the ACO curve.

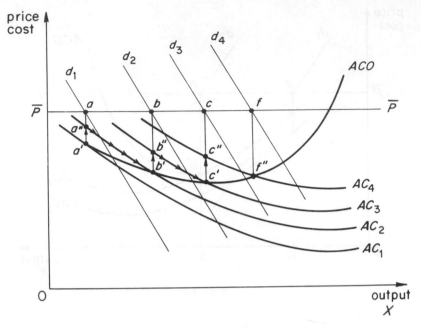

Figure 1.3

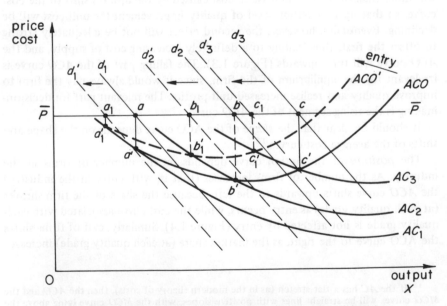

Figure 1.4   Upward shift of the *ACO* curve with entry

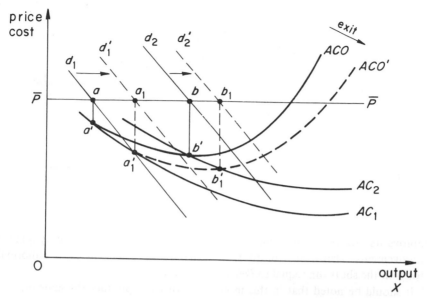

Figure 1.5   Downward shift of the *ACO* curve with exit

(figure 1.5). These shifts of the *ACO* curve are relevant for the long-run equilibrium of the firm, since in the short run the number of firms in the industry is fixed.

We next derive the *marginal cost option curve (MCO)*, which shows the rate at which cost changes in order to supply an *additional unit of output of improved quality*. The *MCO* curve intersects the *ACO* curve at its lowest point.[19] Thus the *MCO* curve lies above the *ACO* curve (over the relevant rising range of the latter), showing that at higher levels of output the firm must incur expenses at an increasing rate in order to improve the quality enough to make possible an additional unit sale.

The behaviour of the profit-maximising firm is marginalistic. That is, the firm reaches equilibrium at the point of intersection of the *MCO* with the price line (point *e* in Figure 1.6). The firm will produce the quality implied by the average cost curve *AC**, and will be selling quantity *X** (on the demand curve *d**) at the market price $\bar{P}$. Note that with price given, $\bar{P} = MR$. Hence the equilibrium condition of the firm is

$$P = MR = MCO \tag{1.1}$$

Profit is at a maximum (shaded area in Figure 1.6) because: to the left of *e* profits have not reached their maximum ($MCO < P$) and the firm will further

---

[19] The relationship between the *ACO* and *MCO* curves is equivalent to the relationship between the *ATC* and *MC* curves of the theory of costs. See Koutsoyiannis, *Modern Microeconomics*.

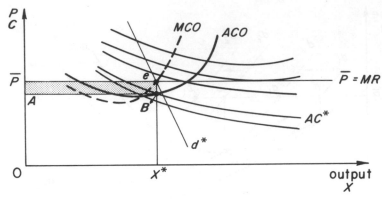

Figure 1.6

improve its quality; to the right of e, $MCO > P$, and profit is reduced by quality improvements. Hence at e profit is at a maximum. The firm earns abnormal profits in the short run (equal to $\bar{P}eBA$ in Figure 1.6).

It should be noted that in this model all firms will produce the same quality grade (implicit in AC^*), given the assumption of identical costs and identical price. However, within this grade there will be as many varieties (horizontal differentiation) as the number of existing firms in the industry.

The horizontal quality variation is due to the appeal of each firm's product to different buyers; each firm has its own clientele because each produces (with the same cost) a variety with attributes (style, colour, etc.) which appeal more to some buyers in the market. Given our assumption of evenly distributed preferences of buyers within each (vertical) grade, all firms will have an identical market share, equal to OX^* (Figure 1.6). The market equilibrium output, if there are n firms in the industry, at price $\bar{P}$, is thus

$$n \times OX^* \tag{1.2}$$

(iii) *Long-run equilibrium*

Abnormal profits will attract entry, and while the cost curves are unaffected, the market share of each firm declines as the number of firms increases.[20] The firm's demand curves shift backwards to the left, giving rise to new ACO and MCO curves. These new curves intersect the given price line to the left of the original equilibrium point, showing that the firm's unit costs increase as its share declines: the firm is producing a smaller quantity of the same quality level, sliding backwards on its initial cost curve (AC^*). If at the new equilibrium abnormal profits are still earned, new firms will enter the industry and the

[20] It is assumed that the market demand (size of the market) is given. Alternatively, one may assume that the market size increases as quality improves, but the increase is such that the share of all firms is reduced.

process of adjustment will repeat itself. Entry will stop, and long-run equilibrium will be reached when the *ACO* curve shifts upwards until it becomes tangent to the price line. The long-run equilibrium is denoted by point e' in Figure 1.7. The condition for long-run equilibrium is defined by the expression

$$P = MCO = ACO \tag{1.3}$$

In the long-run equilibrium the following results emerge.

The total volume of output in the market will be the same as before entry, given that the price did not change. However, this output will be produced by a larger number of firms, and, while the quality level remains unchanged, the variety will increase.

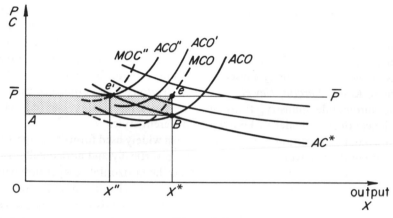

Figure 1.7

Excess profits are eliminated, due to the increased average cost resulting from a reduction in the plant size following the increased number of firms in the industry, which results in a smaller market share ($X'' < X^*$ in Figure 1.7).

The number of varieties within the same quality grade has increased (given that the number of firms is larger, and, by our assumptions, each firm produces a single variety).

In summary. The consumers benefit by the product competition, because a wider choice becomes possible, due to the increase in the number of firms and the consequent increase in horizontal differentiation. Thus, given $\bar{P}$, product competition increases the welfare of consumers who buy the product. However, product competition leads to a decrease in the size of firms, and hence to unexhausted economies of scale.

It should be clear that product competition with fixed price brings about similar results to price competition conducted with a fixed product.[21]

---

[21] These results are the consequence of the 'tangency solution' of the model of *monopolistic competition*. See Koutsoyiannis, *Modern Microeconomics*, ch. 8.

B.   A Model of Horizontal Quality Competition

This model examines how firms reach equilibrium (maximum profit) by adjusting the variety of their product within a given quality grade. This is the case of *pure horizontal product* competition.

To illustrate the meaning of pure horizontal product competition consider the following examples: (a) competing firms produce the same quality of carpets, but each firm's product has a different colour or design; (b) electrical-appliance firms produce the same quality kettles but of different style (dome design, or flat-top design); (c) recording firms produce records or tapes of the same quality but with different types of music (classical, jazz, rock-'n'-roll, disco, etc.); (d) cosmetics firms produce deodorants of the same quality but with different scents; (e) clothing firms produce the same quality of T-shirts or pullovers, but of different colour or style; (f) in the food industry firms produce breakfast cereals of the same quality but of different flavour or ingredients; (g) movie corporations (and TV channels) produce the same type of films (e.g. comedy serials, police serials, family-stories serials) but with different characters (*The Avengers, Kojak, Baretta, Hawaii–5–O, The Waltons, The Jeffersons*, etc.); (h) in the automobile industry, firms produce the same quality car (e.g. eight-cylinder car or six-cylinder car) but with a different style.

Horizontal competition is probably the most widely used form of competition. Of course in the real world firms compete both vertically and horizontally. However, the most intense form of competition is the horizontal competition within each quality grade. Horizontal competition is usually combined with some innovational element, a new feature or modification of existing features, so as to adapt the product to the tastes of the different buyers of a certain quality grade. The analysis abstracts from both vertical and innovational differentiation in order to examine the adjustments that take place in horizontal competition alone.

(i) *Assumptions of the model*

(1) The quality grade is given. Firms have made their choice as to what quality grade to produce with an earlier decision, for example luxury neckties, or records of the same quality standard but with different kinds of music. The price is given for all firms, who are free to offer different varieties within the given quality grade. For example, the price of high-quality records is $4–5, irrespective of the type of music.

(2) Horizontal variation may refer to differences in one or more characteristics of the product (within the given grade) which do not give rise to major differences in costs. For example, luxury neckties may differ in colour, length, width, design, type of material, and so on. It is assumed that all firms produce a product which differs only in one attribute (for example, colour of neckties, or type of music). All other characteristics are given. (This assumption will be relaxed at a later stage.)

(3) Each firm produces only one variety (e.g. luxury neckties of a particular colour, records of classical music, or jazz music).

(4) Technology is given. Costs are U-shaped, and do not vary with the variety produced. Thus all firms have identical costs.

(5) It is assumed that the possible varieties can be ranked in order along a given scale. For example, colours can be ranked from the lightest to the darkest shades; or music records can be ranked from classical music to disco music (see Figure 1.8).

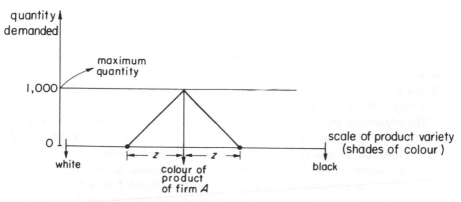

Figure 1.8

(6) Consumers have perfect knowledge of the available varieties (e.g. colours or types of music) and can rank their preferences for these varieties. Furthermore, buyers' preferences are distributed evenly along the horizontal quality scale. (This assumption also will be relaxed at a later stage.)

(7) It is assumed that the demand for a firm's product is a decreasing function of the product's difference from the buyer's 'ideal' variety on the quality scale. For example, if a buyer has strong preference for light (modern) music, he will decrease his purchases as the type of records offered on the market becomes more classical. This behaviour is compatible with the traditional utility theory: the greater the difference between the variety actually offered and the one most desirable ('optimal'), the less the utility attained by the buyer. The demand function under the above assumptions is given by the expression

$$q = m \left(1 - \frac{d}{z}\right) \tag{1.4}$$

where q = quantity demanded

m = maximum quantity, that is, the quantity that would be bought if the variety was to the complete satisfaction of the buyers

d = deviation of the actual variety from the one considered optimal

z = deviation of actual from optimal variety at which demand drops to zero — when $d = z$, $q = 0$ — That is, z is the maximum tolerable deviation of the variety offered from what the consumer considers 'ideal' for his tastes.

(8) The scale representing horizontal quality variability is a closed curve. (This avoids the instability that would arise by the adjustment process of firms producing the 'extreme' ('end') varieties.)[22]

(ii) *Short-run equilibrium*

It is assumed that the number of firms is fixed, and is such that some excess profit (less than the maximum level) is earned.

Thus firms, in order to maximise profits, would seek an increase in their sales volume, given the market price $\bar{P}$. In summary, the problem of the firm is to choose to produce a variety (colour of luxury neckties) which would maximise its volume sales (and its profits, given $\bar{P}$ and the firm's costs).[23]

The adjustment process can be illustrated diagrammatically. On the horizontal axis we depict the scale of horizontal variations of the product. On the vertical axis we measure the quantity demanded of the different varieties.

Since consumers' preferences are evenly distributed among the different varieties, we can indicate *the maximum quantity demanded* of each variety by a horizontal line at an appropriate height above the quality-scale axis. For example, in Figure 1.8 it is assumed that the maximum number of neckties demanded of each colour is 1,000. The saleable output of a firm which would face no rivalry ('unopposed producer', or 'unrivalled producer') can be shown by the area of an isosceles triangle whose apex is directly above the variety it produces (colour A in Figure 1.8) and whose base is $2z$.

If a firm has rivals, they can only be its two adjacent producers (the one to its left, producing lighter-colour neckties, and the one to its right, offering a darker colour than shade A), and their markets would overlap to a certain extent. Given the assumption of evenly distributed preferences of buyers, the overlapping segment of the market would be equally divided between the rivals producing adjacent varieties. The market share of each rival would be demonstrated by vertical lines drawn from the points midway between the adjacent varieties of rival firms: to consumers whose 'ideal' variety is shown by these points, the two adjacent varieties are equally unsatisfactory. In Figure 1.9 firm A is 'rivalled' on both sides. A's share (sales volume) is shown by the shaded area $abcde$.

---

[22] See Abbott, *Quality and Competition*.
[23] By definition the profit is the difference between total revenue ($R = XP$) and total cost (C), that is

$$\Pi = XP - C$$

where X = volume of output. If price and total cost is given (the firm works with a given budget), it is apparent that profit, π, is maximised if X, the volume of output, is maximised.

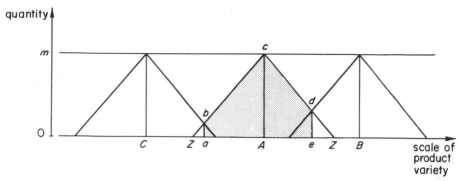

Figure 1.9

We will show that firms are in equilibrium when the varieties produced are such that the difference between them (as measured on the horizontal scale) is equal, and all firms have identical market shares.

Suppose that initially the varieties produced differ by different degrees. In Figure 1.10 the variety of A's product differs less than that of firm C's (i.e. $AB < AC$). Firm A is rivalled only by firm B: the two firms share equally the overlapping segment of their market $z0y$. (The triangles $z0x$ and $x0y$ are equal.) Firm A's sales volume is shown by the dotted area $x0bz'$ in Figure 1.10. This situation is not a stable equilibrium, because firm A can increase its sales (and profits) by changing its variety so that it is equally 'distant' from the varieties of the two adjacent firms. In Figure 1.11 firm A shifts its variety to A', so that $A'B = A'C$. With the change in variety the firm becomes unrivalled on both sides, and its sales volume increases by the area hfk in Figure 1.11. (Firm A's total sales are shown by the area of the triangle $yb'k$.) Firm A is now in equilibrium, because, by changing its variety (to A'), it maximizes its sales and its profits, given the price and the firm's costs.

To explore further this equilibrium, we may start from a situation in which the varieties produced by the rival firms are 'equi-distant', and show that any change of variety of the firm in the middle will result in a reduction in its sales (and profits). This is shown in Figure 1.12. Initially $AB = AC$, and the sales of firm A are shown by the dotted area $LTFQN$. Assume that firm A changes its variety so that its product is closer to that of firm B's. (In Figure 1.12 it is seen that $A'B < A'C$). With this move firm A loses sales equal to the striped area $(FGWMNQ)$, but at the same time it gains customers, denoted by the dotted area $(KRYEGTL)$. From elementary geometry it is seen that the loss of sales is greater than the gain in sales. In Figure 1.12 the firm's *net* loss of buyers is shown by the area of the triangle XYR.

In summary, equilibrium will be reached when the varieties have changed so that the difference between them (as measured on the horizontal scale) is equal, and all firms have identical market shares. So long as a producer's variety lies close enough to the varieties of the two adjacent rivals, so that his sales are

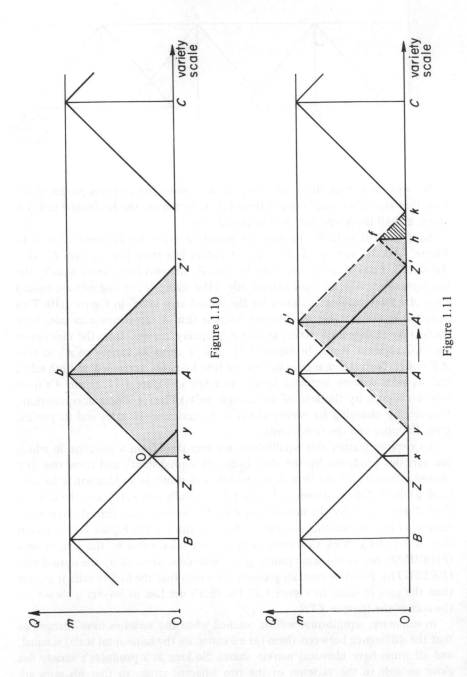

Figure 1.10

Figure 1.11

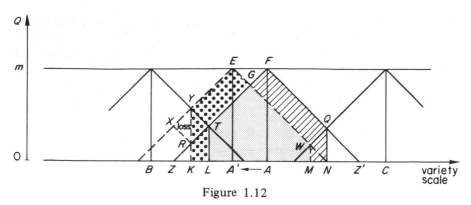

Figure 1.12

restricted by their products, but his variety is more similar to one of the adjacent varieties than to the other, it will pay the firm to move to a variety that is *exactly in the middle* of the varieties of adjacent rivals. This is so because the buyers it will gain are more than those it will lose in the process of adjustment of its variety. So long as the vertical lines that divide the firm's market from that of its adjacent rivals have different heights, the buyers lost are less than the buyers gained. In equilibrium the rival firms will produce equi-distant varieties.

The distribution of varieties along the variety scale depends on the distribution of buyers' preferences. With the assumption of evenly distributed preferences, the varieties produced in equilibrium are 'equi-distant': varieties are different by equal degrees. If the assumption of evenly distributed preferences is abandoned, the type of varieties produced in equilibrium will be different. Thus, if there is some form of concentration of preferences for some varieties (mass preferences), it can be shown that more firms will be producing these varieties, and that the difference in their qualities will be smaller (adjusted to the mass preferences): firms' varieties will bunch together more closely in the market segments with the mass preferences.[24] Firms may or may not have the same shares, depending on the distribution of preferences. What is certain is that firms whose products have the greatest popular appeal will face stronger competition than firms whose products appeal only to a small minority of buyers.

(iii) *Long-run equilibrium*

If firms earn abnormal profits, new firms will enter the market, up to the point when excess profits are eliminated. With evenly distributed preferences of buyers and identical cost structures, firms will have equal market shares, and in equilibrium they will be earning just normal profits.

---

[24] This conclusion is also reached by Peter O'Steiner in his study of the programme of radio broadcasting of the USA ('Program Patterns and Preferences, and the Workability of Competition in Radio Broadcasting', *American Economic Review*, 1953). His model bears striking similarities to the analysis of this section. See p. 27.

For example, assume that the given quality grade is sold at price $\bar{P}$ and gives rise to the cost curves shown in Figure 1.13. If the existing firms in the industry reach horizontal equilibrium at an output OX_1, the abnormal profits (*ab* per unit of output in Figure 1.13) will attract entrants, who will produce a variety chosen at random.[25] At first entrants would be too close to adjacent rivals to attain profit maximisation. Firms will start changing their varieties until the difference in their products became equal (products would be 'equi-distant' in variety). The process would continue until all firms produced an output level equal to OX_2 (where $\bar{P} = AC$ and normal profits are earned).

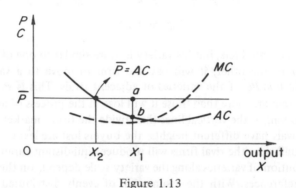

Figure 1.13

Although the above model implies competition only between adjacent rivals, it can be extended to rivalry between other firms as well, if the assumption of one-dimensional difference in variety is relaxed. If we assume that products (within the same quality grade) differ in more than one attribute (e.g. colour and length), the number of rivals would increase and competition would take place among as many firms as the aspects of product that are assumed to differ.

The above model of horizontal quality competition is limited in its scope. It bears little resemblance to real-world situations. However, it is useful as an illustration of the complexity of the problem of quality competition.

The model shows how horizontal quality competition leads to results similar to those of vertical quality competition and price competition (given the quality of the product). Thus with horizontal competition excess profits are eliminated, the number of varieties increases, but also costs are higher as the size of firms declines, and each is pushed backwards on its *AC* curve, giving rise to the highly controversial issue of unexhausted economies of scale.[26]

The model shows some of the most important determinants of horizontal quality competition: (a) the distribution of buyers' preferences, (b) the nature

[25] If firms were earning abnormal profits, but were still in quality disequilibrium, the new entrant would produce a variety in between those adjacent varieties most widely differing.

[26] See Koutsoyiannis, *Modern Microeconomics*, ch. 8.

of interdependence between buyers' tastes and the ability of firms to affect the choice by creating mass markets (mass preferences), (c) the cost structure, (d) the concentration of firms in the industry, and (e) the goals of the firm.

An interesting application of the theory of horizontal product competition has been attempted by Peter O'Steiner in his analysis of the type of programmes of the radio broadcasting industry of the USA.[27] He assumes that the goal of the stations is revenue maximisation attained by maximising their audience (listener-hours). Listeners' preferences are assumed to be ranked on a program-type scale. Steiner concludes that the number of programmes (horizontal varia-tion) at any one time depends on: (a) the distribution of listeners' preferences − the more unequal the distribution, the greater the programme diversity; and (b) the size of the stations (national networks, local stations) − the more equal the size of stations, the less the diversity of the programmes at any one time. A larger difference in preferences would increase competition among equally sized stations. Listeners would be worse off as their choice at any one time would be restricted (by similarity of programmes).

III. MANAGERIAL MODELS OF PRODUCT COMPETITION

In this section the goal of profit maximisation is abandoned. Managers are assumed to be growth seekers, because maximisation of the growth of the firm leads to the maximisation of the managerial utility function.[28]

We will develop three growth models of product competition. In the first model firms compete vertically, each aiming at the maximisation of its sales. The second and third models deal with the case of 'product wars': firms compete vertically or horizontally, with the aim of eliminating rivals.

A. Vertical Quality Equilibrium with Sales Maximisation

The assumptions of this model are the same as in the first model of section II, with the exception of the goal of the firm, which is now assumed to be sales maximisation subject to the condition of earning at least a normal profit at all stages of the adjustment process. It is also assumed that the number of firms remains fixed: firms do not eliminate rivals by aggressive quality competition, and new firms do not enter the industry during the adjustment process.

---

[27] O'Steiner, 'Program Patterns and Preferences, and the Workability of Competition in Radio Broadcasting', *American Economic Review*, 1953.

[28] See R. Marris, *Theory of Managerial Capitalism* (Macmillan, 1964); J. K. Galbraith, *Economics and the Public Purpose* (Houghton Mifflin, 1973); W. J. Baumol, *Business Behav-iour, Value and Growth*, rev. edn (Macmillan, 1967).

Under the above conditions a sales maximiser will reach equilibrium by choosing to produce a quality grade such that

$$P = ACO < MCO \tag{1.5}$$

The equilibrium of a sales maximiser is shown by point e' in Figure 1.14. We saw in the previous section that a profit maximiser will reach equilibrium when $MCO = \bar{P}$ (point e in Figure 1.14). However, a sales maximiser will use the excess profit to improve the quality of his product, so as to increase his sales. The firm's demand and cost curves will shift upwards to the right. The firm will continue improving its quality until all excess profits are exhausted. This occurs when the (shifted) demand curve intersects the ACO curve on the price line (point e'). At this point the firm earns just normal profits.

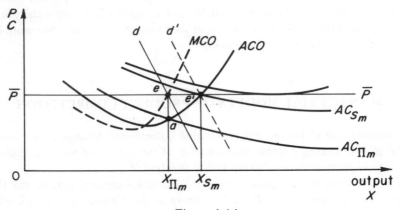

Figure 1.14

It is interesting to compare the equilibrium of a profit maximiser with that of a sales maximiser under vertical quality competition.

(1) The sales maximiser will produce a larger level of output than the profit maximiser ($X_{\Pi m} > X_{\Pi m}$) at the given market price.

(2) The quality grade of the sales maximiser will be higher than that of the profit maximiser (AC_{Sm} lies above $AC_{\Pi m}$, implying an improvement in the quality grade).

(3) The profits of a sales maximiser are lower than those of a profit maximiser. As we said, the sales maximiser earns just normal profit (since $\bar{P} = ACO$ at e').

(4) With given price, the goal of sales maximisation can be attained only by improvements in quality which absorb the excess profits.

(5) Sales maximisation via quality competition leads to a shift of the market demand curve upwards to the right. At equilibrium the market output under sales maximisation is $n \times OX_{Sm}$, where n is the number of firms in the industry.

(6) The number of varieties offered in the market will be the same (given n), but their quality grade will be higher.

(7) Under the assumed cost structure, the increase in output leads to a better utilisation of the plant: production moves closer to the minimum point of the *AC* curve. However, the unit cost will be higher due to the improved quality.

(8) With sales maximisation the buyers in the market are better off: they can buy a larger quantity of an improved quality product at the same (fixed) price.

B. Vertical Quality Competition with Aggressive Sales Maximisation: a Model of Cut-throat Product Competition

Assume that each firm believes that an improvement in quality (beyond point e' in Figure 1.15) will force some competitor(s) out of the market and is willing to undergo temporary losses for the sake of eventual increase in sales. Under these conditions a quality war will emerge until the financially weaker firms are eliminated, and the survivors attain a larger market share. It is assumed here that the total industry demand does not expand with the quality war. Alternatively one may assume that if the market expands, the aggressive firms will capture the increase in demand, because they offer a better quality.

Let us examine the above process in some detail.

Assume that the improvement in quality shifts the cost curve to AC'' in Figure 1.15. Associated with this quality improvement is the demand curve d''. Under these demand and cost conditions, and given the market price $\bar{P}$, the firm should sell quantity X'' in order to break even, covering all its costs and earning normal profits. However, with the quality implied by AC'', buyers demand

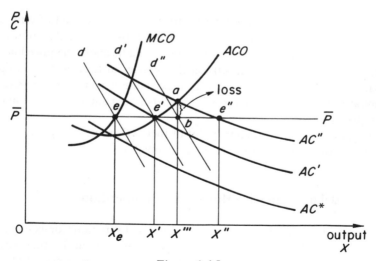

Figure 1.15

quantity X''' (at price $\bar{P}$), which is smaller than X''. (In other words, in order to sell OX'' at $\bar{P}$, the firm should further improve its quality.) Thus sales remain temporarily below the break-even point, and losses are incurred (equal to ab per unit) until some firm(s) leaves the industry. With exit, the demand of the remaining firms shifts to the right. However, an aggressive seller would not stop at the break-even point e'' (which would be gradually reached as firms were eliminated and his individual demand would shift to the right). Such a firm (or firms) would further improve quality, and the process would be repeated until the improvements in quality shift the AC curve to a point of tangency with the given price line. As exit takes place, the ACO curve shifts to the right, and at equilibrium it cuts the price line at its tangency with the AC curve. This equilibrium is denoted by point e^* in Figure 1.16.

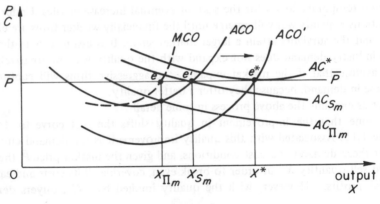

Figure 1.16

The firms would earn just normal profit on an enlarged level of output of a higher quality. There would be no incentive for further quality improvement because the corresponding (higher) AC curve would lie above the price line.

With cut-throat quality competition the number of firms will be smaller (as compared with the models of profit maximisation and non-aggressive sales maximisation). Hence the buyers will have to choose among fewer brands of a higher quality.

Firms produce at the minimum point of their AC curve, so that all economies of scale are exhausted, and profits are just normal.

C.   A Model of Aggressive Horizontal Competition

In this model it is assumed that horizontal product variation (for example, style change) increases the minimum optimal scale of production. Furthermore, it is assumed that firms have unequal market shares. Under these conditions frequent style changes may be used as an aggressive policy by large firms to eliminate the smaller rivals, given the market price.

Assume that the minimum optimal scale of production in the industry is $\bar{x}$. (Recall that the minimum optimal scale is the level of output at which all the known economies of scale are exhausted.) Small firms produce at this scale due to their small market share, while large firms produce at a larger scale (x_L in Figure 1.17). The price in the market is given ($\bar{P}$ in Figure 1.17). Under these conditions all firms earn abnormal profits. Assume next that the larger firms adopt a policy of frequent style changes, as for example in the automobile industry of the USA. Such changes require replacement of dies (which are an insert in a large metal stamping press) which are indivisible. This change in technology is reflected by an increase in the minimum optimal scale. If the output of the smaller firms remains unchanged, they will be eventually eliminated. In Figure 1.17 small firms can survive (producing $\bar{x}$ at price $\bar{P}$) only so long as the change in the minimum optimal scale is not beyond $\bar{x}'$: at point e small firms break even, producing at a sub-optimal scale ($\bar{x} < \bar{x}'$). If, however, the style change shifts the *LAC* to the right of $\bar{x}'$ (e.g. LAC_3 with minimum optimum scale $\bar{x}''$), the small firms, producing $\bar{x}$, cannot cover their unit costs, given the market price $\bar{P}$, and hence are driven out of business. Thus style changes can be used as a deliberate method of cut-throat product competition by large firms to eliminate small rivals.

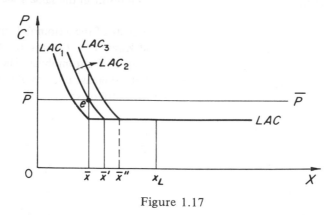

Figure 1.17

Menge[29] has argued that the yearly style changes of automobiles in the USA resulted in the elimination of the smaller firms (Packard, Dodge, Studebacker, etc.) which unwittingly followed the style-change competition of the 'big three' (General Motors, Ford, Chrysler). His argument runs as follows. The large automobile firms are able to use their dies and wear them out within one year, while

[29] J. A. Menge, 'Style Change Costs as a Market Weapon', *Quarterly Journal of Economics*, 1962.

smaller firms need three or more years for such complete depreciation. Thus large firms can change the style of their cars yearly without any change in their unit cost, due to the volume of their yearly production, while small firms' unit costs rise sharply, given their low level of output. The style war in the automobile industry resulted, according to Menge, in the elimination of the smaller car producers.

Elimination of small firms by a style war requires the fulfilment of several assumptions. First, technology has strong indivisibilities which increase the minimum optimal scale as style changes take place. Second, the market share of smaller firms may remain constant or increase, but is smaller than the increasing minimum optimal plant scale. Third, small firms follow style changes of large firms and in the same direction (imitation of styles). Fourth, the price is given.

If some of these assumptions are violated, small firms can still survive a style war of large firms. For example, small firms can adopt a policy of infrequent style changes and sell their product at a lower price. Another possible strategy is change of style and of other aspects of the product in different directions to the large firms' changes in product. Menge argues that AMC (American Motors Company) managed to survive because it followed such a policy, concentrating on compact models. How long it will survive remains to be seen, in view of the production of compact models by the 'big three' (and the increased competition of imported small cars). The large firms have adopted yearly changes of style for the compact models as well, and this may well result in the same scale disadvantage for AMC.

In view of the findings of a study of the costs of the automobile industry of the USA conducted by Fisher, Griliches and Kaysen,[30] it seems that Menge has exaggerated the importance of style-change costs of automobiles. The results of this study show that between 1949 and 1961 the increase in costs of the 'average' car amounted to $683, which is accounted for as follows:

1. Cost of higher horse power, greater lengths, greater weight, etc.	$454
2. Cost of optional equipment	$116
3. Costs of retooling	$ 99
4. Costs of increased advertising	$ 14
Total	$683

These costs have been passed on to the buyers via increased prices. Thus Menge's hypothesis is not supported by the available empirical evidence. Style

[30] F. Fisher, Z. Griliches and K. Kaysen, 'The Costs of Automobile Model Changes since 1949', *American Economic Review*, 1962.

cost changes may have contributed to the process of elimination of small car makers, but other factors seem to have been operative, such as sub-optimal output levels prior to the style war, different efficiencies of firms (absolute cost advantages of larger firms prior to the style war), loss of share due to less successful style changes, poor distribution channels, and so on.

The model of style-change competition can be extended in various directions. One can change the assumption of identical costs (prior to change of style), and can also introduce an upward shift of the *AC* curve as the product changes. These conditions would not basically alter the analysis: small firms would still be eliminated by style changes so long as their market share remains smaller than the optimal plant scale, and the price in the market is fixed. The process of elimination would actually be accelerated if efficiency differentials are introduced into the model.

Some interesting implications of this model should be noted.

If firms are of unequal size, small firms should not follow the style changes of their large rivals. Their differentiation should take a different direction, stressing other parameters of the product. For example, in the case of cars, important aspects of the product would be economy in fuel and in maintenance, durability, manoeuvrability, and so on.

If firms are of equal size, a style war will have little effect on market shares. Cost increases associated with style changes would affect all rivals equally, and would result in lower profits and higher prices, which endanger the position of the industry by increased competition from imports. Firms of equal size would sooner or later recognise the defects of such a code of behaviour and would gradually change it with or without collusion. This seems to be happening in the automobile industry.

Firms with sub-optimal scales are vulnerable not only to product competition but also to price competition of larger firms operating at efficient levels of output. The former could sooner or later be eliminated by an aggressive price or product strategy of larger rivals.

IV. SOME REMARKS ON MAXIMISING MODELS OF PRODUCT COMPETITION

The pure-quality equilibrium models are useful as a first step in building a general-equilibrium model of the behaviour of the firm in which all the the policy variables (price, product, advertising, etc.) are simultaneously determined.

These models are also of interest in analysing the competitive behaviour of firms in those markets where prices are rigid (sticky) while product varies. Such markets form a substantial part of the modern oligopolistic world.

The models developed in the earlier sections can explain situations in which, with given price, abnormal profits can be earned, if barriers to entry exist.

The models can deal with different goals of the firm. Of course, depending on the goal, the emerging equilibrium will differ in the total level of output (at the given price), the number of firms and their size, the number of available quality standards, and varieties in each quality grade.

The previous analysis can be applied to illustrate how product competition may lead to elimination of firms: that is, how product changes may be used as an aggressive weapon of competition for the elimination of smaller, weaker firms.

The models can be extended to encompass situations in which improved quality may lead to a smaller volume of output produced by the firm (at the given market price), by causing a shift to the left of the individual demand curves (as quality standards are raised). For example, the increase in the durability of razor blades may reduce the volume of sales.

Finally, the models can explain how excessive product competition may result eventually in deterioration of the quality of the product. For example, a style war among firms of similar size, given the market price, is bound to shift upwards the cost curves of the firms. Given the market price, the squeeze on profit margins will lead to a general reduction of quality standards.

The weakness of the above models is related to their partial approach to the behaviour of the firm and to their assumptions of perfect knowledge and given technology. Firms are assumed to have knowledge of all available possibilities of products and processes. They thus know their demand and cost structures for all quality improvements.

Most changes in products have some innovational element. Innovation is by its nature risky and uncertain. The demand and cost curves of innovational product changes cannot be known with certainty.

Equilibrium models ignore all the organisational complexities of the firm, and the effects of behaviour in organisations on the goals, decision-making process, and performance of the firm.

The assumption of perfect knowledge and rational behaviour of buyers is also highly unrealistic. In most real-world situations the assumption of imperfect knowledge or even of complete ignorance would be more realistic.[31]

Yet quality equilibrium models make clear something that is usually ignored in economic analysis: that quality competition performs essentially the same functions as price competition. Product competition when price is fixed can bring about elimination of excess profits (with free entry) in the same way as price competition does when the product is fixed.

Thus price rigidity does not necessarily imply excess profits or lack of competition. Only if quality is also rigid (and there are no secret price concessions) is price rigidity indicative of lack of competition. Product variations may well supplant price competition, but still they constitute competition. Whether the results of pure product competition (with fixed price) are more desirable than

---

[31] E. Chamberlin, 'The Product as an Economic Variable', *Journal of Political Economy*, Vol. LXVII, 1953, pp. 1–29. For an opposite view see Harry Townsend, 'Big Business and Competition', in *A New Era in Competition*, ed. T. M. Rybczynski (Blackwell, 1972).

the results of pure price competition (with product fixed) so far as the allocation of resources is concerned hinges on the problem of whether quality competition is excessive or not.[32] Abbott argues that vertical quality competition cannot be excessive, while the other types (horizontal and innovational) can be excessive.[33] Of course, this conclusion is derived from the assumption of perfect knowledge, which does no hold in the real world. Results become more obscure when horizontal and innovational competition are combined with vertical competition, and when advertising and other selling activities enter the picture. We will return to this point later.

V. A BEHAVIOURAL MODEL OF PRODUCT STRATEGY

Over the last fifteen years product decisions have attracted the interest of economists in business schools. The literature on this topic has increased rapidly. Its main features are a behavioural approach to product decisions and the stressing of the importance of product planning for the efficient operation of the firm. Most of the work in this field has strong overtones of normative prescription for 'optimal' decision-making regarding the product mix of the firm. In this section we will present Ansoff's 'strategic theory of the firm' as a sample of the current trend in the analysis of product decisions.[34]

Ansoff considers the firm as an organisation-coalition which seeks the attainment of a set of goals. Its operations are designed and controlled by the top management. In seeking the attainment of its goals top management is involved in three types of decisions: strategic decisions, administrative decisions and operating decisions.

Strategic decisions relate to the determination of the relationships between the firm and its environment. They are in their essence planning decisions. Strategic decisions are of three types: those which determine the relationship between the firm and the market(s) in which it sells its products, those which determine the relationship between the firm and the markets in which it buys its factors of production, and those which determine the relationship between the firm and its social and political environment. The most important of these strategic decisions (according to Ansoff) are its product decisions. *The core problem of a business strategy is the selection of the product-market portfolio of the firm.* Ansoff's analysis concentrates on product strategic decisions.

Administrative decisions relate to the setting up of the firm, the organisation of its managerial hierarchy and of its various departments.

---

[32] Chamberlin, 'The Product as an Economic Variable', and M. Clark, *Competition as a Dynamic Process* (Brookings Institution, 1961), have explained the process of 'product inflation' and 'product adulteration'.

[33] Abbott, *Quality and Competition.*

[34] H. I. Ansoff, 'Toward a Strategic Theory of the Firm', *Economies et sociétés*, 1968; reprinted in *Business Strategy*, ed. H. I. Ansoff (Penguin, 1969).

Operating decisions relate to the determination of the values of the variables under the control of the firm (price, output levels) at any one time.

Operating decisions are short-run decisions, which are taken repetitively and as a routine, while strategic decisions are long-run planning decisions.

Table 1.1 includes the main types of decisions within each one of the above broad groups.

Table 1.1   Types of decisions of the firm

Strategic decisions	Administrative decisions	Operating decisions

1. Objectives
2. Product strategy
   Growth strategy:
   method, direction,
   timing
4. Finance strategy
5. Administrative
   strategy
	1. Hierarchical structure
	   (i) Delegation of
	        authority
	   (ii) Flow of information
	2. Structure of production process
	   (i) Production flow
	   (ii) Organisation of
	        production work
	3. Structure of selling process
	   (i) Distribution system
	   (ii) Organisation of selling
	        operations
	4. Structure of buying process
	   (i) Acquisition of finance
	   (ii) Recruiting of personnel
	   (iii) Acquisition of equipment
	        and raw materials
		1. Operating objectives
		2. Price levels
		3. Output levels
		4. Production process
		5. Selling (marketing)
		   process
		6. Inventory decisions
		7. R & D activities
		8. Control of operations

Ansoff argues that the most important decisions are the strategic decisions. Traditional microeconomic theory has concentrated on operating decisions and has considered only *economic variables*, such as prices and quantities of inputs and outputs. The behavioural theory of Cyert and March[35] has also concentrated on operating decisions, but has stressed the importance of *behavioural variables* (which describe the motivation of people in the firm and the effects of such behaviour on the operations of the firm), and *informational variables* (which describe the degree of knowledge available to the various members of the firm-coalition).

Ansoff attempts to build a 'strategic theory of the firm' in which strategic decisions only are analysed. His exposition consists of two sets of hypotheses: *descriptive hypotheses*, which describe how strategic decisions are actually taking place in large firms; and *prescriptive hypotheses*, which are of normative nature, relating to how strategic decisions *should* be taken for the successful operation of the firm.

[35] Cyert and March, *A Behavioural Theory of the Firm.*

Ansoff deals only with product strategy. We will present below only his 'positive theory': that is, his descriptive set of hypotheses. Normative prescriptions are beyond the scope of this book.

The various types of decisons compete for the time of top management.

The available empirical evidence[36] shows that:

(1) Firms are not continuously preoccupied with strategic decisions. Product strategy is attended to only at rather infrequent periods. This implies that firms fail to see the importance of strategic decisions.

(2) Top management is mainly preoccupied with operating decisions. This is the result of historical evolution. First, operating decisions are brought to the attention of top management by lower-level managers as a routine procedure. Operating decisions are large in volume and frequent. Solutions must be given to problems brought to the top managers' attention. Second, most top managers have reached their administrative position by promotion within the firm (or in other firms with a similar hierarchy); thus they are familiar with operating decisions from their previous training at lower hierarchical levels, where operating decisions are the only type of decisions taken. Thus most top managers are not familiar with strategic decisions; they are not aware of their importance or of the ways to deal with them. Third, most firms have not delegated authority for strategic planning either to specific top managers or to a specific department within the firm. Thus strategic decisions are competing with operating and administrative decisions for the limited time of top management; and for the above (historical) reasons, operating decisions tend to take priority over strategic decisions.

(3) Decisions are taken by firms *serially*. This means that when a crisis (problem) arises, top management first considers it as an operating problem, and attempts its solution by changing previous operating decisions (for example, changing the selling strategy, or the level of price and output). If the crisis is not resolved by operating decisions, the top management concentrates on administrative decisions (reorganisation of the firm is a common phenomenon following some failure in the operation of the firm). Only if operating and administrative decisions fail to solve the crisis does the top management examine its strategy, looking for changes in the market environment as possible causes of the crisis. In short, serial decision-making, which is typical of most firms in the real world, considers any problem initially as due to operating deficiencies, secondly as administrative, and only lastly as strategic deficiencies.

However, since the early 1950s the environment has been changing very fast (new products, new processes became available with the fast post-war technological progress). Firms became increasingly aware of the need for adjusting their product strategy to the changing environment and have developed various methods for exploiting these changes. Ansoff states that in recent years an

[36] A. D. Chandler, *Strategy and Structure* (MIT Press, 1962); R. A. Smith, *Corporations in Crisis* (Doubleday, 1963).

increasing number of firms has become aware of the importance of product strategy, and are devoting attention to strategic decisions. Ansoff's hypotheses are based on observation of the process by which product strategy is formulated in large firms. Thus his analysis belongs to the behavioural school.

Ansoff is concerned with the organisational process by which the firm handles strategic change. He examines three aspects of product strategy:

(A) The determinants of the involvement of top management in strategic decisions.

(B) The stages involved in a change in product strategy and the top management actions in each stage.

(C) The role of top management in two types of strategic change: *expansion*, which is an extension of the current product activities of the firm; and *diversification*, which is a radical departure from the current product policies.

A.   Determinants of the Degree of Involvement of Top Management in the Strategic Decisions

There are several factors which determine the time and effort of top management devoted to strategic decisions, some internal and some external to the firm.

Internal factors include:

(i) The gap between goals and past achievement. A series of failures in the market is bound to cause pressure for strategic changes.

(ii) Past patterns of decision-making. The historical evolution of the decision-making process determines to a large extent the attitude of top managers towards strategic planning.

(iii) The internal organisation of the firm and the degree of delegation of authority.

External factors determining strategic decisions include:

(i) Past experience of the strategic tactics of competitors.

(ii) The rate of technological change.

(iii) The position attained by the firm in the industry as a result of its past actions and the counteractions of competitors.

(iv) The general economic and competitive conditions of the environment of the firm.

The internal organisational factors (internal constraints) and environmental pressures (external constraints) define the strategic behaviour of top managers.

Three types of strategic behaviour are distinguished.

Defensive strategy. This implies a lag-response to changes in the environment. Change is detected after it has occurred and action is taken to adjust to the change. Usually actions are imitations of the activities of successful rivals, who have been the initiators or the first to exploit the change in the environment (invention or adoption of a new product or new method of production). The firm fails to anticipate environmental changes which require a change in the product-mix. The firms seek remedial action after the change has occurred.

Anticipatory strategy. This implies forward planning to foresee significant changes in the environment and preparedness to meet (adjust to) such changes as soon as they occur.

Aggressive strategy. This implies continuous planning for initiating changes which create growth and expansion opportunities.

If operating decisions are given priority, defensive strategy is almost inevitable, given that strategic decisions compete with operating decisions for top managers' time and attention. If there is a strong entrepreneurial propensity (and training) of top management for strategic planning, strategic behaviour will be more aggressive. Similarly, if the environment changes fast and/or the competition of rivals is strong, or rivals follow aggressive product tactics, strategy will be attended to continually.

B. Types of Strategic Change (or Growth)

It is implicitly assumed that firms seek (alongside their other goals) to grow.

Growth can take two forms: *expansion* of existing lines and markets; and *diversification*, which involves introduction of new products. There is a natural tendency in the firm for priority to be given to expansion. Diversification from within the firm will be generated from the R & D or design department. New ideas (about new products and processes) will be developed only if these departments allocate time to such research or design. However, other departments (marketing, production) will be pressing the R & D department for improvements of existing products, so as to satisfy demands of customers or meet competition or rivals in existing product lines and markets. Thus there is an inevitable conflict in which strong pressures favour expansion against diversification.

Ansoff next postulates that growth (strategic change) takes place in most firms regardless of whether top management devotes special attention to planning or controlling it. This is due to dynamic forces within and outside the firm: internal pressure arises from various groups or individuals in pursuing their own aspirations and goals; external pressures arise from rivals' tactics, demands from customers, technological progress, general business conditions. This dynamic autonomous expansion allows firms to survive in a changing environment even without an explicit product strategy, provided that the environment is not strongly competitive. However, unless the top management directs strategic change, the latter will normally take the form of expansion of existing products and strengthening of existing markets.

Both types of strategic change (expansion and diversification) may take place either from within the firm or by acquisition from outside. Acquisition may include purchase of products developed by others, licensing, acquisition of firms.

Ansoff postulates that:

(a) Expansion occurs from within, due to the 'natural dynamics of the firm'. Lower-level managers deal with internal and external stimuli to this type of expansion as a matter of their normal duties. Thus they tend to concentrate on the existing within-the-firm capacities and potential for further growth. They normally have neither the knowledge nor the stimulus to look for expansion through acquisition. Thus expansion through acquisition will take place only if top management guides this process.

(b) Diversification, either from within or through acquisition, will take place normally only through top management action.

In general, therefore, if the firm wants to expand through acquisition, it has to set up a special organisational unit, because the existing departments will not normally have the expertise in looking for and judging promising opportunities for acquisition.

In summary, strategic change occurs in a majority of firms independently of top management involvement, but it can only be 'optimal' if top managers consciously direct such change. If left unplanned, strategic change will not be optimal either in timing or in the form it takes: it will be biased by the 'politics' and 'influence processes' inherent in the firm's organisation. Even when planned, strategic change takes place under conditions of imperfect knowledge: top management has limited information, limited time and limited ability in comparing alternative product strategies. The involvement of top management in the process of strategic product change can vary from simple allocation of budget funds to the relevant departments (mainly the R & D or design and marketing departments), to detailed guidelines.

The determinants of strategic change are complex. They may be grouped into internal factors and external stimuli.

Internal factors include:

(i) The attitude (and training) of top management towards exploitation of opportunities (within the firm, or created by technological change).
(ii) The attitude of top management towards risk.
(iii) The skills available within the firm (particularly in the marketing, design and R & D departments).
(iv) The funds available for searching for promising strategic changes. This determines the amount of knowledge which will be available to top management.
(v) Existence of areas of high *synergy*, that is, areas where a new product will use mainly skills and equipment (or other facilities) already available in the firm but not exploited to their full potential, and areas where the new product(s) will create complementarity of skills or facilities in the production and/or distribution of old and new products (for example, the acquisition by a firm, with a strong R & D department, of another firm which has poor R & D facilities but has well-established production and distribution departments).

(vi) Aspirations and ambitions of the persons or groups involved in the search activity.

(vii) Past search patterns of the firm.

External factors include:

(i) Rate of technological change.

(ii) Rivalry of competitors.

(iii) Desires and needs of the firm's customers.

(iv) Glamour of certain growth areas as perceived by society as a whole at any one time.

(v) Position of the firm in the industry, attained by historical evolution through past competitive moves and counter-moves of the firm and its competitors.

C. Stages of Strategic (Product) Change

Strategic change is defined as the change of the product-portfolio mix and/or the markets in which the firm operates.

Strategic change follows a definite chronological pattern. Initially the firm passes through a period of search, during which several alternative new ideas (about products and/or markets) are investigated. Given the limited search capacity of the firm (especially skills in the marketing, design and R & D departments), and the costs and time required for such activity, only the most promising alternatives are explored (hence the limited information by which top management acts). During this stage estimates of risk and profitability are obtained.

The search period is followed by a stage of product development during which pilot production and/or marketing studies take place in order to verify the initial profitability estimates. The most profitable alternative is chosen for exploitation.

The next stage involves building up full-scale facilities for the production and marketing of the new product. Once this stage is completed the firm enters the exploitation period of the new product.[37]

The exploitation period of all products exhibits a *natural life cycle* which is determined by demand and cost conditions. At the initial stages of the introduction of a product, demand rises at a fast rate, economies of scale are reaped and profits are high. Gradually competitors imitate the successful product, and demand for the product of the individual firm slows down. Eventually the market is saturated. Then comes an eventual decline in demand, which will necessitate discontinuation of the product (when profits are very low or losses occur). Such a natural life cycle is shown in Figure 1.18.

The length of the life cycle varies from industry to industry. The longest life cycles are observed in extractive industries and industries producing intermediate

---

[37] See also C. F. Carter and B. R. Williams, *Investment in Innovation* (Oxford University Press, 1958).

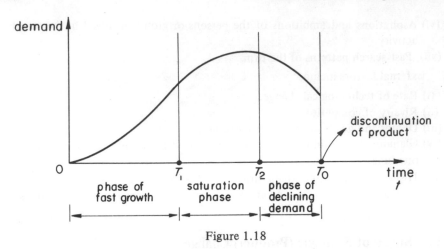

Figure 1.18

standardised products. The shortest life cycles are observed in consumers' 'fashion goods'. In the post-war period there has been a trend towards a shortening of the life cycles of products due to refined technological progress and deliberate action of firms, which exploit the imperfect knowledge of consumers, avail themselves of the power they have in manipulating consumers' preferences and induce obsolescence of goods by introducing new varieties.

The natural life cycle may be affected in two ways.

(1) If there is a major technological breakthrough, the product becomes obsolete before it reaches maturity. In these conditions the life cycle is distorted. Demand declines rapidly and discontinuation of the product is accelerated. This situation is shown in Figure 1.19. Normally the product would be discontinued at period T_0. With technological change at T the product is discontinued at period T_0'.

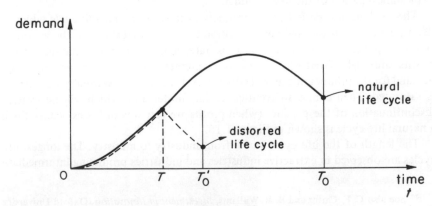

Figure 1.19

(2) If technological change is slow, the life cycle can be extended in two ways. One way is to penetrate markets hitherto not reached. The other way is to introduce minor changes which enhance the demand by creating a replacement demand or by making the product attractive to a wider range of buyers (without necessitating replacement). This is shown in Figure 1.20.

The firm introduces minor changes of the product or taps new markets at the time periods denoted by t, t_1, t_2. The product remains basically the same, but the changes attract additional buyers, thus prolonging the normal life cycle of the product.

This 'expansion form' of change is typical for many products in most firms. It is automatically stimulated by pressures of rivals, demands from buyers, and ideas developed within the firm (in the production, marketing and R & D departments). This process takes place in most firms regardless of whether there is an explicit product strategy (see also p. 40).

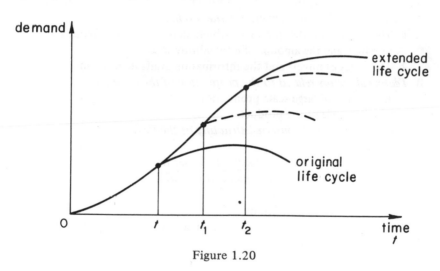

Figure 1.20

D. Critique of Ansoff's Behavioural Model

Ansoff presents a set of hypotheses which are descriptive (he maintains) of the behaviour of firms in the real world. He has adopted a behavioural approach which, however, differs from that of Cyert and March in that these latter writers concentrate on operating decisions, while Ansoff stresses strategic decisions.

In its present form Ansoff's set of hypotheses does not constitute a theory of the firm. Nor is it a theory of product-portfolio selection. It contains some of the factors that influence product decisions, while ignoring the crucial relationships between strategic and operating decisions. By replacing operating decisions, which deal with the current activities of the firm, with strategic decisions, which deal with the future (long-run) development of the operations of the firm,

Ansoff fails to see the interaction of present and future and the trade-offs which must be made between them.[38]

Another shortcoming of Ansoff's approach is the lack of analysis of the relation between external and internal constraints. The goals of the firm are not explicitly stated, and without a precise formulation of the relationships between the various determinants of the behaviour of the firm no simulation is possible, and hence no predictions can be made regarding the reaction of the firm to changes in the environment.[39]

VI.   DETERMINANTS OF PRODUCT VARIATION

In this section we will summarise the various determinants of product variation, drawing on the discussion of the preceding sections.

We may group the factors affecting product diversity in various categories.

A. *Factors related to the demand for the product.*
  1. The nature of the product, which determines the frequency of the purchase and the amount of expenditure involved.
  2. The types of buyers and the information available to them.
B. *Technical factors related to the production of the commodity.*
  1. Economies of large-scale production.
  2. The life cycle of the product.
C. *Factors related to the internal structure of the firm.*
  1. Goals of the firm.
  2. Availability of managerial skill and other resources.
D. *Factors related to the environment of the firm.*
  1. Technological progress.
  2. General business conditions.
  3. Rivalry of competitors, which is related to the relative position of the firm in the industry.

A.   Factors related to the Demand for the Product

One of the main determinants of product diversity is the nature of the product itself.

Consumer goods change more frequently than producers' goods. Intermediate goods are usually standardised; they are produced to the specifications of the buying industries. Machinery and equipment are defined by the state of technology and changes in these products are determined by technological progress.

---

[38] See also S. Tilles, *Making Strategy Explicit* (Boston Consulting Group, 1966).
[39] For an example of product strategy see A. P. Sloan Jr, *My Years with General Motors* (Matson, 1964). Chapter 4 of this book is reprinted in *Business Strategy*, ed. H. I. Ansoff (Penguin, 1969).

Consumer-goods industries are characterised by extensive product differentiation and product variability. Within the group of consumer goods, changes are more frequent for non-durables than for durables. Consumers are more willing to experiment with new brands of non-durables, because they are subject to frequent repeat purchases, which, individually, involve relatively small expenditures. For durables, which are bought infrequently and involve large expenditures, the consumers will usually spend some time to 'shop around', comparing the available brands and gathering information from friends and relatives who have bought similar commodities.

The degree of the variability of products is also determined by the type of buyers and the amount of information they possess and are willing to use. Consumers in general are less informed than industrial buyers. The buying departments of firms are well informed about the alternative sources of supply of industrial commodities, and it is their job to make effective use of all available information in order to minimise the purchasing costs of the firm. Consumers have limited information. Firms, unless coerced by law, tend to limit information to the level that increases the appeal of their product. When specifications are required by law, firms usually present the information in technical terms, most often not very helpful to the consumer.

Consumers are more vulnerable than industrial buyers to advertising and other selling gimmicks adopted by firms. Furthermore, consumers do not act under the pressure of cost minimisation, which is the main criterion for efficient performance of the buying departments of firms. Firms adopt selling strategies which manipulate consumers' choices not only of non-durable commodities but of durables as well. Through frequent product changes they quickly render the 'stock of knowledge' of consumers obsolete. In addition, advertising and other marketing policies stress the prestige associated with the ownership or the consumption of new products. Consumers are further enticed by such tactics as guarantees of performance, refund or exchange of faulty or 'unsatisfactory' products, free servicing, and so on. In summary, firms exploit the inertia (lagresponse), ignorance and gullibility of consumers, and indulge in product-differentiation activities which are to a large extent excessive and wasteful of resources (see pp. 47–50).

B. Factors related to the Production of the Commodity

Technological progress enhances product diversity, by making possible the production of new products to satisfy new wants, and the improvement of existing commodities. Thus product variation is more frequent in industries characterised by fast rates of technical change.

The decision to produce a new commodity which will satisfy a new want is fairly straightforward. However, the production of commodities which will substitute for currently produced goods, or the incorporation of technical improvements to existing lines of brands, involve complex considerations, related to the 'optimal life cycle' of the products. The length of this cycle depends on: (a) the extent of possible economies of scale; (b) the wish of firms to meet the desire of buyers for change in the products; and (c) the anticipated product strategy of rivals or the established code of product change in the industry. For example, in the automobile industry, yearly changes of style (and other features of cars) has been (in the USA) the accepted tradition. In general, frequent changes which do not allow the full exploitation of economies of scale are resisted by firms, unless rivals adopt similar policies and buyers do not react unfavourably to the higher cost associated with such a strategy.

C. Factors related to the Internal Structure of the Firm

The rate of product change (as well as its direction) is to a large extent determined by the goals of the firm, the attitude of top management towards change, and the available managerial skills and other resources of the firm.

Product diversity will in general be greater if the goal of the firm is maximisation of its growth (*ceteris paribus*). Furthermore, product changes will be more frequent if top management has the aspiration of being the innovation leader in the industry. The goals and attitudes of managers to change will shape the product strategy of the firm.

The available talent in managerial skills and R & D activities are major determinants of product change. Powerful marketing, design and R & D departments will generate pressures for frequent product changes. Of course, there is a limit to the rate of introduction of new products, set by the capacity of the managerial and the R & D teams of the firm. Pressures to introduce changes at rates faster than the capacity of the firm are bound to lead to declining effectiveness of the expansion process of the firm.[40]

D. Factors related to the Environment of the Firm

We have already discussed the effect of the technical change on product diversity. Industries with rapid technical progress are typically characterised by extensive product variation.

Products also tend to change at different rates and in different directions during the various phases of economic activity. In periods of expansion, there will be incentives for frequent product changes to meet the demands for higher standards of living. Quality standards are improved as a result of intensive com-

---

[40] See Edith Penrose, *The Theory of Growth of the Firm* (Blackwell, 1959). Also R. Marris, *The Theory of 'Managerial' Capitalism* (Macmillan, 1964).

petition. During recessions the opposite tendency is observed: changes in products are less frequent, and, when undertaken, they are often used as a method of 'hidden' quality deterioration. Price controls during inflationary periods have normally the same effect. Firms tend to absorb the increasing costs by lowering the quality of their product, in an attempt to keep prices within the reach of the decreasing purchasing power of the mass of consumers.

Finally, the behaviour of rivals and the past performance of the firm will affect its product strategy. The decisions of the firm are shaped in the light of its present position in the industry, which is the result of its past actions and the rivals' reactions. Product leadership, if attained, tends to have cumulative effects. The initiating firm will tend to keep ahead of rivals, by continuous R & D activities. The imitators of successful products usually survive, but lag behind the innovating leader. This tends to be the typical pattern in markets where one or a small number of firms have large R & D departments. These produce the new ideas, which lead to patented inventions. The other firms which buy the right to use the patent may introduce some changes to their product, which may give them some breathing-space. However, the initiator will usually keep abreast of product innovation.

VII. EFFECTS OF PRODUCT VARIATION ON MARKET CONDUCT AND PERFORMANCE

A. Product Competition and Quality Standards

It is generally agreed that the impressive rise in the living standards over the post-war period would not have been possible without the development of new products and the improvement of existing ones.

However, quality standards have deteriorated over the same period, especially in consumer-goods industries. It has been argued that this deterioration of quality is to a large extent attributable to excessive product competition. The argument runs as follows. Imitation of successful products leads to *product inflation*: that is, a proliferation of close substitutes. This reduces market shares, prohibits the exploitation of economies of scale, and leads inevitably to increased costs. If prices are rigid (either by industry practice or government control), firms will be coerced to lower the quality of their product, especially in ways which are not obvious to the buyer. Limits to product deterioration are set, of course, by technological factors (for example, minimum strength of wires and fibres, rubber content in rubber tyres and tubes), by laws which are legislated for the protection of consumers, by such knowledge that consumers have and can use, and by considerations of the reputation and goodwill of the firms. However, intensive product competition may well be expected to result in a lowering of quality standards, if the higher cost associated with this policy cannot be passed on to the consumer by charging a higher price for various reasons.

This of course does not mean that new products are always worse products than the existing ones. Furthermore, a certain degree of quality deterioration may be desirable in some cases. For example, a decrease in the durability of materials used in clothing and other fashion goods is probably the 'second-best' alternative, given the extremely short life cycle of these items.

In summary. Intensive product competition usually results in lower quality standards, as the high-quality, high-price products are competed out of the market by low-price, low-quality varieties. Whether this is a desirable result from society's point of view depends on the type of product and on one's subjective concept of what are the 'right social priorities'.

B.   Product Diversity and Technical Progress

It is often argued that product competition enhances R & D activities and thus leads to rapid technical progress and higher rates of growth.

Although a strong correlation has been observed between product diversity and the R & D activities of large firms, one cannot deduce from it the direction of causality. Furthermore, in many of the industries where the phenomenon of product inflation has been obviously excessive (cosmetics, various drugs, soaps and detergents, soft drinks, gum and sweets, fashion goods) the rate of technical advance has been negligible. It is likely that there is a two-way causation between product diversity and technical progress in most industries where the latter has been fast, but a high degree of product variability does not always imply high innovative activity.

C.   Product Diversity and Consumers' Expenditure

Product proliferation has been strongly attacked by Galbraith (among others),[41] who has argued that this policy of firms encourages excessive consumption. As society becomes more affluent, new commodities satisfy less important needs, with the result of wasteful use of resources and promotion of materialistic aspirations in individuals. There is a lot of truth in this argument, as evidenced by the number of available close substitutes in all consumer-goods industries. We will discuss further Galbraith's thesis in Chapter 2 in connection with advertising, which he considers as the sustaining factor of this 'undesirable' development.

D.   Product Variation and Industry Concentration

Some writers have argued that product competition results in the elimination of the weaker firms and the increase of the monopoly power of the survivors. For

[41] J. K. Galbraith, *The Affluent Society* (Houghton Mifflin, 1958).

example, Menge maintains that the frequent style changes in the automobile industry eliminated the smaller car producers and resulted in the concentration of car production in four firms. As we said in section III, Menge's analysis is limited. Although in principle style changes may increase the minimum optimal scale of production, the conditions which must be fulfilled for this result to occur are difficult to visualise in real-world situations.

Industrial concentration is fundamentally influenced by the conditions of entry. Bain in his study of the barriers to entry in twenty manufacturing industries of the USA found that product differentiation was the most important barrier to entry.[42] However, his study examined entry by completely new firms, which naturally are faced by preference barriers, created by consumers' brand loyalty. In the modern business world the typical entrant is not a new firm, but an already existing firm, established in the same or a different industry. Product differentiation under these conditions enhances rather than deters entry. An existing firm is likely to be successful in entering a new market by launching a product differentiated in some respect(s) from the products of other firms in this market. In conclusion, product variation may not have been a deterrent to entry.

E.   Product Variation and Competition

As we said in section I, product changes have become the most important weapon of competition in oligopolistic markets. There is some evidence supporting the Schumpeterian hypothesis, that product competition (especially from entry of large firms in a market) erodes the monopoly profits of established firms. However, little is known about the lags involved in the product-competition process. Furthermore, it is not known whether this method of elimination of excess profits is the most effective or the most efficient. From casual observation it seems that the process of product competition is costly, and may have wasted a considerable amount of resources.

F.   Product Variation and Price Competition

Product changes have been used increasingly as an alternative weapon to price competition, which is avoided by firms for various reasons (see pp. 2–4).

Product changes are a common method for absorbing changes in cost conditions, when firms cannot or do not want to change the existing price structure. Thus product variation can explain the observed price rigidity in certain markets.

It is also probable that product variations have slowed down the inflationary process in many markets, though such changes are often used as an excuse for a price rise.

[42] J. Bain, *Barriers to New Competition* (Harvard University Press, 1956).

G.   Product Variation and Economies of Scale

Product changes are usually associated with shifts in the cost curve. However, such changes may also result in an increase of the scale of production, thus allowing the reaping of economies which could not be realised at lower levels of output. New varieties of products may appeal to untapped segments of the market and create the demand required for efficient production. Beyond a certain point, however, an increase in the rate of product changes results in higher costs, which will affect the quality standards and/or the price of the commodity.

It should be evident from the above discussion that much work has to be done before we can draw any definite conclusion regarding the effects of product variations on market conduct and performance.

2. The Advertising Decision of the Firm

I. INTRODUCTORY REMARKS

Advertising and other selling activities aim at shifting the demand curve for the product of the firm and making it less elastic.

Advertising does not alter the product. Its aim is to change demand conditions, to change the position, the shape and the slope of the firm's demand curve.

Advertising is only one means of sales promotion. Another major promotional technique is sales networks (salesmen). A third type of selling effort is the distribution of free samples, coupons, special offers and similar techniques for attracting customers. These selling activities are substitutable for each other, in varying degree, depending on the type of the product (consumer goods, producer goods, etc.), as well as on the type of buyer (consumer, other firms, government, institutional buyers, etc.). In general, advertising is more important for consumer goods. For producers' goods advertising can do little, since industrial buyers have special purchasing departments with skilled personnel, capable of evaluating the products they buy.

Of all the selling activities advertising is the most controversial and has attracted a lot of academic and non-academic interest since the 1960s. The controversy is centred on the effects of advertising on resource allocation and consumer welfare. These effects will be discussed in detail in section VII.

A. Advertising as a Weapon of Competition

Advertising has become a major means of competition in the modern oligopolistic world.

In pure competition selling expenses are irrelevant. The price is given, and the firm can sell (at that price) any amount of output it wishes. So there is no incentive for firms to advertise.

In pure monopoly, selling expenses can have some use. The monopolist may advertise in order to reduce the market elasticity of demand, raise his price and increase his profits. In general, however, the monopolist does not have much incentive to advertise.

In monopolistic competition advertising is one of the major means of product differentiation. Advertising is assumed to decrease the price elasticity of each firm's demand, allowing it to raise its price and increase its profits. However, monopolistic competition is not a relevant model for real-world situations.[1]

It is in oligopoly that advertising is a particularly attractive competitive weapon. The reasons have been discussed briefly on pages 2–4. Advertising helps the introduction of new products. It involves lags (competitors can undertake counter-advertising, but this takes time, and in any case it is not certain that they will be equally successful). Price competition can lead to price wars, from which all rivals lose, while advertising by all may increase the over-all market, thus allowing larger sales for all firms even though shares may not be affected. However, because all oligopolists have the same incentives for advertising, a substantial part of it becomes self-cancelling: defensive advertising has become a routine for oligopolists. Advertising has become essential for maintaining one's market share. The advertising largely cancels itself out mutually among the firms, while market shares remain virtually constant in the long run (for the large corporations).

B.   Advertising Expenditures

Advertising in its present form is a relatively new activity. It emerged in the 1920s with the spreading of the radio and the increase of magazine circulation. It boomed in the post-war period (1945–55) with the advent of television, and has grown at a fast rate ever since.

Tables 2.1 and 2.2 show the advertising expenditure in the United Kingdom and the USA for some selected years. From the data of these tables is is seen that both in the United Kingdom and the USA advertising expenses have increased by approximately 9 per cent annually over the last twenty years.

In the USA advertising increased from $5 billion in 1949 to $28 billion in 1975. After adjusting for the price changes, advertising expenditures in real terms more than tripled in the post-war period as compared with the doubling of real personal consumption expenditures.[2] In the United Kingdom the increase in advertising expenditure has been more spectacular. It reached £590 million in 1965 and, compared with £121 million in 1948, this was a rise of 388 per cent over the period 1948–65. Despite its faster rate of increase, advertising expenditure in the United Kingdom was 2.6 per cent of consumers' expenditure, as compared with 3.5 per cent in the USA in the year 1965.

---

[1] See A. Koutsoyiannis, *Modern Microeconomics*, 2nd edn (Macmillan, 1979) ch. 8.
[2] J. Backman, *Advertising and Competition* (New York University Press, 1966).

Table 2.1   United Kingdom: advertising expenditures

	1948	1956	1960	1962	1964	1965
Advertising expenditure (£m.)	121	309	457	488	568	590
Advertising as % of net national income	2.0	1.8	2.2	2.1	2.1	2.1
Advertising as % of consumers' expenditure	2.2	2.2	2.7	2.6	2.7	2.6

Source: The Economists Advisory Group, *The Economics of Advertising* (London, 1967), p. 15.

Table 2.2   USA: advertising expenditures

	1949	1958	1960	1965	1975
Advertising expenditures ($ m.)	5,000	10,300	11,960	15.256	28,320
Advertising as % of net national income	2.6	2.8	2.9	2.7	2.3
Advertising as % of consumers' expenditure	2.8	3.6	3.9	3.5	2.9

Sources: US Census Bureau, *Statistical Abstract of the United States*; F. M. Scherer, *Industrial Market Structure and Economic Performance* (Rand McNally, 1970) p. 326; W. G. Shepherd, *The Economics of Industrial Organization* (Prentice-Hall, 1979), p. 373; *Economic Report of the President* (Washington, D.C., 1977).

C.   Advertising by Media

Advertising expenditures both in the United Kingdom and in the USA have increased over time for all major media (newspapers and magazines, radio and television). However, the largest growth has been observed for TV advertising, whose share in total advertising has increased at the expense of all other media. Still, advertising in newspapers is by far the most important way of advertising. This is due to classified advertising, and the increased use (in the USA) of local newspapers by local advertisers, particularly the retail trade (see Table 2.3).

The fast increase in TV advertising in particular has been the main source of the controversial issue related to the extent to which advertising is 'useful', 'beneficial' or 'desirable' for consumers' welfare and resource allocation. Traditional theory distinguishes two forms of advertising: *informative*, which aims at supplying consumers with information about existing alternative products (their price, quality, conditions of sale); and *persuasive*, which aims at manipulating the tastes of consumers and making them *believe* that some products are 'superior'

Table 2.3   Advertising expenditures by media

Media	United Kingdom		USA								
	Year 1965		Year 1960		Year 1965		Year 1970		Year 1977	
	£ million	%	$ million	%	$ million	%	$ million	%	$ million	%
Newspapers	220	37.3	3,681	30.8	5,162	33.8	8,450	29.8	12,443	32.7
Radio	2	0.3	693	5.8	917	6.0	2,020	7.1	2,586	6.7
Television	106	18.0	1,627	13.6	2,515	16.5	5,325	18.8	7,612	20.0
Magazines	62	10.5	909	7.6	1,199	7.9	1,475	5.2	2,162	5.6
Direct mailings (catalogues, free samples)	65	11.0	1,830	15.3	2,324	15.2	4,125	14.6	5,333	14.0
Other	135	22.9	3,219	26.9	3,139	20.6	6,925	24.5	7,924	21.0
Total	£590m.	100%	$11,959m.	100%	$15,256m.	100%	$28,320m.	100%	38,060	100%

Sources: US Census Bureau, *Statistical Abstract of the United States*; F. M. Scherer, *Industrial Market Structure and Economic Performance* (Rand McNally, 1980), p. 377; P. Doyle, 'Economic Aspects of Advertising: A Survey', *Economic Journal*, 1968.

in some sense to others.[3] There is consensus that the informational part of advertising is socially beneficial, up to the point at which its marginal social benefits equal its cost. Informative advertising increases or improves the consumers' 'stock of knowledge', which is imperfect or becomes obsolete with invention and innovation (new products are brought to the attention of the public). By spreading valuable knowledge, informative advertising widens the choice of consumers, enhances competition and improves the allocation of resources. Persuasive advertising, on the other hand, attempts to change consumers' preferences by stressing the 'image' of a product rather than facts (price, quality, etc.). Thus persuasive advertising is wasteful, because it impairs consumer choice and leads to misallocation of resources.

While the distinction between informative and persuasive advertising is theoretically valid, in practice it is difficult to implement and measure, because almost all advertising messages have both elements. Some crude estimate of the informative content of total advertising expenditure has been attempted by various writers both in the United Kingdom and the USA. In Table 2.4 we show a breakdown of the advertising outlays for 1965 which is often used for determining the informational content of advertising.

Table 2.4   Advertising expenditures in 1965

Type of advertisement	United Kingdom		USA	
	£ m.	%	$ m.	%
Classified advertising	57	9.7	1,200	7.9
Financial, business, technical	46	7.8	705	4.6
Sales promotion (catalogues, samples, exhibitions)	121	20.5	2,321	15.2
Display advertising (TV, magazine, press, posters)	336	56.9	9,870	64.7
Administration, etc.	30	5.1	1,160	7.6
Total	£590m.	100%	$15,256m.	100%

Sources: P. Doyle, 'Economic Aspects of Advertising', *Economic Journal*, 1968; F. M. Scherer, *Industrial Market Structure and Economic Performance* (Rand McNally, 1970), p. 326.

There is a general consensus that classified advertisements and financial, business and technical published messages are basically informative. Most writers

---

[3] See E. Chamberlin, *The Theory of Monopolistic Competition* (Harvard University Press, 1933); Joan Robinson, *The Economics of Imperfect Competition* (Macmillan, 1933). Alfred Marshall made a similar distinction, using the terms 'constractive' and 'combative' expenditure respectively; see R. R. Kerton, 'Consumer Search Capital', *Journal of Public Policy*, 1981.

would also concede that sales promotion expenditures are predominantly informative. The controversial items are display advertising (on TV, magazines, newspapers, outdoor posters and signs, and the like) and the administration expenses, which include such expenditures as the cost of corporate advertising departments, art work and engravings, etc. Scherer argues that display advertising is at least partly informative, so that, over all, 'half of all advertising expenditures cover messages of a primarily informative character, while the other half serve largely to persuade'.[4] It would be dangerous, however, to conclude, as Scherer implies, that half of the advertising expenditures are beneficial to buyers because they are informative in their nature. Before drawing conclusions one should examine whether the information is 'excessive' in the Kaldor sense:[5] that is, whether information provided by advertising messages is more than buyers desire (and hence wasteful). Furthermore, one should examine the degree to which the information provided by advertising messages is accurate and helpful to the buyer. We will discuss these issues in detail in section VII.

D. Advertising Expenditures by Product

The most common measure of advertising intensity is the ratio of advertising outlays to the value of sales (the advertising–sales ratio).

In 1965 the most heavily advertised products in the USA were:[6] (a) drugs and cosmetics, (b) soaps and cleaners, (c) soft drinks, and (d) gum and candies. For the above four groups of products the advertising–sales ratio exceeded 10 per cent in 1965.

Relatively less heavily advertised (with an A/S ratio between 5 and 10 per cent) were: (e) cigarettes, (f) foods, (g) liquor, (h) beer.

Even less advertised (with an A/S ratio between 2 and 5 per cent) were: (i) airlines, (j) paper products, (k) photographic equipment.

The least advertised products (with an A/S ratio less than 2 per cent) were: (l) automobiles, (m) tyres, (n) oil, (o) appliances, (p) chemicals, (q) metals.

The advertising–sales ratio is not a very good indicator of advertising intensity, because it conceals the *absolute amounts* spent on advertising. For example, the less than 2 per cent advertising–sales ratio for automobiles does not reveal the fact that the sales value of cars is a gigantic number, and that even a small percentage of this turnover of car-makers spent on advertising would command a large amount of time on TV and a large space in magazines and newspapers.[7] A more accurate measure of the intensity of advertising would be the frequency of

[4] F. M. Scherer, *Industrial Market Structure and Economic Performance* (Rand McNally, 1970) p. 326.

[5] N. Kaldor, 'The Economic Aspects of Advertising', *Review of Economic Studies*, vol. 18, 1950, p. 20.

[6] Backman, *Advertising and Competition*.

[7] Advertising of automobiles absorbs about $700 million each year; yet because automobile sales are extremely high, this is less than 1 per cent of sales.

messages and their time duration or space occupied in the media. Since the rates charged by the media vary with the time duration (on TV and radio) and the space covered (in magazines and newspapers) it is obvious that the A/S ratio does not represent adequately the intensity of advertising.

Advertising expenditures are heavily concentrated. In 1977 the 100 largest advertisers spent about $9 billion or 27 per cent of the total $33 billion spent on advertising in that year. Table 2.5 shows the advertising expenditures of some of the most intensive advertisers in 1977.

The information of Table 2.5 confirms our earlier observation that the advertising—sales ratio is a misleading indicator of advertising intensity. The absolute

Table 2.5   Selected intensive advertisers, 1977, USA

Ranking in terms of $ spent	Firm/advertiser	Type of product area	Advertising expenditure ($m.)	A/S
1	Proctor & Gamble	Soaps	460.0	5.7
2	General Motors	Autos	312.0	0.5
3	General Foods	Food	300.0	5.6
4	Sears	Merchandising	290.0	1.7
5	K-Mart	Merchandising	210.0	2.1
6	Bristol—Myers	Drugs	203.0	9.3
7	Warner—Lambert	Drugs	201.0	7.9
10	American Home Products	Drugs	171.0	8.7
12	Ford	Autos	157.3	0.6
13	Richardson—Merrell	Drugs	148.8	17.8
15	Mobil Oil	Oil	142.8	0.4
22	McDonald's	Fast foods	122.2	3.8
23	Colgate—Palmolive	Soaps	120.0	3.1
31	Chrysler	Autos	97.4	0.5
32	CBS	Broadcasting	96.3	3.5
37	Gilette	Cosmetics	90.0	5.7
43	Revlon	Cosmetics	80.0	9.9
45	Anheuser—Bush	Brewing	75.4	3.4
48	Kellogg	Cereals	69.8	4.6
62	Avon	Cosmetics	55.0	5.7
73	Nissan	Autos	49.3	*
74	Time Inc.	Magazines	45.9	3.7
75	Volkswagen	Autos	45.5	2.3
78	Toyota	Autos	41.7	*
83	Noxell	Cosmetics	33.3	24.2
87	American Motors	Autos	31.5	*
88	Block Drug	Drugs	31.0	22.8
92	American Airlines	Air travel	28.9	1.2
*	Honda	Autos	20.6	*

* Not available.
Source: adapted from J. V. Koch, *Industrial Organisation and Prices*, 2nd edn (Prentice-Hall, 1980) pp. 301—2.

level of dollars spent implies the following ranking of the various advertised products:

Drugs	$754 million
Autos	$710 million
Soaps and detergents	$580 million
Merchandising (retailing)	$500.0 million
Cosmetics	$258.3 million

The information and discussion of this section gives some idea of the importance of the advertising decision and the extent of the advertising expenditures.

In sections II–V we will present several theoretical models of the advertising decision.

In section VI we will discuss some empirical studies of the advertising decision.

Finally, in section VII we discuss the main effects of advertising.

II. MARGINALISTIC, PROFIT-MAXIMISING MODELS OF THE ADVERTISING DECISION

As we said in the preceding section, advertising is a part of the broader category of 'selling costs', which, apart from advertising, include salaries of personnel in the marketing department of the firm, value of free samples, coupons, and in general all expenses related to the selling effort of the firm. We will concentrate our analysis on advertising expenses, but the results will, in general, be valid for most other items of the broader category of selling costs.

In this section we will present some models of the advertising decision within the framework of the profit-maximisation hypothesis. We will start by a partial-equilibrium model in which price and product (style) are given, and the optimum (profit-maximising) selling expenditure is determined under the usual *ceteris paribus* clause. We will next present a model in which price and advertising expenditures are simultaneously determined, while 'product' is assumed to be given. Finally, we will present a 'general' model in which price, product style and selling expenditure are allowed to vary simultaneously. This approach has analytical advantages. Assuming that the goal of the firm is profit maximisation, the model of 'advertising equilibrium' is relevant in the case where prices are given by industry practice and the product-style decision has been taken at an earlier stage, and the entrepreneur would adjust his selling effort without disturbing the price structure. The model of price and selling-cost adjustments is relevant in situations where the type of the product has been determined by an earlier decision of the firm, and managers are concerned with the determination of the optimal price and optimal selling outlay, so as to attain maximum profit. This situation is quite common with durable commodities. For example, in the auto-mobile industry the style and technical characteristics of the models of every period are determined by a series of decisions taken well in advance of the pricing and advertising decisions of the firm. Although product decisions are not completely independent of pricing decisions, the latter are finalised at a later stage, together with the advertising and other selling decisions of the firm. It should be stressed that the example illustrates the timing of the various decisions. The models of this section assume profit maximisation, an assumption which does not seem to hold in the real world (see Koutsoyiannis, *Modern Microeconomics*). Still, these models provide the stepping-stone for the development of the managerialist models of advertising, as we shall see in section III.

The first two models will be presented initially with diagrams and then in a simple mathematical form. This will facilitate the development of the 'general' model (as well as other models) where a diagrammatic presentation would be too complicated. The mathematical exposition will be presented in smaller print so that the non-mathematically inclined reader can omit it without loss of continuity.

A.   A Simple Model of the Advertising Decision

The first systematic analysis of selling costs was attempted by Chamberlin.[8] However, his exposition is somewhat sketchy, and in some parts inconsistent.[9] The following model is a formalised presentation of Chamberlin's basic ideas.

In this model advertising is the only policy variable of the firm. The type of the product and the price are given by an earlier decision, and the firm is faced with the problem of choosing the advertising outlays, A, so as to maximise its profit.

The assumptions of the model are:

(1) The goal of the firm is profit maximisation.

(2) The type of the product and its price are given, defined by an earlier decision.

(3) Advertising shifts outwards the firm's demand curve, so that at the given price, $\bar{P}$, more output is sold. In other words, advertising increases the quantity demanded, but does not affect the firm's monopoly power, so that it cannot charge a higher price.

(4) To each demand curve there corresponds a given total amount of advertising outlay. In other words, the firm, in order to shift its demand curve at a certain level (position), must incur a specific advertising expenditure. Hence the *average*

---

[8] Chamberlin, *The Theory of Monopolistic Competition*.
[9] See Yale Brozen, 'Entry Barriers: Advertising and Product Differentiation', in *Industrial Concentration: The New Learning*, ed. H. Goldschmid, H. Mann and J. F. Weston (Little, Brown & Co., 1974).

advertising cost curve, associated with the corresponding demand curve, is a hyperbola (like any kind of average fixed cost curve).

(5) The average production cost curve is U-shaped. Production costs are independent of the advertising costs. The latter affect only the demand conditions, but not the production process of the firm, as defined by its production function.

(6) Firms have identical costs and identical demands. (This is a simplifying assumption, which allows the use of a single diagram to show the equilibrium of the firm and the industry.)

(7) Firms act atomistically, each adjusting its advertising outlays independently from the others so as to maximise its profit. This is the basic framework of the monopolistic competition model.

The equilibrium process is shown in Figure 2.1. Without advertising the demand curve of the firm is d_0. The firm is at equilibrium at point e, charging a price $\bar{P}$, and earning excess unit profits equal to ab. With advertising (which gives rise to the average advertising cost AAC) the firm's demand curve shifts to d_1. The summation of the APC and the AAC gives the average total cost (ATC) of the firm. The marginal cost is not affected by the advertising activity of the firm (from assumption 5). The firm is now in equilibrium at e' (where $MC = MR_1$). It sells a larger output $(X_2 > X_1)$ at the given price $\bar{P}$, and realises excess unit profit equal to hg, which is higher than the profit prior to advertising.

If the firm increases its advertising $(AAC_2$ in Figure 2.2), its demand will shift to d_2. While the MC curve remains unaffected, the average total cost is now higher. The firm sells a higher quantity $(X_3 > X_2)$ at the given price, and realises

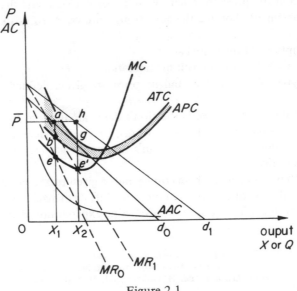

Figure 2.1

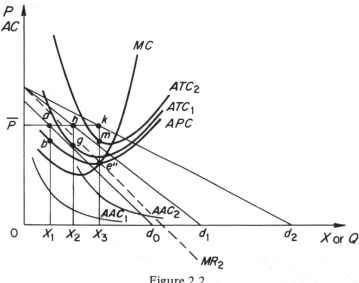

Figure 2.2

a unit profit equal to km. As the various curves are drawn, $km < hg$. Hence the firm has surpassed the advertising level which maximises its per unit profit.

It is easier to show the optimal advertising expenditure, using total cost and total revenue curves. In Figure 2.3 each advertising level generates a higher total revenue and a higher total cost curve. For each advertising level we find the maximum profit, which is the largest (vertical) distance between the corresponding total cost and total revenue curves.

An advertising level of A_1 gives rise to the total curves TR_1 and TC_1, and the total profit $\Pi_1 = AB$. Similarly an advertising outlay of A_2 yields a higher total profit of $\Pi_2 = HG$. A further increase of advertising expenditure (equal to A_3) reduces the total profit ($MK < GH$). In this particular example the optimal advertising expenditure is A_2.

Note that the price remains constant at all levels of advertising. The price is the slope of the line OP in Figure 2.3.

It should be clear that the optimal (profit-maximising) level of advertising depends on the slope of the production cost curve (reflected in the slope of the TC curves in Figure 2.3), and the slope and shift of the demand curve as advertising takes place.

$$*\qquad\qquad *\qquad\qquad *$$

Mathematical presentation of the simple advertising model

The firm wants to maximise its profit

$$\Pi = R - C - A \tag{2.1}$$

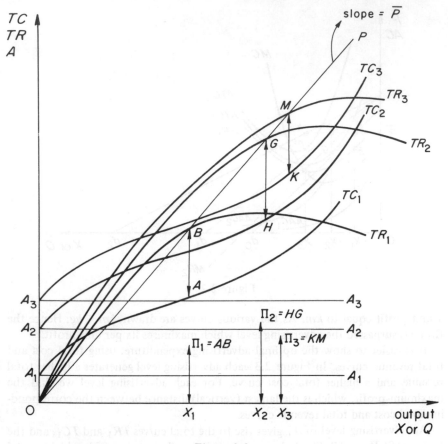

Figure 2.3

where Π = profit

      R = total revenue = PQ

      C = total production cost

      A = total advertising expenditure

From the assumptions of the model, we have:

      (a) $Q = f(P, A)$ (2.2)

or, in a simpler form

    $Q(P, A)$ (2.2a)

$$\frac{\partial Q}{\partial P} < 0; \quad \frac{\partial Q}{\partial A} > 0 \qquad\qquad\qquad\qquad\qquad (2.3)$$

In words, the demand curve is downward-sloping and shifts outwards with advertising.

(b) The price is given, so that

$$\frac{\partial P}{\partial A} = 0 \tag{2.4}$$

(c) The production cost is a function of output, which is a function of advertising.

$$C = g(Q) = g[f(P, A)] \tag{2.5}$$

or, in a simpler form

$$C[Q(P, A)] \tag{2.5a}$$

However, the production cost is not a function of the advertising activity of the firm, so that

$$\frac{\partial C}{\partial A} = 0 \tag{2.6}$$

Given the above assumptions, the profit function may be written in the form

$$\Pi = \bar{P}\,[Q(\bar{P}, A)] - C[Q(\bar{P}, A)] - A \tag{2.7}$$

Since price, $\bar{P}$, and the type of the product are given, the firm has to decide how much to spend on advertising so as to maximise its profit.

The first condition for a maximum requires that the derivative $\partial\Pi/\partial A = 0$.[10]

---

[10] In taking derivatives we will use the following three elementary rules of differentiation:

(i) *Basic rule of differentiation*

If $y = ax^n$, then $y' \equiv \dfrac{dy}{dx} = nax^{n-1}$ $\tag{2.8}$

For example, assume $y \equiv 3x^5$. Then $y' = 15x^4$

(ii) *Multiplication rule of differentiation*

If $y = uv$, where $u = f_1(x)$ and $v = f_2(x)$, then

$y' \equiv \dfrac{dy}{dx} = u\dfrac{dv}{dx} + v\dfrac{du}{dx}$ $\tag{2.9}$

For example, assume $y = \underbrace{(3x + 5 + x^2)}_{u}\ \underbrace{(3x^3 + 2x)}_{v}$

Then $y' = (3x + 5 + x^2)(9x^2 + 2) + (3x^3 + 2x)(3 + 2x)$

(iii) *The 'chain rule' of differentiation (or rule of 'a function of a function')*

If $y = f_1(u)$ and $u = f_2(x)$, then

$y' \equiv \dfrac{dy}{dx} = \dfrac{dy}{du}\dfrac{du}{dx}$ $\tag{2.10}$

For example, assume $y = (5x^4 + 6x^2 + 3x)^3 = u^3$. Then

$y' = (3u^2)\dfrac{d(5x^4 + 6x^2 + 3x)}{dx} = 3(5x^4 + 6x^2 + 3x)^2\,(20x^3 + 12x + x)$

Taking the derivative of (2.7) and equating to zero, we obtain

$$\frac{\partial \Pi}{\partial A} = \left(P \frac{\partial Q}{\partial A} \right) - \left(\frac{\partial C}{\partial Q} \frac{\partial Q}{\partial A} \right) - \frac{\partial A}{\partial A} = 0 \qquad (2.11)$$

Rearranging, we have

$$P \frac{\partial Q}{\partial A} = \left(\frac{\partial C}{\partial Q} \frac{\partial Q}{\partial A} \right) + 1 \qquad (2.12)$$

Note that

$$\frac{\partial A}{\partial A} = \text{marginal cost of advertising} = 1. \qquad (2.13)$$

Also

$$\frac{\partial C}{\partial Q} = \text{marginal production cost} \equiv MC \qquad (2.14)$$

Expression (2.12) can be expressed in terms of elasticity concepts, with which economics students are familiar. Thus, multiplying through expression (2.12) by A/Q, we find

$$P \left(\frac{\partial Q}{\partial A} \frac{A}{Q} \right) = \frac{\partial C}{\partial Q} \left(\frac{\partial Q}{\partial A} \frac{A}{Q} \right) + \frac{A}{Q} \qquad (2.15)$$

The terms in brackets are the advertising elasticity of demand, $\eta_{Q,A}$. Hence we may write

$$P(\eta_{QA}) = \{ MC \, \eta_{QA} \} + \frac{A}{Q}$$

or

$$\eta_{QA} = \left(\frac{MC}{P} \eta_{QA} \right) + \frac{A}{PQ} \qquad (2.16)$$

Noting that $PQ = R$, we may rearrange expression (2.16) to obtain

$$\frac{A}{R} = \eta_{QA} \left(\frac{\bar{P} - MC}{\bar{P}} \right) \qquad (2.17)$$

The term in brackets is known as 'the Lerner index of monopoly power'. It measures the 'power' of the firm to raise its price above the marginal cost.

Thus we may conclude that the firm maximises its profit (given $\bar{P}$ and the style of its product) by setting its advertising–sales ratio (A/R) equal to the advertising elasticity of demand multiplied by the Lerner index of monopoly power.

It is seen from expression (2.17) that the advertising expenditure depends on three factors. (1) *The advertising elasticity of demand*: the greater the responsiveness of consumers to advertising, the greater the advertising expenditure will be. (2) *The firm's sales revenue*: the greater R, the larger the advertising expenditure will be. (3) *The firm's monopoly power*: the greater the power of the firm to raise price above marginal cost, the greater the advertising expenditure will be.

It can be shown that Lerner's index is equal to the inverse of the price elasticity of demand:[11]

$$\frac{P - MC}{P} = \frac{1}{\eta_{QP}} \qquad (2.18)$$

Hence the equilibrium condition (expression 2.17) may be written as follows:

$$\frac{A}{R} = \frac{\eta_{QA}}{\eta_{QP}} \qquad (2.19)$$

or

$$\frac{A}{R} = \frac{(dQ/Q)/(dA/A)}{(dQ/Q)/(dP/P)}$$

and

$$\frac{A}{R} = \frac{dP/P}{dA/A} = \eta_{PA} \qquad (2.20)$$

We may now state the equilibrium condition as follows. The firm maximises its profit by setting its advertising–sales ratio equal to the elasticity of price with respect to advertising. Expression (2.20) implies that the greater the sensitivity of the price to advertising expenditures, the greater will be the advertising–sales ratio of the profit-maximising firm.

*   *   *

Advertising as a rule of thumb

It has been observed that firms in practice set their advertising budgets according to the rule of thumb

$$A = kR \qquad (2.21)$$

[11] PROOF

$$\frac{P - MC}{P} = 1 - \frac{MC}{P}$$

But

$$MC = MR = P\left(1 - \frac{1}{\eta_{QP}}\right)$$

Hence

$$\frac{P - MC}{P} = 1 - \frac{P(1 - 1/\eta_{QP})}{P} = \frac{1}{\eta_{QP}}$$

QED

that is, advertising is set equal to a proportion, k, of the firm's sales revenue. (This is known as 'the percentage-of-sales' rule of thumb.) The problem then arises whether this behaviour is compatible with the profit-maximisation hypothesis. Some writers[12] argue that the behaviour implied by the above rule of thumb 'proves' that firms are profit maximisers. It is apparent that this is not necessarily true. Expression (2.21) implies that the advertising—sales ratio is constant:

$$\frac{A}{R} = k$$

From expression (2.17) we have

$$\frac{A}{R} = \eta_{QA} \left(\frac{P - MC}{P} \right)$$

Under the assumptions of the simple advertising model, the Lerner index is constant, given that the price is constant, $\bar{P}$, and $MC \neq f(A)$. However, the elasticity of demand with respect to advertising is not necessarily constant. Rasmussen[13] argues that η_{QA} is a variable whose determinants are:

(1) *The amount of money already spent on advertising.* We said that advertising shifts the demand curve, thus increasing the quantity demanded at the given price, $\bar{P}$. The relationship between advertising expenditure and quantity demanded is likely to be as implied by the curve AE (advertising expenditure curve) in Figure 2.4.[14]

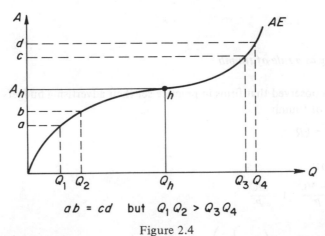

$$ab = cd \quad \text{but} \quad Q_1 Q_2 > Q_3 Q_4$$

Figure 2.4

[12] See, for example, R. Schmalensee, *The Economics of Advertising* (North-Holland, 1972).

[13] A. Rasmussen, 'The Determination of Advertising Expenditure', *Journal of Marketing*, 1952, pp. 439—46.

[14] See ibid.

The shape of the advertising expenditure curve implies that, initially, advertising shifts the demand at an increasing rate. However, beyond a certain level of advertising (A_h in Figure 2.4) demand increases at a decreasing rate. The economic meaning of the sigmoid shape is the following. At low levels of advertising expenditure, its effect on the quantity demanded is negligible, as the number of advertising messages and/or the number of media is small. As advertising increases, consumers are attracted in great numbers. However, beyond some level of advertising it becomes more difficult to pursuade new consumers to buy the firm's brand. In other words, up to a certain level of advertising, the advertising elasticity of demand, $\eta_{QA} = (dQ/Q)/(dA/A)$ increases, but eventually decreases.

(2) *The η_{QA} depends on the quantity sold (demanded).* This is a corollary of the first determinant, and needs no further explanation.

(3) *The type of commodity.* The η_{QA} is greater for luxuries than for necessities. It is also larger for new products than for old. It is larger for commodities for which few precise claims can be made by the firm (due to the technology of the product). It is greater for low-priced goods: if goods are high-priced, then buyers will not rely on advertising for information, but will undertake direct search. η_{QA} is greater for frequently bought goods. Finally, η_{AQ} is smaller for non-durables.

(4) *The share of market of the firm.* The greater the share, the less the η_{QA}.

(5) *The advertising reactions of competitors.* If rival firms counter-advertise, the initiating firm's advertising is likely to be less effective.

(6) *The cyclical phase of the economy*, or, we may say, *the income elasticity of the good.* Advertising has shown a clear pro-cyclical pattern over time, increasing in booms and declining in recessions.

Since η_{QA} changes, if the firm adheres to a constant A/R ratio, it most probably does not maximise its profit.

B.   Buchanan's Advertising—Price Model[15]

In this model the type of the product is given, and the firm chooses the advertising expenditure *and* the price which maximise its profit.

The assumptions of the model are as follows:

(1) The goal of the firm is profit maximisation.

(2) Product is given, defined by an earlier decision of the firm.

(3) The firm can sell a certain quantity without any advertising. Furthermore, it is assumed that there is a certain minimum selling expenditure below which it has no effect on the level of sales. Above this minimum level, advertising outlay yields initially increasing returns and subsequently decreasing returns. Increasing returns to advertising imply a situation in which an increase in advertising expenditure leads to an increase in sales at a faster rate (at any given price). Diminishing

[15] See N. S. Buchanan, 'Advertising Expenditures', *Journal of Political Economy*, 1942, pp. 537–57.

returns imply that an increase in advertising expenditure results in an increase in sales but at a decreasing rate. Thus, given the price, an increase in the level of advertising will always shift the demand curve to the right, initially at an increasing rate, but subsequently at a declining rate. In summary, demand is a positive non-linear function of the level of advertising expenditure, as shown in Figure 2.4.

(4) There is a given level of advertising associated with any particular demand curve. Thus the *average advertising cost* (corresponding to the particular demand curve) is a rectangular hyperbola, similar to all other fixed costs of the firm.

(5) Average production costs are U-shaped. (The analysis, however, would not be substantially altered if the production cost per unit of output is assumed constant.) (See below, pp. 78–9.)

(6) It is assumed that the firm acts in isolation from its rivals. Furthermore, it is assumed that all rivals act identically, changing advertising and selling expenditure concurrently (but without collusion). This behaviour is consistent with the assumption that all firms have identical costs and identical demands. From these assumptions it follows that firms have equal market shares.

(7) In the short run there is no entry. The number of firms is such that abnormal profits are earned. Firms make adjustments of their price and selling expenditures so as to maximise their profit.

(8) The firm is assumed to have complete knowledge of the effectiveness of advertising in shifting the demand for its product, and of the advertising cost curve. That is, the firm is assumed to know its shifting demand and its shifting cost curves with certainty. It is also assumed that the firm considers all possible pairs of demand and cost curves associated with the possible levels of advertising, that for each demand–cost pair it estimates the optimum level of price and output (that price–output level which maximises profit for the corresponding advertising level), and that it finally chooses among these optima the one that yields the highest profit.

(9) It is assumed that consumers react 'rationally' to the advertising campaigns of firms, and do not change brand loyalties, since all firms indulge in the same selling efforts concurrently. Shares are constant as advertising takes place.

(10) Technology is given, and the prices of inputs are fixed.

Short-run equilibrium in Buchanan's model

The number of firms is less than that required for elimination of abnormal profits. Each will adjust its price and advertising so as to attain maximum profit. Entry does not take place in the short run. Finally, it is assumed that total market (industry demand) expands by the concurrent advertising of all the firms in the industry.

Under these conditions we can show the equilibrium adjustments in a single figure. (At equilibrium all firms will have reached identical solutions with equal price and equal shares, and will be earning abnormal profits).

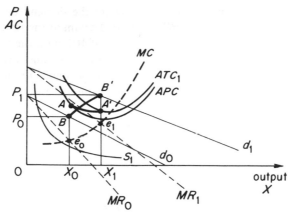

AA' is the Average Advertising Option *Cost* curve of the firm
BB' is the Average Advertising Option *Revenue* curve of the firm

Figure 2.5

In Figure 2.5 let d_0 be the demand curve confronting the firm with zero advertising. The corresponding marginal revenue curve is MR_0 and the average and marginal production costs are APC and MC respectively. The equilibrium of the firm is defined by the intersection of MR_0 and MC (point e_0 in Figure 2.5). The quantity and price is X_0 and P_0 respectively. As we have drawn the curves, the firm suffers losses, since the average production cost is higher than the price. (The loss is equal to AB per unit of output.)

Assume now that the firm attempts to improve its position by advertising. By incurring advertising expenses equal to S_1 it induces a shift of the demand curve (and the MR curve) to d_1 (and MR_1). Given that the advertising outlay is a fixed amount (S_1), the average advertising curve is a rectangular hyperbola, which will give rise to total average cost curve ATC_1 when added to the APC. However, neither APC nor the marginal cost curve (MC) are affected by advertising. The new equilibrium of the firm is determined by the intersection of the given MC with the new (shifted) marginal revenue curve MR_1 (point e_1 in Figure 2.5). With advertising outlay S_1 the firm will maximise its profit by producing X_1 and selling it at price P_1.

This process may be repeated with higher advertising expenditures. Thus there will be a whole family of demand curves (and related MR curves) higher to the right, corresponding to larger advertising expenditures ($S_1 < S_2, \ldots, < S_n$). The latter will form a family of average advertising costs (hyperbolas) which, when added to the production cost, will give a family of average total cost curves ($ATC_2, ATC_3, \ldots, ATC_n$). Each ATC will lie higher and to the right of the preceding one. The increasing advertising expenditures, however, will not affect the marginal cost curve (MC), which is determined by the production cost only. Once it is decided to make advertising expenses of a certain amount, the rectangular hyperbola of the average advertising cost, S_i, does not affect the marginal cost. The only effect that S_i has is to generate the demand curve d_i and the corresponding marginal revenue, MR_i. The equilibrium of the firm for each level of advertising, S_i, is defined by the intersection of MR_i with the given MC curve. We may locate the optimal price–output pairs corresponding to each advertising level by the points of intersection of the successive marginal revenue curves with the marginal cost curve. Such points are, for example, the points e, e_1, e_2 in Figure 2.6.

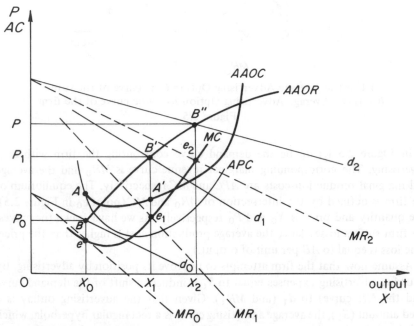

$AAOC$ = average advertising option *cost* curve
$AAOR$ = average advertising option *revenue* curve
Figure 2.6

If we join all the equilibrium prices corresponding to the different advertising levels, we obtain the locus of equilibrium average revenues of the firm (associated with the different advertising expenditure levels). We will call this curve the *average advertising option revenue curve (AAOR)*. Each point on the $AAOR$ is the point on a particular demand curve, generated by a corresponding advertising expenditure, at which maximum profit is attained, given this specific level of advertising outlay of the firm.

If we join all the points on the average total cost curves, corresponding to the profit-maximising price–output solution for each level of advertising, we obtain the locus of unit costs associated with each advertising option. We will call this curve the *average advertising option cost curve (AAOC)*. Each point on the $AAOC$ belongs to an average total cost curve: it is that point corresponding to the profit-maximising price—output combination associated with the relevant level of advertising.

It is important to discuss the shape and the position of the *AAOR* and the *AAOC* curves. The shape and the position of these curves are determined by two factors: first, the effect of advertising on the demand curve for the product of the firm (whether it becomes more elastic or less elastic as it gradually shifts to the right with the increasing levels of advertising expenditures); second, the behaviour of the production cost and the average total cost as the firm increases its output to meet the increased demand following the increase in advertising expenditure.

Let us examine the *AAOC* and the *AAOR* curves in some detail.

The shape and position of the AAOC curve

(a) *Shape of the AAOC curve.* The *AAOC* curve will be U-shaped given the assumption of a U-shaped average production cost curve. As advertising increases, there will be two effects on the unit cost of the firm. First, the average total cost curve shifts upwards, showing that with advertising unit costs increase at all levels of output. Second, the amount of output increases (due to the shift in demand), and hence the firm moves along the (shifted, higher) average total cost curve, so that unit costs will fall. If initially there are strong technical economies of production, the second effect will more than offset the first, so that the *AAOC* curve will decline. Eventually, however, technical economies are exhausted and the *AAOC* curve turns up, for two reasons: because of increasing advertising (which shifts upwards the *ATC* curve), and (at some point) because of increasing production costs. In Figure 2.7 we see that with advertising expenditures S_1 the average total cost curve shifts upwards (as shown by the ATC_1 curve). If output were to remain at the level X_0, the unit costs would increase by AM. However, advertising shifts the demand curve outwards (d_1), and as output increases (to X_1) unit costs fall to A'. The fall in costs (movement along the ATC_1 curve from M to A') is greater than the increase in costs (by AM) due to advertising. Hence the *AAOC* declines, as shown by the segment AA' in figure 2.7. However, with the increased advertising S_2, the increase in unit costs (by $A'L$) is stronger than the decline ('sliding' from L to A'') in costs from production economies, so that the *AAOC* curve turns upwards (segment $A'A''$ in Figure 2.7).

(b) *Position of the AAOC curve.* The position of the *AAOC* curve is affected by the entry or exit of firms in the industry. The curve shifts upwards to the left as new firms enter the industry and the market share of each rival declines at any one price. This is shown in Figure 2.8. With entry, the demand curves of the firm (associated with the different levels of advertising) shift downwards to the left $(d'_1, d'_2,$ etc.), while the *ATC* curves remain unchanged. As a result of the smaller demand after entry, the firm 'slides backwards' on its *ATC* curves, and the *AAOC* curve shifts to the position AGG' in Figure 2.8.

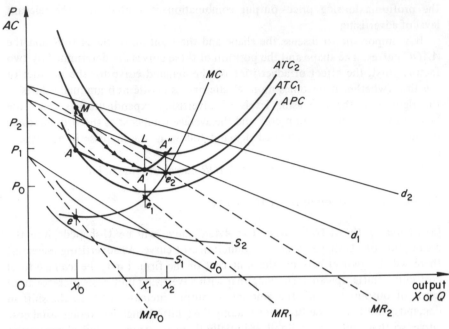

Figure 2.7

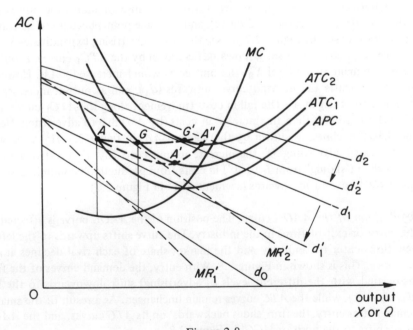

Figure 2.8

Similarly, the *AAOC* curve shifts downwards with exit of firms from the industry.

The shape and position of the AAOR curve

(a) *The shape of the AAOR curve.* The *AAOR* curve will in general have a positive slope, because of the change in the price elasticity as the demand curve shifts with advertising. It can be shown that if the (linear) demand curve shifts outwards and becomes flatter, then the elasticity decreases.* This means that advertising will increase the monopoly power of the firm, enabling it to charge a higher price.[16] As price rises with advertising, the *AAOR* curve (being the locus of the profit-maximising prices at the various levels of output) will have a positive slope. (Note that in Figure 2.6 we have drawn the *AAOR* rising continuously. Thus we have ruled out the possibility of a reduction in price as a result of increased advertising.)

*   *   *

* PROOF

The equation of a linear demand curve is

$$Q = a - bP \tag{1}$$

The elasticity at price P is

$$\eta = \frac{dQ}{dP} \times \frac{P}{Q}$$

But $dQ/dP = -b$. Hence

$$\eta = -b \left(\frac{P}{a - bP} \right) = \frac{-bP}{a - bP} \tag{2}$$

where a = intercept on the Q-axis
       b = slope (w.r.t. the Q-axis)

From (2) it is apparent that if a increases, then η decreases. Similarly if $|b|$ decreases (i.e. the demand curve becomes flatter), then η decreases.

For example, assume $Q = 50 - 2P$. This is shown by the line d_1 in Figure 2.9. If the demand shifts to d_2, the intercept increases to 100, but the slope remains

---

[16] It is conceivable, however, that the shift and change of slope of the demand curve are such that the elasticity increases, so that price falls (after the advertising has taken place). This will cause the *AAOR* curve to turn downwards. However, this cannot continue indefinitely, because there is a limit to the increase of elasticity, reached when $\eta = \infty$: that is, when the demand curve becomes a horizontal line. At this point (i.e. when $\eta = \infty$) the *AAOC* stops falling. Further increases in advertising shift the (horizontal) demand upwards, and, given $MC > 0$, price will rise. Thus eventually the *AAOR* curve will turn upwards.

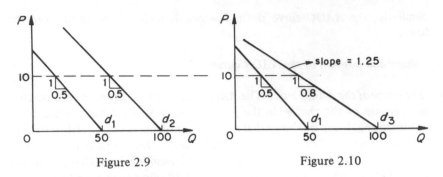

Figure 2.9   Figure 2.10

constant, so that d_2 is parallel to d_1. The elasticity at, say, $P = 10$ on d_1 is

$$\eta_1 = (-2)\frac{(10)}{50 - 2(10)} = \frac{-20}{30} = -\frac{2}{3} = -0.66$$

and on d_2

$$\eta_2 = (-2)\frac{(10)}{100 - 2(10)} = \frac{-20}{80} = -\frac{1}{4} = -0.25$$

i.e. $\eta_2 < \eta_1$.

Consider next d_3 in Figure 2.10, where the intercept has increased to 100 and the demand curve has become flatter, with $|b| = 1.25$. The elasticity at $P = 10$ on d_3 is

$$\eta_3 = -1.25\frac{(10)}{100 - 1.25(10)} = \frac{-12.5}{87.5} = -0.14$$

that is, the price elasticity (η_3) has further decreased.

            *   *   *

(b) *The position of the AAOR curve.* The position of the *AAOR* curve is affected by the number of firms in the industry. With the entry of new firms to the industry, the demand curve of each firm shifts backwards as the market is shared among a larger number of rival firms. Hence, with entry, the *AAOR* curve shifts downwards to the right. This is shown in Figure 2.11. Entry shifts the *AAOC* curve from BB'' to BH''.

Similarly, if there is exit of firms, the share of each one of the remaining firms will increase and the *AAOR* curve will shift upwards to the left.

The relationship between the AAOC and AAOR curves

We made the assumption of initially increasing returns to advertising but subsequently decreasing returns. This assumption seems plausible in most real-world situations. At the initial stages of advertising a firm can fairly easily attract

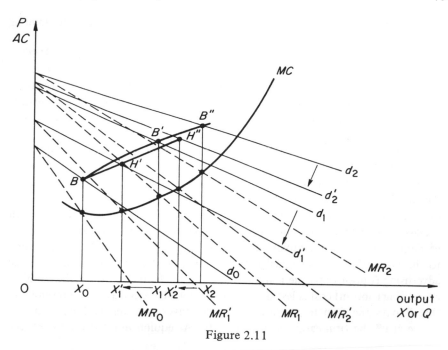

Figure 2.11

additional buyers (not previously in the market), so that the shift in demand is faster than the shift in average total cost. Consequently, over the range of increasing returns to advertising, the distance between the *AAOC* and *AAOR* curves will be increasing. At larger levels of output, however, it becomes increasingly difficult to attract additional customers by additional advertising. Thus, eventually, increasing amounts of advertising bring in additional buyers at a decreasing pace. Thus the *AAOC* curve rises steeply and the distance between this curve and the *AAOR* curve decreases, until the *AAOC curve cuts the AAOR* curve from below. Beyond that point the *AAOR* curve lies below the *AAOC* curve.[17]

The marginal curves in Buchanan's model

Given that we assumed the *AAOC* and the *AAOR* curves to be continuous, we may derive for each of them a *marginal* (or 'incremental') curve.

Recall, from elementary principles, that (a) to each 'average curve' there corresponds a marginal curve; (b) if the average curve is rising, the corresponding marginal curve will lie above it, while if the average curve is falling, the corresponding marginal will lie below it; (c) if the average curve is U-shaped, the

---

[17] Note that the *AAOC* and *AAOR* curves may intersect at more than one point. This would occur if, as advertising outlays increase, the firm adopts different methods of advertising which open up segments of the market previously untapped. For example, the switching from a local TV station to a national TV network might have this effect. Thus the distance between the two curves may widen again before it eventually declines.

marginal will also be U-shaped, while if the average is concave, the corresponding marginal will have a similar shape.

In Buchanan's model the 'marginal advertising option revenue' curve (*MAOR*) shows *the rate of change* of price (average revenue) resulting from the increase in advertising. Similarly, the 'marginal advertising option cost' curve (*MAOC*) shows *the rate of change* of the cost per unit of output as a result of increasing advertising. In other words, the marginal curves show the slope of the *AAOR* and *AAOC* curves respectively as output expands due to advertising.

Part of the *MAOC* and the *MAOR* curves are drawn in Figure 2.12. Given the shapes of the *AAOR* and *AAOC* curves, the respective marginal curves must intersect. The point of intersection of the *MAOC* and *MAOR* curves defines the equilibrium of the firm. At this point price, output and advertising are at their optimal levels, yielding the maximum (*maximorum*) level of profit. The relevant average and marginal cost and revenue curves are shown in Figure 2.12. Point e^* defines the short-run equilibrium of the firm. This is an equilibrium, because to the right of e^* the marginal advertising (option) cost exceeds the marginal advertising (option) revenue and profit is reduced. To the left of e^* the marginal advertising (option) cost is less than the marginal advertising (option) revenue, so that it pays the firm to increase further its advertising outlay (and its price). Hence at e^* the firm earns maximum profit. At equilibrium the price is P^*, the

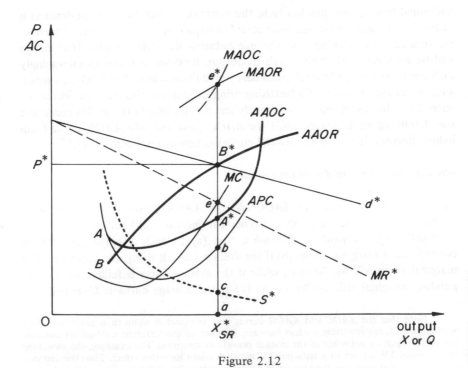

Figure 2.12

output is X^*, the average production cost is ab and the average advertising expenditure is bA^* ($= ac$). With entry not occurring in the short run, firms in the industry earn abnormal profits (equal to A^*B^* per unit of output in Figure 2.12).

Long-run equilibrium in Buchanan's model

Abnormal profits attract entry. As new firms enter the industry the share of each rival declines. The individual demand curve facing the firm (and the associated *MR* curve) shifts to the left. We said that, given the average and marginal production cost curves, the *AAOC* shifts upwards while the *AAOR* will tend to move downwards as entry occurs. This reflects the fact that a given level of advertising is associated now with a lower demand curve, as the market is shared among a larger number of sellers. In other words, each firm produces a lower level of output and increases its advertising cost per unit of output. It is reasonable to assume that the elasticity of demand also increases with entry, so that the firms will reduce their price. Although (a) average production costs decrease (from b to b' in Figure 2.13), (b) advertising unit costs rise, and this, combined with (c) the fall in price, leads to the reduction of excess profits. Entry will stop when the *AAOC* and *AAOR* curves become tangent. The long-run equilibrium of the firm (and the industry) is shown by point E in Figure 2.13. Given our assumptions about the (increasing) costs and the effects of entry on the elasticity of

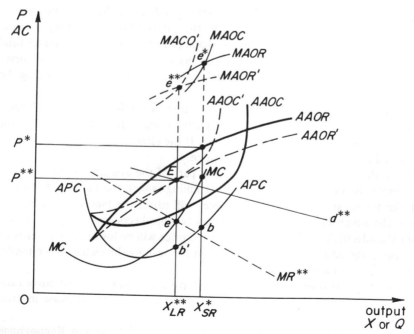

Figure 2.13

demand (increasing elasticity), the price will be lower, the advertising cost will be higher $(=b'E$ per unit of output), the output of each firm will be smaller, and abnormal profits are eliminated.

The implication of the long-run equilibrium is that all advertising ($b'E$ per unit of output) becomes *competitive advertising*: that is, each firm *must* advertise by the same amount in order to avoid losses and retain its market share. Advertising expenditures of each firm 'cancel out' the effects of advertising of rivals. So far as the consumer is concerned, the price will be higher (and the quantity smaller) than would be the case if firms advertised to a smaller extent. A considerable amount of advertising expenditure becomes necessary in order to avoid losses, simply because other rivals advertise.

Critique of Buchanan's model

The above model has the advantage over Chamberlinian analysis in that it considers explicitly simultaneous changes in price *and* advertising. Typically a firm would be interested in the *increase* in sales resulting from an increase in advertising expenditure. Managers would be interested to know 'how much more can we sell and at what price if we spend different amounts of money on advertising?'

The model is based on marginalistic concepts analogous to the ones usually employed in the traditional models of the firm.

The model in its general form does not lend itself to precise predictions. For example, we cannot deduce from it how an increase in advertising will affect the price and output in the market. Predictions depend on the shape and position of the *AAOR* and *AAOC* curves, which, in turn, depend on the shifting demand and advertising costs, as well as on the shape (and position) of the average (and marginal) production costs. Obviously the shapes and positions of these curves can be numerous. However, some general statements can be made regarding the determinants of *AAOR* and *AAOC*.

(1) Advertising may well be expected to decrease the price elasticity of demand as the curve shifts to the right. The less advertising reduces the elasticity, the less, *ceteris paribus*, will be the rise in price. If the elasticity increases, advertising might lead to a reduction in the market price.

(2) If the firm operates on the falling part of the average production cost, the steeper the slope of this curve (on its falling range), the more probable it is that the technical (production) economies will offset the increase in total cost due to the advertising expenditures. Strong technical economies may more than offset the advertising costs, in which case the price will be lower after advertising has created the additional demand required for reaping the technical economies of large-scale production.

(3) If the firm operates on an L-shaped average production cost curve (and there is sufficient evidence supporting this assumption),[18] the increase in price

---

[18] See J. Johnston, *Statistical Cost Analysis* (McGraw-Hill, 1960) Also, Koutsoyiannis, *Modern Microeconomics*.

resulting from advertising will be lower than if the firm operates with increasing production costs. Over the flat range of the average production cost, the *MC* curve is a straight line, and hence its intersection with the upward shifting marginal revenue curves will give rise to a smaller increment in price (as compared with the case of rising *MC*).

(4) There is evidence that in many industries (especially consumer-goods industries) the *AAOC* curve lies above the *AAOR* curve at low levels of output. This implies that if firms did not advertise at all, production could take place only at a loss, since the demand (without advertising) lies below the *APC* at all levels of output. Advertising enables the firms to reach the range of profitable operation. This is particularly true if some of the rivals do advertise. However, if advertising becomes of the 'cancelling-out' type, a cut in advertising by all rivals might lower the price and increase profits.

(5) There is also some evidence that the law of diminishing returns starts operating at fairly low levels of output. This implies that the *AAOC* curve rises fast and cuts the *AAOR* curve before very high levels of production are reached, reducing the possibilities of excessive profits (from advertising) over a wide range of output. Although the atomistic behaviour of firms and the long-run tangency solution may not be realistic, it also seems probable that the range (and amount) of short-run excess profits is much smaller than implied by Figures 2.5–2.13.

The above marginalistic model suffers from the usual defects of all marginalistic models. Four limitations are particularly serious. First, the model assumes perfect knowledge of the effects of advertising on the demand and cost curves of the firm. Second, the assumption that firms ignore their interdependence is implausible. Third, the model does not take into account the lags involved in the process of adjustment of demand to the advertising effort. Fourth, the goal of profit maximisation is unrealistic.

C.   A Note on Advertising as an Investment

In recent years several writers have argued that advertising should be treated as an investment,[19] because it yields returns over several periods of time. Advertising (and product differentiation) are the main means by which a firm builds its name and goodwill gradually over time.[20] This has implications for the advertising decision, as well as for the assessment of its effects on the profits of the firm.

(1) An advertising campaign should be evaluated on the basis of its costs as well as its stream of future earnings. In Chapter 4 we examine in detail the procedures for evaluating investment projects. We note here that according to a widely used criterion (the internal rate of return criterion, IRR), an advertising

---

[19] For example, Kristian Palda, *The Measurement of Cumulative Advertising Effects* (Prentice-Hall, 1964).

[20] Richard Heflebower, 'The Theory and Effects of Non-price Competition', in *Monopolistic Competition: Studies in Impact*, ed. R. E. Kuenne (Wiley, 1967) pp. 177–201.

project should be accepted if its yield (rate of return) is higher than the market interest rate. If this condition is satisfied, advertising will increase the value of the firm and, hence, the wealth of owner-shareholders. (See Chapter 4.) Thus treating advertising as an investment implies a different type of decision than that of the earlier-presented profit-maximising behaviour.

(2) Although advertising has the characteristics of an investment, firms usually consider it as a current expense, which is amortised in the year in which it is incurred. From empirical studies,[21] it has been found that advertising effects last for five to seven years. Accordingly the book value of the firm's assets should be increased by the advertising expenditures (as is done with investment in fixed assets), which then should be amortised over five to seven years. Since most firms treat advertising outlays as current expenditures, the book value of their assets is understated. As a consequence, the profit rate on assets is overestimated (see section VII below). If advertising (and other product-differentiating activities) were viewed as investments yielding depreciable assets similar to the investments in fixed capital, then part of the higher profit rates reported by firms that spend large amounts on product-differentiating activities would disappear.

$$* \qquad\qquad * \qquad\qquad *$$

D. The Dorfman—Steiner Mathematical Version of the Price— Advertising Model[22]

This model is the mathematical formulation of Buchanan's graphical analysis. It is of interest because it expresses the equilibrium conditions in terms of elasticities.

We will use the notation adopted in the simple advertising model.

The firm's profit function is

$$\Pi = R - C - A$$

or

$$\Pi = P\,[Q(P,\,A)] - C(Q) - A \tag{2.22}$$

The firm has to choose the P and A which will maximise its profit.

The first-order conditions for maximum profit are

$$\frac{\partial \Pi}{\partial A} = \left(P \times \frac{\partial Q}{\partial A}\right) - \left(\frac{\partial C}{\partial Q} \times \frac{\partial Q}{\partial A}\right) - 1 = 0 \tag{2.23}$$

and

$$\frac{\partial \Pi}{\partial P} = \left[P \times \frac{\partial Q}{\partial P} + Q \times \frac{\partial P}{\partial P}\right] - \left[\frac{\partial C}{\partial Q} \times \frac{\partial Q}{\partial P}\right] = 0 \tag{2.24}$$

It is convenient to express the above conditions in terms of elasticities.

[21] Leonard Weiss, 'Advertising, Profits and Corporate Taxes', *Review of Economics and Statistics*, vol. 51, 1969, p. 421; Y. Peles, 'Rates of Amortization of Advertising Expenditures', *Journal of Political Economy*, vol. 79, 1971, p. 1032.

[22] R. Dorfman and P. O. Steiner, 'Optimal Advertising and Optimal Quality', *American Economic Review*, vol. 44, December 1954, pp. 835—46. This version of the Buchanan model can be omitted without loss of continuity.

Expression (2.23) yields the condition for the optimal (profit-maximising) advertising decision

$$\frac{A}{R} = \eta_{QA} \left(\frac{P - MC}{P} \right) \tag{2.25}$$

PROOF

Expression (2.23) may be written in the form

$$\frac{\partial Q}{\partial A} (P - MC) = 1$$

Multiplying through by A/PQ, we obtain

$$\left(\frac{\partial Q}{\partial A} \frac{A}{Q} \right) \left(\frac{P - MC}{P} \right) = \frac{A}{PQ}$$

Given that the first term in brackets is the advertising elasticity of demand, and $PQ = R$, we may write the above equation in the form

$$\frac{A}{R} = \eta_{QA} \times \left(\frac{P - MC}{P} \right)$$

QED

This is the same as expression (2.17), which we derived from the simple advertising model (p. 64).

Expression (2.24) yields the optimal (profit-maximising) product–price decision

$$\frac{P - MC}{P} = \frac{1}{\eta_{QP}} \tag{2.26}$$

*   *   *

PROOF

Multiplying expression (2.24) through by P/Q, we obtain

$$\left[P \times \left(\frac{\partial Q}{\partial P} \frac{P}{Q} \right) + Q \frac{P}{Q} \right] - \frac{\partial C}{\partial Q} \left(\frac{\partial Q}{\partial P} \frac{P}{Q} \right) = 0 \tag{2.27}$$

Given $(\partial Q/\partial P)$ (P/Q) is the price elasticity of demand $-\eta_{QP}$, we may write expression (2.27) in the form

$$P(-\eta_{QP}) + P - MC(-\eta_{QP}) = 0 \tag{2.28}$$

or

$$(-\eta_{QP})(P - MC) = -P \tag{2.29}$$

Dividing through by P, we obtain

$$\frac{P - MC}{P} = \frac{1}{\eta_{QP}}$$

QED

This is, of course, the familiar marginalistic rule

$$MR = MC \tag{2.26a}$$

PROOF

To see this, we work as follows

$$\frac{P - MC}{P} = 1 - \frac{MC}{P} = \frac{1}{\eta_{QP}} \tag{2.30}$$

Rearranging, we find

$$\left(1 - \frac{1}{\eta_{QP}}\right) = \frac{MC}{P} \tag{2.31}$$

or

$$P\left(1 - \frac{1}{\eta_{QP}}\right) = MC \tag{2.32}$$

From elementary principles we know that the left-hand side is marginal revenue. Hence $MR = MC$.

QED

   In summary. A profit-maximising firm will set its advertising expenditure on the basis of expression (2.25)

$$\frac{A}{R} = \eta_{QA}\left(\frac{P - MC}{P}\right)$$

and its output and price at the level where

$$MC = MR$$

If we substitute (2.26) in (2.25), we obtain

$$\frac{A}{R} = \frac{\eta_{QA}}{\eta_{QP}} \tag{2.33}$$

This expression combines the advertising decision and the product decision in one rule: the firm maximises its profit if it sets its advertising–sales ratio equal to the ratio of the two demand elasticities. Expanding expression (2.33) we find

$$\frac{A}{R} = \frac{(dQ/Q)/(dA/A)}{(dQ/Q)/(dP/P)} = \frac{(dQ/Q)(dP/P)}{(dQ/Q)(dA/A)}$$

or

$$\frac{A}{R} = \left(\frac{dP}{P}\right)\bigg/\left(\frac{dA}{A}\right) = \eta_{PA} \tag{2.34}$$

That is, the optimal advertising is attained by setting the advertising–sales ratio equal to the elasticity of price with respect to advertising. Thus the two-variable model (where price and advertising are the policy decisions of the firm) implies that the greater the sensitivity (responsiveness) of price to advertising expenditures, the greater will be the advertising budget of the firm.

It is useful to restate the optimal advertising decision in terms of the marginal cost of advertising and the marginal revenue of advertising.

Expression (2.23) may be written in the form .

$$\frac{\partial \Pi}{\partial A} = \frac{\partial R}{\partial A} - \frac{\partial C}{\partial A} - \frac{\partial A}{\partial A} = 0 \tag{2.35}$$

We observe that

$$\frac{\partial R}{\partial A} = \text{marginal revenue of advertising}$$

$$\frac{\partial C}{\partial A} = \frac{\partial C}{\partial Q}\frac{\partial Q}{\partial A} = \begin{array}{l}\text{change in production costs due to the higher} \\ \text{output induced by advertising}\end{array}$$

$$\frac{\partial A}{\partial A} = 1 = \text{cost of an additional 'unit' of advertising}$$

However, the *total change in cost* (when advertising changes) is partly due to the change in the advertising expenditure ($\partial A/\partial A = 1$), and partly to the change in output induced by the shift in demand, that is

$$MC_A = 1 + \frac{\partial C}{\partial A} \tag{2.36}$$

From expression (2.35) it follows that the optimal level of advertising is set at the level where

$$\frac{\partial R}{\partial A} = 1 + \frac{\partial C}{\partial A} \tag{2.37}$$

or

$$MR_A = MC_A = 1 + \frac{\partial C}{\partial A} \tag{2.38}$$

E.   A 'Generalised' Model, with Price, Style-Variety and Advertising Simultaneously Determined

(This model can be omitted without loss of continuity.) The Buchanan–Dorfman–Steiner model has been extended by this author to incorporate the product-style decision.

Let V_i represent the expenditure required to product the ith variety-style. It is assumed that this expenditure is a given amount of money for each variety. Thus the 'average variety cost curve' is a hyperbola (like the S_i curve in Buchanan's model). This curve shifts upwards with a change in the variety or style of the product. Thus we have a family of average V_i curves, which generates a set of (upward-shifted) total unit costs and demand curves.

The crucial assumptions of this model are that:

(1) Quantity depends on all the three policy variables

$$Q(P, A, V) \tag{2.39}$$

$$\frac{\partial Q}{\partial P} < 0; \quad \frac{\partial Q}{\partial A} > 0; \quad \frac{\partial Q}{\partial V} > 0$$

(2) Production costs are dependent on Q, which, in turn, depends on advertising and on product style. In symbols

$$C = g(Q) = g[Q(P, A, V)] \tag{2.40}$$

Hence

$$\frac{\partial C}{\partial A} = \frac{\partial C}{\partial Q} \times \frac{\partial Q}{\partial A} \tag{2.41}$$

In words, total production costs change as a result of the increased demand, induced by the increase in advertising.

(3) Similarly, since quantity depends on the product variety expenses, we have

$$\frac{\partial C}{\partial V} = \frac{\partial C}{\partial Q} \times \frac{\partial Q}{\partial V} \tag{2.42}$$

In words, total production costs change, due to the shift in demand induced by a change in the type or variety of the product.

(4) Finally

$$P = f(Q) = f[Q(P, A, V)] \tag{2.39a}$$

The profit function of the firm is

$$\Pi = R - C - A - V$$

where $R = PQ = P\,[Q(P, A, V)]$

$$C = g(Q) = f[Q(P, A, V)]$$

Hence

$$\Pi = P[Q(P, A, V)] - C[Q(P, A, V)] - A - V \tag{2.43}$$

The firm must choose P, A and V so as to maximise its profit.

The first-order conditions for maximum profit are

$$\frac{\partial \Pi}{\partial A} = \left(P \times \frac{\partial Q}{\partial A} \right) - \left(\frac{\partial C}{\partial Q} \times \frac{\partial Q}{\partial A} \right) - 1 = 0 \tag{2.44}$$

$$\frac{\partial \Pi}{\partial P} = \left[\left(P \times \frac{\partial Q}{\partial P} \right) + Q \right] - \left(\frac{\partial C}{\partial Q} \times \frac{\partial Q}{\partial P} \right) = 0 \tag{2.45}$$

$$\frac{\partial \Pi}{\partial V} = \left(P \times \frac{\partial Q}{\partial V} \right) - \left(\frac{\partial C}{\partial Q} \times \frac{\partial Q}{\partial V} \right) - 1 = 0 \tag{2.46}$$

The next step is to express these conditions in terms of elasticities. This is attained by the following algebraic manipulations.

(a) We multiply expression (2.44) through by A/PQ. This yields

$$\frac{P - MC}{P} = \frac{1}{\eta_{QA}} \times \frac{A}{R} \tag{2.47}$$

or

$$\frac{A}{R} = \eta_{QA} \left(\frac{P - MC}{P} \right) \tag{2.47a}$$

This is the same as expression (2.17) of the simple advertising model, and expression (2.25) of the optimal advertising decision.

(b) We multiply expression (2.45) through by P/Q. This yields

$$\frac{P - MC}{P} = \frac{1}{\eta_{QP}} \tag{2.48}$$

This is the same as expression (2.26) of the Buchanan–Dorfman–Steiner model, which gives the optimal price–output decision rule $MC = MR$.

(c) We multiply expression (2.46) through by V/Q. This yields

$$P \left(\frac{\partial Q}{\partial V} \times \frac{V}{Q} \right) - \frac{\partial C}{\partial Q} \left(\frac{\partial Q}{\partial V} \times \frac{V}{Q} \right) - \frac{V}{Q} = 0$$

Noting that the expressions in brackets are the elasticity of demand w.r.t. the change in product variety, η_{QV}, we may write

$$\eta_{QV}(P - MC) = \frac{V}{Q}$$

Multiplying through by $1/P$, we obtain

$$\eta_{QV} \left(\frac{P - MC}{P} \right) = \frac{V}{PQ} = \frac{V}{R}$$

Rearranging, we obtain

$$\frac{P - MC}{P} = \frac{1}{\eta_{QV}} \times \frac{V}{R} \tag{2.49}$$

or

$$\frac{V}{R} = \eta_{QV} \left(\frac{P - MC}{P} \right) \tag{2.49a}$$

This gives the optimal 'product-variety' decision: the firm maximises its profit by setting its V/R ratio according to expression (2.49).

We can now combine all three policy decisions in a single rule. Thus, equating expressions (2.47), (2.48) and (2.49), we obtain the profit-maximising (equilibrium) condition

$$\frac{A}{V} = \frac{(\eta_{QA})(\eta_{QV})}{\eta_{QP}} \tag{2.50}$$

The firm maximises its profit if it sets the ratio of advertising expenditures to product-change expenditures equal to $(\eta_{QA})(\eta_{QV})/\eta_{QP}$.

It is apparent that this equilibrium depends on the three elasticities of demand, with respect to the three policy variables, A, P, V. One can think of V as the research and development expenses required for a change in the product of the firm.

In summary. In the three-variable model the three decisions of the profit maximiser are taken as follows:

Production decision

$$\frac{P - MC}{P} = \frac{1}{\eta_{QP}} \quad (\text{or } MR = MC)$$

Advertising decision

$$\frac{A}{R} = \eta_{QA} \left(\frac{P - MC}{P} \right)$$

Product-variety decision

$$\frac{V}{R} = \eta_{QV} \left(\frac{P - MC}{P} \right)$$

F.   Schmalensee's Model of Oligopoly Advertising

(This model may be omitted without loss of continuity.) Schmalensee developed a simple advertising model in which oligopolistic interdependence is recognised by rival firms.[23]

The price and the type of the product are given, and the firm has to choose its advertising expenditure, A_i, so as to maximise its profit. The firm takes into account that the effectiveness of its advertising depends on rivals' advertising, A_0.

[23] Schmalensee, *The Economics of Advertising*.

The assumptions may be summarised as follows.

(1) Rivals react to the firm's advertising. In symbols we have

$$A_0 = f(A_i)$$

where A_i = advertising of the ith firm

A_0 = advertising of rivals

This is the assumption of oligopolistic interdependence.

(2) Price is given in the market.

(3) The advertising expenditure is not directly linked with price, so that

$$\frac{\partial P}{\partial A_i} = 0 \tag{2.51}$$

(4) The demand function of the ith firm is

$$q_i = f(A_i, A_0, P)$$

Hence, we have

$$P = f(q_i) = f[q_i(A_i, A_0, P)] \tag{2.52}$$

(5) Production cost is a function of output

$$C_i = g(q_i) = g[q_i(A_i, A_0, P)] \tag{2.53}$$

The firm wants to choose the advertising expenditure, A_i, which will maximise its profit

$$\Pi = Pq - C_i - A_i$$

or

$$\Pi = P[q_i(A_i, A_0, P)] - C_i[q_i(A_i, A_0, P)] - A_i \tag{2.54}$$

The first-order condition for maximum profit is

$$\frac{\partial \Pi}{\partial A_i} = P\left[\frac{\partial q_i}{\partial A_i} + \left(\frac{\partial q_i}{\partial A_0} \times \frac{\partial A_0}{\partial A_i}\right)\right] - \frac{\partial C_i}{\partial q_i}\left[\frac{\partial q_i}{\partial A_0} + \left(\frac{\partial q_i}{\partial A_0} \times \frac{\partial A_0}{\partial A_i}\right)\right] - 1 = 0 \tag{2.55}$$

Rearranging, we obtain

$$\left[\frac{\partial q_i}{\partial A_i} + \left(\frac{\partial q_i}{\partial A_0} \times \frac{\partial A_0}{\partial A_i}\right)\right](P - MC) = 1 \tag{2.56}$$

where $\partial A_0/\partial A_i$ is the conjectural (expected) response of competitors to an increase in the firm's advertising.[24]

In order to express condition (2.56) in terms of elasticities, we multiply the first term in brackets by $A_i q_i/A_i q_i$, and the second term by $(A_0 q_i/A_0 q_i) \times$

[24] The second-order conditions for a maximum are satisfied if the marginal cost, $(\partial C_i/\partial q_i)$, is non-decreasing and there are diminishing returns to advertising.

$(A_0 A_i / A_0 A_i)$. Thus we obtain

$$\left[\left(\frac{\partial q_i}{\partial A_i} \times \frac{A_i}{q_i} \right) \frac{q_i}{A_i} + \left(\frac{\partial q_i}{\partial A_0} \times \frac{A_0}{q_i} \right) \frac{q_i}{A_0} \left(\frac{\partial A_0}{\partial A_i} \times \frac{A_i}{A_0} \right) \frac{A_0}{A_i} \right] (P - MC) = 1$$

We observe that

$$\frac{\partial q_i}{\partial A_i} \times \frac{A_i}{q_i} = \text{elasticity of demand w.r.t. firm's advertising} = \eta_{q_i A_i}$$

$$\frac{\partial q_i}{\partial A_0} \times \frac{A_0}{q_i} = \text{elasticity of demand with respect to rivals' advertising}$$

$$= \eta_{q_i A_0}$$

and

$$\frac{\partial A_0}{\partial A_i} \times \frac{A_i}{A_0} = \text{conjectural response elasticity, i.e. proportionate change in rivals' advertising as the } i\text{th firm changes its advertising} = \eta_{A_i A_0}$$

Thus we may write

$$\left[(\eta_{q_i A_i}) \frac{q_i}{A_i} + (\eta_{q_i A_0})(\eta_{A_0 A_i}) \frac{q_i}{A_i} \right] (P - MC) = 1$$

Rearranging, we find

$$[(\eta_{q_i A_i}) + (\eta_{q_i A_0})(\eta_{A_0 A_i})] (P - MC) = \frac{A_i}{q_i}$$

Dividing through by P, we obtain

$$\frac{A_i}{R_i} = \left(\frac{P - MC}{P} \right) [(\eta_{q_i A_i}) + (\eta_{q_i A_0})(\eta_{A_0 A_i})] \qquad (2.57)$$

Thus the oligopolistic firm maximises its profit by setting its advertising–sales ratio according to expression (2.57).

It can be shown that the simple advertising model and the Buchanan–Dorfman–Steiner model are special cases of Schmalensee's model.

(a) If $\eta_{q_i A_0} = 0$, expression (2.57) reduces to the simple marginalistic advertising model, in which

$$\frac{A_i}{R_i} = \left(\frac{P - MC}{P} \right) \eta_{q_i A_i}$$

that is, expression (2.17). This implies that the advertising of rivals does not affect the demand for the product of the ith firm.

(b) If the price is not given, and $\eta_{q_i A_0} = 0$, then we have a firm operating in a monopolistically competitive framework (the Buchanan–Dorfman–Steiner case). The firm will set its production–price decision according to the usual marginalistic rule

$$MC = MR$$

which is equivalent to[25]

$$\frac{P - MC}{P} = \frac{1}{\eta_{q_i P}}$$

and its advertising decision on the basis of expression (2.25)

$$\frac{A_i}{R_i} = \eta_{q_i A_i} \left(\frac{P - MC}{P} \right)$$

Schmalensee argues that in oligopolistic markets $\eta_{A_0 A_i} = 0$: that is, oligopolists do not react to the advertising campaigns of rivals. His argument may be summarised as follows. (1) It takes time to increase promotional expenses, so that any firm increasing its advertising could expect a sizeable lag before its competitors responded. (2) The impact of any advertising campaign depends on the nature of the 'pitch' as well as on the level of advertising spending. A firm which feels it has developed a particularly good campaign might well doubt the ability of its competitors to respond with equally effective promotional campaigns. (3) There is some empirical evidence[26] suggesting that managers are afraid of retaliation by competitors if they advertise above acceptable levels.

Thus Schmalensee concludes that the assumption that $\eta_{A_0 A_i} = 0$ is generally a good approximation to reality.[27] With this assumption, Schmalensee modifies his model so as to take into account the number of rivals in oligopolistic markets. He proves[28] that if there are N firms in an industry, then the ith oligopolist maximises his profit (assuming $\eta_{A_0 A_i} = 0$, and that all firms have identical production costs) by setting its advertising budget according to the expression

$$\frac{A_i}{q_i P} = \frac{A_i}{R_i} = \left(\frac{P - MC}{P} \right) \left(\frac{\eta_{QA} + (N - 1)}{N} \right) \tag{2.58}$$

where η_{QA} = elasticity of *industry sales* with respect to total *industry advertising*

N = total number of firms in the industry

If $(P - MC)/P$ is independent of N, then the above model implies that the advertising–sales ratios increase with N. Even if $\eta_{QA} = 0$, there will be advertising if N is greater than one, since the oligopolists compete for market shares.

If average cost is constant, expression (2.58) implies that profits will fall to

---

[25] Note that this expression is the familiar

$$MC = P \left(1 - \frac{1}{e_{q_i P}} \right) = MR$$

[26] R. W. Jastram, 'Advertising Outlays Under Oligopoly', *Review of Economics and Statistics*, vol. 31, 1949, pp. 106–9; W. Taplin, 'Advertising Appropriations Policy', *Economica*, 1959, pp. 227–39.

[27] See also L. J. Simon, 'A Simple Model for Determining Advertising Appropriations', *Journal of Marketing Research*, 1965, pp. 285–92; L. J. Simon, 'The Effect of the Competitive Structure upon Expenditures for Advertising', *Quarterly Journal of Economics*, 1967, pp. 610–27.

[28] Schmalensee, *Economics of Advertising*.

zero as N rises, regardless of P. Free entry and advertising competition may eliminate monopoly profit.

Schmalensee's modified model suffers from its restrictive assumptions. Casual observation shows that a lot of advertising is undertaken routinely by oligopolists, for defensive purposes. Furthermore, not all firms can be assumed to be equally efficient in production.

*   *   *

III.   A MANAGERIALIST MODEL OF ADVERTISING: THE BAUMOL–HAWKINS–BUSHNELL–KAFOGLIS STATIC MODEL

In this section we will examine a model of advertising based on the hypothesis that the goal of the firm is sales-revenue maximisation.

This is a static, single-period model, developed by Baumol and extended by Hawkins, Bushnell and Kafoglis.[29]

A.   A Diagrammatic Presentation of the Model

The basic assumptions of the static model

(1) The time-horizon of the firm is a single period.

(2) During this period the firm attempts to maximise its total sales revenue (not physical volume of output).

(3) There is a minimum profit constraint, which is exogenously determined by the demands and expectations of the shareholders, the banks and other financial institutions. The firm must realise a minimum level of profits to keep shareholders happy and avoid a fall of the prices of shares on the stock exchange. If profits are below this exogenously determined minimum acceptable level, the managers run the risk of being dismissed, since shareholders may sell their shares and takeover raiders may be attracted by a fall of the price of shares. The minimum profit constraint is denoted by a line parallel to the X-axis in the diagrams to follow.

(4) The policy variables of the firm are price and advertising. The firm has to choose the price and advertising expenditure so as to maximise its sales revenue, subject to the given minimum profit constraint.

(5) Advertising shifts the firm's demand curve to the right, thus enabling the firm to increase the volume of its sales *and* its revenue.

---

[29] W. Baumol, *Business Behaviour, Value and Growth* (Harcourt, Brace & World, 1967); C. J. Hawkins, 'The Revenue Maximisation Oligopoly Model: Comment', *American Economic Review*, 1970; M. Kafoglis and R. Bushnell, 'The Revenue-Maximisation Oligopoly Model: Comment', *American Economic Review*, 1970).

(6) Production costs vary proportionally with output. Thus the total production cost function is a straight (positively sloping) line through the origin.

(7) Advertising expenditure may change but is independent of the level of output. Thus a given level of advertising is presented by a straight line parallel to the Q-axis.

The total cost function is the summation of the production cost (C), the advertising expenditure (A_i) and the minimum profit constraint ($\bar{\Pi}$). Given the production cost function and the minimum profit constraint, a change in advertising (A_i) will generate a family of total-cost curves which will be upward-sloping (with their slope equal to the slope of the production cost function). Such a family of total cost curves is shown in Figure 2.14.

The total revenue curve has the usual shape, initially increasing but at a decreasing rate, reaching a maximum (where $MR = \partial R/\partial Q = 0$), and then decreasing.

The total revenue curve shifts upwards as advertising is increased. Thus, by changing advertising, we may generate a family of total revenue curves, each representing the relationship of total revenue to output at different levels of advertising expenditure. Such a family of total revenue curves is shown in Figure 2.15. Curve R_1 is drawn on the assumption that advertising expenditure is A_1. Curve R_2 implies an advertising expenditure of A_2, and so on.

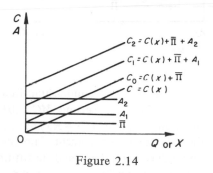

Figure 2.14   Figure 2.15

Equilibrium of the firm

If we superimpose Figures 2.14 and 2.15 and join the points of intersection of total cost and total revenue curves corresponding to the same amount of advertising expenditure, we obtain a curve which is called by (Haveman and DeBartolo)[30] the '$TC = TR$' curve. It is the dotted curve in Figure 2.16. The firm is in equilibrium when it reaches the highest point of this curve. The equilibrium of the firm is at point e, with the total costs C^*, total revenue R^*, output Q^*, advertising A^* (not shown in Figure 2.16), and price equal to OR_e/OQ_e.

[30] R. Haveman and G. DeBartolo, 'The Revenue-Maximisation Oligopoly Model: Comment', *American Economic Review*, 1968, pp. 1355–8.

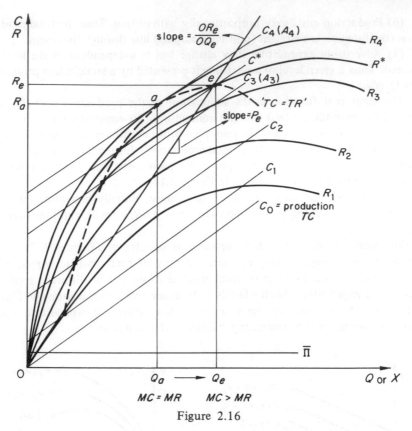

Figure 2.16

It should be clear that two conditions must be satisfied for equilibrium: first, the firm must operate on some point of the '$TC = TR$' curve, second, $MC > MR$ *at equilibrium.* Thus at point a the first condition is fulfilled ($C_4 = R_4$) but the second condition is violated, since at a the two curves are tangent, implying $MC = MR$. Thus if the sales maximiser were to produce at Q_a, he would substitute production expenditure for advertising expenditure (a reallocation of resources from advertising to increased production) until output increased to Q_e. In the process of adjustment price would fall, but the loss in revenue from this cause would be more than offset by the additional revenue from the increased output sold. In Figure 2.16 we see that $R_e > R_a$.

*   *   *

B. A Mathematical Presentation of Baumol's Model

(This section can be omitted without loss of continuity.) In a single period, the firm's goal is the maximisation of its sales revenue

$$R = f(P, A) \tag{2.59}$$

subject to a minimum profit constraint

$$\Pi \geqslant \bar{\Pi} \tag{2.60}$$

It is assumed that:

(1) The marginal revenue of advertising is positive:

$$\frac{\partial R}{\partial A} > 0 \tag{2.61}$$

That is, advertising always increases sales revenue. This assumption ensures that the profit constraint is operative. Since advertising always increases sales revenue, it will always pay the sales maximiser to increase his advertising expenditure until he is stopped by the profit constraint.[31] Thus the constraint takes the form

$$\Pi = \bar{\Pi} \tag{2.62}$$

(2) The demand curve is negatively sloping and shifts outwards with advertising:

$$\frac{\partial Q}{\partial P} < 0; \quad \frac{\partial Q}{\partial A} > 0 \tag{2.63}$$

Hence, we may write

$$R \equiv PQ = P[Q(P, A)] \tag{2.64}$$

$$\frac{\partial R}{\partial P} = P\left(\frac{\partial Q}{\partial P}\right) + Q \tag{2.65}$$

$$\frac{\partial R}{\partial A} = P\left(\frac{\partial Q}{\partial A}\right) \tag{2.66}$$

(3) The production cost is a function of output,[32] which, in turn, is a function of advertising:

$$C = g(Q) = g[O(P, A)] \tag{2.67}$$

$$\frac{\partial C}{\partial Q} > 0 \tag{2.68}$$

$$\frac{\partial C}{\partial A} = \frac{\partial C}{\partial Q} \frac{\partial Q}{\partial A} \tag{2.69}$$

Baumol *et al.*'s model is a constrained-maximisation problem, which can be solved by the Lagrangian multiplier method. Given

$$\Pi = R - C - A \tag{2.70}$$

the constraint may be written in the form

$$\lambda(\Pi - \bar{\Pi}) = 0$$

[31] Alternatively, the assumption $\partial R/\partial Q > 0$, that is, demand is elastic ($\eta_{QP} > 1$) for any relevant output, would alone ensure that the constraint is operative.

[32] The production cost function can be linear or non-linear. In the geometric presentation of the model we assumed for simplicity that the production cost function was linear.

or

$$\lambda(R - C - A - \bar{\Pi}) = 0 \tag{2.71}$$

where $\lambda(< 0)$ is the Lagrangian multiplier.

The 'composite' function to be maximised is

$$\phi = R - \lambda(\Pi - \bar{\Pi})$$

or

$$\phi = R - \lambda(R - C - A - \bar{\Pi}) \tag{2.72}$$

This expression may be written in the form

$$\phi = P[Q(P, A)] - \lambda\{P[Q(P, A)] - C[Q(P, A)] - A - \bar{\Pi}\} \tag{2.73}$$

The first-order conditions for maximum ϕ are

$$\frac{\partial \phi}{\partial P} = \left[\left(P \times \frac{\partial Q}{\partial P}\right) + Q\right] - \lambda\left[\left(P \times \frac{\partial Q}{\partial P}\right) + Q\right] + \lambda\left[\frac{\partial C}{\partial Q} \times \frac{\partial Q}{\partial P}\right] = 0 \tag{2.74}$$

$$\frac{\partial \phi}{\partial A} = \left(P \times \frac{\partial Q}{\partial A}\right) - \lambda\left(P \times \frac{\partial Q}{\partial A}\right) + \lambda\left(\frac{\partial C}{\partial Q} \times \frac{\partial Q}{\partial A}\right) + \lambda = 0 \tag{2.75}$$

$$\frac{\partial \phi}{\partial \lambda} = -(\Pi - \bar{\Pi}) = 0 \tag{2.76}$$

Expression (2.76) gives the constraint

$$\Pi = \bar{\Pi}$$

Expression (2.74) yields the equilibrium production decision of the firm

$$\left.\begin{aligned} \frac{\partial R}{\partial Q} &= \left(\frac{\lambda}{\lambda - 1}\right)\frac{\partial C}{\partial Q} \\[2em] \text{or} \\[1em] MR &= \left(\frac{\lambda}{\lambda - 1}\right)(MC) \end{aligned}\right\} \tag{2.77}$$

PROOF

Expression (2.74) may be written in the form

$$\left[\left(P \times \frac{\partial Q}{\partial P}\right) + Q\right](1 - \lambda) + \lambda\left(\frac{\partial C}{\partial Q} \times \frac{\partial Q}{\partial P}\right) = 0$$

Multiplying through by P/Q, we find

$$\left[P\left(\frac{\partial Q}{\partial P} \times \frac{P}{Q}\right) + Q\frac{P}{Q}\right](\lambda - 1) = \lambda\frac{\partial C}{\partial Q}\left(\frac{\partial Q}{\partial P} \times \frac{P}{Q}\right)$$

Given that $(\partial Q / \partial P) \times (P/Q) = -\eta_{QP}$, we have

$$P(-\eta_{QP}) + P = \left(\frac{\lambda}{\lambda - 1} \right) (MC) (-\eta_{QP})$$

Dividing through by $-\eta_{QP}$, we find

$$P - \frac{P}{\eta_{QP}} = \left(\frac{\lambda}{\lambda - 1} \right) (MC) \qquad (2.77a)$$

or

$$P \left(1 - \frac{1}{\eta_{QP}} \right) = \left(\frac{\lambda}{\lambda - 1} \right) (MC)$$

From the basic principles of economics, we know that the left-hand side is the marginal revenue. Hence

$$MR = \frac{\lambda}{\lambda - 1} (MC)$$

QED

In other words, the constrained sales maximiser will set his output where condition (2.77) is satisfied.

Given that $\lambda < 0$ (by the way in which the constrained ϕ function is written) it follows that

$$0 < \left(\frac{\lambda}{\lambda - 1} \right) < 1 \qquad (2.78)$$

Expression (2.78), in conjunction with (2.77), implies that $MR < MC$: that is, a sales maximiser will produce a greater output than a profit maximiser.

Given that the right-hand side of expression (2.77) is positive, it follows that $\partial R / \partial Q$ (or MR) must also be positive. Since $MR = P(1 - 1/\eta_{QP})$, it follows that

$$MR > 0 \quad \text{if} \quad |\eta_{QP}| > 1 \qquad (2.79)$$

Thus the constrained sales maximiser, like a profit maximiser, will produce at the elastic part of his demand curve. (However, the elasticity of a profit maximiser will be larger than the elasticity of a sales maximiser.)

Finally, expression (2.75) yields the condition for optimal advertising expenditure of a sales maximiser

$$\frac{A}{R} = \left(\frac{\lambda - 1}{\lambda} \right) \times \frac{\eta_{QA}}{\eta_{QP}} \qquad (2.80)$$

PROOF

Expression (2.75) can be written in the form

$$\left(P \times \frac{\partial Q}{\partial A} \right) (1 - \lambda) + \lambda \left(\frac{\partial C}{\partial Q} \times \frac{\partial Q}{\partial A} \right) = -\lambda$$

Multiplying through by A/Q, we find

$$P\left(\frac{\partial Q}{\partial A} \times \frac{A}{Q}\right)(\lambda - 1) - \lambda\,(MC)\left(\frac{\partial Q}{\partial A} \times \frac{A}{Q}\right) = \lambda\,\frac{A}{Q}$$

Given that $\dfrac{\partial Q}{\partial A} \times \dfrac{A}{Q} = \eta_{QA}$, we have

$$P(\eta_{QA})(\lambda - 1) - \lambda(MC)(\eta_{QA}) = \lambda\,\frac{A}{Q}$$

or

$$\eta_{QA}\,[P(\lambda - 1) - \lambda(MC)] = \lambda\,\frac{A}{Q}$$

Dividing through by $\lambda - 1$, we obtain

$$\eta_{QA}\left[P - \left(\frac{\lambda}{\lambda - 1}\right)(MC)\right] = \left(\frac{\lambda}{\lambda - 1}\right)\frac{A}{Q}$$

Substituting (2.77a) in the above expression, we find

$$\eta_{QA}\left[P - P\left(1 - \frac{1}{\eta_{QP}}\right)\right] = \left(\frac{\lambda}{\lambda - 1}\right)\frac{A}{Q}$$

Dividing through by P, we get

$$\eta_{QA}\left[1 - \left(1 - \frac{1}{\eta_{QP}}\right)\right] = \left(\frac{\lambda}{\lambda - 1}\right)\frac{A}{QP}$$

or

$$\eta_{QA}\left(\frac{1}{\eta_{QP}}\right) = \left(\frac{\lambda}{\lambda - 1}\right)\frac{A}{R}$$

and

$$\frac{A}{R} = \left(\frac{\lambda - 1}{\lambda}\right) \times \frac{\eta_{QA}}{\eta_{QP}}$$

QED

From expression (2.78), it follows that

$$\left(\frac{\lambda - 1}{\lambda}\right) > 1 \tag{2.81}$$

Hence, expression (2.80) implies that the sales maximiser will advertise more (will have a higher A/R ratio) than the profit maximiser.

It is useful to express the condition for optimal advertising expenditure in terms of the changes in total costs and total revenue: that is, in terms of marginal cost and marginal revenue of advertising. Thus expression (2.75) may be written in the form

$$\frac{\partial R}{\partial A} - \lambda \left[\frac{\partial R}{\partial A} - \frac{\partial C}{\partial A} - \frac{\partial A}{\partial A} \right] = 0 \qquad (2.82)$$

Rearranging, we obtain

$$\frac{\partial R}{\partial A} (1 - \lambda) = -\lambda \left(\frac{\partial C}{\partial A} + 1 \right) \qquad (2.83)$$

or, given that $\partial C/\partial A + 1$ is the change both in production costs *and* advertising (MC_A),

$$MR_A = \left(\frac{\lambda}{\lambda - 1} \right) MC_A \qquad (2.84)$$

This may be written as

$$MR_A \left(\frac{\lambda - 1}{\lambda} \right) = MC_A \qquad (2.85)$$

which shows that $MR_A < MC_A$ (given $[\lambda - 1]/\lambda > 1$): that is, the sales maximiser will incur higher advertising expenditures than the profit maximiser.

Kafoglis and Bushnell[33] have extended Baumol's mathematical model as follows.

(1) Expression (2.77) may be written as

$$\frac{MC}{MR} = \frac{\lambda - 1}{\lambda} \qquad (2.86)$$

When advertising takes place ($A > 0$), then expression (2.85) holds. It may be written in the form

$$\frac{MC_A}{MR_A} = \frac{\lambda - 1}{\lambda} \qquad (2.87)$$

Combining (2.86) and (2.87), we obtain

$$\frac{MC}{MR} = \frac{MC_A}{MR_A} \qquad (2.88)$$

which implies that any 'surplus profit' (i.e. profit above the minimum constraint $\overline{\Pi}$) will be devoted partly to advertising and partly to increased production.

(2) If we make no assumption about advertising expenditures, then expression (2.87) is no longer valid. Instead we have

$$\frac{MC_A}{MR_A} \geqslant \frac{\lambda - 1}{\lambda} \qquad (2.89)$$

---

[33] Kafoglis and Bushnell, 'The Revenue-Maximisation Oligopoly Model'.

This expression, combined with (2.86), yields

$$\frac{MR}{MC} \geqslant \frac{MR_A}{MC_A} \qquad\qquad (2.90)$$

The inequality sign implies that an extra money unit spent on producing additional output adds more to the total revenue than if it were spent on additional advertising. Thus all 'surplus profit' will be spent on increased production and no advertising will take place.

In any case (Kafoglis and Bushnell conclude) price will always be lower and advertising expenditure smaller than when all 'surplus profit' is allocated to advertising.

In conclusion, Baumol's mathematical version of his single-period advertising model allows for 'excessive' production expenditure and lower price as well as for the more commonly accepted case of 'excessive' advertising and higher price. In fact, Baumol's model is even compatible with strong price competition, which may result in a price lower than the MC. This can be easily seen if in the equilibrium condition

$$MC > MR$$

we substitute

$$MR = P\left(1 - \frac{1}{e}\right)$$

to obtain

$$MC > P\left(1 - \frac{1}{e}\right)$$

With appropriate values of e it is possible that

$$MC > P > MR \qquad\qquad (2.91)$$

This is shown in Figure 2.17. It should be clear that for this result to obtain the elasticity of the sales maximiser must be greater than unity but less than the elasticity of a profit maximiser.

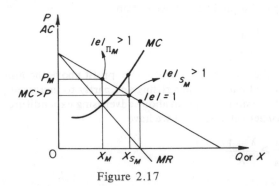

Figure 2.17

IV. A MODEL OF ADVERTISING BARRIERS: WILLIAMSON'S MODEL OF ADVERTISING AS AN ENTRY-PREVENTION STRATEGY

Oliver Williamson has developed a model in which an oligopolistic firm uses advertising in order to prevent entry.[34] Thus the goal of the firm is to forestall entry by choosing an appropriate level of advertising and charging a price which impedes entry of new rivals in the industry. Once this is attained, the oligopolist wants to reap as much profit as possible.

A. The Equilibrium Conditions

In Williamson's model the firm has two policy variables, price P, and selling expense A. The problem facing the firm can be viewed as a constrained profit-maximisation problem: the firm must choose the price and selling expense which maximise its profit, subject to the constraint that entry be prevented.

Three conditions must be fulfilled:

First. Price must be set at an entry-preventing level. In symbols

$$P = P_L \tag{2.92}$$

where P_L = limit price, or entry-preventing price.

Second. The output produced must be set at a level where marginal cost is greater than marginal revenue. In symbols

$$\frac{\partial C}{\partial Q} > \frac{\partial R}{\partial Q} \quad \text{or} \quad MC > MR \tag{2.93}$$

In the theory of entry prevention, the price is higher than the purely competitive price but lower than the profit-maximising price. Hence the firm's output is larger than that of a profit maximiser.[35] This means that a firm whose goal is entry-forestalling will produce beyond the level where $MC = MR$, that is, in the range where the marginal cost is higher than the marginal revenue.

Third. The amount of money spent on advertising must be set at a level where the marginal cost of advertising is larger than the marginal revenue of advertising. In symbols

$$\frac{\partial R}{\partial A} < MC_A \tag{2.94}$$

where MC_A = marginal cost of advertising.

---

[34] O. E. Williamson, 'Selling Expense as a Barrier to Entry', *Quarterly Journal of Economics*, vol. 77, 1963, pp. 112–28.

[35] See Koutsoyiannis, *Modern Microeconomics*, chs 13 and 14.

We established in section II (page 83) that a profit maximiser will set his advertising at the level where

$$MR_A = MC_A$$

or

$$\frac{\partial R}{\partial A} = 1 + \frac{\partial C}{\partial A}$$

When advertising is used as a means of barring entry, advertising expense will be higher, that is, the amount spent on advertising will be at a level where $MC_A > MR_A$.

In Williamson's model the output of the firm does not change with advertising. The only thing advertising does is to enable the firm to charge a higher price. In other words, as advertising takes place, the shift of the demand curve and the change in its slope is such that the quantity remains constant, while price rises. Since output does not change with advertising, we have $\partial C/\partial A = 0$, so that the marginal cost of advertising is equal to 1. Thus we may write condition (2.94) in the form

$$\frac{\partial R}{\partial A} < 1 \quad \text{or} \quad MR_A < 1 \tag{2.95}$$

where $1 = \partial A/\partial A$ = marginal cost of advertising, with quantity constant.

B.   The 'Tools' of the Model

In order to explain (derive) the equilibrium of the firm, we must develop two 'tools': the 'line-constraint', and isoquants, drawn on the price—advertising space.

(i) The 'line-constraint'

The constraint $P = P_L$ is shown by the curve $\bar{P}_L P_L$ in Figure 2.18. It is assumed that the barriers to entry increase with the amount of advertising expense. Hence the price limiting entry, P_L, is an increasing function of advertising. In symbols we may write

$$\frac{\partial P_L}{\partial A} > 0 \tag{2.96}$$

where $\partial P_L/\partial A$ is the slope of the line $\bar{P}_L P_L$, which denotes the constraint (that the price is set at a level to forestall entry).

Any point on the $\bar{P}_L P_L$ curve and below it implies a price—advertising decision which impedes entry. At any point above the $\bar{P}_L P_L$ curve the price—advertising decisions are such that entry is *not* prevented. We will see presently that in equilibrium the firm will choose a point (a price and advertising expense) on the 'line-constraint'.

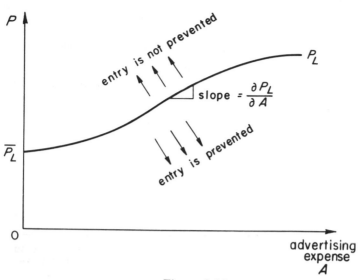

Figure 2.18

The intercept, $\bar{P}_L$, is the limit price without advertising. It reflects barriers arising from scale economies and absolute cost advantage. As advertising increases, so does the entry barrier, and hence the price P_L which the advertising firm can charge without attracting entry.

The *shape* of the $\bar{P}_L P_L$ curve implies that low levels of advertising would not erect high barriers, since potential entrants can match these expenditures fairly easily. At higher levels of advertising, however, the burden on potential entrants from selling expense increases; the barrier increases and so does P_L. However, eventually the curve flattens out. When the potential entrant believes that with a certain selling expense most of the essential information and other customer services have been provided, he is insensitive to selling expenses (by existing firms) in excess of this level. In other words, there is some limit to the effectiveness of advertising in deterring entry.

The *position* of the curve depends on the nature of the product. Three curves, corresponding to Bain's 'high', 'substantial' and 'low' barriers to entry,[36] are shown in Figure 2.19.

Cosmetics, drugs, liquor, soft drinks, for example, would have a 'high' P_L curve, since for such products advertising can create strong buyer preferences. On similar grounds one could argue that canned food, furniture and household appliances would have a 'substantial' P_L curve, and that rayon fabrics would have a low P_L curve.

(ii) *Isoquants on the price–advertising space*

An isoquant drawn on the price–advertising space shows the same level of output

[36] J. Bain, *Barriers to New Competition* (Harvard University Press, 1956).

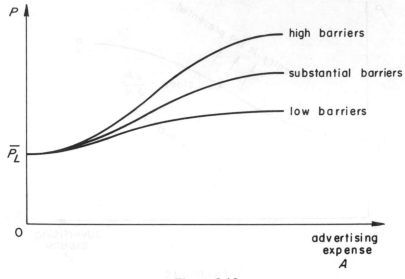

Figure 2.19

that can be sold with different combinations of price and advertising. A family
of such isoquants is shown in Figure 2.20. These isoquants have the following
properties.

(a) *The slope of the isoquant is positive*

$$\frac{\partial P}{\partial A} > 0 \tag{2.97}$$

This reflects the fact that advertising enables the firm to charge a higher price,
and still sell the same amount of output.

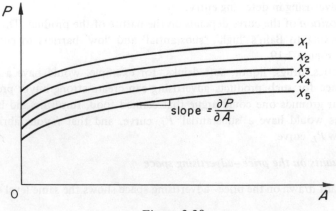

Figure 2.20

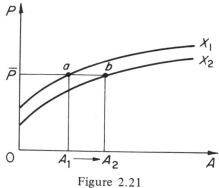

Figure 2.21

(b) *The isoquants do not intersect*, otherwise we would have a point (the point of the intersection) that would represent two different levels of output, which, of course, is impossible.

(c) *The isoquants are concave to the horizontal axis.* The curvature of the isoquant reflects the decreasing 'power' of advertising in maintaining customers' loyalty. As the firm increases its advertising, it can also increase its price, but at a decreasing rate, because higher prices weaken the brand loyalty of buyers.

(d) *The lower the isoquant, the greater the level of output it denotes.* At a given price, $\bar{P}$, the firm can sell a greater amount of output by increasing its selling expenditures. In Figure 2.21 we see that, as advertising increases from A_1 to A_2, the firm can sell $X_2 > X_1$. Similarly, with a given level of advertising expense, $\bar{A}$, the firm can sell more of its product, if it lowers its price. In Figure 2.22 it can be seen that, as price is reduced from P_1 to P_2, the firm can sell a larger output ($X_4 > X_3$), with the same advertising expense $\bar{A}$.

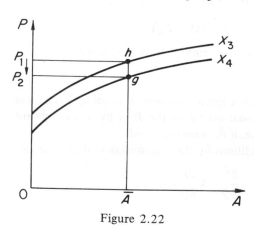

Figure 2.22

Before we proceed with the graphical (geometric) presentation of Williamson's model, it is useful to derive the equilibrium conditions in a formal way. This will facilitate the understanding of the economic meaning of the slopes of the various curves, which we shall use at a subsequent stage.

The firm wants to maximise its profit

$$\Pi = R - C - A \tag{2.98}$$

subject to

$$P = P_L$$

From the assumptions of the model we have

(a) $P_L = f(A)$ $\qquad$ (2.99)

$$\frac{\partial P_L}{\partial A} > 0$$

(b) $P = f(Q, A)$ $\qquad$ (2.100)

$$\frac{\partial P}{\partial Q} < 0; \quad \frac{\partial P}{\partial A} > 0$$

(c) $C = f(Q)$ $\qquad$ (2.101)

$$\frac{\partial C}{\partial Q} > 0; \quad \frac{\partial C}{\partial A} = 0$$

To solve the above constrained maximisation problem we use the familiar Lagrangian multiplier technique, writing the constraint in the form

$$P = P_L = 0$$

The 'composite' function to be maximised is

$$\phi = \Pi - \lambda(P - P_L)$$

or

$$\phi = R - C - A - \lambda(P - P_L) \tag{2.102}$$

where λ is the Lagrangian multiplier. It is assumed

$$\lambda > 0 \tag{2.103}$$

In this model λ has a specific economic meaning: λ is a measure of the marginal benefits which would accrue to the firm by a unit upward shift of the entire 'line-constraint', i.e. if $\bar{P}_L$ were increased.

First-order conditions for the maximisation of (2.102) yield

$$\frac{\partial \phi}{\partial Q} = \frac{\partial R}{\partial Q} - \frac{\partial C}{\partial Q} - \lambda \frac{\partial P}{\partial Q} = 0 \tag{2.104}$$

$$\frac{\partial \phi}{\partial A} = \frac{\partial R}{\partial A} - 1 - \lambda \left(\frac{\partial P}{\partial A} - \frac{\partial P_L}{\partial A} = 0 \right) \tag{2.105}$$

$$\frac{\partial \phi}{\partial \lambda} = (P - P_L) = 0 \tag{2.106}$$

Expression (2.106) gives $P = P_L$. That is, the constraint is operative in equilibrium, which means that the firm will choose a point on the 'line-constraint' (shown in Figure 2.18).

From expression (2.104) we obtain the optimal production condition

$$\frac{\partial R}{\partial Q} = \frac{\partial C}{\partial Q} + \lambda \frac{\partial P}{\partial Q} \tag{2.107}$$

Given that $\lambda > 0$ and $\partial P/\partial Q < 0$, it follows that the firm will produce at a range where

$$\frac{\partial C}{\partial Q} > \frac{\partial R}{\partial Q} \quad (\text{or } MC > MR) \tag{2.108}$$

Finally, from expression (2.105) we obtain the optimal advertising condition

$$\frac{\partial R}{\partial A} = 1 + \lambda \left(\frac{\partial P}{\partial A} - \frac{\partial P_L}{\partial A} \right) \tag{2.109}$$

where $1 = MC_A$ (with output constant).

It is apparent from (2.109) that the third equilibrium condition

$$\frac{\partial R}{\partial A} < 1 \quad (\text{or } MR_A < 1)$$

will be fulfilled only if

$$\frac{\partial P}{\partial A} < \frac{\partial P_L}{\partial A}$$

or

slope of isoquant < slope of the line-constraint

The meaning of this condition can be better understood if we superimpose the $\bar{P}_L P_L$ curve on the isoquant map. This is done in Figure 2.23. At point e' the line-constraint has a greater slope than the isoquant (X_4), because the former intersects the latter from above. Hence point e' is *not* an equilibrium point, since the isoquant is steeper than the line constraint.[37] Given that at this point $MR_A > MC_A$, the firm would be induced to increase its advertising expense along the same isoquant (X_4 in Figure 2.23). In so doing, however, the firm finds itself above the $\bar{P}_L P_L$ constraint, where its price–advertising policies do not deter entry. For example, at point Z entry will take place because the price is too high. To return on the constraint (at the higher advertising level A_2) the firm should reach point W: that is, the firm should lower its price, which would enable it to increase its output. (Note that W lies on isoquant X_5, which denotes

---

[37] At e' we have $(\partial P/\partial A) > (\partial P_L/\partial A)$. Thus expression (2.109) yields $(\partial R/\partial A) > 1$, or, $MR_A > MC_A$, which implies an advertising level lower than that of a profit maximiser, and, of course, lower than the advertising of a firm seeking to forestall entry, using advertising as a barrier.

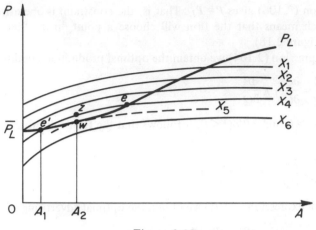

Figure 2.23

a higher level of output than X_4.) However, point W also is not an equilibrium position: although entry at this point is barred, profits are not maximised, because output is now too large (and price too low). At W the slope of the isoquant is equal to the slope of the line-constraint, so that $MC_A = 1$. But this apparent advantage of increasing advertising is offset by the increased production cost involved, given that, by the first equilibrium condition, $MC > MR$, and profit is reduced. The firm is now induced to move along the line-constraint, increasing further its advertising and its price, and reducing its output (reaching a higher isoquant). At any point to the right of W on the line-constraint the second equilibrium condition is satisfied, that is, the slope of the isoquant is steeper then the slope of the constraint

$$\frac{\partial P}{\partial A} > \frac{\partial P_L}{\partial A}$$

and we have $\partial R/\partial A < 1$.

C.   The Equilibrium of the Firm

From the above discussion it is apparent that there are many price—advertising levels which satisfy the two equilibrium conditions

$$MR < MC$$

$$MR_A < 1$$

Any point on the price—advertising space which satisfies these conditions is called (constitutes) a *feasible solution*. Among all the feasible solutions, the firm will choose the one that yields the maximum profit *and* satisfies the entry constraint.

We will first derive the set of feasible solutions open to the firm, and then we will explain how the firm reaches equilibrium.

The set of feasible solutions: the shape and position of isoprofit curves

In order to define the area of feasible solutions we make use of isoprofit curves.

In Figure 2.24 we show an isoprofit map drawn on the advertising–quantity space.

An isoprofit curve (drawn on the $A \leftrightarrow Q$ space) shows the same level of profit, attained with different amounts of quantity sold and advertising expenditure.

The shape and position of the isoprofit curves is determined by (a) the relationship between advertising and quantity (this relationship has in general the shape shown in Figure 2.4 above, which reflects the declining elasticity of demand w.r.t. advertising); (b) the price elasticity of demand; and (c) the shape of the production cost curve.

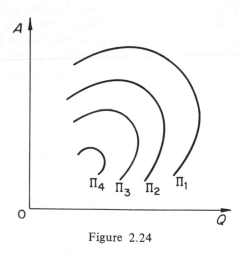

Figure 2.24

The shape of the isoprofit curves

The isoprofit curve (on the $A \leftrightarrow Q$ space) is concave to the origin. This implies that initially the firm can increase both its advertising and its output and still maintain the same level of profit. That is, over a certain range the slope of the isoprofit curve is positive. Consider point a on the isoprofit curve shown in Figure 2.25. At this point the firm spends A_1 on advertising and sells quantity Q_1. The firm can increase its advertising and its output (moving closer to a') and still maintain the same level of profit. Up to point a', advertising shifts the demand curve in such a way that the firm can sell a larger quantity at a higher

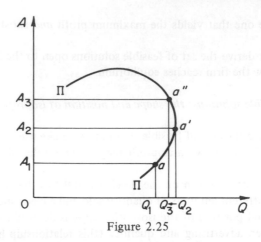

Figure 2.25

price.[38] Costs of production may also be declining due to technical economies. Beyond point a', however, if the firm increases further its advertising expense (say to A_3) and wants to maintain the same level of profit, it must reduce its output: advertising at such high levels does not allow any substantial increase in price. Furthermore, the firm might be producing at the rising part of its production cost (incurring technical diseconomies). A reduction in output will reduce production costs and offset the increase in advertising costs, so that the profit level is maintained. Thus beyond point a' the isoprofit curve turns backwards (acquires a negative slope).

The position of isoprofit curves

The closer to the origin the isoprofit curve is, the higher the level of profit that it signifies and vice versa: the further up the isoprofit curve, the lower the level of profit will be.

Consider point b (in Figure 2.26), which is the point of tangency of isoprofit curve Π_4 and a line vertical to the Q-axis. At b the output is $\bar{Q}$, and the advertising expense (A^*) is *the optimal level* (for that quantity of the product), given that at b we have $\partial A/\partial Q = 0$, that is, a change in advertising does not change the quantity sold.[39] Optimal advertising is the profit-maximising level of advertising, that is, the level where $MR_A = MC_A$ or $\partial R/\partial A = 1$. This is shown by point b^* in Figure 2.27. To the left of b^* (i.e. at a lower advertising level $A' < A^*$, given $\bar{Q}$) we have $MR_A > MC_A$, so that profit is not maximised for the given level of

---

[38] Recall that $\partial P/\partial A > 0$. Thus as A increases, so does the price. This will tend to reduce Q, given that $\partial P/\partial Q < 0$. That is, there will be a movement upwards on the demand curve of the firm. However, advertising shifts the firm's demand outwards, enabling the sale of a larger volume. The second effect is stronger than the first, so that the firm sells more at a higher price.

[39] Note that $\partial A/\partial Q$ is the slope of the vertical line through b, and this slope is, of course, equal to zero.

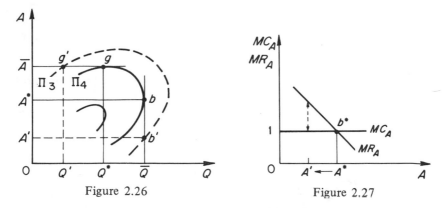

Figure 2.26   Figure 2.27

output $\bar{Q}$. In other words, as advertising is reduced, price falls ($\partial P/\partial A > 0$), and, given $\bar{Q}$, profit is reduced. In Figure 2.26, we see that the (lower) advertising level A' (given $\bar{Q}$) cuts the vertical line at point b', which lies on the isoprofit curve Π_3, showing a profit smaller than Π_4.

Similarly, consider point g (in Figure 2.26), which is the point of tangency of isoprofit curve Π_4 and a line vertical to the A-axis. Point g implies that given the advertising expense $\bar{A}$, the optimal level of output is Q^*. Optimal output is the profit-maximising output (given $\bar{A}$), that is, the output level where $MC = MR$ (or $\partial C/\partial Q = \partial R/\partial Q$). This point corresponds to point g^* in Figure 2.28. If the firm maintains the same advertising expense $\bar{A}$ but reduces its output (choosing, for example, Q' to the left of Q^* in Figure 2.28), then $MR > MC$, and the profit is not maximised (given $\bar{A}$). In Figure 2.26, we see that the lower output Q' (given $\bar{A}$) cuts the vertical (to the A-axis) line at point g', which lies on the isoprofit curve Π_3. Thus this curve, although above Π_4, shows a profit lower than Π_4.

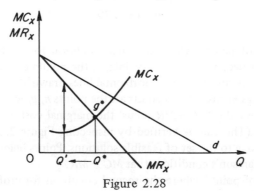

Figure 2.28

We next locate on the isoprofit map the points which satisfy the profit-maximising conditions

$$\frac{\partial C}{\partial Q} = \frac{\partial R}{\partial Q} \quad \text{(or } MC = MR)$$

and

$$\frac{\partial R}{\partial A} = 1 \qquad (\text{or } MR_A = MC_A)$$

This is done in Figure 2.29. In this figure point K represents the profit of a profit maximiser. Hence at this point both conditions are simultaneously satisfied.

However, for any lower (than K) level of profit, the two conditions are *not* fulfilled at the same price–advertising point.

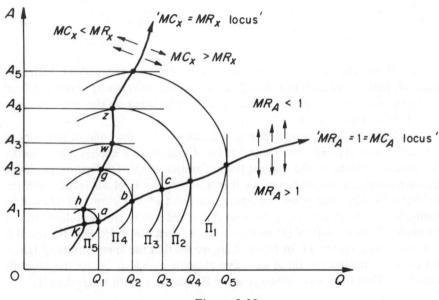

Figure 2.29

(1) The locus of points, where the first condition for profit maximisation ($MC = MR$) is satisfied, is obtained by joining the points of tangency between the isoprofit contours and a series of horizontal lines drawn at successively higher levels of advertising expense. (Such points are the points h, g, w, z in Figure 2.29.) At any point above the '$MC = MR$ locus' the marginal cost is smaller than the marginal revenue. (This can be verified by inspecting Figure 2.28.) Hence these points do not belong to the set of feasible solutions. Points below the '$MC = MR$ locus' satisfy Williamson's condition, that $MC > MR$.

(2) The locus of points, where the second condition for profit maximisation ($MR_A = 1 = MC_A$) is satisfied, is obtained by joining the points of tangency between the isoprofit contours and a series of vertical lines at consecutively higher levels of output. (Such points are the points $a, b, c,$ in Figure 2.29.) At any point below the '$MR_A = 1$ locus', the marginal revenue of advertising is greater than unit. (This can be verified by inspecting Figure 2.27.) Hence such

points violate the second condition of Williamson's model (and do not belong to the set of feasible solutions). However, at any point above the '$MR_A = 1$ locus' Williamson's second condition is met (i.e. $MR_A < 1$).

(3) The two loci intersect at point K, which denotes the profit of a profit maximiser. The intersection implies the simultaneous fulfilment of the two conditions for profit maximisation ($MC = MR$ and $MR_A = 1$).

It follows from the above analysis that the set of feasible solutions in Williamson's model is shown by the area 'bounded' by the two loci, to the right of their intersection at point K (shaded area in Figure 2.30).

It should be noted that at every level of output (to the right of the output corresponding to point K) the optimum selling expense (i.e. the profit-maximising level of A) is less than the selling expense for which the marginal revenue is equal to the marginal cost of production. For example, consider the level of output $\bar{Q}$ in Figure 2.30. The level of advertising A (at which $MR_A = 1$) is lower than A' (at which $MC = MR$). *Hence the price along the* '$MC = MR$ *locus' is everywhere higher than it is along the locus* '$MR_A = 1$'.[40]

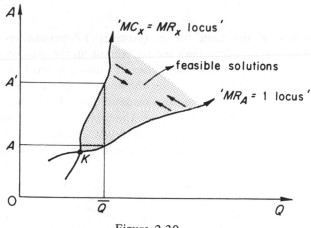

Figure 2.30

The next step is to draw the set of feasible solutions on the price–advertising space. This is attained by mapping the points of the two loci in the $A \leftrightarrow Q$ space of Figure 2.29, to the $P \leftrightarrow A$ space of Figure 2.31. In this figure the '$MC = MR$ locus' lies *above* the '$MR_A = 1$ locus' at all levels of output (to the right of point K', which denotes the profit of a profit maximiser). This is so because the price is higher along the '$MC = MR$ locus' than along the '$MR_A = 1$ locus'.

The set of feasible solutions on the $P \leftrightarrow A$ space is shown by the shaded area in Figure 2.31. It should be clear that $\Pi_5 > \Pi_4 > \ldots > \Pi_1$. That is, on the $P \leftrightarrow A$ space, the higher the isoprofit is, the larger the level of profit will be.

[40] Recall that if A increases, so does P, since, *ex hypothesi*, $\partial P / \partial A > 0$.

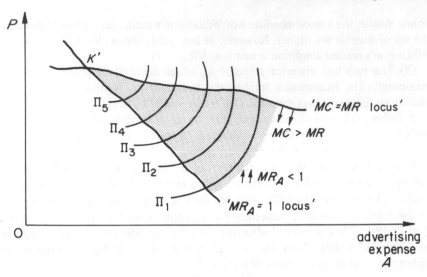

Figure 2.31

We now have all the 'tools' for the (geometric) determination of the equilibrium of the firm in Williamson's model. Among all the feasible solutions, the firm will choose the one which maximises its profit and which at the same time bars entry. This solution is defined by the point of tangency of the limit-price constraint ($\overline{P}_L P_L$ curve) to the highest isoprofit curve. In Figure 2.32 the equilibrium of the firm is denoted by point e. The firm incurs advertising expenses of an amount equal to A_L^*. It produces the output denoted by the isoquant Q_L^*, and sells it at the price P_L^*. This is an entry-preventing price, since it lies on the

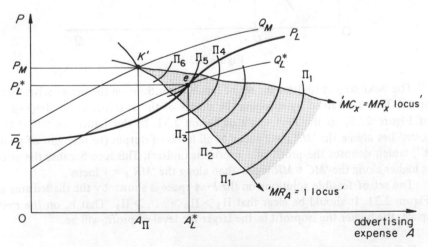

Figure 2.32

'line-constraint' curve, $\bar{P}_L P_L$. The firm's (constrained) profits are denoted by the isoprofit contour Π_5.

From the above analysis it is apparent that an optimal entry-prevention strategy combines a lower price with higher advertising expense and greater output as compared with an unconstrained profit-maximising strategy. From Figure 2.32 we see that

$$P_L < P_M$$

$$A_L > A_M$$

$$Q_L > Q_M$$

$$\Pi_L < \Pi_M = K$$

(where the subscript M denotes the equilibrium magnitudes of an unconstrained profit maximiser).

V. DISTRIBUTED-LAG MODELS OF THE ADVERTISING DECISION: NERLOVE'S STOCK-ADJUSTMENT HYPOTHESIS AND KOYCK'S GEOMETRIC LAG

Various writers have argued that firms pursue a 'target advertising' policy. The most common approach in this line of thought has been the extension of Nerlove's 'stock-adjustment' principle to the advertising decision.

The firm has a target (or desired) advertising level A^*, which depends on its current level of sales

$$A_t^* = b_0 + b_1 R_t + u_t \tag{2.110}$$

where u is a random disturbance. In any one period the firm adjusts its current advertising to the desired target level, but the adjustment is gradual, due to various reasons (e.g. capital-market imperfections, uncertainty in the product and factor markets, etc.). This adjustment mechanism may be approximated by the following function

$$[A_t - A_{t-1}] = \delta[A_t^* - A_{t-1}] \qquad 0 < \delta < 1 \tag{2.111}$$

where δ is the 'adjustment coefficient', measuring the speed of adjustment of the actual to the desired level of advertising.

Substituting A_t^* from (2.110) in (2.111) and rearranging, we obtain

$$A_t = (\delta b_0) + (\delta b_1)R_t + (1 - \delta)A_{t-1} + u_t^*$$

or

$$A_t = a_0 + a_1 R_t + a_2 A_{t-1} + u_t^* \tag{2.112}$$

In this model the current level of advertising depends on current sales *and* on the past level of advertising.

It should be noted that the lagged variable A_{t-1} appears as a determinant in other distributed lag models, derived by a Koyck scheme.[41] Such a scheme implies that past values of the explanatory variables affect the current level of advertising with a geometrically declining weight. For example, assume that the advertising level depends on the current and past level of sales:

$$A_t = a_0 + b_0 R_t + b_1 R_{t-1} + b_2 R_{t-2} + \ldots + u_t \tag{2.113}$$

Koyck's scheme assumes that the *b*s decline geometrically, that is, the influence of past levels of sales becomes smaller the more remote they are. In symbols, we may write

$$\left. \begin{aligned} b_1 &= \gamma b_0 \\ b_2 &= \gamma^2 b_0 \\ b_3 &= \gamma^3 b_0 \end{aligned} \right\} \tag{2.114}$$

and in general

$$\left. b_i = \gamma^i b_0 \right\}$$

where $0 < \gamma < i$.

Substituting (2.114) in (2.113), we obtain

$$A_t = a_0 + b_0 R_t + (\gamma b_0) R_{t-1} + (\gamma^2 b_0) R_{t-2} + (\gamma^3 b_0) R_{t-3} + \ldots \tag{2.115}$$

Lagging for one period, we obtain

$$A_{t-1} = a_0 + b_0 R_{t-1} + (\gamma b_0) R_{t-2} + (\gamma^2 b_0) R_{t-3} + \ldots \tag{2.116}$$

Subtracting (2.116) from (2.115) we find

$$A_t [a_0 (1 - \gamma)] + b_0 R_t + \gamma A_{t-1} + (u_t - \gamma u_{t-1})$$

or

$$A_t = c_0 + c_1 R_t + c_2 A_{t-1} + v_t \tag{2.117}$$

Thus the Koyck distributed-lag mechanism yields a model which is the same as Nerlove's 'stock-adjustment' principle. In both models[42] advertising in the current period is determined by current sales and the past level of advertising:

$$A_t = f(R_t, A_{t-1}) \tag{2.118}$$

---

[41] For a detailed discussion of the Koyck lag scheme see A. Koutsoyiannis, *Theory of Econometrics*, 2nd edn (Macmillan, 1977) ch. 13.
[42] See ibid for the estimation problems of these two models.

VI.   EMPIRICAL STUDIES OF THE ADVERTISING DECISION

From the theoretical models developed in the previous sections we may draw the following list of determinants of the advertising decision:

1. The goal of the firm.
2. The nature of the commodity (consumer good, producer good, etc.).
3. The amount of output sold (prior to advertising).
4. The price of the commodity.
5. The number of firms in the industry.
6. The amount of rivals' advertising expense.
7. The past level of advertising expense of the firm.
8. The general business conditions in the economy. It has been observed that the level of advertising has a definite pro-cyclical pattern, increasing in booms and declining in recessions.[43]
9. The tax treatment of advertising outlays. Under the present law, advertising outlays can be amortized in the year in which they are incurred, and this may induce firms to advertise excessively.

In symbols, we may write

$$A_t = f(Q_t, P_t, Q_{t-1}, N_t, A_{0,t}, A_{t-1}, B) \tag{2.119}$$

where Q_t = current quantity sold by the firm

P_t = current price of the commodity of the firm

Q_{t-1} = lagged quantity, sold by the firm in period $t - 1$

N = number of firms in the industry

A_0 = advertising expense of rivals

A_{t-1} = lagged advertising by the firm

B = an index of 'general business conditions'

Usually Q_t and P_t are combined in the single factor 'sales revenue', R_t.

Expression (2.119) implies that the factors appearing on the right-hand side are independent from advertising: the way of causation goes *from* these factors *to* advertising. Economic theory,[44] however, and empirical evidence[45] suggest that there is a two-way causation between advertising and sales revenue. In other words, sales (R_t) affect and are affected by advertising expense (A_t). This has

---

[43] N. H. Borden, *The Economic Effects of Advertising* (Irwin, 1942); J. M. Cover *et al.*, 'Department Store Sales and Advertising', *Journal of Business*, 1931; Schmalensee, *The Economics of Advertising*; L. Wagner, 'Advertising and the Business Cycle', *Journal of Marketing*, 1941; C. Y. Yang, 'Industrial Production: The Key to Advertising Volume', *Advertising Age*, 1962; D. M. Blank, 'Cyclical Behaviour of National Advertising', *Journal of Business*, 1962, pp. 14–27.

[44] See Schmalensee, *The Economics of Advertising*.

[45] Borden, *The Economic Effects of Advertising*; R. W. Jastram, 'Advertising Outlays Under Oligopoly', *Review of Economics and Statistics*, 1949, pp. 106–9; Taplin, 'Advertising Appropriations Policy'; H. J. Bullen, '1961 Industrial Ad Budgets: How Big, What Goes Into Them', *Industrial Marketing*, 1961, pp. 31–9.

implications for the method of estimating the advertising decision function. In particular, one should use simultaneous-equation methods, otherwise the estimates of the coefficients will be biased and inconsistent.[46]

In the real business world it has been observed that firms widely use the 'percentage-of-sales' rule of thumb in deciding their advertising budget.[47] That is, firms usually set advertising as a proportion of their sales revenue:

$$A_t = kR_t$$

Some writers have argued that this behaviour provides evidence for the profit-maximisation hypothesis. This interpretation is not necessarily true, as we explained in section II. The 'percentage-of-sales' rule is compatible with profit maximisation only under very restrictive assumptions which are not likely to hold in the real world.

Very few empirical studies have been conducted to test the alternative hypotheses pertaining to the explanation of the advertising decision. Most of the empirical research in the area of advertising has focused on the *effects* of advertising. We will discuss the findings of this research in the next section. In the remainder of the present section we shall discuss four studies of the advertising decision.

A. Melrose's Study

Melrose[48] estimated several advertising decision functions of the form

$$A_t = f(R_t, A_{t-1}) \qquad\qquad\qquad (2.120)$$

Recall that underlying this formulation is Nerlove's stock-adjustment principle or Koyck's geometric lag (see section V).

The results of one of Melrose's functions are

$$A_t = -56.6036 + 0.3069\,R_t + 0.4578\,A_{t-1} \qquad\qquad (2.121)$$

$$\text{s.e.} \quad (72.38) \quad (0.051) \quad\quad (0.087)$$

$$R^2 = 0.812 \quad d = 1.77$$

Both current revenue, R_t, and lagged advertising expense, A_{t-1}, appear to be significant explanatory variables of the advertising decision. However, the advertising function has been estimated by the method of *Ordinary Least Squares*, which yields biased and inconsistent estimates of the coefficients, given the simultaneous

[46] For the consequences of using single-equation methods when they are not appropriate, see Koutsoyiannis, *Theory of Econometrics*.

[47] Schmalensee, *The Economics of Advertising*; Rasmussen, 'The Determination of Advertising Expenditures'.

[48] K. B. Melrose, 'An Empirical Study of Optimising Advertising Policy', *Journal of Business*, 1969, pp. 282–92.

relationship between A_t and R_t. Furthermore, the function is mis-specified, in that most of the important *a priori* determinants of the advertising decision are not included in the estimated model.

B. Schmalensee's Study

Schmalensee[49] estimated a function, similar to Melrose's advertising function, for the Pinkham Medicine Company. The only difference between the two models is that Schmalensee introduced in the function a dummy variable, Z, to take into account the fact that Pinkham did not cut A during the recession years 1926–36. Z takes the value of 1 for this period and zero elsewhere. Schmalensee's results are

$$A_t = 22.8797 + 0.6400\,(Z_t R_t) + 0.4564\,[(1 - Z_t)R_t] + 0.0015\,A_{t-1}$$

(2.122)

s.e.   (63.265) (0.841)   (0.054)   (0.122)

$R^2 = 0.869$ $d = 1.54$

The coefficient of A_{t-1} is not significant in Schmalensee's function. In general his study suffers from the same defects as that of Melrose's.

C. Bass's Study

Bass[50] conducted a simultaneous-equation study of the regular and filter cigarette consumption in the USA. His model for each of these two categories of cigarettes is of the form:

$$R_j = f(A_j, A_0, Y, P_c/P_I)$$

(2.123)

$$A_j = f(R_j, A_0)$$

(2.124)

where S_j = sales of cigarettes of the jth type
       A_j = advertising of cigarettes of the jth type
       Y = personal disposable income
       P_c = price of non-filter cigarettes
       P_I = consumer price index
       A_0 = advertising of the other type of cigarettes

Both equations are estimated in log-linear form, which implies constant elasticities. Bass's study has the advantage that it takes into account the two-way causation

[49] Schmalensee, *The Economics of Advertising*.
[50] F. M. Bass, 'A Simultaneous-Equation Regression Study of Advertising and Sales of Cigarettes', *Journal of Marketing*, 1969, pp. 291–300.

between advertising and sales. However, Bass's advertising function does not include many of the important (*a priori*) determinants of the advertising decision.

D.   Bass and Parsons's Study

Bass and Parsons[51] conducted a simultaneous-equation study for RH2, a product belonging to the category of frequently purchased goods predominantly sold in supermarkets. A four-equation system was estimated, relating sales and advertising of RH2 and of the 'remainder' (defined as all other established brands):

$$R_{(RH2)t} = f_1 \left[A_{(RH2)t}, A_{(0)t}, A_{(N)t}, R_{(RH2)t-1}, R_{(0)t-1}, R_{(N)t} \right]$$

$$A_{(RH2)t} = f_2 \left[S_{(RH2)t-1}, A_{(0)t-1}, A_{(RH2)t-1}, A_{(0)t-1} \right]$$

$$R_{(0)t} = f_3 \left[A_{(0)t}, A_{(RH2)t}, A_{(N)t}, R_{(0)t-1}, R_{(RH2)t-1}, R_{(N)t} \right]$$

$$A_{(0)t} = f_4 \left[R_{(0)t-1}, R_{(RH2)t-1}, A_{(0)t-1}, A_{(RH2)t-1} \right]$$

where $R_{(0)}$ and $A_{(0)}$ refer to the 'remainder' (other existing) brands, and R_N and A_N refer to the sales and advertising of *new* brands being on the market less than one year (both variables are exogenous). In this model only one advertising variable (in the demand—sales equations) is statistically significant.

Bass and Parsons conducted a similar study for RH2 and SL6. For each of these a four-equation log-linear model is presented which contains demand and advertising decisions equations for the brand under study and for the 'remainder'. In both cases specifications are identical to those discussed above. For the new brand (SL6), structural estimation yielded three significant advertising coefficients.

The above survey of the empirical literature has not produced any impressive results. Single-equation models fail to take into account the simultaneous relationship between the variables, while the results of simultaneous-equation models are not satisfactory. Both types of studies do not include most of the theoretically important explanatory variables of the advertising decision. It is apparent that more empirical research is required for testing the alternative hypotheses regarding the determinants of the advertising decision.

VII.   EFFECTS OF ADVERTISING

The effects of advertising have been strongly debated in economic literature. In this section we shall present the main issues of the controversy and summarise the available empirical evidence in each case.

[51] F. M. Bass and L. J. Parsons, 'Simultaneous-Equation Regression Analysis of Sales and Advertising', *Applied Economics*, 1969, pp. 103–24.

A. Advertising and Concentration

Economic theory suggests that there is a two-way causation between advertising
and concentration: advertising sets into motion forces which push an industry
towards an oligopolistic organisation; conversely, high concentration encourages
increases in advertising expenditures.

First. Given some initial distribution of the size of firms, as all firms engage in
advertising it is likely that market shares will change. Some firms will be more
successful in their selling strategy than others. The former will expand at the
expense of the latter,[52] and there will be a change in shares, either because of a
shift of customers to the more successful firms, given industry demand, or
because the more successful firms will capture a larger proportion of the enlarged
market following the shift in industry demand induced by the general increase
in advertising. The increase in concentration will be stronger if there exist economies of scale in advertising (see p. 123).

Second. In oligopolistic markets, firms prefer to compete with weapons like
product changes and/or advertising. Even if firms are profit maximisers, it is
likely that advertising expenditures will exceed joint profit-maximising levels,
because oligopolists are likely to believe that they can strengthen their market
position by being more effective with their advertising or product strategies. A
large part of the advertising outlays becomes 'self-cancelling', because rival firms
adopt similar strategies, and the intended benefit at the expense of the rivals is
not materialised.[53] Of course, advertising outlays will be higher if oligopolistic
firms are growth seekers.[54]

Several writers have explored empirically the relationship between advertising
and concentration.

Telser[55] correlated advertising intensity (the ratio of advertising expenditure
to sales revenue) and the four-firm concentration ratio in a sample of forty-two
consumer goods industries in three years (1947, 1954 and 1958). Telser's correlation coefficients were 0.163, 0.165 and 0.169 for these years respectively, and
all were insignificant at the 0.05 level. From this finding Telser concluded that
the relationship between advertising and concentration is 'unimpressive'.

Telser's findings were questioned by Mann.[56] He argued that Telser's data
(from the US Internal Revenue Service) refer to very broad market classifications,
which include markets that should be separated because they include widely
dissimilar products. More important, Telser's low correlations seem to be due to

[52] Kaldor, 'The Economic Aspects of Advertising', p. 13
[53] William Fellner, *Competition Among the Few* (Augustus Kelley, 1965) p. 186.
[54] See the discussion of Baumol's advertising model in section III.
[55] Lester G. Telser, 'Advertising and Competition', *Journal of Political Economy*, vol. 72,
1964, p. 544.
[56] H. M. Mann, 'Advertising, Concentration, and Profitability: The State of Knowledge
and Directions for Public Policy', in *Industrial Concentration: The New Learning*, ed. H.
Goldschmid, H. M. Mann and J. F. Weston (Little, Brown & Co., 1974).

a few extreme observations in his sample. To avoid this shortcoming, Mann estimated the rank correlation coefficients using Telser's sample. The rank correlation coefficients were 0.292, 0.362 and 0.300 for the same years, and were all significant at the 0.05 level (or better).

Else,[57] using a cross-section of forty-four non-durable consumer-goods industries in the United Kingdom, argued that the advertising—sales ratios in 1951 and 1954 were correlated with the degree of sellers' concentration.

Mann et al.,[58] in an attempt to overcome the broad classification defect of Telser's study, selected a sample of forty-two large firms from fourteen narrowly defined industries. Applying correlation analysis, they found fairly high correlations between advertising—sales ratios and four-firm concentration ratios (the value of R ranged from 0.41 to 0.72 in six cases). The years 1954, 1958 and 1963 were examined, and two sets of estimates of advertising were employed. The correlation coefficients were statistically significant.

The above findings led to considerable controversy.

Ekelund and Maurice,[59] Telser[60] and Ekelund and Gramm[61] have argued that no significant correlation between advertising intensity and concentration exists in the USA.

Doyle,[62] Reekie,[63] and Schnabel[64] report similar negative findings with UK data.

However, Marcus,[65] Mann et al.,[66] and Mann and Meehan[67] have contended that there is a significant correlation between advertising—sales ratios and concentration.

[57] P. K. Else, 'The Incidence of Advertising in Manufacturing Industries', *Oxford Economic Papers*, 1966, pp. 88–105.

[58] H. M. Mann et al., 'Advertising and Concentration', *Journal of Industrial Economics*, 1967, pp. 81–4.

[59] R. B. Ekelund and C. Maurice, 'An Empirical Investigation of Advertising and Concentration: Comment', *Journal of Industrial Economics*, 1969, pp. 76–80.

[60] L. Telser, 'Another Look at Advertising and Concentration', *Journal of Industrial Economics*, 1969.

[61] R. B. Ekelund and W. Gramm, 'Advertising and Concentration: New Evidence', *Antitrust Bulletin*, 1970.

[62] P. Doyle, 'Advertising Expenditure and Consumer Demand', *Oxford Economic Papers*, 1968, pp. 394–416.

[63] W. D. Reekie, 'Some Problems Associated with the Marketing of Ethical Pharmaceutical Products', *Journal of Industrial Economics*, 1970, pp. 33–49.

[64] M. Schnabel, 'A Note on Advertising and Industrial Concentration', *Journal of Political Economy*, 1970, pp. 1191–4.

[65] M. Marcus, 'Advertising and Changes in Concentration', *Southern Economic Journal*, 1969, pp. 117–21.

[66] H. M. Mann et al., 'Testing Hypotheses in Industrial Economics: A Reply', *Journal of Industrial Economics*, 1969, pp. 81–4; H. M. Mann et al., 'Statistical Testing in Industrial Economics: A Reply on Measurement Error and Sampling Procedure', *Journal of Industrial Economics*, 1969, pp. 95–100.

[67] H. M. Mann and J. W. Meehan, 'Advertising and Concentration: New Data and an Old Problem', *Antitrust Bulletin*, 1971, p. 101.

In recent years a study by Guth,[68] one by Ornstein, Weston, Intrilligator and Shrieves[69] and one by Mueller and Hamm[70] have also found a positive and significant relationship between advertising intensity and concentration. Mueller and Hamm report that industries with high advertising intensity (advertising–sales ratios of 10 per cent or higher) have shown significantly greater increases in concentration over the years 1947 to 1970 than industries with moderate or low advertising intensity.

A study by Greer[71] has a given a different twist to the advertising–concentration controversy. Greer postulated that the relationship between advertising and concentration is quadratic (see Figure 2.33).

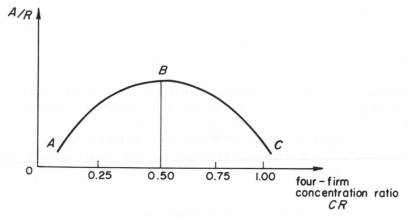

Figure 2.33

According to Greer, the quadratic form implies a two-way causation. Up to a certain point advertising can increase concentration (section *AB* of the quadratic function in Figure 2.33). However, once concentration has reached a certain level (the four-firm concentration ratio is beyond 0.45–0.50) there is a feedback effect of concentration upon advertising, because of tacit collusion between oligopolists, which reduces the amount of advertising expenditures. Greer cites Fellner's *Competition Among the Few* as the theoretical basis for his quadratic function. Fellner does indeed predict the possibility of tacit collusion, where non-price variables are concerned, but only for what he calls 'completely mature' oligopolies. It is questionable whether Greer's sample of forty-one three-digit

[68] L. Guth, 'Advertising and Market Structure Revisited', *Journal of Industrial Economics*, vol. 19, 1971, pp. 179–200.

[69] S. Ornstein, J. F. Weston, M. D. Intrilligator and R. E. Shrieves, 'Determinants of Market Structure', *Southern Economic Journal*, vol. 39, 1973, pp. 612–25.

[70] W. F. Mueller and L. G. Hamm, 'Trends in Industrial Market Concentration', *Review of Economics and Statistics* (forthcoming).

[71] D. F. Greer, 'Advertising and Market Concentration', *Southern Economic Journal*, vol. 38, 1971, pp. 19–32.

industries contains any mature oligopoly (in the Fellner sense), and hence his theoretical framework is rather shaky. Greer's hypothesis can better be rooted on Fellner's assertion that non-price competition is preferable to oligopolists, and on the observed fact that in the real world large corporations compete with non-price variables. Apart from its theoretical shortcomings, Greer's empirical results are very sensitive to the presense of one observation. Greer estimated twelve correlations, nine of which do not pass the conventional tests for statistical significance when one observation is omitted from his sample. Thus Greer's evidence cannot be considered convincing.

Several studies in subsequent years have attempted to test Greer's quadratic advertising–concentration hypothesis. The most important are one study by Ornstein (who found no evidence of a quadratic relationship)[72] and one by Strickland and Weiss (who found evidence supporting a quadratic function).[73] The controversy has become highly technical, centred upon econometric techniques[74] and data deficiencies.

In summary:

(1) Most studies to date indicate that there is a positive (usually significant) relationship between advertising intensity and concentration for consumer-goods industries.

(2) Theory and some statistical evidence suggest that there is a dual causation (two-way causation) between advertising and concentration. The issues, however, have not been settled.

B.   Advertising, Barriers to Entry, and Profitability

Economic theory suggests that advertising may contribute to the perpetuation of oligopolistic market structures, by creating or strengthening existing barriers to entry.[75]

(1) *Advertising and the preference barrier.* Advertising is one of the most important ways of differentiating a product. To the extent that advertising creates brand loyalty, potential entrants face a significant obstacle to attracting customers from existing firms.

(2) *Advertising and absolute cost advantage.* A new entrant must incur some

[72] S. I. Ornstein, 'The Advertising–Concentration Controversy', *Southern Economic Journal*, vol. 43, 1976, pp. 892–902. See also T. S. Friedland, 'Advertising and Concentration', *Journal of Industrial Economics*, vol. 26, 1977, pp. 151–60.

[73] A. Strickland and L. Weiss, 'Advertising, Concentration and Price–Cost Margins', *Journal of Political Economy*, vol. 84, 1976, pp. 1109–21.

[74] Schmalensee, *The Economics of Advertising*, argues that if there is a two-way causation, the existing studies are inappropriate, because they use the method of ordinary least squares (OLS), which is a single-equation technique. See pp. 115–16.

[75] The analysis of this section follows the theoretical argument of W. S. Comanor and T. A. Wilson, 'Advertising, Market Structure and Performance', *Review of Economics and Statistics*, vol. 49, 1967, pp. 423–40.

penetration costs in order to establish himself in a market. In general, penetration costs represent an investment in establishing a market position. They consist mainly of extra advertising outlays which are required for entry. (If the entrant is forced to set a price lower than that of the existing firms, then penetration costs include this price differential times the amount of sales of the new entrant.) Established firms need not incur penetration costs, while an entrant must advertise (and/or charge a lower price) in order to break buyers' brand loyalty and inertia. The unit costs of market penetration are likely to increase as output expands, because it becomes increasingly more difficult to attract customers who are more inert, or loyal, with strong brand preferences. This effect of advertising creates an absolute cost advantage for established firms.

(3) *Advertising and scale economies*.[76] There are real and pecuniary economies of scale of advertising. There is a range of outputs where the marginal effect of advertising on sales is rising due to the increasing effectiveness of advertising messages per unit of output (real advertising scale economies). Furthermore, there is a range over which the cost for each advertising message purchased by the firm on the TV or in the press decreases (pecuniary economies of mass advertising).[77] In each industry there is a certain amount of advertising expense which must be incurred by each firm in order to stay in the market and maintain its share. Larger firms have the advantage of being able to spread this cost over a larger output, so that the unit cost of advertising is less for larger firms than for smaller firms. This advantage creates economies of scale at the firm level, since an established firm does not have to spend twice as much on advertising to maintain a market share which is twice that of a rival. As a result, smaller firms, including most entrants, are placed at a strong disadvantage. Unit advertising costs also decline when the 'price' of advertising messages is lower for larger amount of advertising messages.[78] The scale disadvantage of a new entrant will be greater if the established firms react to entry by increasing their advertising.

In summary, there is a minimum optimal scale of advertising, which, if superimposed on to production scale economies, may result in a larger amount of output which the entrant must sell in order to reap all the economies of scale (production and advertising). Thus advertising may increase the minimum efficient plant size.

(4) *Advertising and the initial capital requirements barrier*. The market penetration costs increase the capital requirements of a new entrant. If also there exist economies of scale in advertising, the need to obtain funds for advertising will further increase. Furthermore, the investment in market penetration is a

---

[76] Backman, *Advertising and Competition*.

[77] The extent of discounts given to large advertisers is documented in Federal Trade Commission *vs* The Procter & Gamble Company, Brief for the Federal Trade Commission in the Supreme Court of the United States (December 1966), pp. 12–13.

[78] Strickland and Weiss, 'Advertising, Concentration and Price–Cost Margins'. The authors found evidence of substantial economies of scale in advertising expenditures.

particularly risky use of funds, since it does not generally create tangible assets which can be resold in the event of failure.[79] Thus the financing of advertising will not only require additional initial funds but will also be more costly.

The above effects of advertising on the various barriers are shown in Figure 2.34.

Curve *APC* is the average production cost for established and prospective firms, and $\bar{x}$ is the minimum efficient scale of production (in the absence of advertising).

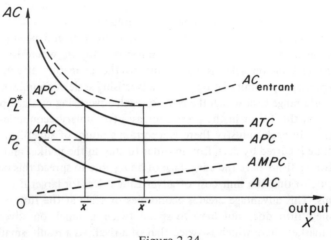

Figure 2.34

Curve *AAC* is the average advertising cost for established firms and for new entrants after they have became established. It is the unit cost required to stay in the market and maintain the attained market share. (Note that if the established firms react to entry with increased advertising, the *AAC* curve would be higher.)

Curve *ATC* is the summation of the *APC* and *AAC* (excluding penetration costs) curves. If production and advertising scale economies are combined, the minimum efficient scale of plant increases to $\bar{x}'$.

Curve *AMPC* is the average market penetration cost. If it is added to the *ATC*, it gives rise to the average total cost curve of the potential entrant (*AC* in Figure 2.34). The minimum efficient plant size when all the effects of advertising are taken into account is $\bar{x}'$. (The minimum efficient scale might be smaller than $\bar{x}'$ (but higher than $\bar{x}$) if penetration unit costs rise sharply with output.)

As a result of the effects of advertising on industry concentration and barriers to entry, established oligopolistic firms acquire a considerable monopoly power. From Figure 2.34 it can be seen that firms which are heavy advertisers can charge

<hr />

[79] See Comanor and Wilson, 'Advertising, Market Structure and Performance'.

a higher price (P_L^*) without attracting entry. P_L^* would not be possible in the absence of advertising. Thus advertising impedes competition and leads to misallocation of resources.

Direct evidence of advertising as a barrier to entry has been provided by Bain, and by Comanor and Wilson.

Bain, in his classic study *Barriers to New Competition*, found that product differentiation (attained mainly by intensive advertising and other selling activities) is the most important barrier to entry.

Comanor and Wilson[80] also found that advertising poses a considerable barrier, allowing firms to earn half as much as firms operating in industries with low advertising intensity.

Comanor and Wilson's findings were criticised on the grounds that they measured profitability in terms of book asset values or book equity, and treated advertising as a current expense rather than as an investment. This argument requires some attention, since many economists argue that advertising is similar to investment in fixed assets. (See also section II of this chapter.)

It is argued that advertising is appropriately viewed as constituting investment that yields returns both currently and in the future.[81] Accordingly a profit-maximising firm should undertake advertising up to the point where the internal rate of return on advertising is equal or greater than the firm's cost of capital funds, which, under certainty, is equal to the market interest rate.[82]

Although advertising expenditures have the properties of an investment, most firms do not treat them as investments. They usually charge them as outlays in the year in which they are incurred, and no allowance is made for the image, goodwill and future profit prospects that advertising creates.[83] Hence the book value of most firms' assets is understated, because no adjustment is made to take

[80] Ibid.

[81] Heflebower, 'The Theory and Effects of Non-Price Competition', in *Monopolistic Competition: Studies in Impact*, ed. Kuenne, pp. 177–201; also Hans Brems, *Product Equilibrium Under Monopolistic Competition* (Harvard University Press, 1951) pp. 116–31.

[82] We will see in Chapter 4 that the internal rate of return of an investment project (IRR) is the rate of discount which equates the stream of future earnings from the investment to the initial cost of the investment. If we denote by S_t the future stream of earnings expected from an advertising project which costs $£A$, the IRR is found from the expression

$$A = \sum_{t=1}^{n} \frac{S_t}{(1 + \text{IRR})^t}$$

The advertising should be undertaken if its IRR is greater than the market interest rate, under certainty. (See Chapter 4.)

[83] Palda found that the Lydia Pinkham Medicine Company realised 95 per cent of the advertising-generated sales within approximately seven years. See Palda, *The Measurement of Cumulative Advertising Effects*. A similar time lag between advertising expenditures and sales was estimated in the cigarette market by Telser. He found that advertising expenditures built up a fund of goodwill that depreciated at a rate of 15 to 20 per cent per year. See L. Telser, 'Advertising and Cigarettes', *Journal of Political Economy*, vol. 70, 1962, pp. 471–99.

into account the increase in the value of the firm's assets as a result of advertising expenditures. Profitability studies often report high profit rates being earned by firms that advertise intensively, because they compute the profit rate using book value of assets. If advertising expenditures were treated as investments in physical assets, the firm's value of assets would be much higher, and so part at least of the higher reported profit rates for firms that spend large amounts on advertising might disappear.[84]

Weiss[85] attempted to correct the methodological deficiency of the Comanor and Wilson study. He capitalised the advertising expenditures over a six-year period, which seems reasonable in the light of the studies of Palda, Telser and other researchers. Weiss found that even when advertising was treated as an investment expenditure, there still remained a positive relationship between advertising and profit rates.

The Comanor–Wilson results have been substantiated by several other studies.[86] These studies, however, suffer from the same methodological deficiency as that of the Comanor–Wilson study.

One of the most vehement critics of the studies that purport to find a positive relationship between advertising and profitability is Jules Backman.[87] He attacks the statistical relationship between advertising and profitability on methodological grounds, but he fails to produce empirical evidence to the contrary.

Bloch[88] re-did a study by the Federal Trade Commission (FTD), using actual advertising expenditures and treating them as an investment. His findings refuted the FTD results. Bloch reports that the firms used in the FTD study do not show a positive relationship between advertising and profit rates.

Yale Brozen[89] also criticises the statistical positive relationship between profitability and advertising, on the grounds that the researchers did not treat advertising as an investment.

On balance, the statistical evidence is that the profit rates are positively related to advertising, though the issue is not yet settled.

[84] J. V. Koch, *Industrial Organization and Prices*, 2nd edn (Prentice-Hall, 1980), pp. 307–10.

[85] Weiss, 'Advertising, Profits and Corporate Taxes'.

[86] R. Sherman and R. Tollison, 'Advertising and Profitability', *Review of Economics and Statistics*, vol. 53, 1971, pp. 397–407; L. Esposito and F. Esposito, 'Foreign Competition and Domestic Industry Profitability', *Review of Economics and Statistics*, vol. 53, 1971, pp. 343–53; W. G. Shepherd, 'The Elements of Market Structure', *Review of Economics and Statistics*, vol. 54, 1972, pp. 25–37; R. A. Miller, 'Market Structure and Industrial Performance: Relation of Profit Rates to Concentration, Advertising Intensity, and Diversity', *Journal of Industrial Economics*, vol. 17, 1970, pp. 104–24; Federal Trade Commission, *Economic Report on the Influence of Market Structure on the Profit Performance of Food Manufacturing Companies* (Washington, D.C., 1969).

[87] Backman, *Advertising and Competition*.

[88] Harry Bloch, 'Advertising, Competition, and Market Performance', Ph.D. dissertation, University of Chicago, 1971.

[89] Yale Brozen, 'Entry Barriers: Advertising and Product Differentiation', in *Industrial Concentration: The New Learning*, ed. Goldschmid, Mann and Weston, pp. 115–137.

Studies of profitability have to resolve many complex methodological problems. (1) The lagged effects of advertising must be taken into account (i.e. advertising must be treated as an investment). (2) Profitability is not influenced only by advertising but also by other sources of market power. (3) The existing tax laws encourage firms to engage in excessive advertising, since such expenditures are viewed as current outlays and are tax deductible. This has lead Mann to the rather extreme statement that

> Further investigation may find that intense advertisers do not earn rates of return markedly different from modest advertisers. This would not mean that heavy advertising is not a barrier to entry. Rather, the meaning is that the tax laws reinforce the oligopolistic tendency to inflate advertising expenditure excessively.[90]

(4) Finally, most studies of the relationship between profitability and advertising use cross-industry samples, which require a very carefully specified set of regressors. Most of the used specifications leave much to be desired. Hence some economists consider such studies misleading.[91]

Up to this point we have presented the theoretical basis and the empirical evidence of the hypothesis that advertising raises or increases barriers to entry. The opposite view is also put forward by several writers. For example, Brozen[92] argues that advertising is used as a means of entry: that is, advertising can break the existing brand loyalty of consumers and create a market for a new entrant. Brozen bases his thesis on the following observations: (1) New products are advertised more intensively than old products. (2) Firms with the largest market share are not always the most intensive advertisers. (3) Brand loyalty of customers is lower in markets with heavy advertising than in markets with less intense advertising. According to Brozen, none of these facts supports the view that advertising is a barrier to entry or is used to create a barrier to entry. On the contrary, these observations show that advertising is a means which facilitates entry.

A closer examination of Brozen's arguments shows that his claim is not valid. *First*, new products are more heavily advertised irrespective of whether they are introduced by existing firms or new entrants. *Second*, large firms need not be the most intense advertisers, because of the cumulative effects of advertising and the economies associated with size. *Third*, the fact that heavily advertised products have less stable market shares than do less advertised products tells us nothing about the degree of rivalry or the ease of entry. Lipsey and Steiner have

---

[90] H. M. Mann, 'Advertising, Concentration and Profitability', in *Industrial Concentration: The New Learning*, p. 146.

[91] P. Cattin and D. R. Sittink, 'Industry Differences in the Relationship between Advertising and Profitability', *Industrial Organization Review*, vol. 4, 1976, pp. 156–64.

[92] Brozen, 'Entry Barriers: Advertising and Product Differentiation', in *Industrial Concentration: The New Learning*.

argued that established firms may proliferate brands (introduce new brands of the same product) in order to forestall entry.[93] The barrier would be stronger if continual new product introduction becomes part of the pattern of competition, because buyers may cease to switch randomly, and begin to choose only after strong persuasive advertising of the newly introduced products. There is evidence that advertising expenditures increase with new products.[94] Since advertising is positively related to concentration, and heavy advertising is associated with new product offerings, it follows that the established oligopolists are the chief promoters of the new products, not new entrants.

C.   Advertising and Prices

There are two schools of thought regarding the relationship between advertising and price.

The one school assumes that advertising is informative: it informs consumers about price, quality and the terms of sale. Informed consumers, in turn, select the sellers with the lowest price. Thus advertising drives prices down. Brozen[95] argues that due to imperfect knowledge of consumers about price and quality differentials, a firm's demand is inelastic. Advertising improves information, spreads knowledge and makes the demand for a seller's product more elastic. Telser[96] adds that advertising attracts customers with weaker brand preferences who are sensitive to price, thus further increasing the elasticity of demand. Finally, Demsetz[97] has shown that under certain assumptions, the demand curve of a firm is more elastic in the presence of advertising as compared with that existing in the absence of advertising.

---

[93] If a certain fraction of customers switches brands periodically on a random basis, a new entrant can expect to attract a smaller portion of these switchers as the number of brands offered by the established firms rises. For example, assume that there are three firms in an industry, selling only one brand each. If 40 per cent of the total buyers choose brands in a random way each year, a new firm can expect to attract 25 per cent of these 'random customers', since it will be selling one brand out of a total of four available brands. This would give the new entrant a share of 10 per cent of the total market (25 per cent of the 40 per cent 'random customers'). If, however, each of the three existing firms is selling four brands, there would be twelve brands available on the market (before entry), and a new entrant selling only one brand could expect to catch only one-thirteenth of the 40 per cent random switchers, that is, the share of the new entrant would be 3 per cent of the total market (= [1/13] × [0.40] = 0.03). See R. Lipsey and P. Steiner, *Economics*, 2nd edn (Harper & Row, 1966) p. 320.

[94] R. D. Buzzell and R. E. M. Nourse, *Product Innovation in Food Processing, 1954–1964*, Graduate School of Business, Harvard University, 1967.

[95] Brozen, 'Entry Barriers: Advertising and Product Differentiation', in *Industrial Concentration: The New Learning*, pp. 115–137.

[96] L. Telser, 'Advertising: Economic Aspects', *International Encyclopedia*, 1968, pp. 106.

[97] H. Demsetz, 'The Nature of Equilibrium in Monopolistic Competition', *Journal of Political Economy*, vol. 67, 1959, pp. 21–30; H. Demsetz, 'Do Competition and Monopolistic Competition Differ?', *Journal of Political Economy*, vol. 76, 1968, pp. 146–8.

There is some evidence which supports the view that advertising leads to a reduction in prices. The most important case studies refer to eye glasses,[98] liquor,[99] legal services,[100] toys,[101] and detergents.[102]

Benham[103] found that the average price of eye glasses in the USA in 1963 in states where advertising was completely banned was $37.48, whereas the price was $17.98 in states with no restriction on advertising.

In a study of toy-manufacturing firms Steiner[104] found that prior to the mid-1950s the 'typical' toy had a price tag of $5.00 (approximately). After the mid-1950s, in cities where toy manufacturers began to use TV advertisements, the price dropped to $3.49, while in cities where no TV advertising was undertaken the price remained unchanged.

Polanyi[105] presented to the English Monopolies Commission evidence that advertising and other selling activities brought about a substantial decrease in retailer mark-ups and in prices of detergents.

The English Monopolies Commission also showed that intensive advertising in the chocolate and cocoa market in England was accompanied by low retailer mark-ups in contrast to high retailer mark-ups on the Continent, where chocolate and cocoa were not intensively advertised by manufacturers.[106]

Arnould[107] found, among others, that, following the assertion of the Federal Commission and the US Supreme Court that lawyers can advertise the prices of their services, the price of a simple, uncontested divorce has fallen from about $600 to about $150 in the Washington, D.C., suburbs.

The other school of thought suggests that advertising is usually undertaken by firms in order to *decrease the price elasticity of demand* of consumer goods, thus enabling firms to increase their price.[108] In other words, advertising confers upon the firms some monopoly power. Furthermore, advertising can raise barriers to entry, so that firms can maintain prices persistently at high levels without attracting entry, and thus pushes industry structure in an oligopolistic direction.

Most existing evidence points to higher prices as a result of advertising. For

[98] L. Benham, 'The Effect of Advertising on the Price of Eyeglasses', *Journal of Law and Economics*, vol. 15, 1972, pp. 337–52.

[99] W. Luksetich and H. Lofgren, 'Price, Advertising and Liquor Prices', *Industrial Organization Review*, vol. 4, 1976, pp. 13–25.

[100] R. J. Arnould, 'Pricing Professional Services: A Case Study of the Legal Services Industry', *Southern Economic Journal*, vol. 38, 1972, pp. 495–507.

[101] R. L. Steiner, 'Does Advertising Lower Consumer Prices?', *Journal of Marketing*, vol. 37, 1973, p. 24.

[102] G. Polanyi, *Detergents: A Question of Monopoly*, Institute of Economic Affairs Research Monograph No. 24 (Transatlantic, 1972).

[103] Benham, 'The Effect of Advertising on the Price of Eyeglasses'.

[104] Steiner, 'Does Advertising Lower Consumer Prices?'.

[105] Polanyi, *Detergents*.

[106] Brozen, 'Entry Barriers: Advertising and Product Differentiation', p. 123.

[107] Arnould, 'Pricing Professional Services'.

[108] Robinson, *The Economics of Imperfect Competition*, pp. 90–101; Chamberlin, *The Theory of Monopolistic Competition*, pp. 213–14. See also section II of this chapter.

example, a report of the US National Commission on Food Marketing[109] found that nationally advertised brands were selling from 4 to 35 per cent above the private or local branded goods. In pharmaceuticals, the differences in prices are even more striking. Walker[110] discovered in a study of 656 medicines that the prices of branded advertised preparations were 66 per cent (on average) higher than the prices of comparable items sold under their generic chemical names. More recent evidence is provided by Kotulak.[111] A sample of the most frequently prescribed drugs in a large Chicago drug store showed that there is a substantial price difference between brand-named drugs and equivalent generic drugs (see Table 2.6). There is also evidence that the recommended price for the heavily advertised ordinary Bayer aspirins was 1.7 times as high than it was for a lightly advertised brand, while children's aspirins of both brands, that were equally advertised, were selling at identical prices (see Table 2.7).[112] Another striking example is the no-brand groceries. Their prices are substantially lower than the trade-marked equivalent items, and their sales have skyrocketed.[113]

It has been argued by the apologists of advertising that the higher prices of advertised brands can be explained by three factors. First, part of the higher price of advertised over non-advertised goods may be accounted for by the higher level of quality and smaller variability of the advertised commodity.[114] Second, the higher price also reflects at least part of the cost of search of the consumer. Brozen argues (unconvincingly) that those who think that drugs are expensive to the consumer ignore the cost of search: a consumer (Brozen argues) might have to go to a doctor to seek counsel for a drug to get rid of a cough, while having been 'informed' about the existence of non-prescription medicines via advertising he avoids a lot of costs.[115] Third, non-advertised products are cheaper because of the 'spillover' effects of the advertised, more expensive goods. Were it not for the advertising of the more expensive brands, cheaper brands might not exist. Manufacturers of these brands choose to offer their product at lower prices (instead of advertising), relying on (taking advantage of) the information spread by the advertised brands.[116] Only because of 'the free ride' is there an inexpensive, generic version of an advertised brand. The advertising of the product of a

[109] US National Commission on Food Marketing, *Special Studies in Food Marketing*, Technical Study No. 10 (Washington, D.C., US. Government Printing Office, 1966).

[110] H. D. Walker, 'Market Power and Relative Prices in the Ethical Drug Industry', *Abstracts of Econometric Society Papers*, December 1967, pp. 73–4.

[111] R. Kotulak, 'Generic Drug Law Hailed as Boon to Poor: Foes Doubt It', *Chicago Tribune*, (2 October, 1977), section 1, p. 4.

[112] Advertising of Proprietary Medicines (Washington, D.C., US Government Printing Office, 1971).

[113] B. Balsley, 'With New Generic Label Products, Frill is Gone', *Chicago Sun-Times*, 13 April, 1978; also, 'No-Brand Groceries', *Time*, vol. 110, November 1977.

[114] Telser, 'Advertising and Competition'; pp. 537–62; Harry G. Johnson, 'The Economics of Advertising', *Advertising Quarterly*, vol. 1, 1964, pp. 9–14; G. Stigler, 'Price and Non-Price Competition', *Journal of Political Economy*, vol. 76, 1968, pp. 149–54.

[115] Brozen, 'Entry Barriers: Advertising and Product Differentiation'.

[116] 'Effects of Treatment on Morbidity in Hypertension', *Journal of the American Medical Association*, vol. 202, 1973, p. 116.

Table 2.6   Pricing comparisons between brand names and comparable generic drugs, 1977

Drug brand name	Price/quantity	Generic name of drug	Price/quantity
Polycillin	$9.36/40 250-mg capsules	Ampicillin	$4.19/40 capsules
Librium	$7.38/100 10-mg capsules	Chlordiazepoxide	$5.37/100 capsules
Erythrocin	$7.50/40 250-mg tablets	Erythromycin	$3.98/40 tablets
Hydrodurial	$6.08/100 50-mg tablets	Hydrochlorothizide	$4.59/100 tablets
Equanil	$8.28/100 400-mg tablets	Meprobamate	$3.09/100 tablets
Tavabid	$10.47/100 150-mg capsules	Papverine	$6.98/100 capsules
V-cillin K	$5.17/40 250-mg tablets	Penicillin VK	$3.26/40 tablets
Darvon Compound 65	$8.19/100 capsules	Propoxyphene Compound 65	$4.48/100 capsules
Serpasil	$4.98/100 0.25-mg tablets	Peserpine	$1.49/100 tablets
Achromycin V	$4.47/100 250-mg tablets	Tetracydine	$2.77/100 tablets

Source: From a sample of ten of the most frequently prescribed drugs and most popular brand names used, Walgreen's Drug Stores, as reported in Ronald Kotulak, 'Generic Drug Law Hailed as Boon to Poor: Foes Doubt It', *Chicago Tribune*, 2 October, 1977, section I, p. 4.

Table 2.7　Retail aspirin prices and advertising

	Advertising expenditures by manufacturer	Suggested retail price per container
Bayer's		
5-grain	$15.6 million	
50 tablets		$0.63
100 tablets		$0.98
200 tablets		$1.73
Children's		
36 tablets	$2.3 million	$0.39
St Joseph's		
5-grain	$0.7 million	
50 tablets		$0.39
100 tablets		$0.59
200 tablets		$0.98
Children's		
36 tablets	$2.1 million	$0.39

Source: Testimony in hearings before the Subcommittee on Monopoly, Select Committee on Small Business, US Senate, 92nd Congress, 1st session, *Advertising of Proprietary Medicines* (Washington, D.C., US Government Printing Office, 1971) part I, p. 271.

firm makes its demand more elastic than it would be without advertising, by creating the volume which creates a competitor.[117]

There is some truth in these arguments. However, the fact remains that most of the advertising messages do not contain useful information in terms of price, quality or terms of sale. They aim primarily at the creation of 'a special image' for products which are otherwise identical. Within the framework of monopolistic competition, it is impossible to predict unambiguously the effect of advertising on price without detailed *quantitative* information on the shape of the cost functions, price elasticities of demand, and the response of demand to advertising expenditures.[118] In oligopoly, the traditional theory predicts that there will be a tendency for advertising to surpass the joint-profit-maximisation level.[119] Modern oligopoly theory predicts that advertising expenditures will be higher than in the profit-maximisation model.[120] However, neither the traditional nor the modern theories of oligopoly specify the relationship between advertising and price. One requires specific quantitative information on cost and demand

[117] H. Demsetz, 'The Effect of Consumer Experience on Brand Loyalty and the Structure of Market Demand', *Econometrica*, vol. 30, 1962, p. 22.

[118] G. C. Archibald, 'Chamberlin versus Chicago', *Review of Economic Studies*, vol. 29, 1961–2, pp. 2–28. See also section II of this chapter.

[119] Fellner, *Competition Among the Few*.

[120] W. J. Baumol, *Business Behaviour, Value and Growth* (Harcourt, Brace & World, 1967). See also section III of this chapter. Also Williamson's model, in section IV of this chapter.

functions which is not as yet available. Pricing studies are difficult to carry out because of the many factors that enter the pricing decision. While most of the available evidence supports the hypothesis that higher prices result from advertising, more quantitative studies are needed before any firm conclusion is reached. What is fairly well established is that advertising, concentration and profitability are positively correlated, though the direction of causality is still disputed. From this evidence one may infer that, although advertising increases the monopoly power of firms, oligopolistic interdependence may diminish price competition and enhance other forms of competition (like advertising or product competition).

D.   Advertising as a Subsidy to the Mass Communications Media

In recent years the sale of advertising space or time has provided approximately two-thirds of the gross revenues of American newspapers and magazines, and virtually all the revenue of radio and television broadcasters, excluding educational stations and channels.[121] It is often argued that advertising subsidises, and hence is responsible for, the continued existence of independent radio, television, magazines and newspapers.

It is difficult to assess this argument on pure economic criteria, because it involves many complex socio-political considerations.

Subsidies tend to distort the allocation of resources, unless the subsidised commodity generates external benefits or is produced under conditions of declining long-run average cost. In the case of the mass communications media the commodities produced are information and entertainment. On *a priori* grounds unit costs may be expected to be decreasing in the mass-media industries. Whether the quantity and/or the quality of the information, news and entertainment is at the socially desired levels is debatable. As we shall see in a subsequent section, firms' advertising is probably more than what consumers want, and it may be misleading or plainly untruthful. Furthermore, if the social goal of the mass-media industries is the cultivation of a sensitive, cultured and well-informed public, the attainment of this goal is impeded by the very nature of the subsidisation process. Advertising firms favour the media which will transmit their messages to the largest audience. In turn, the media attempt to maximise audience size by providing the material or programmes that appeal to the widest possible public. And what appeals to the wide masses does not necessarily improve cultural or informational standards. (As Scherer observes, many TV programmes are of such low intellectual calibre that the commercials stand out as a refreshingly sophisticated interlude.)[122]

The argument hinges on whether advertising is informative or manipulative. (1) If it is informative, then it is socially desirable. It does not constitute a subsidy:

---

[121] Scherer, *Industrial Market Structure and Economic Performance*, p. 328.
[122] Ibid.

the media provide the supply of space or time, and the advertiser-firms form the demand for such space or time. The supply and demand determine the price of advertising, like in all markets. (2) If advertising is excessive, then it should be restricted. The price of newspapers, magazines and TV would then increase, but the community will not be worse off, since a better (socially more desirable) allocation of resources will be attained. (3) If advertising is excessive, but is permitted to continue as a 'second best' solution as opposed to government subsidies to the mass media, then its standing as a contributor to the material well-being of the community is, to say the least, ambiguous.[123]

E.   Advertising and the Quality of Products

It has been argued that advertising may raise consumer welfare by inducing firms to maintain high quality standards.[124] This is particularly true for consumer durables, which involve fairly large expenditures at infrequent intervals. For such commodities, most consumers base their decisions on the manufacturer's reputation for quality and reliability. This reputation is built up through actual performance and advertising. The advertised brand represents a goodwill asset, and if its quality is not maintained there may be a substantial loss of customers in general. This is particularly true for multi-product firms like General Electric or Sunbeam. Such firms are aware that a poor performance of any single product can affect the sales of other products as well. (Obviously, the bad performance of the Pinto model has considerably damaged the reputation of the Ford Company.)

There is some truth in this argument. However, it is also a fact that there is a 'product inflation' in most oligopolistic markets, and advertising is often used to sustain product proliferation (see Chapter 1). In these cases there is often some deterioration in the product, either in the form of inferior quality and performance, or in the sense that a smaller quantity is sold at the current price. One cannot fail noticing the 'shrinking' of chocolate bars, the smaller number of sweets, cookies or toffees per packet, sold at a certain price. Less noticeable is the decrease in the length of cigarettes in all brands over time.

F.   Advertising and Innovation

Advertising is also credited for enhancing research and development, innovation and growth. Advertising, the argument runs,[125] by informing the public about

[123] The Economists Advisory Group, *The Economics of Advertising* (London, The Advertising Association, 1967).

[124] Borden, *The Economic Effects of Advertising*, pp. 631–2 and 866.

[125] Backman, *Advertising and Competition*. It is interesting to note that Backman's study was commissioned by the Association of National Advertisers.

new products enables innovative firms to tap large markets rapidly, and thus enhances the profits from innovation. In turn, firms are induced to spend more on research and development, with the result of speeding up the process of innovation.

With the exception of prescription drugs, the heavily advertised commodities belong to industries where there is virtually no innovation. (Recall that among the most intensively advertised products are deodorants, frozen dinners, detergents, soaps, other cosmetics and toileteries, dog and cat foods, and margarine!)

Furthermore, advertising facilitates an unnecessary proliferation of products, which are differentiated from one another by trivial features.

To be sure, advertising increases the choice of the consumer (a world without some choice would be, to say the least, dull), but casual observation suffices to persuade one that the affluent Western societies suffer from a serious degree of 'product inflation' (see Chapter 1).

G. Excessive Advertising and the Waste of Resources

Kaldor[126] has argued that firms, in their effort to maximise their profit, indulge in advertising expenditures much in excess of what buyers require. Assume that the supply curve of advertising is SS (in Figure 2.35), and the firm's demand for advertising is D_F. Given these schedules, the firm will undertake A_F of advertising, paying a price of P_F for it. The total advertising expenditure is the area of the rectangle OP_FHA_F.

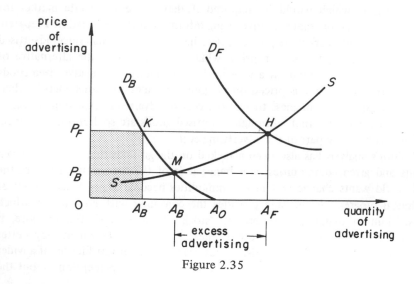

Figure 2.35

[126] Kaldor, 'The Economic Aspects of Advertising'.

The demand for advertising information by buyers is less than that of firms at all prices, and is denoted by the curve D_B in Figure 2.35. This curve intersects the horizontal axis at A_0, showing that buyers' demand for advertising would at most be A_0, when its price is zero. That is, buyers do not want more information than A_0 even if it is provided to them free of charge.

The optimal amount of advertising for the consumers is A_B, for which they are willing to pay a cost price of P_B. There is thus an excess supply of advertising information, equal to $A_B A_F$ in Figure 2.35. Because advertising is jointly supplied with the advertised goods, consumers are forced to take more advertising than they want ($A_F > A_B$). The excess supply of advertising results in a waste of resources. It is seen from Figure 2.35 that consumers cover only part (the shaded area $OP_F K A'_B$) of the total advertising cost, the remaining part ($A'_B K H A_F$) being absorbed by firms, who cannot pass it to their customers (by charging an appropriately high price) because their demand for the product would fall below the profit-maximising level.

In summary, excessive advertising takes place with the consequence of wastage of resources. Furthermore, consumers cannot be charged with the whole cost of advertising, because this would prevent firms from attaining maximisation of their profit. The price of the advertised commodities, although higher than the price of non-advertised commodities, is still set at a level lower than required for optimum allocation of resources. Hence more factors are employed in advertising industries than optimally desired (for maximum consumer welfare).

Kaldor's analysis has been criticised on several grounds.

Telser[127] has argued that Kaldor's argument cannot be conclusive on the point of excessive advertising expenses, because there is no estimate of the cost of advertising which would be required if there were a separate market for attaining information, that is, if advertising information were offered in a separate market from the market of goods. Telser has also argued that since advertised goods are bought at a higher price, while consumers have the alternative of buying unadvertised brands at a lower price, the choice of the advertised goods suggests that advertising is priced on marginalistic rules: the consumers by their choice reveal their willingness to pay the cost of advertising. Apparently, Telser misses Kaldor's point that, although advertised goods are sold at a higher price, consumers pay only part of the advertising cost.

Kaldor's analysis has also been attacked on the grounds that it assumes given wants and given commodities, and hence it is of the 'persuasive' type. In the real world wants change and new commodities become available as a result of technical progress. Advertising provides the consumer with information which assists him in updating his obsolete 'stock of knowledge'. Furthermore, it informs the consumer about the existence of commodities which may better satisfy his wants. Finally, advertising may lead to a fuller satisfaction of a wider number of buyers, each of whom has his own subjective perceptions about the

[127] L. Telser, 'Supply and Demand for Advertising Messages', *American Economic Review*, vol. 56, 1966, pp. 457–66.

usefulness of the various goods. This line of argument hinges on the effect of advertising in shaping the wants and choices of consumers, which is discussed in a subsequent section. We note at this point that, even when the evolution of tastes is taken into account, there seems to be enough evidence that advertising expenditures are largely persuasive and in excess of consumers' demands.

None the less, one should not jump to the conclusion that advertising should be abolished or reduced because it is partly wasteful. We should take into account that advertising is only one aspect of the marketing strategy of the firm. Other alternative marketing methods include personal selling (by salesmen), sales promotion (by mailing catalogues or other pamphlets, free samples, etc.), and other selling activities. If advertising is reduced, firms would most probably intensify other selling activities which may be less efficient and hence more wasteful than advertising. A study by Greyser[128] revealed that out of all firms interviewed 85 per cent stated that 'other selling expenses would take advertising's place if advertising were eliminated'.

H.   Advertising and Consumer Demand

A large number of econometric studies have been conducted in an attempt to measure the effectiveness of advertising on demand (sales). These studies are empirical, since no general theoretical models have been developed to guide the work in this area.[129]

---

[128] S. A. Greyser, 'Business *re* Advertising: Yes, But . . . ', *Harvard Business Review*, 1962.

[129] Some writers have attempted to use utility theory as a framework for analysing the effectiveness of advertising on consumer demand. These attempts have failed to provide any useful model, mainly because the neoclassical consumer theory, derived on the assumption of constant tastes, cannot deal with situations where tastes change, as is the case with advertising (see Schmalensee, *The Economics of Advertising*, pp. 101–103). Other writers have attempted to extend the Weber–Fechner 'law' of psychophysics to advertising* This law relates the *perceived intensity* (*P*) of a stimulus to its *actual intensity* (*A*) with the expression

$$P = a[\log_e (bA)]$$

This law has been questioned by psychologists. Its extension to advertising requires strong assumptions. 'Perceived advertising intensity' may bear no relation to purchasing patterns. It is surely unlikely that this relation is simple. It is even less likely that 'perceived advertising intensity' is related to the advertising expense of firms or even messages purchased by firms in a way as simple as the above 'law' of psychophysics implies. Furthermore, it might be argued that price and income are equally strong stimuli as is advertising. And it is known from a number of studies that the relation between actual prices, perceived value, and purchasing behaviour is quite complex.†

* B. Benjamin and J. Maitland, 'Operational Research and Advertising: Some Experiments in the Use of Analogies', *Operational Research Quarterly*, 1958, pp. 207–17; also B. Benjamin *et al.*, 'Operational Research and Advertising: Theories and Response', *Operational Research Quarterly*, 1960, pp. 205–18.

† D. S. Tull *et al.*, 'A Note on the Relationship of Price and Imputed Quality', *Journal of Business*, 1964, pp. 186–91; A. Gabor and C. W. Granger, 'Price as an Indicator of Quality: Report on an Enquiry', *Economica*, 1966, pp. 43–70; J. E. Stafford and B. M. Enis, 'The Price–Quality Relationship: An Extension', *Journal of Marketing Research*, 1969, pp. 456–8.

We will group the studies in three categories:

(i) Industry studies.
(ii) Firm studies and brand studies.
(iii) Product studies.

(i) *Industry studies*

Several writers have attempted to measure the impact of advertising on *industry sales.* Most of these studies are single-equation models of sales which fail to account for firms' advertising decision rules. We explained in an earlier section that single-equation models impart a bias in the OLS estimates which does not vanish as the sample size increases.

(a) *Single-equation industry studies*

Shoenberg[130] estimated the following demand function for cigarettes, using data for 1923–31:

$$Q_t = 1258.0 - 80.4P_t + 7.9A_t + 47.1t$$

t values   (7.51)   (1.80)   (4.36)

$$R^2 = 0.996$$

where Q_t = *per capita* consumption of cigarettes
 P_t = wholesale price of Camels (per thousand), depicted by the wholesale
    price index
 A_t = total newspaper advertising by the four leading manufacturers
  t = time measured in years

The coefficient of A is significant at the 10 per cent level.

Meissner[131] used annual data on sales of lettuce in the period 1950–51 in twenty-two cities. All observations were pooled together and OLS was applied to a function of the form

$$Q_i = f(Y_i, P_i, T_i, M_i)$$

where Q_i = *per capita* consumption of lettuce
 Y_i = *per capita* income
 P_i = price of lettuce
  T = average maximum temperature
 M_i = seven different measures of marketing activities

---

[130] E. H. Shoenberg, 'The Demand Curve for Cigarettes', *Journal of Business*, 1933, pp. 15–35.
[131] F. Meissner, 'Sales and Advertising of Lettuce', *Journal of Advertising Research*, 1961, pp. 1–10.

The regression explained 66 per cent of the total variation in Q. The signs of the coefficients were correct, but only P, T and one of the seven marketing variables (an 'index of newspaper co-operation') were statistically significant at the 10 per cent level. The joint effect of the seven marketing variables was significant at the 5 per cent level, but the imprecision of the coefficient estimates made it impossible to derive more definite conclusions regarding advertising and other selling activities.

Nerlove and Vaugh[132] carried out a study of the farm sales of oranges. Their estimated log-linear function (for the period 1908–58) is

$$Q_t = -2.929 - 0.390 B_t + 0.924 Y_t + 0.233 A_t + 0.103 \bar{A}_t$$

t values $\qquad (-1.97) \quad (4.84) \qquad (1.86) \qquad (2.29)$

$$R^2 = 0.72$$

where Q = *per capita* oranges sold on farm

$\qquad B$ = *per capita* marketings of oranges in boxes

$\qquad Y$ = *per capita* disposable income

$\qquad A$ = *per capita* advertising by Sunkist Growers and the Florida Citrus Commission

$\qquad \bar{A}$ = ten-year average *per capita* advertising for the ten years preceding year t.

Although this study has the advantage of taking past levels of advertising into account, it has two serious defects: (a) it does not include the price of oranges; (b) when the regression was fitted for the sub-periods 1908–36 and 1937–58, its coefficients were found unstable.

Taylor[133] estimated various specifications for twenty-two categories of consumption, using annual data for the period 1946–64. Of the many specifications only the following gave meaningful results:

'Mens' clothing' $\qquad\left.\vphantom{\begin{matrix}a\\b\end{matrix}}\right\}$ $\quad Q_t = b_0 + b_1 Y_{t-1} + b_2 \bar{A}_t$

'Drug preparations' $\qquad \log Q_t = \log b_0 + b_1 \log Y_{t-1} + b_2 \log \bar{A}_t$

'Airline travel' $\qquad\qquad Q_t = b_0 + b_1 Y_{t-1} + b_2 \bar{A}_t + b_3 P_t$

'Water' $\qquad\left.\vphantom{\begin{matrix}a\\b\end{matrix}}\right\}$ $\quad Q_t = b_0 + b_1 Y_{t-1} + b_2 \bar{A}_t + b_3 P_t$

$\qquad\qquad\qquad\qquad \log Q_t = \log b_0 + b_1 \log Y_{t-1} + b_2 \log \bar{A}_t + b_3 \log P_t$

In general Taylor's results are unimpressive.

[132] M. Nerlove and F. V. Vaugh, 'Advertising without Supply Control: Some Implications of a Study of the Advertising of Oranges', *Journal of Farm Economics*, 1961, pp. 813–37.

[133] W. E. Taylor, 'Industry Advertising and Demand', unpublished honours A. B. thesis, Harvard University.

(b) *Simultaneous-equation industry studies*

Schmalensee[134] estimated the effects of advertising on the demand for cigarettes in the USA, using a variant of the 2-stage least squares (2SLS) method to avoid simultaneous-equation bias. He experimented with various specifications of the form

$$Q_t = f(Y_t, A_t, Q_{t-1}, A_{t-1}, D)$$

where D = dummy variable, taking the value of 1 in 1964 (the year of publication of results linking smoking to lung cancer) and the value of zero elsewhere.

His results may be summarised as follows. In no equation is income (Y_t) or current advertising (A_t) significant. The bulk of the explanation in all estimated models is provided by lagged demand (Q_{t-1}).

In the models where lagged advertising (A_{t-1}) is included, that variable is generally significant, pointing to the presence of a lagged impact of total industry advertising on total demand. In these models, however, current advertising, A_t, is insignificant. The joint effect of A_t and A_{t-1} is tested and found significant. This shows that there may be some impact of advertising on industry demand, but multicollinearity and the values of the coefficients cast some doubt on this result. Actually Schmalensee estimates a function in which A is dropped. The results of this model are

$$\log Q_t = 1.400 + 0.3234 \log Y_t - 0.3156 \log(P_t) + 0.7096 \log Q_{t-1} - 0.06505D$$

$$(2.38) \quad (3.09) \qquad\qquad (-3.28) \qquad\qquad (6.26) \qquad\qquad (-3.11)$$

$$R^2 = 0.942 \qquad d = 1.73 \qquad (t \text{ values in brackets})$$

These results cast further doubt on the hypothesis that advertising affects the total industry demand for cigarettes.

Two other industry studies, one by Bass, and the other by Bass and Parsons, have already been discussed in section VI, because they include demand as well as advertising-decision functions.

In summary, the industry studies did not produce satisfactory results. Most single-equation models failed to yield significant positive advertising coefficients, in spite of the fact that in such models there would be an upward (positive) simultaneous-equation bias. The simultaneous-equation models were not much more impressive in their empirical results.

Many of the econometric studies discussed above include a lagged dependent variable in their regression equations. As we saw in section V, this is equivalent to assuming a distributed lag of the Koyck type. In such a structure, not only advertising but all current-period independent variables have dynamic (lagged) effects. In fact, if demand is expressed as a function of income and advertising,

[134] Schmalensee, *The Economics of Advertising*.

income and advertising are constrained to have precisely the *same* dynamic impact (same lag scheme) on current sales (apart from scale). The main exception to this pattern is the study of Nerlove and Vaugh, where only advertising has lagged effects. Work by Vidale and Wolfe,[135] Benjamin *et al.*,[136] Ozga[137] and Stigler[138] suggests that the Koyck lag structure may be a fair approximation to the dynamic impact of advertising when time periods involved are fairly long, though determining how much time constitutes a 'fairly long' period for particular commodities may not be easy. Very little work seems to have been devoted to the question of whether or not all demand-influencing factors operate through the same lag scheme.

(ii) *Firm and brand studies*

Palda's study[139] is probably the most known of the studies which used firms' data to estimate the effectiveness of advertising on sales.

Palda used a single-equation model to estimate the impact (effectiveness) of advertising (A) on sales for the Pinkham Medicine Company. The model, estimated for the period 1908–60 by OLS, yielded the following results:

$$R_t = 3649 + 1180 \log_{10}(A_t) + 774(D) + 32(T) - 2.83(Y_t) + 0.665R_{t-1}$$

t values   (4.86)   (7.23)   (5.42)   (−4.22)   (10.56)

$R^2 = 0.941$ $d = 1.59$

where R = sales revenue (demand)
     A = advertising expenditure
     T = time trend
     Y = total personal disposable income in current dollars
     D = dummy variable, with value equal to 1 from 1908–1925, and zero thereafter

(The dummy has been designed to measure the impact of an order by the Food and Drug Administration, issued in 1925, requiring the company to reduce drastically its claims for its product.)

The apparent weaknesses of this study are: (a) the omission of price from the set of regressors; (b) the use of a single-equation model, despite the two-way causation between R and A; (c) the autocorrelation of the random term (as

---

[135] M. L. Vidale and H. B. Wolfe, 'An Operations-Research Study of Sales Response to Advertising', *Operations Research*, 1957.

[136] B. Benjamin *et al.*, 'Operational Research and Advertising: Theories and Response', *Operations Research Quarterly*, 1960.

[137] S. A. Ozga, 'Imperfect Markets Through Lack of Knowledge', *Quarterly Journal of Economics*, 1960, pp. 29–52.

[138] G. J. Stigler, 'The Economics of Information', *Journal of Political Economy*, 1961, pp. 213–25.

[139] Palda, *The Measurement of Cumulative Advertising Effects*.

evidenced by the low value of the Durbin—Watson d statistic), which casts doubt on the reliability of the reported significance of the estimates.

Berreman[140] used correlation analysis to examine the impact of advertising on the sale of novels. Most best sellers received more pre-publication advertising than novels which did not sell well. Furthermore, there was a significant relationship between post-publication advertising and sales in the class of best sellers. However, Berreman stressed that correlation does not imply causation. This was one of the earliest statements of the simultaneous relationship between sales and advertising.

Roberts[141] studied the impact of advertising on the sales of two drug products from a cross-section of 1,504 families for six-monthly periods. The dependent variables in his regressions were the total purchases of A and B drugs per family. The regressors were advertising on A and B (measured by the number of magazines carrying advertisements for A or B that were bought by each family), city size, age of head of household, size of family, economic class, education, occupation, region. Unfortunately, advertising of A was strongly correlated ($r = 0.84$) with advertising of B. The over-all R^2 for A was low (0.045). The coefficient of A's advertising was positive and significant, while the coefficient of B's advertising was negative (as expected) but not significant at the 10 per cent level. The over-all R^2 for B was also low (0.035) and neither advertising coefficient was significant. Apparently multicollinearity did not allow the reliable estimate of the advertising coefficients.

Lambin[142] studied the demand for a frequently purchased food product sold in Belgium. His specification was almost identical with that of Palda. The firm was dominant in the industry, so that competitors' advertising was omitted from the function. The set of regressors included disposable income, lagged sales, advertising, rainfall. The over-all R^2 was high (0.974) and all coefficients had the expected signs and were significant. Lambin's study has the same shortcomings as Palda's study.

Peles[143] estimated the effects of advertising on total sales for firms and brands in the beer, cigarette and automobile industries. The impact of A was significant only for motor-cars, but this result is dubious since Peles did not include in his model the stock of cars on the road.

Schmalensee[144] estimated demand functions for the largest six cigarette firms (American Tobacco, Reynolds, Liggett & Myers, Lorillard, Philip Morris, Brown & Williamson). He experimented with linear and log-linear forms including some

[140] J. V. Berreman, 'Advertising and the Sale of Novels', *Journal of Marketing*, 1943, pp. 124—35.
[141] H. V. Roberts, 'The Measurement of Advertising Results', *Journal of Business*, 1947, pp. 131—45.
[142] J. J. Lambin, 'Measuring the Profitability of Advertising', *Journal of Industrial Economics*, 1969, pp. 86—103.
[143] Peles, 'Rates of Amortization of Advertising Expenditures'.
[144] Schmalensee, *The Economics of Advertising*, ch. 6.

or all of the following variables:

$$C_t = f(P_t, Y_t, A_t, A_0, C_{t-1}, D_{1964}, A_{t-1}, A_{(0)t-1}$$

where C = cigarette sales by the jth firm

           P = price (retail or wholesale)

           A = advertising by the jth firm

           Y = disposable income

           A_0 = advertising of competitors

    D_{1964} = dummy for the 1964 Surgeon General's Report

The models were estimated by OLS and a variant of 2SLS[145] for the period 1956–1967. The two methods gave nearly identical results, and if anything the OLS estimates were more reliable. This was interpreted by Schmalensee as a failure to deal with the simultaneous-equation bias. Schmalensee estimated functions for each firm individually (with twelve observations in each sample) and for all firms pooled together (in a sample of seventy-two observations). The individual case studies showed that the same equation does not hold for all firms (the bs are not the same for all firms). In view of this finding it is surprising to see that Schmalensee spends most of his 'firm' study on the pooled sample (which assumes that all firms have the same bs). In any case this pooled sample, including the largest firms, is not expected to yield different results from the 'industry study'. Schmalensee's results for the individual firms are: there is no significant impact of advertising ('own' or 'rivals') on the sales of individual firms; neither price nor real income had a significant coefficient; and the lagged dependent variable was suspiciously important.

The above summarised individual-firm case studies yielded mixed results. Palda, Lambin and Peles found significant impacts of advertising on sales, while Schmalensee did not find any significant impact.

In general, aggregate advertising is adjusted rapidly to changes in sales. There is virtually no lag at all in annual data. If firms adopt a fixed A/R policy (i.e. if the advertising decision function has only R_t as a regressor), then the demand function will not be identified, and any attempt to measure the impact of advertising on sales is bound to fail. Schmalensee seems to believe that this is the case with most firms. This is not in general true. As we saw in sections II–VI, although R_t may be an important determinant of advertising, the firms also take other factors into account in deciding their advertising budgets.

(iii) *Product studies*

Several writers have explored the hypothesis that the effectiveness of advertising depends on the nature of the product.

---

[145] The variant consists of the estimation of a 'reduced form' for A which does not include all the predetermined variables, but only the most important of them. Schmalensee calls this method 'an instrumental variables' method.

Reekie[146] found that advertising is heavier for new than for established products. Advertising is also heavier for products for which few precise claims (for the product) can be made on technological characteristics.

Doyle[147] found that:

(1) Advertising is heavier for low-priced commodities, since for expensive products buyers would rely on direct search for information rather than on advertising; this implies a negative relation between A/S and P.

(2) Advertising is lower for frequently purchased products, since habitual patterns of behaviour develop and since little thought is typically given to brand choice. Since 'frequency of purchase' is directly related to dollar sales volume, Doyle's argument implies a negative relation between A/S and S.

(3) Advertising is much heavier for non-durables, since buyers of durables would rely on direct search for information, rather than on advertising. Furthermore, durables have specialised characteristics, which would be very expensive (and boring for buyers) to include them in advertisements, except in specialised trade publications. If 'durability' is approximated with a dummy variable with a value of one for durables and zero for non-durables, the coefficient of this dummy would be negative.

Nelson[148] distinguishes between 'search goods' (goods whose quality can be assessed by information gathered before purchase) and 'experience goods' (goods which can be evaluated only after the purchase). Nelson provides evidence that 'search goods' would be more heavily advertised in local media (relative to nationwide media).

Schmalensee[149] argues that the cost of advertising is not a significant determinant of A, contrary to the findings of a study by Else.[150]

We may conclude that the effects of advertising on buyers have not been theoretically or empirically established in a satisfactory way.

I. Advertising and Consumers' Sovereignty

The argument can best be presented in terms of what Galbraith has called the 'dependence effect'.[151] Galbraith has argued that the wants of the consumers do not originate in their personality, as traditional theory postulates. Wants are rather shaped by the advertising and salesmanship of firms. Wants thus depend on producers, who create demand for their products by various selling activities.

---

[146] Reekie, 'Some Problems Associated with the Marketing of Ethical Pharmaceutical Products'.

[147] Doyle, 'Advertising Expenditure and Consumer Demand'.

[148] P. Nelson, 'Information and Consumer Behaviour', *Journal of Political Economy*, 1970, pp. 311–29.

[149] Schnalensee, *The Economics of Advertising*, p. 19.

[150] Else, 'The Incidence of Advertising in Manufacturing Industries'.

[151] J. K. Galbraith, *The Affluent Society* (Houghton Mifflin, 1958).

As a result, the sovereignty of consumers, embedded in the theory of free-market enterprise, requires revision. In particular the postulate that firms produce the commodities which give maximum welfare to the society is not tenable, and statements regarding the efficient allocation of resources in a free market system are questionable.

Galbraith's thesis has been widely attacked by several writers. Hayek[152] argues that advertising does not affect consumers, because expenses 'cancel out', and because consumers are intelligent enough to choose rationally between all the different products offered by firms. Similarly, Townsend,[153] though conceding that advertising has some effect on sales promotion, argues that consumers 'are not easy dupes', that is, they cannot be easily fooled by advertising.

I think that there are flaws in such criticisms. In the first place, advertising is usually combined with some 'new' feature(s) of products. Thus the consumer's 'stock of knowledge' becomes fast obsolete with the frequent changes in the product,[154] or is simply inaccurate. Advertising updates consumers' stock of information. Second, the fact that a large proportion of advertising 'cancels out' does not invalidate Galbraith's thesis. If all firms in the industry advertise, the market demand is affected (*ceteris paribus*): it increases in most cases (even if only in the short run), thus absorbing a larger proportion of consumers' income, or it checks an existing falling trend.

In summary. That advertising affects consumers' choice cannot seriously be questioned. Thus Galbraith's 'dependence effect' is at work in Western societies. What is debatable is the strength of this effect, which is a matter of empirical evidence, unfortunately lacking at the present stage, as well as the desirability of the evolved pattern of consumers' choice. The latter is a matter of philosophical and normative conceptions, which are beyond the scope of this book.

J. Advertising and Social Priorities

Galbraith in his *Affluent Society* postulates the 'law of diminishing urgency of human wants'. This 'law' implies that as society becomes more affluent, less urgent human needs are satisfied.

Galbraith maintains that in affluent societies, once the most urgent needs are satisfied, advertising and other selling efforts take over, and, by subtle manipulation, persuade consumers about 'the usefulness' or 'desirability' of various commodities produced by firms which satisfy decreasingly important needs. The very fact, he argues, that advertising is effective in persuading consumers shows

[152] F. A. von Hayek, 'The Non Sequitur of the Dependence Effect', *Southern Economic Journal*, 1961.
[153] H. Townsend, 'Big Business and Competition', in T. M. Rbyczynski (ed.), *A New Era in Competition* (Blackwell, 1971).
[154] Tibor Scitovsky, 'On the Principle of Consumers' Sovereignty', *American Economic Review*, 1962.

that the needs that the advertised commodities satisfy are less urgent, because advertisements 'are effective only with those who are so far removed from physical want that they do not already know what they want. In this state alone men are open to persuasion.' The conclusion of Galbraith's argument is that 'consumerism' is encouraged, and hedonistic values are promoted at the expense of more worthy cultural aspirations.

Hayek's[155] attack is again misplaced. He argues that all culture and civilisation would be impossible without the consumers becoming aware of the existence of goods which firms produce:

> The innate wants are probably confined to food, shelter, and sex. All the rest we learn to desire because we see others enjoying various things. To say that a desire is not important because it is not innate is to say that the whole cultural achievement of man is not important.

This materialistic philosophy is precisely what Galbraith attacks. Hayek's example of arts (music, painting, literature) barely support his thesis, since arts are not produced or advertised by firms!

Again the argument hinges on philosophical and metaphysical valuations, and as such is beyond the scope of positive economics. The main point of interest to the economist in this respect is that advertising has played some role in shaping the consumption patterns of society, and has thus influenced the allocation of resources. Whether the observed allocation is efficient in the sense of providing maximum welfare is debatable. However, the ample statistical evidence[156] that the average propensity to consume has remained constant over very long periods of time in affluent societies is compatible with Galbraith's view of a gradual prevalence of materialistic culture.

K.   Advertising and Interdependence of Consumers' Utility

The traditional theory of consumer demand is based on the axiom of independence of the utility functions of individual consumers. This implies that each consumer chooses the goods he buys for the qualities inherent in them, and is not influenced by the choices of other consumers. This axiom rules out all the 'external effects on the utility' of the consumer. In particular it ignores what Harvey Leibenstein[157] has called 'bandwagon effects' (which refer to increased demand arising from the desire of people to purchase a commodity in order to

---

[155] Von Hayek, 'The Non Sequitur of the Dependence Effect'.

[156] S. Kuznets, *Uses of National Income in Peace and War* (National Bureau of Economic Research, 1942). Also R. Goldsmith, *A Study of Saving in the United States* (Princeton University Press, 1955).

[157] H. Leibenstein, 'Bandwagon, Snob and Veblen Effects in the Theory of Consumers' Demand', *Quarterly Journal of Economics*, 1950.

'keep in style' or 'to get into the swim of things'), 'snob effects' (which refer to a decrease in demand owing to the fact that others are increasingly buying a commodity, in an attempt 'to be exclusive' or 'to be different from the herd'), 'Veblen effects' (which refer to the phenomenon of conspicuous consumption, arising from an urge to buy things of a higher price just in order 'to keep up with the Joneses'), 'speculative' demand, and 'irrational demand' (which refers to purchases unplanned, decided 'on the spur of the moment' in order to satisfy sudden whims and desires). Advertising is at least partly responsible for encouraging bandwagon and Veblen effects in Western societies. Leibenstein has shown how such effects can be meaningfully incorporated into the theory of consumer demand,[158] without, however, dwelling on the thorny aspects of the desirability of such 'externalities'. Once again we are faced with value judgements, which we will avoid, keeping our discussion on the lines of positive economics. From this standpoint it is interesting to examine the effects of advertising in enhancing Veblenesque and bandwagon effects as well as 'irrational' demand. Casual observation suffices to assert that advertising and salesmanship have enhanced conspicuous consumption in the Western capitalistic countries. This has resulted in some misallocation of resources, the extent of which it is not easy to assess. Unless one accepts the dubious view of Hayek, that 'keeping up with the Joneses does not matter since this makes people happier',[159] one is bound to question the usefulness of advertising on the grounds of its effects on shaping the future culture of society. As Keynes noted,[160] the needs arising from efforts to keep abreast of one's fellow human beings 'may indeed be insatiable; for the higher the general level [of consumption] the higher still are they'. Thus advertising might well be expected to affect further the allocation of resources and to shape the form of future civilisation — whether for the better or for the worse hinges upon normative issues which are beyond the scope of this book.

[158] Ibid.
[159] Von Hayek, 'The Non Sequitur of the Dependence Effect'.
[160] J. M. Keynes, *The General Theory of Employment, Interest and Money* (Macmillan, 1936).

PART TWO

The Growth Decision
of the Firm

Introduction

A firm may pursue growth either in a national market or by investing directly in a foreign country and acquiring the status of a multinational corporation. In both cases the expansion or growth can be attained either by *internal expansion*, that is, building a new plant or adding new capacity to its existing plant, or by *external expansion*, that is, by mergers with other existing firms or by taking them over.

Internal expansion (either at home or abroad) can take the form of:

(1) Increasing the share of the market by increasing the quantity of existing products or by differentiation of the produced commodities. We saw in Chapter 1 that product differentiation can be attained by changing the technical characteristics of the product, its style, the services associated with it, or by advertising and other selling activities. It should be clear that differentiation refers to changes (real or imaginary) of some aspects of the *same* basic product.

(2) *Vertical integration*. This involves the undertaking of production of a different product at a previous stage ('upstream' or backward integration) or a subsequent stage ('downstream' or forward integration) of the same productive process. For example, an oil refinery may decide to become fully vertically integrated by buying oil fields and producing crude oil as well as by building petrol stations for the distribution of its refined products. It should be stressed that, although vertical integration involves different products, these products are technologically related since they belong to the same productive process.

(3) *Diversification*. This involves the introduction of a new product totally different from the one already produced. The firm enters a different market, where the product is completely unrelated with its current productive activity. For example, a firm in the clothing industry diversifies by undertaking the production of cosmetics. A firm in the automobile industry diversifies by entering the market of electrical products (cookers, refrigerators, etc.). Diversification refers to growth via the production of commodities which are completely unrelated (technically or otherwise). Diversification is also called *conglomerate expansion*: a firm with diversified products and activities is called a conglomerate. Strictly speaking, vertical integration is a form of diversification, since it involves different products; however, these products, as we said, are related technologically because they belong to different stages of the same productive activity. Thus we

will use the term 'conglomerateness' to cover products or activities in unrelated lines.

External expansion (either at home or abroad) is expansion by merger with, or takeover[1] of, another existing firm(s). It can take the form of:

(1) *Horizontal integration*. This involves the combination or merger of two or more firms that produce the same commodity: the firms are at the same stage of the same productive process. For example, horizontal integration was a widespread phenomenon in the textile industry.

(2) *Vertical integration*. This has been defined above. It involves the combination or merger of two or more firms that produce different products within the same productive process. A typical example of vertical integration is steelmaking, which consists of at least the eight separate stages listed below:

Mining	coal, iron ore, limestone
Input preparation	coke, ore concentrates
Smelting	pig iron
Refining	ingot steel
Rolling	semi-finished steel, e.g. rods
Finishing	finished steel products, e.g. pipe
Fabrication	manufactured steel products, e.g. buildings
Distribution	

Many steel firms have combined into one corporation several of the early stages of steelmaking. For example, US Steel owns and controls considerable iron-ore deposits, and also the means to transport such ore to the required locations. This type of vertical integration, which is in the direction of factor inputs, is called 'upstream' or 'backward' vertical integration. Integration of a 'downstream' or 'forward' direction involves the acquisition of a stage of production which is closer to the final buyer. For example, some steel companies have acquired their own plant and equipment for rolling, finishing and fabricating of steel products. There are many other examples of vertical integration. The petroleum industry, as we pointed out earlier, is vertically integrated in both an upstream and a downstream direction. Oil refiners own oil reserves (upstream) and retail petrol stations (downstream). The automobile manufacturers produce many of the components of automobiles (upstream) and at the same time own and control many retail sales outlets (or have exclusive retail agreements with agencies) for automobiles.

(3) *Conglomerate merger*. This involves the combination or merger of two or more firms which produce completely unrelated products. It is diversification by merging or taking over other already established firms that produce completely different products or are involved in other totally different activities. Conglomerate diversification[2] has increased at a striking rate in recent years. Striking

---

[1] The difference between a merger and a takeover will be discussed in Chapter 5.
[2] Recall that vertical integration is, strictly speaking, a diversification activity. However, we will examine it later, retaining here the term 'diversification' only for products or activities completely unrelated.

examples of conglomerates in the USA are ITT, Litton Industries and Gulf & Western. Litton Industries own banking and insurance companies, weapons industries, consulting firms, hotels, electrical equipment companies, paper-product companies and many other lines of production and activities. Gulf & Western has acquired firms as disparate as Paramount Pictures and New Jersey Zinc. This conglomerate began in the 1960s as a manufacturer of automobile bumpers, with sales of $8.4 million. In 1968, after some eighty takeovers, Gulf & Western's sales revenue exceeded $1.3 billion. Howard Hughes enterprises are another typical example of a conglomerate empire, formed via mergers and acquisitions (takeovers).

Growth by foreign direct investment can be internal or external, as we saw above, and it can take any of the forms described earlier. Multinationals may be established in a foreign market to produce the same product as the parent company (differentiation), a new product (conglomerate diversification), or in order to provide upstream or downstream vertical integration to the operations of the parent company. Multinationals can also be established by mergers and takeovers of firms already operating in a foreign country.

The methods and types (forms) of growth of a firm are shown schematically in the figure opposite.

We shall examine the growth strategy of the firm in five chapters.

In Chapter 3 we introduce some basic concepts of the theory of valuation of the firm. The valuation models of this chapter underlie the analysis of all subsequent chapters. In Appendix 3.1 to Chapter 3 we present the elementary theory of portfolio selection. This explains the rationale of the substitution of the goal of owner-shareholder wealth maximisation for the traditional goal of profit maximisation in most of the literature on the investment decision and the financing decision.

In Chapter 4 we examine the investment decision of the firm under certainty. The investment decision under risk and uncertainty is postponed until Part Four, because it requires knowledge of several topics (such as the optimal capital structure, the optimal dividend-retention policy, and the cost of capital to the firm) which will be discussed in Part Three.

In Chapter 5 we develop alternative theories of mergers and takeovers. We also survey the extensive empirical work conducted on the causes and the effects of mergers and acquisitions.

In Chapter 6 we consider various issues arising from the decision of the firm to integrate vertically its operations. In this respect the most important decision relates to the determination of the transfer price, that is, the price that a producing division of the firm will charge to other buying divisions so that the profit of the firm as a whole is maximised. Another crucial decision of a vertically integrated firm is the decision to close down a particular (producing or buying) division, if its operation does not contribute to the over-all profitability of the firm. We conclude this chapter with a brief discussion of the effects of vertical integration on the degree of competition and on resource allocation.

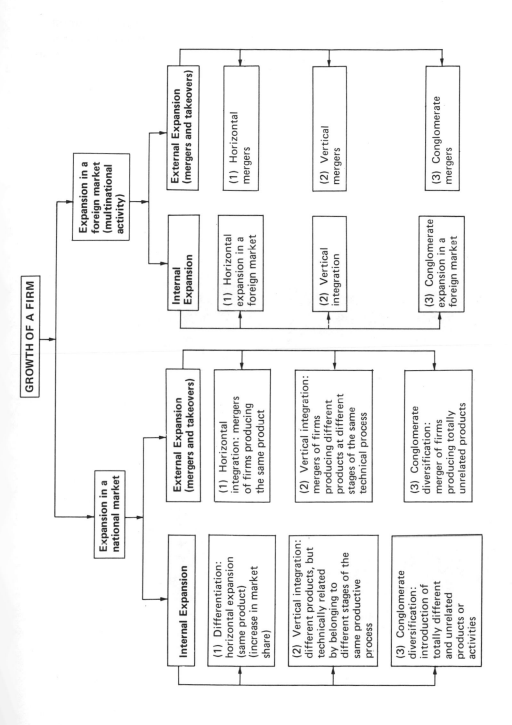

GROWTH OF A FIRM

Expansion in a national market

Internal Expansion

(1) Differentiation: horizontal expansion (same product) (increase in market share)

(2) Vertical integration: different products, but technically related by belonging to different stages of the same productive process

(3) Conglomerate diversification: introduction of totally different and unrelated products or activities

External Expansion (mergers and takeovers)

(1) Horizontal integration: mergers of firms producing the same product

(2) Vertical integration: mergers of firms producing different products at different stages of the same technical process

(3) Conglomerate diversification: merger of firms producing totally unrelated products

Expansion in a foreign market (multinational activity)

Internal Expansion

(1) Horizontal expansion in a foreign market

(2) Vertical integration

(3) Conglomerate expansion in a foreign market

External Expansion (mergers and takeovers)

(1) Horizontal mergers

(2) Vertical mergers

(3) Conglomerate mergers

Finally, in Chapter 7, we examine the firm's decision to grow by investing directly in a foreign country, thus acquiring the status of a multinational corporation. We first present several hypotheses about the causes of foreign direct investment. We next discuss the economic effects of foreign subsidiaries in host countries. We end the chapter with a survey of the empirical work on the causes of foreign direct investment and its effects.

3. Basic Concepts in Valuation Theory

In the remainder of the book we will be concerned with the growth decision, the financing decision and the dividend decision of the firm.

The growth decision relates to (a) investment in the same line of products or in new product lines, (b) mergers and takeovers, (c) foreign direct investment, that is, the establishment of production facilities in another country.

The financing decision involves the determination of the capital structure of the firm, that is, the proportion of debt that the firm should use to finance its long-run operations.

The dividend decision involves the determination of the proportion of earnings to be distributed as dividends, and, hence, the proportion to be retained for reinvestment.

Most of the literature in these areas assumes that the goal of managers is the maximisation of the market value of the equity of the current shareholders. In other words, it is assumed that the growth, financing and dividend decisions are taken so as to lead to the maximisation of the price of the shares of the current owner-stockholders.

The prices of stocks (and other securities) are determined in the capital market, where individual investors buy and sell securities. Thus we must examine how investors value securities in general, and stocks in particular.

In the first section of this chapter we discuss the goal of maximisation of the equity of the stockholders. In the second section we explain some basic concepts of valuation. In the third section we use these concepts to develop various models of valuation of stocks.

I. THE GOAL OF MAXIMISATION OF THE VALUE OF THE FIRM

A. The Rationale of the Maximisation of the Value of the Firm

The neoclassical theory of the firm postulates that in the modern business world, where ownership is separated from control, the managers should take decisions which maximise the utility of owner-shareholders. However, the aggregation of individual utility functions into a global utility function, representing the preferences of all shareholders, poses serious conceptual problems. In general, there is no way of directly combining the preference functions of individual shareholders into a single aggregate preference function which satisfies all the axioms of rational choice.[1]

To avoid these difficulties, the goal of utility maximisation has been replaced by the goal of maximisation of the market value of the common stock, which, in general,[2] leads to the maximisation of the wealth of owner-shareholders. Once managers have attained this goal, each stockholder can pursue the maximisation of his own utility.[3]

From the standpoint of the economy as a whole, the goal of maximisation of the value of the firm, or, assuming constant number of shares, of the price of the stock, is rationalised on the grounds that it results in the efficient allocation of savings in an economy from ultimate savers (investors in the capital market) to ultimate users of funds (firms mostly) who invest in real assets (plant, equipment, construction). The allocation of savings to the users of funds (firms) occurs on the basis of the prices of securities which are determined by investors on the basis of the securities' expected return and risk. As we will see in the next section, maximisation of the stock price or the value of the firm, keeping risk constant, implies maximisation of the return or yield on the share. Rational investors will be buying the stocks with the highest yields (*ceteris paribus*). High yields, in turn, accrue to firms with promising investment opportunities. Hence the savings in the economy will be allocated to those firms which have the most promising investment opportunities if managers take decisions (growth, financing, dividend decisions) that maximise the market value of the firm (or the price of shares). (See also Appendix 3.1, as well as Chapters 4 and 12.)

---

[1] See K. J. Arrow, *Social Choice and Individual Values* (Wiley, New York, 1951). Arrow argues that only under some special conditions is it possible to construct a social utility function which has the properties of the individual utility functions. In general, however, such a function cannot be constructed. See also R. Wilson, 'The Theory of Syndicates', *Econometrica*, vol. 36, 1968, pp. 119–32.

[2] Maximisation of the value of the common stock results always in the maximisation of the wealth of the stockholders if the prices of the different securities traded in the stock market are independent. If this condition is not fulfilled, and dependent securities are in the portfolio of a stockholder, maximisation of the value of the stock of one firm might reduce the wealth of the stockholder. Thus the goal of maximisation of the value of the equity (and the associated maximisation of stockholder wealth) implicitly assumes that the prices of securities are independent.

[3] This is explained in Appendix 1 to this chapter. Each stockholder can use the capital market, lending funds (buying securities) or borrowing funds (selling securities), so as to maximise his own utility. Investors who prefer current consumption may borrow funds using their common stock as collateral, or they may sell a part of their stock. Others, who prefer future consumption, may reinvest the dividends of their stocks, or sell these stocks and buy shares of other firms which pay out a lower proportion of their earnings as dividends. (See H. Bierman and S. Smidt, *The Capital Budgeting Decision*, 4th edn (Macmillan, 1975).) This is further disscussed in Appendix 3.1, where we explain the basic process of portfolio selection by individuals as well as by a firm.

B. Profit Maximisation versus Market Value of Equity Maximisation

In the *traditional theory of the firm* it is assumed that the rational entrepreneur's goal is profit maximisation. In a multi-period analysis profit is a *flow concept*. The entrepreneur is assumed to maximise the stream of profits in all time periods, which are assumed to be independent and homogeneous. Under these assumptions profit maximisation in the short run leads to profit maximisation in the long run.

As we mentioned earlier, in the *traditional theory of finance* the goal of managers is assumed to be the maximisation of the value of the shares of common shareholders. The market value of the owners' equity is a *stock variable*.

Profit maximisation and maximisation of the market value of the equity of existing shareholders are not incompatible goals if profits grow continuously over time: clearly if profits increase in every time period, the market value of the firm is raised, because this value is in effect a weighted sum of the profits per period (see section II). When, however, profits, although maximised in each period, show an irregular pattern over time, the two goals are not equivalent. In the real world it is generally true that increases of profits in some periods imply decreases in other periods, and vice versa. The timing of the profits is mostly ignored in conventional price theory, under the convenient assumption of independent and identical time periods. In the real world, however, smooth profit streams are rarely observed. In these conditions the maximisation of the market value of the equity of owners is a more appropriate criterion than profit maximisation. Failure to recognise the importance of the timing of profits and the interdependence of decision-making over time has been responsible for the confusion about the relationship between the two sets of goals.[4]

It should be noted that the goal of maximisation of the market value of equity is subject to the same criticisms as the goal of profit maximisation. In particular, the separation of ownership and management of the firm has seriously undermined the validity of either goal. The managerial utility function includes variables such as job security, growth, high salaries, power, prestige, etc., while the utility function of owner-shareholders includes mainly profits.[5] While the 'market-value' criterion is still the most widely accepted goal of managers, in recent years some writers have formulated models based on the goal of managerial utility maximisation.[6]

II.   BASIC CONCEPTS IN VALUATION THEORY

Individual investors have in general a time preference, that is, they place a higher value on money received in the current period than money received in a future

---

[4] See E. Fama and M. Miller, *The Theory of Finance* (Holt, Rinehart & Winston, 1972).

[5] See A. Koutsoyiannis, *Modern Microeconomics*, 2nd edn (Macmillan, 1979) ch. 11.

[6] See A. Koutsoyiannis, 'Managerial Job Security and the Capital Structure of Large Firms', *Manchester School*, 1978.

period. Thus, if they are to be persuaded to save and lend some of their current income, they must be compensated by an appropriate interest rate. The further away the time of receiving back the money they lend, the greater the interest rate will be.[7] Thus money has a definite value for savers, who become the suppliers of funds in the stock market.

In this section we will develop some concepts associated with the time value of money which are essential for understanding the valuation of securities in the capital market.

A.   Compound Value (or Future Value or Terminal Value)

Compound value (X_t) is the sum to which an initial amount of money, X_0, will grow over t periods when interest is earned (and reinvested, or compounded) at the rate of i per cent per period. The compound value is calculated from the expression

$$X_t = X_0(1 + i)^t \tag{3.1}$$

This is derived as follows. If the initial amount of money is lent for one year, at the end of the year the lender (investor) will receive

$$X_1 = X_0(1 + i)$$

If the investor lends this amount for another year, he will receive

$$X_2 = X_1(1 + i) = X_0(1 + i)(1 + i) = X_0(1 + i)^2$$

Similarly,

$$X_3 = X_2(1 + i) = X_0(1 + i)^3$$

And, in general, the compound amount at the end of any year t is

$$X_t = X_0(1 + i)^t$$

For example, if a person lends $1,000 for five years at a (compound) interest rate of 5 per cent, at the end of the fifth year he will receive $1,276. The calculations for each period are

$$X_1 = (\$1,000)(1 + 0.05) = \$1,050$$

$$X_2 = (\$1,050)(1 + 0.05) = (\$1,000)(1 + 0.05)^2 = \$1,102$$

$$X_3 = (\$1,102)(1 + 0.05) = (\$1,000)(1 + 0.05)^3 = \$1,158$$

$$X_4 = (\$1,158)(1 + 0.05) = (\$1,000)(1 + 0.05)^4 = \$1,216$$

$$X_5 = (\$1,216)(1 + 0.05) = (\$1,000)(1 + 0.05)^5 = \$1,276$$

---

[7] Assuming that the term structure of interest rates is increasing with time.

Fortunately, tables of compound values of $1 for different years and interest rates have been compiled, so that the compound value of any (initial) amount of money can be easily estimated without going through the above tedious calculations. The compound value of $1 is called the *compound value interest factor* (CVIF) or 'future value interest factor'. A compound value table is reproduced in Appendix 3.2. (Table 1 on page 200). With the aid of this table we can find the future value of any initial amount for a specified interest rate and time period. For example, if a person lends $5,000 at 6 per cent for ten years, the compound value at the end of the tenth year is

$$X_{10} = \$5,000 \left\{ \begin{matrix} \text{CVIF } n = 10 \\ i = 0.06 \end{matrix} \right\}$$

$$= \$5,000 \ (1.7908) = \$8,954$$

The CVIF (= 1.7908) was found from Table 1 of Appendix 3.2.

B. Present Value (Discounting)

(i) *Present value of a future amount of money*

The present value of an amount Y_t received at the end of t periods is the amount (V_0) which, if a person had it now and invested it at the specified interest rate i, would equal Y_t, that is,

$$V_0(1 + i)^t = Y_t$$

or

$$V_0 = \frac{Y_t}{(1 + i)^t} \tag{3.2}$$

The interest rate i in this case is called the *discount rate*. It is apparent from the above expression that the present value V_0 of a given future amount Y_t declines as the discount rate increases.

The valuation expression may be written as follows:

$$V_0 = Y_t \left[\frac{1}{(1 + i)^t} \right] \tag{3.2a}$$

The term in brackets is the present value of $1 discounted at i per cent. It is called the *present-value interest factor* (PVIF). Tables of PVIFs have been compiled for different years and interest rates. A present-value table is reproduced in Appendix 3.2. Using this table we can estimate the present value of any future amount of money. For example, assume that we want to find the present value of $6,000 to be received after five years, discounted at 7 per cent. From Table 2 of Appendix 3.2 we see that the PVIF, for $n = 5$ and $i = 0.07$, is 0.7130. Hence

$$V_0 = \$6,000 \times \frac{1}{(1 + 0.07)^5} = \$6,000 \,(0.7130) = \$4,278$$

(ii) *Present value of a stream of earnings*

If we have a stream of (unequal) amounts of earnings over n periods (Y_1, Y_2, $\ldots$, Y_n), its present value is

$$V_0 = \frac{Y_1}{(1 + i)} + \frac{Y_2}{(1 + i)^2} + \ldots + \frac{Y_n}{(1 + i)^n}$$

$$V_0 = \sum_{t=1}^{n} \frac{Y_t}{(1 + i)^t} \tag{3.3}$$

To estimate the present value of such a stream, we can use the PVIF table, finding the present value of the amount for each year, and then summing them up. For example, assume a three-year stream of earnings ($Y_1 = \$300$, $Y_2 = \$100$, $Y_3 = \$200$). Its present value, with a discount rate of 4 per cent, is

$$V_0 = \frac{\$300}{1 + 0.04} + \frac{\$100}{(1 + 0.04)^2} + \frac{\$200}{(1 + 0.04)^3}$$

$$V_0 = \$300 \left\{ \begin{matrix} \text{PVIF } n = 1 \\ i = 0.04 \end{matrix} \right\} + \$100 \left\{ \begin{matrix} \text{PVIF } n = 2 \\ i = 0.04 \end{matrix} \right\} + \$200 \left\{ \begin{matrix} \text{PVIF } n = 3 \\ i = 0.04 \end{matrix} \right\}$$

$$V_0 = \$300 \,(0.9615) + \$100 \,(0.9246) + \$200 \,(0.8890) = \$558.71$$

(iii) *Present value of an annuity*

An annuity is a stream of earnings with equal yearly amounts of money ($Y_1 = Y_2 = \ldots = Y_n = Y$). The present value of an annuity is

$$V_0 = Y \left[\sum_{t=1}^{n} \frac{1}{(1 + i)^t} \right] \tag{3.4}$$

The term in brackets is the present-value interest factor of a one-dollar annuity (PVIF$_A$). A table of PVIF$_A$ values is reproduced in Table 4 of Appendix 3.2. It shows the present value of a one-dollar annuity for different years and interest rates. Using this table we can estimate the present value of any annuity. For example, if we have a three-year stream of earnings, with a yearly amount of $\$1,000$ ($Y_1 = Y_2 = Y_3 = \$1,000$), its present value (with a 4 per cent discount rate) is

$$V_0 = \$1{,}000 \left(\Sigma \frac{1}{(1 + 0.04)^3} \right)$$

$$V_0 = \$1{,}000 \left(\text{PVIF}_A \begin{array}{l} n = 3 \\ i = 0.04 \end{array} \right)$$

$$V_0 = \$1{,}000 \, (2.7751) = \$2{,}775$$

We could find the above present value by hand calculations, as follows:

$$V_0 = \frac{1{,}000}{1 + 0.04} + \frac{1{,}000}{(1 + 0.04)^2} + \frac{1{,}000}{(1 + 0.04)^3}$$

$$= \$1{,}000 \left\{ \frac{1}{1.04} + \frac{1}{(1.04)^2} + \frac{1}{(1.04)^3} \right\}$$

$$= \$1{,}000 \, (0.9615 + 0.9246 + 0.8890)$$

$$= \$1{,}000 \, (2.7751) = \$2{,}775$$

Note that 0.9615 is the present value of $1 to be received after one year, discounted by $i = 0.04$; 0.9246 is the present value of one dollar to be received after two years (at $i = 0.04$), and 0.889 is the present value of one dollar to be received after three years (at $i = 0.04$). Thus 0.9615, 0.9246 and 0.8890 are PVIFs which can be obtained directly from Table 2 of Appendix 3.2.

(iv) *Present value of an infinite stream of earnings*

If we have a stream of (unequal) earnings over an infinite time horizon (Y_1, Y_2, ..., Y_n, ..., Y_∞), its present value is

$$V_0 = \frac{Y_1}{(1 + i)} + \frac{Y_2}{(1 + i)^2} + \ldots + \frac{Y_\infty}{(1 + i)^\infty}$$

or

$$V_0 = \sum_{t=1}^{\infty} \frac{Y_t}{(1 + i)^t} \tag{3.5}$$

The present value of such a stream requires estimation of the present value of each term separately, using the present-value table (Table 2 of Appendix 2). This, apparently, is a very tedious process. However, expression (3.5) can be simplified if the stream of earnings is uniform, that is, if the amounts to be received in each future period are equal (perpetuity). (See the next section.)

(v) *Present value of a perpetuity*

A perpetuity is a uniform stream of earnings, that is, a stream of equal amounts, equally spaced over an infinite time horizon:

$$Y_1 = Y_2 = \ldots = Y_n = \ldots = Y_\infty = \bar{Y}$$

The present value of a perpetuity is

$$V_0 = \frac{\bar{Y}}{i} \tag{3.6}$$

*   *   *

PROOF

From expression (3.5) we have

$$V_0 = \sum_{t=1}^{\infty} \frac{\bar{Y}}{(1+i)^t} = \bar{Y} \sum_{t=1}^{\infty} \frac{1}{(1+i)^t}$$

or

$$V_0 = \bar{Y} \left\{ \frac{1}{(1+i)} + \frac{1}{(1+i)^2} + \ldots + \frac{1}{(1+i)^\infty} \right\}$$

Given that $i > 0$, the expression in brackets is a declining geometric progression with common ratio $1/(1+i)$. Its sum can be estimated from the expression

$$1 \int_{}^{\infty} = \frac{A}{1-\lambda}$$

where A = first term of the declining progression
       λ = common ratio

Thus the present value of a perpetuity is

$$V_0 = \left[\frac{1/(1+i)}{1 - \{1/(1+i)\}} \right] = \frac{\bar{Y}}{i}$$

QED

*   *   *

For example, if a person has a bond of an indefinite maturity, from which he receives \$200 per year, the present value of this bond, at a discount rate of 5 per cent, is

$$V_0 = \frac{\$200}{0.05} = \$4,000$$

(NOTE: In the context of finding the present value of a stream of earnings, we are dealing with a *flow* of earnings over time. By discounting, we find the present value of this stream, and this is a *stock* variable, or 'capital', concept. Thus the discount rate i is also called the *capitalisation rate*, because it turns a 'flow' concept into a 'capital' concept.)

C. Relation Between Present Value and Compound (or Future) Value

A thorough understanding of discounting is essential in order to follow the remainder of this book. Thus it is useful to examine in more detail compounding and discounting.

Recall that the basic equation of discounting

$$V_0 = \frac{Y_t}{(1 + i)^t}$$

was derived from the compounding expression

$$V_0(1 + i)^t = Y_t$$

We mentioned that:

(a) The term $(1 + i)^t$ is the compound or future value of \$1 (that we called CVIF).
(b) The term $1/(1 + i)^t$ is the present value of \$1 (that we called PVIF).

Consequently

$$\text{PVIF} = \frac{1}{\text{CVIF}} \tag{3.7}$$

Thus we may find the present value in two ways:

(a) either by multiplying Y_t by the PVIF:

$$V_0 = Y_t(\text{PVIF}) = Y_t \left[\frac{1}{(1 + i)^t} \right] \tag{3.8}$$

(b) or by dividing Y_t into the CVIF:

$$V_0 = \frac{Y_t}{\text{CVIF}} = \frac{Y_t}{(1 + i)^t} \tag{3.9}$$

The second form is more useful, because it shows that the present value declines as the discount rate increases.

D. Estimating Compound Rates or Discount Rates

(i) *Compound rates*

In many cases the initial amount and its compound value (at the end of n years) are known but the interest rate involved is not. In these instances the (compound) interest rate is found by using the expression for compounding

$$X_t = X_0(1 + i)^t \qquad\qquad (3.10)$$

and the compound value table (Table 1 of Appendix 3.2). For example, assume that a person borrows $2,000 from a bank, with the obligation of paying back to the bank $2,434 after five years. The interest that the bank is charging is found by solving expression (3.10) for $(1 + i)^5$. That is,

$$\frac{X_t}{X_0} = (1 + i)^t$$

$$\frac{2,434}{2,000} = 1.217 = (1 + i)^5$$

We next look (in Table 1 of Appendix 3.2) across the row corresponding to the fifth year, and we find that the CVIF value 1.217 implies an interest rate of 0.04.

(ii) *Discount rates*

Similarly, in many cases we know the present value and the even stream of earnings of an annuity, but we do not know the discount rate involved. We can estimate it from the expression

$$V_0 = Y \left\{ \sum_{t=1}^{n} \frac{1}{(1 + i)^t} \right\}$$

and the present-value table for annuities (PVIF$_A$ in Table 3 of Appendix 3.2). For example, assume that a person buys a three-year bond for $5,550, which yields $2,000 at the end of each of the three years. The discount rate is found as follows. We first solve the present-value expression for the PVIF$_A$ term:

$$\left\{ \sum_{t=1}^{n} \frac{1}{(1 + i)^t} \right\} = \frac{V_0}{Y} = \frac{5,550}{2,000} = 2.775$$

We next look at the present value of an annuity table (Table 3 of Appendix 3.2) across the row corresponding to $n = 3$, and find that the PVIF$_A$ value of 2.775 implies a discount rate of 0.04 per cent.

E.   Yield (or Internal Rate of Return)

The yield or internal rate of return of any investment (for example, buying a bond) is the discount rate that equates the present value of the expected earnings over the lifetime of the investment (V_0) to the original cost of the investment C_0 (e.g. the cost of buying the bond). Mathematically, the yield, k, is estimated from the expression

$$C_0 = V_0$$

$$C_0 = \sum_{t=1}^{n} \frac{Y_t}{(1+k)^t} \tag{3.11}$$

or

$$C_0 = \frac{Y_1}{(1+k)} + \frac{Y_2}{(1+k)^2} + \ldots + \frac{Y_n}{(1+k)^n} \tag{3.12}$$

If the stream of earnings is even over time (i.e. if we have an annuity), the yield (or internal rate of return) is found from the $PVIF_A$ table (Table 3 of Appendix 3.2), as explained in the previous paragraph. However, if the annual earnings are not equal, k can be found either by an *iterative procedure*, or by appropriate computer programs.

To illustrate the iterative procedure, assume that the initial cost of a two-year investment is $12,337, and that the stream of earnings are $10,000 for the first year and $5,000 for the second year. We want to find the rate of discount, k, that equates the sum of the present values of the above stream of earnings to the original outlay of $12,337. We choose *arbitrarily* an initial rate of discount, say 5 per cent, and we estimate the present value of the stream of earning, using the present-value table (PVIF, Table 2 of Appendix 3.2), as follows:

Year	*Earnings*	x	*PVIF*	=	*Present value*
1	10,000	x	0.9524	=	9,524
2	5,000	x	0.9070	=	4,535
			Total present value		$14,059

Since $V_0 = \$14,059$ and $C_0 = \$12,337$, we must choose a higher discount rate (so as to decrease the present value of future earnings and bring it closer to C_0). Assume that we choose $k = 0.20$. With this discount rate, we find the following present value of the stream of earnings:

Year	*Earnings*	x	*PVIF*	=	*Present value*
1	10,000	x	0.8333	=	8,333
2	5,000	x	0.6944	=	3,472
			Total V_0 =		$12,805

Now $V_0 < C_0$, indicating that the 20 per cent rate of discount is too high. Hence we try a discount rate between 0.05 and 0.20. In fact we must choose a value closer to 0.20 than to 0.05, since the difference $V_0 - C_0$ is smaller when $k = 0.20$.

Let us try $k = 0.16$. The present value is now:

Year	Earnings	x	PVIF	=	Present value
1	10,000	x	0.8621	=	8.621
2	5,000	x	0.7432	=	3,716
					$V_0 = \$12,337$

We observe that $V_0 = C_0$ when the discount rate is 0.16. Hence $k = 0.16$ is *the yield* or *internal rate of return* of the investment with initial outlay of \$12,337.

The iterative procedure for finding the yield or internal rate of return, k, is tedious. However, with some experience, the number of iterations can be reduced significantly. And, of course, iterations are not needed if we have access to appropriate computer programs.

F.   Certainty and the 'Time Value of Money'

In the above discussion of compounding and discounting it was assumed implicitly that individual investors live in a world of certainty. The stream of future earnings of an investment (in real or financial assets) was assumed known with certainty. In the absence of risk, the purpose of discounting is to take into account (consideration) the time preference of investors, that is, the fact that one dollar received today has a greater value for individuals than a dollar received in a future period. Under certainty, the rate of discount, i (or the yield of an investment, k), measures 'the time value of money'. Put it another way, i is the riskless rate of interest, the interest rate at which funds can be lent without any risk of default. Risk and uncertainty affect the valuation of securities. We will discuss the effects of uncertainty and risk on the behaviour of investors in Chapter 12. However, at this stage it is necessary to discuss the sources of risk (and uncertainty), and develop methods or expressions for measuring it.

G.   Risk and its Measurement

In order to understand risk and its measurement, we must explain the concept of a probability distribution and its two main characteristics: the mean (or expected value) and the standard deviation.

(i) *The probability distribution of an uncertain stream of earnings*

In a world of uncertainty the future stream of earnings of an investment is not known with certainty. Earnings may assume any value (within a certain range, usually), each having some probability of being realised. The total of possible values with their associated probabilities form the probability distribution of the (uncertain) stream of earnings.

A usual assumption of the theory of decision-making under uncertainty (see Chapter 12) is that individual investors can form *subjective expectations* about the future (uncertain) stream of earnings (of a firm or of an investment) and assign (subjective) probabilities to this stream. These subjective probability distributions are based on information about the future prospects of the firms, on information about the 'general business conditions' in the economy in any one period, and on the experience and intuition of individual investors. Decisions of investors under uncertainty are based on such probability distributions.

For example, assume that an individual considers buying shares of two firms, *A* and *B*. Presumably, he is interested (amongst other things) in the average future earnings of these shares and their variability. This information can be obtained from the probability distributions of the earnings of the two firms. The individual, taking into account any available information and using his intuition and experience, forms the subjective probability distributions of the earnings of the two firms (see Table 3.1).

Table 3.1 Subjective probability distributions of earnings of firms *A* and *B*

Subjective probability distribution of earnings of firm *A*		Subjective probability distribution of earnings of firm *B*	
Earnings (*A_i*)	Probability	Earnings (*B_i*)	Probability
$0	0.50	$220	0.50
$350	0.30	$350	0.50
$1,000	0.20		

The information conveyed by the probability distribution can be conveniently summarised by two characteristics: the mean (or expected value) and the standard deviation.

The mean (or expected value) is a measure of the average earnings. It is defined as the sum of all possible earnings multiplied by their respective probabilities. In general, if the possible earnings are denoted by X_i, their mean (or expected value) is given by the expression

$$E(X) = \sum_{i=1}^{n} X_i \, [Pr(X_i)] \tag{3.13}$$

The standard deviation is a measure of the dispersion of the various values of earnings around their mean. It is the square root of the variance of earnings, σ_x^2, which is defined as the weighted average of the squared deviations of the various values of earnings from their mean, with weights being the probabilities of the different levels of earnings. Mathematically, the variance is given by the expression

$$\text{var}(X) = \sigma_x^2 = \Sigma [X_i - E(X)]^2 [Pr(X_i)] \tag{3.14}$$

The standard deviation is the square root of the variance

$$\text{s.d.} = \sqrt{\sigma_x^2} = \sigma_x \tag{3.14a}$$

In our example, the mean, variance and standard deviation of the probability distribution of earnings of the two firms are

$$E(A) = \sum_{i=1}^{3} A_i [Pr(A_i)] = \$350 \qquad \sigma_A^2 = \$143,723 \qquad \sigma_A = \$379.11$$

$$E(B) = \sum_{i=1}^{2} B_i [Pr(B_i)] = \$285 \qquad \sigma_B^2 = \$3,075 \qquad \sigma_B = \$55.45$$

Decisions of investors under uncertainty are based on these two following characteristics:

(a) *The mean of future earnings, which is a measure of the expected (average) profitability of the firms' operations.*
(b) *The standard deviation, which is a measure of risk of the stream of earnings*: the greater the variability of earnings, as measured by the standard deviation, the riskier the stream of earnings.[8]

In the next section we will show that there is a trade-off between expected (mean) profitability and risk: as risk increases, investors will require a higher profitability (yield, return) to compensate them for the increase in risk. The trade-off curve between risk and return is the basic tool for decision-making under uncertainty (see Chapter 12).

(ii) *Business risk and its measurement*

There are two types of risk which face the buyer of a share: the *business risk*, and the *financial risk*. Business risk refers to the production activity of the firm, while financial risk is associated with the use of debt for financing the operations of the firm. In this paragraph we will examine the determinants and the measurement of business risk.

---

[8] For a further discussion of the use of the variance as a measure of risk see Chapter 12. The variance as a measure of risk has several shortcomings. The most serious is that it measures deviations on both sides of the mean. Obviously an investor is concerned with negative deviations from the expected mean return. Values of returns greater than the mean are apparently desirable. Such considerations can be captured by a measure of the skewness of the probability distribution of the earnings, but the measure of skewness is difficult in practice. For a discussion of other shortcomings of the variance as a measure of risk, see J. C. van Horne, *Financial Management and Policy*, 3rd edn (Prentice-Hall, 1975) pp. 29–31.

Business risk arises from the uncertainty of the realisation of the (subjectively) estimated total earnings of the firm, before payment of interest on the existing debt and corporate taxes. In finance literature these earnings are denoted by the word EBIT (from the initials of the expression 'earnings before interest and taxes'). They are the difference between total revenue and total cost:[9]

$$X = \text{EBIT} = TR - TC = TR - TVC - TFC \tag{3.15}$$

The business risk is measured by the standard deviation of EBIT. To find the determinants of business risk, it suffices to derive the mean and variance of the probability distribution of earnings.

Expression (3.15) may be rearranged as follows:

$$X = PQ - (AVC)Q - TFC$$

or

$$X = -TFC + (P - AVC)Q \tag{3.16}$$

The determinants of earnings are:

(1) The quantity of output sold, Q. It is assumed that Q is a random variable, that is, it can take a value within a certain range (Q_{min} and Q_{max}), each value having some probability of being realised. The distribution of sales (Q) depends on the market demand for the product. Investors are assumed to know (subjectively) the distribution of Q, that is, the various possible levels of sales with their probabilities.

(2) The price of the commodity produced, P. It will be assumed that P is constant.

(3) The cost structure of the firm, as reflected in TVC (or AVC) and TFC. It will be assumed that TFC increases and AVC decreases with the capital intensity of the method of production used by the firm.

Expression (3.16) implies that earnings (X) are a linear function of the quantity sold (Q). The intercept of this relation is $-TFC$, and its slope is $(P - AVC)$.

The cost structure of the firm (as measured by the proportion of fixed costs to total costs) determines the speed and flexibility with which the firm can reduce its costs when total sales decline.[10] If the firm's cost structure is dominated by fixed costs, the total cost will not be very responsive to changes in the volume of sales. In this case, the earnings (EBIT) are greatly affected by changes in the volume of sales. The firm does not have much flexibility in reducing its total costs when sales decline. In fact, the cost structure of the firm affects both the mean and the variability of earnings.

---

[9] Note that EBIT differs from the economist's profit, because total costs do not include normal profit and other opportunity costs.

[10] See Ezra Solomon, *The Theory of Financial Management* (Columbia University Press, 1963) p. 70.

(a) *Cost structure and the variability of earnings*

The variability of earnings increases with an increase in *TFC*.

If the firm uses a capital-intensive technique, the fixed costs will be large relative to the variable costs. Thus the average variable cost will be relatively low. The relation between EBIT and the level of sales, Q, is defined by the expression

$$X_1 = \underbrace{-TFC_1}_{\text{intercept}} + \underbrace{(\bar{P} - AVC_1)Q}_{\text{slope}} \qquad (3.17)$$

If the firm chooses a labour-intensive technique, the EBIT line

$$X_2 = -TFC_2 + (\bar{P} - AVC_2)Q \qquad (3.18)$$

will have a smaller slope, given $AVC_2 > AVC_1$, and a smaller (negative) intercept $(TFC_2 > TFC_1)$.

The two EBIT lines, corresponding to the two different cost structures, are shown in Figure 3.1. It is apparent from this graph that the variability of earnings is greater the more capital intensive the technique, or, equivalently, the greater the proportion of fixed costs to total costs (given the price of the output, $\bar{P}$). Since variability is a measure of risk we conclude that business risk increases with an increase in capital intensity, *ceteris paribus*.

The relation between risk and the cost structure can be seen from the variance of EBIT. Assuming that P and AVC are known with certainty, expression (3.17) gives:[11]

$$\text{var}(X) = (P - AVC)\,\text{var}(Q)$$

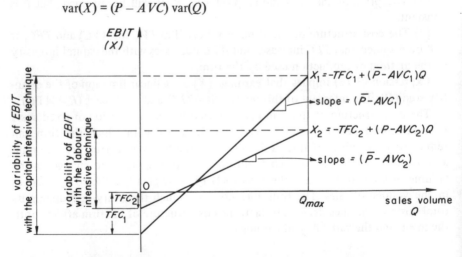

(It is assumed that the firm can sell a maximum quantity, $Q_{\max}$)

Figure 3.1

[11] See Chapter 12 for an explanation of this expression.

or

$$\sigma_x^2 = (P - AVC)\sigma_Q^2 \tag{3.19}$$

The variance of earnings is negatively related to AVC, which, in turn, is negatively related to the capital intensity and the corresponding TFC. An increase in TFC implies a decline in AVC, which leads to an increase in the variance of earnings (EBIT).

(b) *Cost structure and expected (mean) earnings*

The cost structure also affects the mean of earnings, $E(X)$. From expression (3.17) we obtain:[12]

$$E(X) = (P - AVC)[E(Q)] - TFC \tag{3.20}$$

The influence of the cost structure on the mean earnings stems from the TFC and the AVC, which, *ex hypothesi*, move in opposite directions. Thus, in general, under our assumptions an increase in the proportion of fixed costs will initially raise the mean earnings; eventually, however, the mean earnings will decline.

From the above discussion it can be seen that there is a trade-off between risk and mean (expected) earnings. This trade-off can best be illustrated by the following numerical example.

Assume that the firm's sales (volume) distribution has a mean $E(Q) = 100$ units of output, and a standard deviation $\sigma_Q = 20$ units of output. Assume further that the sales price is given ($P = \$1.00$). There are three methods of production with different capital intensities (and different cost structures). The $E(X)$ and σ_x corresponding to these methods of production are shown in Table 3.2.

From the contents of Table 3.2 we see that while business risk, as measured by σ_x, increases continuously with the increase in capital intensity (and the resulting different cost structure), the mean earnings, $E(X)$, initially increase and then fall. This trade-off between risk and expected earnings is shown in Figure 3.2. The trade-off curve shows combinations of risk and expected earnings resulting from different cost structures.

Apparently the managers of the firm will choose a cost structure corresponding to the positive segment of the trade-off curve (segment AB). (The negatively sloping segment CB implies a higher risk for a reduced level of expected earnings. Clearly, points on CB are inferior choices for the firm as compared with points on AB.) (See also Chapter 12.) The cost structure should be chosen by managers so as to maximise the market value of the firm to its stockholders.

In summary. Business risk arises from many factors related to the current production operations of the firm, which determine its total revenue, its total

---

[12] Idem.

Table 3.2 Mean earnings, $E(X)$, and risk, σ_X, of different techniques

Method of production	TFC ($)	TVC ($)	$E(Q)$ (units of output)	σ_Q (units of output)	AVC ($)	P ($)	$(P - AVC)$ ($)	$E(X) = (P - AVC)E(Q) - TFC$	$\sigma_X = (P - AVC)\sigma_Q$
Method A	$10	$800	100	20	$0.80	$1.00	$0.20	$10	$ 4
Method B	$40	$400	100	20	$0.40	$1.00	$0.60	$20	$12
Method C	$70	$200	100	20	$0.20	$1.00	$0.80	$10	$16

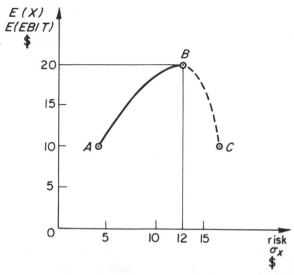

Figure 3.2 Trade-off curve between business risk and expected earnings

costs as well as its cost structure. The above analysis focused on the cost structure. However, business risk is defined by other factors which appear in the
standard deviation of earnings:

$$\sigma_x = (P - AVC)\sigma_Q \qquad (3.21)$$

Thus changes in the conditions of supply and demand in the market of the
product will affect P as well as the standard deviation of the level of sales. Similarly, changes in the market conditions of inputs will affect the AVC, and hence
the risk of the firm's earnings. The same factors will affect the expected value of
earnings. Managers must choose a combination of risk–expected earnings so as
to maximise the price of shares to the existing stockholders.

We have used the standard deviation of earnings as a measure of the basic
business risk. The standard deviation by itself, however, is not an adequate
measure of risk, because it does not take into account the scale (size) of operation of the firm which changes the expected earnings of the firm. Business risk
is not simply the variability of earnings but the variability in conjunction with
the level (size) of earnings. For example, consider two firms, a large firm A and a
small one B, whose earnings have the same variability

$$\sigma_{x_A} = \sigma_{x_B} = \$5 \text{ million}$$

but different expected earnings

$$E(X_A) = \$50 \text{ million} \qquad E(X_B) = \$20 \text{ million}$$

Apparently an investor will judge the riskiness of the firms by taking into account both the variability and the mean value of their earnings streams.

A measure of the business risk which incorporates both the variability and the mean earnings is the *coefficient of variation*, defined by the expression

$$CV_x = \frac{\sigma_x}{E(X)} \tag{3.22}$$

The coefficient of variation is an index of *business risk*. It is a measure of 'normalised' variability that adjusts the standard deviation for the scale (size) of operations of the firm. Thus an increase in total fixed costs (relative to the total costs) does increase σ_x, but may also increase $E(X)$, so that the coefficient of variation may remain constant or even decrease.

(iii) *Financial risk and its measurement*

The *financial risk* includes the business risk as well as the additional risk that arises from the decision of managers to use debt for financing (in part) the firm's operations. As indebtedness increases, the fixed costs for servicing the debt (F) rise. Since bondholders have a priority claim on the earnings of the firm, the existence of debt (and/or its increase) reduces the amount of *earnings available to shareholders*. Thus debt creates an uncertainty regarding the amount of earnings available to shareholders after deduction of fixed charges. Furthermore, the use of debt exposes shareholders to a potential loss of their total equity if earnings (EBIT) fall below the fixed charges of debt, that is, if the firm becomes insolvent, a situation which may lead to legal bankruptcy.[13]

In summary, financial risk arises from the uncertainty about the amount of earnings available to shareholders (after interest payments) and the danger of cash insolvency which may lead to bankruptcy.

The earnings available to shareholders are

$$X - F$$

where F = fixed charges of debt. The probability distribution of these earnings has a mean

$$E(X - F) = E(X) - F \tag{3.23}$$

and a variance

$$\sigma^2_{(X-F)} = \sigma^2_X + \sigma^2_F - 2 \operatorname{cov}(XF) = \sigma^2_X \tag{3.24}$$

given $\sigma^2_F = 0$, and cov (XF) = covariance of X and $F = 0$.[14]

---

[13] See Solomon, *The Theory of Financial Management*.

[14] A constant (such as *TFC*) does not vary: its variance is zero. Furthermore, its covariance with any other variable is zero: a constant does *not* vary together (does not covary) with variables. See Chapter 12 for the derivation of expressions (3.23) and (3.24).

If we compare the *distribution of total earnings* (EBIT) to the *distribution of earnings available to stockholders* we observe that both have the same variance (and standard deviation), but different means, hence different coefficients of variation. Thus the financial risk as measured by the ratio

$$\frac{\sigma_x}{E(X) - F} \tag{3.25}$$

is obviously larger than the pure business risk (= $\sigma_x/E(X)$). We may then write

$$\begin{bmatrix} \text{Financial} \\ \text{risk} \end{bmatrix} = \begin{bmatrix} \text{Pure} \\ \text{business} \\ \text{risk} \end{bmatrix} + [\text{Premium}] \tag{3.26}$$

where the premium is required to compensate the common shareholders for the danger of default and the higher chance that they will receive no income after fixed obligations are met.

To illustrate the concept of financial risk consider two firms which are identical in all respects except leverage: firm A is unlevered, while firm B has some debt in its capital structure. The operating earnings (EBIT) are identical, with a mean of, say, $100,000 and a standard deviation of $20,000. The interest payments of firm B amount to $30,000. The pure business risk of both firms is the same:

$$\frac{\sigma_x}{E(X)} = \frac{20,000}{100,000} = 0.2$$

The financial risk of the two firms, however, is different. For the unlevered firm A, the distribution of earnings available to shareholders has a coefficient of variation

$$CV_A = \frac{\sigma_x}{E(X)} = 0.2$$

while the distribution of earnings available to the stockholders of the levered firm B gives rise to a coefficient of variation of

$$CV_B = \frac{\sigma_x}{E(X) - F} = \frac{20,000}{100,000 - 30,000} = 0.29$$

This is shown in Figures 3.3 and 3.4.

Note that business risk is not a function of financial risk. The probability distribution of *total* earnings is not affected by the different ways of financing the operating decisions (production and investment decisions) of the firm, which alone generate this distribution. The effect of the financing decision is to shift to the left the probability distribution of *earnings available to common shareholders*,

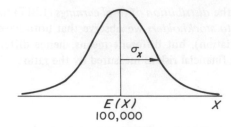

Figure 3.3   Distribution of total
earnings of both firms

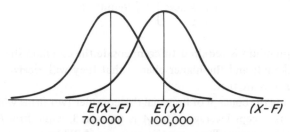

Figure 3.4   Distribution of earnings
available to shareholders of the two
firms

and thus increase their total risk, as defined by the coefficient of variation: $\sigma_x/$
$[E(X) - F]$. Thus financial risk is a function of business risk and of the amount
of fixed charges of debt, which depend on the capital structure of the firm. (The
capital structure of the firm is discussed in Chapter 8.)

III.   STOCK VALUATION MODELS

A.   The General Dividends Model

In the previous section we defined the yield of an investment as the rate of
discount which equates the cost of the investment to the present value of its
future stream of earnings. In this section we will use this general concept to
develop some models of valuation of common stock which are widely used for
the *measurement* of the discount rate of the stream of earnings of the common
stock.

The yield or expected return of a stock of common equity, k_e, is the rate of
discount that equates the present value of all future expected dividends per share
to the present price of the common stock.

It is generally agreed that the stream of earnings of a share consists of all the
future expected dividends, even though an investor may resell the stock after a

certain period.[15] The capital gains he may realise are due to expectations of the new buyers about future dividends of the stock. Thus a dividend valuation model may be expressed either in terms of a stream of dividends in perpetuity, or as the sum of a stream of dividends over a given period plus capital gains realisable at the end of this period. The dividends model can explain the behaviour of investors who intend to hold the stock in perpetuity, as well as the behaviour of investors who plan to sell their stock at some time in the future and realise a capital gain.

Formally the dividends model may be presented as follows.[16]

In a world of uncertainty the earnings of a firm are not known with certainty. They are a random variable, that is, earnings may assume several values, each associated with some probability. It is assumed that investors can form subjective expectations regarding the earnings of the firm, based on information about the firm's production and investment decisions, as well as on assessment of the general economic and political conditions, specific conditions in the markets of outputs and inputs, and so on. (These factors, as we said in the previous section, define the *basic business risk* of individuals who consider the purchase of the firm's shares.) It is also assumed that from this and other information (for example, from managers' reports) the investor can form expectations about the future dividends and changes in the price of the share. It is not necessary that the expectations be realised. It is simply *assumed* that investors can and do form such expectations.

If an investor holds a share for one period, he expects to earn at the end of the period the current dividend plus any capital gain from possible appreciation of the share. In other words his expected earnings (for one year) are

$$dv_1 + [P_1 - P_0] \tag{3.27}$$

The rate of return on the share is the discount rate, k_e, which equates the current market price of the share to the expected earnings:

$$P_0 = \frac{dv_1 + [P_1 - P_0]}{k_e} = \frac{dv_1 + P_1}{1 + k_e} \tag{3.28}$$

[15] Various views have been expressed by different writers regarding what shareholders pay for when purchasing a stock. The most widely discussed in the theory of corporate finance are (a) the dividends approach, (b) the dividends plus capital-gains approach, (c) the cash-flow approach, and (d) the earnings approach. However, all these approaches are equivalent, provided that the appropriate definitions are given to the concepts and variables used in each approach. This equivalence has been established by various writers. See, for example, F. Modigliani and M. Miller, 'The Cost of Capital, Corporation Finance, and the Theory of Investment', *American Economic Review*, 1958. An excellent discussion of the various approaches is included in Fama and Miller, *The Theory of Finance*, pp. 86–92.

[16] In this chapter we adopt a partial-equilibrium approach, that is, we concentrate on the determinants of the share price of one firm assuming that all other stock prices are given. Under this approach the riskiness of that firm's share is traditionally measured by the *coefficient of variation*. In a general-equilibrium approach, however, the riskiness of a share is measured by its effect on the risk of the *portfolio* of investors, which normally consists of several securities. The theory of portfolio selection is presented in Chapter 12.

If the investor holds the share for two periods, the expected rate of return is estimated from the expression:

$$P_0 = \sum_{t=1}^{2} \frac{dv_t}{(1+k_e)^t} + \frac{P_2}{(1+k_e)^2} \tag{3.29}$$

If the investor holds the share for ten years, the expected return, k_e, is found from the expression:

$$P_0 = \sum_{t=1}^{10} \frac{dv_t}{(1+k_e)^{10}} + \frac{P_{10}}{(1+k_e)^{10}} \tag{3.30}$$

If the stock is held indefinitely (in perpetuity), the investor's expected return is estimated by solving the following expression for k_e:

$$P_0 = \sum_{t=1}^{\infty} \frac{dv_t}{(1+k_e)^t} \tag{3.31}$$

Note that P_0 is the market price of a single share. The market value (or present value) of all outstanding shares (that is, the present value of the equity capital of the firm) is found by multiplying the above expression by N, the number of existing shares:

$$S_0 = (N)(P_0) = \sum_{t=1}^{\infty} \frac{N(dv)_t}{(1+k_e)^t} = \sum_{t=1}^{\infty} \frac{Dv_t}{(1+k_e)^t} \tag{3.32}$$

where S_0 = present (market) value of the equity capital of the firm, and Dv_t = total dividends of the firm.

Of course, the period for which an individual may hold a security is unknown. However, investors who hold a security only for a certain period expect to sell at a higher price than what they paid for it. This assumes that at that time there will be other buyers willing to pay the price. These investors will formulate their expectations based on future dividends and future selling price. The latter will depend upon other investors at that time wanting to buy the stock. The price they will be prepared to pay will depend upon their expectations of dividends and reselling value. This process will continue, assuming that the firm is expected to survive indefinitely. Since the total of cash earnings of all successive investors is the sum of dividends paid, including any liquidating value,[17] it is evident that cash dividends are all that stockholders as a whole receive from buying a share. Consequently it is assumed that dividends are what investors discount when estimating the price of shares.

If in any period a firm does not pay any dividend, this does not mean that its

---

[17] The liquidating value can be viewed either as a liquidating dividend or a terminal price for the share.

price will fall to zero. It simply implies that investors rely on (discounting) the reselling price alone, expecting that the firm will eventually pay dividends. In the meantime investors are satisfied with the expectation that they can resell it in the future at a higher price based on future expected dividends. The firm, by retaining all its earnings and reinvesting them, is expected to earn higher earnings and distribute larger dividends in the future.[18]

The measure of k_e (which, as we will see in Chapter 11, is the cost of equity capital) from the general valuation expression (3.31) is extremely tedious. In most of the finance literature k_e is estimated by simpler expressions, derived from the general valuation expression, under some assumptions regarding the future stream of dividends. In the remainder of this section we examine two models which are commonly used for *measuring* k_e.

B.   The Constant Dividend Stream Model

Under the assumption that the components of the stream of dividends do not grow and are equal in all periods ($dv_0 = dv_1 = \ldots = dv_t = dv$), the general valuation expression (3.31) reduces to

$$P_0 = dv \sum_{t=0}^{\infty} \frac{1}{(1 + k_e)^t} \tag{3.33}$$

or

$$P_0 = \frac{dv}{k_e} \tag{3.34}$$

The market value of the total equity capital of a firm is found by multiplying the above expression by N, the number of outstanding shares. Thus

$$S_0 = (N)(P_0) = \frac{N(dv)}{k_e} \quad \text{or} \quad S_0 = \frac{Dv}{k_e} \tag{3.35}$$

where S_0 = present value (market value) of all the outstanding shares, that is, the present value of equity capital, and Dv = total dividends of the firm.

The required rate of return of the share in this case is the 'dividend–price' ratio

$$k_e = \frac{Dv}{P_0} = \text{dividend–price ratio} \tag{3.36}$$

---

[18] This explains the so-called 'Petersburg Paradox', that is, the case of shares selling at high prices although their current dividend is zero. See David Durand, 'Growth, Stocks and the Petersburg Paradox', *Journal of Finance*, 1957, pp. 348–63.

If all earnings, $\bar{X}$, are distributed (zero retentions), $Dv = \bar{X}$, so that

$$k_e = \frac{\bar{X}}{P_0} = \text{price--earnings ratio} \tag{3.37}$$

that is, k_e is equal to the 'price--earnings' ratio in this model.

C. The Constant Growth (or the Gordon--Shapiro) Model of Valuation

In the real world dividends (and earnings) usually grow over time. If the rate of growth is not uniform, k_e, can be estimated from the general expression (3.31), in which the components dv_t are assumed to be subjectively estimated by investors, and differ over time.

To simplify the valuation model in conditions of growth Gordon and Shapiro[19] have developed the 'constant growth model', which is very popular in applied research because of its convenient mathematical form.

It is assumed that dividends grow at a constant rate g per cent per period of time. With this assumption expression (3.31) reduces to

$$P_0 = \frac{dv_0(1+g)}{(1+k_e)} + \frac{dv_0(1+g)^2}{(1+k_e)^2} + \ldots + \frac{dv_0(1+g)^\infty}{(1+k_e)^\infty} \tag{3.38}$$

or

$$P_0 = dv_0 \sum_{t=0}^{\infty} \left(\frac{1+g}{1+k_e}\right)^t = dv_0 \left[\left(\frac{1+g}{1+k_e}\right) + \left(\frac{1+g}{1+k_e}\right)^2 + \ldots + \left(\frac{1+g}{1+k_e}\right)^\infty\right] \tag{3.39}$$

If $g < k_e$, the geometric progression in the brackets is declining at a common ratio $(1+g)/(1+k_e)$. Summing the progression,[20] we obtain

$$P_0 = dv_0 \left(\frac{1+g}{k_e - g}\right) \tag{3.40}$$

or

$$P_0 = \frac{dv_1}{k_e - g} \tag{3.41}$$

Solving for k_e we find

$$k_e = \frac{dv_1}{P_0} + g \quad \text{or} \quad k_e = \frac{dv_0(1+g)}{P_0} + g \tag{3.42}$$

given that $dv_1 = dv_0(1+g)$.

[19] Myron Gordon and Eli Shapiro, 'Capital Equipment Analysis: The Required Rate of Profit', *Management Science*, 1956, pp. 102--10.
[20] The relevant expression is $\int_1^\infty = A/(1-\lambda)$ (see p. 162), where A is the first term of the declining geometric progression and λ is the common ratio.

The constant-growth model is mathematically very convenient. However, it is based on stringent assumptions, of which the reader should be aware. This model assumes that: (a) investors expect a constant growth rate of dividends, g, *ad infinitum*: (b) $dv > 0$; and (c) $g < k_e$. If assumptions (b) and (c) are not fulfilled, the model breaks down. If $dv_0 = 0$, then $P = 0$, and the 'Petersburg Paradox' cannot be explained. If $g \geqslant k_e$ the model predicts an infinitely large price.

D. General Growth Models

The assumption of constant g has been relaxed by various writers who have developed models capable of dealing with differential rates of growth.[21] For example, assume that for ten years the growth is expected to be very high, g_1, while for all subsequent years growth drops to g_2 ($g_2 < g_1$). Then the growth model becomes

$$P_0 = \sum_{t=1}^{10} Dv_0 \frac{(1+g_1)^t}{(1+k_e)^t} + \sum_{t=11}^{\infty} \frac{Dv_{10}(1+g_2)^{t-10}}{(1+k_e)^t} \tag{3.43}$$

This model is obviously mathematically less convenient than the constant-growth model. None the less, it is often used in practice.

E. A Note on the Determinants of the Discount Rate k_e

The above valuation models are used for *the measurement* of the discount rate, k_e, of a stream of future dividends. (As we will see in Chapter 11, k_e is the cost of equity capital, which is essential for the determination of the supply of funds to the firm.) We saw that, mathematically, k_e is an implicit function of the share price in the general valuation model, expression (3.31), and the general growth models, expression (3.43). In the other two models k_e was expressed as an explicit function of the price of shares.

Measuring k_e, however, is a different matter from establishing its determinants. In general, k_e is determined by *the time value of money* for investors (the riskless rate of interest), *and* the risk or uncertainty of the future dividend stream. The uncertainty arises from the total *financial risk*, which, as we saw in the previous section, includes the basic business risk as well as the risk from using debt for

---

[21] See B. G. Malkiel, 'Equity Yields, Growth, and the Structure of Share Prices', *American Economic Review*, 1963, pp. 1004–31; E. Brigham and J. L. Pappas, 'Duration of Growth, Changes in Growth Rates and Corporate Share Prices', *Financial Analysts Journal*, 1966, pp. 157–62; W. Scott Bauman, 'Investment Returns and Present Values', *Financial Analysts Journal*, 1969, pp. 107–18; P. F. Wendt, 'Current Growth Stock Valuation Methods', *Financial Analysts Journal*, 1965, pp. 3–15; C. C. Holt, 'The Influence of Growth Duration on Share Prices', *Journal of Finance*, 1962, pp. 465–75.

financing the operations of the firm. Thus we may write

$$k_e = i + \theta \qquad\qquad (3.44)$$

where i = the riskless interest rate, or time value of money (see also Chapter 12)

  θ = risk premium, for changes in business conditions and from the use of debt

As we saw in section II, the time value of money is the riskless interest rate, which is usually taken to be equal to the yield of long-term government bonds, on the presumption that the government is the most trustworthy borrower.

  In the partial-equilibrium approach, adopted in this chapter, the riskiness of a share is measured by the variability of the future stream of earnings available to stockholders, after payment of the fixed charges of debt ($X - F$, in the notation of section II).

  Total earnings (X or EBIT) are determined by the operating decisions and the investment and other growth decisions of managers. The operating decisions include the production decision, the pricing of output, the style of the product decision, and the advertising (and other marketing strategies) decision. The price–output decision is examined by the general theory of the firm.[22] The style of the product decision and the advertising decision were examined in Chapters 1 and 2 respectively. The investment decision is examined in Chapters 4 and 12. The other growth decisions (mergers and takeovers, vertical integration, foreign direct investment) are examined in Chapters 5, 6 and 7 respectively.

  The amount of fixed charges of debt, F, depends on the capital structure of the firm, or the financing decision of managers, which is examined in Chapter 8. Managers also decide the amount of dividends, and hence the amount of retained earnings. This decision is examined in Chapter 9. Thus, given the production and investment decisions of the firm, both the financing and the dividend decisions affect the actual dividend stream which stockholders expect to receive in the future. In Chapters 8 and 9 we examine how these decisions affect investors' valuation of common stock.

APPENDIX 3.1   INTRODUCTION TO THE THEORY OF PORTFOLIO SELECTION (INTERTEMPORAL ALLOCATION OF INCOME OR RESOURCES)[23]

The determination of the prices of securities (bonds or stocks) in a capital market is the result of the interaction of investors in the process of selection of their portfolios of various assets. In this appendix we will examine the elements of the theory of portfolio selection by individuals under certainty).

---

[22] See Koutsoyiannis, *Modern Microeconomics*.
[23] In this appendix we assume certainty. The theory of portfolio selection under conditions of uncertainty is discussed in Chapter 12.

A. Portfolio Selection by Individuals

In conditions of certainty portfolio selection involves the determination of the proportion of income which will be consumed in the current period and the proportion of income which will be invested in securities.

Thus inherent in portfolio selection is the problem of the allocation of financial resources by individuals over time with the aim of maximisation of their utility. When an individual investor buys a security (bond or stock) he gives up current consumption in order to attain a higher level of consumption and an improved standard of living in the future. This will become possible by the yield of the security and/or a capital gain from the sale of the security at a price higher than the original purchase price. At any one period of time we can think of the investor as having a stream of incomes which he attempts to allocate between current and future consumption so as to maximise his utility. In this sense the allocation of financial resources over time is an application of the general theory of choice. The determination of the equilibrium of the investor requires the determination (i) of the opportunity locus, that is, of the range of options available to him, and (ii) of his indifference map, which represents his preferences between current and future consumption.

Assumptions

1.   *Investors' rationality*. It is assumed that the investor aims at the maximisation of his utility by an appropriate allocation of his financial resources over time. The investor's utility depends on consumption levels over time.

$$U = f(c_1, c_2, c_3, \ldots, c_t) \tag{3.45}$$

2.   *Perfect capital markets*. Such markets have the following characteristics:
 (i) All traders have the same costless and complete information.
 (ii) Traders are price-takers.
 (iii) There are no transaction costs, such as brokerage fees, flotation costs, transfer taxes.

We will develop in detail a simple two-period model. The extension of this model to t periods is dealt with only briefly at the end of this section.

The indifference map of the investor

In the simple two-period model we may construct the investor's indifference map on a two-dimensional graph on the axes of which we measure the levels of consumption in the two periods. The indifference map under certainty reflects *the time preference of the investor*.

Under certainty we can construct an investor's indifference curves on the basis of the four basic axioms of the general theory of choice:

Axiom 1   *Ranking of preferences.* The individual is assumed to be able to rank his preferences when presented with various 'baskets' of commodities. In the present context the 'baskets' consist of different levels of current and future consumption (C_1 and C_2).

Axiom 2   *Transitivity.* It is assumed that if 'basket' A is preferred to 'basket' B, which is preferred to 'basket' C, then 'basket' A is preferred to 'basket' C.

Axion 3   *Non-satiation of wants.* The individual is assumed to prefer a bundle A to any other bundle B, if A contains more of any commodity and no less of the others.[24]

Axion 4   *Convexity of indifference curves.* The indifference curves are assumed to be convex to the origin.

Under the above assumptions the indifference curves appropriate for the allocation of wealth over time have the usual properties: they have a negative slope; they do not intersect; they show higher satisfaction, the further away from the origin. A family of such indifference curves is shown in Figures 3.5 and 3.6. Figure 3.5 depicts the indifference map of an individual with strong preference for future consumption, while Figure 3.6 shows the indifference map of an individual with strong preference for current consumption. To acquire a future increment in consumption equal to ab, investor A is prepared to give up a substantial amount of current consumption (cd). For the same increment of future consumption, investor B is prepared to give up only a small amount of current consumption (ef in Figure 3.6). In general, the steeper the slope of the investor's indifference curves the stronger his preference for present consumption.

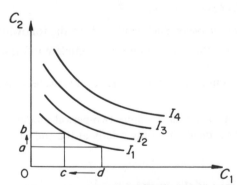

Figure 3.5   Indifference map of an
individual with strong preference for
future consumption

[24] It is assumed that all commodities have a positive utility. If a commodity has disutility for the consumer (e.g. contaminated mineral water, polluted land, etc.), this statement does not hold.

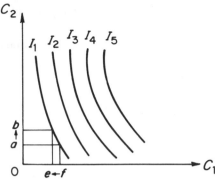

Figure 3.6   Indifference map of an
individual with strong preference for
current consumption

The investor's opportunity locus

It is assumed that the income of the individual investor in the two periods (y_1
and y_2) is given exogenously. The choice facing the investor is the allocation of
these incomes in the two periods to consumption levels c_1 and c_2 such as to
maximise his total utility:

$$U = f(c_1, c_2) \tag{3.46}$$

The opportunity frontier (locus), which is the constraint in this maximisation
problem, is determined by the total amounts y_1 and y_2, and their allocation
over time. In a perfect capital market the investor can lend funds (buy securities)
and borrow funds (sell securities), all of which are riskless: in a perfect capital
market *all assets* and *cash* have the same yield, i, the market interest rate. It is
convenient to conduct the analysis in terms of lending and borrowing at the
market rate of interest, i.

In the two-period model the individual's opportunity frontier is defined by
y_1, y_2 and the allocation of y_1 between present consumption c_1 and investment
(lending or buying a riskless asset) in period 1. If $c_1 < y_1$, the individual can
lend an amount equal to $y_1 - c_1$, which in period 2 will bring him a yield of
$i(y_1 - c_1)$ and a *total amount of money* equal to $a_2 = (y_1 - c_1)(1 + i)$. His total
financial resources, to be consumed in period 2, are

$$y_2 + a_2 = c_2$$

Substituting for a_2, we obtain

$$c_2 = \underbrace{[y_2 + y_1(1 + i)]}_{\text{intercept}} - \underbrace{(1 + i)}_{\text{slope}} c_1 \tag{3.47}$$

This is the equation of the opportunity frontier or constraint. It shows the trade-off between current and future consumption. Its slope is $-(1 + i)$ and its intercept on the C_2 axis is $[y_2 + y_1(1 + i)]$.

If we solve the equation of the constraint for c_1 we obtain

$$c_1 = \left[y_1 + \frac{y_2}{1 + i} \right] - \frac{c_2}{1 + i} \qquad (3.48)$$

which shows that the intercept of the opportunity frontier on the C_1 axis is:[25]

$$y_1 + \frac{y_2}{1 + i}$$

A hypothetical opportunity frontier is shown in Figure 3.7. Point w is the point showing that the income earned in each period is also consumed in that period, that is, w is defined by the values $c_1 = y_1$ and $c_2 = y_2$. This point is called the *endowment point*.

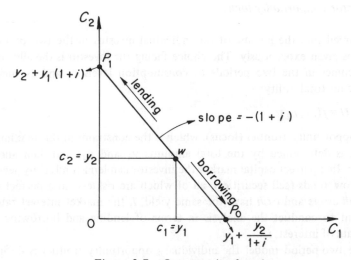

Figure 3.7   Opportunity frontier

Any point on the opportunity frontier shows a particular allocation of total available financial resources between consumption levels in periods 1 and 2:

(a) At the 'endowment point' w the individual consumes in each period all his earned income: that is, $c_1 = y_1$ and $c_2 = y_2$ at the 'endowment point' w.

[25] The intercept on the horizontal axis is *the present value* of the total income of the investor. The intercept on the vertical axis is the *future value* of the total income of the investor, that is, the value of his income in period 2 if all his income in period 1 is loaned at the market interest rate, i. Thus the opportunity frontier is the locus of points of total income (in both periods) which can be either consumed in the present period or in the future (period 2). In other words, the points on the opportunity frontier show consumption levels in the two periods which exhaust all the income of the investor.

(b) To the left of w, $c_1 < y_1$: the individual lends the difference $(y_1 - c_1)$ at an accumulation rate $(1 + i)$.

(c) To the right of w, $c_1 > y_1$: the individual borrows money (at the market interest rate i) to attain a higher current consumption.

(d) At point P_0 the individual consumes all his resources in the current period, by borrowing an amount equal to the discounted value of his income in period 2. Thus P_0 is the present wealth (or *the present value* of the resources) of the individual

$$P_0 = y_1 + \frac{y_2}{1 + i}$$ (3.49)

(e) At point P_1 the individual consumes all his resources in the final (second) period by lending all his current income at an accumulation rate of $(1 + i)$. Thus P_1 is the *terminal value* of the resources of the individual

$$P_1 = y_2 + y_1(1 + i)$$ (3.50)

We may rewrite the equation of the opportunity frontier, expression (3.47), as follows:

$$\left[c_1 + \frac{c_2}{1 + i} \right] = \left[y_1 + \frac{y_2}{1 + i} \right]$$ (3.51)

In this form we see that the opportunity frontier consists of combinations of consumption levels in the two periods such that

$$\left[\begin{matrix} \text{Present value of total consumption} \\ \text{in the two periods} \end{matrix} \right] = \left[\begin{matrix} \text{Present value of total financial} \\ \text{resources in the two periods} \end{matrix} \right]$$

The optimal allocation of financial resources among consumption levels in the two periods is defined by the point of tangency of the highest indifference curve with the efficient opportunity frontier (point e in Figure 3.8).

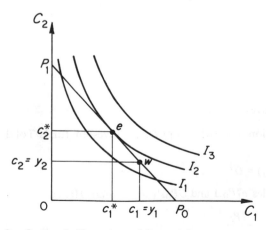

Figure 3.8 Optimal allocation of financial resources over time

The position that the investor will choose on the opportunity frontier defines the proportion (x) of his total income that he will invest in securities. That is

$$x \equiv \frac{\text{Invested funds}}{\text{Total funds}} \tag{3.52}$$

For example, assume that the investor chooses point A in Figure 3.9. This point is drawn (in our hypothetical example) to lie three-quarters of the way along the line towards P_1, i.e. $AP_0/P_1P_0 = 3/4$. Thus in our example the investor devotes one-third of all his income (OP_0) to current consumption, and two-thirds to investment in securities.

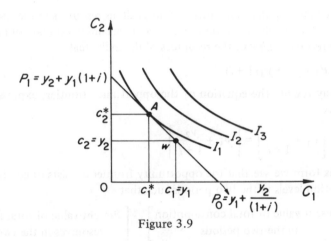

Figure 3.9

It can be shown that in general the proportion x of total available income (OP_0) devoted to investment is equal to the ratio AP_0/P_1P_0, that is,

$$x = \frac{AP_0}{P_1P_0} \tag{3.53}$$

$$* \qquad\qquad * \qquad\qquad *$$

PROOF

We want to prove $x = AP_0/P_1P_0$:

(1) By definition $x = (OP_0 - c_1^*)/OP_0$ = Invested funds/Total funds. It follows that

$$x(OP_0) = OP_0 - c_1^* \tag{3.54}$$

(2) The triangles $c_1^*P_0A$ and OP_0P_1 are similar. Hence

$$\frac{AP_0}{P_1P_0} = \frac{c_1^*P_0}{OP_0} \tag{3.55}$$

But from Figure 3.9 we see that

$$c_1^* P_0 = OP_0 - c_1^* \tag{3.56}$$

Substituting expression (3.54), we have

$$c_1^* P_0 = x(OP_0) \tag{3.57}$$

Substituting (3.57) in (3.55) we find

$$\frac{AP_0}{P_1 P_0} = \frac{c_1^* P_0}{OP_0} = \frac{x(OP_0)}{OP_0} = x$$

QED

*   *   *

We have shown that under certainty and within a two-period time horizon the investor maximises his utility by considering his total resources (funds, income)

$$OP_0 = y_1 + \frac{y_2}{(1+i)}$$

and devoting a proportion x to investment and the remainder $(1-x)$ to consumption in the first period. In other words, *the portfolio* that maximises the utility of the investor will consist of current consumption c_1^*, which absorbs the proportion

$$(1-x) = \frac{c_1^*}{OP_0}$$

and from investment $(OP_0 - c_1^*)$, which absorbs the proportion

$$x = \frac{OP_0 - c_1^*}{OP_0} = \frac{AP_0}{P_1 P_0}$$

The two proportions sum to unity, since the total income of the investor is allocated.

Extension of the certainty model of portfolio selection to a t-period time horizon

The extension of the two-period model to a time horizon consisting of t periods is straightforward.

The investor's utility function is

$$U = f(c_1, c_2, \ldots, c_t)$$

The investor wants to maximise this utility function subject to the constraint that total consumption be equal to total income. Thus we have the constrained maximisation problem

$$\text{maximise } U = f(c_1, c_2, \ldots, c_t) \tag{3.58}$$

subject to

$$\left[c_1 + \frac{c_2}{(1+i)} + \frac{c_3}{(1+i)^2} + \ldots + \frac{c_t}{(1+i)^{t-1}} \right] = \left[y_1 + \frac{y_2}{(1+i)} + \ldots + \frac{y_t}{(1+i)^{t-1}} \right]$$

(3.59)

Using Lagrangian multipliers we maximise the function

$$\phi = U - \lambda \left[c_1 + \frac{c_2}{(1+i)} + \ldots + \frac{c_t}{(1+i)^{t-1}} - y_1 - \frac{y_2}{(1+i)} - \ldots - \frac{y_t}{(1+i)^{t-1}} \right]$$

(3.60)

Setting the first derivatives of this function w.r.t. c_t equal to zero, we obtain t equations:

$$\left.\begin{array}{lll} \dfrac{\partial U}{\partial c_1} - \lambda & = 0 & \text{where } \dfrac{\partial U}{\partial c_1} = MU_{c_1} \\[3mm] \dfrac{\partial U}{\partial c_2} - \lambda \dfrac{1}{(1+i)} & = 0 & \text{where } \dfrac{\partial U}{\partial c_2} = MU_{c_2} \\[3mm] \qquad . \qquad\quad . \qquad . \qquad\quad . \\[2mm] \qquad . \qquad\quad . \qquad . \qquad\quad . \\[2mm] \qquad . \qquad\quad . \qquad . \qquad\quad . \\[2mm] \dfrac{\partial U}{\partial c_t} - \lambda \dfrac{1}{(1+i)^{t-1}} = 0 & & \text{where } \dfrac{\partial U}{\partial c_t} = MU_{c_t} \end{array}\right\}$$

(3.61)

Solving the t equations for λ, we find

$$\left.\begin{array}{l} \lambda = \dfrac{\partial U}{\partial c_1} \\[4mm] \lambda = \dfrac{\partial U}{\partial c_2}(1+i) \\[4mm] \lambda = \dfrac{\partial U}{\partial c_3}(1+i)^2 \\[4mm] \qquad . \qquad\quad . \qquad . \\[2mm] \qquad . \qquad\quad . \qquad . \\[2mm] \lambda = \dfrac{\partial U}{\partial c_t}(1+i)^{t-1} \end{array}\right\}$$

(3.62)

Equating these expressions we obtain the equilibrium condition

$$\frac{\partial U}{\partial c_1} = \frac{\partial U}{\partial c_2}(1+i) = \frac{\partial U}{\partial c_3}(1+i)^2 = \ldots = \frac{\partial U}{\partial c_t}(1+i)^{t-1}$$

(3.63)

This shows that in a multi-period model the investor will maximise his utility by allocating his total income to consumption levels

$$c_1, c_2, \ldots, c_t$$

such that the marginal utilities from the consumption levels (appropriately adjusted for the time value of money) are equal.

B. Optimal Portfolio Selection by Firms under Certainty

In this section we extend the model of intertemporal allocation of resources to firms. We will develop only a two-period model under the assumption of perfect capital markets. This analysis will clarify several issues relating to the goal of maximisation of the wealth of shareholders which is adopted in the traditional theory of finance.

The single-owner firm

The extension of the basic certainty model of individual investors to the behaviour of firms is fairly straightforward if we assume that the firm is owned by a single individual who has a clearly defined utility function describing his time preferences. The case of the multi-owner corporations is more complex, and will be examined after the development of the single-owner model.

The owner of the firm is assumed to aim at the maximisation of his utility by an appropriate use of his productive resources. The determination of the equilibrium of the owner-entrepreneur requires simultaneous choices of optimal investment and consumption patterns over time.

Optimal investment choice

Our first step is the introduction of *physical capital assets* which are held in the firm's portfolio. We can visualise the owner of the firm (decision-maker) as having an amount of productive resources which he can (a) liquidate immediately in the current period, (b) invest and receive their proceeds at the end of the second period, or (c) partly liquidate and partly invest in the first period in order to receive higher proceeds in the second period.

If we accept the neoclassical assumption of diminishing marginal returns of investment in capital assets, the opportunity frontier (or transformation curve) of the firm is a curve concave to the origin (Figure 3.10). Point K' represents the present (current) value of the resources, while point K represents the terminal value of the resources if all of them are invested in the current period. Any intermediate point of the KK' frontier denotes an investment strategy. For example, at point A the firm decides to withdraw a cash amount (liquidate an amount of its resources) equal to OA and invest the remaining resources, AK'. This strategy

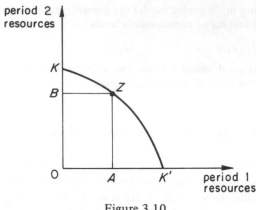

Figure 3.10

will yield proceeds of *OB* to be consumed in period 2. It should be clear that each investment strategy yields a different combination of proceeds in the two periods. These proceeds can be allocated to consumption in the two periods by lending or borrowing money (buying or selling of bonds) at the prevailing market interest rate *i*. The lending–borrowing opportunities are defined, *for each point on the KK' production transformation curve*, by drawing a straight line *through that point* with slope $-(1 + i)$. This line is called the 'present-value line', because its intercept on the horizontal axis shows the value in terms of current (present-period) resources of any combination of resources lying on the line.[26] For example, the consumption opportunity line or present-value line corresponding to point *K'* is the line *WK'* (Figure 3.11), with slope $-(1 + i)$. Since at point *K'* investment is zero, the owner-entrepreneur can attain a higher utility level only by using the capital market to lend (buy bonds) a part of his liquidated resources, thus securing larger proceeds (for consumption) in the second period.

Consider next a point such as *z* (in Figure 3.11) on the production transformation frontier, which implies the positive level of investment *AK'* and the withdrawal of the amount *OA* which can be used in the capital market for borrowing or lending so as to attain an allocation of consumption in the two periods that would maximise the utility of the decision-maker. Note that the choice of the investment policy implied by point *A* increases the present value of the resources $(OV' > OK')$: the present-value line (or consumption opportunity locus) is the line *YV'* through *Z*, which dominates that for the strategy of complete liquidation (denoted by point *K'*). The present value of the proceeds from strategy *z* is *OV'*. If the owner wishes to attain a level of current consumption higher than

[26] This line is also called the 'consumption opportunity line', because it shows the consumption possibilities open to the owner-entrepreneur if he adopts the investment strategy of that particular point of the production frontier.

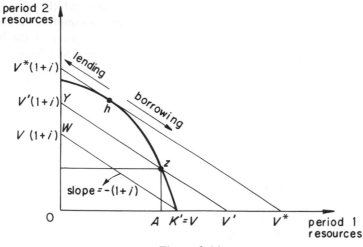

Figure 3.11

the withdrawal OA, he can borrow the required funds at the market interest rate i. If he has a preference for a lower (than OA) current consumption, he can lend part of the withdrawn amount of his wealth and enjoy a higher income in the second period.

By repeating the above process for strategies including higher investment levels, we generate a family of present-value lines, each corresponding to a particular point on the production-possibility frontier.[27] Clearly the owner-entrepreneur will choose the investment strategy with the highest present value, that is, the point of tangency of the production frontier with the highest possible present-value line (point h in Figure 3.11). This point represents the optimal investment strategy, because it maximises the present value of the resources of the firm. Formally, the condition for an optimal investment decision is that *the slope of the production frontier be equal to the slope of the consumption opportunity frontier.*[28]

Optimal consumption choice by the owner-manager

The determination of the optimal production—investment strategy is the first stage in defining the equilibrium of the owner of the firm. We must next locate

[27] See W. J. Baumol, *Portfolio Theory: The Selection of Asset Combinations* (General Learning Press, 1970). Also Fama and Miller, *The Theory of Finance,* Ch. 2.

[28] Or, equivalently, the internal rate of return on investment must be equal to the market rate of interest. See Chapter 4 for an explanation of the equivalence of these two statements of the condition for an optimal investment decision.

the point of the highest consumption opportunity line at which the entrepreneur maximises his utility. This is determined by using the consumption indifference map of the decision-maker and finding the point of tangency of the highest attainable consumption frontier with the highest possible indifference curve.

Two possible equilibrium positions are shown in Figures 3.12 and 3.13.

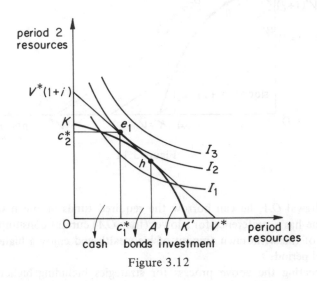

Figure 3.12

In Figure 3.12 the shape of the indifference curves implies a strong preference of the owner-entrepreneur for future consumption. He reaches equilibrium at point e_1, where the following decisions have been made: (i) withdrawal of OA cash, (ii) investment equal to AK', (iii) current consumption Oc_1^*, (iv) lending (buying bonds) the remaining cash withdrawal c_1^*A, (v) consumption of Oc_2^* in the second period.

In Figure 3.13 the shape of the indifference curves implies a preference for current consumption. The owner-entrepreneur maximises his utility at point e_2, where he borrows an amount equal to Bc_1^* from the capital market.

In summary. The equilibrium of an owner-entrepreneur requires simultaneous choices as to both investment and consumption levels over time. His equilibrium is defined by a *double tangency solution*:

(1) The optimal investment decision is defined by the tangency of the highest present-value line with the production opportunity frontier. This decision does not require any subjective preference (utility) considerations. It is based on objectively given information about the firm's technology and the market interest rate.

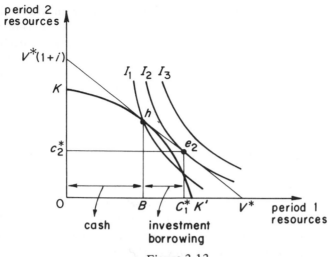

Figure 3.13

(2) The optimal consumption pattern is defined by the tangency of the highest present-value line with the highest possible consumption indifference curve. This choice is based on the subjective utility function of the owner-entrepreneur.

The multi-owner corporation

In the preceding model the ultimate criterion for optimal choice was the maximisation of the utility of the owner of the firm. This criterion, however, is not readily applicable when the firm is owned by many shareholders, each of whom has his own time preference for consumption.

We said at the beginning of this chapter (p. 156) that the aggregation of individual utility functions into a global utility function, representing the time preference of all shareholders, presents serious conceptual problems.

Another problem arises from the separation of ownership and control in the large corporations. In principle shareholders have the power to control the managers, to whom they have delegated the authority to run the operations of the firm in the best interests of stockholders. In practice, however, managers have a certain degree of discretion in goal-setting.[29] Managers have their own utility functions, which, in general, include different variables from the utility

---

[29] For a summary of the debate regarding the discretion of managers see M. F. Scherer, *Industrial Market Structure and Economic Performance* (Rand McNally, 1970). See also Koutsoyiannis, *Modern Microeconomics*, ch. 11.

functions of shareholders. Under these conditions it is not clear what is the utility function that managers should seek to maximise or how it can be constructed.

These difficulties can be avoided if we assume *perfect capital markets*. With this assumption the utility-maximisation criterion can be replaced by another, which (a) does not require the use of the utility functions of the individual shareholders, and (b) leads to the same production–investment decisions which would be reached if each stockholder were the only manager or decision-maker. This alternative criterion is *the maximisation of the market value of the equity (shares) of existing stockholders*, or, briefly, the 'market-value criterion'. This criterion implies that the maximisation of the *present value of the productive resources* of the firm (the attainment of the first tangency, of the production frontier with the highest present-value line), which, as we saw, is a technological problem, leads to the maximisation of the *market value of the equity* of share-holders. In other words, *the maximisation of the present value of the firm's resources by appropriate production–investment decisions is equivalent to the maximisation of the value of the shares of the existing shareholders*. This is so because in a perfect capital market the present value of the resources of the firm is necessarily equal to the market value of the equity, given that there is a unique interest rate. Hence, if the managers attain the first tangency, the wealth of owner-shareholders is maximised. Once this point has been reached, each stock-holder can be left alone to use the capital market, lending or borrowing funds as required to maximise his own utility. That is, the first tangency (optimal invest-ment decision) is attained by managers, while the second tangency (optimal consumption patterns) is pursued by each investor individually according to his own time preferences.

The 'market-value criterion' can in principle be implemented, because it requires 'objective' knowledge of the technology of the firm and the current interest rate. As a consequence, *optimal investment decisions can be taken inde-pendently from the preferences (tastes) of shareholders*.

To illustrate the 'market-value criterion', assume that the technology of the firm and the prevailing market interest rate give rise to the optimal investment strategy z in Figure 3.14. This investment decision would be reached by any 'rational' decison-maker, manager or individual shareholder whose goal would be the maximisation of the present value of the resources of the firm. Once the first optimality condition has been met, the second one can be sought individually by each investor, depending on his own time preference. In Figure 3.14 share-holder A maximises his utility at point a, by lending some of his cash withdrawals (dividends) from the firm, while shareholder B maximises his utility at point b, by borrowing funds in addition to his cash withdrawals. These lending and bor-rowing operations by shareholders are of no consequence to managers, whose goal is to take the investment decisions implied by point z: *optimal investment decisions on the basis of the 'market-value criterion' can be made by managers independently from the shareholders' preferences and tastes*.

It should be stressed that, if the assumption of perfect capital markets does

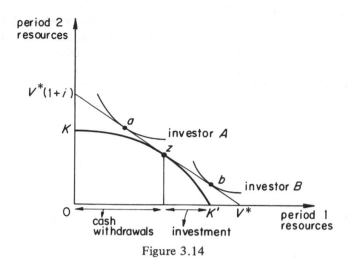

Figure 3.14

not hold, the criterion of maximisation of the present value of the resources of the firm is *not* a substitute for the criterion of maximisation of the utility of shareholders, because it does not lead to the same investment decisions. For example, assume that market imperfections result in the lending interest rate to be lower than the borrowing rate ($i_B > i_L$). Under these conditions borrowers and lenders will have present-value lines (or consumption opportunity lines) with different slopes (see Figure 3.15). For borrowers (i.e. investors with strong preference for current consumption) the optimal investment is BK', while for lenders (i.e. investors with strong preference for future consumption) the optimal

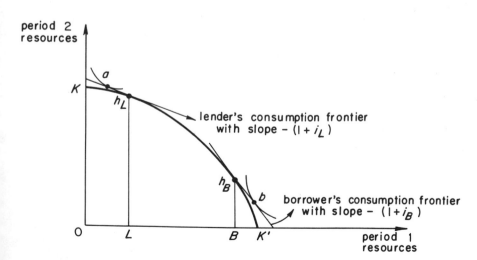

Figure 3.15

investment level is $LK' > BK'$. Thus *in imperfect capital markets there is no longer a unique investment decision*: each stockholder would reach a different investment decision, influenced by his own time preferences. If the capital markets are imperfect, the investment decisions are not separable (independent) from investors' preferences.

APPENDIX 3.2   MATHEMATICAL TABLES

Table 1   Compound Value of $1

Future Value of $1

Period \ i	1%	2%	3%	4%	5%	6%	7%	8%	9%	10%
1	1.0100	1.0200	1.0300	1.0400	1.0500	1.0600	1.0700	1.0800	1.0900	1.1000
2	1.0201	1.0404	1.0609	1.0816	1.1025	1.1236	1.1449	1.1664	1.1881	1.2100
3	1.0303	1.0612	1.0927	1.1249	1.1576	1.1910	1.2250	1.2597	1.2950	1.3310
4	1.0406	1.0824	1.1255	1.1699	1.2155	1.2625	1.3108	1.3605	1.4116	1.4641
5	1.0510	1.1041	1.1593	1.2167	1.2763	1.3382	1.4006	1.4693	1.5386	1.6105
6	1.0615	1.1262	1.1941	1.2653	1.3401	1.4185	1.5007	1.5869	1.6771	1.7716
7	1.0721	1.1487	1.2299	1.3159	1.4071	1.5036	1.6058	1.7138	1.8280	1.9487
8	1.0829	1.1717	1.2668	1.3686	1.4775	1.5938	1.7182	1.8509	1.9926	2.1436
9	1.0937	1.1951	1.3048	1.4233	1.5513	1.6895	1.8385	1.9990	2.1719	2.3579
10	1.1046	1.2190	1.3439	1.4802	1.6289	1.7908	1.9672	2.1589	2.3674	2.5937
11	1.1157	1.2434	1.3842	1.5395	1.7103	1.8983	2.1049	2.3316	2.5804	2.8531
12	1.1268	1.2682	1.4258	1.6010	1.7959	2.0122	2.2522	2.5182	2.8127	3.1384
13	1.1381	1.2936	1.4685	1.6651	1.8856	2.1329	2.4098	2.7196	3.0658	3.4523
14	1.1495	1.3195	1.5126	1.7317	1.9799	2.2609	2.5785	2.9372	3.3417	3.7975
15	1.1610	1.3459	1.5580	1.8009	2.0789	2.3966	2.7590	3.1722	3.6425	4.1772
16	1.1726	1.3728	1.6047	1.8730	2.1829	2.5404	2.9522	3.4259	3.9703	4.5950
17	1.1843	1.4002	1.6528	1.9479	2.2920	2.6928	3.1588	3.7000	4.3276	5.0545
18	1.1961	1.4282	1.7024	2.0258	2.4066	2.8543	3.3799	3.9960	4.7171	5.5599
19	1.2081	1.4568	1.7535	2.1068	2.5270	3.0256	3.6165	4.3157	5.1417	6.1159
20	1.2202	1.4859	1.8061	2.1911	2.6533	3.2071	3.8697	4.6610	5.6044	6.7275
21	1.2324	1.5157	1.8603	2.2788	2.7860	3.3996	4.1406	5.0338	6.1088	7.4002
22	1.2447	1.5460	1.9161	2.3699	2.9253	3.6035	4.4304	5.4365	6.6586	8.1403
23	1.2572	1.5769	1.9736	2.4647	3.0715	3.8197	4.7405	5.8715	7.2579	8.9543
24	1.2697	1.6084	2.0328	2.5633	3.2251	4.0489	5.0724	6.3412	7.9111	9.8497
25	1.2824	1.6406	2.0938	2.6658	3.3864	4.2919	5.4274	6.8485	8.6231	10.8340
26	1.2953	1.6734	2.1566	2.7725	3.5557	4.5494	5.8074	7.3964	9.3992	11.9180
27	1.3082	1.7069	2.2213	2.8834	3.7335	4.8223	6.2139	7.9881	10.2450	13.1100
28	1.3213	1.7410	2.2879	2.9987	3.9201	5.1117	6.6488	8.6271	11.1670	14.4210
29	1.3345	1.7758	2.3566	3.1187	4.1161	5.4184	7.1143	9.3173	12.1720	15.8630
30	1.3478	1.8114	2.4273	3.2434	4.3219	5.7435	7.6123	10.0620	13.2670	17.4490
40	1.4889	2.2080	3.2620	4.8010	7.0400	10.2850	14.9740	21.7240	31.4090	45.2590
50	1.6446	2.6916	4.3839	7.1067	11.4670	18.4200	29.4570	46.9010	74.3570	117.3900
60	1.8167	3.2810	5.8916	10.5190	18.6790	32.9870	57.9460	101.2500	176.0300	304.4800

Note: CVIF is the abbreviation of 'Compound Value Interest Factor'. In many managerial finance textbooks the term FVIF is used instead, as the abbreviation of 'Future Value Interest Factor'.

(CVIF)

at the End of *n* Periods

$$CVIF = (1 + i)^t$$

12%	14%	15%	16%	18%	20%	24%	28%	32%	36%
1.1200	1.1400	1.1500	1.1600	1.1800	1.2000	1.2400	1.2800	1.3200	1.3600
1.2544	1.2996	1.3225	1.3456	1.3924	1.4400	1.5376	1.6384	1.7424	1.8496
1.4049	1.4815	1.5209	1.5609	1.6430	1.7280	1.9066	2.0972	2.3000	2.5155
1.5736	1.6890	1.7490	1.8106	1.9388	2.0736	2.3642	2.6844	3.0360	3.4210
1.7623	1.9254	2.0114	2.1003	2.2878	2.4883	2.9316	3.4360	4.0075	4.6526
1.9738	2.1950	2.3131	2.4364	2.6996	2.9860	3.6352	4.3980	5.2899	6.3275
2.2107	2.5023	2.6600	2.8262	3.1855	3.5832	4.5077	5.6295	6.9826	8.6054
2.4760	2.8526	3.0590	3.2784	3.7589	4.2998	5.5895	7.2058	9.2170	11.7030
2.7731	3.2519	3.5179	3.8030	4.4355	5.1598	6.9310	9.2234	12.1660	15.9160
3.1058	3.7072	4.0456	4.4114	5.2338	6.1917	8.5944	11.8050	16.0590	21.6460
3.4785	4.2262	4.6524	5.1173	6.1759	7.4301	10.6570	15.1110	21.1980	29.4390
3.8960	4.8179	5.3502	5.9360	7.2876	8.9161	13.2140	19.3420	27.9820	40.0370
4.3635	5.4924	6.1528	6.8858	8.5994	10.6990	16.3860	24.7580	36.9370	54.4510
4.8871	6.2613	7.0757	7.9875	10.1470	12.8390	20.3190	31.6910	48.7560	74.0530
5.4736	7.1379	8.1371	9.2655	11.9730	15.4070	25.1950	40.5640	64.3580	100.7100
6.1304	8.1372	9.3576	10.7840	14.1290	18.4880	31.2420	51.9230	84.9530	136.9600
6.8660	9.2765	10.7610	12.4670	16.6720	22.1860	38.7400	66.4610	112.1300	186.2700
7.6900	10.5750	12.3750	14.4620	19.6730	26.6230	48.0380	85.0700	148.0200	253.3300
8.6128	12.0550	14.2310	16.7760	23.2140	31.9480	59.5670	108.8900	195.3900	344.5300
9.6463	13.7430	16.3660	19.4600	27.3930	38.3370	73.8640	139.3700	257.9100	468.5700
10.8030	15.6670	18.8210	22.5740	32.3230	46.0050	91.5910	178.4000	340.4400	637.2600
12.1000	17.8610	21.6440	26.1860	38.1420	55.2060	113.5700	228.3500	449.3900	866.6700
13.5520	20.3610	24.8910	30.3760	45.0070	66.2470	140.8300	292.3000	593.1900	1178.6000
15.1780	23.2120	28.6250	35.2360	53.1080	79.4960	174.6300	374.1400	783.0200	1602.9000
17.0000	26.4610	32.9180	40.8740	62.6680	95.3960	216.5400	478.9000	1033.5000	2180.0000
19.0400	30.1660	37.8560	47.4140	73.9480	114.4700	268.5100	612.9900	1364.3000	2964.9000
21.3240	34.3890	43.5350	55.0000	87.2590	137.3700	332.9500	784.6300	1800.9000	4032.2000
23.8830	39.2040	50.0650	63.8000	102.9600	164.8400	412.8600	1004.3000	2377.2000	5483.8000
26.7490	44.6930	57.5750	74.0080	121.5000	197.8100	511.9500	1285.5000	3137.9000	7458.0000
29.9590	50.9500	66.2110	85.8490	143.3700	237.3700	634.8100	1645.5000	4142.0000	10143.0000
93.0500	188.8800	267.8600	378.7200	750.3700	1469.7000	5455.9000	19426.0000	66520.0000	*
289.0000	700.2300	1083.6000	1670.3000	3927.3000	9100.4000	46890.0000	*	*	*
897.5900	2595.9000	4383.9000	7370.1000	20555.0000	56347.0000	*	*	*	*

* CVIF > 99999.

Table 2   Present Value of

Present Value

Period \ i	1%	2%	3%	4%	5%	6%	7%	8%	9%	10%
1	.9901	.9804	.9709	.9615	.9524	.9434	.9346	.9259	.9174	.9091
2	.9803	.9612	.9426	.9246	.9070	.8900	.8734	.8573	.8417	.8264
3	.9706	.9423	.9151	.8890	.8638	.8396	.8163	.7938	.7722	.7513
4	.9610	.9238	.8885	.8548	.8227	.7921	.7629	.7350	.7084	.6830
5	.9515	.9057	.8626	.8219	.7835	.7473	.7130	.6806	.6499	.6209
6	.9420	.8880	.8375	.7903	.7462	.7050	.6663	.6302	.5963	.5645
7	.9327	.8706	.8131	.7599	.7107	.6651	.6227	.5835	.5470	.5132
8	.9235	.8535	.7894	.7307	.6788	.6274	.5820	.5403	.5019	.4665
9	.9143	.8368	.7664	.7026	.6445	.5919	.5439	.5002	.4604	.4241
10	.9053	.8203	.7441	.6756	.6139	.5584	.5083	.4632	.4224	.3855
11	.8963	.8043	.7224	.6496	.5847	.5268	.4751	.4289	.3875	.3505
12	.8874	.7885	.7014	.6246	.5568	.4970	.4440	.3971	.3555	.3186
13	.8787	.7730	.6810	.6006	.5303	.4688	.4150	.3677	.3262	.2897
14	.8700	.7579	.6611	.5775	.5051	.4423	.3878	.3405	.2992	.2633
15	.8613	.7430	.6419	.5553	.4810	.4173	.3624	.3152	.2745	.2394
16	.8528	.7284	.6232	.5339	.4581	.3936	.3387	.2919	.2519	.2176
17	.8444	.7142	.6050	.5134	.4363	.3714	.3166	.2703	.2311	.1978
18	.8360	.7002	.5874	.4936	.4155	.3503	.2959	.2502	.2120	.1799
19	.8277	.6864	.5703	.4746	.3957	.3305	.2765	.2317	.1945	.1635
20	.8195	.6730	.5537	.4564	.3769	.3118	.2584	.2145	.1784	.1486
21	.8114	.6598	.5375	.4388	.3589	.2942	.2415	.1987	.1637	.1351
22	.8034	.6468	.5219	.4220	.3418	.2775	.2257	.1839	.1502	.1228
23	.7954	.6342	.5067	.4057	.3256	.2618	.2109	.1703	.1378	.1117
24	.7876	.6217	.4919	.3901	.3101	.2470	.1971	.1577	.1264	.1015
25	.7798	.6095	.4776	.3751	.2953	.2330	.1842	.1460	.1160	.0923
26	.7720	.5976	.4637	.3607	.2812	.2198	.1722	.1352	.1064	.0839
27	.7644	.5859	.4502	.3468	.2678	.2074	.1609	.1252	.0976	.0763
28	.7568	.5744	.4371	.3335	.2551	.1956	.1504	.1159	.0895	.0693
29	.7493	.5631	.4243	.3207	.2429	.1846	.1406	.1073	.0822	.0630
30	.7419	.5521	.4120	.3083	.2314	.1741	.1314	.0994	.0754	.0573
35	.7059	.5000	.3554	.2534	.1813	.1301	.0937	.0676	.0490	.0356
40	.6717	.4529	.3066	.2083	.1420	.0972	.0668	.0460	.0318	.0221
45	.6391	.4102	.2644	.1712	.1113	.0727	.0476	.0313	.0207	.0137
50	.6080	.3715	.2281	.1407	.0872	.0543	.0339	.0213	.0134	.0085
55	.5785	.3365	.1968	.1157	.0683	.0406	.0242	.0145	.0087	.0053

Note: PVIF is the abbreviation of 'Present Value Interest Factor'.

$1 (PVIF)

of $1

$$PVIF = \frac{1}{(1+i)^t}$$

12%	14%	15%	16%	18%	20%	24%	28%	32%	36%
.8929	.8772	.8696	.8621	.8475	.8333	.8065	.7813	.7576	.7353
.7972	.7695	.7561	.7432	.7182	.6944	.6504	.6104	.5739	.5407
.7118	.6750	.6575	.6407	.6086	.5787	.5245	.4768	.4348	.3975
.6355	.5921	.5718	.5523	.5158	.4823	.4230	.3725	.3294	.2923
.5674	.5194	.4972	.4761	.4371	.4019	.3411	.2910	.2495	.2149
.5066	.4556	.4323	.4104	.3704	.3349	.2751	.2274	.1890	.1580
.4523	.3996	.3759	.3538	.3139	.2791	.2218	.1776	.1432	.1162
.4039	.3506	.3269	.3050	.2660	.2326	.1789	.1388	.1085	.0854
.3606	.3075	.2843	.2630	.2255	.1938	.1443	.1084	.0822	.0628
.3220	.2697	.2472	.2267	.1911	.1615	.1164	.0847	.0623	.0462
.2875	.2366	.2149	.1954	.1619	.1346	.0938	.0662	.0472	.0340
.2567	.2076	.1869	.1685	.1372	.1122	.0757	.0517	.0357	.0250
.2292	.1821	.1625	.1452	.1163	.0935	.0610	.0404	.0271	.0184
.2046	.1597	.1413	.1252	.0985	.0779	.0492	.0316	.0205	.0135
.1827	.1401	.1229	.1079	.0835	.0649	.0397	.0247	.0155	.0099
.1631	.1229	.1069	.0930	.0708	.0541	.0320	.0193	.0118	.0073
.1456	.1078	.0929	.0802	.0600	.0451	.0258	.0150	.0089	.0054
.1300	.0946	.0808	.0691	.0508	.0376	.0208	.0118	.0068	.0039
.1161	.0829	.0703	.0596	.0431	.0313	.0168	.0092	.0051	.0029
.1037	.0728	.0611	.0514	.0365	.0261	.0135	.0072	.0039	.0021
.0926	.0638	.0531	.0443	.0309	.0217	.0109	.0056	.0029	.0016
.0826	.0560	,0462	.0382	.0262	.0181	.0088	.0044	.0022	.0012
.0738	.0491	.0402	.0329	.0222	.0151	.0071	.0034	.0017	.0008
.0659	.0431	.0349	.0284	.0188	.0126	.0057	.0027	.0013	.0006
.0588	.0378	.0304	.0245	.0160	.0105	.0046	.0021	.0010	.0005
.0525	.0331	.0264	.0211	.0135	.0087	.0037	.0016	.0007	.0003
.0469	.0291	.0230	.0182	.0115	.0073	.0030	.0013	.0006	.0002
,0419	.0255	.0200	.0157	.0097	.0061	.0024	.0010	.0004	.0002
.0374	.0224	.0174	.0135	.0082	.0051	.0020	.0008	.0003	.0001
.0334	.0196	.0151	.0116	.0070	.0042	.0016	.0006	.0002	.0001
.0189	.0102	.0075	.0055	.0030	.0017	.0005	.0002	.0001	*
.0107	.0053	.0037	.0026	.0013	.0007	.0002	.0001	*	*
.0051	.0027	.0019	.0013	.0006	.0003	.0001	*	*	*
.0035	.0014	.0009	.0006	.0003	.0001	*	*	*	*
.0020	.0007	.0005	.0003	.0001	*	*	*	*	*

* The factor is zero to four decimal places.

Table 3   Compound Value of an Annuity of $1

Sum of Annuity of $1

Periods \ i	1%	2%	3%	4%	5%	6%	7%	8%	9%	10%
1	1.0000	1.0000	1.0000	1.0000	1.0000	1.0000	1.0000	1.0000	1.0000	1.0000
2	2.0100	2.0200	2.0300	2.0400	2.0500	2.0600	2.0700	2.0800	2.0900	2.1000
3	3.0301	3.0604	3.0909	3.1216	3.1525	3.1836	3.2149	3.2464	3.2781	3.3100
4	4.0604	4.1216	4.1836	4.2465	4.3101	4.3746	4.4399	4.5061	4.5731	4.6410
5	5.1010	5.2040	5.3091	5.4163	5.5256	5.6371	5.7507	5.8666	5.9847	6.1051
6	6.1520	6.3081	6.4684	6.6330	6.8019	6.9753	7.1533	7.3359	7.5233	7.7156
7	7.2135	7.4343	7.6625	7.8983	8.1420	8.3938	8.6540	8.9228	9.2004	9.4872
8	8.2857	8.5830	8.8923	9.2142	9.5491	9.8975	10.2590	10.6380	11.0280	11.4350
9	9.3685	9.7546	10.1590	10.5820	11.0260	11.4910	11.9780	12.4870	13.0210	13.5790
10	10.4620	10.9490	11.4630	12.0060	12.5770	13.1800	13.8160	14.4860	15.1920	15.9370
11	11.5660	12.1680	12.8070	13.4860	14.2060	14.9710	15.7830	16.6450	17.5600	18.5310
12	12.6820	13.4120	14.1920	15.0250	15.9170	16.8690	17.8880	18.9970	20.1400	21.3840
13	13.8090	14.6800	15.6170	16.6260	17.7130	18.8820	20.1400	21.4950	22.9530	24.5220
14	14.9470	15.9730	17.0860	18.2910	19.5980	21.0150	22.5500	24.2140	26.0190	27.9750
15	16.0960	17.2930	18.5980	20.0230	21.5780	23.2760	25.1290	27.1520	29.3600	31.7720
16	17.2570	18.6390	20.1560	21.8240	23.6570	25.6720	27.8880	30.3240	33.0030	35.9490
17	18.4300	20.0120	21.7610	23.6970	25.8400	28.2120	30.8400	33.7500	36.9730	40.5440
18	19.6140	21.4120	23.4140	25.6450	28.1320	30.9050	33.9990	37.4500	41.3010	45.5990
19	20.8100	22.8400	25.1160	27.6710	30.5390	33.7600	37.3790	41.4460	46.0180	51.1590
20	22.0190	24.2970	26.8700	29.7780	33.0660	36.7850	40.9950	45.7620	51.1600	57.2750
21	23.2390	25.7830	28.6760	31.9690	35.7190	39.9920	44.8650	50.4220	56.7640	64.0020
22	24.4710	27.2990	30.5360	34.2480	38.5050	43.3920	49.0050	55.4580	62.8730	71.4020
23	25.7160	28.8450	32.4520	36.6170	41.4300	46.9950	53.4360	60.8930	69.5310	79.5430
24	26.9730	30.4210	34.4260	39.0820	44.5020	50.8150	58.1760	66.7640	76.7890	88.4970
25	28.2430	32.0300	36.4590	41.6450	47.7270	54.8640	63.2490	73.1050	84.7000	98.3470
26	29.5250	33.6700	38.5530	44.3110	51.1130	59.1560	68.6760	79.9540	93.3230	109.1800
27	30.8200	35.3440	40.7090	47.0840	54.6690	63.7050	74.4830	87.3500	102.7200	121.0900
28	32.1290	37.0510	42.9300	49.9670	58.4020	68.5280	80.6970	95.3880	112.9600	134.2000
29	33.4500	38.7920	45.2180	52.9660	62.3220	73.6390	87.3460	103.9600	124.1300	148.6300
30	34.7840	40.5680	47.5750	56.0840	66.4380	79.0580	94.4600	113.2800	136.3000	164.4900
40	48.8860	60.4020	75.4010	95.0250	120.7900	154.7600	199.6300	259.0500	337.8800	442.5900
50	64.4630	84.5790	112.7900	152.6600	209.3400	290.3300	406.5200	573.7600	815.0800	1163.9000
60	81.6690	114.0500	163.0500	237.9900	353.5800	533.1200	813.5200	1253.2000	1944.7000	3034.8000

Note: FVIF$_A$ is the abbreviation of 'Future Value Interest Factor of an Annuity'.

(FVIF$_A$)

per Period for n Periods

$$FVIF_A = \sum_{t=1}^{n} (1 + i)^{t-1} = \frac{(1 + i)^{t-1}}{i}$$

12%	14%	15%	16%	18%	20%	24%	28%	32%	36%
1.0000	1.0000	1.0000	1.0000	1.0000	1.0000	1.0000	1.0000	1.0000	1.0000
2.1200	2.1400	2.1500	2.1600	2.1800	2.2000	2.2400	2.2800	2.3200	2.3600
3.3744	3.4396	3.4725	3.5056	3.5724	3.6400	3.7776	3.9184	4.0624	4.2096
4.7793	4.9211	4.9934	5.0665	5.2154	5.3680	5.6842	6.0156	6.3624	6.7251
6.3528	6.6101	6.7424	6.8771	7.1542	7.4416	8.0484	8.6999	9.3983	10.146
8.1152	8.5355	8.7537	8.9775	9.4420	9.9299	10.9800	12.1350	13.4050	14.7980
10.0890	10.7300	11.0660	11.4130	12.1410	12.9150	14.6150	16.5330	18.6950	21.1260
12.2990	13.2320	13.7260	14.2400	15.3270	16.4990	19.1220	22.1630	25.6780	29.7310
14.7750	16.0850	16.7850	17.5180	19.0850	20.7980	24.7120	30.3690	34.8950	41.4350
17.5480	19.3370	20.3030	21.3210	23.5210	25.9580	31.6430	38.5920	47.0610	57.3510
20.6540	23.0440	24.3490	25.7320	28.7550	32.1500	40.2370	50.3980	63.1210	78.9980
24.1330	27.2700	29.0010	30.8500	34.9310	39.5800	50.8940	65.5100	84.3200	108.4300
28.0290	32.0880	34.3510	36.7860	42.2180	48.4960	64.1090	84.8520	112.3000	148.4700
32.3920	37.5810	40.5040	43.6720	50.8180	59.1950	80.4960	109.6100	149.2300	202.9200
37.2790	43.8420	47.5800	51.6590	60.9650	72.0350	100.8100	141.3000	197.9900	276.9700
42.7530	50.9800	55.7170	60.9250	72.9390	87.4420	126.0100	181.8600	262.3500	377.6900
48.8830	59.1170	65.0750	71.6730	87.0680	105.9300	157.2500	233.7900	347.3000	514.6600
55.7490	68.3940	75.8360	84.1400	103.7400	128.1100	195.9900	300.2500	459.4400	700.9300
63.4390	78.9690	88.2110	98.6030	123.4100	154.7400	244.0300	385.3200	607.4700	954.2700
72.0520	91.0240	102.4400	115.3700	146.6200	186.6800	303.6000	494.2100	802.8600	1298.8000
81.6980	104.7600	118.8100	134.8400	174.0200	225.0200	377.4600	633.5900	1060.7000	1767.3000
92.5020	120.4300	137.6300	157.4100	206.3400	271.0300	469.0500	811.9900	1401.2000	2404.6000
104.6000	138.2900	159.2700	183.6000	244.4800	326.2300	582.6200	1040.3000	1850.6000	3271.3000
118.1500	158.6500	184.1600	213.9700	289.4900	392.4800	723.4600	1332.6000	2443.8000	4449.9000
133.3300	181.8700	212.7900	249.2100	342.6000	471.9800	898.0900	1706.8000	3226.8000	6052.9000
150.3300	208.3300	245.7100	290.0800	405.2700	567.3700	1114.6000	2185.7000	4260.4000	8233.0000
169.3700	238.4900	283.5600	337.5000	479.2200	681.8500	1383.1000	2798.7000	5624.7000	11197.9000
190.6900	272.8800	327.1000	392.5000	566.4800	819.2200	1716.0000	3583.3000	7425.6000	15230.2000
214.5800	312.0900	377.1600	456.3000	669.4400	984.0600	2128.9000	4587.6000	9802.9000	20714.1000
241.3300	356.7800	434.7400	530.3100	790.9400	1181.8000	2640.9000	5873.2000	12940.0000	28172.2000
767.0900	1342.0000	1779.0000	2360.7000	4163.2000	7343.8000	22728.0000	69377.0000	*	*
2400.0000	4994.5000	7217.7000	10435.0000	21813.0000	45497.0000	*	*	*	*
7471.6000	18535.0000	29219.0000	46057.0000	*	*	*	*	*	*

FVIF$_A$ > 99999.

Table 4   Present Value of an Annuity

Present Value of an Annuity of

Periods i	1%	2%	3%	4%	5%	6%	7%	8%	9%
1	0.9901	0.9804	0.9709	0.9615	0.9524	0.9434	0.9346	0.9259	0.9174
2	1.9704	1.9416	1.9135	1.8861	1.8594	1.8334	1.8080	1.7833	1.7591
3	2.9410	2.8839	2.8286	2.7751	2.7232	2.6730	2.6243	2.5771	2.5313
4	3.9020	3.8077	3.7171	3.6299	3.5460	3.4651	3.3872	3.3121	3.2397
5	4.8534	4.7135	4.5797	4.4518	4.3295	4.2124	4.1002	3.9927	3 8897
6	5.7955	5.6014	5.4172	5.2421	5.0757	4.9173	4.7665	4.6229	4.4859
7	6.7282	6.4720	6.2303	6.0021	5.7864	5.5824	5 3893	5.2064	5.0330
8	7.6517	7.3255	7.0197	6.7327	6.4632	6.2098	5.9713	5.7466	5.5343
9	8.5660	8.1622	7.7861	7.4353	7.1078	6.8017	6.5152	6.2469	5.9952
10	9.4713	8.9826	8.5302	8.1109	7.7217	7.3601	7.0236	6.7101	6.4177
11	10.3676	9.7868	9.2526	8.7605	8.3064	7.8869	7.4987	7.1390	6.8052
12	11.2551	10.5753	9.9540	9.3851	8.8633	8.3838	7.9427	7.5361	7.1607
13	12.1337	11.3484	10.6350	9.9856	9.3936	8.8527	8.3577	7.9038	7.4869
14	13.0037	12.1062	11.2961	10.5631	9.8986	9.2950	8.7455	8.2442	7.7862
15	13.8651	12.8493	11.9379	11.1184	10.3797	9.7122	9.1079	8.5595	8.0607
16	14.7179	13.5777	12.5611	11.6523	10.8378	10.1059	9.4466	8.8514	8.3126
17	15.5623	14.2919	13.1661	12.1657	11.2741	10.4773	9.7632	9.1216	8.5436
18	16.3983	14.9920	13.7535	12.6593	11.6896	10.8276	10.0591	9.3719	8.7556
19	17.2260	15.6785	14.3238	13.1339	12.0853	11.1581	10.3356	9.6036	8.9501
20	18.0456	16.3514	14.8775	13.5903	12.4622	11.4699	10.5940	9.8181	9.1285
21	18.8570	17.0112	15.4150	14.0292	12.8212	11.7641	10.8355	10.0168	9.2922
22	19.6604	17.6580	15.9369	14.4511	13.1630	12.0416	11.0612	10.2007	9.4424
23	20.4558	18.2922	16.4436	14.8568	13.4886	12.3034	11.2722	10.3711	9.5802
24	21.2434	18.9139	16.9355	15.2470	13.7986	12.5504	11.4693	10.5288	9.7066
25	22.0232	19.5235	17.4131	15.6221	14.0939	12.7834	11.6536	10.6748	9.8226
26	22.7952	20.1210	17.8768	15.9828	14.3752	13.0032	11.8258	10.8100	9.9290
27	23.5596	20.7069	18.3270	16.3296	14.6430	13.2105	11.9867	10.9352	10.0266
28	24.3164	21.2813	18.7641	16.6631	14.8981	13.4062	12.1371	11.0511	10.1161
29	25.0658	21.8444	19.1885	16.9837	15.1411	13.5907	12.2777	11.1584	10.1983
30	25.8077	22.3965	19.6004	17.2920	15.3725	13.7648	12.4090	11.2578	10.2737
35	29.4086	24.9986	21.4872	18.6646	16.3742	14.4982	12.9477	11.6546	10.5668
40	32.8347	27.3555	23.1148	19.7928	17.1591	15.0463	13.3317	11.9246	10.7574
45	36.0945	29.4902	24.5187	20.7200	17.7741	15.4558	13.6055	12.1084	10.8812
50	39.1961	31.4236	25.7298	21.4822	18.2559	15.7619	13.8007	12.2335	10.9617
55	42.1472	33.1748	26.7744	22.1086	18.6335	15.9905	13.9399	12.3186	11.0140

Note: PVIF$_A$ is the abbreviation of 'Present Value Interest Factor of an Annuity'.

of $1 (PVIF$_A$)

$1 per Period for *n* Periods

$$\text{PVIF}_A = \sum_{t=1}^{n} \frac{1}{(1 + i)^t}$$

10%	12%	14%	15%	16%	18%	20%	24%	28%	32%
0.9091	0.8929	0.8772	0.8696	0.8621	0.8475	0.8333	0.8065	0.7813	0.7576
1.7355	1.6901	1.6467	1.6257	1.6052	1.5656	1.5278	1.4568	1.3916	1.3315
2.4869	2.4018	2.3216	2.2832	2.2459	2.1743	2.1065	1.9813	1.8684	1.7663
3.1699	3.0373	2.9137	2.8550	2.7982	2.6901	2.5887	2.4043	2.2410	2.0957
3.7908	3.6048	3.4331	3.3522	3.2743	3.1272	2.9906	2.7454	2.5320	2.3452
4.3553	4.1114	3.8887	3.7845	3.6847	3.4976	3.3255	3.0205	2.7594	2.5342
4.8684	4.5638	4.2883	4.1604	4.0386	3.8115	3.6046	3.2423	2.9370	2.6775
5.3349	4.9676	4.6389	4.4873	4.3436	4.0776	3.8372	3.4212	3.0758	2.7860
5.7590	5.3282	4.9464	4.7716	4.6065	4.3030	4.0310	3.5655	3.1842	2.8681
6.1446	5.6502	5.2161	5.0188	4.8332	4.4941	4.1925	3.6819	3.2689	2.9304
6.4951	5.9377	5.4527	5.2337	5.0286	4.6560	4.3271	3.7757	3.3351	2.9776
6.8137	6.1944	5.6603	5.4206	5.1971	4.7932	4.4392	3.8514	3.3868	3.0133
7.1034	6.4235	5.8424	5.5831	5.3423	4.9095	4.5327	3.9124	3.4272	3.0404
7.3667	6.6282	6.0021	5.7245	5.4675	5.0081	4.6106	3.9616	3.4587	3.0609
7.6061	6.8109	6.1422	5.8474	5.5755	5.0916	4.6755	4.0013	3.4834	3.0764
7.8237	6.9740	6.2651	5.9542	5.6685	5.1624	4.7296	4.0333	3.5026	3.0882
8.0216	7.1196	6.3729	6.0472	5.7487	5.2223	4.7746	4.0591	3.5177	3.0971
8.2014	7.2497	6.4674	6.1280	5.8178	5.2732	4.8122	4.0799	3.5294	3.1039
8.3649	7.3658	6.5504	6.1982	5.8775	5.3162	4.8435	4.0967	3.5386	3.1090
8.5136	7.4694	6.6231	6.2593	5.9288	5.3527	4.8696	4.1103	3.5458	3.1129
8.6487	7.5620	6.6870	6.3125	5.9731	5.3837	4.8913	4.1212	3.5514	3.1158
8.7715	7.6446	6.7429	6.3587	6.0113	5.4099	4.9094	4.1300	3.5558	3.1180
8.8832	7.7184	6.7921	6.3988	6.0442	5.4321	4.9245	4.1371	3.5592	3.1197
8.9847	7.7843	6.8351	6.4338	6.0726	5.4510	4.9371	4.1428	3.5619	3.1210
9.0770	7.8431	6.8729	6.4642	6.0971	5.4669	4.9476	4.1474	3.5640	3.1220
9.1609	7.8957	6.9061	6.4906	6.1182	5.4804	4.9563	4.1511	3.5656	3.1227
9.2372	7.9426	6.9352	6.5135	6.1364	5.4919	4.9636	4.1542	3.5669	3.1233
9.3066	7.9844	6.9607	6.5335	6.1520	5.5016	4.9697	4.1566	3.5679	3.1237
9.3696	8.0218	6.9830	6.5509	6.1656	5.5098	4.9747	4.1585	3.5687	3.1240
9.4269	8.0552	7.0027	6.5660	6.1772	5.5168	4.9789	4.1601	3.5693	3.1242
9.6442	8.1755	7.0700	6.6166	6.2153	5.5386	4.9915	4.1644	3.5708	3.1248
9.7791	8.2438	7.1050	6.6418	6.2335	5.5482	4.9966	4.1659	3.5712	3.1250
9.8628	8.2825	7.1232	6.6543	6.2421	5.5523	4.9986	4.1664	3.5714	3.1250
9.9148	8.3045	7.1327	6.6605	6.2463	5.5541	4.9995	4.1666	3.5714	3.1250
9.9471	8.3170	7.1376	6.6636	6.2482	5.5549	4.9998	4.1666	3.5714	3.1250

4. The Investment Decision of the Firm Under Certainty

Investment refers to commitment of resources for fixed assets (plant, machinery and buildings)[1] used in production.

The characteristic of an investment decision is that the purchase and use of capital goods involve costs and revenues that are spread out over several periods of time. The use of capital goods by firms introduces an important time element into the production process, because the services embodied in them cannot be utilised at the moment the capital good is produced or purchased, but must be drawn upon over several time periods. Thus the time value of money must be considered in order to evaluate the investment alternatives correctly. Furthermore, the risk in investment decisions is much greater than in the other decisions of the firm. Since fixed capital goods are commonly used over several time periods, there is greater risk that expected revenues will not be attained than in the case of other decisions. All decisions require prediction of the future, but in the case of investment goods the predictions must usually extend to distant future periods where uncertainty is greater.

In this chapter we will assume certainty, and we will concentrate on the time aspects of the investment decision. In particular we will assume that the stream of costs and revenues over the lifetime of each project (the cash flows of prospective investments) are known with certainty. The firm has the relevant engineering and marketing information which allows the estimation of the costs and revenues of each project with certainty. Risk and uncertainty will be considered in Chapter 12.

Throughout this chapter it will be assumed that the goal of the firm is the maximisation of stockholders' wealth. Thus the motivation for investment is

[1] Inventory investment will not be considered, because its treatment would require an explicit account of the dynamics of the production process, an area of analysis that is beyond the scope of this book.

the increase in the value of the firm to its existing stockholders (see Appendix 3.1 of Chapter 3).

Given this goal, we will establish that the optimal amount of investment (the investment that maximises stockholder wealth) is defined by the intersection of the demand schedule for investment goods and the supply schedule of capital funds of the firm.

In this chapter we will concentrate on the derivation of the demand schedule for investment goods. The supply schedule for (investable) funds will be examined in detail in Chapters 11 and 12.

Before we start our analysis we will give some definitions.

I.   TYPES OF INVESTMENT

A.   Replacement Investment and New Investment

Some investment is designed to replace existing capital goods which have either worn out physically or have become economically obsolete.

New investment may be undertaken for *capital-widening* purposes, that is, to increase the total stock of capital goods used, without changing the capital intensity of the production process. For example, a transport firm that has twenty trucks buys another ten of the same type. This kind of investment depends primarily upon the rate of change of sales. If the firm has reached the point of full capacity utilisation, and sales continue to grow, purchase of additional equipment may be advantageous to produce the greater output.

New investment may also be undertaken for *capital-deepening*, that is, in order to attain more intensive use of capital relative to labour. Such a change in the capital/labour ratio may be advantageous if wages increase faster than the cost of new equipment.

Finally, investment may be undertaken in order to take advantage of technological progress. The above types of investment may be advantageous even though the state of technology remains unchanged. However, if technological change occurs, the firm will often find it profitable to invest so as to take advantage of new products and/or new methods of production.

B.   Independent and Dependent Investment Projects

Independent projects are projects whose costs and revenues are independent of one another. For example, building a warehouse for storing the final product and installing a new machine for producing the output of the firm are independent projects. However, installing machinery for producing a new commodity and machinery for obtaining by-products are dependent investments, since their costs (and possibly the revenues) are interdependent.

C. Mutually Exclusive Investment Projects

Mutually exclusive projects are alternative investments, that is, investment projects such that if one is undertaken, the other must be rejected. For example, a firm may use (in its warehouse) either a conveyor belt on which products are moved, or fork trucks. These are mutually exclusive projects, since accepting one implies rejection of the other.

D. Conventional and Non-Conventional Investments

A conventional investment is defined as an investment having one or more periods of outlays followed by periods of cash revenues. In other words, the cash flow of a conventional investment has initially one or more terms with a negative sign, while its subsequent terms are positive. A non-conventional investment is an investment whose cash flow has terms with interchanging signs: in some periods the net proceeds are positive, while in others they are negative. Consider the cash flows (streams of net earnings, i.e. total revenue minus total costs) of projects A and B in Table 4.1. Project A is a conventional investment, while project B is a non-conventional investment.

Table 4.1

Cash flow (in thousand dollars)

	Period 1	Period 2	Period 3	Period 4	Period 5
Project A	−1,000	800	500	300	200
Project B	−500	700	−100	−150	1,500

II. THE INVESTMENT DECISION USING THE INTERNAL RATE OF RETURN APPROACH (OR THE MARGINAL EFFICIENCY OF INVESTMENT)

A. The Demand for Capital Goods Schedule

It is assumed that the earnings (cash flows) of the investment projects available to the firm are known with certainty.

The demand for capital goods schedule relates the amounts of investment to their profitability. Derivation of this schedule requires the ranking of investment projects on the basis of their profitability. We will discuss two criteria which are used in the traditional theory of investment *for the ranking* of investments: the internal rate of return (or marginal efficiency of investment) criterion; and the net present value criterion.

Under some conditions both criteria give the same ranking of projects. However, in many real-world situations the ranking of the same set of investments differs, depending on the adopted criterion.

The internal rate of return criterion (IRR) or the marginal efficiency of investment criterion (MEI) carries with it the prestige of some of the great names of economics. Keynes was among those who employed this measure of profitability of an investment. In fact, this criterion works satisfactorily in many case, but we shall see that it has several theoretical shortcomings, and leads to incorrect ranking of projects in situations frequently observed in the real business world.

The internal rate of return (IRR) or marginal efficiency of an investment good (MEI) is the rate of discount which makes the present value of the expected stream of future earnings from the particular investment good equal to the initial expenditure required for the acquisition of that investment good.

Let C_j be the acquisition cost of the jth investment project, which has the expected stream of earnings

$$X_1, X_2, \ldots, X_n$$

where n is the number of years of life of the jth project. The internal rate of return, r, of this project can be estimated directly from the equation

$$\left[\frac{X_1}{(1+r)} + \frac{X_2}{(1+r)^2} + \ldots + \frac{X_n}{(1+r)^n} \right] = C \tag{4.1}$$

$$[\text{Present value of expected earnings}] = \left[\begin{array}{c} \text{Initial} \\ \text{acquisition} \\ \text{cost} \end{array} \right]$$

Expression (4.1) can be written in the slightly different form

$$\left[\frac{X_1}{(1+r)} + \frac{X_2}{(1+r)^2} + \ldots + \frac{X_n}{(1+r)^n} \right] - C = 0$$

or

$$\sum_{t=1}^{n} \frac{X_t}{(1+r)^t} - C = 0 \tag{4.2}$$

The left-hand side is the net present value of the project. From expression (4.2) we can say that the internal rate of return (or marginal efficiency of investment) is the rate of discount which makes the sum of present values of the terms of the investment's cash flow, or *the net present value*, equal to zero.

The internal rate of return can be calculated from expression (4.2). We know the value of C and also the values of $X_1, X_2, \ldots, X_n$, and we can solve for the unknown r. There are n values (roots) for r that may be obtained, but normally there will be just one positive (real) value that satisfies this equation.

In practice, the value of r can be calculated (computed) by a trial-and-error method of search. We first choose arbitrarily a discount rate to compute the present value of the stream of future earnings. If the present value thus obtained is greater than the investment's acquisition cost, we choose a higher discount rate (in order to lower the present value of the stream of earnings) and go through the process again. Conversely, if the present value is lower than the cost, we choose a lower discount rate. The process is repeated until the present value of the stream of earnings is equal to the cost of the investment project.

To illustrate the above trial-and-error method, consider an investment project whose initial cost is $12,930 and has the following stream of revenues

$$X_1 = 1,000 \qquad X_2 = 10,000 \qquad X_3 = 5,000$$

Assume that we choose an 11 per cent discount rate. This gives the following present value:

Period	Cash flows	Present-value factors	Present value
1	1,000	$1/(1+0.11) = 0.9009$	$ 900.9
2	10,000	$1/(1+0.11)^2 = 0.8116$	$ 8,116.0
3	5,000	$1/(1+0.11)^3 = 0.7312$	$ 3,656.0
			$12,672.9

We observe that the present value of expected earnings is smaller than the cost of acquisition ($12,930), resulting in a negative net present value. We thus must choose a lower rate of discount, so as to increase the present value of earnings (cash flows). Assume we select $r = 0.09$. The calculations are shown below:

Period	Cash flows	Present-value factors	Present value
1	1,000	$1/(1+0.09) = 0.9174$	$ 917.4
2	10,000	$1/(1+0.09)^2 = 0.8417$	$ 8,417.0
3	5,000	$1/(1+0.09)^3 = 0.7722$	$ 3,861.0
			$13,195.4

With a 9 per cent discount rate the present value of future earnings is larger than the initial cost of the investment. Apparently we must choose a discount rate between 11 per cent and 9 per cent. Assume we choose a 10 per cent rate of discount. The present value of the stream of earnings is shown below:

Period	Cash flows	Present-value factors	Present value
1	1,000	$1/(1+0.10) = 0.9090$	$ 909.0
2	10,000	$1/(1+0.10)^2 = 0.8264$	$ 8,264.0
3	5,000	$1/(1+0.10)^3 = 0.7513$	$ 3,757.0
			$12,930.0

Thus the 10 per cent discount rate is the internal rate of return of the investment project, because it makes the net present value equal zero (i.e. the expected stream of the investment's earnings is equal to the initial cost).

If we calculate the internal rate of return for all investments available to the firm and we rank them in descending order of this return (or yield), we obtain the demand schedule for investment goods. This is often called *the marginal efficiency of investment (MEI) schedule.* Assuming that investment projects are infinitely divisible, the MEI schedule will have the shape of Figure 4.1.

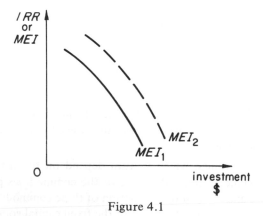

Figure 4.1

The MEI schedule has a negative slope. The shape of the investment schedule reflects the cost conditions of producing capital goods, as well as the development of prices of commodities produced by the investment goods which preclude the continuous increase in fixed capital assets at the same rate of profit. The reasons for this are that, on the one hand, the rate of return (profit rate or prospective yield) of any type of fixed capital asset will fall as more units of it are produced, and, on the other hand, the supply price (acquisition cost) of the asset will rise (unless some units have been unemployed in the past). The prospective profit will fall because, as more fixed capital goods are produced, the supply of commodities which they make will increase, and hence their price will fall. The supply price (cost of acquisition) is likely to rise because of rising costs in the industry making the particular fixed investment good. (Costs usually rise in the short run, even if they do not in the long run.) This holds for each individual type of fixed capital, so that we can generalise in the same way for the marginal efficiency of investment of the firm, and derive the MEI schedule of Figure 4.1.

The *position* of the MEI curve shows the size of the available investment opportunities. The further away from the origin, the greater the investment opportunities open to the firm. The schedule MEI_2 in Figure 4.1 implies greater investment opportunities than those of MEI_1.

In the real world, investments are not infinitely divisible. Investment expenditures are characterised by lumpiness, so that the MEI will typically have the

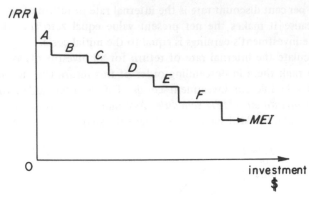

Figure 4.2

shape of Figure 4.2, where *A, B, C, D*, etc., denote individual investment projects.

From the above discussion we may say that the determinants of the demand for investment goods are:

(1) The expected earnings, which in turn depend on the firm's expectations about the volume of sales, the price of the commodities produced by the capital goods, and the cost of production of these commodities.

(2) The supply price or acquisition cost of the fixed capital goods.

B.   The Supply-of-Funds Schedule of the Firm

The supply-of-funds schedule relates the amounts of funds available for investment to their cost. It will be discussed in detail in Chapter 11. For the purposes of the present analysis we note the following.

There are three sources of funds for financing the investments of a firm: debt financing (issue of new bonds), equity financing (issue of new stock), and internal financing from retained earnings.

The cost of funds (money capital) to the firm is the weighted average of the individual costs of these sources of finance, with weights equal to the proportions of each type of finance in the optimal capital structure of the firm. (The optimal capital structure is examined in Chapter 8.)

Under the assumption of certainty, the cost of capital to the firm is simply the long-term interest rate. Since under certainty all securities (traded in the same competitive market) must have the same yield in equilibrium, there is only a single market rate of interest, and it is a directly observable magnitude. In a world of certainty there is no need to distinguish between the alternative sources of funds, since all securities (shares, stocks) have the same return. Thus, given our assumption of certainty, the supply of funds of the firm will be a straight line parallel to the horizontal axis, cutting the vertical axis at the height of the

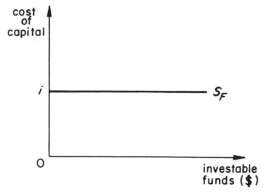

Figure 4.3   Supply-of-funds schedule under certainty

long-term market interest rate, i (Figure 4.3). (The long-term interest rate is the yield of long-term government bonds.) This implies that the firm can find any amount of finance at a constant cost, equal to the market interest rate.

C.   The Investment Decision on the Basis of the IRR

We may now combine the demand for investment schedule, MEI, with the supply of funds schedule, S_F, to determine the optimal amount of investment, that is, the amount of investment which maximises the value of the firm to its existing stockholders. The optimal amount of investment is defined by the intersection of the two schedules (Figure 4.4). The firm should invest up to the point where the internal rate of return (or marginal efficiency of investment) is equal to the market interest rate. (This assumes that the investment projects are not mutually

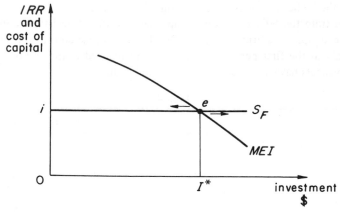

Figure 4.4

exclusive.) If the internal rate of return exceeds the cost of funds to finance a project (points to the left of *e* in Figure 4.4), a surplus is left over after paying for the capital. This surplus accrues to the firm's stockholders, so that undertaking of the project increases the value of the firm. If the internal rate of return is less than the cost of funds (points to the right of *e* in Figure 4.4), taking on the project results in a loss for the existing stockholders, so that in this case deciding to undertake the project leads to a reduction of the value of the firm. Hence at point *e* the value of the firm is maximised: the optimal investment of the firm is *OI** in Figure 4.4.

III.   THE INVESTMENT DECISION USING THE NET PRESENT VALUE (NPV) CRITERION

The net present value approach (to the investment decision) involves the following steps:

Step 1. Use the firm's cost of capital (which, under certainty, is the market rate of interest) to estimate the present value of the expected earnings of each project.

Step 2. Use the firm's cost of capital to estimate the present value of the acquisition expenditures of each investment project. (If all the acquisition expenditures are made in the first period, then the present value of these expenditures is equal to the actual amount spent for obtaining the investment good).

Step 3. Subtract the present value of the acquisition cost(s) from the present value of the expected earnings, to find the net present value of each project, *j*:

$$NPV_j = \sum_{t=1}^{n} \frac{X_{j,\,t}}{(1+i)^t} - C_j \tag{4.3}$$

Step 4. Accept all independent projects whose net present value is greater or equal to zero (NPV $\geqslant$ 0). If two (or more) projects are mutually exclusive, the one with the higher net present value should be chosen.

To illustrate the NPV criterion for optimal investment decisions, consider the four projects open to a firm shown in Table 4.2. It is assumed that the acquisition cost is paid in the first period, the earnings are realised at the end of each year, and the projects have a zero salvage or terminal value.

Table 4.2

Project	Acquisition cost ($)	Expected earnings ($)	
		Period 1	Period 2
Project *A*	10,000	$10,000	0
Project *B*	10,000	10,000	1,100
Project *C*	10,000	3,762	7,762
Project *D*	10,000	5,762	5,762

Assume that the market interest rate (which under certainty is the firm's cost of capital) is 6 per cent. The net present value of the four projects is shown in Table 4.3.

Table 4.3

	Present value of earnings			Present value of acquisition cost	NPV
Project A	$\dfrac{10,000}{(1+0.06)} + \dfrac{0}{(1+0.06)^2} =$	$10,000(0.9434) +$	$0(0.8900) = 9,434$	10,000	−566
Project B	$\dfrac{10,000}{(1+0.06)} + \dfrac{1,100}{(1+0.06)^2} =$	$10,000(0.9434) + 1,100(0.8900) = 10,413$		10,000	413
Project C	$\dfrac{3,762}{(1+0.06)} + \dfrac{7,762}{(1+0.06)^2} =$	$3,762(0.9434) + 7,762(0.8900) = 10,457$		10,000	457
Project D	$\dfrac{5,762}{(1+0.06)} + \dfrac{5,762}{(1+0.06)^2} =$	$5,762(0.9434) + 5,762(0.8900) = 10,564$		10,000	564

According to the NPV criterion, if the goal of the firm is the maximisation of stockholder wealth, projects B, C and D should be undertaken, since they have a positive NPV, while project A should be rejected, assuming that the projects are independent. If the four projects are mutually exclusive, project D should be selected, because it has the highest NPV.

The rationale of the NPV criterion is that the value of the firm is a composite of the values of its parts. Thus, when the firm undertakes an investment project with a positive NPV, the value of the firm should increase by the amount of the NPV. In our example (assuming that the projects are independent), the value of the firm would increase by $1,434 if it took on projects B, C and D. The increase of the value of the firm from its investment for a year is the sum of the NPVs of all accepted projects. If the projects are mutually exclusive, selection of the project with the highest net present value maximises the value of the firm to its existing shareholders.

Because the present value of an investment will depend upon the rate of interest used, there is not a single present value for each project, but an array of net present values, depending on the prevailing rate of interest. The graph of present values of an investment (sometimes called the *net present value profile* of the investment) is one of the more useful devices for summarising the profitability characteristics of an investment. To obtain the net present value graph of a project we use a two-dimensional diagram, on the horizontal axis of which we measure discount rates and on the vertical axis the net present value of the investment. To construct the graph we compute the NPV for several discount rates, from zero to some reasonably large rate. Note that at a zero discount rate the NPV is simply the sum of the undiscounted expected earnings less the cost of the project. This NPV is the intercept of the net present value line on the vertical axis. Next note that the net present value line will cross the horizontal axis when the NPV of the project is zero. The discount rate at this point is the internal rate of return of the investment, since the IRR is defined as the rate of discount which makes the NPV equal to zero.

To illustrate the construction of the net present value graph, we will use two mutually exclusive projects: project Z is the installation of a conveyor-belt system in a warehouse; while project W involves buying fork trucks for the warehouse. Each project costs $10,000 but each has different expected returns, as shown in Table 4.4.

Table 4.4

	Project Z	Project W
Period 1	$500	$100
Period 2	$400	$300
Period 3	$300	$400
Period 4	$100	$600

The net present value of these projects is estimated with discount rates, 3, 5, 8, 10, 12, 15 and 18 per cent. The computations are shown in Table 4.5.

The NPV lines for the two investment projects are shown in Figure 4.5. From Figure 4.5 we see that at low discount rates ($i < 7.1$ per cent) project W has a higher NPV, while at high discount rates ($i > 7.1$ per cent) project Z has a higher

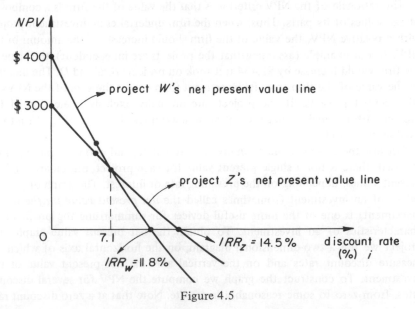

Figure 4.5

NPV. The fact that the NPV line of project W has a steeper slope than the NPV line of project Z indicates that project W's NPV is more sensitive to changes in the discount rate than is the NPV of project Z: a change in the discount rate has a larger effect on the NPV of project W.

In general, if a project has earnings coming in early years, its NPV will not be seriously affected if the discount rate increases, but a project whose earnings come late will be severely penalised by high discount rates. Thus project W, which has its largest earnings in the later years, is ranked higher than project Z when the interest rate is low, but is ranked lower than project Z when the interest rate is high.

The economic implications of Figure 4.5 are interesting. A high cost of capital implies that the firm must pay a high price for obtaining funds. Thus projects with relatively fast payback periods will tend to be attractive when the cost of capital is high, while long-term, slow-payback projects tend to be attractive when the cost of capital is low.

Figure 4.5 is helpful in comparing the two methods of ranking projects, the IRR method and the NPV method.

IV. A COMPARISON OF THE IRR AND NPV APPROACHES

A. Conventional, Independent Investments

For conventional, independent investments the IRR and the NPV methods lead to identical investment decisions. (Recall that a conventional investment is an investment with a cash flow whose initial terms are negative and are followed by subsequent positive terms. Independent investments are investments whose cash flows do not affect one another. For example, an investment in an office building has cash flows that are independent of the cash flows of an investment in an oil tanker.)

To see this it suffices to look at the net present value line of a project. Consider our earlier example of a project which costs $12,930 and whose expected earnings are

$$X_1 = \$1,000 \qquad X_2 = \$10,000 \qquad X_3 = \$5,000$$

We saw that the IRR of this project is 10 per cent, since at this discount rate the present value of the earnings is

$$909 + 8,264 + 3,757 = 12,930$$

that is

$$PV = 12,930 = C$$

or

$$NPV = PV - C = 0$$

Table 4.5

	Present value of earnings	Acquisition cost	NPV
i = 0%			
Project Z	$\frac{500}{(1+0.0)} + \frac{400}{(1+0.0)^2} + \frac{300}{(1+0.0)^3} + \frac{100}{(1+0.0)^4} = 500 + 400 + 300 + 100 = \$1,300$	$1,000	$300
Project W	$\frac{100}{(1+0.0)} + \frac{300}{(1+0.0)^2} + \frac{400}{(1+0.0)^3} + \frac{600}{(1+0.0)^4} = 100 + 300 + 400 + 600 = \$1,400$	$1,000	$400
i = 0.03: The PVIF are: $\frac{1}{(1+0.03)} = 0.9701;\ \frac{1}{(1+0.03)^2} = 0.9426;\ \frac{1}{(1+0.03)^3} = 0.9151;\ \frac{1}{(1+0.03)^4} = 0.8885.$			
Project Z	$\frac{500}{(1+0.03)} + \frac{400}{(1+0.03)^2} + \frac{300}{(1+0.03)^3} + \frac{100}{(1+0.03)^4} = 500(0.9701) + 400(0.9426) + 300(0.9151) + 100(0.8885) = \$1,225.47$	$1,000	$225.47
Project W	$\frac{100}{(1+0.03)} + \frac{300}{(1+0.03)^2} + \frac{400}{(1+0.03)^3} + \frac{600}{(1+0.03)^4} = 100(0.9701) + 300(0.9426) + 400(0.9151) + 600(0.8885) = \$1,278.93$	$1,000	$278.93
i = 0.05: The PVIF are: $\frac{1}{(1+0.05)} = 0.9524;\ \frac{1}{(1+0.05)^2} = 0.9070;\ \frac{1}{(1+0.05)^3} = 0.8638;\ \frac{1}{(1+0.05)^4} = 0.8227.$			
Project Z	$\frac{500}{(1+0.05)} + \frac{400}{(1+0.05)^2} + \frac{300}{(1+0.05)^3} + \frac{100}{(1+0.05)^4} = 500(0.9542) + 400(0.9070) + 300(0.8638) + 100(0.8227) = \$1,180.41$	$1,000	$180.41
Project W	$\frac{100}{(1+0.05)} + \frac{300}{(1+0.05)^2} + \frac{400}{(1+0.05)^3} + \frac{600}{(1+0.05)^4} = 100(0.9524) + 300(0.9070) + 400(0.8638) + 600(0.8227) = \$1,206.48$	$1,000	$206.48
i = 0.08: The PVIF are: $\frac{1}{(1+0.08)} = 0.9259;\ \frac{1}{(1+0.08)^2} = 0.8573;\ \frac{1}{(1+0.08)^3} = 0.7938;\ \frac{1}{(1+0.08)^4} = 0.7350.$			
Project Z	$\frac{500}{(1+0.08)} + \frac{400}{(1+0.08)^2} + \frac{300}{(1+0.08)^3} + \frac{100}{(1+0.08)^4} = 500(0.9259) + 400(0.8573) + 300(0.7938) + 100(0.7350) = \$1,117.51$	$1,000	$117.51
Project W	$\frac{100}{(1+0.08)} + \frac{300}{(1+0.08)^2} + \frac{400}{(1+0.08)^3} + \frac{600}{(1+0.08)^4} = 100(0.9259) + 300(0.8573) + 400(0.7938) + 600(0.7350) = \$1,108.30$	$1,000	$108.30
i = 0.10: The PVIF are: $\frac{1}{(1+0.10)} = 0.9091;\ \frac{1}{(1+0.10)^2} = 0.8264;\ \frac{1}{(1+0.10)^3} = 0.7513;\ \frac{1}{(1+0.10)^4} = 0.6830.$			

Project Z $\dfrac{500}{(1+0.10)} + \dfrac{400}{(1+0.10)^2} + \dfrac{300}{(1+0.10)^3} + \dfrac{100}{(1+0.10)^4} = 500(0.9091) + 400(0.8264) + 300(0.7513) + 100(0.6830) = \$1,078.8$ $1,000 $78.80

Project W $\dfrac{100}{(1+0.10)} + \dfrac{300}{(1+0.10)^2} + \dfrac{400}{(1+0.10)^3} + \dfrac{600}{(1+0.10)^4} = 100(0.9091) + 300(0.8264) + 400(0.7513) + 600(0.6830) = \$1,049.15$ $1,000 $49.15

$i = 0.11$: The PVIF are: $\dfrac{1}{(1+0.11)} = 0.9009; \quad \dfrac{1}{(1+0.11)^2} = 0.8116; \quad \dfrac{1}{(1+0.10)^3} = 0.7312; \quad \dfrac{1}{(1+0.11)^4} = 0.6587.$

Project Z $\dfrac{500}{(1+0.11)} + \dfrac{400}{(1+0.11)^2} + \dfrac{300}{(1+0.11)^3} + \dfrac{100}{(1+0.11)^4} = 500(0.9009) + 400(0.8116) + 300(0.7312) + 100(0.6587) = \$1,060.32$ $1,000 $60.32

Project W $\dfrac{100}{(1+0.11)} + \dfrac{300}{(1+0.11)^2} + \dfrac{400}{(1+0.11)^3} + \dfrac{600}{(1+0.11)^4} = 100(0.9009) + 300(0.8116) + 400(0.7312) + 600(0.6587) = \$1,021.27$ $1,000 $21.27

$i = 0.12$: The PVIF are: $\dfrac{1}{(1+0.12)} = 0.8929; \quad \dfrac{1}{(1+0.12)^2} = 0.7972; \quad \dfrac{1}{(1+0.12)^3} = 0.7118; \quad \dfrac{1}{(1+0.12)^4} = 0.6355.$

Project Z $\dfrac{500}{(1+0.12)} + \dfrac{400}{(1+0.12)^2} + \dfrac{300}{(1+0.12)^3} + \dfrac{100}{(1+0.12)^4} = 500(0.8929) + 400(0.7972) + 300(0.7118) + 100(0.6355) = \$1,042.42$ $1,000 $42.42

Project W $\dfrac{100}{(1+0.12)} + \dfrac{300}{(1+0.12)^2} + \dfrac{400}{(1+0.12)^3} + \dfrac{600}{(1+0.12)^4} = 100(0.8929) + 300(0.7972) + 400(0.7118) + 600(0.6355) = \$994.47$ $1,000 –$5.53

$i = 0.15$: The PVIF are: $\dfrac{1}{(1+0.15)} = 0.8696; \quad \dfrac{1}{(1+0.15)^2} = 0.7561; \quad \dfrac{1}{(1+0.15)^3} = 0.6575; \quad \dfrac{1}{(1+0.15)^4} = 0.5718.$

Project Z $\dfrac{500}{(1+0.15)} + \dfrac{400}{(1+0.15)^2} + \dfrac{300}{(1+0.15)^3} + \dfrac{100}{(1+0.15)^4} = 500(0.3696) + 400(0.7561) + 300(0.6575) + 100(0.5718) = \$991.67$ $1,000 –$8.33

Project W $\dfrac{100}{(1+0.15)} + \dfrac{300}{(1+0.15)^2} + \dfrac{400}{(1+0.15)^3} + \dfrac{600}{(1+0.15)^4} = 100(0.8696) + 300(0.7561) + 400(0.6575) + 600(0.5718) = \$919.87$ $1,000 –$80.13

$i = 0.18$: The PVIF are: $\dfrac{1}{(1+0.18)} = 0.8475; \quad \dfrac{1}{(1+0.18)^2} = 0.7182; \quad \dfrac{1}{(1+0.18)^3} = 0.6086; \quad \dfrac{1}{(1+0.18)^4} = 0.5158.$

Project Z $\dfrac{500}{(1+0.18)} + \dfrac{400}{(1+0.18)^2} + \dfrac{300}{(1+0.18)^3} + \dfrac{100}{(1+0.18)^4} = 500(0.8475) + 400(0.7182) + 300(0.6086) + 100(0.5158) = \$945.19$ $1,000 –$54.81

Project W $\dfrac{100}{(1+0.18)} + \dfrac{300}{(1+0.18)^2} + \dfrac{400}{(1+0.18)^3} + \dfrac{600}{(1+0.18)^4} = 100(0.8475) + 300(0.7182) + 400(0.6086) + 600(0.5158) = \$853.13$ $1,000 –$146.87

To draw the net present value of this investment project we note that:

(1) At a zero rate of discount the net present value of the investment is $3,070 (the sum of the undiscounted earnings, $16,000, minus the acquisition cost, $12,930). Thus $3,070 is the intercept of the net present value line on the vertical axis (Figure 4.6).

(2) At a 10 per cent discount rate, the net present value of the project is zero. Thus 0.10 is the point where the NPV line cuts the horizontal axis, and, by definition, 0.10 is the internal rate of return of the project.

(3) At discount rates between 0 and 0.10 the net present value is positive. For example, at $i = 0.06$ the NPV = $1,111.

(4) At discount rates greater than 10 per cent, the net present value is negative.

The net present value of this particular investment project is shown in Figure 4.6.

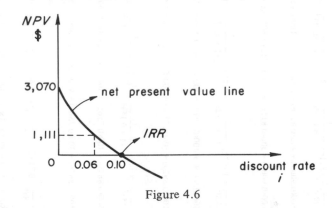

Figure 4.6

Note that the NPV is positive (and, according to the NPV criterion, the project would be accepted) when the cost of capital (which is equal to the market rate of interest i under certainty) is less than the IRR. Thus, if an investment is accepted on the basis of the NPV criterion, it would also be accepted on the IRR criterion, because a positive NPV implies that the cost of capital (used to estimate the NPV) is less than the IRR. Using the IRR criterion, we would decide to accept the project if the IRR > cost of capital, which is the case when NPV > 0.

In summary, the NPV method and the IRR method will lead to identical investment decisions for conventional, independent investments.

However, investment decisions may be different (a conflict in ranking of the same investment projects may result) if projects are mutually exclusive, or if investments are non-conventional and have multiple internal rates of return. We shall examine these two cases in some detail.

B.   Mutually Exclusive Investments

We said that a set of mutually exclusive investments is a group of projects such that the acceptance of one implies rejection of the others. For example, a construction firm can use a particular piece of land either for building an apartment complex, or an office building, or a parking garage. The piece of land can be used only for one of these alternative projects. Similarly, an oil company can transport oil either by a fleet of tankers or by pipeline. Adopting one method implies rejection of the other.

For mutually exclusive investments the NPV method is more reliable than the IRR method. Consider the two mutually exclusive investments, A and B, shown in Table 4.6.

Table 4.6

Project	Acquisition cost	Expected earnings		
		Period 1	Period 2	Period 3
Project A	$12,930	$1,000	$10,000	$5,000
Project B	$3,198	0	0	$5,000

The net present value lines of these projects are shown in Figure 4.7. We observe that project A has an internal rate of return of 0.10, while project B has an internal rate of return a little higher than 0.16. Hence, on the basis of the IRR method project B would be selected. However, if we use the NPV method, project A would be selected if the cost of capital, i, was lower than 0.07. Under these conditions the NPV method should be used. As we mentioned at another point, if the goal of the firm is the maximisation of stockholder wealth, the important consideration is the net present value. Hence, for mutually exclusive investments, the firm should choose the one with the highest NPV, estimated by using the cost of capital as the discount rate. The project which has the largest NPV, by definition, makes the largest contribution to the wealth of the firm's stockholders.

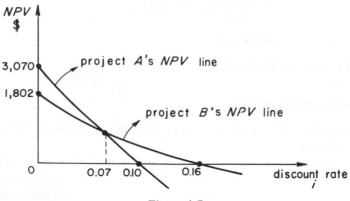

Figure 4.7

C. Multiple Internal Rates of Return

The IRR method breaks down when non-conventional investments have more than one internal rate of return.

We saw that the equation used to estimate the IRR is

$$\frac{X_1}{(1 + r)} + \frac{X_2}{(1 + r)^2} + \ldots + \frac{X_n}{(1 + r)^n} - C = 0$$

This is a polynomial of degree n. Therefore, there are n different roots, or solutions, to this equation. If the investment is conventional (i.e. the project has one period or more of negative earnings followed by a series of positive earnings), then only one of these roots will be positive: that is, a conventional investment has a unique IRR. If, however, the investment is non-conventional (the stream of costs and earnings interchange, so that we have positive and negative interchanging terms in the cash flow), the following possibilities exist:

(a) there is *no* positive IRR;
(b) there may be *one* positive IRR;
(c) there may be more than one positive IRR.

In the case of multiple rates of return the method breaks down.

To illustrate the problem of multiple internal rates of return, consider a project which requires an expenditure of $1.6 million to develop a strip mine. The mine will produce earnings of $10 million at the end of year 1. Then, at the end of year 2, the firm must spend $10 million to restore the land to its original appearance. Thus the project's cash flow is

Period 0	Period 1	Period 2
−$1.6 million	+$10 million	−$10 million

Substituting these values in the above equation we obtain

$$\text{NPV} = -\$1.6 \text{ m.} + \frac{\$10 \text{ m.}}{(1 + r)^1} - \frac{\$10 \text{ m.}}{(1 + r)^2} = 0$$

Solving for r we obtain two values:

$$r_1 = 0.25 \text{ (or 25 per cent)}$$

and

$$r_2 = 4.00 \text{ (or 400 per cent)}$$

This means that NPV = 0 when r = 25 per cent and also when r = 400 per cent. The project has two IRR.

The net present value line of this project is shown in Figure 4.8. The NPV line crosses the horizontal axis at two points, corresponding to the two internal rates of return. The IRR method breaks down, because it is impossible to decide which rate of return to choose.

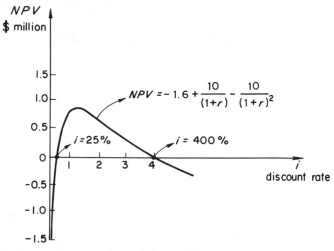

Figure 4.8

However, the NPV method still applies. The criterion for investment would be: accept the project for a cost of capital between 25 and 400 per cent.

As another example consider the following investment:

Period	Cash flow
0	−100
1	+300
2	−200

The NPV = 0 if $i = 0$ or $i = 100$ per cent. Since a 0 per cent return is bad and a 100 per cent return is very good, it is not obvious what decision should be reached.

Figure 4.9, however, shows that if we apply the NPV method the investment

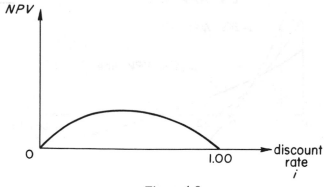

Figure 4.9

should be accepted if the cost of capital is between 0 and 100 per cent, since the NPV is positive for any discount rate within that range.

Multiple IRR situations cannot be solved using only the IRR of the investment. We must resort to the NPV method.

From the above analysis it is apparent that the NPV method is more general and more reliable than the IRR method. Yet the IRR approach is conceptually easier to use for the derivation of the demand for investment schedule (or the MEI schedule). To avoid the two shortcomings of the IRR method, that is, the case of mutually exclusive investments and situations of multiple internal rates of return, we may proceed as follows.

(1) Mutually exclusive investments are compared by using the graph of net present values. Given the prevailing market interest rate (which, under certainty, is the cost of capital), we find the project which has the highest net present value. The IRR of this project is then used for ranking it in the demand for investment schedule. For example, consider the three mutually exclusive projects, whose present-value lines are shown in Figure 4.10. If the prevailing market interest rate is 3 per cent, project B has the highest NPV, and, hence, is preferable to either project A or project C, though B has the lowest internal rate of return (= 0.10). Project B's internal rate of return (0.10) will be used in order to include B in the firm's demand for investment schedule (its MEI curve).

Note that if the cost of capital changes, a re-examination of the mutually exclusive investments is required, since their ranking may be affected. For example, if $i = 0.11$, project A has the highest NPV, and should be included in the MEI schedule with an internal rate of return of 0.20.

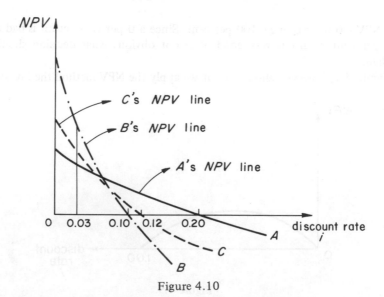

Figure 4.10

(2) If an investment project has multiple internal rates of return, the firm may reach a ranking as follows. The firm may use its average rate of return on existing assets to estimate the present value of the stream of future earnings. (This implies that the firm expects the new project to have a profitability equal to the average profitability of existing capital goods.) The IRR is then defined as the rate of discount which equates the thus estimated present value of expected future earnings to the initial (acquisition) cost of the fixed investment project.[2]

With the above modifications, we may use the IRR method to derive the demand for investment schedule of the firm. The optimal amount of investment is then defined by the point of intersection of that curve with the supply-of-funds schedule, S_F, as earlier explained (see p. 215).

V. THE PAYBACK METHOD FOR INVESTMENT DECISIONS

Prior to the 1960s the payback method was the most commonly used method for project evaluation and investment decisions. It is still widely used because of its simplicity, but as we will presently see it has two serious shortcomings which disqualify it as a general method for reaching optimal investment decisions.

The payback period is defined as the length of time (number of time periods) required for the stream of expected earnings of an investment to equal the initial acquisition cost of the investment. In other words, the payback period is the number of years (periods) it takes the firm to recover the original cost of an investment from the earnings generated by that investment.

The payback method involves the following steps:

(1) Find the payback period of the investment projects available to the firm. The payback period is determined by adding up the earnings in successive years until the sum is equal to the original cost.

(2) Define some maximum payback period, which is considered desirable for any reason.

(3) Reject all investment projects for which the payback period is greater than this maximum.

The payback-period criterion ranks the investment projects on the basis of how fast the firm recovers the cost of these projects. A project with a four-year payback period is generally preferred to a five-year payback investment, and two projects with the same payback period are equally attractive to the firm.

The payback-period method has two serious weaknesses. First, it does not take into account earnings that accrue after the payback date. For example, consider the two projects shown in Table 4.7. Both projects have the same payback period (two years), and, hence, according to the payback criterion, both are equally desirable. However, it is obvious that project A is a better investment, because its total earnings are larger than those of project B.

---

[2] See Eugene F. Brigham, *Financial Management*, 2nd edn (Dryden Press, 1979) p. 386.

Table 4.7

Project	Initial cost	Expected earnings			
		Period 1	Period 2	Period 3	Period 4
Project *A*	$7,000	$5,000	$2,000	$1,000	$500
Project *B*	$7,000	$3,500	$3,500	0	0

Second, the payback criterion completely ignores the time pattern of the expected earnings, that is, it fails to take into account the time value of money. Consider the investment projects *C* and *D* in Table 4.8. Since both have the same payback period, the firm should view them with indifference. Yet it is clear that most firms will not be indifferent between the two projects, and they would prefer project *C*, because it 'brings back' the invested money much faster than project *D*.

Table 4.8

Project	Initial cost	Expected earnings		
		Period 1	Period 2	Period 3
Project *C*	$10,000	$7,000	$2,000	$1,000
Project *D*	$10,000	$1,000	$2,000	$7,000

We may conclude that the payback-period criterion is a crude rule of thumb which fails to take into account crucial aspects of the investment decision, such as the total earnings of the prospective projects and their timing. Sometimes the payoff criterion is defended as a simple and inexpensive device for dealing with risk.[3] However, its shortcomings may make it a very costly decision rule.

The analysis of this chapter refers to the investment decision under certainty. The investment decision under conditions of risk and uncertainty is not examined until Chapter 12, because it requires knowledge of several topics which are developed in subsequent chapters.

[3] The investment decision under conditions of risk and uncertainty is examined in Chapter 12.

5. Growth by Merger and Takeover

I. INTRODUCTION

A. Preliminary Remarks

It is generally agreed that mergers and takeovers have played an important role in shaping the modern capitalistic economies. Yet, until recently, economists did not attempt to develop a formal theory of mergers and takeovers, explaining the decision of one firm to merge with or take over another. There is an enormous literature on mergers and acquisitions, but it is mostly descriptive. At a theoretical level economists were mostly preoccupied with the examination of mergers and takeovers *at the industry level*. The interest was centred on the effects of mergers and takeovers on market structure and market conduct, and their consequences for market performance (allocation of resources). To a large extent this is the result of the general concern about the social desirability of large firms that possess significant market power, which distorts the market mechanism by reducing competition and leads to misallocation of resources. *At the firm level*, economic literature contains a number of scattered suggestions about the motives for mergers and acquisitions, without a systematic attempt to relate these motives to specific behavioural hypotheses.

In this chapter we will present the motives of mergers and takeovers in the framework of three competing hypotheses: the profit-maximisation hypothesis of the neoclassical model of the firm, the growth-maximisation hypothesis of the managerialist school, and the 'valuation-discrepancies' hypothesis. We will also attempt to evaluate the explanatory power of these alternative hypotheses in the light of the available empirical evidence.

B. Distinction Between Mergers and Takeovers

Most writers distinguish between mergers and takeovers (or acquisitions) on a purely legal basis. An acquisition or takeover of firm B by firm A occurs when company A acquires more than 50 per cent of the equity of company B; company B ceases to exist as a separate *legal* entity (B is considered as having legally died and is recorded as such in statistical sources). A merger between companies A and B occurs when the two companies amalgamate to form a *new legal entity*. In this event in a legal sense both A and B are considered (in statistical records) as dead and a new legal entity emerges.

This legal distinction between mergers and takeovers is of little interest from an economic point of view, since the legal form of the amalgamation (consolidation) has little to do with broader economic considerations, such as the motives for, or the effects of, the amalgamation.

An economically more meaningful distinction between mergers and takeovers is the way in which these two types of amalgamation takes place.[1] A merger between two companies A and B takes place when the managers of A approach B's managers directly; they negotiate the conditions of the amalgamation and they agree upon a mutually satisfactory price; then B's managers use their influence and proxy power to persuade their stockholders to approve the merger. In short, a merger takes place with the mutual agreement of the managements of the merging companies. A takeover (or acquisition) occurs when the managers of firm A directly make a tender offer and buy the shares of the stockholders of firm B at a price, which is usually substantially higher than the current share price on the stock market. Such a takeover usually takes place with opposition from B's managers. In other words, a takeover involves a direct transaction between the managers of A (the acquiring firm) and the stockholders of firm B (the acquired firm).

Another difference between mergers and takeovers is that takeovers require funds for the acquisition of one firm by another, while mergers usually take place by an exchange of the shares of the merging firms with shares of the new legal entity.

These differences are relevant to the causes of mergers and takeovers, as we will presently see. In this chapter we will be using the word 'merger' as a generic term covering amalgamations of all forms: takeovers, acquisitions, mergers.

C.   Historical Notes: Merger Waves

The American economy has experienced three distinct waves of mergers during the twentieth century.

The first wave may be dated approximately as having taken place between 1885 and 1905. This wave consisted predominantly of horizontal mergers. Thus in this period we have an increase in concentration in industrial markets. Mergers were particularly strong in the steel, rubber and tobacco industries.

---

[1] This distinction has been adopted by Dennis C. Mueller, 'A Theory of Conglomerate Mergers', *Quarterly Journal of Economics*, 1969, pp. 643–59.

The second wave may be dated approximately as having occurred during the period 1916–30, with the peak during the late 1920s. Horizontal mergers continued to be predominant, but vertical ones and conglomerates in particular started being important. Significant merger activity took place in petroleum, primary metals and food products.

The third period started in the 1940s, after the Second World War, and is still with us. Over that period a striking change in the form of merger took place. Horizontal and vertical mergers have declined in importance while conglomerate mergers have become predominant, as can be seen from the data shown in Table 5.1.

Table 5.1   The changing pattern of mergers

Type of merger	1926–30	1940–7	1951–5	1956–60	1961–5	1966–75
Horizontal	75.9%	62.0%	39.2%	30.1%	22.5%	11.9%
Vertical	4.8%	17.0%	12.2%	14.9%	17.5%	7.9%
Conglomerate	19.3%	21.0%	48.6%	55.0%	60.0%	80.2%
	100.0%	100.0%	100.0%	100.0%	100.0%	100.0%

Sources: Federal Trade Commission, *Economic Report on Corporate Mergers and Hearings on Economic Concentration* (US Government Printing Office, 1969). Also, Federal Trade Commission, *Statistical Report on Mergers and Acquisitions* (US Government Printing Office, 1977).

A common characteristic (feature) in all periods has been the positive correlation of merger activity with the movements in stock markets: mergers are intensified in booming stock markets, while merger activity declines in depressed stock markets. Some possible reasons for this phenomenon are:

(1) Firms which want to be acquired 'stick on' a little longer (in recessions), waiting for a higher price of their shares.
(2) Acquiring firms can find funds more easily and at a lower cost in a booming capital market.
(3) The acquiring firms' expectations are more optimistic in a booming stock market.

These hypotheses will be further discussed in section III below.

II.   MERGERS AND THE PROFIT-MAXIMISATION HYPOTHESIS

In this section we examine the profit-maximisation hypothesis as a working hypothesis capable of explaining the observed merger movement.

It is assumed that the goal of managers is the maximisation of stockholders' wealth, that is, the maximisation of the market value of the firm.[2] We saw in Chapter 3 that if the capital market is perfect (in the sense that there is certainty, perfect (complete) information, and no transaction costs such as brokerage fees, flotation costs, etc.), the maximisation of the stock-market value of the firm is equivalent to the maximisation of the profit of the firm.

Given this goal, a merger or takeover should take place if the market value of the merged firm is greater than the market values of the firms operating as separate independent entities. In symbols, a merger is justified (assuming profit maximisation as the goal of managers) only if

$$V_C > V_A + V_B$$

where V_C = market value of the merged firm
V_A = market value of firm A
V_B = market value of firm B

To see whether this condition is fulfilled in any particular situation, we must examine how the merger can affect the various factors that determine the market value of the firm.

From the single-period general valuation expression of a levered firm (which will be explained in Chapter 8) we have

$$V_L = \frac{\bar{X}(1 - t_c)}{k_e} + Dt_c \tag{5.1}$$

where V_L = market value of a levered firm, that is, a firm that uses an amount of debt equal to D in its capital structure
$\bar{X}$ = expected earnings of the firm, before interest payments to bond-holders, and before corporate tax payments
t_c = corporate tax rate
D = amount of debt (in the capital structure of the firm)
k_e = subjective discount rate of stockholders reflecting the business and financial risk they undertake by buying the shares of the firm.

*   *   *

The valuation of a levered firm will be discussed in detail in Chapter 8. At this stage it is helpful to explain briefly the derivation of the valuation expression (5.1).

The market value of a firm (in a single-period context) is the present (dis-counted) value of its earnings, irrespective of whether these earnings accrue to the bondholders (as interest payments to them by the firm) or to the sharehold-ers. Interest payments are costs and are tax-deductible, while other earnings are taxed at the prevailing corporate tax rate, t_c. The total earnings, $\bar{X}$, are thus

---

[2] The valuation of the firm in the stock market has been examined in Chapter 3. The valuation of a levered firm will be explained in Chapter 8.

split into two components: rD = interest payments to bondholders; and $\bar{X} - rD$ = earnings after interest payments. Since the latter are taxed at the rate of t_c, stockholders will eventually receive only $(\bar{X} - rD)(1 - t_c)$, assuming no retentions.

Thus we may write:

[total earnings after corporate taxes] $= (\bar{X} - rD)(1 - t_c) \quad + \quad rD$

$$= \left[\begin{array}{c} \text{Stockholders} \\ \text{expected earnings} \end{array} \right] + \left[\begin{array}{c} \text{Bondholders} \\ \text{earnings} \end{array} \right]$$

Rearranging, we obtain

$$[\text{Total earnings after taxes}] = \bar{X}(1 - t_c) - rD(1 - t_c) + rD$$

$$= \bar{X}(1 - t_c) + rDt_c$$

To find the present value of these two income components we must discount them by an appropriate discount rate. The interest payments, rD, are a *sure* income for the bondholders, who have a priority claim on the earnings of the firm; hence the appropriate rate of discount for this income is the market bond interest rate r, which is a purely time discount rate. However, the stockholders' expected income is uncertain, given the business and financial risk of the firm. Hence this part of earnings is discounted by the stockholders' (subjective) discount rate, k_e, which is greater than r and reflects the over-all risk (business and financial) which they have by owning the shares of the firm. Hence the value of a levered firm is

$$V_L = \frac{\bar{X}(1 - t_c)}{k_e} + Dt_c$$

* * *

Given the above valuation expression, we will examine the effects of a merger or takeover on each of the factors that determine the market value of a merged firm.

A. Effects of a Merger on Expected Earnings, $\bar{X}$

There are several ways in which a merger can increase the expected earnings of the merged firm. The most important are briefly discussed below.

(i) *Increase in market power*

The typical argument here is that the acquiring firm, by taking over a firm, reduces competition. Or a reduction in competition occurs with mergers, which increase industry concentration. In both cases there is an increase in market power, which allows the charging of higher prices and the reaping of monopoly profits.

There is a lot of confusion surrounding this argument. To clarify the issues it is essential to discuss the effects of mergers and takeovers on competition for the three types of mergers, horizontal, vertical and conglomerate, separately.

(1) Horizontal mergers and takeovers do result in elimination of competitors and an increase in concentration. Hence they lead to increased market power. In some cases acquisitions and mergers have been used as a means to put an end to price-cutting and 'establishing industry discipline'. As we mentioned previously, horizontal mergers were the predominant form of mergers during the first major merger wave around the turn of the century. Concentration increased spectacularly during that period, and was followed by a reduction in competition that prompted the US government to anti-trust legislation which prohibits horizontal mergers between firms which have or may acquire (after the merger) even a modest proportion of a market.[3]

Horizontal mergers have decreased considerably in recent years. Thus we can infer that acquisition of market power via horizontal mergers is not at present an important determinant of the expected earnings of the merged firm.

(2) It is generally agreed that vertical mergers do have the potential to increase market power. Downstream mergers are most often formed in order to ensure a market for the final product, by foreclosing competitors from it. For example, during the period 1959—67 cement manufacturers acquired (took over) sixty-five cement users (mixed-concrete firms or concrete-product manufacturers). These acquisitions represent the foreclosed part of the market of cement users from other competing cement producers, since the acquired firms used the cement of their acquirers. This was an aggressive use of vertical integration, aiming at the reduction in the number of customers of competing cement manufacturers. Subsequently the latter started an extensive acquisition of cement users in an attempt to foreclose a portion of the cement market for themselves. Thus this second vertical integration movement was primarily defensive: a reaction of competitors to the initial aggressive vertical integration policy of the first downstream vertical integration.[4]

Upstream vertical integration may also be used for acquiring market power, via increasing or creating barriers to entry and/or placing competitors at a cost disadvantage. This has been the case with Alcoa in the aluminum industry.[5] In the 1940s Alcoa, an aluminum product corporation, became the greatest producer of ingot, and charged its competitors exceptionally high prices for this key material. Alcoa used its monopoly power in the ingot market to put its competit-

[3] See F. M. Scherer, *Industrial Market Structure and Economic Performance* (Rand McNally 1970) Ch. 20.

[4] W. F. Muller, 'Public Policy Toward Vertical Mergers', in J. Fred Weston and Sam Pelzman (eds), *Public Policy Towards Mergers* (Goodyear, 1969).

[5] Merton J. Peck, *Competition in the Aluminum Industry* (Harvard University Press, 1961).

ors at a cost disadvantage and to prevent entry into the aluminium ingot market for more than thirty years.

In conclusion, vertical mergers can increase market power, and hence the expected earnings of the integrated corporation. However, vertical mergers have been only a small proportion of the total merger activity in the US economy.

(3) Conglomerate mergers are a form of *cross-entry*: a firm established in one industry merges with or takes over another firm established in another unrelated industry. Thus conglomerate mergers do not give market power of the same form as horizontal or vertical mergers. However, conglomerates acquire other forms of market power which usually increase their expected earnings. The most important effects of such economic market power arise from the ability of conglomerates to pursue several policies which affect their earnings. Such policies are: reciprocal buying agreements with customer-firms, predatory pricing, 'tie-in sales' agreements, exclusive dealing agreements, cross-subsidisation of the various branches of the conglomerate, and prevention of potential competition. Let us examine in some detail these practices and their effect on a conglomerate's earnings.

Conglomerates have increased power to enter into reciprocal buying agreements. That is, a conglomerate has the power to coerce its suppliers to buy the products of its different branches under the threat that it will stop buying from them. As Koch[6] puts it, reciprocity is the practice of one firm stating to another that 'I will buy your products if you will buy mine'. A good example of reciprocity is provided by the Consolidated Foods Corporation, which took over Gentry Inc., a firm producing dehydrated onion and garlic. After the acquisition Consolidated Foods pressed its suppliers (especially those making soups and related products) to buy and use Gentry onion and garlic. Although the acquisition and the exercise of reciprocal purchasing pressure increased Gentry's market share slightly (from 32 per cent to 35 per cent in ten years), the Supreme Court (in 1965) ordered Consolidated Foods to divest itself of Gentry.[7] Reciprocal agreements are quite common in the chemical, petroleum and steel markets. However, in these industries there is the countervailing power of conglomerates, so that the effects of such agreements may not be too damaging to competition. In general, however, reciprocity can destroy price competition, and increase the expected earnings of conglomerates.

Predatory pricing is price-cutting aimed at the elimination of (usually) smaller firms if they do not follow policies set by the conglomerate. It is a price policy with threatening (predatory) intent. A conglomerate may have the power to pursue predatory pricing which may well enhance its earnings.

Tie-in sales are agreements by which a firm can coerce another to buy more than one of its products. It is the sort of agreement in which firm *A* says to firm

[6] James V. Koch, *Industrial Organization and Prices*, 2nd edn (Prentice-Hall, 1980).
[7] Federal Trade Commission *vs* Consolidated Foods Corp. *et al.*, 380 US 592(1965).

B that 'if you want my product *x*, you must also buy my product *y*'. Conglomerates have a larger power for imposing such agreements as compared with independent individual firms. These agreements may increase the sales of conglomerates and hence their expected earnings.

Exclusive dealing is the power of forcing customers to buy the products of the conglomerate rather than that of a competitor. Such agreements may increase the market share of the conglomerate and its expected earnings.

A conglomerate can and does cross-subsidise the operations of its various branches. By engaging in selective price discrimination a large conglomerate may monopolise one or more markets, while maintaining its prices at 'competitive levels' in all other markets.[8] Such practices may increase considerably the earnings of the conglomerate.

Finally, a conglomerate may prevent a potential entrant from entering its markets by taking over the firm. This increases the market power of the merged firm and may result in greater expected earnings.[9]

(ii) *Economies of scale and expected earnings*

Here we have to distinguish between *real* and *pecuniary* economies of scale.[10] Real economies arise from a reduction in the factor inputs per unit of output, while pecuniary economies are economies realised from paying lower prices for factor inputs, due to bulk transactions.

Real economies may arise from (a) the production activity of the firm; (b) the technological (R & D) activities; (c) synergistic effects; (d) marketing and distribution activities; (e) transport, storage, inventories; and (f) managerial economies.

Theoretically mergers can result in the realisation of most of the above types of economies of scale, with the exception of real production economies. Real production economies normally result from building a larger new plant. That is, such economies are realised at the plant level, not at the firm level. If two or more plants are to be merged, no real production economies can be expected. The plants are already built and cannot be unbuilt in order to increase and make their scale more efficient. However, mergers do offer, in theory, opportunities for the other types of real scale economies. Among the more obvious possible sources of such economies of scale are lower marketing and distribution costs, lower transportation costs, and reduction in inventories. It is also possible, by general reorganisation of the operations of the merged firms, to consolidate the

---

[8] F. Machlup, 'Characteristics and Types of Price Discrimination', in G. J. Stigler (ed.), *Business Concentration and Price Policy* (Princeton University Press, 1955). Also R. C. Brooks Jr, 'Price Cutting and Monopoly Power', *Journal of Marketing*, 1961, pp. 44–9.

[9] For a general discussion of the various policies which enhance the economic power of conglomerates, see James H. Lorie and Paul Helpern, 'Conglomerates: The Rhetoric and the Evidence', *Journal of Law and Economics*, 1970, pp. 149–66.

[10] See A. Koutsoyiannis, *Modern Microeconomics*, 2nd edn (Macmillan, 1979) ch. 3.

functions of production, research and development, marketing, purchasing, administration and accounting, so as to eliminate duplication of facilities and under-employment of personnel. Theoretically such production, marketing, transportation, inventory and R & D economies are more readily attainable with horizontal mergers, where the activities of the firms are of the same nature and can be easily streamlined. Realisation of such economies are hard to see in vertical mergers, and even harder in conglomerate mergers, where the merging firms belong to unrelated activities.

However, synergistic economies, managerial economies and pecuniary economies may be realised with all types of mergers.

Synergy is said to exist when the combination of firms or activities results in a situation where the total is more than the sum of the individual parts. It is often described as the '2 + 2 greater than 4' case. Synergy results from *complementary* activities, or from spreading of existing managerial skills over a larger concern (operation). One firm may have a strong R & D team, while the other may have a very efficiently organised production department. The combination of the two firms increases the efficiency of the consolidated entity. Similarly, one firm may have well-established products (brands) but may have a poor marketing department. If such a firm merges with (or takes over a) firm with a strong marketing organisation, the merged concern will be more efficient than the individual firms.[11]

While synergistic effects arising from complementarity of functions within firms are theoretically attainable in all types of mergers, synergy from managerial talent is more likely to be attained in horizontal mergers, because management is experienced (specialised) in running a certain line of business. Vertical mergers and conglomerates involve firms producing different commodities or services which normally require different managerial skills and experience. Thus if managerial economies are to be realised with conglomerate (or even vertical) mergers, the managerial ability must be of a special kind: the managers of the acquiring company must be equally efficient in running operations of highly diversified type, that is, they must be a sort of super-management, men of much greater talent than the managers of the corporations they absorb. This implicitly assumes that managerial talent is an amorphous non-specialised ability which can be applied with equal success to totally unrelated lines of business.[12]

Pecuniary economies may be realised by all types of mergers, from lower prices for factor inputs owing to bulk transactions. Such economies are most important for horizontal mergers. For vertical and conglomerate mergers the most important pecuniary economy is that of cheaper finance. It is argued that a large conglomerate has a large cash flow with which it can cross-finance its various branches. Furthermore, it has access to outside finance (bonds and issue

---

[11] J. Fred Weston, 'The Nature and Significance of Conglomerate Firms', *St John's Law Review*, 1970.
[12] See Mueller, 'A Theory of Conglomerate Mergers'.

of new stocks) at the lowest attainable rates. Hence a small firm can benefit from being absorbed by a larger firm by gaining access to cheaper capital. This financial advantage is examined critically in section V.

(iii) *Fast growth and expected earnings,* $\bar{X}$

It is often argued that an acquisition of another firm enables the acquiring company to enter a new market quickly, avoiding the delays associated with building a new plant and establishing the new line of product. Internal growth is time-consuming, requiring research and development, organisation of production, market penetration and in general a smoothly working organisation. Through merger a company can quickly obtain an already established firm in the new market. This is true. The main limit to growth by merger is the likelihood that too many acquisitions may create substantial managerial diseconomies: the management of the conglomerate may become unable to control efficiently, co-ordinate and motivate the newly acquired firms.

Whatever the long-run effects of such fast growth, it is almost certain that it will enhance investors' expectations about the expected earnings of the conglomerate in the short run. Speed of entry is an advantage of a merger.

B.   Tax Effects on the Merged Firm

Under certain conditions it is possible to observe an increase in the market value of a firm acquiring another which has a large tax-loss carry forward. Tax laws allow income deferral. Thus the loss of the acquired firm can be subtracted (for tax purposes) from the current income, the previous year's income, or be carried forward (and be subtracted from the future income) for up to five years. It is argued that this tax-loss carry forward may reduce the taxable income of the merged entity, making it fall into a lower tax bracket, with the attendant reduction in the tax rate. From the valuation expression (5.1) it is seen that the marginal tax rate appears with a negative sign in the first term on the right-hand side, implying that if t_c decreases the after-tax expected earnings will increase. Dewey[13] has argued that many mergers take place because the tax laws encourage firms to acquire unprofitable firms in order to obtain a tax write-off. However, Boyle[14] has conducted statistical tests that give little support to this hypothesis.

In considering the effect of a lower corporate tax rate on the market value of a merger, one must take into account not only the above tax-loss carry forward advantage but also the disadvantage of such a lower t_c associated with the fact

---

[13] Donald J. Dewey, 'Mergers and Cartels: Some Reservations about Policy', *American Economic Review*, 1961, pp. 255–62.

[14] Stanley E. Boyle, 'Pre-merger Growth and Profit Characteristics of Large Conglomerate Mergers in the United States', *St John's Law Review*, 1970, pp. 152–70.

that interest payments on debt are tax-deductible. Recall that t_c also appears with a positive sign in the second term (Dt_c) of the valuation expression (5.1). This implies that a reduction in t_c reduces the tax advantage of financial leverage (debt financing). In other words, although a reduction in the corporate tax rate improves the firm's earnings after taxes, it also reduces the tax advantage of debt. Thus the net effect of a reduction in t_c on the value of the merger cannot be known on *a priori* grounds.

In general it does not seem that tax laws create sufficient inducements for merger. For example, merger intensities (as we pointed out earlier) vary widely among industries. This cannot be explained by the tax laws. Moreover, merger frequencies have varied sharply over time with no change in the tax structure. Indeed, some of the periods of high merger activity preceded the present period of high corporate and personal taxes.[15]

C.   Effects of Mergers on Risk and on Investors' Discount Rate

It is often argued that one of the greatest advantages of mergers, especially conglomerate mergers, is the reduction in business risk through the diversification of the activities of the firm. A reduction in business risk, if attained, reduces the discount rate of the merger (k_e) and hence increases its market value: as risk is lowered, the market value of the merged firm exceeds the values of the companies operating independently. If the firm wants to diversify its activities, the argument runs, it is safer (less risky) to do it by merger with an existing firm, established in the new product, with established distribution channels and accumulated product-differentiation advantage. The internal development and promotion of new products requires time, new know-how and probably extensive (and expensive) R & D effort as well as marketing effort.

Let us examine this argument in some detail.

Risk, as we saw in Chapter 3, is measured by the variability of earnings. The most commonly used measure of risk is the variance or standard deviation of earnings:

$$\text{var}(x) = s_x^2 = \frac{\Sigma(X_i - \bar{X})^2}{n} \text{ and } s = \sqrt{\frac{\Sigma(X_i - \bar{X})^2}{n}} \tag{5.2}$$

The higher the standard deviation, the greater the variability of earnings, and hence the greater the risk, *ceteris paribus*.

Two issues relating to the reduction in the risk via merger need stressing.

(1) It is commonly believed that, unless the earnings (returns) of the merging firms are perfectly positively correlated, the merger will result in a lower dispersion of the expected earnings of the merged company. This is not necessarily true, as the following example shows.

[15] Michael Gort, 'An Economic Distrubance Theory of Mergers', *Quarterly Journal of Economics*, 1969, p. 625.

Table 5.2   Profitability of firms *A, B*, and the merger *A & B*

Year	Firm *A* Profit rate (%)	Firm *B* Profit rate (%)	Merger *A & B* Profit rate (%)
1	6.0	6.0	6.0
2	7.0	3.0	5.0
3	8.0	2.0	5.0
4	5.0	7.0	6.0
	Mean profit = 6.5%	Mean profit = 4.5%	Mean profit = 5.5%
	s = 1.12%	*s* = 2.06%	*s* = 0.50%

In Table 5.2 we show the profitability of two firms, *A* and *B*, over a four-year period. The last column of the table shows the profitability of the merged firm *A & B*. It is obvious that the profit of the merged firm has a smaller standard deviation than that of either of the individual firms. The merger has, therefore, reduced the risk in this particular example. Since investors are risk-averse (see Chapter 11), they will consider this an advantage of the merger, and will apply a lower discount rate to the expected earnings of the merged entity *A & B*.

In Table 5.3 we show the effect of the merger of the same firm *A* and another firm *C*. It is seen that when these firms merge into firm *A & C* the standard deviation of the merged firm's profits is larger than that of the profits of firm *A* prior to merger. Hence such a merger would increase the risk of the stockholders of firm *A*. This result is due to the fact that the variability of earnings of the acquired firm *C* is substantially larger than the variability of firm *A*'s profits. The variability of profits of *C* is so large that a merger between *A* and *C* increases the risk to the stockholders of firm *A*.

Table 5.3   Profitability of firms *A, C*, and the merger *A & C*

Year	Firm *A* Profit rate (%)	Firm *C* Profit rate (%)	Merger *A & C* Profit rate (%)
1	6.0	6.0	6.0
2	7.0	1.0	4.0
3	8.0	0.0	4.0
4	5.0	11.0	8.0
	Mean profit = 6.5%	Mean profit = 4.5%	Mean profit = 5.5%
	s = 1.12%	*s* = 4.39%	*s* = 1.66%

In general the reduction of the risk via a merger depends (a) on the correlation coefficient between the profits of the merging companies, and (b) on the relative size of the standard deviation of the profits of the two firms.[16] Reduced variability of profits is possible via merger, but it is not a necessary outcome of

[16] For a rigorous discussion of the relation between the standard deviation of the merged firm and the correlation and the standard deviations of the profits of the merging firms, see W. W. Alberts, 'The Profitability of Merger', in W. W. Alberts and Joel E. Segall (eds), *The Corporate Merger* (University of Chicago Press, 1966) pp. 262–72.

merger. It should also be stressed that the above example assumed that the variability of the earnings of the merging firms would remain the same after the merger. This may not be a valid assumption. After the merger has taken place it is quite possible that the profit performance and the variability of earnings of the individual firms may change in a direction that may reduce or increase the risk of the stockholders of *A* prior to the merger.

There is some empirical evidence[17] that provides no conclusive support for the hypothesis that acquiring firms reduce their risk (as measured by the variability of earnings) by merging with other firms.

(2) The second point that must be stressed in relation to the reduction of risk by means of merger is the following. Even if the merger reduces the variability of earnings of the stockholders of *A*, it is an expensive way of attaining this result, due to the heavy costs of acquisition. The stockholders of *A* can achieve the same risk-reduction effect by diversifying their own investment portfolios, at a lower cost and with a greater flexibility. The typical premium paid by an acquiring firm in a merger is 10–20 per cent above the market price of the acquired firm's stock before the merger.[18] To this one must add the costs of bringing the two firms together, the costs of assimilating the acquired firm into the parent company's organisation.[19] Finally, the acquisition of the entire firm *B* requires 'lumpy' investment, and the acquiring firm *A* loses the flexibility to divest (disengage) itself from *B* quickly (if the merger turns out to be unsuccessful) and at low cost. The stockholders can achieve the same risk reduction by purchasing some of the stock of both firms and at a much lower cost than is involved in the acquisition of firm *B* by firm *A*.[20] Thus a valid argument can be made that a conglomerate is less efficient at diversification than the individual investor. Therefore, investors will be prepared to pay less for the conglomerate than for the merging firms as separate entities.[21] In other words, since the investors can individually attain the same reduction in risk as the merged firm, but at a lower cost and with greater flexibility, they will value the new entity less than the two firms separately. Yet another point to be stressed in this connection is that the acquisition or merger is negotiated by management and is more or less forced on the stockholders, while by selecting portfolios themselves they can achieve a more desirable balance between risk and return, thus attaining a higher level of satisfaction.

[17] See Thomas F. Hogarty, 'Profits and Merger: The Evidence of Fifty Years', *St John's Law Review*, 1970, pp. 378–91.

[18] See James B. Walker Jr, *Financing the Acquisition*, Financial Management Series, No. 114 (University of Chicago Press, 1970).

[19] E. Penrose, *The Theory of the Growth of the Firm* (Oxford University Press, 1959).

[20] Investors who invest only a small amount of money and cannot acquire a fully diversified portfolio can always buy shares of trust funds or mutual funds which are expert in portfolio selection, have lower transactions costs and offer greater flexibility than the conglomerate firm.

[21] K. V. Smith and J. C. Schreiner, 'A Portfolio Analysis of Conglomerate Diversification', *Journal of Finance*, 1969, pp. 413–28.

In summary, the advantage from a possible reduction in the variability (risk) of earnings of the merger may be offset by the high costs and other disadvantages of conglomerate firms, so that the discount rate which investors apply to the earnings of the merged firm may in fact increase, resulting in a lower market value of the new entity. A merger does not necessarily result in a reduction in the investors' discount rate and the increase of the market value of the merged firm.

D.   Effects from Increased Debt Capacity

The second term in the valuation expression (5.1) includes the debt used in the capital structure of the firm. The question is whether a merger can raise Dt_c for the merged firm above the sum of Dt_c for the individual firms prior to merger. If it can, then there are financial advantages of the merger which increase its market value above the sum of the values of the separate firms.

Such financial advantages are possible in two cases.

(1) It is possible that one of the firms was not using enough debt financing. As we will see in Chapter 8, the market value of a firm increases with increased use of debt, up to the point of its debt capacity (or debt limit).[22] This is due to the tax-deductibility of the interest payments to bondholders. If a firm's use of debt is below its debt limit, it will be undervalued in the capital market. If this firm is acquired by another, which increases the amount of debt to its limit, the market value of the merged firm will exceed the market values of the firms as separate independent units.

Although this is a possible source of financial advantage to the merger, it does not seem to be important in the real world. If a firm is undervalued because of its low debt/equity ratio, it is bound to be 'discovered', not only by aggressive takeover raiders, but by other investors in the market (insurance companies, trust funds, mutual funds, etc.). Given the time required to consummate a merger, it is more likely that other investors will start buying the stock of the under-levered firm, thus bidding up its market value. In fact, the announcement or even the rumour of the possibility of merger is likely to attract attention to the stock and cause it to be bid up to a level such that it is no longer undervalued.

(2) It has been suggested by Lewellen[23] that a merger increases the debt capacity of the merged firm. The amount that creditors are prepared to lend a corporation depends, among other things, upon their estimate of the likelihood that the corporation will default, that is, the probability that the firm's earnings will be lower than its required payments on debt. A merged corporation can

---

[22] See A. Koutsoyiannis, 'Managerial Job Security and the Capital Structure of the Firm', *Manchester School*, March 1978.

[23] W. G. Lewellen, 'A Pure Financial Rationale for the Conglomerate Merger', *Journal of Finance*, 1971, pp. 521–37.

divert cash from one of its divisions to another, if the latter's earnings are insufficient to cover its debt payments. Hence lenders of a conglomerate face a smaller risk of default, and are prepared to provide more capital to the merged entity than they would give to the two individual separate firms. Whereas a conglomerate's diversification does nothing for its stockholders that they cannot do for themselves, it can provide a greater security to creditors than creditors can provide for themselves when dealing with the 'constituent' separate firms. Thus lenders are willing to provide relatively more debt to a merged firm than to the independent firms. This advantage of merger is greater for conglomerates than for horizontal mergers, since the returns (profits) of the various branches of a conglomerate are less correlated in any one period. With a greater use of debt the value of the merged firm should be greater than the sum of the values of the individual firms, and we have a rational financial justification for merger.

In summary, the profit-maximisation hypothesis postulates that mergers take place when the market value of the merged company is higher than the value of the individual separate entities.

The market value of the merged company increases if one of the following conditions attains:

(1) The merged firm acquires increased market power, which enables it to charge a higher price and reap monopoly profits.
(2) The merger gives rise to economies of scale, real or pecuniary.
(3) The merged company attains an increased rate of growth.
(4) The merged firm attains some tax advantage which the independent firms did not have.
(5) The merger reduces the variability of earnings and, hence, the risk of stockholders, but at a cost that does not exceed the expense which stockholders would have if they themselves attained the same reduction in risk by diversifying their individual portfolios.
(6) The merger increases the debt capacity of the new entity.

III. MERGERS AND THE VALUATION-DISCREPANCIES HYPOTHESIS

The basic premise of this hypothesis is that the real world is a world of uncertainty. Capital markets are imperfect, and hence different investors may well be expected to reach different valuations of the same firm(s). Such valuation discrepancies are the cause of mergers and acquisitions.

In perfect capital markets valuation discrepancies cannot persist in the long run. However, when uncertainty, incomplete knowledge and other market imperfections are taken into account, valuation discrepancies are likely to be a common phenomenon. We saw that the value of the stocks of a firm depends on the expectations of both buyers and sellers regarding the future earnings of the firm.

Expectations are affected by uncertainty, incomplete information, and the attitudes, temperaments and other personal attributes and characteristics of investors. Expectations in stock markets are particularly sensitive to real or rumoured events or prospective events. We thus must distinguish between the purposeful manipulation of expectations of investors by merger promoters, and valuation discrepancies arising from the different assessment of the available information and prevailing conditions by the various individual investors.

A.   Manipulative Effects of Expectations of Investors

We shall examine two ways in which investors' expectations can and have been affected by merger promoters in the stock market. One practice is known as 'stock watering'. The other is sometimes referred to as 'the price/earnings ratio game'.

'Stock watering' involves spreading misleading information, planting rumours and tampering in general with the stock market to convince investors about non-existing monopoly power or economies-of-scale prospects. This enables promoters to sell the stock of newly consolidated firms at prices which far exceed their economic value. Promoters, in this case, hasten to sell their stock before the bubble bursts. And such 'bubble-bursts' were very frequent during the frenzied merger movement in the 1897—9 and 1926—9 periods.[24] Subsequent US legislation (the Securities Act of 1933 and the Stock Exchange Act of 1934) curbed the power of merger promoters to spread misleading information. But new ways have been invented to reap speculative gains through promoting a merger, and without breaking the law.

The most spectacular examples are the 'go-go' mergers of the 1960s based on the 'price/earnings ratio game' or 'bootstrapping'. The method adopted by merger promoters was to convince investors that conglomerates have a kind of perpetual growth. The following example is used to illustrate the conditions under which investors' expectations can be manipulated so that they maintain the belief that the earnings of a continuously growing (via further acquisitions and mergers) conglomerate may well be expected to increase, and hence the price of its shares will rise, yielding lucrative capital gains.[25]

Assume that conglomerate A has 1,000,000 shares outstanding and has net profits of $10,000,000, that is, $10 per share. Investors believe (or are led to

---

[24] Shaw Livermore, 'The Success of Industrial Mergers', *Quarterly Journal of Economics*, 1935, pp. 68—96.

[25] This example has been adapted from 'The Conglomerates', *Wall Street Journal*, 25 July, 1968.

believe) that the conglomerate has a high growth potential, so that its stock is selling at a price/earnings ratio of 30; that is, a share of A has

$$P_A/10 = 30$$

and sells at the price $P_A = \$10 \times 30 = \$300$.

The conglomerate sets out to acquire another firm, B, which has the same number of shares (1,000,000) and the same net profits ($\$10,000,000$). But investors are not very impressed by the past growth performance of this firm, so that its shares sell at a price/earnings ratio of 10 that is,

$$P_B/10 = 10$$

or $P_B = \$100$.

The conglomerate makes a direct bid to the stockholders of B, offering to exchange one share of B with one-half share of A. The offer is apparently attractive, since one-half share of A has a value of $\$150$. The acquisition is agreed, and A issues 500,000 new stocks which it exchanges with the 1,000,000 shares of the acquired firm B. After the transaction, conglomerate A has

1,500,000 shares

$\$20,000,000$ net (combined) profit

$\$13.33$ earnings per share

If investors continue to believe in the same high growth potential of conglomerate A, and hence value it at the initial price/earnings ratio of 30, the price of the shares of this conglomerate will increase from $\$300$ to $\$400$:

$$P_A/13.33 = 30$$

or $P_A = \$400$.

Everyone is better off, though the total combined earnings have not increased at all!

In general, the price of the shares of a conglomerate will continue to increase provided that the two following conditions are fulfilled: (i) the acquired firm has a lower price/earnings ratio than the conglomerate; and (ii) investors continue to maintain the same expectations about the price/earnings ratio of the conglomerate. It is quite conceivable that the growth performance of A may deteriorate, having absorbed a firm with a less spectacular growth achievement. If investors, however, are led to believe that this will not occur, that A will continue to equal its original performance, then the price of the shares of A will rise.

Although such cases have occurred in the past, there is a limit to their attainment. If a 'go-go' merger policy has been successful, it will soon be imitated. Thus the price/earnings ratios of the potential acquirable firms will be bid up, and their number will decline. At the same time, the conglomerate which has pursued such a 'go-go' game may well be expected to have a lower profitability and develop considerable managerial diseconomies. Hence such manipulative effects cannot be expected to last for long.

B. Valuation Discrepancies of Expected Earnings

Mergers can occur when the acquiring firm (A) estimates the present value of the earnings of B to be greater than the present value of these earnings as estimated by B itself. This discrepancy may arise *either* because the expected earnings of B as perceived by A are larger than firm B thinks, or because the stockholders of A use a lower discount rate than the stockholders of B. In symbols, let

$\bar{X}_B^B$ = firm B's expected earnings as perceived by the stockholders of firm B

$\bar{X}_B^A$ = firm B's expected earnings as perceived by the stockholders of firm A

k_A = discount rate (for risk) of the stockholders of firm A

k_B = discount rate of the stockholders of firm B

The price that the acquiring firm A is prepared to pay for the acquisition cannot exceed the present value of the expected earnings of B as estimated by A that is, the demand price for firm B (by the potential acquirer A) is

$$[A\text{'s demand price for } B] = \frac{\bar{X}_B^A}{k_A} \tag{5.3}$$

The price that firm B is prepared to sell is the present value of the expected earnings of B as estimated by the stockholders of B, that is,

$$[B\text{'s supply (selling) price}] = \frac{\bar{X}_B^B}{k_B} \tag{5.4}$$

A valuation discrepancy exists if the price that firm A is willing to pay for acquiring firm B is greater than the price firm B itself is willing to accept. Thus a merger will take place (due to valuation discrepancies) if:

(i) both discount rates are the same ($k_A = k_B$), but the earnings of B as estimated by A's stockholders exceed these earnings as estimated by B's stockholders ($\bar{X}_B^A > \bar{X}_B^B$); or

(ii) the expected earnings of B are estimated at the same level both by the stockholders of A and the stockholders of B ($\bar{X}_B^A = \bar{X}_B^B$), but A's stockholders have a lower discount rate than the stockholders of B ($k_A < k_B$).

In perfect capital markets such valuation discrepancies cannot arise, because arbitrage would eliminate them. Let us see how the mechanism of a perfect capital market eliminates valuation discrepancies. First, assume that all investors have the same discount rates, but there is a divergence in expectations among stockholders regarding the future earnings of firm B ($\bar{X}_B^A > \bar{X}_B^B$). Under these conditions A's stockholders will find that the shares of B are *underpriced.*[26] This will induce them to buy shares of B, thus bidding their price up. As B's stockholders see the price of their shares increasing, they will adjust (upwards) their estimation of the prospective earnings of their firm. This will continue until all stockholders maintain the same expectations about the future earnings of firm B. Second, assume that $\bar{X}_B^A = \bar{X}_B^B$, but the marginal stockholder of A has a lower discount rate than the marginal stockholder of B. Under these conditions the stockholder of A will consider B's shares underpriced. This will cause him to begin buying shares of firm B. If we make the simplifying assumption that a stockholder of firm A obtains the money to do this by selling shares of firm A, then, following the arbitrage transaction, the price of shares A will fall, while the price of shares of B will rise, and, given $\bar{X}_B^A = \bar{X}_B^B$, the discount rate of the marginal stockholder of A will be increased while the discount rate of the marginal stockholder of B will be reduced, until $k_A = k_B$. In short, valuation discrepancies of the above type cannot persist in perfect capital markets, where there is certainty, complete information and no transactions costs or other imperfections.

However, in the real world capital markets are not perfect, and hence valuation discrepancies do occur. Gort[27] has developed a theory of mergers, based on the assumption that valuation discrepancies are inevitable, due to several factors which give rise to *systematic variations* in such discrepancies in valuation. In particular, Gort argues that in periods of (a) fast technological progress, (b) fast market growth, and (c) frequent fluctuations of prices of shares, the 'stock of information' of investors becomes obsolete. Different investors perceive events and developments in different ways, and hence they can reach different valuations of the prospects of firms.

Changes in technology may lead either to new products or to new methods of production. Demand for new products, as well as their costs, are difficult to estimate from past data. Given that cost changes will affect prices, future prices

---

[26] The price that a marginal stockholder of A is willing to pay for a share of firm B will be equal to

$$\left(\frac{\bar{X}_B^A}{k_A}\right) \Big/ N_B$$

where N_B is the number of shares of firm B outstanding. This is higher than the value that stockholders of B put for their shares which is

$$\left(\frac{\bar{X}_B^B}{k_B}\right) \Big/ N_B$$

Apparently

$$\left(\frac{\bar{X}_B^A}{k_A}\right) \Big/ N_B > \left(\frac{\bar{X}_B^B}{k_B}\right) \Big/ N_B$$

if $k_A = k_B$, because in this case $\bar{X}_B^A > \bar{X}_B^B$.

[27] Gort, 'An Economic Disturbance Theory of Mergers'.

and levels of output cannot be easily forecast. In summary, when technology changes rapidly, past information and experience are of little assistance in estimating future streams of earnings. Consequently differences in the valuations of investors arise, and this may increase merger activity.

Rapid changes in the price of a firm's share confuses investors, and makes it difficult to use past changes to form expectations about future changes in stock prices. Information on past price/earnings ratios becomes largely irrelevant. Consequently one may well expect that the differences in the values of these shares estimated by various investors will increase. According to Gort, the increase in merger activity during booming stock markets can be attributed to valuation discrepancies of this type: in booming capital markets speculators tend to overvalue stocks. Furthermore, potential acquiring firms tend to be more optimistic about the prospects of firms which they want to take over. The latter, in turn, tend to 'hold on' to their stocks, expecting further increases in their price. Hence mergers are likely to be far more frequent in periods of high than in periods of low security prices.

Finally, Gort argues that the growth of the market may affect merger intensity. As we pointed out earlier, mergers are a faster way of attaining growth. Hence one may expect mergers to increase when markets are growing rapidly. Market growth, furthermore, enhances expectations about future earnings, and hence provides an additional stimulus to mergers.

Gort has tested the valuation-discrepancies hypothesis using a sample of 5,534 mergers recorded by the US Federal Trade Commission during the years 1951 to 1959. His results are discussed in section V below.

C.   Differences in the Discount Rates of Stockholders of Acquiring and Acquired Firms

Valuation discrepancies may also arise because the discount rate of the stockholders of the acquiring firm is lower than that of the stockholders of the acquired firms.

There are several cases in which firms *want* to be acquired or *want* to merge with another company. Their stockholders (or managers) have a high discount rate which makes them willing to sell at a price lower than the true value of the firm. The most frequently cited motives of the acquired firms are the following.

(1) *Lack of management succession.* If a firm is owner-managed and the owner approaches retirement or wants to avoid the stress of running the business, he may decide to sell the firm, especially if there is no family heir to succeed him. The discount rate of the owner-manager in this case will be high; his valuation of the worth of the firm is affected by the lack of a successor in the management of the firm. This is a common motive for small firms.

(2) *Establishing a value for the firm for tax purposes.* An owner-manager knows that if he dies, his firm (together with all other estate) will be evaluated

by the tax authorities for inheritance-tax purposes. Tax authorities may tend to overvalue the firm, so that more taxes are paid. If, however, the firm is sold before the owner's death, then a market valuation has been established for the firm.

(3) *Ageing management*. The managers of a firm will have a relatively high discount rate just before they retire. In this case they may be willing to promote a merger (or selling) of the firm in exchange for bonuses and stock options of the new entity.

(4) *Threat of a hostile takeover bid*. The managers of a firm will have a short time horizon (high discount rate) if they think they are about to be dismissed through a takeover bid. Since the threatened managers will have little control over their positions should the takeover bid be successful, they may be willing to see their firm merge with a third company at a price below the 'normal' selling price, if they can ensure for themselves better positions in the newly merged entity than they could expect following a hostile successful takeover. Seeking out a new merger partner is becoming an increasingly popular defensive strategy for avoiding takeover bids.[28] This strategy is equivalent to the managers increasing their discount rate (by lowering their selling price to another buyer-firm).

IV. MERGERS AND THE GROWTH-MAXIMISATION HYPOTHESIS: MUELLER'S MODEL OF CONGLOMERATE MERGERS

Although the speeding up of growth has been suggested by various economists as a motive for mergers, it was Dennis Mueller[29] who presented a formal model of mergers in which the merger activity is attributed to the growth-maximisation goal of managers.

Mueller adopts the managerialist school of thought.[30] According to this school the utility functions of managers differ from those of stockholders. Stockholders are mainly interested in the profits of the firm, while managers want job security, power, status, high salaries and other perquisites. Empirical studies suggest that both the pecuniary and non-pecuniary goals of managers are closely related to the growth rate of their firm. Managerial salaries, bonuses, stock options and promotions all tend to be more closely related to the growth of the firm than to its profits. Similarly, the prestige and power of managers

---

[28] Samuel L. Hayes and Russel A. Taussig, 'Tactics of Cash Take-over Bids', *Harvard Business Review*, 1967.

[29] Mueller, 'A Theory of Conglomerate Mergers'.

[30] W. J. Baumol, *Business Behaviour, Value and Growth* (Macmillan, 1959); J. K. Galbraith, *The New Industrial State* (Houghton Mifflin, 1967); J. K. Galbraith, *Economics and the Public Purpose* (Houghton Mifflin, 1973); R. Marris, *The Economic Theory of Managerial Capitalism* (Macmillan, 1964); Edith Penrose, *The Theory of the Growth of the Firm* (Oxford University Press, 1959); J. Williamson, 'Profit, Growth and Sales Maximisation', *Economica*, 1966.

are directly related to the size and the growth of the company, not to its profitability. Thus managers are more interested in the size and growth of the firm
than in its profits. The separation of ownership from management in the large
corporations gives some discretion to managers in setting the goals of the firm
and they may use it to maximise their own welfare. Given the close correlation
between growth and the magnitudes in which managers are interested, they set
as their goal the maximisation of the growth of the firm. This is a radical departure from the basic premise of the neoclassical theory of the firm, which assumes
that the goal of managers is the maximisation of the profit or the welfare of
stockholders.

The pursuance of growth maximisation by managers affects their investment
policy in general, because their motivation for growth makes them apply a lower
discount rate than that of stockholders in evaluating the future profitability of
alternative investment opportunities open to the firm at any one time.

In Figure 5.1 we show the demand and supply schedules for investable funds.
The S_{Fs} curve is the supply of funds as perceived by stockholders. (The supply-
of-funds schedule is explained in Chapters 10 and 11.) It relates various amounts
of capital to their unit cost (marginal cost of capital, MCC). The horizontal part
of this curve corresponds to the amount of internal funds, from profits and
depreciation.[31] The cost of these funds to the stockholders is their opportunity
cost, that is, the return that stockholders expect to earn from investing in the
shares of another firm (or portfolio of firms) of comparable risk. It should be
clear (from Chapter 3) that the stockholders' opportunity cost is the rate of

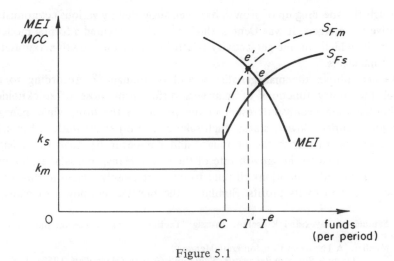

Figure 5.1

<hr />

[31] The straight part of the supply curve also includes any change in debt (bonds outstanding) which is required to maintain the leverage of the firm (its debt/equity ratio) to its
target level. The target debt/equity ratio relates to the financing decision of the firm and is
discussed in Chapter 8.

discount (k_s) which they apply to evaluate the present value of future streams of earnings which they might have from alternative investment in securities of other firms. The rising part of the S_{Fs} curve shows the increased cost of external finance (see Chapters 10 and 11). If the firm needs capital beyond its internally generated funds, it will have to raise it from the capital market, by issuing new stocks or new bonds. The cost of raising additional debt is higher than k_s, because the firm will have to pay transaction costs *and* an ever larger risk premium to its lenders, as the risk of default increases with increasing leverage. The cost of raising capital through new equity is even higher, because, apart from the transactions costs of the new issue, new stocks are usually sold at a lower price than their nominal value.

The S_{Fs} curve is the relevant marginal cost of capital curve if the goal of the firm is the maximisation of profits or the maximisation of stockholder welfare.

The dashed curve S_{Fm} is the supply of funds as perceived by managers, who are growth maximisers. The opportunity cost of internal funds is much lower for such managers than for stockholders, because managers, who are keen to maximise the growth of the firm, will tend to ignore (or at least discount heavily) investment opportunities in securities of other firms, since these will not contribute to the expansion of the size of the firm.[32] Hence the marginal cost of capital schedule (the supply-of-funds curve — see Chapters 10 and 11) as perceived by managers lies below that of the stockholders over the range of the internally generated funds of the firm. The distance between the two supply curves over that range depends (a) on the outside opportunities of the stockholders, (b) on the threat of mass dismissal of the management from dissatisfied stockholders (who resent the deviation of managers from profit maximisation), or (c) on a successful takeover raid following the adverse effect on stock prices of an aggressive growth-maximisation policy at the expense of profit maximisation.[33] The rising part of the supply-of-funds curve of growth-maximising managers will lie above the supply-of-funds curve of stockholders, because the risk (to investors in the capital market) associated with growth-maximising policies is higher than the risk of profit-maximising projects. Accordingly, investors in the market will be prepared to provide capital to growth-maximising firms at a higher cost.

The *MEI* curve is the familiar marginal efficiency of capital schedule of the firm, its demand for investable funds (see Chapter 4). It shows the internal investment opportunities open to the firm, with their expected rate of return. In particular this curve excludes opportunities for expansion via merger or acquisition of other firms. As shown in Figure 5.1, the MEI schedule implies that the firm has large internal investment opportunities which exceed its internally generated funds. This is the case of new firms with high internal growth potential.

---

[32] Market interest rates will not be completely ignored, of course, since interest earned today can be internally invested to produce future growth. However, the more distant the time period for the realisation of growth by this means, the more heavily the prospects of interest earnings will be discounted.

[33] Marris, *The Theory of 'Managerial' Capitalism*, pp. 29–40.

For these firms the equilibrium level of investment both for stockholders and managers is defined by the point of intersection of the *MEI* and the S_{Fs} curves (point *e* in Figure 5.1). The divergence of interests and of goals of owners and managers of such young firms with high internal growth potential does not affect the amount of 'optimal' investment. The same amount of investment (I^e in Figure 5.1) maximises the welfare of stockholders *and* the growth of the firm. In general, so long as the *MEI* intersects the rising part of the marginal cost of capital curve, the profit-maximisation hypothesis and the growth-maximisation hypothesis lead to the same equilibrium level of investment. If managers equated the *MEI* with the marginal cost of capital implied by their S_{Fm} curve, they would be inconsistent to their goal, because they would undertake less investment (I' in Figure 5.1), and hence the firm would grow at a slower rate than the stockholder-welfare-maximising firm. Thus under these circumstances managers attain growth maximisation by maximising stockholder welfare: for young firms with high internal growth potential, there is no conflict of interests between managers and stockholders, so that their decisions and policies coincide. For a young firm of this type the optimal policy will be to retain all its profits (pay no dividends) and raise outside capital until its marginal cost (as measured by the stockholders' discount rate) equals the firm's marginal return on (internal) investment. In Figure 5.1 the optimal level of investment would be financed with an amount of *OC* internal funds, and with CI^e external capital.

As the firm expands and matures, its internal funds will increase, and this will cause a shift of the supply-of-funds curves to the right (see Figure 5.2).

The *MEI* schedule will be also shifting to the right, but at a decreasing rate, because the firm's opportunities for internal expansion gradually reach a limit in a maturing industry (see Figure 5.3).

The different rates of shift of the supply and demand for capital curves means that at some point in time the firm's *MEI* schedule will intersect the supply-of-capital curves in their flat stretch. In Figure 5.4 the *MEI* curve intersects the

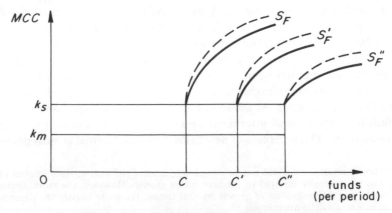

Figure 5.2   Shifting supply-of-funds curves

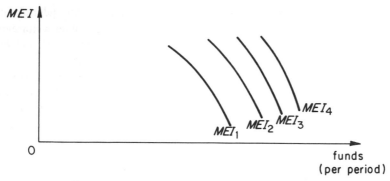

Figure 5.3 Shifting demand-for-funds curves

supply curves at points e_s and e_m respectively. If managers maximise stockholder welfare, they would undertake an investment level of $I_{\Pi m}$, they would pay out dividends equal to ah ($= I_{\Pi m}C$), and would not resort to outside finance.[34] With declining internal investment opportunities, the management would see that shareholders will be better off if they receive part of the profits in the form of dividends and invest it elsewhere.

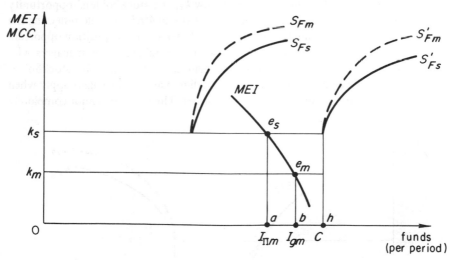

Figure 5.4

[34] Note that only long-run investment and dividend policies are implied in Figure 5.4. In any one period the firm may very well borrow to finance lumpy investment projects or some exceptional investment opportunities. These loans, however, will be repaid quickly, so that the firm maintains its target debt/equity ratio. But a stockholder-welfare-maximising firm will not adopt a long-run policy of paying dividends and constantly issuing new equity or increasing its leverage ratio.

However, if managers aim at growth maximisation, they will undertake more internal investment ($I_{gm} > I_{\Pi m}$ in Figure 5.4) than a stockholder-welfare-maximising firm, they would pay less in dividends ($bh < ah$ in Figure 5.4), and would tolerate a lower rate of return on the marginal investment project.

The above equilibrium refers to internal investment opportunities. However, if managers are growth-seekers, they will not limit themselves to internal expansion alone. They will be looking at external investment opportunities, not in the form of some of the securities of other firms, but in opportunities of acquiring other firms in their entirety. Purchase of part of the shares of other firms does not contribute to the growth of the size of the firm. For this goal to be attained the other (outside) firms must be acquired and 'internalised', that is, become an integral part of the organisation of the firm. The demand schedule, when such external acquisition opportunities are taken into account, will not only shift to the right, but will also change shape: it will become much flatter, below the stockholders' opportunity cost (discount rate k_s). This is the result of the high costs of acquisition. If management were interested in buying only part of the stock of other firms, its opportunity cost would be the same as that of the stockholders (k_s). But, as we pointed out earlier, the acquisition of firms involves high costs (payment of a premium on the shares of the acquired firm, plus costs of assimilating it in the parent's organisational unit). Hence the flattening out of the *MEI* schedule, as greater resort to outside investment (acquisition) opportunities is made, will occur at a point below k_s, the stockholders' opportunity cost. A growth-maximising management will have an *MEI* schedule reflecting the fact that there is a seemingly boundless set of merger and acquisition opportunities. The essence of the difference between the behaviour of managers who maximise growth and the behaviour of managers who maximise stockholder welfare is the lower discount rate that growth-maximising managers apply when evaluating the various investment opportunities. Thus a firm cannot completely

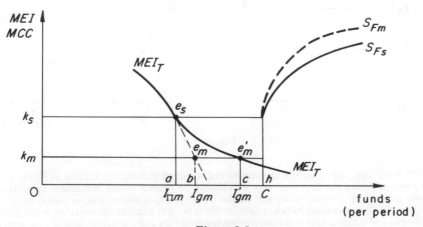

Figure 5.5

avoid the risk of being taken over by pursuing a policy of stockholder-welfare maximisation, because its market value will always be less than what the managers with a growth-maximising motivation think, since these managers apply a lower discount rate than the stockholders of the potentially acquirable firm. Thus even if the managements of all other firms maximised stockholder welfare, these firms would still be attractive candidates for a takeover raid by a growth-maximising management. The marginal efficiency of investment schedule including external acquisition and merger opportunities is denoted by the curve MEI_T in Figure 5.5. With external acquisition and merger opportunities the total investment of a growth-maximising firm will be I'_{gm} (greater than I_{gm}, the level of internal investment projects).[35]

A direct test of the growth-maximisation theory of mergers is almost impossible to carry out, because it requires information about the non-observable magnitudes of the relative rates of discount of managers and stockholders, as well as about the expected rates of returns. However, the observed pattern of mergers over time as well as the control and running of acquired firms may be compared with the predictions of the three competing hypotheses about the merger decision of firms. In the next section we attempt to summarise the available empirical evidence, and to discuss various observed facts, with the intention of finding out whether these facts can provide support for or refute the competing hypotheses.

V. EMPIRICAL EVIDENCE

In this section we shall examine various studies and other evidence related to the verification of the competing hypotheses pertaining to the explanation of the merger and takeover decision of the firm.

With the exception of a study by Gort,[36] empirical work on mergers has been concentrated on examining certain characteristics of the merger process. The majority of studies do not include formal specifications which would allow testing one hypothesis against another.

In this section the empirical work on mergers will be presented under four headings:

A. The profitability of merged firms.

[35] Note that an acquisition may be financed by newly borrowed funds. However, such loans will be repaid quickly, so that the firm retains its target debt/equity ratio. It is also possible that conglomerates will increase their target leverage, if this will further increase their growth. Lewellen ('A Pure Financial Rationale for the Conglomerate Merger') has suggested that conglomerates have a greater debt capacity. He also cites evidence that conglomerates are in fact more levered than other firms. In either case the intersection of the MEI_T schedule with the supply-of-funds curve will always occur over the flat stretch of the latter, since this part includes not only internally generated funds but also any change in debt necessary to reach the firm's target debt/equity ratio.

[36] Gort, 'An Economic Disturbance Theory of Mergers'.

B. Gort's test of the valuation-discrepancies theory.
C. Studies of the characteristics of the acquired and non-acquired firms.
D. Observed facts and their compatibility with the competing hypotheses of
    profit maximisation *vs* growth maximisation.

A.   Studies of the Profitability of Mergers

We saw that profitability through merger can increase either due to attainment
of market power or the realisation of scale economies.

Three studies of the first merger wave of the turn of the century are of particular interest, because the mergers of that period were predominantly horizontal
mergers which had resulted in a considerable increase in concentration in various
industries, and hence to an increase in the market power of the merged corporations. The question tackled by the researchers was whether the profitability of
the merged entities had increased as a consequence of their increased market
power.

The earliest study in this area was conducted by Arthur Dewing.[37] From a
sample of firms belonging to various industries, Dewing concluded that the
earnings of the merged firm were lower than the earnings of the individual firms
in the first year following the merger; the average earnings of merged firms over
the ten years after merger were less than their earnings during the first post-
merger year; the earnings of the first year were somewhat greater than those of
the tenth year after the merger took place. These findings suggest that the profitability of mergers is lower than that of non-merging firms, and it declines over
time.

Dewing's findings were questioned by Shaw Livermore.[38] Livermore used
two cross-section samples. The first included 156 firms from various industries
which were judged as having achieved a great increase of market power. The
second consisted of 172 firms, which, according to Livermore, had not achieved
a high degree of market control. For the first sample Livermore concluded that
40.4 per cent of the merged firms failed to increase their profitability, 10.9 per
cent were doubtful in their success, and 48.7 per cent were successful in terms of
profitability. The second sample showed similar results: 48.3 per cent of the
mergers were successes in terms of profitability, and 45.3 per cent were failures.
In summary, only half of the mergers of Livermore's study increased their profitability, and this result seems unrelated to the market power attained by the
merged firms.

Nelson's study[39] included thirteen large merged companies of the turn of

[37] Arthur S. Dewing, 'A Statistical Test of the Success of Consolidations', *Quarterly
Journal of Economics*, 1921, pp. 231–58.
    [38] Livermore, 'The Success of Industrial Mergers'.
    [39] Ralph Nelson, *Merger Movements in American Industry, 1895–1956* (Princeton
University Press, 1959).

the century. His conclusions were similar to those of Livermore: approximately half of the mergers were successful, while the other half were considered as failures in terms of profitability.

The above three studies have several shortcomings. The most important is the use of cross-section samples of firms belonging to different industries, without 'keeping constant' inter-industry differences in merger intensity and other characteristics, such as industry growth, concentration, barriers to entry, etc.[40] Despite their shortcomings, however, their common finding that the turn-of-the-century mergers were not particularly profitable, irrespective of the degree of market power attained, does not support the profit-maximisation hypothesis.[41]

Several recent studies reached the same conclusion: merged firms do not seem to have attained increased profitability.

The first study of the post-1945 merger wave was conducted by Kelly,[42] with a sample of twenty-one firms selected from *Fortune*'s 500 largest companies. The sample was divided into two sub-samples, one including firms with high merger activity (i.e. firms which had increased their sales by at least 20 per cent through merger), and the other including firms with little or no merger activity (i.e. firms which had increased their sales through merger by less than 5 per cent). Kelly compared the profitability of these two groups during the 1946—60 period and concluded that 'the form of investment, internal versus external, does not have a significant impact on profitability'. In other words, mergers had no perceptible effect on profitability.

A large-sample study was conducted by Samuel Reid.[43] Reid's study may be considered as an indirect test of the growth-maximisation hypothesis. Reid explored the hypothesis that the intensity of merger activity is more closely related to variables which appear in the managerial utility function (such as sales, assets, number of employees) than to variables appearing in the stockholder utility function (such as profitability, price of common stock, etc.)

Reid worked with a sample of 478 firms from *Fortune*'s list of the 500 largest industrial corporations for the year 1961. These firms had acquired more than 3,300 other firms through merger during the 1951—61 period. Reid divided his sample in four groups depending on the number of mergers that the firms had undertaken. Table 5.4 shows some of Reid's results.

It is evident from these results that merger intensity is positively correlated with growth of sales (a managerial variable), and negatively correlated with profitability and share price (both stockholder variables).

---

[40] See Brian Hindley, 'Recent Theory and Evidence on Corporate Mergers', in Keith Cowling (ed.), *Market Structure and Corporate Behaviour: Theory and Empirical Analysis* (Gray-Mills, 1972).

[41] For a critical evaluation of the results of the pre-war studies see Jesse Markham, 'Survey of the Evidence and Findings on Mergers', in *Business Concentration and Price Policy*, Conference of the Universities/National Bureau Committee for Economic Research (Princeton, 1955).

[42] Eaman Kelly, *The Profitability of Growth Through Mergers* (Pensylvania State University Press, 1967).

[43] Samuel Reid, *Mergers, Managers and the Economy* (McGraw-Hill, 1968).

Table 5.4   A summary of Reid's study

	48 firms (with no mergers)	214 firms (with 1—5 mergers)	142 firms (with 6—10 mergers)	74 firms (with 11 or more mergers)
% increase in sales 1951—61	160	121	201	341
% increase in share price 1951—61	680	230	245	307
% increase in profits (return per $ of 1951 assets) realised by 1951 (original) stockholders	12.1	3.2	2.3	2.2

Reid's study has several shortcomings:

(i) Only one year (1961) is examined, and this year is before the conglomerates became predominant.

(ii) A mere count of the number of acquisitions does not necessarily measure the merger intensity. One large merger, for example, may outweigh many small ones.

(iii) The study ignores inter-industry differences. Edward Heiden, in a paper presented at the annual meeting of the Econometric Society in 1968, reported the results of a study of seventy-five corporations which suggest that the profitability of merged firms had increased, once size of firm, industry concentration and market growth had been taken into account.

Despite its shortcomings, Reid's study provides support for the growth-maximisation hypothesis. The negative relation between merger intensity and profitability shows that managers sacrifice profits in order to attain a higher rate of growth via merger.[44]

A cross-section study of firms from various industries has been recently conducted by Ansoff, Brandenburg, Partner and Radosevich.[45] Their findings are similar to those of Reid. Covering a twenty-year period the writers conclude that 'acquisitions do not pay and, in fact, are an inferior method of growth'. However, the researchers found that high-growth acquirers were distinctly superior to non-acquirers on both price/earnings and price/equity ratios.

---

[44] Scherer, *Industrial Market Structure and Economic Performance*.
[45] H. I. Ansoff, R. G. Brandenburg, F. E. Partner and R. Radosevich, *Acquisition Behaviour of US Manufacturing Firms, 1946—1965* (Vanderbilt University Press, 1971).

The results of the above studies (with the exception of Heiden's) are limited by the fact that the researchers ignored the effects on merger intensity of industry differences. The market structure and growth conditions affect the decision to merge and should be taken into account before reaching valid conclusions about the profitability of mergers. For example, assume that growth-seeking acquiring firms belong to a declining industry, where their assets have a low return (before the merger), while non-acquiring firms (pursuing profit maximisation via internal expansion) belong to growing industries, where profitability is high. If the growth-maximising raiders did not merge with firms in the growing industry, their profitability would be substantially worse than that of non-acquirers. The empirical finding that acquirers and non-acquirers have roughly the same performance may reflect the *high* profitability of acquisition, which offsets the *low* profitability of the raider's original assets.

Such difficulties may be avoided by comparing acquiring and non-acquiring firms *in the same industry*, where presumably all firms are faced with similar conditions and opportunities. This approach has been adopted by several researchers in recent years.

Hogarty conducted three empirical studies on mergers. In one study[46] he examined three measures of profitability of shareholders and the stock price performance of merged corporations. His analysis was based on forty-three corporations which engaged heavily in merger activity during the years 1953–64, randomly selected from the 1965 edition of *Moody's Industrial Manual*. The firms in the sample were widely differing in size (their assets range from \$2 million to over \$700 million) and belonged to twenty-nine (three-digit) industries. Hogarty compared three measures of stockholders' return with corresponding indexes of the average returns of the industry group to which the firm belonged. In this way inter-industry differences were 'kept constant'.

The first measure is the 'total return' accruing to the original stockholder from owning a share. An investor who bought a share in any time period has a total current wealth which consists of two things: (i) the current market price of the share, and (ii) the total cash dividends he has received during the period he owns the share. Thus the return on the money he paid to buy the share is found by dividing this current wealth by the purchase price. In Hogarty's study the return on the money invested in a share of an acquirer is

$$\frac{P_{1964} + \sum_{T=t-1}^{1964} D_T}{P_{t-2}}$$

where t is the year in which the first acquisition was completed. (Hogarty used the price prevailing two years before the merger to eliminate the effects of merger

[46] Thomas F. Hogarty, 'The Profitability of Corporate Mergers', *Journal of Business*, 1970, pp. 317–27.

announcements on market price). This return for the jth firm in the ith industry was compared with the Fisher—Lorie index of return for the same industry. In particular, Hogarty estimated the average difference

$$\left[\left(\frac{P_{1964} + \sum\limits_{T=t-1}^{1964} D_T}{P_{t-2}} \right)_{j,I} - \frac{(F \& L)_{1964,I}}{(F \& L)_{t-2,I}} \right] \bigg/ n$$

where F & L = Fisher—Lorie return index defined by the expression (for any two consecutive periods 0 and 1)

$$\frac{P_1 + D_1}{P_0}$$

and n = number of years between $t - 2$ and 1964.

If the difference is positive, the merger is considered a 'success', since its return is higher than the industry average return. Conversely, if the difference is negative, the merger is considered a failure. Hogarty found that only ten of the forty-three firms in his sample can be considered as successful.

The second measure of return is the earnings per share. Hogarty computed the average difference

$$\left[\left(\frac{EPS_{1964}}{EPS_{t-2}} \right)_j - \frac{ESP (S \& P)_{I,1964}}{ESP (S \& P)_{I,t-2}} \right] \bigg/ n$$

where EPS = earnings per share

EPS (S & P) = Standard & Poor's earnings per share index

j = jth firm

I = ith industry

A positive difference implies a return performance better than the industry average. Hogarty found that sixteen out of thirty-seven merged firms in his sample had a better EPS performance than the industry group.

Finally, Hogarty compared the stock-price index of the jth firm with the Standard & Poor's stock price index of the industry to which the jth firm belonged. He found that twenty out of the forty-three active acquirers of his sample performed better than the industry average.

The above results provide strong evidence against the stockholder-wealth-maximisation hypothesis. On the grounds of the first finding of this study we can conclude that the return to original stockholders of heavily merging firms is generally worse than the average return of firms in their respective industries. On the basis of the other two tests we may conclude that mergers have at best a neutral impact on the profitability (EPS) and the capital gains of original stockholders. In summary, mergers do not benefit original stockholders.

In another study[47] Hogarty attempted to test the hypothesis that managers

---

[47] Hogarty, 'Profits from Mergers: The Evidence of Fifty Years'.

pursue sales growth via merger at the sacrifice of profits. For this he compared the actual sales of the merged entity with an estimate of the aggregate sales that the individual firms would have realised in the absence of merger. From a sample of forty-one firms Hogarty found that in only fifteen cases were the sales of the merged firm greater than the sum of the sales that could 'reasonably' have been expected from the individual firms without the merger.

Although this finding does not support the growth-maximisation hypothesis, it does not refute it either. With merger the absolute size of the firm increases, and there is substantial evidence that size yields a positive utility to managers, not only because it is related positively to the pecuniary and non-pecuniary rewards that managers pursue, but also because size is a deterrent to takeover raiders and hence enhances managerial job security, which, according to managerialist theorists (e.g. Marris and Galbraith),[48] is the most important argument of the managerial utility function.

It should also be stressed that the measure of probable sales of the merged firms in the absence of merger used by Hogarty can be questioned on several grounds. Thus the findings of his study are rather limited.

In another study Gort and Hogarty[49] found that 'most mergers do not appear to raise the value of the combined properties of the merging firms'. Using the Fisher—Lorie industry-return indexes, the researchers argue that merger has a roughly neutral effect on the profitability of the joined firms. However, 'while most acquirers did not profit from merger, the stockholders of most of the selling firms gained by the acquisition'. In other words, mergers tend to result in a net transfer of wealth from the owners of buying firms to the owners of the sellers.

Ajit Singh,[50] in a recent study of takeovers in five UK manufacturing industries, found that acquirers are not significantly more profitable than non-acquirers. When inter-industry differences are 'kept constant', merger activity does not have a perceptible effect on profitability. However, acquiring firms had a higher rate of growth and all the other attributes associated with growth-maximisers: higher retention ratio, higher gearing ratio and less liquidity. Thus Singh's results seem to support the growth-maximisation hypothesis: raiders and non-merging firms have similar profitability records (in the same industry), but the former have a higher rate of growth. Apparently the goal of growth-maximisation does not adversely affect the profitability of raiders relative to non-merging firms.

Singh also investigated the profitability of merged firms after acquisition. The profitability (on assets) of each acquiring firm after acquisition was compared with the combined profitability of both the acquiring and the acquired firm before amalgamation. To take into account industry effects as well as the effects

[48] Marris, *The Theory of 'Managerial' Capitalism*; Galbraith, *Economics and the Public Purpose*.

[49] Michael Gort and Thomas F. Hogarty, 'New Evidence on Mergers', *Journal of Law and Economics*, 1970, pp. 167—84.

[50] Ajit Singh, *Take-overs* (Cambridge University Press, 1971) pp. 158—66.

on profitability of the general state of the economy, Singh divided the firm's
profitability by the average profitability of firms in the same industry/year. Thus,
in fact, Singh compared the *relative* profitability of an acquiring firm in the year
of acquisition and for one and two years after acquisition with the combined
(weighted average) relative profitability of both the acquiring and the acquired
firm before acquisition. His results show that both for the individual industries
and for all industries together there was in the majority of cases a decline in the
relative profitability of the acquiring firms over time. For three years after
acquisition, 77 per cent of all firms showed a decline in relative profitability.
Singh considers the one- or two-year period after merger as 'optimal', in the sense
that a shorter period may be inadequate for the full absorption of the acquired
entity, while a longer period might involve more acquisitions and external developments in the industry or the economy which could affect the firm's profitability. Singh concludes that although the more dynamic and 'efficient' firms
tend to acquire the relatively weak and inefficient ones, in at least half of the
cases there is a fall in profitability (on either the combined assets of the amal-
gamating firms, or the assets of the acquiring firms). Thus mergers do not
increase profitability:

> The weight of the evidence indicates that the take-over process is at best
> neutral in this respect. It could be argued, however, that some of the acquiring
> firms whose relative profitability falls after take-over are sacrificing profits to
> growth. It is possible that these firms might have been able to maintain their
> profitability records if they had not indulged in take-overs.

In summary, Singh's study can be considered as providing some evidence in
support of the growth-maximisation hypothesis.

B. Gort's Test of the Valuation-Discrepancies Theory of Merger

Gort's[51] is the only empirical study designed to test the valuation-discrepancies
hypothesis against two versions of the profit-maximisation hypothesis: the
'reduced competition' (or 'increased market power') hypothesis, and the 'economies of scale' hypothesis.

Gort adopted the following empirical specifications for the three hypotheses
that he wanted to test.

(i) *The test of the 'valuation-discrepancies' hypothesis*

We saw that in Gort's theory merger activity is determined by the rate of technological change, the growth of industry demand, changes in stock prices, industry

---

[51] Gort, 'An Economic Disturbance Theory of Mergers'.

concentration and entry barriers. Rapid movement in stock prices, as well as fast technical change and market growth, render the 'stock of knowledge' of investors obsolete and give rise to a random re-ordering of expectations of individuals. As a result, some shareholders will come to value the assets of the firm less highly than other investors in the market, and these discrepancies in valuation of firms lead to mergers.

The empirical specification of the valuation-discrepancies hypothesis adopted by Gort is

$$Y = b_0 + b_1 T + b_2 G + b_3 P + b_4 C + u$$

where Y = merger rate, measured by the ratio of acquisitions in an industry divided by the total number of firms in the industry

T = a measure of technological change

G = industry growth rate, measured by an index of physical production

P = share price

C = concentration ratio, measured by the proportion of industry output produced by the four largest producers (C is considered to reflect the influence of concentration as well as of entry barriers)

On the basis of his theory Gort expected

$$b_1 > 0; \quad b_2 > 0; \quad b_3 > 0; \quad b_4 > 0$$

Gort estimated the above model by OLS, using a cross-industry sample of forty-six observations, obtained by classifying 5,534 acquisitions (listed by the US Federal Trade Commission during the years 1951–9) by industry at the three-digit level of detail. The acquisitions cover large firms (with assets exceeding $500,000). Gort estimates that these acquisitions represent 65–80 per cent of *all* acquisitions in manufacturing industries. This implies that mergers and acquisitions are taking place mostly among large firms. (This fact has further implications for the various competing hypotheses of merger, and will be discussed in some detail in the next section.)

Gort experimented with various measures and combinations of independent variables. His 'best' regression was

$$\hat{Y} = -1.6426 + 0.0373T + 0.0591G + 0.4393C$$

s.e. (4.52)   (0.01)   (0.03)   (0.10)

$$R^2 = 0.70, n = 46$$

The coefficient estimates are statistically significant and the explanatory power of the regression is fairly high.

Gort was unable to introduce stock prices in his model due to lack of data. However, he refers to two other studies which established a positive relation between stock prices and merger intensity. Nelson,[52] using quarterly data for

[52] Nelson, *Merger Moverments in American Industry, 1895–1956.*

1895–1904, found a strong positive correlation between an index of industrial stock prices and the number of mergers. Weston[53] obtained the same result for the interwar period using annual data.

On the basis of his own estimated regression and the above two studies Gort concludes that the evidence supports his valuation-discrepancies theory.

Although the estimated regression gives a fairly good statistical fit, the omission of stock prices is bound to give rise to some mis-specification bias to the parameter estimates. Furthermore, the results of Nelson and Weston cannot be accepted as a verification of Gort's hypothesis, because correlation does not necessarily imply causation.[54]

(ii) *The test of the 'monopoly-power' hypothesis*

To derive a suitable empirical specification for the 'reduced-competition' hypothesis, Gort argues as follows.

(1) An increase in market power is likely to be attained if the industry has a fairly high degree of concentration. If there are many firms in an industry (low concentration), a few acquisitions are not likely to give rise to increased market power. Similarly, if there are barriers to entry, mergers will be enhanced, because the excess profits enjoyed from the reduced competition will be likely to continue post-merger. If the concentration ratio is an indication of monopoly power and barriers to entry, one would expect a positive relation between the merger rate and the concentration ratio.

(2) If the goal of mergers is to increase market power, one would expect a positive relationship between the rate of merger and the *change in the concentration* of firms in an industry.

(3) Market growth is expected to be negatively related to merger intensity if the goal of merger is the attainment of increased market power. This is explained as follows. The firm's profits increase by growth, which can be attained either internally or externally through merger. In either case the firm would not like to cause a fall in price if its goal is the reaping of monopoly profits. In a growing industry a firm will find it easier to grow by adding to its capacity (i.e. grow internally) without depressing the market price. In a stagnant market, however, any addition to existing capacity is bound to lead to a decrease in price. To avoid this effect firms will tend to grow through merger in markets which do not expand. Hence the negative relation between market growth and the merger rate.

On the basis of the above reasoning Gort adopted the following specification

[53] J. Fred Weston, *The Role of Mergers in the Growth of Large Firms* (University of California Press, 1953).

[54] See A. Koutsoyiannis, *Theory of Econometrics*, 2nd edn (Macmillan, 1977) chs 3 and 11. The same criticism is raised by Hindley, 'Recent Theory and Evidence on Corporate Mergers'.

for the 'reduced-competition' hypothesis:

$$Y = a_0 + a_1 C + a_2 \frac{\Delta C}{C} + a_3 G + u$$

With $a_1 > 0; a_2 > 0; a_3 < 0$. From the same data sources Gort obtained a sample of 101 three-digit industry observations, from which he estimated the above model. His chosen function was

$$\hat{\hat{Y}} = -0.9672 + 0.4279C - 3.8790 \frac{\Delta C}{C} + 0.1425G$$

s.e.   (9.44)   (0.073)   (7.938)   (0.025)

$R^2 = 0.414, n = 101$

Given the 'wrong' signs of the coefficients of G (growth) and $\Delta C/C$ (change in concentration ratio), Gort concludes that his sample refutes the 'monopoly-power' hypothesis.

It does not seem that the empirical specification adopted by Gort is suitable for testing the 'reduced-competition' hypothesis. In particular, Gort's argument about the negative relation between the rate of mergers and the growth of the market ignores the direct positive effect of growth on the merger rate. Acquiring firms will prefer to merge with firms in growing markets. Gort attempts to capture the relation between merger activity and the price of the commodity via the growth rate. Given the expected direct positive relation between market growth and merger activity, Gort's findings are not surprising. Furthermore, the change in concentration is the result rather than the cause of the merger activity. Hence inclusion of the variable $\Delta C/C$ in the set of regressors seems inappropriate.

(iii) *The test of the 'economies-of-scale' hypothesis*

Gort postulates that if mergers were aimed at the realisation of economies of scale, one would expect a positive relation between the rate of merger and the change in the average size of firm. Furthermore, the rate of merger should be positively related to entry conditions as measured by the change in the number of firms in the industry: the larger the number of *new* firms (i.e. the lower the entry barriers), the higher the likelihood that these firms will be entering at inefficient scales (*ceteris paribus*), and hence the greater the incentive for merger (of the inefficient small firms).

Finally, the rate of merger would be negatively related to the growth of the industry, if economies of scale were the goal of merging. This is so, Gort argues, because with rapidly growing demand it is easier to reach the minimum optimal scale through construction of new capacity (internal expansion), while in a stagnant industry firms of sub-optimal scale could grow only via merger.

Based on the above arguments Gort adopted the following empirical specification for testing the 'economies-of-scale' hypothesis:

$$Y = \beta_0 + \beta_1 \frac{\Delta A}{A} + \beta_2 \frac{\Delta N}{N} + \beta_3 G + u$$

where $\Delta A/A$ = change in average size of firm
   $\Delta N/N$ = change in number of firms
   $\beta_1 > 0; \quad \beta_2 > 0; \quad \beta_3 < 0$

Gort's regression analysis (from his sample of 101 industry observations) gave the following results:

$$\hat{\hat{Y}} = 1.1421 + 8.3015 \frac{\Delta A}{A} - 7.5302 \frac{\Delta N}{N} + 0.1786 G$$

s.e. (6.99)   (4.141)   (4.297)   (0.036)

$R^2 = 0.261, n = 101$

Gort rejected the 'economies-of-scale' hypothesis on the grounds that the coefficients of growth (G) and change in the number of firms ($\Delta N/N$) appeared with the 'wrong' sign.

It seems that Gort's specification of the 'economies-of-scale' hypothesis has several shortcomings.

(1) The measurement of entry introduces a spurious negative relation between this variable and the rate of merger. In particular Gort measures entry by the ratio

$$\frac{N + E - M}{N}$$

where N = initial number of firms in the industry
   E = number of *new* entrants in the industry
   M = number of amalgamations within the industry.

Since the dependent variable, the rate of merger, is

$$\frac{M + C}{N}$$

(where C is the number of acquisitions within the industry) a negative regression coefficient is not surprising.[55]

(2) The omission of the concentration ratio is surprising, given that it is a 'noise' variable in cross-industry samples.

(3) Gort's reasoning about the negative sign of market growth may be valid for horizontal mergers but it is not for conglomerate mergers, which are the predominant form of merger in the post-war period.

[55] See Hindley, 'Recent Theory and Evidence on Corporate Mergers'.

(4) The same criticism holds for the change in the number of firms: Gort's argument is valid for horizontal mergers but not for conglomerates.

In summary, Gort's disposal of the 'monopoly-power' and 'economies-of-scale' hypotheses is not convincing, given the serious misspecification of his respective empirical models.

C. Studies of the Characteristics of Acquired versus Non-Acquired Firms

A number of researchers have attempted to explore the various hypotheses about the determinants of the merger and takeover decision of the firm by studying the characteristics of firms that have been taken over and firms which have not been taken over.

Two extensive studies of takeovers in the United Kingdom are of particular interest because they reach similar conclusions, even though they use different approaches and statistical methods. Both studies concentrate on mergers and takeovers during the late 1950s and 1960s. In the United Kingdom most of the acquisitions and mergers were of the horizontal type during that period, and hence the findings of these studies are of great importance for the controversy about the goals of management.

The studies were conducted by Ajit Singh[56] and Douglas Kuehn.[57] The researchers examined the factors that determine the chance (probability) of being taken over. Both were greatly influenced by Robin Marris's *Theory of 'Managerial' Capitalism*, in which the threat of takeover is considered as a constraint on the managerial discretion to pursue growth at the sacrifice of profit.

Both Singh and Kuehn adopt as the theoretical framework of their research Marris's theory of merger. Marris postulates that the various causes for mergers and takeovers (suggested by different writers) can be subsumed and conceptualised in one variable, the valuation ratio, defined as

$$v = \frac{\text{Market value of the firm's equity}}{\text{Book value of the firm's equity assets}}$$

The denominator reflects the value of the resources employed by the firm, while the numerator expresses the market's valuation of the earning potential of these resources. According to Marris, an acquisition will take place if there is a valuation discrepancy, that is, if the acquiring firm A puts a higher valuation ratio on the acquired firm B than the market (M) does, that is, when

$$v_B^A > v_B^M$$

---

[56] Singh, *Take-overs.*
[57] Kuehn, *Take-overs and the Theory of the Firm* (Macmillan, 1975).

where v_B^A = valuation ratio of firm B as perceived by firm A
       v_B^M = valuation ratio of firm B as perceived by the capital market

If the capital market is perfect, $v = 1$. But with market imperfections $v \neq 1$ for most publicly quoted firms.

In this form Marris's theory cannot be tested, because the subjective valuation ratio (v_B^A) is not observable.

However, Marris uses the threat of takeover as a constraint on the discretion of managers to pursue growth and deviate from profit maximisation (or stockholder-welfare maximisation). Marris posits an inverse relationship between the valuation ratio and the threat of takeover: the lower the valuation ratio, the greater the probability of being taken over. Marris also states that unless the firm attains a certain level of its valuation ratio it is bound to be taken over. The inverse relation postulated by Marris can be tested by an appropriate comparison of the valuation ratio of taken-over and not-taken-over firms. This approach has been adopted by both Singh and Kuehn.

(i) *Kuehn's study*

Kuehn used a sample of 3,566 companies (out of a total population of 4,057 companies quoted on the UK stock exchange market). Annual data for all the companies were collected for the thirteen-year period 1957–69.

Kuehn conducted two studies, an aggregate study of all 3,566 firms, and an industry study in which the 3,566 firms were classified in sixty-seven industries.

(a) *Industry analysis: 'The valuation-ratio model'*

For each of the sixty-seven industries Kuehn estimated (by OLS) the model

$$Z = a_0 + a_1 v + a_2 S + u$$

where Z = a dummy variable with values, $Z = 1$ for a firm that has been taken
       over, $Z = 0$ for a firm that has *not* been taken over
    v = valuation ratio
    S = size (assets) of the firm

This technique is known as a *linear probability function*. The estimated value of the dependent variable (Z) is an estimate of the probability of the firm being taken over.

On the basis of Marris's hypothesis, the sign of the coefficient of v is expected to be negative.

Similarly, the sign of the coefficient of size, S, is expected to be negative, on the grounds that the larger the firm, the fewer the number of potential raiders, and the greater the financial and organisational difficulties that its acquisition posits.

From this study Kuehn found that the coefficient of the valuation ratio had the expected negative sign and was statistically significant in most industries. The coefficient of size had the 'correct' negative sign in all but ten industries, but its statistical significance was very poor. Kuehn concluded that the valuation ratio is an important determinant of the probability of being taken over, while 'size' was a rather weak explanatory variable.

The negative relationship between the valuation ratio and the probability of being taken over is compatible with both the profit-maximisation and the growth-maximisation hypotheses. This relationship is a necessary condition for Marris's and the other managerialist theories, but not a sufficient one, because one would also expect a profit-maximising firm to choose undervalued firms as takeover candidates on the expectation of increasing the stockholder-wealth after the merger. Only if the inverse relation were perfect would the managerialist theories be invalidated. An imperfect relationship satisfies a necessary condition of the Marris hypothesis but does not give any guide as to whether the goal of managers is profit maximisation, growth maximisation or something else.

The low explanatory power of Kuehn's regressions imply that the takeover mechanism is 'inefficient', in the sense that there are many additional determinants (apart from v and S) of the probability of being taken over. There is a large number of firms with low v which were *not* taken over, as well as a large number of firms with a high v which were taken over. This, according to Hindley,[58] is evidence against both the growth-maximisation and the profit-maximisation hypotheses. Hindley bases his thesis on the view that growth-maximisers should be more eager to acquire undervalued firms (i.e. firms with low v) than profit-maximisers, so that presumably for undervalued firms to survive suggests that neither goal is commonly pursued by most firms. Hindley states that: 'Demonstration of an inefficient takeover system would therefore be a major step towards rejecting growth-maximising models in favour of some form of non-aggressive "easy-life" managerial model of the firm.'

(b) Industry analysis: the 'financial-characteristics model'

Kuehn also estimated (for each of the sixty-seven industries) a linear probability function in which the valuation ratio was replaced by its determinants, which, according to Kuehn, are: profit rate, growth rate, retention ratio and liquidity ratio. Thus the second model estimated by Kuehn is

$$Z = b_0 + b_1(PR) + b_2(g) + b_3(RR) + b_4(LR) + u$$

where Z = the dichotomous variable earlier defined
     g = growth rate
   PR = profit rate
   RR = retention ratio
   LR = liquidity ratio

[58] Hindley, 'Recent Theory and Evidence on Corporate Mergers'.

On *a priori* grounds Kuehn expects

$$b_1 < 0; \quad b_2 < 0; \quad b_3 > 0; \quad b_4 > 0$$

It is surprising that Kuehn did not include leverage and firm size in this model.

Kuehn found that: (a) profits or growth or both appear to be significant determinants of takeover; (b) the firm's retention ratio is a weak explanatory variable; (c) the liquidity ratio appears with a negative sign, contrary to Kuehn's original expectations. However, Kuehn accepts this result on the basis of an 'obscure' explanation, which makes him change his mind. Marris[59] argues that the sign of the liquidity ratio is indeterminate on *a priori* grounds. It is surprising that Kuehn did not draw on Marris's arguments regarding the liquidity of the firm.

(c) Kuehn's aggregate analysis

In this study all 3,566 firms are considered as a single sample, on the expectation that inter-industry differences are random and hence will be absorbed by the disturbance term u. Kuehn uses probit analysis, which yields fifteen grouped observations. Using these grouped data Kuehn estimated again his 'valuation-ratio model' (omitting 'size', S, on the grounds that it was insignificant in the industry analysis), as well as his 'financial-characteristics model'.

The results of the aggregate analysis reinforce those obtained from the industry analysis. Thus: (a) the valuation ratio emerges as an important determinant of the probability of takeover; (b) profitability and growth are important determinants in the second model; (c) retentions and liquidity fail to emerge as significant influences on whether or not a firm will be taken over; and (d) inter-industry differences are not important in the takeover mechanism. Kuehn concludes that variables significant in the linear probability models continue to be significant when industry classes are ignored in the probit models.

Kuehn maintains that these results, while revealing some of the determinants of the takeover activity, do not throw any light on the controversial issue of the goal of the managers of large corporations.

To test the profit-maximisation hypothesis *vs* the growth-maximisation hypothesis he selects a sample of 117 raiders which had undertaken three or more successful raids within the sample period. Kuehn next sets out predictions about the proportion of raiders expected to achieve values of three financial variables (g, PR, RR), and of the valuation ratio greater or less than that of the industry median for the two alternative goals. We will not examine these predictions in detail, as some of them appear dubious on theoretical grounds. We only mention that from the comparison of the proportions obtained from the sample of 117 firms to the 'predicted' proportions, Kuehn concludes that the evidence

[59] R. Marris, 'A Model of the Managerial Enterprise', *Quarterly Journal of Economics*, 1963.

is consistent with the growth-maximisation hypothesis. Raiders tend to have a higher rate of growth, lower profitability, lower retentions (higher dividend payout ratios), but similar valuation ratios as compared with the corresponding median industry values.

Kuehn's general conclusion is that firms are growth-maximisers, and they attain growth via mergers:

> raiding leads to growth, security through safe levels of the valuation ratio, and size, all of which are valued for themselves by managers and also for the rewards, both pecuniary and non-pecuniary associated with growth and size.[60]

(ii) *Singh's study*

Singh applied *discriminant analysis*[61] to test the null hypothesis that there is no difference between the valuation ratio and the economic and financial characteristics of taken-over and not-taken-over firms.

Singh compared the two groups of firms in five UK industries during the 1954—60 period. The industries studied were: food, drink, non-electrical engineering, clothing and footwear, and electrical engineering. By adopting the industry approach, Singh eliminates the influence of inter-industry differences on the takeover mechanism.

Singh compared the two groups of firms (acquired and non-acquired) on the basis of the following variables:

Profit rate
Size (assets)
Growth of assets
Liquidity ratio
Debt/equity ratio (leverage)
Retention ratio
Valuation ratio

Profitability and growth are, according to Singh, measures of the past performance of the firm. On *a priori* grounds these variables should be negatively related to the probability of being taken over.

The liquidity ratio, the debt/equity ratio and the retention ratio are the financial characteristics of the firm. On *a priori* grounds leverage and retentions should be positively related to the likelihood of being taken over. Regarding liquidity, Singh, like Marris, argues that on theoretical grounds the relationship

---

[60] Kuehn, *Take-overs and the Theory of the Firm*, p. 152.

[61] It has been proved that discriminant analysis is formally equivalent to the linear probability function. See R. A. Fisher, *Statistical Methods for Research Workers*, 9th edn (Blackwell, 1944). Also G. W. Ladd, 'Linear Probability Functions and Discriminant Functions', *Econometrica*, 1966.

between the probability of being taken over and the liquidity ratio can be either positive or negative.

Size, according to Singh, acts as a deterrent to takeover raids. Large companies are more expensive to acquire and more difficult to absorb in the existing organisation of the acquiring company. Hence the larger the firm, the smaller the probability of being taken over, *ceteris paribus*. The relationship between size and the probability of being taken over is expected to be negative.

The valuation ratio is considered by Singh as a measure of the future expected performance of the firm. Singh, following Marris, expects a negative relationship between v and the probability of being taken over. It should be noted that although Singh is correct in postulating the above relationship, he seems to ignore the fact that the valuation ratio is to a large extent determined by the other variables in his analysis. Thus v should not be included in the set of discriminant factors.

In a univariate analysis (in which firms were grouped on the basis of one factor at a time) Singh found that:

(1) The taken-over firms on the whole had a worse performance than not-taken-over firms in terms of profitability, growth and valuation ratio.
(2) The average taken-over firm was significantly smaller than the average not-taken-over firm.
(3) Taken-over firms had a significantly greater proportion of their profits retained as compared with not-taken-over firms.
(4) With respect to liquidity and leverage, the two groups of firms were statistically indistinguishable.

In summary, Singh's univariate analysis suggests that the most important determinants of takeover are profitability, size, growth, retention ratio and valuation ratio. Leverage and liquidity did not emerge as significant discriminating factors of the two groups of firms.

However, there was a big overlap between the two groups. A large number of firms with above-average valuation ratios had been taken over. Similarly, a large number of firms with below-average valuation ratio were not taken over. This suggests that the takeover mechanism of the stock market is far from perfect.

In a multivariate analysis Singh found that size and profitability (and to a lesser extent growth) were the only important discriminating factors of the two groups of firms. Singh analyses these two factors separately in great detail. His conclusions may be summarised as follows.

(a) Size

The comparison of the two groups of firms revealed a negative non-linear relation between size of the firm and probability of acquisition. For small and medium-sized firms the probability of acquisition declined only slightly with an increase in size, while for the large firms the probability of being taken over (i) was much smaller and (ii) declined sharply and monotonically with an increase in firm size.

(b) Profitability

(1) Short-run profitability. In general there is a negative relation between profitability in the short run and the probability of being taken over. However, this relation is not monotonic, but has a peculiar non-linear shape: for very small firms with a poor profitability record and for very large firms (with a high profit rate) the negative relation between profitability and probability of acquisition is clear. There is, however, a wide range of in-between profitability over which the probability of being taken over remains practically constant. This implies that once firms have reached a 'satisfactory' level of profits, their chance of survival increases very little with an increase in profitability.

In sum, there is at work in the capital market a selection (survival) mechanism, on the basis of profitability, for firms which have extremely low or extremely high profitability. But for a very large number of firms with in-between profits the selection on the basis of profitability does not work. However, there is a large number of firms with excellent profitability records which are acquired, and a large number of firms with very poor profitability that survive. These results suggest that the takeover mechanism is imperfect: not all firms are induced (by the threat of takeover) to pursue profit maximisation.

Singh's analysis of profitability of acquirers and non-acquirers provides strong evidence against the profit-maximisation hypothesis. The existence of a wide profitability range over which the probability of acquisition is almost constant shows that firms, once they have reached the lower part of this profitability range, are not under any pressure to increase their profit further in order to reduce the danger of takeover. On the other hand, these results seem to support the managerialist theories which postulate that once the firms have achieved a certain 'satisfactory' level of profit, they are able to pursue growth or whatever goals they want without greatly affecting the risk of takeover.

(2) Long-run profitability. Examining the long-run profitability of the two groups of firms Singh found that: (i) the probability of being taken over is the same for *all* firms that have a profitability below the industry median profitability; (ii) the probability of being taken over is the same for *all* firms with above the median profitability, but this probability is half that for firms with below-average profitability.

These findings suggest that while for firms which already have average profitability there is no incentive to increase profit further in order to avoid being taken over, firms with lower than average profitability have a reasonably strong incentive to increase profit. Thus in the long run the takeover mechanism provides some discipline for firms with a below-average record of long-term profits.

(c) Profitability and size

The results from the separate analyses of size and profitability led Singh to the following 'joint' conclusions.

Given the ample evidence that there is little relationship between size and profitability of firms, Singh suggests that his findings relating to size, in conjunction with the findings relating to profitability, lead to the following general conclusions about the best strategies for survival (not being taken over) for firms of various sizes. First, for most *small* firms with a poor record of long-run profitability the best strategy is to improve their profits performance to a level above the industry average. (The alternative course of increasing size is not of much use to such firms, since they would have to become several times larger before they could attain any substantial reduction in the chances of being acquired.) It should be stressed that it is necessary for this improvement in profitability to be continuous, since a temporary (short-run) improvement for a year or two would make the firm more vulnerable in the future. Second, for *large* firms with a poor record of long-run profits the best strategy (in order to survive) is to increase their size. The alternative strategy of increasing profitability would not reduce appreciably the probability of being taken over, unless the large firms attained a very large proportionate increase in their rate of profit. Unlike the small firms, large firms will find it easy to increase their chances of survival by becoming bigger. The increase in size need not be large, since the probability of acquisition for these firms falls sharply and continuously with an increase in firm size. The evidence clearly indicates that it is in general possible for large firms to decrease their chances of acquisition, while maintaining their poor profitability record or even with a worse profitability, provided that they can achieve a sufficient increase in size.

To sum up. The takeover mechanism on the stock market provides a measure of discipline, i.e. an inducement to increase profitability for small firms with low profitability. In other words, such firms must maximise profit in order to survive. However, large firms are not subject to such market discipline. Large firms are not compelled to maximise profit (or pursue profits vigorously) in order to reduce the danger of takeover, since they can achieve this objective by becoming larger, without increasing their profitability. Thus the results of Singh's study support the growth-maximisation hypothesis of mergers (and the managerialist school). Large firms pursue growth via a merger in order to avoid a takeover raid. The threat of takeover, rather than being a constraint on managerial discretion, encourages firms to grow bigger and faster.

Singh's findings show that the capital market is not perfect. There is a basic asymmetry in the takeover process in the real world. With given rates of profit it is much easier for a large firm to acquire a small one than the other way around. As a large firm becomes bigger, it becomes more immune to takeover: the potential raiders require more funds and face more difficulties in assimilating such big acquisitions in their organisation. This assymetry makes it possible for large firms to deviate from profit maximisation.

The stock market, through its takover mechanism, is a poor disciplinarian: it provides a measure of discipline for small firms with low profitability. However, small firms which have attained a 'satisfactory' level of profit are not forced or induced by the takeover mechanism to be profit-maximisers.

Large firms (and medium-sized firms) with low profitability can more easily reduce the chances of takeover by pursuing growth rather than profit.

Over all, Singh's study provides evidence against the profit-maximisation hypothesis, and in support of the growth-maximisation hypothesis.

D. Observed Facts and their Compatibility with the Competing Hypotheses

The shortcomings of Gort's empirical study show the difficulties encountered when one attempts to test one hypothesis against another. It is almost impossible to test rigorously the growth-maximisation and the stockholder-welfare-maximisation hypotheses and discriminate between them,[62] because the variables required for such a test are the subjective expected profitabilities and discount rates of the managers and stockholders, which are non-observable. However, Mueller[63] argues that the observed recent developments in merger activity can be explained by the growth-maximisation hypothesis, while they are mostly incompatible with the predictions of the profit-maximisation hypothesis.

(1) Firms with synergistic and economies-of-scale potential will be the first to be acquired, either by a profit-maximising or by a growth-maximising management. Once synergistic merger opportunities are exhausted, the profit-maximisation hypothesis predicts that merger frequency (activity) would decline, while the growth-maximisation hypothesis predicts that no such decline will take place. Instead, the *direction* of a firm's acquisition efforts will change: that is, the growth-maximising firm will turn to mergers and acquisitions of firms with no synergistic potential (after such opportunities have dried up). Given the intensive merger activity since the turn of the century, one may well argue that synergistic opportunities have been greatly depleted. Yet merger activity has intensified. This is consistent with the growth-maximisation hypothesis, but not with the profit-maximisation hypothesis.

(2) The anti-trust laws have effectively blocked horizontal mergers. There is a *per se* prohibition of mergers which may lead to a moderate or even small restriction of competition, and arguments of economies of scale are not any more easily accepted as a justification for mergers. Under these conditions the profit-maximisation hypothesis predicts a decline in the frequency of merger, which has not been observed. In 1966 mergers were taking place at roughly nine times the rate that had immediately preceded the Second World War, and at two and a half times the level of the 1946–7 peak. The main impact of the anti-trust legisla-

---

[62] John R. Meyer, 'An Experiment in the Measurement of Business Motivation', *Review of Economics and Statistics*, 1967.

[63] Mueller, 'A Theory of Conglomerate Mergers', pp. 657–9.

tion appears to have been to substitute conglomerate for horizontal mergers (see Table 5.1, p. 231). These developments seem to be consistent with the growth-maximisation hypothesis.

(3) In recent years acquisitions have increasingly taken the form of takeovers rather than mergers. Recall that mergers are usually agreed between the managements of the merging firms, while takeovers take place through a direct cash tender offer to the stockholders of the acquired firm, often against the will of the defensive management. Between 1962 and 1965 the ratio of stock takeovers to the total number of mergers more than doubled.[64] This development suggests that opportunities for mergers with firms whose management has a high discount rate (due, for example, to approaching retirement age, or extremely cautious attitudes) have been greatly depleted. The increase in takeover activity is compatible with the growth-maximisation hypothesis, which postulates that managers have a lower discount rate than stockholders, and hence all firms are attractive buys at their stockholder selling price. The increase in takeover frequency (relative to merger frequency) cannot be explained adequately by the profit-maximisation hypothesis, which requires that the managers of the acquired firms have a higher discount rate than the managers of the acquiring firm.

(4) In the post-war period merger activity (rate of) has been higher for large-size firms as compared with small and medium-size firms. One of the major causes of merger, according to the profit-maximisation hypothesis, is the realisation of scale economies. Thus this hypothesis predicts that the rate of merger activity would be higher between small firms than between large firms because it is the small firms which will attain such economies by merging. The post-war history of mergers contradicts this prediction.[65] On the other hand, the growth-maximisation hypothesis can explain this development.

(a) If firms are growth-maximisers, it is the largest firms which can pursue this goal more successfully, since few other firms will have the financial resources to attempt to acquire them. Small and medium-sized firms will have to pursue stockholder-welfare-maximising behaviour to a greater extent, in order to try to keep the stock price up and thereby avoid takeover raids.

(b) The largest firms will also be the more mature ones, having exhausted internal profitable investment opportunities, and hence looking to outside opportunities (mergers and acquisitions) to achieve growth. Thus the growth-maximisation hypothesis provides the theoretical explanation of the observed higher rate of mergers between large firms.[66]

[64] Ibid, p. 658.

[65] Gort ('An Economic Disturbance Theory of Mergers', p. 632) states that according to the US Internal Revenue Service, about four-fifths of all manufacturing firms had assets of less than $500,000 in the mid-1950s. The Federal Trade Commission reported mergers for firms with assets exceeding $500,000; these mergers accounted for more than 65—80 per cent of all merger activity. Hence the merger rate for small firms must have been very much less than for larger firms, and in absolute terms, quite low.

[66] John McGowan found that the proportion of a firm's growth which stems from mergers is positively related to the size of the firm. See J. McGowan, 'The Effect of Alternative Antimerger Policies on the Size Distribution of Firms', *Yale Economic Essays*, vol. V, Autumn 1965.

(5) It has been observed that some of the most aggressive conglomerate merger firms look for companies whose managements are able and willing to continue to run the acquired company after it has been assimilated into the conglomerate's organisational structure.[67] Empirical studies have found that less than half of the board of directors has been replaced within the first two years after the acquisition.[68] These findings are contrary to the 'managerial economies' predicted by the profit-maximisation hypothesis. If this hypothesis were correct, one would expect that the conglomerate's managers would dismiss the management of the acquired firm, in the belief that they would be more successful in running the newly acquired entity. That such mass dismissals have not been observed suggests that the management of the growth-maximising conglomerate is aware that it does not have the 'super-managerial skills' implied by the profit-maximisation hypothesis. The fact that the conglomerate lets the existing, experienced management continue to run the acquired firm provides evidence that conglomerate mergers do not attain managerial economies. This is evidence against the profit-maximisation hypothesis, while it is not inconsistent with the growth-maximisation hypothesis.[69]

(6) The growth-maximisation hypothesis can provide a rational explanation of the acquisition of small firms that are short of cheap finance. The profit-maximisation hypothesis cannot explain such mergers and acquisitions. If small firms need cheap finance, a profit-maximising management would not acquire them, but would instead buy some of the small firms' new stock or bond issues, since this is much less costly than the acquisition of the entire firm. However, if management is growth-orientated it will be willing to finance the operations of the small firms only after their acquisition. Buying bonds or stocks of smaller firms does not contribute to the growth of the (acquiring) company. Only after the two firms have been merged and the small company's investment opportunities have been internalised will the managers of the acquiring firm supply it with its low-cost capital, because the acquisition *does* contribute to the growth of the acquiring firm.

---

[67] Gilbert Burck, 'The Perils of the Multi-Market Corporation', *Fortune*, vol. LXXV February 1967.

[68] Singh, *Takeovers*, pp. 147–9. The actual replacement of members of the board of directors must be even smaller than that reported by Singh, since his study is based on a simple comparison of the constitution of the boards of directors prior to merger. A change in members may be attributed to several factors other than deliberate dismissal by the acquirer, for example death of a director, ageing, voluntary retirement, etc.

[69] See Mueller, 'A Theory of Conglomerate Mergers'.

6. Growth by Vertical Integration

I. BASIC CONCEPTS AND DEFINITIONS

Vertical integration is widespread. Nearly all firms engage in more than one stage of the same productive process. An example is the steel industry, where the larger firms embrace all stages of production: mining, shipping ores, blast furnaces, rough rolling, finished rolling, and fabricated products. In all industries most firms are vertically integrated to some degree. However, it is an observed fact that in the same industry some firms have a high degree of integration, while their rivals have much less integrated operations. The reason for this is that most of the advantages of integration may be attained by other means, such as the exercising of monopsony power, signing of long-term contracts, adjacent location, or other devices between separate companies.

Despite its widespread existence, vertical integration has attracted relatively little attention in economic theory. This may be attributed to several reasons. Vertical integration is a many-dimensional phenomenon and much more complex than the extension of horizontal integration, and hence it is harder to study. Another reason is the fact that vertical integration has been less important than horizontal expansion. Finally, vertical integration is considered to be less harmful to competition and resource allocation than horizontal integration.

In this chapter we will discuss systematically the causes and effects of vertical integration. However, we will be mostly concerned with the theory of transfer pricing, which has not yet seen its way into economics textbooks. Yet the determination of the transfer price (i.e. the price at which a division will sell or transfer its product to a subsequent division) has serious implications for the divisionalised firm as well as for government policy.

A. Types of Vertical Integration

There are two types of vertical integration: backward or 'upstream' integration; and forward or 'downstream' integration.

Backward integration occurs when a firm undertakes to produce raw materials and intermediate inputs which it was previously buying from independent producers.

Forward integration involves the extension of the operations of the firm from earlier stages of production towards processing of the outputs of these stages (raw materials or intermediate inputs) into final products and distributing them via wholesaling and retailing. For example, the big petroleum firms are highly integrated: they own extensive oil reserves, refining plants, pipelines through which crude oil and refined products flow to their markets, and in many cases they also own networks of retail petrol stations. On the other hand, small transistor manufacturers have a low degree of vertical integration. They buy raw materials from the chemical and metal industries and sell their product (transistors) to electrical equipment firms. These produce radios, television sets or tape recorders and sell them to wholesalers or retailers.

B. Measures of Vertical Integration

Vertical integration is difficult to measure, though conceptually its meaning is straightforward.

A crude way of measuring vertical integration is to count the 'stages of production'. The greater the number of stages, the greater the integration. However, the definition of a 'stage' often involves subjective judgement, and has led to long debates. A 'stage' may include many individual steps which could be done by separate firms.

Another measure of the degree of vertical integration is the ratio of value added to sales. Recall that the difference between value added and sales is the value of intermediate goods and raw materials bought. Thus the greater the ratio of value added to sales, the greater the degree of vertical integration. This ratio, however, has several shortcomings. Some one-stage industries (such as brick-making) have a high value added, while other industries have many stages but a low total value added. Thus this measure should be used with caution when one is interested in making inter-industry comparisons.[1]

A better measure of vertical integration has been suggested by Gort.[2] On the basis of qualitative analysis he identified for each of 111 large corporations the 'primary production operations' and the 'auxiliary operations', the latter being activities which either supplied inputs into the primary production operation or contributed to further 'downstream' processing or distribution of the primary

---

[1] See M. A. Adelman, 'Concept and Statistical Measurement of Vertical Integration', in *Business Concentration and Price Policy*, ed. G. Stigler (Princeton University Press, 1955) pp. 281–322.

[2] M. Gort, *Diversification and Integration in American Industry* (Princeton University Press, 1962).

product(s). For example, in a petroleum corporation the primary operation is the refining process, while the extraction of crude oil and the distribution of the products of the refineries are auxiliary activities. Once the distinction between primary and auxiliary operations is identified, a measure of the degree of vertical integration is provided by the ratio of the percentage of employment in auxiliary activities to total company employment. The greater this ratio, the higher the degree of vertical integration. Gort's estimates ranged from 9.7 per cent in transportation to 67.3 per cent in petroleum.

Three empirical studies have shown that the degree of vertical integration (in the US economy) has not been increasing: Adelman[3] examined the period 1849–1951; Laffer[4] examined the period 1929–65; Tucker and Wilder[5] examined the period 1954–72. All studies concluded that vertical integration was not changing perceptibly in the USA.

In his study Laffer investigated the vertical-integration activity over the various phases of the business cycle. He did not find any significant relationship between vertical integration and the cycle.

Nelson[6] found that vertical integration is unrelated to market size. Finally, Gort[7] found no evidence of any relation between vertical integration and firm size.

II. THE DETERMINANTS OF THE DECISION TO GROW BY VERTICAL INTEGRATION

There are several causes why firms integrate the various stages of their production. We shall discuss briefly the most important of them.

A. Economies of Vertical Integration

In traditional price theory the attainment of economies is the only motive for vertical integration. In perfect markets with complete information, integration would be done only if it yields cost reductions. Integration does not affect competition. This is often called 'the Adelman–Spengler hypothesis', after the names of the authors who expounded it.[8] It holds under the assumptions of

[3] Adelman, 'Concept and Statistical Measurement of Vertical Integration'.

[4] Arthur B. Laffer, 'Vertical Integration by Corporations, 1929–1965', *Review of Economics and Statistics*, vol. 51, 1969, pp. 91–3.

[5] Irwin B. Tucker and Ronald P. Wilder, 'Trends in Vertical Integration in the US Manufacturing Sector', *Journal of Industrial Economics*, vol. 26, 1977, pp. 81–94.

[6] Ralph L. Nelson, *Merger Movements in American Industry, 1895–1956* (Princeton University Press, 1959).

[7] Gort, *Diversification and Integration in American Industry*.

[8] Morris A. Adelman, 'Integration and Antitrust Policy', *Harvard Law Review*, vol. 63, 1949, pp. 27–77; Joseph J. Spengler, 'Vertical Integration and Antitrust Policy', *Journal of Political Economy*, vol. 58, 1950, pp. 347–52.

perfect product and input markets, functioning under certainty, with no barriers to entry.

The economies from vertical integration may be grouped in five categories.

(1) *Technical production economies.* Factor inputs can be reduced if the integrated firm can perform different successive production stages more efficiently than they could be performed by separate firms. Such economies are more likely to be realised when the various stages of production are technologically complementary. For example, in the steel industry the integration of furnacing operations with milling operations saves reheating costs.

(2) *Co-ordination economies.* Even if the successive stages of production are not technologically complementary, economies can be attained from better co-ordination of the various operations of a vertically integrated firm. An example is provided by the automobile industry. Big automobile manufacturers produce steel, various components, assemble the components into the finished product, and distribute their automobiles through their exclusive dealers. In such cases the firm attains the elimination of purchasing and selling expenses by moving the intermediate commodities from one stage to the next.

(3) *Inventory economies.* The co-ordination of the successive production stages results in the reduction of the intermediate inventories. (The firm also avoids delays of deliveries, which may slow down its operations.)

(4) *Managerial and R & D economies.* With vertical integration a firm may attain a more efficient utilisation of its managerial team and the R & D department.

(5) *Pecuniary economies.* The integrated firm may, by its size, attain discounts from its suppliers.

In general, the importance of the economies from vertical integration depends on how important is the stage which is being integrated; on whether or not the production of the final product will absorb most or all of the intermediate product(s); and on the potential scale economies in production at successive production stages. For example, tin-can manufacturers do not produce the steel strip they need, because as a raw material steel is a small fraction of the value of the final product, and because steel producers can attain substantial scale economies from producing several products, which enable them to sell steel strip to the can-makers at a price lower than it would cost the can-makers to produce steel themselves. Similarly, manufacturers of breakfast cereals do not have their own retail outlets, because such forward integration is uneconomical: breakfast foods are only a small fraction of all food items, which are handled more efficiently by grocers.[9]

B. Reduction of Uncertainty in Input Markets

The assumptions of the Adelman–Spengler hypothesis are not met in the real world. Uncertainty is inherent in the economic environment. The uncertainty in

[9] See J. Bain, *Industrial Organization* (Wiley, 1958), p. 178.

the markets of inputs may be reduced by vertical integration. The supply of some raw materials (like oil, bauxite, wheat) is often highly volatile in nature. Furthermore, suppliers may be few and have strong monopoly power, capable of imposing high prices on the buying firms. In addition, a disruption of the production of the suppliers (e.g. from a strike) may lead to a disruption of the operations of the buying firms. For example, in the United Kingdom strikes of the Lucas Company (which produces most of the electrical parts and accessories of the automobile industry) have often caused slowdowns in the production of car manufacturers. Such uncertainties can be eliminated by backward integration, which ensures that supplies of raw materials and other inputs will be available in time, and provides protection from high prices by monopolistic suppliers.

C.   Reduction of Uncertainty in the Product Market

Forward integration provides protection from a foreclosure (being shut out from the market) by powerful buyers or traders (wholesalers and retailers). An example is provided by the *Brown Shoe Case*. Brown Shoe, which produced approximately 4–10 per cent in various shoe markets in 1955, attempted to merge with Kinney, a shoe producer and retailing chain with 2 per cent of US retail shoe sales. The Supreme Court prohibited the merger in 1962, largely because Brown's past behaviour indicated that there was the possibility of 'vertical foreclosure' in the retail shoe market. (Brown was requiring newly acquired retail chains to shift their purchasing to Brown products.) The merger would have given Brown the opportunity to channel Kinney's purchases towards Brown shoes, to the exclusion of other shoe manufacturers. Had the merger been allowed, other shoe-makers would probably seek forward integration (acquiring shoe retail outlets) as a defensive action against market foreclosure.

D.   Attaining Monopoly Power in the Product Market

If the share in the forward market is substantial, the firm may acquire considerable monopoly power in price-setting.

E.   Attaining Monopoly Power in Input Markets

If a firm acquires the source of a raw material, it can squeeze the profit margin of its competitors by charging them a higher price, and can force them to close down. This practice has allegedly been adopted by the large vertically integrated oil companies, which squeezed the small independent retail petrol stations out of the market.[10]

[10] See M. D. de Chazeau and Alfred Kahn, *Integration and Competition in the Petroleum Industry* (Yale University Press, 1959).

F.   Creation or Intensification of Barriers to Entry

Vertical integration can be used as a means of forestalling entry.

(1) As we said above, an integrated firm, owning ores or other indispensable inputs, may withhold them from others (absolute entry barrier) or may sell to other firms at a sufficiently high price, and this puts rivals at an absolute cost disadvantage.

(2) Vertical integration increases the initial capital requirements for setting up a firm with the same degree of integration as that of the existing firms. Unless capital markets are perfect, the rise in capital requirements can increase barriers substantially.

(3) Vertical integration may increase the scale barrier. That is, it may result in an increase of the minimum optimal scale at which some of the integrated production activities must be performed for best over-all efficiency. Suppose that at a certain production stage the minimum optimal scale either (a) requires more inputs, from a preceding stage, than a minimum optimal scale plant in that stage will supply, or (b) produces more output than the subsequent stage can absorb, if it operates at its minimum optimal scale. In this event the preceding or the succeeding production stage will need to be increased above its own minimum optimal scale in order for the firm to attain the greatest over-all efficiency. This, apparently, results in an increased scale barrier at the relevant stage.

In summary, while traditional price theory assumes that the only cause for vertical integration is the attainment of cost reductions, in the real world, where managers have their own goals and do not necessarily pursue cost minimisation, where product and input markets are imperfect, and uncertainty is a prevalent characteristic, firms may seek growth by vertical integration for reasons other than cost reductions.

Although in most cases vertical integration results in greater economic efficiency,[11] it is clear that it can also create market power and increase the size of barriers to entry of new competitors. A study by Clevenger and Campbell[12] provides some evidence that vertically integrated firms have a higher rate of profit. The two researchers examined the buying and selling patterns in input markets for twenty two-digit industries for the years 1963 and 1967. They found that industries where monopsony power was present earned higher profit rates, while industries that purchased inputs from other industries which were highly concentrated earned lower profit rates.

In subsequent sections we shall examine two of the main decisions facing a vertically integrated firm: (a) the determination of the transfer price, that is, the

---

[11] John S. McGee and Lowell R. Bassett, 'Vertical Integration Revisited', *Journal of Law and Economics*, vol. 19, 1976, pp. 17–38.
[12] T. S. Clevenger and G. R. Campbell, 'Vertical Integration: A Neglected Element in Market–Structure–Profit Models', *Journal of Industrial Organization*, vol. 5, 1977, pp. 60–7.

price at which products of an intermediate stage are 'transferred' to subsequent divisions; and (b) the decision to close down a particular division.

III. THEORY OF TRANSFER PRICING

One of the major decisions of a vertically integrated firm is the determination of the transfer price, that is, the price of goods and services transferred from one division to another within the firm.

The determination of the transfer price has serious implications for the integrated firm. The modern industrial world is made up of many large, multi-product, multi-plant corporations. As these giant firms have expanded, it has become generally recognised that the best way for their management is not by a central top management but by decentralisation, that is, by setting up more or less autonomous decision-making divisions or 'profit centres' within the firm. These centres should operate within certain guidelines set by the top management so as to attain the maximisation of the aggregate profit of the firm (or other goals of the firm). As we will see below, the maximisation of the profit of each division independently of the others does not in general maximise the profit of the firm as a whole. The determination of 'correct' transfer prices gives division managers both the economic basis and the incentives for 'correct' decisions. Such prices also provide top management with profit and loss information which is essential for the evaluation of the results of complex combinations of managerial skills and diverse divisions. 'Correct' transfer prices are the basis for attaining the smooth co-operation of the various divisions and the successful decentralisation of the operation of complex corporations.

In the earlier stages of the development of divisionalised firms the difficulties of defining a transfer price acceptable to the relevant divisions were so great that many firms decided to abolish transfer prices completely. This practice is no solution at all. Abolition of transfer prices prevents meaningful measurement of the profits of individual divisions and estimation of the returns on proposed investments in different operating centres.

In most cases the employed methods for setting transfer prices are inadequate, in that they keep many losses hidden at various stages and thus inhibit rational decision-making by top management.

The theory of transfer pricing provides the apparatus for the analysis of the behaviour of large multi-division corporations. In this section we will develop four models of transfer pricing which differ on the assumptions regarding the market conditions of an 'intermediate' division, i.e. a division which is the supplier of other divisions within the firm.[13]

---

[13] The discussion of this section is based on two articles by Jack Hirshleifer: 'On the Economics of Transfer Pricing', *Journal of Business*, vol. 39, 1956; 'Economics of the Divisionalized Firm', *Journal of Business*, vol. 40, 1957, pp. 96–108.

Large corporations are divisionalised, that is, they have several divisions, some producing final products, others producing intermediate goods for the former. The costs of such divisionalised firms can be grouped in four categories:

(1) *Joint fixed costs.* These are costs common to all divisions (for example, expenses of top management). As such they affect only the decision as to whether or not to close down the entire firm. They are irrelevant to the problem of transfer pricing and closing down a particular division. So they do not enter the subsequent analysis.

(2) *Separable fixed costs.* These are the fixed costs that can be identified as arising from particular divisions. These costs are not relevant for the pricing—output decisions of the division. They are relevant only to the decision as to whether or not to close down the particular division, and will be considered for this purpose in section IV of this chapter.

(3) *Separable variable costs.* These are the variable costs associated with a particular division. They define the marginal costs of each division. Separable variable costs include all production costs except the cost of materials bought from other divisions within the firm. It is assumed that the separable variable costs (or operating costs) of each division are independent of those of other divisions. This is *the assumption of technical independence.* The condition that some variable costs are separable and independent of the operating costs of other divisions is almost a necessary condition for divisionalisation, that is, the delegation of decision-making power among autonomous profit centres, each producing one product or a group of products.

(4) *Joint variable costs.* These are the variable costs of the division(s) which supplies jointly other divisions within the firm. For simplicity we assume that there exists only one supplying division within the firm, which may be regarded as an autonomous decision centre (or autonomous profit centre).

The theory of transfer pricing deals with the determination of the price of the supplying division, i.e. the price which the common supplier must charge to the final product division(s), so as to attain the maximisation of the aggregate profit of the firm. Thus the core of this section is the problem of dealing with the joint variable costs, or costs of internally produced intermediate products, which will be used by other divisions. In a separate model we consider the case where the joint-supplier division can also sell to outside buyers.

A. Model 1: There is no External Market for the Intermediate Product of the Firm, which has only one Final-Product Division

(i) *Assumptions*

(1) It is assumed in this model that the firm has two divisions, a manufacturing division (A), and a distribution division (B).

(2) The goal of the top management is the maximisation of the profit of the firm as a whole.

(3) The top management imposes the restriction that division A produces only for division B, and the latter is not allowed to buy from sources other than the internal division A. Under these conditions we have a bilateral monopoly inside the firm, but the top management, aiming at the maximisation of the aggregate profit of the firm, does not allow either division to exploit the other by exercising monopolistic or monopsonistic power (see below).

There are several conditions under which the top management would require the production division A to produce only for the internal division B. First, there might be no outside market for the 'intermediate' product at all, in which case there is no way for the manufacturing division A to dispose of a surplus, or for the distribution division B to buy from outside if the supply from A is inadequate. Second, there might be a strong technological interdependence between the production operations of the two divisions, such that the marginal costs of either division increase sharply if they are free to have transactions with outside firms. For example, take an integrated steel firm, with two divisions, the one transferring to the other molten iron. If the manufacturing division produces more than the needs of the distribution division, it will incur high handling costs in order to sell the surplus to outside firms. Similarly, if the production of molten iron is less than the requirements of the distribution division, the latter will have to buy from outside sources, incurring high reheating costs. Third, top management may want to control the supply of the 'intermediate' product in order to keep rivals at a cost disadvantage. The last case is excluded from the present analysis, unless such a policy maximises the aggregate profit of the integrated firm.

To simplify the analysis at this stage we assume technological independence of the two divisions, that is, we assume that the operating (separable variable) costs of each division, and hence their marginal costs, are independent.

(4) Since there is no external market for the manufacturing division A, we can assume that the operations of this division cannot affect the demand for the final product of division B. That is, we assume demand independence (as well as technical independence).

(5) To simplify the diagrammatic presentation of the model, it is assumed that the output of both divisions is measured in a common unit. In some cases there exists an obvious common unit of measurement, as, for example, pairs of shoes transferred from the shoe-manufacturing division to the shoe-retailing division. If the intermediate product is different from the final product (e.g. copper and copper products), a common unit of measurement can be technically worked out (the copper products are measured in tonnes of copper contained in them).

Under the above assumptions both divisions will produce an equal amount of output. This amount can be determined by the central management as follows. The central management computes the total marginal cost of the firm, by adding the marginal cost curves of the two divisions at each level of output:

$$MC_T = MC_A + MC_B \tag{6.1}$$

Having obtained the total marginal cost curve, the central management acts marginalistically, equating this MC_T with the marginal revenue of the final output.

(a) If the market of the final product is perfectly competitive, the equilibrium of the firm is determined by the condition

$$\overline{MR}_x = MC_T$$

or equivalently

$$\overline{P}_x = MC_A + MC_B \tag{6.2}$$

(b) If the market for the final product is imperfectly competitive, the central management sets output where

$$MR_x = MC_A + MC_B \tag{6.3}$$

The above centrally defined equilibrium is shown in Figures 6.1 and 6.2. In Figure 6.1 it is assumed that the market for the final product is perfectly competitive. In Figure 6.2 the market for the final product is imperfectly competitive. In either case both divisions will produce an output equal to OX_e. The transfer price is P_e^*. The dotted area is the gross profit of the firm (before subtraction of the fixed costs of each division). The contribution of each division to the aggregate profit can be found by drawing lines vertical to the Y-axis, passing through the points a and b of intersection of the line through the equilibrium point e and the individual MC curves.

The same equilibrium solution can be reached by autonomous decisions of the two divisions, if an appropriate transfer price is established. In this event decentralisation secures the maximisation of the aggregate profit of the firm. The initiative for setting the transfer price may be delegated to the final-product

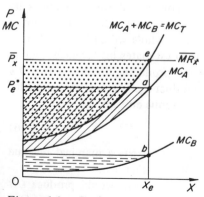

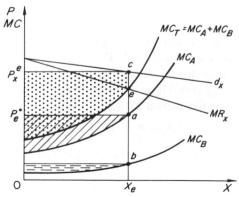

Figure 6.1   Perfect market for the final product

Figure 6.2   Imperfect market for the final product

division or to the 'intermediate' division. We will show that in either case the profit of the firm as a whole is maximised, provided that the individual divisions do not exercise their monopoly or monopsony power.

(ii) *The transfer price is set by the final-product division*

Assume that the transfer-price decision is delegated to the distribution division B, under the condition that it will not exploit the manufacturing division by exercising its monopsonistic power. This is attained if the central management instructs division B to act as follows.

(1) Obtain from A information on the latter's supply curve. That is, division B asks division A what quantity the latter would sell at different prices, P_i^*. (The asterisk will be used throughout the analysis to denote the transfer price.) Assuming that the intermediate (production) division A is a profit-maximiser, it sets $P_i^* = MC_A$. Thus the supply curve of A is its marginal cost curve MC_A.

(2) The distribution division adds the MC_A to its own operating MC_B curve to obtain its total marginal cost curve MC_T.

(3) The distribution division B finds its level of output setting

$$MR_x = MC_T = MC_A + MC_B \tag{6.4}$$

or, if the product market is perfectly competitive,

$$\bar{P}_x = MC_T = MC_A + MC_B \tag{6.5}$$

In Figure 6.1 (or 6.2) the output of B is OX_e.

(4) The distribution division B offers to the manufacturing division A a transfer price P_e^*, equal to the MC_A corresponding to B's equilibrium.

(5) The producing (intermediate) division A will produce OX_e, defined by it setting $P_e^* = MC_A$ (see Figure 6.1 or 6.2).

Thus both divisions produce OX_e each, and the aggregate profit is maximised with *autonomous decisions* of the decentralised divisions.

It should be noted that if the distribution division were allowed to exercise its monopsonistic power, it would offer a lower transfer price to the manufacturing division, and the aggregate profit of the firm as a whole would be less. This is shown in Figure 6.3. The distributor (division B) estimates his 'average revenue curve' by subtracting what he has to pay to the producing division A (i.e. A's MC_A curve) from the market price of the final product P_x. (Assume for simplicity a perfect market for x.) In symbols, B's average revenue curve is

$$AR_x = P_x - MC_A = P_x - P_i^* \tag{6.6}$$

Corresponding to this average revenue curve, there exists a marginal revenue curve for B. This is shown by the dashed curve MR_x in Figure 6.3.

The distributor (division B), acting as a monopsonist, would produce OB (setting $MC_B = MR_x$), and would offer to the manufacturing division (A) a transfer price $P_e^{*'}$. The latter would also produce OB (setting $MC_A = P_e^{*'}$). From

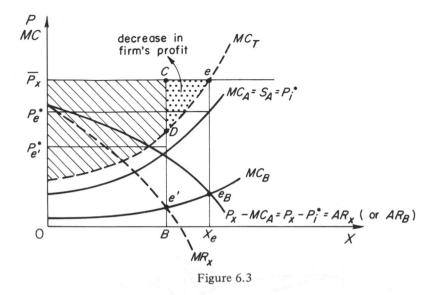

Figure 6.3

Figure 6.3 it can be seen that the output of each division would be lower and the aggregate profit would be reduced by the area *CDe*,[14] if the final-product division were to exercise its monopsony power, maximising its own profit.

(iii) *The transfer price is set by the producing division*

In the previous analysis we assumed that the transfer price is set by the distribution division. However, the central management may delegate the decision of the transfer price to the manufacturing division, with the proviso that it will not exploit the distribution division by exercising its monopolistic power. In this case the equilibrium of the firm and the transfer price will be identical, as previously, but the process of reaching this equilibrium will be different. The manufacturing division asks the distribution division B how much it would buy of the intermediate good at various prices, P_i^*. The distribution division (B), assuming it is a rational profit-maximiser, would work on the basis of the marginalistic rule:[15]

$$\bar{P}_x = MC_B + P_i^* \tag{6.7}$$

[14] Note that the original equilibrium can be reached by the distributor if he sets

$$MC_B = AR_x = P_x - P_i^*$$

[15] It is assumed for simplicity that the market for the final product x is perfectly competitive.

Thus B's demand for the intermediate product (which shows A's average revenue) is

$$P_i^* = P_x - MC_B = AR_A \tag{6.8}$$

With this information the manufacturing division A (without exercising its monopolistic power) defines its output setting

$$MC_A = (P_x - MC_B) = AR_A \tag{6.9}$$

He will produce OX_e (in Figure 6.4), and offer to sell to B at the transfer price P_e^*.

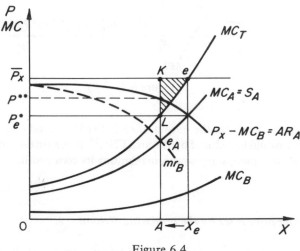

Figure 6.4

Given this transfer price, the distributor B would also produce OX_e, applying the profit-maximising rule:[16]

$$P_x = MC_B + P_e^* = MC_B + MC_A = MC_T \tag{6.10}$$

Thus the equilibrium of the firm can be reached by an independent decision of the producing (intermediate) division A, if it is not allowed to exercise its monopolistic power. If the manufacturing division acts as a monopolist, attempting to maximise its own profit, then the profit of the firm as a whole will be reduced. In this event, division A would derive a marginal revenue curve (MR_A in Figure 6.4) corresponding to its average revenue curve, and he would apply the marginalistic rule

$$MC_A = MR_A$$

[16] It is assumed for simplicity that the market for the final product x is perfectly competitive.

The equilibrium of the monopolist A is shown by point e_A in Figure 6.4. He would produce the (smaller) quantity OA, quoting a transfer price P^{**} to the distributing division B. The latter would also be forced to produce an output equal to OA, and the profit of *the firm as a whole* would decrease by the dotted area KLe. (Note that if both divisions were left to determine the transfer price by bargaining (as in the pure bilateral monopoly model), the profit of the firm as a whole would be even smaller.)

B. Model 2: There is no External Market for the Intermediate Product, which is Sold to Two Final-Product Divisions with Interdependent Demands

In this model we assume that the manufacturing division A supplies two internal divisions, which in turn produce two commodities whose demands are interdependent. Thus the firm has three independent divisions: the supplier division A, which produces some intermediate commodity, and two final-product divisions. The two final products can be substitutes or complements. In both cases we have demand interdependence, since the sales of one division will affect the sales of the other.

For example, consider a firm which produces cameras in one division (X), and film in another division (Y). Both these divisions buy the services of the R & D department of the firm, which we will call 'the supplier division'. The cameras and films are complementary commodities on the demand side, and have some joint costs, arising from the supplier division (R & D). As another example assume that a car manufacturer produces two types of cars, in two separate divisions. The final products are substitutes. Each of the two divisions has its own separable operating costs, but also some joint variable costs, consisting of the transfer price P_e^* which they will pay to a third independent division that produces body parts. A third example is a chain of grocery stores. The marginal cost of the operations of each store is substantially independent of the costs of the other stores; however, all stores buy from a central supplier division, paying the transfer price that this supplier division charges. Another example is the autonomous export divisions set up by many firms. The export costs are separable from the costs of the divisions which sell in the home market, but all divisions have to pay the transfer price of the production division.

The distinguishing feature of this model is that the final products have interdependent demands. This affects the marginal revenue accruing *to the firm* from each product. (If the price of one automobile model is reduced, the sales of the other model(s) will decline. Similarly, if the price of cameras is reduced, more films will be sold.) Thus we must find the 'corrected' marginal revenue that each product has for the firm.

The total revenue of the firm as a whole is

$$R = P_x Q_x + P_y Q_y$$

We assume that $P_x = f(Q_x, Q_y)$ and $P_y = f(Q_y, Q_x)$. Thus the 'corrected' marginal revenue for each of the two products is

$$
\left.
\begin{aligned}
MR_x^* = \frac{\partial R}{\partial Q_x} = \left[P_x + Q_x \frac{\partial P_x}{\partial Q_x} \right] + \left[Q_y \frac{\partial P_y}{\partial Q_x} \right] \\
MR_y^* = \frac{\partial R}{\partial Q_y} = \left[P_y + Q_y \frac{\partial P_y}{\partial Q_y} \right] + \left[Q_x \frac{\partial P_x}{\partial Q_y} \right]
\end{aligned}
\right\}
\tag{6.11}
$$

The first term in the brackets is the simple marginal revenue for each product, without taking into account their demand interdependence. The second term in brackets takes into account this interdependence, and may be called the 'cross marginal revenue': it shows the change in the total revenue *of the firm* received for one product when an additional unit is sold of the other product. The 'cross marginal revenue' will be negative for substitute commodities, and positive for complementary goods.

The above 'corrected' marginal revenue may be written in terms of elasticities, with which students of economics are familiar. Let

e_x = 'own' price elasticity of commodity x
e_y = 'own' price elasticity of commodity y
e_{xy} = cross-elasticity of demand for x w.r.t. the price of y
e_{yx} = cross-elasticity of demand for y w.r.t. the price of x

It can be shown (see below) that the marginal revenues of the two commodities are

$$
MR_x^* = \frac{\partial R}{\partial Q_x} = \left[P_x \left(1 + \frac{1}{e_x} \right) \right] + \left[P_y \frac{Q_y}{Q_x} \frac{1}{e_{xy}} \right]
$$

and

$$
\left.
\begin{aligned}
 \\
MR_y^* = \frac{\partial R}{\partial Q_y} = \left[P_y \left(1 + \frac{1}{e_y} \right) \right] + \left[P_x \frac{Q_x}{Q_y} \frac{1}{e_{yx}} \right]
\end{aligned}
\right\}
\tag{6.12}
$$

*   *   *

We shall prove that

$$
MR_x^* = \left[P_x \left(1 + \frac{1}{e_x} \right) \right] + \left[P_y \frac{Q_y}{Q_x} \frac{1}{e_{xy}} \right]
$$

From expression (6.11) we have

$$
MR_x^* = \left[P_x + Q_x \frac{\partial P_x}{\partial Q_x} \right] + \left[Q_y \frac{\partial P_y}{\partial Q_x} \right]
$$

We multiply the term $\left(Q_x \dfrac{\partial P_x}{\partial Q_x} \right)$ by $\dfrac{P_x}{P_x}$, and the term $\left(Q_y \dfrac{\partial P_y}{\partial Q_x} \right)$ by $\dfrac{Q_x\, P_y}{Q_x\, P_y}$

$$MR_x^* = \left[P_x + Q_x \left(\frac{\partial P_x}{\partial Q_x} \times \frac{P_x}{P_x} \right) \right] + \left[Q_y \frac{\partial P_y}{\partial Q_x} \frac{Q_x\, P_y}{Q_x\, P_y} \right] \tag{6.13}$$

Rearranging, we obtain

$$MR_x^* = \left[P_x + P_x \left(\frac{\partial P_x}{\partial Q_x} \frac{Q_x}{P_x} \right) \right] + \left[P_y \frac{Q_y}{Q_x} \left(\frac{\partial P_y}{\partial Q_x} \frac{Q_x}{P_y} \right) \right] \tag{6.14}$$

We note that

$$\frac{\partial P_x}{\partial Q_x} \frac{Q_x}{P_x} = \frac{\partial P_x/P_x}{\partial Q_x/Q_x} = \frac{1}{e_x} \tag{6.15}$$

and

$$\frac{\partial P_y}{\partial Q_x} \frac{Q_x}{P_y} = \frac{\partial P_y/P_y}{\partial Q_x/Q_x} = \frac{1}{e_{xy}} \tag{6.16}$$

Substituting (6.15) and (6.16) in (6.14), we find

$$MR_x^* = \left[P_x \left(1 + \frac{1}{e_x} \right) \right] + \left[P_y \frac{Q_y}{Q_x} \frac{1}{e_{xy}} \right]$$

QED

In a similar way it can be shown that

$$MR_y^* = \left[P_y \left(1 + \frac{1}{e_y} \right) \right] + \left[P_x \frac{Q_x}{Q_y} \frac{1}{e_{yx}} \right]$$

*   *   *

It is assumed that all three divisions have independent separable variable costs, so that the marginal operating costs of each division are independent. However, the two final-product divisions will pay the transfer price P_e^* to the supplier division, so that they must add this common variable cost to their own operating marginal cost:

$$\left. \begin{array}{l} MC_x^* = MC_x + P_e^* \\[4pt] MC_y^* = MC_y + P_e^* \end{array} \right\} \tag{6.17}$$

where MC_x^* = 'corrected MC' of division X
        MC_y^* = 'corrected MC' of division Y
        MC_x = operating (separable) MC of X
        MC_y = operating (separable) MC of Y
        P_e^* = equilibrium transfer price

Each autonomous division is required to act so as to maximise the aggregate profit of the firm, *not* its own profit. Thus, if an autonomous division sets its *MC* equal to its *simple MR*, the total profit of the firm may suffer. For example, the division that produces cameras, in setting its price, should consider that the marginal revenue *to the firm* is not limited to the change in receipts from cameras but also to the change in receipts from the probable change in the demand for film. This would tend to make the firm willing to accept a lower price for its cameras than it would require if it were producing only cameras. The equilibrium of each of the two final-product divisions is found by equating the 'corrected' marginal cost to the 'corrected' marginal revenue:

$$\left. \begin{aligned} MC_x^* &= MR_x^* \\[1em] \text{and} \\[1em] MC_y^* &= MR_y^* \end{aligned} \right\} \qquad (6.18)$$

where the asterisk indicates the 'corrected' marginal cost and marginal revenue of each division.

We will next examine how the manufacturing division sets its transfer price, P_e^*. We will show that the transfer price is determined by the intersection of the marginal cost curve of the supplier division (MC_A) with the total demand for its (intermediate) product.

The total demand for the product of the supplier division is the horizontal summation of the individual demands of each final division. The supplier asks the buying (final) divisions what amount they would buy at various prices, P_i^*. Each buyer division, acting rationally, sets its demand by the profit-maximising rule

$$\left. \begin{aligned} MR_x^* &= MC_x + P_i^* && \text{or} && P_i^* = MR_x^* - MC_x = d_{Ax} \\ MR_y^* &= MC_y + P_i^* && \text{or} && P_i^* = MR_y^* - MC_x = d_{Ay} \end{aligned} \right\} \quad (6.19)$$

In other words, each final division estimates the demand for the intermediate product by subtracting its simple *MC* from its 'corrected marginal revenue'. These curves are shown in Figures 6.5 and 6.6, which assume an imperfectly competitive market for the final products, x and y.

The supplier division adds horizontally the individual demands for its own product, and, forbidden by the central management to exercise its monopoly power (arising from the fact that it is the only supplier of the two other divisions), sets a price corresponding to the intersection of its marginal cost curve, MC_A, and the total demand for its product

$$D_A = d_{Ax} + d_{Ay}$$

The equilibrium of the supplier division is shown in Figure 6.7. The supplier division produces a total output of OX_A^e and sells it to the buying divisions at the transfer price P_e^*. This price absorbs the supplier's output: division X, faced with the transfer price P_e^*, buys a quantity OA_x, and division Y buys (at P_e^*) the

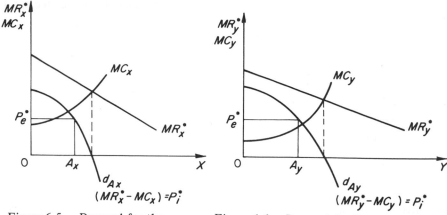

Figure 6.5 Demand for the
intermediate product
by division X

Figure 6.6 Demand for the
intermediate product
by division Y

quantity OA_y, so that the total quantity produced by the 'intermediate' division is sold. In Figure 6.7 it is seen that $OX_A^e = OA_x + OA_y$.

In summary, the equilibrium of the firm (the position with the maximum aggregate profit) is reached by the following steps:

(1) The final-product divisions estimate their 'corrected' marginal revenue curves (from information of the sales of the respective divisions in the past).

(2) The final-product divisions communicate to the supplier division their demand for the intermediate product, estimated by the following subtraction:

$$MR_x^* - MC_x = d_{Ax}$$

$$MR_y^* - MC_y = d_{Ay}$$

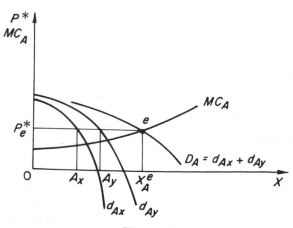

Figure 6.7

(3) The supplier division adds the individual demands to obtain the total demand for its product (at each price P_i^*):

$$D_A = d_{Ax} + d_{Ay}$$

(4) The transfer price is set at the level corresponding to the condition

$$MC_A = D_A$$

(5) The transfer price P_e^* is added by each buying division to its simple (separate) MC to obtain the 'corrected MC' curve:

$$MC_x^* = MC_x + P_e^*$$

$$MC_y^* = MC_y + P_e^*$$

(6) The buying divisions set their price and output at the level defined by the conditions

$$MR_x^* = MC_x^* \quad \text{or} \quad MC_x + \begin{bmatrix} \text{Cross} \\ \text{marginal} \\ \text{revenue} \end{bmatrix} = MC_x + P_e^*$$

and

$$MR_y^* = MC_y^* \quad \text{or} \quad MR_y + \begin{bmatrix} \text{Cross} \\ \text{marginal} \\ \text{revenue} \end{bmatrix} = MC_y + P_e^*$$

This sequence leads to the maximisation of the aggregate profit of the firm as a whole.

The crucial features of this model are: (a) there is no outside market for the intermediate product, so that there is only one supplier to the other autonomous divisions of the firm; and (b) the demands of the final-product divisions are interdependent.

Note that the above model is relevant to the pricing decisions of the three autonomous decision centres. In these decisions only marginal magnitudes are important. However, this model is not suitable for other decisions such as the closing down of a division. For such a decision the fixed costs must also be considered (see section IV below).

C. Model 3: There is a Perfectly Competitive External Market for the Intermediate Product of the Firm

In this model we assume that there is a perfectly competitive external market for the intermediate product, so that the manufacturing division can sell either to other internal divisions or to outside buyers. Similarly, the distribution divisions are free to buy either from the internal supplier A or from outside suppliers. For simplicity we assume that the firm has only one final-product division, B, which we will call 'the distributing division'.

The market for *the final product* can be either perfectly competitive or imperfectly competitive. The distinctive feature of this model is that the market for *the intermediate product* is perfectly competitive.

It is assumed that the marginal cost of each division is independent of the marginal cost of the other. Under this assumption of technological independence, each division is indifferent between trading the intermediate commodity within or outside the firm. As a first approximation assume that the market for the final product is also perfectly competitive.

The price in the market of the intermediate commodity is $\bar{P}^*$, and the price for the final product is $\bar{P}_x$. Both divisions are price-takers. Each, without the intervention of the central management, will produce an amount of output defined by the intersection of the given market prices and the corresponding marginal costs. Note that the total marginal cost for the distribution division is its own marginal cost (MC_B) plus the market price of the intermediate commodity, $\bar{P}^*$.

In Figure 6.8 the equilibrium of the manufacturing division A is defined by point e_A, given the price $\bar{P}^*$ for its product. The total marginal cost of division B is the curve $MC_{TB} = MC_B + \bar{P}^*$. The equilibrium output of this division is OB, given $\bar{P}^*$ and $\bar{P}_x$. The distribution division will need a quantity of intermediate product equal to OB (under the assumption of commensurate units of measurement of the output of the two divisions). The manufacturing division produces

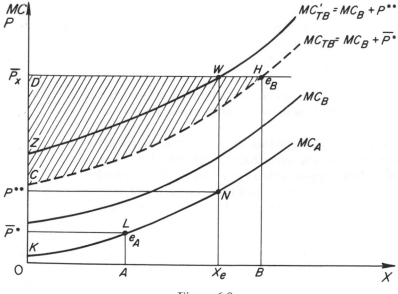

Figure 6.8

only OA and is prepared to sell it internally at a transfer price equal to the external market price $(\bar{P}^*)$. If division B pays this price, it will buy OA internally and AB from outside sellers.

The total gross profit of the firm (with or without internal trading) is the dotted area CDH in Figure 6.8.

If the central management interferes and imposes the restriction that both divisions produce an equal product greater than OA, the transfer price will have to be higher than the market price $\bar{P}^*$, say P^{**}. At this transfer price the total MC of division B will be $MC'_{TB} = MC_B + P^{**}$. The equilibrium output for both divisions would be OX_e. The gross profit of the manufacturing division has increased, but the over-all profit of the firm has been reduced to the area ZWD. This is due to the fact that the distribution division B is coerced by the central management to buy the intermediate product internally at a transfer price P^{**} higher than the external market price $\bar{P}^*$. The manufacturing division over-produces $(OX_e > OA)$, while the distributing division underproduces $(OX_e < OB)$.

The assumption of a perfectly competitive market for the *final* commodity is not essential to the above analysis. If we assume that the distribution division faces a downward-sloping demand curve, we merely need substitute a downward-sloping MR_x instead of the straight line $\bar{P}_x$: the distribution division will set its output by equating its total marginal cost $(MC_{TB}$ and $MC'_{TB})$ to its marginal revenue.

In summary. If the intermediate market is perfectly competitive, the transfer price should be the market price, irrespective of the competitive conditions in the market of the final product.

It should be noted that in all the models examined up to this point the 'correct' transfer pricing is the marginal cost pricing, i.e. setting P^* equal to the marginal cost of the intermediate division.

D. Model 4: There is an Imperfectly Competitive External Market for the Intermediate Product of the Firm

In this model we assume that there is an external market for the intermediate commodity, which is imperfectly competitive. We will show that under these conditions the supplier division will adopt a discriminating policy, selling at the internal division at a price equal to its marginal cost, while charging to outside buyers the market price, which is higher than its marginal cost.

For simplicity we assume that the firm has only one buying division, B, producing a final product whose market is imperfectly competitive. (The analysis would not be essentially affected if the final-product market is perfectly com-petitive—see, for example, Model 1 above.) It is further assumed that there is demand independence of the two divisions. In other words, sales of the inter-mediate division in the external market do not reduce the demand for the final product of the distribution division, and, conversely, internal sales do not reduce the external demand for the intermediate product.[17] The intermediate supplier division is in the position of a discriminating monopolist: it sells its output in two markets, in the external market and to the internal distributor.

The equilibrium of the *firm*, if reached by decisions of the central management, involves the determination of (a) the price and output of the final product of division B; (b) the total amount of the intermediate product; (c) the amount of the intermediate product to be sold to the internal division B and the appropriate transfer price P_e^*; and (d) the amount of the intermediate product to be sold in the external market at a profit-maximising price P_A. This equilibrium can be reached by the following procedure.

The central management knows the marginal separable costs of each division, the external demand curve for the intermediate product, and the demand curve for the final product. This information is shown in Figures 6.9 and 6.10. (It is assumed that the intermediate and final products are measured in commensurate units.)

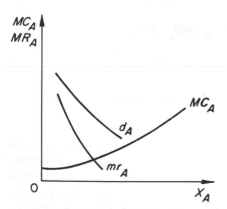

Figure 6.9 External market demand and marginal cost of supplier division A

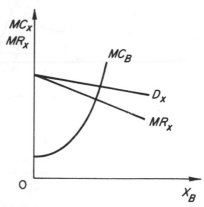

Figure 6.10 Market for the final product of division B

The central management estimates B's demand for the intermediate product of A, at various transfer prices, P_i^*, by subtracting B's marginal cost (MC_B) from its marginal revenue (MR_x) at each level of output. That is, on the assumption that division B is a profit-maximiser, when it is faced with a given P_i^*, it would

---

[17] In many cases the assumption of demand independence is unrealistic. For example, if the intermediate division produces and sells shoes both internally and in the external market, one would expect the demands of the two divisions to be interdependent to a certain extent. But in many cases the assumption of demand independence holds. For example, the intermediate division may sell (shoes) to foreign markets, while the distribution division's operations are confined to the domestic market. Similarly, a division producing copper sells to external buyers, who produce final copper products different from those produced by the internal distributor.

buy the quantity of intermediate product (which *ex hypothesi* is equal to the quantity of the final product) corresponding to the profit-maximising condition

$$MR_x = MC_B + P_i^* \qquad (6.20)$$

Thus the demand of the final division (*B*) for the intermediate product of the supplying division is

$$P_i^* = MR_x - MC_B \qquad (6.21)$$

This demand is shown by the curve d_B in Figure 6.11.

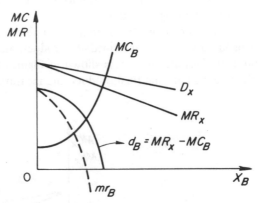

Figure 6.11   *B*'s demand for the intermediate product of *A*

To *B*'s d_B curve corresponds a marginal revenue curve (dashed curve mr_B in Figure 6.11). If the central management allowed *A* to act as an independent discriminating firm, this division would add the two separate marginal revenue curves (mr_A and mr_B) to form its total marginal revenue curve. However, the central management does not allow any monopolistic exploitation of *B* by division *A*. Thus the total 'marginal revenue' curve of *A* is defined by the horizontal summation of mr_A and d_B, and *A*'s 'restricted'[18] equilibrium is determined by equating *A*'s *MC* to this total 'marginal revenue' curve:

$$MC_A = mr_A + d_B \qquad (6.22)$$

The equilibrium of the supplier division is shown by point e_A in Figure 6.12. Drawing a vertical line from this point to the *Y*-axis, the central management defines the quantity to be sold to the internal buyer (*OD*) at the transfer price $P_e^* = MC_A$, and the quantity to be sold in the external market (*OM*) at the price P_A (determined by $mr_A = MC_A$) on the d_A curve.

Given that, *ex hypothesi*, the units of X_A and X_B are the same, division *B*

[18] *A* is restricted in the sense that it is not allowed to exercise its monopolistic power on the internal buyer division *B*.

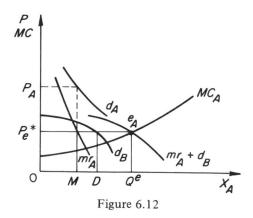

Figure 6.12

will produce an output equal to OD, and will sell it at the corresponding price P_x^e (in Figure 6.13). Note that this equilibrium of B can be defined in two ways:

(a) By setting $P_e^* = d_B$ (point a in Figure 6.13).

(b) By setting $MR_x = MC_A + MC_B$ (point b in Figure 6.13).[19]

The equilibrium of the external market of A is shown in Figure 6.14. A quantity OM will be sold to external buyers at the price P_A. Obviously $P_A > P_e^*$, a fact that puts the external buyers at a cost disadvantage.

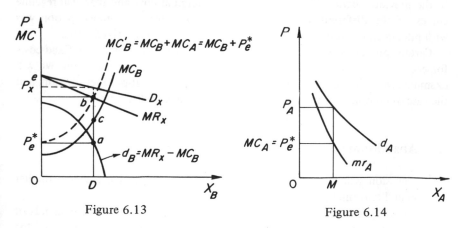

Figure 6.13   Figure 6.14

The above equilibrium can be reached by independent decisions of the two divisions, acting within some rules defined by the central management. The procedure may be outlined as follows:

[19] It can be seen from Figure 6.13 that $Dc = MC_B$ and $cb = MC_A$ at the equilibrium output OD.

Step 1. The final-product division B estimates its demand d_B for the intermediate product and conveys this information to the manufacturing division A.

Step 2. The manufacturing division determines its total 'marginal revenue' curve by summing d_B to mr_A.

Step 3. Division A produces the quantity where $MC_A = (mr_A + d_B)$.

Step 4. Division A establishes a transfer price P_e^*, equal to its MC_A (at the equilibrium position e_A in Figure 6.12).

Step 5. Division A establishes the price P_A for the external market, along the demand curve d_A. P_A corresponds to the point where $MC_A = mr_A$. The quantity sold in the external market at P_A is OM (Figure 6.14).

Step 6. Given the transfer price P_e^*, the final-product division B buys a quantity equal to OD (Figure 6.12).

Step 7. Division B will produce a final product equal to OD (Figure 6.13). This equilibrium is reached either by setting $P_e^* = d_B$ or $MR_x = MC_A + MC_B$, where MC_A is the marginal cost of A at the level of output OD (Figure 6.12).

The price of the final product, P_x, is similarly defined by either of the equilibrium conditions given under Step 7.

IV.   THE DECISION TO CLOSE DOWN A PARTICULAR DIVISION

In the previous section we made use of the marginal cost and marginal revenue curves of the different divisions of the firm, because our preoccupation was with pricing and output decisions, which are not affected by fixed costs.

Certain problems require, however, consideration of the separable fixed costs for each division. Such a problem is whether to close down a division. We will examine two cases below, the case of closing down a final-product division, and the case of complete or partial abandonment of the supplier division.

A.   Abandonment of a Final-Product Division

The discussion will be confined to the case where a firm has a single supplier division and two final-product divisions.

To simplify the analysis we will assume in this section that the demands of the final products are independent. Thus the marginal revenue curves of the two final divisions are the simple marginal revenues MR_x and MR_y. With this assumption the demand curves of these divisions for the intermediate product of the supplier division are mutually consistent at all levels of output (while with demand interdependence these curves are consistent only at the equilibrium points). Thus we can use the areas under these curves to find total revenues, costs and gross profits of the various divisions. These are shown in Figure 6.15.

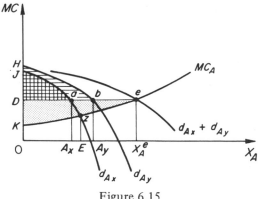

Figure 6.15

Recall that

$$d_{Ax} = MR_x - MC_x$$

and

$$d_{Ay} = MR_y - MC_y$$

Given the MR and MC curves of the two final-product divisions, we can find the gross profit of all the divisions:

(a) *Division X.* The division's equilibrium is at point a in Figure 6.15. Its total marginal revenue is the area $OJaA_x$, its total cost for the intermediate product is $ODaA_x$, and its total gross profit (i.e. profit before the subtraction of the fixed cost) is the difference DJa (cross-hatched area in Figure 6.15).

(b) *Division Y.* The division's gross profit is the horizontally striped area $DHb = OHbA_y - ODbA_y$.

(c) *Supplier division A.* The gross profit of this division is the dotted area $kDe = ODeX_A^e - OKeX_A^e$.

The decision of whether to close down any particular final-product division must be taken on the basis of its own (separate) profit plus its contribution to the profit of the common supplier division. Assume, for example, that division Y has separable fixed costs equal to its gross profit (horizontally striped area), so that its own net profit is zero. However, this division contributes a gross profit equal to the area aze to the supplier division's gross profit. If division Y is closed down (because it has no profit from its own operations), the output of the supplier division would be reduced to OE and the *firm's* profit would be reduced by aze. Thus division Y, although not profitable on its own, should be maintained for its contribution to division A's profit. Even if division Y had a net loss, it should still be maintained, so long as this loss is less than the area aze.

We may conclude that the decision to abandon a final-product division should be based on that division's contribution to the operations of the firm as a whole.

Consideration of the separate profits alone may lead to the reduction of the aggregate profit of the firm.

B. Partial or Complete Abandonment of the Supplier Division

The shape of the marginal cost curve of the supplier division A, and also its separable fixed costs, are crucial in this case.

Assume that the MC_A curve is rising (Figure 6.16). If division A charges the transfer price P_e^*, it will have a gross profit equal to KDR. If the intermediate product can be bought from outside firms at a fixed price equal to the transfer price, the supplier division should be maintained so long as its fixed cost is less than its gross profit.

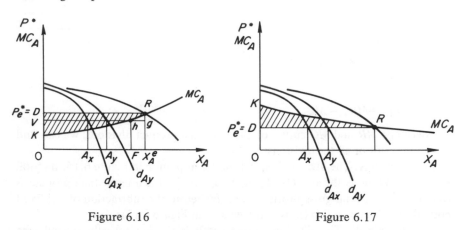

Figure 6.16   Figure 6.17

If the outside price is, however, lower than the optimal transfer price, say $OV < P_e^*$, the firm should allow the supplier division to produce only OF,[20] and buy externally the quantity FX_A^e, saving an amount equal to the area Rhg. In addition to this saving, the over-all profit of the firm will be increased, since the reduced marginal cost of the intermediate product will lead to a reduction of the marginal cost of the final divisions, which will in turn increase their output.[21]

If the MC_A curve is declining (Figure 6.17), the correct transfer price continues to be $P_e^* = OD$. At this equilibrium the supplier division makes a loss equal to DKR, over and above its separable fixed cost. Thus the firm should abandon the intermediate division completely, if it can buy externally the good produced by A at a price equal to $OD = P_e^*$.

---

[20] Provided that the gross profit VKh is greater than the fixed cost of A.
[21] This analysis assumes that the external market is perfectly competitive, so the firm can buy any quantity of the intermediate product at a fixed price. If the firm is a monopsonistic buyer, the analysis needs modification.

V. EFFECTS OF VERTICAL INTEGRATION

Vertical integration may have various effects, some of which are desirable for competition and resource allocation, while others are adverse to the economy.

Desirable effects are associated with the realisation of cost reductions. As we saw in section II, such reductions may be attained from technical production economies, co-ordination economies, inventory economies, managerial economies, research and development economies, and pecuniary economies. It is argued by several writers that in most cases vertical integration results in such economies, which are clearly beneficial to the economy.[22]

Such benefits should be compared with possible adverse effects that vertical integration may have on competition and resource allocation. These have been the subject of a long controversy, which still goes on. We shall discuss briefly the effects of vertical integration on market shares and concentration, and on various aspects of market structure, such as product differentiation, minimum optimal scale, and barriers to entry arising from absolute cost advantage and initial capital requirements.

A. Vertical Integration, Market Foreclosure and Concentration[23]

It is often argued that the most undesirable effect of a vertical merger is the foreclosure of competitors at both stages of integrated production. An integrated firm may acquire substantial leverage over non-integrated firms which are *competitors* at one stage of production, *suppliers* at another stage, or *customer-buyers* at a different stage. Thus an integrated firm can impose a price squeeze on single-stage (non-integrated) firms, and this reduces their profit margins and may force them to close down.

A classical example of a price squeeze occurred in the aluminum industry in the 1920s, when Alcoa, a vertically integrated firm, had a virtual monopoly in the production of the basic metal. Alcoa charged a high price for aluminum ingot to its competitors, whose profitability was squeezed. As some of these firms were driven out of the market of fabricated aluminum products, Alcoa increased its share in that market.

The degree of foreclosure is used to measure the extent of the market which is removed from competitors at both stages of production. For example, if a firm with 50 per cent of the market at an early stage acquires another firm which holds a 10 per cent share at the next production stage, then, as a result of the

[22] See D. L. Kaserman, 'Theories of Vertical Integration: Implications for Antitrust Policy', *Antitrust Bulletin,* vol. 23, 1978, pp. 483–510; Also McGee and Bassett, 'Vertical Integration Revisited'.

[23] The discussion of this section is based on W. S. Comanor, 'Vertical Mergers, Market Power and the Antitrust Laws', *American Economic Review*, Papers and Proceedings, 1967, pp. 254–65.

merger, rivals of the acquired firm are said to be potentially foreclosed from half of the supplying market, while rivals of the acquiring firm are foreclosed from 10 per cent of the market for their output, because the acquired firm will be supplied by the acquiring firm.

However, foreclosure provides a poor measure of the change in market shares which may occur with vertical integration. In the example above the acquired firm at the second production stage may well be able to expand its market share to 50 per cent. This will be attained if the integrated firm refuses to supply its 'intermediate' product or raw material to external firms at the second stage. (If the integrated supplier continues to sell to these rivals, it will almost certainly charge them a higher price, so that their market position will deteriorate, while the market share of the integrated firm in the second stage will expand.) At the same time, the integrated supplier will stop other firms from selling to its second-stage operation. Thus the share of the firm in the first stage will also increase (unless it was the only supplier of the acquired firm prior to merger).

Another cause of change in market shares is oligopolistic interdependence: if an oligopolist undertakes vertical integration, rivals may develop competing patterns of vertical integration as a defensive strategy. The ultimate impact on market shares of the initial 'triggering' vertical move may be large. (This behaviour has been observed in the cement industry in the USA.)

In summary, vertical integration is likely to increase market shares in some or all the stages of production. Hence concentration is increased as a result of vertical integration.

B. Vertical Integration and Entry Barriers

As we saw in section II, vertical integration has an impact on all major barriers to entry.

(i) *Product differentiation*

Forward integration between manufacturing and distribution stages of production serves frequently to enhance product differentiation. Professor Bain[24] found that the integration of retail dealer–service organisations by manufacturers, either through ownership or exclusive dealing agreements, creates an important barrier to entry, by enhancing product differentiation.

(ii) *Absolute cost advantage*

We have already discussed the various kinds of economies (cost reductions) that usually arise from vertical integration. A new entrant, in order to attain a similar

---

[24] J. Bain, *Barriers to New Competition* (Harvard University Press, 1956).

favourable cost structure, must enter with the same degree of integration. However, even in this case, the potential entrant may be in a position of an absolute cost disadvantage for two reasons: (a) the existing vertically integrated firms are usually granted special discounts by their suppliers, who are unlikely to do the same for new unknown entrants; (b) most important, the vertically integrated firm is likely to charge a higher price for products it will supply to the new entrant. On both accounts, the costs of a new entrant are likely to be higher than the cost of an established integrated firm. This behaviour is known as 'price-squeezing', and will be discussed further below.

(iii) *Absolute capital requirements*

Vertically integrated firms usually limit their supply and purchasing relationships to internal sources and refrain from dealing with external suppliers and customers. Under these conditions prospective entrants must begin operations at both stages of production. This necessarily raises the amount of capital required for entry. Given that risk is higher at a larger (vertically) aggregate size, it is likely that a prospective entrant will have to incur a higher cost for acquiring the initial capital required. Thus vertical integration, by raising the amount of initial capital requirements, makes entry more difficult and more costly.

An example is provided by the automobile producers who 'tied up' almost all of the retail auto distributive dealers, under a system of franchises which precludes the sale of the automobiles of different manufacturers by the same dealer. This erected a considerable barrier to the entry of new automobile manufacturers.

(iv) *Scale barrier*

If an integrated concern is to attain best efficiency, there must be a 'reconciliation' of the differences in the minimum optimal scale plant at each stage.

The *critical* optimal scale is the largest minimum optimal scale plant, and this critical scale is imposed on the whole integrated operation if over-all efficiency is to be maximised. The following example illustrates this point.[25]

In the automobile industry there is a two-stage integration, including (a) the production of components (engines, body parts, etc.), and (b) the assembly of components into finished automobiles. Assume that the minimum optimal scale in the first stage is the production of components for 1,000,000 automobiles (or 15 per cent of the entire automobile market), while the minimum optimal scale for an assembly plant is 100,000 units per year (or 1.5 per cent of the entire market). Under these conditions *the minimum efficient scale of the integrated firm* is 15 per cent of the entire automobile market (assuming no diseconomies of large-scale production in the assembly line). Thus, for optimal efficiency, the integrated firm should have one plant for components and ten assembly plants.

---

[25] Adapted from Bain, *Industrial Organization*, pp. 179–80.

In general, we may expect that vertical integration imposes requirements of greater scale (for optimal efficiency) on some of the stages of production absorbed by integration.[26]

If an integrated firm attains the over-all optimal efficient scale, entry barriers will be increased for some stages of production. In summary, vertical integration may increase considerably the entry barriers at various stages of the production process.

C.   Vertical Integration and Cost Structure

Vertical integration, by internalising costs which would have been variable if incurred by independent suppliers or distributors, increases the overhead costs (fixed costs become a greater proportion of total costs). This renders the operations of the integrated company more susceptible to general business recessions, because the firm loses its flexibility as its fixed costs increase relative to its variable costs. (See Chapter 3, p. 170.)

D.   Vertical Integration and Pricing Behaviour

We saw that vertical integration increases concentration as well as the barriers to entry. Hence the integrated firm acquires increased market power. Whether this market power will lead to higher prices depends on the competitive conditions prior to integration and on the goals of the firm.

It should be clear from the various models of transfer pricing, developed in section III, that output will be larger (and price lower) if prior to integration (a) suppliers had monopoly power, imposing high supply prices to the integrating firm, (b) buyers had monopsony power, forcing the integrating firm to sell its product at prices yielding below-normal profit, and (c) elements of bilateral monopoly existed in intermediate markets. Under these conditions, vertical integration results in higher output and lower price, which is beneficial to the economy.[27]

However, the fact remains that the vertically integrated firm acquires monopoly power, which it can then use to reduce or eliminate competition or bar entry at some stage(s) of the integrated operation.

(1) An integrated firm may adopt selective price discrimination in the final-product market to eliminate non-integrated rivals, using its financial power to cross-subsidise its various activities.[28]

---

[26] See ibid.

[27] It should be noted that long-term contracts with suppliers and/or customers could in principle attain the same result. However, such long-term agreements are difficult to reach. Furthermore, even when reached, they may be difficult to implement.

[28] This is sometimes called the 'deep-pocket' effect.

(2) Monopolisation of distributive outlets allows the integrated firm to charge non-integrated rivals a higher price in order to attain access to the market. An example is provided by the acquisition or control by the largest twenty petroleum refiners in the USA of nearly all trunk pipelines and most tankers for transporting crude oil and refined products for the American market. These firms charged smaller independent crude oil producers and refiners a high price for the use of their transport and distribution facilities. Eventually some of these firms incurred substantial financial outlays to equip themselves with transport facilities.

(3) An integrated firm may adopt a price-discrimination policy when it monopolises a key raw material. In this case actual or potential competitors may be excluded or operate at a cost disadvantage. There have been many instances of this pricing behaviour. A good example is the gradual acquisition, from 1910 to 1940 or later, by the Aluminum Company of America (ALCOA) of the richest deposits of bauxite (aluminum ore). Alcoa set the aluminum ingot price at a high level, squeezing the profits of firms in the finished aluminum products market and forcing many of them to close down.

There is no systematic empirical research on the effects of vertical integration. This is in part explained by the fact that vertical integration is a complex phenomenon which is very difficult to measure (see section I). In the present state of knowledge the only general conclusion that can be drawn from the literature on the subject is that vertical integration is beneficial to the economy when it results in cost reductions and the elimination of monopolistic or monopsonistic power existing prior to the integration. However, casual observation suggests that in many cases vertical integration has been undertaken for acquisition of market power, and cannot be justified on the basis of cost savings. This is apparently true in three instances: first, in the case of integration of distributive facilities by manufacturing firms (as in the example of the exclusive-dealer retailing system of the car manufacturers); second, in the case of integration of resource deposits by processing firms (as in the case of acquisition of iron ores by steel manufacturers, of bauxite ores by aluminum processors, of copper ores by copper-product manufacturers, and petroleum deposits by oil refiners and distributors); and third, in the case of monopolisation of specialised transport facilities by processing firms (as in the case of iron ore and petroleum).

7. Growth by Foreign Direct Investment: The Decision to Invest Abroad

I. INTRODUCTION

In this chapter we shall examine the decision to establish production facilities in another country as a method of expansion of the operations of the firm. We will be concerned with the initial decision to invest abroad (foreign direct investment).[1]

The growth in recent years of foreign direct investment (the growth of the multinational corporation) has generated a considerable body of literature. Much of this literature is largely descriptive. A considerable portion is normative, relating to the problem of 'national sovereignty'. Only a relatively small fraction relates to economic-theoretical issues, such as the motivation for foreign direct investment and the effects on the host country.

A. Types of Foreign Direct Investment

A firm's expansion by foreign direct investment can take any of three forms: *horizontal expansion* (producing the same products as in the domestic market), *vertical expansion* (adding a stage in the production process that comes before or is subsequent to the firm's principal processing activity), or *conglomerate expansion* (producing different goods from those for the domestic market).

---

1 This decision is theoretically different from the decision to expand the production facilities of an already established foreign affiliate (subsidiary). See Edith Penrose, 'Foreign Investment and the Growth of the Firm', *Economic Journal*, vol. 66, June 1956, pp. 220–35. See also J. David Richardson, 'Theoretical Considerations in the Analysis of Direct Foreign Investment', *Western Economic Journal*, vol. 9, March 1971, pp. 87–98. In this chapter we do not examine the issues relating to investment in expanding an existing subsidiary.

The greatest part (in terms of value) of foreign direct investment involves either horizontal expansion to produce the same or a similar line of goods abroad, or vertical integration backwards into the production of some raw material(s).[2] Foreign direct investment of the conglomerate type is very rare.[3] Thus we concentrate on the horizontal form and on the vertical backward integration of the parent company.

B.   Alternatives to Foreign Direct Investment

If a firm wants to penetrate a foreign market, it can do so by exporting, by licensing a foreign producer, or by establishing production facilities in the foreign market, that is, undertaking foreign direct investment (FDI).

Exporting is usually undertaken prior to establishing production facilities in a foreign market. Exports are probably the best way for exploring the profitability of foreign direct investment (see p. 330).

The choice between licensing and FDI has not been fully explored in the economic literature.[4] Some general observations, however, can be made. First, the greater the transaction costs for licensing, the stronger the incentive for foreign direct investment. Second, foreign direct investment is more profitable than licensing if the advantage of the firm consists of a continuous flow of innovative knowledge. Third, foreign direct investment is more risky than licensing and requires commitment of funds. A profit-maximising firm will evaluate each strategy on the basis of the returns and costs involved in each case. Fourth, foreign direct investment will be preferred to licensing if the firm possesses not only a technological advantage but also has funds and managerial skills in excess of its domestic needs (see section III of this chapter).

In the next section we shall present various hypotheses pertaining to the causes (determinants) of foreign direct investment. These hypotheses may be classified in four groups.

(1) *Strictly economic theories.* These theories stress purely economic factors as determinants of foreign direct investment. Prominent among them is the 'specific-advantage' hypothesis, which postulates that the cause of foreign direct investment is some advantage that the multinational firms have which gives them

---

[2] In many cases foreign subsidiaries take the form of sales agencies, constituting a vertical integration forwards. However, the capital investment in them is small, and they will not be examined in this chapter.

[3] E. R. Barlow and I. T. Wender, *Foreign Investment and Taxation* (Prentice-Hall, 1955).

[4] C. P. Kindleberger, *American Business Abroad: Six Lectures on Direct Investment* (Yale University Press, 1969); J. H. Dunning (ed.), *International Investment* (Penguin Books, 1972); R. F. Mikesell (ed.), *US Private and Government Investment Abroad* (Academic Press, 1962) ch. 5; Kingman Brewster, *Antitrust and American Business Abroad* (Holt, Rinehart & Winston, 1958) ch. 7.

a lead over host-country producers. Such advantage may stem from a technologically superior product or process, managerial skills, multi-plant economies, internal financial resources from retained earnings, and the like.

(2) *Strictly subjective theories.* These theories stress the subjective attitudes of management towards foreign direct investment. Foreign direct investment is explained by behavioural factors relating to the preferences of managers for establishing operations in foreign markets.

(3) *Dynamic theories of foreign direct investment.* These theories concentrate on the patterns of foreign direct investment over time. The most important of these theories is the 'product-cycle' hypothesis, which postulates that there is a rigid cycle of foreign market exploitation. Exporting and investment abroad are separate stages in the dynamic process by which multinational firms expand into foreign markets. In particular, foreign investment is the successor to foreign trade (exporting): foreign investment is undertaken to protect the share attained in a foreign market by exports. This sequence is inevitable in the life cycle of a product and cannot be reversed.

(4) *'Generalised' theories.* These theories combine strictly economic factors, subjective-behavioural factors and dynamic considerations in explaining the foreign investment decision. Neither economic factors nor behavioural factors alone can provide a realistic theory of foreign direct investment. And the 'product-cycle' hypothesis does not have the degree of generality required by a theory, though as a rule exporting does precede foreign direct investment in most cases. Thus general models which combine economic and non-economic aspects, and are compatible with the observed sequence of exporting and direct investment activities, are of particular interest.

In section III we shall discuss the main *economic* effects of foreign direct investment in the host country. Normative aspects, relating to the trade-off between economic benefits and national sovereignty, will not be discussed.

Finally, in section IV, we shall present the results of the most important empirical studies on the causes and effects of foreign direct investment.

II.   CAUSES OF FOREIGN DIRECT INVESTMENT

A.   Preliminary Remarks

The existing body of theory on multinational corporations has been developed by drawing upon several branches of economic theory. Dunning,[5] Caves[6] and others have convincingly argued that there is no need for a special theory of the multinational corporation, because the establishment and operation of such

---

[5] J. H. Dunning (ed.), *Multinational Enterprise and Economic Analysis* (Allen & Unwin, 1974).

[6] R. E. Caves, 'International Corporations: The Industrial Economics of Foreign Investment', *Economica*, 1971, pp. 1–27.

firms, as well as the effects of their activities, can be adequately explained by the existing body of economic theory. In particular, the causes and effects of foreign direct investment can be analysed in the framework of the general theory of the firm, the theory of investment, the theory of location, the theory of industrial organisation, and the theory of international trade. This can be understood if we look at the distinctive features (nature) and behaviour of the multinational firm.

(1) It is an observed fact that horizontal direct investment is undertaken by oligopolistic firms, which tend to be large in size, more profitable, more advertising- and research-orientated and more diversified than firms which do not invest abroad.[7] In other words, oligopoly with product differentiation prevails in domestic industries, whose large firms become multinational.[8]

(2) Similarly, oligopoly, not necessarily differentiated, in the domestic market is typical in industries which undertake vertical direct investment in foreign countries.[9]

(3) In the case of horizontal investments, multinationals tend to populate foreign industries which are oligopolistic with strong barriers to entry. The investing parent firm, being established in the home market, enjoys the usual advantages that create barriers to new entry. Thus they can break the barriers of foreign markets, but they expect these barriers to be maintained after they penetrate the foreign market, so as to ensure excess profits in the long run. Short-run opportunities (typical of easy entry) do not provide adequate inducement for foreign direct investment. Thus foreign direct investment extends the recognition of mutual interdependence (the basic characteristic of oligopoly) beyond national boundaries.[10] The market conduct of multinationals can be analysed within the theory of industrial organisation.

(4) Foreign direct investment involves movements of factors of production to the host country. In particular, foreign investment transmits equity capital, entrepreneurship and technological knowledge (in new products or processes) to another country in the form of an industry-specific package.[11] Furthermore, foreign direct investment is an alternative method of exploiting any advantage (technological, managerial, financial) to exporting or licensing. Factor movements, as well as the choice between such transfers of factors, exporting and licensing, involve tariff and other trade restrictions, factor-cost differentials between two countries, that is, considerations covered by the theory of international trade.

(5) The international corporation's plans to make horizontal or vertical investments in a foreign market are directly comparable with the firm's decisions of similar (horizontal or vertical) expansions in the domestic market.

[7] R. Vernon, *Sovereignty at Bay: The Multinational Spread of US Enterprises* (Basic Books, 1971).

[8] Caves, 'International Corporations'.

[9] Ibid.

[10] R. E. Caves, 'Multinational Firms, Competition, and Productivity in Host-Country Markets', *Economica*, 1974, pp. 176–93.

[11] Caves, 'International Corporations'.

(a) *Horizontal* foreign direct investment is analogous to the decision of becoming a multi-plant firm in the domestic country. Relevant factors in such a decision are technical, marketing, managerial, storage, transport, inventory and other forms of scale economies associated with a *single plant*, as well as similar *multi-plant* economies. These factors are analysed by the theory of production, the theory of investment and the theory of location. Furthermore, horizontal foreign direct investment constitutes entry to a foreign market, analogous to the entry of an established firm in a certain area to another region (market) of the same country. The implications of entry for the decision-making of the firm has attracted considerable attention in the modern theory of the firm,[12] as well as in the field of industrial organisation.[13]

(b) *Vertical* foreign investments are analogous to 'backward' integration in the domestic market. For the competing producers in the host country, this type of entry forecloses a part of the former market for the output of this stage. That is, competing independent producers in the host country lose the sales to the parent company, which will be supplied by its own subsidiary, irrespective of price conditions.

Taking into account the above distinctive nature of the multinational corporation, it is not surprising that economists have drawn on the existing body of economic theory to provide an explanation of the causes and effects of foreign direct investment.

B.   Causes of Horizontal Foreign Investment

Several hypotheses have been postulated to explain why corporations undertake horizontal investments abroad in order to produce in foreign markets the same general line of commodities as they produce in their domestic market. The most important are outlined below.

(i) *The 'Specific-Advantage' Hypothesis*

Most writers attempt to explain the foreign investment decision in terms of a specific advantage that the investing firms have relative to the producers of a foreign (host) country. They argue that a firm undertaking production in a foreign country has disadvantages as compared with a local entrepreneur. A native entrepreneur has accumulated knowledge about the economic, social, political, legal and cultural conditions in his home market and 'knows where to look'. The foreign entrepreneur has to pay for the acquisition of such knowledge, and to that extent, due to his alien status, he operates at a cost disadvantage.[14]

[12] See A. Koutsoyiannis, *Modern Microeconomics*, 2nd edn (Macmillan, 1979) chs 13 and 14.
[13] See J. Bain, *Industrial Organization* (Wiley, 1958).
[14] H. C. Eastman and S. Stykolt, *The Tariff and Competition in Canada* (Macmillan, 1967).

Furthermore, he runs the risk of foreign-exchange instability and expropriation. To offset such disadvantages the foreign firm must possess some advantage.

The 'specific-advantage' hypothesis was originally postulated by Hymer,[15] extended by Kindleberger[16] and Caves,[17] and rendered dynamic by Vernon.[18]

Caves[19] has classified the sources of specific (unique) advantages in three groups.

(1) *Technological advantage in products or processes.* The large oligopolistic firms, that undertake direct foreign investment, have a specific (unique) asset in the form of a patented differentiated product or a patented new method of production. It is assumed that firms having such unique assets are profit-maximisers, and hence will establish production facilities abroad only if by investing abroad they can earn a higher yield than by exporting or licensing.

It should be noted that not all types of technological advantage will lead to foreign direct investment. Only under two conditions will a new product or process be exploited by producing directly in a foreign market:

(a) The unique asset must be readily transferable from one country to another within the firm at no extra cost (or very little additional cost), i.e. without the firm having to incur the sunk costs of the initial invention.

(b) Its imitation by competitors must be very difficult (for example, introduction of a close substitute may be too expensive), or impossible (for example, the product is protected by a patent). In other words, the unique asset must have the characteristics of a public good within the firm and must be enterprise-specific.[20]

If the transfer of the asset involves considerable costs and/or other firms can easily imitate it, the advantage of the parent company over host-country producers will be negligible, or may even become negative.[21]

Caves stresses product differentiation as the main source of technological advantage. Differentiation may be due to physical differences (different technical characteristics) of the product, 'brand name', differences in 'style', differences in services associated with the product (prompt delivery or repair services), or it can be created by advertising and other selling activities of the firm.[22]

---

[15] S. Hymer, 'International Operations of National Firms: A Study of Direct Foreign Investment', unpublished Ph.D. disseration, M.I.T., 1960.

[16] Kindleberger, *American Business Abroad*; and Kindleberger (ed.), *The International Corporation* (M.I.T. Press, 1970).

[17] Caves, 'International Corporations'.

[18] R. Vernon, 'International Investment and International Trade in the Product Cycle', *Quarterly Journal of Economics*, vol. 80, 1965, pp. 190–207.

[19] R. E. Caves, 'Causes of Direct Investment: Foreign Firms' Shares in Canadian and UK Manufacturing Industries', *Review of Economics and Statistics*, 1974, pp. 279–93.

[20] Harry Johnson, 'The Efficiency and Welfare Implications of the International Corporation', in *The International Corporation*, ed. Kindleberger, ch. 2.

[21] S. Kardasz, 'The Causes and Consequences of Direct Investment: A Review of Selected References', unpublished paper, University of Waterloo, 1974.

[22] See E. H. Chamberlin, *The Theory of Monopolistic Competition* (Harvard University Press, 1933) ch. 4. Also Koutsoyiannis, *Modern Microeconomics*.

(2) *Entrepreneurial excess capacity*. Several writers have argued that the cause of foreign direct investment is under-utilised entrepreneurial resources of the firm. The firm expands abroad (becomes multinational) in order to give full employment to its fixed stock of managerial talent. Unique managerial skills (in production or marketing) do not create product differentiation, but they can be the source of higher efficiency relative to foreign producers. It should be stressed that the firm's management must have specific skills, associated with the production and/or marketing activities of the parent company. If the firm has excess capacity in managerial personnel whose skills are not related to a particular product, the firm would prefer to use such personnel for conglomerate expansion at home rather than becoming multinational, since the alien environment of an unfamiliar foreign market may well be expected to reduce the efficiency of management.

The managerial-advantage hypothesis provides theoretical support to the widely held view that the success of US multinational firms is due to the higher quality (efficiency) of American entrepreneurial talent.[23] It also seems to support the suggestion that multinational corporations become those firms which have managerial teams 'with international decision horizons', i.e. management which takes a world-wide view of the profit opportunities open to the firm.[24]

(3) *Multi-plant economies*. Some writers attribute direct foreign investment to multi-plant economies. It is argued that large corporations, having exhausted all possible economies within single plants, can attain further reductions in their costs by becoming multi-plant in the domestic market. If the economies to the multi-plant are not exhausted in the home market, the natural development is to establish new plants in other countries. Thus the multinational corporation, according to this argument, becomes simply a species of the multi-plant firm: a firm with plants operating in different countries.[25]

The main sources of multi-plant economies are marketing economies, advertising economies,[26] administrative economies from co-ordination of input purchases or output distribution (transport and inventory economies, for example), or economies from spreading the cost of R & D over larger outputs.

(ii) *The 'Capital-Abundance' Hypothesis*

This stems from the factor-endowments theory of international trade. According

[23] J. J. Servan-Schreiber, *The American Challenge* (Atheneum, 1968).

[24] Barlow and Wender, *Foreign Investment and Taxation*; Also J. N. Behrman, *Some Patterns in the Rise of the Multinational Enterprise*, Research Paper No. 18, Graduate School of Business, University of North Carolina, 1969.

[25] This explanation has been advanced by Eastman and Stykolt, *The Tariff and Competition in Canada*. A similar view is held by J. C. McManus, 'The Theory of the Multinational Firm', in *The Multinational Firm and the Nation State*, ed. G. Paquet (Collier-Macmillan, 1972) pp. 66–93.

[26] J. Bain, *Barriers to New Competition* (Harvard University Press, 1956). Also W. S. Comanor and T. A. Wilson, *Advertising and Market Power* (Harvard University Press, 1974).

to this hypothesis, flows of direct investment move from countries well endowed to countries poorly endowed with money (equity) capital.[27] There is not much evidence to support this hypothesis. A casual review of the available information on capital flows reveals that such flows take place between countries where profit rates are high. Surely capital does not flow out of the USA because profitability is low there! As we mentioned earlier, foreign investments involve transfer of several factors simultaneously – in a 'package'. A foreign investment transmits equity capital as well as entrepreneurship and technological or other knowledge. Thus equity capital is only one of the factors involved, and in most cases it is not the most important consideration in the decision to invest abroad.

(iii) *The 'Research and Development' Hypothesis*

Several writers have argued that the cause of foreign direct investment is the research intensity of the firm or the industry. For example, Gruber, Mehta and Vernon[28] have found that the share of American subsidiaries in Western Europe is strongly correlated with the research intensity of the industries of the parent companies. The greater the R & D expenditures in an industry, the greater the share of the subsidiaries of parent corporations in such industry in the foreign markets of Western Europe. Horst[29] reaches a similar conclusion for the share of US manufacturing firms in the Canadian market. His sample included eighteen two-digit manufacturing industries for the year 1963. Horst found that both the exports and the FDI of the various industries were positively correlated with the research and development expenditure in the corresponding industries. Also, research and development expenditures on new products have been found related to the amount of FDI of the USA.[30] If one takes into account the fact that most research and development expenditure is devoted to new products, one can plausibly argue that the 'research and development' hypothesis is subsumed in the 'specific-advantage' hypothesis: research and development activities result in superior products and/or processes which give a definite advantage to investing firms over the local producers in foreign countries. However, as we mentioned earlier, R & D is not the only way for attaining a specific advantage. Thus the 'R & D' hypothesis is supplementary to the 'specific-advantage' hypothesis, the latter being built on a wider basis, and hence being able to provide a better explanation of the flow of foreign direct investment.

[27] This view is expressed by Hugh G. J. Aitken, *American Capital and Canadian Resources* (Harvard University Press, 1961).

[28] W. Gruber, D. Mehta and R. Vernon, 'The R & D Factor in International Trade and International Investment of US Industries', *Journal of Political Economy*, vol. 75, 1967, pp. 20–37.

[29] Thomas Horst, 'The Industrial Composition of US Exports and Subsidiary Sales to the Canadian Market', *American Economic Review*, 1972, pp. 37–45.

[30] Robert Lacroix, 'Pour une théorie de l'investissement direct étranger dans l'industrie manufacturière', unpublished MS, University of Montreal, 1970, ch. 2.

(iv) *The 'Barriers to Entry' Hypothesis*

The 'specific-advantage' hypothesis stresses product differentiation as the main cause of foreign direct investment (apparently product differentiation is one of the most powerful barriers to entry),[31] as well as other advantages, such as a patented process, economies of scale, absolute cost advantage, ability to secure the initial capital, multi-plant economies, excess managerial skills, and excess liquidity of the parent company.

However, foreign direct investment can take place even when the investing firm has no specific advantage *vis-à-vis* the local producers of host countries, so long as there are barriers to entry in the foreign markets which are expected to persist in the long run. The firm is equally efficient as its potential foreign competitors, enjoying the same advantages that create the barriers to entry in the host country. If such a firm has excess liquidity (abundant retained earnings from its operations at home), or excess technological knowledge, or excess managerial talent, which can yield a higher return when employed abroad (in a market protected by long-run entry barriers) rather than at home, foreign direct investment will take place. A firm, in other words, which has excess supply of some key factor (such as excess liquidity, excessive technological knowledge and under-utilised managerial personnel) has several alternatives. For example

(1) Use them for conglomerate expansion (diversification) at home.
(2) Dismiss the personnel, or dispose of other assets that are in excess of its needs.
(3) Use these excess resources for producing abroad, i.e. enter a foreign market where barriers give rise to excess profits. The firm, having the same (or very similar) advantages as the local producers, can break these barriers, capture a share of the market and secure part of the excess profits which were previously accruing to the local producers.

It follows that seller concentration (and the associated barriers to entry in the foreign market), as well as the size and growth of the foreign market, may well explain the amount of foreign investment in some industries, even when the investing firms have no specific advantage whatsoever over their foreign (host-country) competitors.

(v) *The 'Tariff' Hypothesis*

Several writers have argued that tariffs are a powerful determinant of the foreign investment decision. High tariffs impede exports in protected foreign markets. To offset this trade barrier and maintain the share of sales, firms install production facilities in the foreign market.[32] There is considerable survey evidence

---

[31] Bain, *Barriers to New Competition*. See also all earlier references to the writings of economists stressing the 'specific-advantage' hypothesis.

[32] A theoretical treatment of the effect of tariffs on the foreign investment decision can be found in T. Horst, 'The Theory of the Multinational Firm: Optimal Behaviour Under Different Tariff and Tax Rates', *Journal of Political Economy*, vol. 79, 1971, pp. 1059–72.

pointing to the influence of tariffs on foreign direct investment.[33] Several econometric studies[34] have also provided evidence of the effects of the height of tariffs on foreign investment activity. Finally, there is some indirect evidence of the impact of tariffs, from data showing that foreign subsidiaries (in Canada and Australia) have higher production costs than their parent companies at home. This should be due to the tariff structure in host countries, since the same surveys indicate that subsidiaries tend to be profitable relative to their parents.[35] Higher profitability, when production costs are higher, may well be explained by high tariffs in foreign markets.

A final point on tariffs should be made. A high tariff wall or an increase in tariffs will not necessarily increase the inflow of foreign direct investment. If tariffs protect markets where productivity and profitability is high, foreign investment will be attracted: the tariffs reduce imports; thus firms, in order to defend the share they had attained through their exports, undertake direct production in the foreign market. Furthermore, multinationals are attracted to foreign markets with high profitability (arising from higher efficiency or lower costs, or from monopoly power associated with the offered product). This profitability may well be greater after the increase (or imposition) of the tariff, a fact that will enhance the inflow of foreign direct investment. However, if a tariff is imposed to protect an inefficient industry, where profitability is low, foreign investment will not be enhanced by such a tariff, especially if entry to that industry is easy. An efficient firm could establish a subsidiary in such a foreign market, but its profitability would be short-lasting, as new entrants may well imitate its product or organisation. Such transient (temporary) profits are not an adequate incentive to offset the disadvantages of the alien status of the subsidiary.

In summary, the impact of tariffs is closely related to the 'specific-advantage' hypothesis. Such advantage is the cause of expecting high returns in the long run, and a tariff would reinforce such expectations. Tariffs have an impact when combined with product differentiation. If there is no product differentiation, a tariff may have no impact on foreign direct investment. For example, in countries such as Canada and Australia, tariff protection is pervasive in all manufacturing industries. Yet direct investment is much stronger in differentiated industries (such as automobiles, consumer durables, scientific instruments, chemicals, rubber), and much less common in undifferentiated industries (like textiles and steel).

[33] Eastman and Stykolt, *The Tariff and Competition in Canada*; D. T. Brash, *American Investment in Australian Industry* (Australian National University Press, 1966); and Barlow and Wender, *Foreign Investment and Taxation*.

[34] Horst, 'The Industrial Composition of US Exports and Subsidiary Sales to the Canadian Market'; also D. Orr, 'The Industrial Composition of US Exports and Subsidiary Sales to the Canadian Market', *American Economic Review*, 1978.

[35] A. E. Safarian, *Foreign Ownership of Canadian Industry* (McGraw-Hill, 1966); A. E. Safarian, *The Performance of Foreign-owned Firms in Canada* (Private Planning Association of Canada, 1969); 'The Gray Report', or *Foreign Direct Investment in Canada* (Information Canada, 1972); Brash, *American Investment in Australian Industry*, ch. 7.

(vi) *The 'Lower Production Costs' Hypothesis*

It is sometimes argued that large corporations establish a foreign subsidiary in order to avail themselves of lower production costs and reap 'efficiency' profits in the foreign market. This is the familiar comparative cost advantage theory of international trade, and is relevant to the choice between producing at home and exporting in the foreign country or establishing direct production abroad.

There is some confusion regarding this argument; thus some clarifications become necessary.

First, the reader should be clear about the difference between the *specific advantage* that investing firms have relative to their foreign competitors, and the *comparative advantage* of international trade theory. As we saw, a specific advantage may arise from a new, superior product, a technologically more efficient method of production, skilled managerial or other personnel, multi-plant economies from marketing and/or buying skills, or rationalisation of the administration of the various plants, of excess liquidity, etc. The traditional 'comparative cost advantage' of the theory of international trade refers to factor-cost differences between countries. The typical types of such costs are the labour costs, raw-material costs, cost of finance and scale economies.

Second, if factor costs are lower in the host country, they are presumably accessible to local entrepreneurs. The question then arises why domestic producers do not take advantage of these cost advantages. Several explanations have been advanced.

(a) The cost of finance is higher for local producers. Multinational corporations usually have abundant internal funds, and there is evidence that subsidiaries have access to the parent company's funds at a lower cost relative to the financing cost of host-country producers.

(b) Scale economies (minimum optimal scale) are easier to attain by foreign subsidiaries, because they can supply not only the foreign market but other third countries, or even ship back part of their output to the home country, provided that the cost savings of production are higher than the transportation and other export costs.

(c) Foreign investing companies are likely to enjoy specific advantages over host-country producers. There is considerable evidence that investing firms have superior knowhow and sophisticated products as well as more efficient managerial personnel relative to domestic competitors. Foreign direct investment may use local raw materials and unskilled or semi-skilled labour, but the subsidiary will use the superior technology of the parent company and will employ skilled management and other technical personnel from the reserves of the parent company or hired by it in the 'parent' country.

(d) Raw materials in the host country are important for vertically integrating multinationals (these will be discussed later).

(e) Intermediate products will often be imported from the parent company, at a lower cost than the local producers can attain.

(f) Labour costs are not always lower in host countries. But even if they are, the cost differential may be due to lower productivity, so that they are not a real advantage to the investing multinational.

Surveys of investing companies have tended to show that actual average production cost is, if anything, a minor motivation to invest in a foreign market.[36] As we will see later, the existence of profitable (low-cost) investment opportunities is not a sufficient condition for 'going abroad'.[37]

Third, factor-cost differences may be offset by other considerations. For example, several writers have argued that cost differences are not decisive in the decision regarding foreign direct investment. As we will see later, Vernon[38] and others postulate that foreign direct investment is the natural successor of exporting: exports are initially used to test a foreign market, but eventually firms switch to local production through a subsidiary, for better adaptation of the product to the needs of the local market, or for providing better and/or lower-cost service to the local customers. The marketing advantages of having production and servicing facilities 'on the spot' are particularly important for producer goods, but they are also crucial for consumer goods. Exports may be difficult to expand, for the sole reason that foreign customers feel that a source of supply which must cross oceans and national boundaries is inherently more risky than a local source of supply. Hence buyers may choose local products rather than imported ones. American firms have reported considerable increases in foreign sales solely for this reason when they switch to direct production in foreign markets.[39]

(vii) *The 'Foreign Government Inducements' Hypothesis*

A popular belief is that foreign direct investment has been influenced by various measures of host-country governments. Such measures are in fact policy-motivated cost reductions in the form of various concessions to foreign investors. The most common forms of such concessions are (a) tax differentials and incentives, (b) depreciation allowances, and (c) favourable interest rates and credit conditions. These are tools which are widely used, especially by developing countries, to promote foreign investment. The available evidence shows that these policies have had minor influences on the decision of multinationals.[40] Richardson provides a

---

[36] Brash, *American Investment in Australian Industry*, p. 46.

[37] J. D. Richardson, 'On "Going Abroad": The Firm's Initial Foreign Investment Decision', *Quarterly Review of Economics and Business*, 1971, pp. 7–22.

[38] Vernon, 'International Investment and International Trade in the Product Cycle', pp. 190–202.

[39] Behrman, *Some Patterns in the Rise of the Multinational Enterprise*.

[40] Lawrence B. Krause and Kenneth W. Dam, *Federal Tax Treatment of Foreign Income* (Brookings Institute, 1964) pp. 92–3; Judd Polk, Irene W. Meister and Lawrence A. Veit, *US Production Abroad and the Balance of Payments* (National Industrial Conference Board, 1966) pp. 50, 64–5; Barlow and Wender, *Foreign Investment and Taxation*, pp. 215–17; Brash, *American Investment in Australian Industry*, p. 48; H. Hughes and You Poh Seng (eds), *Foreign Investment and Industrialisation in Singapore* (University of Wisconsin Press, 1969) pp. 158–9, 183–5.

plausible explanation of the failure of policy-motivated cost reductions in enhancing the inflow of foreign investment in underdeveloped countries (see below, p. 346).

(viii) *'The Multinational Fad' Hypothesis*

A large number of references to the 'bandwagon effect', the 'multinational fad' and 'follow-the-leader behaviour' exist in the economic literature on multinationals.[41] Foreign direct investment is, according to this view, influenced by the behaviour of other firms in the same or other industries. The 'group-behaviour' hypothesis is gaining ground in economic literature. There is substantial evidence that firms imitate their rivals in various policies.[42] Firms tend to comply to standards and norms established in the industry.[43] Such 'group motivation' is particularly strong for the investment decision, given that the large corporations are growth-seekers, and hence very sensitive to relative market shares. If some close competitor makes a successful foreign investment, this is bound to affect the foreign investment decisions of other firms in the industry. Oligopolistic interdependence enhances imitative behaviour. Investments motivated for such competitive reasons are often referred to as 'defensive' investments. We will return to this point when examining Richardson's model (see below, p. 328).

(ix) *Vernon's 'Product-Cycle' Hypothesis*

Vernon[44] and others[45] consider foreign direct investment as a natural stage in the life cycle of a product.

According to Vernon, the theory of comparative advantage of international trade, as well as the various hypotheses pertaining to the explanation of the

[41] Kindleberger, *American Business Abroad*, p. 57; J. N. Behrman, 'Foreign Investment Muddle: The Perils of Ad Hoccery', *Columbia Journal of World Business*, 1965, pp. 51–8; L. Gordon and E. L. Grommers, *United States Manufacturing Investment in Brazil* (Harvard University Press, 1962) p. 149; C. F. Karsten, 'Should Europe Restrict US Investments?', *Harvard Business Review*, 1965, pp. 53–61; R. N. Farmer and B. M. Richman, 'International Business: Form and Motivation', in *International Economics and Business: Selected Readings*, ed. W. Krause and F. J. Mathis (Houghton Mifflin, 1968).

[42] H. Leibenstein, 'Allocative Efficiency vs *X*-efficiency', *American Economic Review*, 1966. Leibenstein argues that firms are not cost-minimisers. Firms adjust their unit cost of production to the 'weighted average' unit cost of the industry as a whole.

[43] A. Koutsoyiannis, 'Managerial Job Security and the Capital Structure of Firms', *Manchester School*, 1978. Here it is argued that firms set their target debt equity ratio to the most recently observed 'industry average debt equity ratio'. See also A. Koutsoyiannis, *A Managerialist Theory of Capital Structure: Some New Evidence*, University of Waterloo, Economics Research Series, 1981. And also it is generally accepted that the firm's dividend payout is set at the level of other similar firms in the industry to which the firm belongs (see Chapter 9).

[44] Vernon, 'International Investment and International Trade in the Product Cycle'.

[45] Gruber, Mehta and Vernon, 'The R & D Factor in International Trade and International Investment of US Industries'.

flows of foreign direct investment, although relevant in some cases, cannot provide an adequate explanation of trade and international investment. In particular, Vernon argues that the theory of factor endowments and comparative cost advantage, while providing a simple elegant model of capital movements, lacks realism. Thus Vernon sets less emphasis upon the comparative-cost doctrine and more upon the timing of innovation, the uncertainty at the various stages of developing and marketing a new product and the effects of economies of scale. Vernon's contention is that the traditional theory of comparative advantage and factor endowments becomes more realistic (though less elegant) by introducing to it the roles of innovation, scale economies, the accumulating stock of knowledge and reduction of uncertainty in the development of new products, and oligopolistic interdependence between the large multinational corporations.

The basis of Vernon's 'product-cycle' hypothesis is that firms established in the rich developed countries have a strong stimulus to *acquire* a technological advantage over producers in other less developed markets. While other theorists *assume* that multinationals have a specific advantage, Vernon explains theoretically how this advantage is acquired.

A technologically superior product or method of production is created by large corporations which spend more on research and development. There are two reasons why firms in advanced countries have a higher R & D intensity. First, they operate in markets with high *per capita* incomes. As consumers become more affluent, they want better and new products to enjoy their riches. Firms operating in such markets become aware of these needs and respond by devoting more funds to the development of new (and/or higher-quality) products. Proximity of firms to rich markets is a powerful determinant of research and development expenditures. Second, developed economies have in general high labour unit costs and an abundant supply of capital. This makes labour-intensive commodities and techniques relatively expensive. Hence the firms located in such countries have an incentive to develop products and processes which are relatively more capital intensive. For example, the development of drip-dry clothing items and of home washing and drying machines may be attributed to the relative supply of labour and capital, and the same holds true for the development of industrial products such as the fork-lift truck or the introduction of the conveyor belt and automatic control systems, the increasing use of computers at all stages of the operations of firms, and so on.

In summary, Vernon postulates that innovation (investment in the development of new products or methods of production) depends on the ability of firms to be the first to perceive an opportunity for high-income markets or for labour-saving new products and processes.[46] In turn, the perception of the need for a new product or process is a function of spatial proximity. Firms that operate in

---

[46] Similar hypotheses have been discussed by H. G. Barnett, *Innovation: The Basis of Cultural Change* (McGraw-Hill, 1953). Also Albert O. Hirschman, *The Strategy of Economic Development* (Yale University Press, 1958).

high-income markets are more likely to be the first to identify the need for new products. The specific advantage in the form of a new product or process thus depends on the proximity of firms to high-income markets or markets in need of labour-saving products and processes.

The above hypothesis can explain the advantage that large corporations of investing countries acquire in consumer as well as in industrial products. Regarding industrial innovation in general, Vernon hypothesises that industrial producers develop at an earlier time labour-saving methods of production which are more efficient and can be used in foreign markets, putting host-country producers at a cost disadvantage. The same holds for the development of new key raw materials. A classical example is West Germany's outstanding success in the development and use of plastics.[47] This advantage may plausibly be attributed to the timing of the perception of the need for substitute raw materials: West Germany recognised at an early stage that a market existed for synthetic substitutes.

Once a specific advantage (in the form of a new product or a new process) is acquired by the firm, there are, according to Vernon, four separate (distinct) stages in its exploitation.

Stage 1. In the first stage the new commodity will be produced (or the new process applied) in the country where the firm is already located. Cost considerations (of location, production and distribution) are not important at this stage, contrary to the traditional theory of production and location. This is due to several factors.

(a) In the early stages of introduction of a new product there is no or very little standardisation. (Good examples are found in the automobile and the radio industries.) Given this lack of standardisation, producers are very concerned to have the production under close control, so as to be able to secure the appropriate inputs and components. Smooth production, secured by flexibility in the sources of supply, is more essential than cost considerations at this stage. Disruption of production at the early stages of the introduction of a product can be very damaging in establishing it in the market.

(b) Another reason why costs are of lesser importance is that a new product introduced in a high-income market has low price and income elasticities. This gives a high degree of monopoly power to the innovating firm, which can pass the higher costs of production on to the buyers by charging a higher price.

(c) The innovating firm wants to be able to diagnose and deal swiftly with the specific requirements of the customers. Buyers may want some changes in the specifications of the product before they firmly adopt it.

(d) Finally, the firm wants to watch closely its competitors' reactions, to see how successful they are in introducing substitutes or imitating the product.

[47] C. Freeman, 'The Plastics Industry: A Comparative Study of Research and Innovation', *National Institute Economic Review*, vol. 26, 1963; G. C. Hufbauer, *Synthetic Materials and the Theory of International Trade* (Duckworth, 1965).

These considerations imply that a firm at the initial stage of the introduction of a new product is mostly preoccupied with being in close contact with its customers as well as its suppliers. It will also want to be able to 'spy' closely on competitors' reactions when the latter are faced with the challenge of the new product. Hence, in the first stage of the product cycle, the firm will establish production facilities in its original home market.

Stage 2. During this stage the product becomes 'mature'.

(a) A certain degree of standardisation is attained. This has two consequences. First, standardisation opens up possibilities for achieving technical economies of scale, and hence lower unit costs. Second, the supply of components and other inputs presents fewer uncertainties.

(b) Competitors have had the time to develop substitutes. Thus the monopoly power of the innovator declines, its price elasticity is reduced, and cost considerations become more important.

(c) Such cost considerations will usually result in a re-examination of the location of production within the same country, as well as a reconsideration of the various sources of input supplies.

(d) The product begins to be known to foreign markets by the exporting activity of the innovating firm. The share of exports in relatively advanced foreign markets will grow at a high rate if the product has a high income elasticity (or if it is a satisfactory substitute for high-cost labour). Once the share in the foreign market has reached a certain size, firms are bound to consider establishing production in the foreign market (undertake foreign direct investment). There are several reasons for this. Foreign countries may impose a tariff in an attempt to protect local producers. The latter, being more informed about the tastes and preferences of buyers than foreign suppliers, can better satisfy these preferences; thus the competitive power of local producers increases over time, eroding the initial advantage of exports of the innovators.

In summary, in the stage of 'maturity of the product', standardisation leads to scale economies, the firm exports to foreign markets, and it starts considering the profitability of foreign direct investment. If the firm is a profit-maximiser, the firm will choose to continue exporting so long as the marginal production cost, plus the transport cost of the goods exported (including tariffs), is lower than the average cost of prospective production in the foreign market. However, profit considerations are not the only factors that affect the decision to 'go abroad'. In fact, Vernon argues that profitability aspects may be less important than other aims of the firm.

Stage 3. Vernon sees foreign direct investment as an inevitable stage in the exploitation of a new product (or a technological advantage in general). Implicit in his theory is that firms are more preoccupied with servicing best a foreign market than with strict profit maximisation. In particular, Vernon argues that once the share of exports in the foreign market has reached a certain level, several factors lead inevitably to direct foreign investment: (a) tariffs may be imposed to stop a further increase in imports; (b) scale economies from concentrating production in the home country are eventually exhausted – a plant in a foreign market becomes equally efficient as a plant in the domestic market; (c) providing prompt service (repairs, spare parts) to the foreign customers requires establishment of production facilities abroad. Delays in obtaining spare parts or lack of expert repair personnel are serious obstacles in expanding (or even maintaining) the attained share of sales in foreign markets. Foreign direct investment becomes a necessary defensive measure to maintain foreign market shares in an increasingly competitive environment.[48] To be sure, such investment behaviour is not optimising. However, there is substantial empirical evidence that the decision-making sequence in connection with international investments conforms to Vernon's theoretical model.[49] Any threat to the established position of an enterprise is, according to Vernon, a more powerful stimulus for action than profitability. An international investment by an exporter (irrespective of its profitability in strict terms) becomes a 'rational' action, since it forestalls the loss of a market. The profitability of such an investment is not judged in the conventional sense (of the difference between costs and revenues). It includes considerations (calculations of the consequences) of losses of income from a potential shrinkage of the share in the foreign market.

Stage 4. In this stage foreign subsidiaries will not only supply the market in which they are located but under certain conditions they will also export to other countries and possibly ship back part of their production to the parent country. This is more likely if the labour costs in the location of the affiliate are lower than in the country of the parent company. Once a firm has become multinational, producing in several countries, the allocation of production between the different plants will be decided on the basis of costs. There are three main cost items, decisive at this point: the cost of finance, the cost of labour, and scale economies. For an international firm one may plausibly argue that the costs of financing its operations in different locations are not sufficiently different to matter very much. Scale economies may also be considered as not being substantially different in the plants located in several countries, assuming that the minimum optimal plant scale is eventually reached by the affiliates. Consequently, the principal differences in costs between any two locations are likely to be labour costs. If these costs are lower in the countries where the subsidiaries operate, it may be profitable for the multinational firm to begin supplying other

[48] Vernon, 'International Investment and International Trade in the Product Cycle'; Gruber, Mehta and Vernon, 'The R & D Factor in International Trade and International Investment of US Industries'; R. Z. Aliber, 'A Theory of Direct Foreign Investment', in *The International Corporation*, ed. Kindleberger; R. Stobough *et al.*, 'US Multinational Enterprises and the US Economy', mimeo (Harvard Business School, 1972).

[49] See Yair Aharoni, *The Foreign Investment Decision Process* (Harvard Business School, 1966).

countries with exports from the affiliate. And, if labour-cost differences are large enough to offset transport costs, then exports back to the original (parent) country will be profitable.

Vernon's 'product-cycle' hypothesis can explain the widely spread phenomenon of the 'multinational fad' in some industries. Once a foreign investment is undertaken by a firm, other principal (major) competitors see it as a threat to the status quo:

(1) Competitors consider that they lose ground relative to the investing company, because they tend to view their 'share of the market in global terms'.

(2) Competitors cannot have an accurate idea of the profitability of the investing firm, operating as it does in an unfamiliar foreign area; thus they feel uneasy, because they think of the possibility that the rival might eventually import 'cheaper' output from his foreign subsidiary, a fact that might change the status quo in competitive power: the investing firm might start a price competition based on the lower costs of its foreign affiliate. This threat may lead to 'imitative' foreign investment, resulting in what is often called the 'multinational bandwagon' or 'multinational fad'. This is not, apparently, an optimising investment behaviour, but can surely be considered as rational, in view of the concern of firms with potential threats to the status quo.

Some comments on Vernon's 'product-cycle' hypothesis

(1) It should be clear that Vernon's hypothesis does not contradict the 'specific-advantage' hypothesis. It is complementary to it in two ways. First, it explains how the investing firm acquires a specific advantage over the producers in a foreign market. Second, it introduces time considerations in the static 'specific-advantage' hypothesis, thus rendering it dynamic.

(2) Vernon postulates a rigid time sequence in the exploitation of a technological advantage, according to which foreign direct investment is the natural successor to exporting. As we mentioned earlier, there is some evidence supporting Vernon's hypothesis (for automobiles, sewing machines, typewriters, tractors, and electrical and electronic products).

(3) However, the product-cycle hypothesis has not yet been tested adequately (see p. 363). Vernon states that his 'product-cycle' hypothesis is not an optimising investment behaviour. We believe that a more accurate statement is that Vernon's hypothesis is not competing but complementary to the profit-maximisation and sales-maximisation hypotheses: it can be incorporated in both models, enriching their static predictions.[50]

---

[50] T. Horst, 'The Theory of the Firm', in *Multinational Enterprise and Economic Analysis*, ed. J. H. Dunning (Allen & Unwin, 1974).

(x) *Richardson's Generalised Model of Foreign Direct Investment*

(a) *The Concept of Spatial Preference*

Richardson[51] has developed a general model of the initial foreign investment decision which combines the subjective attitudes of the firm's management with purely economic factors. Furthermore, Richardson's model integrates the dynamic aspects of Vernon's product-cycle hypothesis with the static factors of the competing theories of FDI. Richardson's analytical framework allows a more systematic treatment of the determinants of the decision to invest in a foreign country.

Strictly *economic factors*, stressed by most writers, are a necessary but not a sufficient condition for foreign direct investment. The existence of profitable investment opportunities (from a specific technological advantage, managerial expertise, favourable cost conditions in foreign markets, entry barriers or tariff barriers in the foreign markets, which give rise to monopoly power and potential excess profits, etc.) does not necessarily lead to foreign direct investment (a good example is the steel industry). Such expected profits may be offset by *subjective considerations*, which have been ignored in the traditional theory of production and investment. In consumption theory preferences play an important role in explaining consumer behaviour. In contrast, production and investment theory use isoquants which are measurable, and two investors faced with the same set of investment opportunities have been assumed to act identically in the absence of risk. When risk is present, a scale of subjective preferences is often introduced between risk and return. But risk-return models, while common in the theory of portfolio selection (financial investment decisions), have not been used in the theory of investment in plant and equipment.

Richardson introduces subjective factors in the form of a *spatial preference*, which is analogous to the 'time preference' in the theory of consumption. The economic principle of 'time preference' implies that the household has a preference for present consumption over future consumption, and must be paid a premium to induce it to forgo a given amount of current consumption in exchange for the same amount of consumption in a future period of time. The premium increases with time.

In a similar way, the concept of 'spatial preference' implies that the firm has a preference for operations in the location where it is already situated, even in the absence of risk. The firm has a definite aversion to new locations or markets which stems not only from physical distance but also from differences in language, political system, ideological and economic environment, in law and customs which differentiate two geographic areas. To induce the firm to build a plant in a new location, a premium (a higher return or profit) must accrue to the firm, and this premium must be sufficient to overcome the firm's aversion to new

[51] Richardson, 'On "Going Abroad" '.

locations. The degree of this aversion is called the 'rate of spatial preference', and it increases with 'distance'. The markets where the firm is already established have a zero 'rate of spatial preference', that is, the returns from investment in an established market are valued equally with returns from any other market in which the firm operates: no spatial premium must accrue to the firm for expanding its investment in its present location(s). However, 'distant' markets have a positive 'rate of spatial preference', just as distant time periods have a 'rate of time preference'. The more 'distant' the new market, the greater the rate of spatial preference and the greater the premium (return) that must accrue to the firm to break its 'spatial resistance' (or 'spatial inertia').

The consequence of the subjective factors (considerations) implied by the concept of 'spatial preference' is that equal profit opportunities in different markets around the world will not be valued equally by the firm. Potential profit opportunities in new markets must be greater than profit opportunities in the current location of the firm by at least the 'rate of spatial preference' appropriate to the particular market.

The firm evaluates the investment opportunities in each market (current or new market) on the basis of both *economic* factors, which define the profitability of the investment, and on *subjective* factors, which reflect the management's spatial preference. Thus for *each market* we have a valuation expression of the general form

$$U_j = f(\Pi_j, v) \tag{7.1}$$

where Π_j = expected average returns (profits) of prospective investment in the jth market

v = subjective variable, representing the spatial preference or inertial resistance of the management

U_j = returns adjusted for the rate of spatial preference of the managers

These objective functions could presumably by summed across all markets to arrive at a single valuation function for the firm. (This holds for firms which have no intermediate production. The valuation of a vertically integrated firm is discussed later.)

A convenient specific form of the above valuation expression is

$$U = \Pi^v \tag{7.2}$$

where $0 < v \leqslant 1$.

Let us examine the economic and subjective factors included in the above valuation functions.

(b) *Subjective Factors Affecting the Firm's Decision to 'Go Abroad'*

We said that the subjective preferences of the management are represented by the variable v. For markets or areas where the firm already has production operations, $v = 1$. This implies that for existing established markets $U_j = \Pi_j$, that is, the expected profits (Π_j) are the measure of the value of the investment. No adjustment for spatial preference is required for investments in expanding an existing operation.

For new markets or areas, $v < 1$. That is, spatial preference implies that investments in new markets must pay a premium (equal to $\Pi - \Pi^v$) in order to overcome the aversion of managers to new locations.

For markets or areas which for some reason are completely outside the firm's planning horizon, v approaches zero. For example, for small firms v probably approaches zero for any investment in a foreign market. These are firms which do not even consider the possibility of becoming multinationals ('going abroad'), no matter how profitable potential operations might be in foreign markets.

Small values of v for a given firm or industry may be the explanation of why a decision to undertake foreign direct investment is never made.

Being a subjective variable, v cannot be directly observed. However, we can list several factors which determine the spatial preference, and, therefore, if they change, they cause v to change. This is important, because, as we will presently see, v is a crucial determinant of the initial decision to undertake foreign direct investment.

(1) The amount of information about a foreign market affects the firm's spatial preference. Inadequate information gives rise to small values of v, the subjective spatial coefficient. Information can be increased by means of trade fairs, commercial missions and advertising by foreign governments. However, an even better source of increased information are exports to foreign markets. A gradual increase in exports may well be expected to lead to progressively higher values of v.[52]

(2) Spatial preference may be affected by political or exchange instability or government policies in foreign countries, factors which create a poor investment climate. Such factors may not only increase risk, but may also make the value of v very small.

(3) Expected growth opportunities, such as those which arose at the inception of the European Economic Community (EEC), may lead to some reduction in spatial preference, apart from the pure economic effects they have (increase of expected profits and sales). Buoyant foreign expectations reduce the subjective 'distance' between domestic and foreign markets.

(4) The undertaking of foreign investment by close rival firms is bound to have an effect on how a firm views foreign operations. The firm's spatial preference (or inertial resistance) is almost sure to be reduced, especially if competitors' foreign direct investment has been profitable. (These effects on v are additional to any economic effects, for example a reduction in potential demand facing the firm in question.) Investments motivated by competitors' strategic movements are often referred to as 'defensive' investments.

---

[52] But even with a given value of v, increasing exports may lead to foreign direct investment. This is the essence of Vernon's theory. Later we will examine Vernon's hypothesis within Richardson's analytical framework.

(5) In general, the number of firms (even from other industries) which become multinational affects the firm's spatial preferences. In the economic literature there is a large number of references to the 'bandwagon effect', the 'multinational fad' and 'follow-the-leader' behaviour.[53] Such behaviour is to a large extent explained by economic factors. But partly it can be explained by a decrease in spatial preference: the presence, in a foreign market, of familiar corporate suppliers, financial institutions and corporate customers reduces the 'foreignness' of a new market. The subjective impediments to going abroad (as measured by an increasing value of v) are reduced.

In summary, increases in general information about foreign markets, changes in the political or economic climate abroad, increased insight in foreign markets gained by an increased share of exports, growth expectations of foreign markets, the number of other firms (rivals or not) with multinational activities, all affect the spatial preferences of the firm, and hence change the value of the subjective variable v.

(6) Another subjective factor that affects the decision to 'go abroad' is the firm's target returns, U^*. This factor will be discussed in a subsequent paragraph.

(c) *Economic Factors Affecting the Firm's Decision to 'Go Abroad'*

Economic factors affect profitability (Π_j) in foreign markets. Richardson measures profitability in terms of the rate of return on the firm's *internal (scarce) resources*. These are those factors of production which cannot be purchased readily from outside the firm. The more important of these factors are skilled management, and to a lesser extent the availability of internal finance from retained profits.[54] Since a market does not exist for such resources, their amount (supply) is fixed in the short run, and this sets limits to the growth of the firm: the firm can undertake investments only up to the point of optimal employment of its managerial team (including production, marketing, forecasting, R & D and other specialised personnel).

The expected total earnings (returns) of the various prospective investment projects, divided by the number of 'management time units' required for their realisation, give the rate of return to management time. Richardson argues that this rate of return is superior to the conventional profitability measures, such as the rate of return on sales or on assets or on invested capital, since 'management time' is the limiting scarce resource, and the firm should aim at the maximisation of the returns on this resource.

The economic factors that determine the profitability of an investment in a foreign market are the factors that determine the demand and costs in domestic

[53] Kindleberger, *American Business Abroad*, p. 57; Behrman, 'Foreign Investment Muddle', p. 51; Gordon and Grommers, *United States Manufacturing Investment in Brazil*, p. 49; Karsten, 'Should Europe Restrict US Investments?', pp. 53–4; Farmer and Richman, 'International Business: Form and Motivation'.

[54] Internal finance is more important for smaller firms, because of absolute limits on the availability of outside funds.

and foreign markets. A systematic analysis of these factors is essential in order to understand Richardson's analytical framework and the relation between Richardson's model and the thoeretical hypotheses of other writers.

From the basic definition of profit, we have

$$\Pi_F = R_F - C_F = (P_F - AC_F)Q_F \tag{7.3}$$

where Π_F = profit in the foreign market

$R_F = P_F Q_F$ = total revenue in the foreign market

$C_F = (AC_F)Q_F$ = total cost of production in the foreign market

P_F = price in the foreign market

Q_F = amount of production in the foreign market

Two features of foreign direct investment must be stressed in relation to expression (7.3). *First*, foreign direct investment is undertaken by large oligopolistic firms, which have the usual advantages that create barriers to entry (product differentiation, technological knowhow, skilled personnel, internal financial resources, and marketing advantages, as well as buying expertise, which all give rise to pecuniary economies of scale). Such firms do not only have monopoly power in price-setting but they also enjoy substantial cost advantages. *Second*, multinational subsidiaries (affiliates) populate foreign markets which are oligopolistic, well protected by barriers to entry. The investing firm (multinational) can break down these barriers because it is an already established large oligopolist in the domestic market, enjoying all the advantages in unit costs and profitability. However, it expects the barriers to be maintained *post-entry*, so that it reaps monopoly profits in the long run. Short-term profit opportunities do not provide an adequate incentive for foreign direct investment.

A consequence of the above considerations is that a firm which contemplates investing in a foreign country may well be expected to have some control on the price that it can charge in the foreign market, P_F. Furthermore, there is a lower limit to this price below which no direct investment would be undertaken by the firm. Specifically, the firm will most probably have exported the final product to the particular foreign market, and hence it would expect to receive at least its own domestic price plus the costs of exporting (transportation costs, insurance, etc.) plus the tariff in the foreign market, that is

$$P_F \geqslant P_{\min} \tag{7.4}$$

where

$$P_{\min} = P_d + EC + T \tag{7.5}$$

P_d = price in the domestic market

EC = export costs

T = tariff

Assuming mark-up pricing in the domestic market, we may write

$$P_d = AC_d + m_d \tag{7.6}$$

where AC_d = unit cost in the domestic market

m_d = profit margin in the domestic market

The unit costs in the domestic market depend on factor prices, scale economies and the technological knowhow of the firm. The profit margin, m_d, depends on the monopoly power of the firm (concentration in the industry, product differentiation and other local barriers to entry).

Substituting (7.6) in expression (7.5) we obtain

$$P_{\min} = AC_d + m_d + EC + T \tag{7.7}$$

Expressions (7.5) and (7.7) imply that multinational corporations 'price up to the tariff'. There is considerable evidence that this is in fact the case.[55] If barriers in the foreign market are high, or the investing multinational firm has a considerable advantage over host-country producers, it may charge a price P_F higher than $P_{\min}$.

The unit cost in the foreign market, AC_F, depends on factor prices in the foreign country and the technology which the multinational will adopt. The latter depends to a certain extent on the size of the foreign market.

Combining the above relations we may write

$$\Pi_F = (AC_d + m_d + EC + T - AC_F)Q_F \tag{7.8}$$

In summary, the economic determinants of the profitability of direct foreign investment are:

AC_d	the unit costs of domestic production
m_d	the profit margin in the domestic market
EC	export costs
T	tariff in the foreign market
AC_F	the unit cost in the foreign market
Q_F	the scale of operations in the foreign market

A comparison of the above list with the determinants of direct foreign investment discussed by Caves shows that Richardson incorporates in his model all the economic forces which have been suggested by other writers as motives for 'going abroad'. This is further discussed in a subsequent paragraph.

(d) *The Foreign Investment Decision of the Firm*

Richardson describes the foreign investment decision of the firm as follows.

Stage 1. The firm estimates the expected profitability of the foreign investment, r_j.

The firm undertakes a market analysis (a study of cost and demand conditions) for each prospective investment project. This gives information on the expected profitability, Π_j, which the firm adjusts on the basis of the management's spatial

[55] Caves, 'International Corporations', p. 16.

preferences, defined by expression (7.2):

$$U_j = \Pi_j^{\,\nu}$$

The adjusted returns, U_j, if divided by the required (for this particular project) units of internal resources $(IR)_j$ yield the expected rate of return on each prospective investment:

$$r_j = \frac{U_j}{(IR)_j} \tag{7.9}$$

Stage 2. The firm sets a target *rate* of return, r^*. This is defined by the total target return, U^*, which the firm wants (desires) to earn on its total 'internal resources'. In other words, it is assumed that the firm is interested in earning a given total return on its scarce (non-marketable) resources. For example, assume that the only scarce internal resource is skilled management, and the firm has one hundred managerial time units available. If the firm sets as a target the earning of $U^* = \$5,000,000$ in total from the full employment of its managerial talent, the target *rate of* return is

$$r^* = \frac{U^*}{IR} = \$50,000 \text{ per unit of management time} \tag{7.10}$$

It is apparent from expression (7.10) that the target rate of return is inversely related to the availability of 'internal resources'. If the firm has a lot of excess managerial time, it will be satisfied with a lower target rate of return. Similarly, if the firm loses some of its managers, it will require a higher rate of return (less investment will be undertaken). Thus the amount of total investment is positively related to the firm's available 'internal resources'.

Another factor that affects the target return is the behaviour of close rivals. An actual or potential threat of entry in a foreign market will usually reduce U^* (and, hence, r^*).

In summary, we may write:

$$U^* = f(\text{Internal resources, competitors' reactions})$$

Stage 3. On the basis of the information of the previous two stages, the firm makes its decision to invest abroad, applying the following accept—reject criterion. If the expected rate of return exceeds the target rate (that is, if $r_j > r^*$), the investment will be undertaken. Conversely, if $r_j < r^*$, the foreign investment will not be undertaken.

This may not be a maximisation criterion for investment, but there is substantial evidence that this is in fact the way firms make decisions to invest abroad.[56]

---

[56] Behrman, *Some Patterns in the Rise of the Multinational Enterprise*, pp. 8 and 124; Aharoni, *The Foreign Investment Decision Process*, p. 43; Judd Polk, 'The Economic Implications of the Multinational Corporation', in *The Multinational Corporation* (US Department of State, Office of External Research, 1969) pp. 19—20; Polk, Meister and Veit, *US Production Abroad and the Balance of Payments*, pp. 61 and 73; Brash, *American Investment in Australian Industry*, p. 40; Barlow and Wender, *Foreign Investment and Taxation*, pp. 173—4.

Since 'internal resources' are given, the investment decision may be expressed in terms of *total* expected returns (U) relative to *total* target returns (U^*), instead of the expected *rate* of return relative to the *target rate* of return. Thus we can say that an investment will be undertaken if $U > U^*$. Conversely, an investment will be rejected if $U < U^*$.

The above procedure of the foreign investment decision can be formalised by deriving an *investment decision curve* or *investment opportunity frontier*. This is a curve on the $AC_F - Q_F$ space, showing $U = U^*$ at all points. In other words, the investment opportunity frontier is the locus of all combinations of unit costs (AC_F) and output (Q_F) which make an investment in the given foreign market barely attractive.

The investment opportunity frontier is derived by setting $U = U^*$.

Given that, by expression (7.2), $U = \Pi^v$, we may write

$$U^* = \Pi^v = [(P_F - AC_F)Q_F]^v \qquad (7.11)$$

Rearranging, we obtain

$$U^{*\,1/v} = (P_F - AC_F)Q_F \qquad (7.12)$$

We mentioned earlier that multinationals have control over the price they can charge, since direct horizontal investment takes place almost exclusively in oligopolistic markets with differentiated products. Furthermore, there is evidence that multinationals 'price up to the tariff'. Thus we may set $P_F = P_{min}$. Assuming given spatial preferences of the firm, as well as given target returns, and given P_{min}, we see that expression (7.12) is an implicit function of average cost and sales in the foreign market. This function generates a locus of average cost and sales (quantity) such that U is always equal to U^*. This locus is shown in Figure 7.1. This is a *decision curve*, in the sense that it is the *boundary* between investments that will be undertaken and those which will *not* be undertaken.

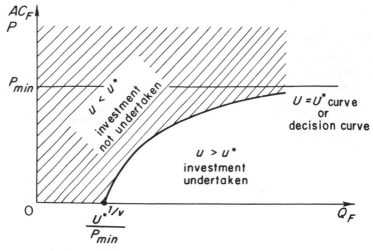

Figure 7.1   Investment opportunity frontier

(1) Points *on* the curve (such as point a in Figure 7.2) show average cost and corresponding sales such that $U = U^*$.

(2) Points *below* the curve show a lower AC_F for the given price (P_{min}) and any given level of output; hence, for investments which have AC_F and Q_F combinations below the curve, $U > U^*$, and such investments will apparently be undertaken. For example, consider point b in Figure 7.2. This point shows the average cost AC_B and the quantity Q_F of the given investment project B. Apparently $AC_B < AC_A$, while P_{min} and Q_F are the same as for project A (denoted by point a on the curve). Thus investment B will have $U_B > U^*$, because of its lower unit cost.

(3) Points *above* the curve imply a higher average cost at any given level of output. For example, project C, denoted by point c, has $AC_C > AC_A$, while sales are the same for both projects. Hence $U_C < U^*$, and project C will not be undertaken.

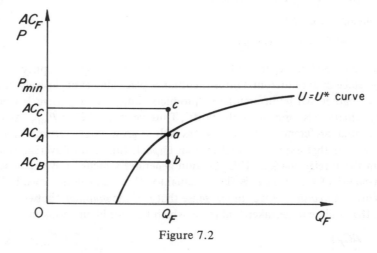

Figure 7.2

Formal derivation of the decision curve
Before we discuss the full implications of the decision curve, it is useful to derive its intercept and slope algebraically. This will show the determinants of the position and the slope of the curve, and hence will enable the exploration of changes in these variables.

The equation of the decision curve is obtained by solving expression (7.12) for the average cost:

$$AC_F = P_{min} - \frac{U^{*1/v}}{Q_F} \tag{7.13}$$

The intercept (on the Q-axis) is obtained by setting $AC_F = 0$. Thus

$$0 = P_{min} - \frac{U^{*1/v}}{Q_F}$$

or

$$\text{Intercept} = Q_F = \frac{U^{*1/v}}{P_{min}} \tag{7.14}$$

The meaning of the intercept is that if $AC_F = 0$, then $Q_F = U^{*1/v}/P_{min}$

The slope of the decision curve is obtained by taking the derivative of (7.13) with respect to quantity, recalling that, by our assumptions, U^*, v and P_{min} are constant. Thus

$$\text{Slope} = \frac{\partial(AC_F)}{\partial Q_F} = 0 - \frac{\partial \dfrac{U^{*1/v}}{Q_F}}{\partial Q_F} = - \frac{\partial(U^{*1/v} Q_F^{-1})}{\partial Q_F}$$

$$= U^{*1/v} Q_F^{-2}$$

$$= \frac{U^{*1/v}}{Q_F^2}$$

Substituting $U^* = \Pi^v = (P_{min} - AC_F)Q_F$, we obtain

$$\text{Slope} = \frac{P_{min} - AC_F}{Q_F} \tag{7.15}$$

It is obvious that the intercept of the curve is very important, since it varies directly with the level of spatial preference (or inertial resistance). Greater spatial aversion, as measured by a smaller v, shifts the whole decision curve to the right, thus reducing the area of acceptable sales–cost combinations. This reduces the likelihood that an investment will be made in this market.

Another implication of the decision curve is that profitable investment opportunities in foreign markets will not be undertaken if they fall outside the decision curve (investment opportunity frontier). In Figure 7.3 all points above the curve

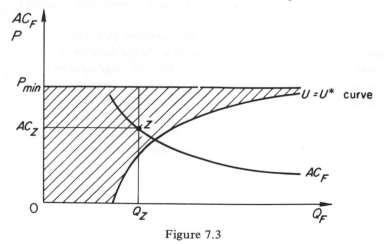

Figure 7.3

$U = U^*$ but below the line $P = P_{min}$ (shaded area) denote profitable investment opportunities, given $AC_F < P_{min}$. For example, point Z shows an extremely profitable investment opportunity, with a unit profit equal to $P_{min} - AC_Z$. Still, this investment will not be undertaken because it falls outside the 'investment horizon' of the firm, as this is defined by the management's spatial preference, v, and given the 'internal resources' of the firm (which determine U^*).

(e) *Predictions of Richardson's Model*

From the above analysis we may write

$$\text{FDI} = f(U^*, v, P_{min}, AC_F) \tag{7.16}$$

We derived the decision curve by assuming that target returns (U^*), price in the foreign market ($P_F = P_{min}$), and the spatial preference or intertial resistance of the firm (v) are constant. However, the values of these factors cannot be expected to be constant. Their changes affect the position and/or the slope of the decision curve, and hence the level of foreign direct investment.

(1) *Changes in target returns, U^**. We said earlier that the target returns depend on the availability of scarce 'internal resources' (IR) and on the conduct of close competitors, that is,

$$U^* = f(IR, \text{Competitors' reactions})$$

As we mentioned earlier, U^* is negatively related to the amount of non-marketable scarce 'internal resources', such as excess managerial talent or excess liquidity. If some key managers leave the firm, the amount of returns that prospective investments must yield will be raised, and hence less over-all investment will be undertaken.

Similarly, successful operations in a foreign market of a rival may well be expected to force the firm to reconsider its target return. This effect is additional to any influence on the firm's v and on the strictly economic variables P_{min} and AC_F.

In general, a change in U^* affects the intercept (but not the slope) of the decision curve. An increase in target returns shifts the decision curve to the right, thus reducing the investment opportunity that the firm considers worth while. On the contrary, a reduction in U^* will shift the decision curve to the left, making the area of acceptable investment projects larger. The amount of foreign direct investment is inversely related to U but positively related to the available (excess) 'internal resources'. It should be stressed that changes in U^* affect the intercept, and hence the position of the decision curve, but not its slope:

Recall that the intercept of the decision curve is

$$\frac{U^{*1/v}}{P_{min}}$$

and its slope is

$$\frac{P_{min} - AC_F}{Q_F}$$

(2) *Changes in the spatial preference of the firm, v.* Like changes in U^*, changes in the spatial preference of the firm affect the intercept of the decision curve, but not its slope (v appears only in the intercept of the decision curve). A high spatial preference implies a high aversion to new markets, that is, a low value of v, and vice versa. As v increases (towards unity), the decision curve shifts to the left and the investment opportunities considered worth while increase: the 'foreignness' of new markets decreases. Thus the amount of foreign direct investment is inversely related to v.

We mentioned earlier that the determinants of v are: (i) the amount of information about the foreign market; (ii) political and economic conditions in foreign markets, and (iii) the number of rival or other firms which have already established profitable operations abroad. An increase in the amount of knowledge about foreign markets (by means of trade fairs, special commissions, and in particular by increased exports), expectations of high growth of foreign markets, and an increase in the number of rival or complementary firms in foreign markets will increase v and cause a shift of the decision curve to the left. Similarly, political and economic instability of foreign markets, poor growth prospects and hostile government attitudes will decrease v and cause a shift of the decision curve to the right, reducing the investment projects which are considered worth while.

In summary, v and the amount of foreign direct investment are positively related.

(3) *Changes in the price in the foreign market, P_F.* Changes in the price, P_F, are more important than changes in either U^* or v, because P_F appears both in the intercept and in the slope of the decision curve.

Recall that

$$P_F = P_d + EC + T$$

or

$$P_{min} = AC_d + m_d + EC + T$$

Thus P_{min} can change either by a change in domestic unit costs, or the profit margin, or in export costs, or in the tariff. An increase in P_{min} shifts the decision curve up and to the left. The intercept is reduced and the slope becomes steeper, so that the area of acceptable cost–sales combinations under the curve becomes larger.

Note, however, that for undertaking FDI a necessary condition is that

$$P_{min} > AC_F \tag{7.17}$$

For the inequality to hold, foreign costs of production need not be lower than domestic costs of production. The inequality may hold even if $AC_d > AC_F$, because of export costs and/or tariffs.

Tariffs have opposite effects to spatial preference. A high level of tariff may be more than enough to offset a strong spatial preference. An increase in tariffs shifts the decision curve to the left (reduces the intercept, by increasing P_{min}). Furthermore, the level of tariffs affects the slope of the decision curve. Thus tariffs can be a very powerful factor in the decision to invest abroad. Several writers have stressed the importance of tariffs in the decision to establish production facilities in a foreign market. A rigorous theoretical analysis of the effects of tariffs on foreign direct investment has been developed by Horst.[57] The same writer has provided empirical evidence supporting the importance of tariffs on the foreign investment decision.[58]

(4) *Changes in foreign production costs, AC_F.* Production costs in the foreign market affect the slope of the decision curve. The amount of foreign direct investment is inversely related to the costs of production in the foreign market. A rise in AC_F reduces the slope of the decision curve and the area of the acceptable cost—sales combinations.

The absolute level of unit costs is also an important determinant of FDI, because of the necessary condition $AC_F < P_{min}$ (expression (7.17)). If foreign unit costs are higher than the minimum price that the firm expects to receive in the foreign market, foreign direct investment will not take place. (This will be further discussed subsequently.)

(f) *Comparison of Richardson's Model with Alternative Hypotheses of Foreign Direct Investment*

Having examined the determinants of FDI in Richardson's model, it is interesting to examine their relation to the determinants suggested by other writers.

(1) Specific advantages of a firm in the form of managerial skills (Kindleberger, Caves) enter into U^*, the target returns which are inversely related to the excess 'internal resources' (the most important of which is trained managerial and other non-marketable personnel).

---

[57] Horst, 'The Theory of the Multinational Firm: Optimal Behaviour Under Different Tariff and Tax Rates'. See also W. M. Corden, 'Protection and Foreign Investment', *Economic Record*, vol. 43, 1967, pp. 209–32; Brash, *American Investment in Australian Industry*, pp. 35–8; Gordon and Grommers, *United States Manufacturing Investment in Brazil*, pp. 23–4.

[58] Horst, 'The Industrial Composition of US Exports and Subsidiary Sales to the Canadian Market'.

(2) Similarly, U^* reflects the availability of excess money capital, which can be used for the initial capital required to establish a plant in a foreign market.

(3) Multi-plant economies are reflected in P_{min}, via the 'residual' profit margin, m. Since AC_F is the production cost in the foreign market, other costs (marketing, R & D, etc.) will be covered by the gross profit margin. If these costs are lowered by foreign direct investment, the net unit profit will be increased.

(4) Specific advantage in the form of a superior differentiated product is reflected in P_F, the price that will be charged in the foreign market. Recall that P_F can be higher than P_{min}. This will depend, among other things, on existing product advantages that the investing firm has over the host-country producers. Even if $P_F = P_{min}$, product advantages (brands, patents, etc.) will be reflected in P_d, the domestic price. A firm that develops a new improved product will be able to charge a higher price than the domestic price, which is the major component of P_{min}.

(5) Specific advantage in the form of superior processes (technology, know-how) is reflected in the unit domestic costs AC_d, which is a determinant of P_{min}.

(6) Comparative cost advantages of the traditional theory of international trade are reflected in the two cost terms, AC_F, the production costs in the foreign market, and AC_d, the production costs in the domestic market.

(7) Similarly, scale economies, as well as other absolute cost advantages of the investing company, are shown in the unit domestic cost, AC_d. If similar advantages exist in the foreign market, they will be shown by AC_F, the unit production costs in the foreign market.

(8) Tariffs (and export costs) work their effects on foreign direct investment via P_F or P_{min}.

(9) Finally, the size of the firm will be reflected in the availability of internal resources, and hence in the target returns U^*. A large supply of internal resources will be shown by a low value of U^*, that is, a small intercept of the decision curve. This implies that large firms have a larger range of potential investments.

Size may also be expected to affect the spatial preference of the firm, v. Large firms are usually better informed about the political and economic conditions prevailing in foreign markets. Such firms will usually have exported in foreign markets, and will thus have direct information about the preferences of buyers in foreign countries.

It is apparent from the above discussion that Richardson's model includes directly or indirectly most of the economic factors which have been suggested by other writers as explaining the foreign direct investment decision. Richardson's contribution lies in his explicit discussion of subjective factors that shape the preferences of managers. Furthermore, Richardson provides a neat framework for the analysis of the initial decision of the firm to become multinational.

(g) *Exports and Foreign Direct Investment*

Up to now exports have been assumed to have an indirect effect on foreign direct investment, by increasing the information about foreign markets and thus increasing v, the coefficient of spatial preference.

However, as we saw earlier, Vernon[59] and others[60] see exporting activity leading naturally to eventual foreign direct investment. Vernon's hypothesis can be analysed within Richardson's theoretical framework. Recall that Vernon's theory is a dynamic analysis of foreign direct investment. As such it is complementary to the static theories of Kindleberger, Hymer and Caves which stress static factors, such as technological advantage (in products or processes), tariff rates, market size and factor costs, as determining the export and direct investment decisions of firms. It is useful to summarise Vernon's 'product-cycle' hypothesis.

According to Vernon, exporting and foreign direct investment are separate sequential stages in the dynamic process by which American firms expand their share in foreign markets. Large US corporations, having superior knowhow and producing for the needs of affluent and sophisticated buyers at home, have the ability and the incentive to develop technically superior products as compared with producers of foreign (host) countries who have neither the knowhow nor the sophisticated customers of US markets. At the earlier stages of the product's development, US firms sell in the domestic market. As the home market becomes saturated, the large corporations attempt to penetrate foreign markets. Initially penetration is attained by exporting, because exports require less capital and are less risky than foreign direct investment. The latter requires the establishment of plant(s), that is, the commitment of resources for a long period of time. But as time moves on the foreign market expands, the product is imitated by foreign producers, and the advantages to US firms diminish. The US firm, wishing to maintain its initial share of the foreign market, is eventually forced to establish marketing, service and production facilities in the foreign market. Thus there is a definite time sequence in the exporting and foreign investment activities: foreign direct investment is the successor to foreign trade.

Let us now see how the Vernon hypothesis can be analysed within Richardson's model.

It is assumed that the decision curve is given, that is, the earlier-discussed determinants of the slope and the intercept remain constant, as export activity is expanding. This assumption in unrealistic, since, as we mentioned, exports affect v. However, we start with this assumption in order to simplify the analysis. At a subsequent stage the constant U-curve assumption will be relaxed.

Exports, within Richardson's model, can start prior to foreign direct investment, because exporting activity has a smaller spatial preference (high v value) than foreign production. Exporting requires limited resources and attention only to the demand side of the market. Moreover, export sales of a product may start

[59] Vernon, 'International Investment and International Trade in the Product Cycle'.

[60] Gruber, Mehta and Vernon, 'The R & D Factor in International Trade and International Investment of US Industries'.

at the initiative of foreign buyers rather than the producing firm. Production abroad requires the commitment of many more resources and attention to both the supply and demand sides of the market. Thus exporting without foreign direct investment is consistent with the concept of spatial preference.

As exports expand and the firm attains a certain share (volume of sales) in the foreign market, it may well decide to switch from exporting to local production, that is, to undertake foreign direct investment. This is shown in Figure 7.4. Once again P_{min} indicates the lowest price which the firm would charge in the foreign market. This is equal to the firm's home price of the product plus the costs of exporting and the level of the tariff in the foreign market. It is assumed that the firm initially has some idea of the minimum conceivable cost of production in the foreign market. This is denoted by the curve AC_{min} in Figure 7.4.

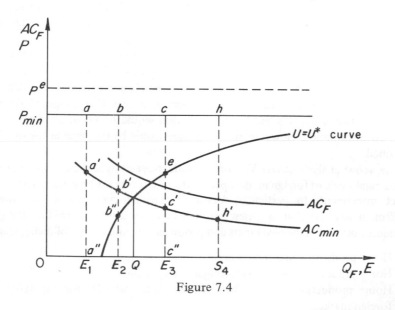

Figure 7.4

In period 1 the firm exports E_1 at the export price P_{min}.[61] With export sales of this amount, the firm does not even consider investing in this market, though the profitability of exports is high (P_{min} is much higher than $AC_{min} = a'$). The firm considers that the share captured by E_1 is far too low; the information or knowledge of the market is inadequate. The cost–sales point a' lies above the decision curve; E_1, is not adequate to break the spatial aversion of the firm. Even if the foreign production cost were zero (point a'' in Figure 7.4), the sales–cost point would still lie outside the decision area. With exports E_1, all the cost–sales combinations would lie on the line aa'', which is outside the decision curve.

[61] The price could be higher, for example p^e, if the firm's product were such as to give it high monopoly power. This would be the case for a new product with no substitutes.

In period 2 the market has grown, and so have the firm's exports, to E_2. Even with this level of sales, however, the firm will not consider direct production in this market, because the sales–cost point b' lies outside the decision curve. Only if the AC_F were lower than b'', would there be an inducement for the firm to invest in this market.

In period 3 the firm's exports have grown to E_3. With this volume of exports there is a range of cost–sales combinations (along the line ec'') which lie below the decision curve. Thus the firm has an inducement to invest in this market.

If the firm estimates that its total sales in the foreign market in period 4 will be S_4 (and given P_{min} and AC_{min}), it will invest abroad, installing a plant to produce at least a quantity OQ. In this event the firm will continue to export a quantity equal to QS_4. Alternatively, the firm may decide to produce S_4 and cover the entire foreign demand by local production. Exports would cease completely. Finally, the firm might decide to produce locally an amount greater than Q, but less than S_4, covering the difference by exports.

Note that once the firm's exports reach the level Q, it may decide to undertake a detailed study of the cost and demand conditions. This study might reveal that the foreign costs are higher, say AC_F (in Figure 7.4), and the demand stronger, so that the firm can charge a higher price, e.g. P^e (in Figure 7.4). The decision between exports and local production would be taken on the basis of this new information. However, the procedure would be the same as the one just described.

The above analysis covers Vernon's 'product-cycle' hypothesis, which postulates a rigid cycle of foreign market penetration: exports lead naturally to foreign direct investment. In particular, Vernon's 'product-cycle' theory of foreign investment suggests that as a new product becomes a mature product the geographical horizons of the developers and producers expand in the following stages:

(1) Home production and marketing.
(2) Home production, home marketing and exporting.
(3) Home production for the domestic market, and FDI for supplying the foreign market.

In Richardson's framework these stages are:

(1) No exports; v is approximately zero, there is no foreign production.
(2) Exports are realised; $0 < v < 1$, and the possibility of foreign direct investment is studied seriously.
(3) Foreign direct investment is undertaken: $v = 1$.

However, Richardson's framework also covers Horst's hypothesis,[62] that exports and foreign direct investment are alternative methods by which firms exploit the same technological advantages over the host-country producers.

---

[62] Horst, 'The Industrial Composition of US Exports and Subsidiary Sales to the Canadian Market'. Horst's hypothesis is critically discussed subsequently.

Exports need not be replaced completely by foreign production. Firms are interested in their total sales in the foreign market, and a given amount of sales can be attained by exporting, by investing abroad, or by both activities simultaneously. The choice between exporting and foreign production in any one period is determined by economic and subjective factors.

The above process, in which exports lead naturally to production abroad, requires implicitly that the AC_F curve lies partly below the P_{min} curve *and* inside the decision area. Thus Vernon's cycle hypothesis cannot explain situations in which the cost curve lies above the P_{min} line.

Assume that initially the AC_F curve lies above the P_{min} line. This is shown in Figure 7.5, where AC_F lies above the P_{min} line. In this case foreign direct investment would not take place, no matter how much exports grew. However, if P_{min} increases[63] sufficiently, the AC_F curve will again lie below the decision curve, because an increase in P_{min} reduces the intercept and increases the slope of the decision curve. That is, the entire decision curve shifts upwards and to the left, so that the given AC_F lies below the (shifted) decision curve. This is also shown in Figure 7.5. Under these conditions FDI will be undertaken once exports have reached (or exceeded) the volume E'. The foreign investment in this case is the result of *both* increased exports *and* economic factors (increase in P_{min}).

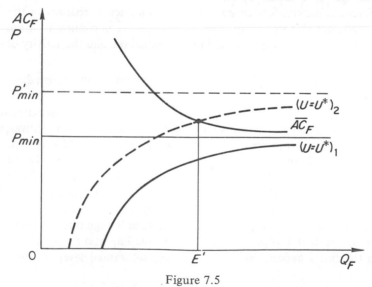

Figure 7.5

<hr />

[63] Recall that $P_{min} = AC_d + m_d + EC + T$, so that P_{min} can increase if any one of its determinants increases. FDI requires $AC_F < P_{min}$, not necessarily $AC_F < AC_d$. In other words, the foreign production costs need not be lower than the unit domestic costs. P_{min} can be higher than AC_F *either* because of higher AC_d *or* a lower domestic cost combined with high transport costs and/or tariffs. Thus FDI can be undertaken even when the foreign costs are higher than the domestic costs, so long as the transport costs or tariffs make $P_{min} > AC_F$. The most common case is a high tariff or an increase in the tariff, which make P_{min} increase, *ceteris paribus*.

Thus we have an 'economic stimulus' explanation of direct investment as a complement to Vernon's explanation (of FDI occurring via the natural growth of exports).

With the above analysis Richardson's static framework has been extended to cover dynamic considerations of increasing export activity over time, which leads naturally to foreign direct investment. The 'dynamic' aspects of Richardson's framework can be further extended if we relax the assumption of a fixed decision curve (given determinants of the intercept and the slope).[64]

When the factors underlying the decision curve are allowed to vary, the predictions that can be drawn from Richardson's framework become much wider. Recall that the intercept of the decision curve is affected by the target returns (U^*), the spatial variable v and the foreign price P_{min}. The latter includes the domestic unit costs (AC_d) the profit margin (m_d), export costs (EC) and tariffs (T). Thus the intercept changes with:

(1) Changes in domestic production costs, the profit margin, export costs and tariffs.
(2) Changes in the 'internal resources' of the firm (which are the main determinant of U^*).
(3) Changes in v, caused by improved communications and information about foreign markets, foreign government inducements, changes in the foreign investment climate, competitors' investments, complementary firms' investments, the general trend toward multinationalism, and the activity of exporting itself.

These predictions can explain several observed facts about foreign direct investment.

For example, it has been observed that various government measures aimed at attracting foreign investment have not been successful.[65] Tax incentives, depreciation allowances, investment credits, low interest rates and credit conditions have had minor influences on the decision as to whether to invest abroad.

Another fact that has puzzled economists and governments is the small importance of lower production costs in foreign countries as an inducement for foreign investment.[66] Richardson's framework provides a plausible explanation of the minor impact of lower production costs in foreign markets. In Figure 7.4 above we see that foreign costs (AC_F) become important only after period 3, when the firm's exports have reached some substantial level at which foreign

---

[64] The shift in the decision curve of the last section was briefly introduced in order to show that the model can explain both Vernon's and Horst's hypotheses. Shifts of the decision curve within a dynamic environment will be discussed in detail in this section.

[65] Krause and Dam, *Federal Tax Treatment of Foreign Income*, pp. 92–3; Polk, Meister and Veit, *US Production Abroad and the Balance of Payments*, pp. 50 and 64–5; Barlow and Wender, *Foreign Investment and Taxation*, pp. 215–17; Brash, *American Investment in Australian Industry*, p. 48; Hughes and Poh Seng (eds), *Foreign Investment and Industrialization in Singapore*, pp. 158–9 and 183–5.

[66] See, for example, Brash, *American Investment in Australian Industry*, p. 46.

production is both feasible and desirable. If the level of exports is too small (e.g. E_1 in Figure 7.4), no level of foreign costs (even zero) could induce foreign direct investment, because at such low export levels all cost—sales points lie outside the decision curve. The spatial preference is too strong (v is too low), so that projects which are profitable (even very profitable, in the sense that P_{min} is above AC_F) are not considered by the firm: management feels that the market is not known enough or stable enough for production facilities to be established in this market. Thus profitable operations may be possible, but will not be seized because of the spatial inertia of the firm. Government policies which reduce foreign production costs under these conditions are bound to fail to attract foreign investors.

In conclusion, most existing hypotheses pertaining at the explanation of the initial direct investment decision can be considered as special cases of Richardson's model. Strictly economic theories[67] assume that subjective factors are constant. At the other extreme, purely subjective theories[68] assume that economic factors are constant. However, in the real business world the initial foreign investment decision can be explained only by a combination of strictly economic and subjective variables. These types of variables are of course interdependent. Thus a realistic theory of the decision to invest abroad must first take into account this interdependence between subjective and economic variables and then determine the relationship of these variables to the decision-making criteria of the firm.

C. Causes of Vertical Foreign Investment

(i) *Economic Factors Influencing Vertical Foreign Investment*

In principle, foreign investment in a vertically integrated stage of production can be analysed within the framework of the theory of optimal vertical integration, which we discussed in Chapter 6. However, in practice we need a less general theory, given that most of the vertical investment in a foreign country is undertaken for the production of a raw material. Firms integrate backwards by investing in foreign countries rich in natural resources, which are used as raw materials by the processing parent companies.

As we saw in Chapter 6, the theory of vertical integration suggests various motives for the decision to undertake direct investment in different stages of the

[67] Hymer, 'The International Operations of National Firms: A Study of Direct Foreign Investment'; Kindleberger, *American Business Abroad*; Caves, 'International Corporations'; Vernon, 'International Investment and International Trade in the Product Cycle'.
[68] Aharoni, *The Foreign Investment Decision Process*.

same production process. The most important of these motives are summarised below.

(1) *Realisation of multi-plant economies.* These may be significant if the various stages involve activities which are technologically related. The available empirical evidence lends little encouragement to the expectation of significant multi-plant economies. This is particularly true for upstream vertical integration aimed at control of raw materials, since the technology at this stage has nothing in common with the subsequent processing stages.

(2) *Securing supplies of raw materials located in less developed countries.* The corporation may integrate backwards to produce raw materials in such countries, where supplies might not be forthcoming, due to lack of the required infrastructure and shortages of local entrepreneurship and finance.

(3) *Avoidance of oligopolistic uncertainty.* This is a powerful motive for vertical investments among the industrialised countries. Markets of natural resources have strong bilateral monopoly characteristics: few buyers are facing few sellers. Under these conditions negotiations become uncertain and agreement on a price may take a long time. In particular, buyer concentration in the domestic market generates uncertainty regarding rivals' actions. Insecurity about forthcoming supplies provides a strong stimulus for buying up the sources of supply.

(4) *Avoidance of business risk.* Investments of the buyers and sellers of raw materials are large, involving an enormous financial commitment for a long period of time. The profitability of such investments depends heavily on the prices expected to prevail over their lifetime, a fact that increases the risk of prospective yields. Another source of market uncertainty is the large minimum optimal scale of plant in resource industries. Finally, many raw materials have neither alternative uses nor close substitutes. Under these conditions much business uncertainty can be eliminated by ownership of the raw materials.

(5) *Increase in market power.* It is generally agreed that vertical integration has the potential to increase market power. In particular, the owners of factor inputs may force competitors to pay higher prices for such inputs, putting them at an absolute cost disadvantage.

(6) *Increase in entry barriers.* Upstream vertical integration can be used to increase barriers to the entry of new competitors. If known supply sources are owned by vertically integrated firms, a new entrant to the processing industry must incur the extra costs and uncertainties of finding and developing his own source of raw materials. The established integrated firms can enjoy excess profits without attracting new rivals.

From the above discussion we may derive the main determinants of vertical foreign direct investment.

(1) *Seller concentration (oligopolistic structure) in the domestic market.* High
   seller concentration is critical for two reasons. It directly generates uncertainty in the market for the raw material, and it motivates the investing firm
   to take actions aiming to raise entry barriers to the industry.

(2) *The size of the firm.* Investments for the development of natural resources are large, and hence the processing firm must initially be of large absolute size.

(3) *The minimum optimal plant size and the durability of the investment in resource exploitation.* These aspects tend to increase market uncertainty and enhance foreign vertical investment.

(4) *The existence of alternative uses of the resources.* Foreign vertical investment will be more attractive if the natural resource acquired can be sold to different users.

The above factors are purely economic in nature. However, subjective factors do affect the decision to invest in a foreign country in order to attain vertical integration. Richardson has modified his 'horizontal FDI model' so as to take into account specific considerations that are important when a firm decides to integrate its operations vertically by investing in a foreign country. Richardson's 'vertical FDI model' is outlined below.

(ii) *Richardson's Model for Vertical Integration by Foreign Direct Investment*

Richardson argues that the valuation expressions used for horizontal foreign investments are not satisfactory for the case of investment in intermediate production (extractive investment or production of an intermediate product in a vertically integrated firm). In such cases the profitability of an investment should include not only the profits from selling to other firms but also the profits on the portion of foreign production which is shipped back to the vertically integrated parent as an input into domestic production. This profit is equal to the cost savings (accruing to the parent company) through not having to buy from other (independent) producers of the particular input. Thus the firm's valuation function for a potential investment in an intermediate or extractive industry takes the general form

$$U = f[(P_{min} - AC_F)Q_1 ; (AC_0 - AC_F)Q_2] \qquad (7.18)$$

where Q_1 = sales of the subsidiary to outside firms
$\quad\quad Q_2$ = shipments to the parent company
$\quad\quad AC_0$ = average cost of alternative domestic suppliers (less the cost of importing from the foreign country where the affiliate is located)

A specific form of the above valuation function is

$$U = [(P_{min} - AC_F)Q_1]^{v_1} + [(AC_0 - AC_F)Q_2]^{v_2} \qquad (7.19)$$

$$0 < v_1 \leqslant 1 \qquad\qquad 0 < v_2 \leqslant 1$$

where v_1 and v_2 are the appropriate spatial preference (or inertial resistance) parameters.

Investment decision curves for such projects (in extractive or intermediate input industries) can be derived in the same way as the decision curves of investment for final production.

The decision curve is derived by setting $U = U^*$ and Q_2 equal to the input requirements of the parent (investing) company. Thus, given U^*, v_1, v_2, P_{min}, AC_0 and Q_2, the valuation function is an implicit function of AC_F and Q_1, the sales volume to outside firms. If we solve this expression for AC_F we obtain the equation of the decision curve. Its intercept is

$$AC_0 - \frac{U^{*1/v_2}}{Q_2} \tag{7.20}$$

and its slope is

$$\frac{P_{min} - AC_F}{Q_1} \tag{7.21}$$

This decision curve is shown in Figure 7.6.

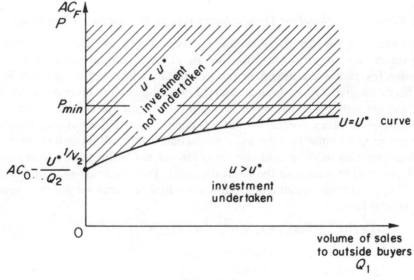

Figure 7.6

Comparing this decision curve with the one derived for horizontal foreign investment, we observe that there is no difference in the slope or concavity of the decision curve. However, the intercept is now positive. The economic meaning of this positive intercept is that sales to outside buyers are no longer always necessary to motivate an investment, as is the case with horizontal investments. The benefits derived from lower costs of inputs into the parent's domestic production process are sufficient to push the valuation of the potential returns of the investment beyond U^*. However, small values of v_2 (the spatial preference parameter) may cause profitable investment opportunities to be rejected for subjective reasons.

The predictions of this model are similar to those of the horizontal investment model and need not be repeated.

The empirical evidence on the motives of vertical foreign direct investment is not impressive. Horst[69] found that resource-intensive industries tend to include a larger number of multinational corporations. This finding, however, does not throw much light on the causes of vertical direct foreign investment. An interesting result, established by Krainer,[70] is that vertical direct investment comprises a greater portion of the total direct investment of a country which has limited natural resources. Krainer's study was based on a comparison of US and UK flows of foreign direct investment.

III. ECONOMIC EFFECTS OF FOREIGN DIRECT INVESTMENT

A. Benefits to the Host Country

We saw in an earlier section that foreign direct investment transplants in the host country capital, managerial skills and technological knowledge (in products or processes) in a package. The effects of the transfer of these resources take diverse forms.

To the extent that the transferred factors are scarce in supply in the host country, they stimulate employment, output and growth. Furthermore, the inflow of capital in countries poorly endowed with this resource is essential for foreign-exchange purposes. These are the main effects of foreign direct investment at the macro level.

At the micro level foreign direct investment has several effects, which are interrelated with the macro effects. The discussion of these will be mainly focused on the horizontal type of foreign direct investment. At the end of this section we will examine briefly the differences between the effects of horizontal and vertical direct investments.

The main gains to the host country of horizontal direct investment are: (a) the revenue from the taxation of profits of the foreign subsidiaries; (b) improvement in the skills of the labour force of the host country; (c) increase in the productivity of factors of production in general; (d) improvement in the allocation of resources of the host country, from the increased competition and the

---

[69] T. Horst, 'Firm and Industry Determinants of the Decision to Invest Abroad', *Review of Economics and Statistics*, 1972, pp. 258–66.

[70] R. E. Krainer, 'Resource Endowment and the Structure of Foreign Investment', *Journal of Finance*, vol. 22, 1967, pp. 49–57.

ensuing pressure on the prices of commodities; and (e) speeding-up of the adoption of technological progress.

We will briefly discuss these economic benefits.[71]

(i) *Corporate income tax*

A direct gain to the host country stems from the tax collected from the profits of subsidiaries. The net benefit is smaller by the amount of the incremental cost of public services supplied to foreign affiliates.

(ii) *Improvement in the skills of the labour force*

To exploit its product-differentiation advantage or its new technology advantage the multinational firm requires skilled labour, which is not usually available in the foreign market. No benefit from manpower training would accrue to the host country if *either* the workers acquired the required skills on their personal initiative, investing in training up to the point where its marginal cost to them equals the present discounted value of its marginal benefit, *or* the multinational firm provided training up to the level that maximises its profit. The available evidence suggests that these conditions do not hold in the real world. Employees underinvest in training on their own initiative. In many countries the required skills cannot be acquired, even if workers are willing to invest in their training, due to lack of appropriate training institutions. Thus the multinational firm undertakes labour-training programmes which are in general more extensive than are required for profit maximisation, due to the fear of running short of skills. Uncertainty about their future needs in skilled labour and personnel turnover induces the multinational corporation to engage in labour training beyond its immediate needs. This training would presumably be in technical, scientific and managerial skills, and would lead to higher wages (a rent to skilled employees).

Several results are possible from the manpower training undertaken by the multinational firm.

(1) The skilled personnel employed by the subsidiary will enjoy higher wages. However, given the excess supply of such personnel, the subsidiary will not pay the full rent of the higher skills to its employees, thus earning higher profit from the higher productivity of its labour force.

(2) The domestic producers (of the host country) may be induced to undertake similar training programmes or the government may establish appropriate training institutions.

(3) The excess supply of skilled personnel created by the subsidiary's training programmes will be absorbed by the domestic producers at no additional training cost. This is a clear benefit to the host country, and it will be larger, the greater the mobility of the labour force from the foreign subsidiary. This mobility in

---

[71] This discussion is based on Caves, 'International Corporations'.

turn will increase with the following factors: (a) the number of local firms producing similar products or using similar processes to those of the foreign subsidiary; (b) the extent to which the trained personnel has skills that can be used by other firms in other industries (that is, the less specific and more general the training is); and (c) the physical proximity of the subsidiary to local firms (if the subsidiary is located in a remote region, local firms will not have much opportunity to attract the subsidiary's personnel).

In summary, the manpower-training programmes provided by the multinational corporations improve the skills of the labour force of the host country at no cost. This increases the production capacity of the economy: there is an outward shift of the production-possibility frontier of the host country stemming from spillovers of the activity of the foreign subsidiaries.

(iii) *Increase in the productivity of factor resources*

The subsidiary's market behaviour may give rise to substantial productivity gains to domestic firms.

Foreign subsidiaries are more efficient than host-country competitors. The latter, being protected by strong barriers to new entry, usually suffer from technical inefficiency: they operate at a sub-optimal scale and/or produce their chosen output with inefficient combinations of factors. In either case the domestic oligopolistic firms will have higher unit costs relative to the foreign subsidiary. If the foreign subsidiary's higher productivity is captured fully in its profits, there is no benefit to the host country apart from the extra tax revenue raised from the higher profits of the subsidiary. Empirical studies suggest, however, that the foreign subsidiaries, intentionally or unintentionally, do not capture the full value of their higher productivity in their profits. Their market behaviour and (in general) their activities affect the productivity of domestic producers in various ways.

(1) Productivity improvement takes place when the excess personnel trained by the subsidiaries is employed by domestic firms, or when employees of the subsidiaries switch to domestic firms. In both cases this skilled personnel forms the basis for the adoption of the superior methods of production or marketing of the foreign subsidiary: the employees have the knowledge and they put pressure for the improvement of the organisation and the operation of the domestic firms.

(2) Foreign subsidiaries often *take the initiative* in improving the efficiency of domestic firms which are their suppliers, their distributors, or their customers. They pass on to them modern techniques of inventory and quality control, induce them to adopt standardisation, and in general to modernise their organisation and operations.[72] Transactions with efficiently organised local firms improve in turn the operations of the foreign subsidiary.

---

[72] Brash, *American Investment in Australian Industry*, ch. 8; J. H. Dunning, *American Investment in British Manufacturing Industry* (Oxford University Press, 1958) ch. 7.

(3) The entry of a foreign subsidiary will *exert an indirect pressure* on home-owned rival firms to improve their productivity, even without the subsidiary engaging in price competition. We saw that subsidiaries have advantages against each of the major sources of entry barriers (see also below). Thus it is unlikely that they will conform to the established patterns of restricted competition between the domestic firms.[73] Even if the subsidiary refrains from competitive price-cutting, non-price competition will be spurred. This is bound to affect the domestic firms' market share and reduce their profit. A squeeze on rivals' profit may also result from the rise in the prices of inputs, which will be bidden up as the foreign subsidiary increases the demand for factors of production. Thus, even if the price of the commodity remains constant, shrivelled profits will induce local producers to improve their productivity and reduce their costs.[74] This may be attained either through the 'demonstration effect' of the multinational firm (the domestic producers copy the subsidiary's superior production or marketing techniques), or through an increased effort of management to reduce costs (cut out 'slack', choice of a more efficient combination of factors of production). Such reductions in X-inefficiency imply a movement from points inside the production transformation curve to (efficient) points on the economy's possibility frontier. These gains are referred to as gains in 'technical efficiency' or 'X-efficiency'.[75]

(iv) *Improvement in the allocation of resources*

The multinational corporations may provide a significant increase in price competition in the host-country market. The establishment of a subsidiary constitutes entry in industries where barriers to entry by new firms are high. Rivals in the country of origin may well be expected to establish their own affiliates as a defensive strategy. With several foreign subsidiaries operating in a market, price may decline, causing an additional reduction in the monopolistic profits of local producers. This will result in the closing down of those home-owned firms which cannot improve their efficiency. The released resources will be absorbed by other more productive sectors. In the long run, the host country will gain from the more efficient allocation of its resources. This allocative efficiency implies a movement along the host country's production-possibility frontier, and this increases consumers' welfare.

(v) *Speeding-up of technical progress*

The subsidiary may speed up the adoption of new methods or products by local

[73] T. Scitovsky, 'International Trade and Economic Integration as a Means of Overcoming the Disadvantages of a Small Nation', in *Economic Consequences of the Size of Nations*, ed. E. A. G. Robinson (Harper & Row, 1960).

[74] W. M. Corden, 'The Efficiency Effects of Trade and Protection', paper given at the Conference on International Trade, Monash University, 1969.

[75] Caves, 'Multinational Firms, Competition, and Productivity in Host-Country Markets'.

producers. Home-owned firms, protected by strong entry barriers, tend to be slow in technological change. The presence of a foreign subsidiary with its superior technical knowledge will provide a stimulus to local firms for more research and development, which will speed up technical progress. The production capacity of the host country is increased by the induced invention and innovation.

In summary, foreign direct investment may benefit the host country in several ways. The host country may have substantial gains from a more efficient allocation of its resources (allocative-efficiency gains), from increases in the productivity of its resources (technical-efficiency or X-efficiency gains), from improvement of the quality of its resources (especially of the skills of its labour force) and from the spurring of technical progress, all of which enlarge the production capacity of the economy: subsidiaries may not only cause movements from points inside the production-possibility curve to efficient points on the frontier but may also push the whole production-possibility frontier outwards.

The above analysis was related to the economic effects in the host country of *horizontal* direct investments.

The economic effects of *vertical* direct investment are similar in general to those of horizontal foreign investment, though their impact is smaller.

The main difference arises in the welfare significance of taxation by the host country of the profits of subsidiaries. These subsidiaries are mostly engaged in the extraction and processing of raw materials, which they ship back to the parent company. The profits of these subisidiaries include a pure return on the capital invested and a rent on the natural-resource deposit which they exploit. The rent should accrue to the native seller of the natural resource, secured in the selling agreement with the multinational corporation. However, native resource owners are usually in a poor bargaining position. The small number of interested (foreign) buyers and the large investment capital required for the exploitation of the resource constrain the ability of the native owners in striking an agreement that will succeed in capturing all rents that will be forthcoming during the exploitation of the resource in future periods. As a consequence, a significant proportion of these rents accrues to the foreign subsidiaries, a fact deeply resented in host countries. The taxation system of the profits of vertical foreign investments could, in principle, be designed to capture the rents which native owners cannot secure for themselves.

Allocative, X-efficiency and technological benefits from extractive subsidiaries are likely to be smaller than for horizontal investment in manufacturing.

(1) Extractive subsidiaries are capital intensive, with little scope for manpower training and skill improvement which could be used by local producers.

(2) Extractive subsidiaries have little contact with other local firms. They buy few local inputs, and they sell their output to the parent company or export it to other countries. Thus local firms cannot avail themselves to any considerable extent of the superior organisation or technical knowledge of extractive subsidiaries.

(3) Finally, benefits from 'demonstration effects' of extractive subsidiaries are not likely to be important, given that the location of such firms is remote to the locations of domestic firms. However, this remoteness may benefit the local labour force: the monopsonistic power of extractive subsidiaries in the labour market may generate significant rents for their workers.[76]

B.   Market Structure and Market Conduct

The *total impact* of foreign direct investment in the host country depends both on the *reasons* for establishing a subsidiary and on the consequences of the operations of the subsidiary on market behaviour (conduct) and on economic performance. The latter has been examined in the preceeding section. Here we discuss some aspects related to market structure and market conduct.

To understand the effects and predict the consequences of foreign direct investment on market structure and conduct it is useful to summarise the chief traits of multinationals and their subsidiaries.

(1) Foreign direct investment originates from differentiated oligopoly in the home market and is directed to foreign markets which are also oligopolistic with product differentiation.[77]

(2) Multinational corporations are large in size. They are oligopolistic firms in the home market, having exhausted all possible sources of economies of scale. A firm would not invest abroad while profitable opportunities remained for the exploitation of scale economies in production or sales in the home market.[78]

(3) Multinationals tend to populate foreign oligopolistic markets which are protected by strong barriers to entry. However, the multinational firm has advantages against each of the major sources of entry barriers.

(a) The product-differentiation advantage has already been discussed in detail. Multinationals develop new superior products which give them a lead over foreign local producers.

(b) The international corporation can attain (or exceed) the minimum optimal scale of plant in a foreign market, for at least two reasons. First, having a better product it may well expect to capture a larger share of the foreign market than the local producers. Second, the subsidiary may start exporting to other countries

---

[76] A. Stonehill, 'Foreign Ownership in Norwegian Enterprises', *Samfunnsokonomiske Studier*, no. 14, Oslo, 1965; R. E. Baldwin, *Economic Development and Export Growth: A Study of Northern Rhodesia 1920–60* (University of California Press, 1966); Kindleberger, *American Business Abroad*.

[77] Dunning, *American Investment in British Manufacturing Industry*, pp. 155–7; M. D. Steuer *et al.*, *The Economic Effects of Inward Investment in the United Kingdom* (Cambridge University Press, 1970) ch. 4; G. Rosenbluth, 'The Relation between Foreign Control and Concentration in Canadian Industry', *Canadian Journal of Economics*, vol. 3, 1970, pp. 14–30; E. L. Wheelwright, 'Overseas Investment in Australia', in *The Economics of Australian Industry*, ed. A. Hunter (Melbourne, 1963) pp. 155–6.

[78] Idem.

and/or ship back part of its output to the home country. Another factor associated with scale economies is that if such economies are important at one stage of the production process, but not in others, the parent company undertakes this stage, and builds subsidiaries for the other stages. It is observed that subsidiaries are less vertically integrated than their parent company.[79] They are organised to carry out only an intermediate part of the parent's product (production of components, assembly operations) for which scale economies are not important.

(c) Initial capital requirements are not a barrier, since the subsidiaries are financed mostly by the retained earnings of the parent corporation. Even when they need external finance, they have easy access to capital markets, having good credit rating as affiliates of well-established multinational firms.

(d) Finally, multinational firms have substantial absolute cost advantages over local foreign producers. Such advantages stem mainly from the lower cost of finance (they have access to the 'pockets' of the parent corporation at a lower opportunity cost), superior technical knowhow, and more efficient and skilled managerial talent.

(4) The above advantages that the foreign firm enjoys, and which enable it to break down barriers in foreign markets are weighted against the disadvantages associated with operations in an alien market. These disadvantages arise (a) from the additional costs of gathering information, (b) exchange-rate fluctuations, and (c) political actions by foreign governments. Thus foreign direct investment is more risky than investment in the domestic market.

(5) The greater risk of foreign direct investment can be born by large firms. Thus the risk factor partly explains the large absolute size of multinational firms.

(6) The greater risk also makes multinationals require a higher rate of profit on foreign investments. The cost of information sets a limit to the amount that the investor would ideally like to possess. He will settle for less of it, and, as a result, uncertainty and business risk will be higher in foreign markets. Accordingly, the required rate of return will be higher. The available evidence from several countries suggests that subsidiaries often have a superior profit performance than domestic firms.[80] This is partly only attributable to the additional risks of foreign operations. To a great extent the greater profitability reflects the transfer of rents (from the parent company to the affiliate) from the use of trade marks (brand names), technical knowhow and managerial expertise for which subsidiaries are not charged.

In summary, the additional risks of foreign operations (arising from the cost of information, foreign exchange-rate changes and the political environment)

---

[79] Irving Brecher and S. S. Reisman, *Canada—United States Economic Relations* (Studies for Royal Commission on Canada's Economic Prospects, 1957); T. R. Gates and F. Linden, *Cost and Competition: American Experience Abroad* (Harper & Row, 1961).

[80] Brash, *American Investment in Australian Industry*; J. H. Dunning, *The Role of American Investment in the British Economy*, PEP Broadsheet, no. 507, 1969, pp. 130–3; Safarian, *The Performance of Foreign-owned Firms in Canada*, chs 6 and 7.

explain several aspects of foreign direct investment, such as:

the prevalence of large firms as foreign investors;
the greater risk of foreign investment;
the observed fact that US multinationals usually start their foreign expansion
in the Canadian market, where the specific (additional) risks of direct investment are smaller;
the higher rate of profit expected from foreign operations;
the higher actual profit performance of subsidiaries relative to their competitors in the host country.

The above analysis refers primarily to the market structure of the industries
of the parent companies. The type of *market structure* that will emerge in the
host country has not been theoretically or empirically explored. However, some
general patterns can be predicted.

(1) The establishment of subsidiaries will decrease industry concentration in
the short run. However, in the long run it seems likely that the more inefficient
local producers will be closed down, so that seller concentration may be higher
than before the establishment of the subsidiaries.

(2) The size of the subsidiaries will tend to be, on average, larger than the size
of the foreign competitors. This is due to the access of the subsidiaries to markets
other than the one in which they are located.

(3) If the establishment of a subsidiary enhances sales due to better service
and/or adaptation of the product to the requirements of the local buyers, other
rivals will be induced to make similar 'defensive' investments. Such oligopolistic
interdependence may result in an excessive number of foreign subsidiaries in the
industry, each operating at sub-optimal scale.

An important issue related to the effects of foreign direct investment is the
market conduct in the host country. No general predictions can be derived from
the existing literature. Some writers have advocated the following behaviour,
which, they maintain, applies at least to Canadian industries.

(1) Barriers to entry continue to be strong after the establishment of the subsidiary, thus securing excess profits for all the firms in the industry.

(2) Price competition is avoided. The local producers are aware of the product-
differentiation advantage (or technological advantage) of the foreign entrants, as
well as of the fact that they have access to the 'deep pockets' of their parents,
which would enable them to survive a price war. Also, foreign subsidiaries do
not have any incentive to start competitive price-cutting. There is substantial
evidence that foreign subsidiaries 'price up to the tariff', that is, they set their
price at the world (external) price (inclusive of transport cost, insurance and
other export costs) plus the tariff.[81]

[81] Eastman and Stykolt, *The Tariff and Competition in Canada*; H. E. English, *Industrial Structure in Canada's International Competitive Position* (Prentice-Hall, 1964) ch. 4.

(3) Given that this price allows excess profits, both domestic and foreign firms will tend to be of sub-optimal scale.[82]

(4) However, non-price competition will most likely be enhanced. The foreign subsidiary will tend to stir up competition more than a local entrant, who will be more likely to follow the 'established code of behaviour in the industry'. As a consequence advertising and product competition will tend to be excessive.

(5) Home-owned firms may be induced to spend more on research and development in their attempt to offset the technological advantage of foreign subsidiaries.

The allocative and welfare implications of the above market conduct cannot be predicted on *a priori* grounds. The analysis should be conducted within the general framework of the theory of industrial organisation.

IV.   EMPIRICAL EVIDENCE

Although theoretical hypotheses pertaining to the decision to invest abroad abound in economic literature, empirical work in this field leaves a lot to be desired. A large number of studies on the activities of multinational corporations have been conducted over the last three decades. However, most of them are descriptive, providing information on the growth of multinationals in various countries, and comparisons of the foreign affiliates with their parent companies and host-country competitors.[83] Econometric work on the causes and effects of foreign direct investment has been very limited. This may be attributed to several factors, such as data availability, difficulties in measuring the relevant variables, the confusing stage of economic theory on multinationals, and the controversial issues arising from the economic dependence of the host country on foreign investment and its effects on the political independence of the host country.

In this section we will discuss briefly the main econometric studies on the causes and effects of multinationals, because they are more relevant to the

---

[82] Eastman and Stykolt, *The Tariff and Competition in Canada*, chs 1 and 3; J. S. Bain, *International Differences in Industrial Structure* (Yale University Press, 1966) p. 39.

[83] Some of the main sources of empirical evidence are: Barlow and Wender, *Foreign Investment and Taxation*; US Department of Commerce, Office of Business Economics, 'US Business Investments in Foreign Countries', supplement to *Survey of Current Business* (Washington, D.C., 1960); Dunning, *American Investment in British Manufacturing Industry*; W. B. Reddaway *et al.*, *Effects of UK Direct Investment Overseas: Final Report*, University of Cambridge, Department of Applied Economics, Occasional Paper No. 15, Cambridge, 1968; Brash, *American Investment in Australian Industry*; Stonehill, *Foreign Ownership in Norwegian Enterprises*; Safarian, *Foreign Ownership of Canadian Industry*; Safarian, *The Performance of Foreign-owned Firms in Canada*; Behrman, *Some Patterns in the Rise of the Multinational Enterprise*; Eastman and Stykolt, *The Tariff and Competition in Canada*; Aitken, *American Capital and Canadian Resources*.

theoretical analysis of the preceding sections. We will group these studies in four classes:

(a) Studies of the characteristics of the firms which become multinational.
(b) Studies of the causes (or motives) of foreign direct investment.
(c) Studies of the 'product-cycle' hypothesis.
(d) Studies of the economic effects of multinational corporations in the host country.

A.   Studies of the Characteristics of the Firms which Undertake Foreign Direct Investment

Studies of this kind provide evidence on the static determinants of foreign direct investment.

Two recent studies of the nature of firms which become multinational are of particular interest.

Vernon[84] conducted a detailed study based on 187 US manufacturing corporations with six or more foreign subsidiaries outside Canada. He found that firms which decide to 'go abroad' have (a) large size, (b) high profitability, (c) high advertising intensity, (d) high R & D intensity, and (e) a substantial degree of diversification.

Horst[83] estimated the following empirical specification, applying OLS to a sample of 1,191 US firms:

$$\begin{bmatrix} \text{Probability} \\ \text{of becoming} \\ \text{multinational} \end{bmatrix} = f\,[\text{Size, Type of industry, Profitability, R \& D,} \\ \text{Advertising, Vertical integration, Product diversity}]$$

From his analysis Horst concluded that the only significant determinants of the decision to invest abroad are the size of the firm and the industry to which the firm belongs. The other structural characteristics are not statistically significant.

Horst attributes these results to the fact that 'size' absorbs all the other factors that appear in his empirical specification. Thus Horst's results do not in fact contradict the findings of Vernon and other researchers.

We note that neither of the above two studies is an adequate test of the alternative hypotheses about the motives of foreign direct investment. The findings of both studies, however, *imply* that specific advantages of various kinds are the cause of foreign direct investment.

---

[84] Vernon, *Sovereignty at Bay*.
[85] Horst, 'Firm and Industry Determinants of the Decision to Invest Abroad'.

B.   Studies of the Causes of Foreign Direct Investment

Caves[86] attempted to test the hypothesis that the causes of foreign direct investment are specific advantages that foreign firms have over host-country producers,
the tariff policy of host countries, comparative cost advantages of the theory of
international trade, and the size of the firm.

Caves's empirical specification may be written in the summary form:

$$\text{FDI} = f[\text{Specific advantages, Size of firm, Tariffs,}$$
$$\text{Comparative cost advantage}]$$

In the group of 'specific advantages' Caves included: (a) product-differentiation advantages, measured by R & D intensity and advertising intensity; (b) lower
cost of finance; (c) scale economies; (d) multi-plant economies; (e) managerial
skill advantages.

Caves estimated his empirical model with two cross-industry samples: a sample
of sixty-four industries of Canada, and a sample of fifty-two industries of the
United Kingdom. He experimented with various subsets of the regressors, and
with different measures for each variable. From his 'experimental' approach
Caves draws the following conclusions.

(1) Product-differentiation advantages are significant determinants of FDI in
both countries.

(2) Multi-plant economies are important in Canada, but not in the UK. This is
attributed to the geographic proximity of Canada to the USA, the principal
foreign investor in Canadian industries.

(3) Given the importance of the R & D ('product') advantage and of the multi-
plant economies, it follows (according to Caves) that multinational firms will
population oligopolistic industries with high concentration and significant barriers
to entry.

(4) Managerial advantages do not appear to be important in explaining foreign
direct investment.

(5) The 'size' variable is a significant determinant of the decision to invest
abroad.

(6) Tariffs do not show any significant effect.

(7) Relative factor costs seem to be a significant determinant of the choice
between FDI and exporting, especially in the Canadian case.

Most of Caves's conclusions are unwarranted, given the estimated functions
which he reports in his article. In the case of Canada, five of the reported regressions contain a coefficient with the 'wrong' *a priori* sign. And it is in these regressions that 'size' appears as a significant factor. In the remaining regressions 'size'
is not included in the set of regressors. Hence Caves's inference about the 'size'

---

[86] Caves, 'Causes of Direct Investment: Foreign Firms' Shares in Canadian and UK
Manufacturing Industries'.

variable is not supported by his results. This is hardly surprising, given that 'size', as Horst suggested, subsumes most of the structural influences (advantages which create entry barriers), and hence its inclusion in the function results in 'double-counting'.

In general, Caves's results must be interpreted with great caution. Theoretically his models suffer from mis-specification, due to the inclusion of 'size' and the exclusion of other variables which would express the 'specific advantages' of multinational corporations. On an empirical basis, Caves's study suffers from the measurement of the various variables. For example, his assumption that the existence of multi-plant firms in the USA is 'proof' that these firms have multi-plant economies is dubious. Professor Bain,[87] in his classic study of entry barriers, found that multi-plant economies are not important in US industries. The 'strong' relation (observed by Caves) between FDI and his measure of multi-plant economies is consistent with other hypotheses[88] and does not seem to reflect the impact of any multi-plant economies on the decision to invest abroad.

The measures of 'managerial skills' are too crude to allow the definite rejection of the 'managerial-advantage' hypothesis. Similar objections can be raised for other measures.

Despite its limitations, however, Caves's study is useful in that it provides a basis for further meaningful econometric work.

The second study on the causes of FDI that is of some interest is one conducted by Horst.[89] He measures FDI not in terms of the production activity of the foreign subsidiaries, as most writers do, but in terms of the intensity of multinational activity. That is, Horst's dependent variable is the proportion of large firms in each (two-digit) manufacturing industry which become multinational by undertaking foreign direct investment. This approach is not quite satisfactory, since it ignores the multinational activity of 'small' firms (which are not included in Horst's sample of *Fortune*'s list of 500 largest US firms).

From the set of 'specific advantages' discussed in the theory of multinationals, Horst selects only two: (a) R & D expenditure, as a proxy for the product-differentiation advantage, and (b) a measure of minimum optimal scale, to account for scale economies.

In order to account for the fact that some firms invest abroad in order to exploit the natural resources of the host country, Horst uses a dummy variable, which takes on the value of unity for five 'resource-intensive industries' (wood, paper, petroleum, non-metallic mineral products, basic metals), and the value of zero for the remaining fifteen industries.

Horst's findings provide evidence in support of the 'specific-advantage' hypothesis: product advantages and scale economies are important determinants

---

[87] Bain, *Barriers to New Competition*.
[88] For example, one may plausibly argue that multi-plant firms in the USA are growth-seekers which, having saturated the domestic market, extended their operations in foreign markets.
[89] Horst, 'Firm and Industry Determinants of the Decision to Invest Abroad'.

of foreign direct investment. The statistical insignificance of the 'resource-intensity' factor is surprising, given the two-digit cross-industry sample used in Horst's study. A puzzling feature of Horst's empirical model is that it does not include tariffs or any measure of comparative cost advantage. Horst does not explain the omission of such factors, though in another study[90] he found that tariffs and comparative cost advantages have an important influence on the decision of the firm to exploit 'specific advantages' by exports or foreign direct investment.

C.   Tests of the 'Product-Cycle' Hypothesis

We will discuss briefly three studies which were conducted with the aim of testing Vernon's 'product-cycle' hypothesis.

(1) Gruber, Mehta and Vernon[91] used a sample of nineteen manufacturing industries (for the year 1962) and which they classified in two groups. The first includes five industries (aircraft and other transport equipment, electrical machinery, instruments, chemicals, non-electrical machinery) which are 'most research intensive', and hence have a strong technological advantage over producers in foreign countries. The second group includes all the other (two-digit) industries which have low research and development activity.

In the first part of their study the authors find a high correlation between exports and the R & D activity of the various industries. They argue that this provides evidence that the strength of US exports is centred on the group of the five industries which, as a result of high R & D activity, produce technologically sophisticated products that can successfully meet competition in other countries.

In the second part of their study the authors examine the foreign direct investment activity of the manufacturing industries in 1962, and conclude that 'the propensity to build facilities or otherwise invest abroad' is higher in the five research-intensive industries than in other US industries. They argue that this is compatible with the 'product-cycle' hypothesis, which predicts that FDI is the final step in a process which starts with local production of technologically superior products, evolves into a strong export position, and ends by the establishment of production facilities in export markets, in an attempt to preserve the foreign market share.

Finally, the authors compare (for the year 1962) the exports of the US industries to the sales of US foreign subsidiaries in Europe and the rest of the world.

---

[90] Horst, 'The Industrial Composition of US Exports and Subsidiary Sales to the Canadian Market'. In this study Horst concludes that the exports of US multinational (parent) corporations are reduced relative to FDI when tariffs increase and Canadian producers have a comparative cost advantage. In other words, tariffs and cost advantages of Canadian firms discourage exports of US firms and induce them to substitute subsidiary production for exporting.

[91] Gruber, Mehta and Vernon, 'The R & D Factor in International Trade and International Investment of US Industries'.

They conclude that the pattern of exports and subsidiary sales of the research-intensive industries suggests that FDI has substituted exports to a large extent, a fact which is compatible with the 'product-cycle hypothesis'. However, the foreign direct investment of the less research-orientated industries cannot be altogether explained by the 'product-cycle' hypothesis. Foreign direct investment by many firms in these industries (especially food-processing and food-distributing) has little to do with defending or salvaging an export position. Alternative hypotheses must be used. The authors suggest that in the less research-orientated industries the most plausible motive for foreign direct investment is the exploitation of a specific advantage.

However, a cross-industry sample in a single year is really inadequate for testing the dynamic aspects of Vernon's 'product-cycle' hypothesis. The conclusions of the authors is based on other knowledge rather than on the 1962 data which they analyse in their study. The substitution of exports by foreign direct investment can be revealed only by a study of these activities over time.

(2) Wells[92] attempted to test four predictions of the 'product-cycle' hypothesis. However, he was interested in the explanation of the exports of the USA rather than in foreign direct investment. Implicit in Wells's analysis is *the assumption* that US industries producing technologically sophisticated consumer durables (such as refrigerators, freezers, cooking stoves, radios, vacuum cleaners, etc.) were, during the 1952–63 period, in the second stage of the product cycle, that is, in the phase of expanding exports prior to foreign direct investment. In this respect his findings are not relevant to the explanation of the motives of foreign direct investment. It is noted that Wells's study suffers from serious methodological shortcomings and data limitations, so that its results are in general questionable.

(3) In a recent article Horst[93] postulated an alternative to Vernon's product-cycle hypothesis.

According to Horst, foreign direct investment is not the successor to exporting to a foreign market. Foreign direct investment is not undertaken to protect or salvage the share attained in a foreign market by previous exporting activity. Rather, exports and foreign direct investment are alternative ways (substitute activities) for exploiting a technological advantage that a firm possesses. The firm is interested in the *total* share in a foreign market, and this can be attained by exporting, by direct investment, or by a combination of both activities at any one time.

The total share of sales of a firm in a foreign market depends, according to Horst, on its technological advantage relative to its competitors in the foreign market. In turn, the firm's technological advantage is determined by its R & D activity.

    [92] L. T. Wells, 'Test of a Product Cycle Model of International Trade: US Exports of Consumer Durables', *Quarterly Journal of Economics*, vol. 83, 1969, pp. 152–62.
    [93] Horst, 'The Industrial Composition of US Exports and Subsidiary Sales to the Canadian Market'.

To test the substitutability of direct investment for exporting, Horst applied regression analysis to a cross-industry sample including eighteen two-digit US manufacturing industries for the year 1963.

Horst measured 'technological advantage' by the ratio of the amount spent by firms in an industry on research and development divided by the total output of the industry.

Horst estimated three regressions: one for the share of US exports in the Canadian market (X_j/C_j), one for the share of subsidiary production (by US affiliates) in the Canadian market (SP_j/C_j), and one for the total share (of exports plus subsidiary production) in the Canadian market $[(X_j + SP_j)/C_j]$. His results are summarised below:

$$\frac{X_j}{C_j} = 0.043 + 5.47 \ (\text{R \& D}) \qquad R^2 = 0.33$$
$$(t = 2.69)$$

$$\frac{SP_j}{C_j} = 0.166 + 14.65 \ (\text{R \& D}) \qquad R^2 = 0.48$$
$$(t = 3.71)$$

$$\frac{X_j + SP_j}{C_j} = 0.209 + 20.69 \ (\text{R \& D}) \qquad R^2 = 0.63$$
$$(t = 5.10)$$

From the higher R^2 of the third regression Horst concludes that the cross-industry pattern of US exports and subsidiary production to the Canadian market 'provides strong, if indirect, support for the hypothesis that exporting and foreign investing represent alternative methods by which US firms exploit the same technological advantages over their Canadian competitors'. Horst infers that his results refute Vernon's product-cycle hypothesis.

It is apparent that Horst's functions are grossly mis-specified. Many important explanatory variables are omitted from the model. Furthermore, a cross-industry sample is not appropriate for studying decisions involving choices over time. Finally, it is not clear why a higher R^2 for the aggregate regression supports Horst's thesis. Horst's approach is surely inadequate for testing Vernon's 'product-cycle' hypothesis.

D.   Studies of the Effects of Foreign Direct Investment

In this section we shall present briefly the results of four econometric studies.

(1) Caves[94] tested two hypotheses about the effects of foreign direct investment on domestic-owned firms competing with foreign subsidiaries. Caves's first hypothesis is that 'subsidiaries serve as an effective competitive force, reducing the [excess] profits earned by domestic competitors and improving allocation

---

[94] Caves, 'Multinational Firms, Competition, and Productivity in Host-Country Markets'.

efficiency'. Using a cross-industry sample (of forty-nine Canadian industries) Caves estimated a profit function for the period 1965–7 from which he found that the profit rates of Canadian-owned firms were inversely related to the 'pressure' of foreign firms (measured by the subsidiary share of sales or assets in an industry). From this finding Caves infers that foreign direct investment has improved the allocative efficiency in manufacturing industry. This conclusion can be challenged on several accounts.

Statistically, Caves's results are rather poor (the adjusted R^2 does not exceed 0.18 in any of his reported regressions and the statistical significance of his estimates is mostly low). However, a more fundamental weakness stems from the use of the profit rate as the dependent variable, and from the omission from the set of regressors of several important explanatory variables.

(a) Profit rates are an accounting residual, which reflects changes both in unit costs and in prices. Profits may be squeezed as a consequence of a price reduction from increased competition, or from a rise in costs (after entry), or from an *increase* in price which is more than offset by cost increases. As we will argue subsequently, foreign presence may result in productivity improvements, which may reduce costs, as well as increased industry competition, which may put pressure on prices and costs. Since Caves's profit function does not include any variable to account for these effects separately, his conclusion is not necessarily valid.

(b) Caves uses a cross-industry sample, which implies that the same mechanism of micro behaviour applies to all industries. However, there are too many non-random inter-industry differences which are not accounted for and which make Caves's results difficult to interpret. In particular, Caves ignores inter-industry risk differentials, as well as the influence of market size and market growth on the profitability of firms, despite the evidence that these are important explanatory variables of profitability. Hence, mis-specification bias may well affect the coefficients of included variables.

(c) It is doubtful whether the measures which Caves uses for his variables are appropriate for his purpose.

(d) Even if one ignores the above criticisms, the fact remains that an inverse relationship between the Canadian profit rates and the competitive pressure of foreign subsidiaries is a *necessary* but not a *sufficient* condition for the improvement of allocative efficiency. No reallocation may take place, despite the squeezed profits, if barriers continue post-entry, enabling all firms to earn some excess profit. The theory of multinationals predicts that this is the general case rather than the exception. Furthermore, even if some Canadian firms are forced to reallocate, it is not certain that there will be an improvement in the allocative efficiency of resources, since these firms may choose an industry where monopolistic distortions are more serious.

The second hypothesis that Caves tested is that foreign direct investment increases the productivity of competing firms, by inducing a higher level of technical efficiency in these firms and speeding up the adoption of new technology. Caves used two sets of data to conduct his test. The first sample includes forty-nine Canadian industries. In his empirical model (for Canada) Caves reverses the causation between 'foreign pressure' and labour productivity of Canadian-owned firms without any explanation. His statistical fit is very poor ($\bar{R}^2$ is 0.01), and the coefficient of the labour-productivity variable turns up with the 'wrong' *a priori* sign. Based on this finding, Caves rejects his maintained hypothesis and infers that foreign subsidiaries do not improve the productivity of Canadian-owned firms. The theoretical foundation of this model and Caves's statistical results cast serious doubts on the validity of this inference for Canada. However, Caves's second sample (for forty-two Australian industries) allowed him to adopt a correct empirical specification, in which labour productivity is the dependent variable, while 'foreign pressure' is included in the set of explanatory variables. For this sample Caves concluded that multinationals have improved the productivity of Australian-owned competing firms.

(2) Globerman[95] adopted a specification similar to that of Caves for the Australian manufacturing industry, but estimated it with a cross-industry sample of thirty-five Canadian industries for the year 1972. Contrary to Caves, Globerman found that the productivity of labour of Canadian firms has improved as a consequence of the activity of foreign subsidiaries. It should be noted that Globerman's specification is more plausible than that of Caves. However, his results, like those of Caves, are difficult to interpret due to the nature of his cross-industry sample, and are limited to the productivity gains of Canadian-owned firms alone.

(3) In a recent paper this author[96] examined the impact of multinationals on the price and cost levels of Canadian manufacturing industries, not on Canadian-owned firms alone. Price and cost functions were estimated for each of the twenty two-digit manufacturing industries, using time-series data for the 1962–75 period. This approach was broader than that of Caves and Globerman, in that the effects of multinationals in each industry as a whole were explored. Furthermore, the time-series data used did not pose the interpretation problems associated with cross-industry samples.

The results of this study may be summarised as follows. First, the estimated price functions suggest that the increase in competition from the operations of foreign subsidiaries in Canada has had a favourable impact on the prices of manufactures over the 1962–75 period. This is compatible with Caves's observed inverse relationship between the profits in Canadian manufacturing industries and the subsidiaries' market share. Second, the estimated cost functions show that during the same period foreign subsidiaries, with their superior technology

---

[95] S. Globerman, 'Foreign Direct Investment and "Spillover" Efficiency Benefits in Canadian Manufacturing Industries', *Canadian Journal of Economics*, vol. XII, 1979, pp. 42–56.

[96] A. Koutsoyiannis, 'The Impact of Multinational Firms on Prices and Costs in Host-Country Markets: The Case of Canadian Manufacturing Industry' (forthcoming).

and greater efficiency, have exerted a downward pressure on the costs of Canadian manfuacturing industries. This finding is contrary to Caves' conclusion, but confirms Globerman's finding that the productivity of Canadian manufacturing sectors has improved, due partly to the operations of foreign firms.

(4) Lall[97] examined the impact of multinational corporations on industry concentration in the host country. Using a cross-section sample of forty-six manufacturing industries of Malaysia for 1972, Lall estimated (with OLS) a function in which the dependent variable was the four-firm concentration ratio, and the set of explanatory variables included various measures of the four barriers to entry (scale economies, absolute cost advantage, product-differentiation barrier and initial capital requirements) and a measure of the 'multinational presence'. From his results Lall concluded that multinationals in Malaysia have a *direct* effect on concentration (they *increase* concentration). This effect may be due to introduction of new products and/or techniques which improve the efficiency of the industrial sector (a beneficial effect), or to predatory conduct or favourable concessions from the government which put smaller, local firms at a disadvantage and may coerce them to close down, a fact that reduces competition (an undesirable effect). Given his data, Lall could not ascertain which of the above effects was more predominant.

Lall next used simple correlation analysis. From the correlation coefficients of the 'foreign-presence' variable with the other explanatory variables, Lall concluded that multinationals, apart from their direct effect on concentration, have an additional *indirect* effect, by increasing the four barriers to entry. This inference is not warranted, given that correlation does not necessarily imply causation. However, the direct effect of foreign subsidiaries on concentration is evident from Lall's results. This finding is contrary to Rosenbluth's[98] results for the Canadian manufacturing industry. Rosenbluth examined the relationship between concentration and the activity of foreign subsidiaries in the 1960s and concluded that there is no discernible relationship between these variables. Lall attributes this finding to the fact that the market structure in developed host countries is fairly similar to that of the investing countries. However, if the host country is underdeveloped, one may well expect a change in concentration brought around by the characteristics and the conduct of the large multinational affiliates.

It should be apparent from the above survey of the empirical work on multinationals that further research is needed before any firm conclusion can be reached on either the motives or the effects of foreign direct investment.

[97] S. Lall, 'Multinationals and Market Structure in an Open Developing Economy: The Case of Malaysia', *Weltwirtschaftliches Archiv*, 1979, pp. 325–49.
[98] G. Rosenbluth, 'The Relation Between Foreign Control and Concentration in Canadian Industry', *Canadian Journal of Economics*, vol. 3, 1970, pp. 14–38.

PART THREE

The Financing Decisions
of the Firm

Introduction

A decision to grow (increase the productive assets of the firm) involves an implicit decision to raise money capital in order to finance the growth. In turn, the way of financing growth defines the cost of capital to the firm, and thus it has a bearing on the amount of investment which will be undertaken by the firm. Hence the financing decisions and the investment decisions of the firm are closely related.

Investment in real assets requires long-term finance.[1] In Part Three we shall examine how the management of large corporations reaches 'optimal' decisions regarding the use of the various sources of funds, in order to finance its long-run operations.

There are three main sources of funds: (a) issues of shares (equity financing); (b) issues of bonds (debt financing); and (c) retained profits. The two first sources of funds constitute *external financing*, while retained earnings are an *internal source of finance*.

The financing decisions involve the determination of the optimal mix of the various sources of funds required for financing the assets of the firm. Given the different sources of funds, the financing decisions imply two separate types of decisions. *First*, management must decide the optimal capital structure of the firm, that is, the optimal proportion of debt in its total capital. The capital structure is reflected in the firm's debt/equity ratio, that is, the proportion of debt to equity in the total assets of the firm. *Second*, management must decide an optimal dividend/payout policy. Determination of the dividend/payout ratio (the ratio of dividends to total earnings available to shareholders after payment of interest

---

[1] Liquidity aspects, although important, are short-run decisions and will not be dealt with in this book. The interested reader is referred to textbooks on managerial finance, e.g. J. C. Van Horne, *Financial Management and Policy* (Prentice-Hall, 1977), and E. F. Brigham, *Financial Management, Theory and Practice* (Dryden Press, 1979).

and corporate taxes) implies the determination of the retention ratio, the proportion of earnings to be retained for financing investment projects which will yield increased earnings in future periods.

In summary, the financing decisions involve the determination of an optimal debt/equity ratio (capital structure decision) and an optimal dividend/payout decision (retention—dividend policy).

The optimality of a decision is related to the goal of the firm. In other words, a decision is considered as optimal if it contributes to the attainment of the goal of the firm. In the traditional theory of finance the goal of the firm is assumed to be the maximisation of stockholder welfare, that is, the maximisation of the market value of the firm to its shareholders.[2] In recent years this goal has been disputed on several grounds.[3] Various alternatives have been suggested by different writers. The most prominent among these alternative goals is the maximisation of the growth of the firm and of the job security of managers.[4] The financing decisions will be examined in the light of the above two alternative hypotheses.

In the real business world, which is characterised by uncertainty, each type of funds has a different cost. The over-all cost of capital to the firm is the weighted average of the costs of the various sources of finance. The determination of the cost of capital is important for two reasons. It defines the supply of investable funds to the firm, and it is widely used as a criterion for investment decisions of the firm (see Chapters 4 and 11).

In Chapter 8 we examine the alternative theories of the capital-structure decision (or 'leverage' decision), and we survey the available empirical evidence in this area.

In Chapter 9 we consider the alternative theories of the dividend decision of the firm, and we summarise the main empirical studies in this field.

In Chapter 10 we discuss in some detail the concept of the cost of capital, its measurement, and its relevance in determining the supply-of-capital schedule to the firm and in taking 'optimal' investment decisions.

[2] The relation between the goal of profit maximisation and the goal of stockholder-wealth maximisation was discussed in Chapter 3, and will be further examined in Chapter 8.

[3] For a summary discussion of the alternative goals of the firm see A. Koutsoyiannis, *Modern Microeconomics*, 2nd edn (Macmillan, 1979) ch. 11.

[4] See R. Marris, *The Theory of 'Managerial' Capitalism* (Macmillan, 1964); J. K. Galbraith, *Economics and the Public Purpose* (Houghton Mifflin, 1973); A. Koutsoyiannis, 'Managerial Job Security and the Capital Structure of Firms', *Manchester School*, 1978.

8. The Capital Structure of the Firm: The Leverage Decision

In this chapter we examine the factors that managers take into account when deciding how much debt to use in the capital structure of the firm. This decision is important, because it determines the cost of capital to the firm, which is a widely used criterion for optimal investment decisions (see Chapter 11).

There are three main theories, based on the goal of stockholder-wealth maximisation, that deserve consideration. All three examine the question as to whether there is a capital structure that maximises the value of the firm to the existing (current) stockholders. The first theory, known as the 'classical' or 'traditional' theory, postulates that there is a *unique optimal capital structure* which maximises the market value of the firm by minimising the average cost of its capital. A version of this theory, developed systematically by Ezra Solomon,[1] postulates that there is a *range of optimal capital structures*, that is, a range of debt/equity ratios over which the discount rate (or the average cost of capital) attains its minimum value, resulting in the maximisation of the market value of the firm (over that range). The second theory was developed by Modigliani and Miller[2] under the assumptions of perfect capital markets and no corporate (or other) taxes. This theory postulates that the value of the firm and, consequently, the wealth position of stockholders is *not* affected by the capital structure (type of financing). The third theory, also developed by Modigliani and Miller,[3] takes into account corporate taxes and postulates that a firm should use as much debt as possible to maximise its value and the wealth position of its stockholders.

---

[1] Ezra Solomon, *The Theory of Financial Management* (Columbia University Press, 1963).

[2] F. Modigliani and M. Miller, 'The Cost of Capital, Corporate Finance and the Theory of Investment', *American Economic Review*, 1958, pp. 261–77.

[3] F. Modigliani and M. Miller, 'Corporate Income Taxes and the Cost of Capital: A Correction', *American Economic Review*, 1963, pp. 433–43.

In a recent article this author developed an alternative theory of 'optimal' capital structure, based on the assumption that the goal of managers is the maximisation of their own utility rather than the maximisation of the wealth of shareholders.[4]

In sections I and II we examine and evaluate each of these theories. In section III we examine how managers in practice decide the proportion of debt and equity in the capital structure of the firm. In section IV we combine the conclusions of the previous analyses and we draw a list of the factors that influence the leverage decision of managers. Finally, in section V we present a critical evaluation of the main empirical studies on the determinants of the capital structure of the firm.

I. THE CAPITAL STRUCTURE OF FIRMS UNDER THE ASSUMPTION THAT THE GOAL OF MANAGERS IS STOCKHOLDER-WEALTH MAXIMISATION

In this section we will present the main theories of capital structure under the assumption that the goal of managers is the maximisation of the market value of the firm to its original stockholders.

Although the capital structure refers to the proportion of all types of securities in the total assets of the firm, we will concentrate for simplicity on the two most important types, common stock and bonds. The capital structure will be reflected in the debt/equity ratio of the firm.

Before embarking on the examination of the various theories we introduce some definitions and assumptions which are common to all of them.

Assumptions

(1) There is a perfect capital market, in the sense that all investors have the same (costless) information, they are price-takers, there are no transaction costs (such as brokerage fees, flotation costs, etc.) and there are no taxes (corporate or personal).

(2) Investors act rationally, in the sense that they behave consistently and they prefer more wealth to less.

(3) Investors are assumed to form (subjective) expectations regarding the stream of future earnings of each firm. These expectations are summarised in the mean $E(X)$ and variance of the stream of earnings (σ_x^2). (These concepts were explained in Chapter 3.)

(4) Investors have homogeneous expectations, that is, all investors maintain

---

[4] A. Koutsoyiannis, 'Managerial Job Security and the Capital Structure of Firms', *Manchester School*, 1978, pp. 51–75.

the same beliefs regarding $E(X)$ and σ_x^2 for the earning stream of each firm, since they have the same information.

(5) The firms distribute all their earnings (left over after the payment of interest) as dividends to common shareholders; there are no retained earnings. This assumption is necessary in order to isolate the effects of leverage from the effects of the dividend/payout policy of the firm. It is relaxed in Chapter 9, where we examine the effects of the dividend policy of the firm.

(6) The stream of earnings is not expected to grow over time. Thus

$$E(X_1) = E(X_2) = \ldots = E(X_n) = \bar{X}$$

(7) The goal of managers is the maximisation of the value of the firm to its stockholders (or, equivalently, the maximisation of stockholder wealth).

Notation and definitions

The following notation will be adopted throughout the analysis:

D = market value of debt

S = market value of common stock

V = total market value of the firm

$\bar{X}$ = expected value of *total earnings* (before interest and taxes, EBIT)

iD = interest payments to bondholders

i = market rate of interest

E = *earnings available to shareholders*, after interest payments (but before taxes). Thus $E = \bar{X} - iD$

From the above notation it follows that

$$V = S + D \tag{8.1}$$

$$\bar{X} = E + iD \tag{8.2}$$

There are three streams of earnings: the total earnings, $\bar{X}$, the earnings accruing to bondholders, iD, and the earnings available to shareholders, $E = \bar{X} - iD$. It is assumed that the market value of debt is the present value of the stream of earnings of bondholders

$$D = \frac{iD}{k_d} \tag{8.3}$$

where k_d is the discount rate which bondholders apply in order to find the present value of the stream of their earnings. Similarly

$$S = \frac{\bar{X} - iD}{k_e} = \frac{E}{k_e} \tag{8.4}$$

where k_e is the discount rate that shareholders apply in order to estimate the present value of their stream of earnings. Finally

$$V = \frac{\bar{X}}{k_o} \tag{8.5}$$

or

$$V = \frac{\bar{X} - iD}{k_e} + \frac{iD}{k_d} \tag{8.5a}$$

where k_o is the over-all discount rate which investors in the market apply in order to find the present value of the firm as a whole, that is, the present value of the stream of *total* earnings of the firm, irrespective of who receives them.

From (8.3), (8.4) and (8.5) we obtain

$$k_d = \frac{iD}{D} = i \tag{8.6}$$

$$k_e = \frac{\bar{X} - iD}{S} \tag{8.7}$$

$$k_o = \frac{\bar{X}}{V} \tag{8.8}$$

k_o reflects the pure business risk that all investors (stockholders or bondholders) associate with the stream of total earnings. Thus

$$k_o > k_d$$

because the chances that the firm will actually earn $\bar{X}$ are lower than the chance that it will earn at least a fraction of $\bar{X}$, i.e. the fraction iD required to pay the fixed-interest charges for its debt.

k_e reflects the *total financial risk of shareholders*, which, as we pointed out in Chapter 3, includes the pure business risk as well as the risk arising from the capital structure. Thus

$$k_e > k_o > k_d$$

The three discount rates are related mathematically with the expression

$$k_o = k_e \frac{S}{V} + k_d \frac{D}{V} \tag{8.9}$$

that is, the over-all discount rate is the weighted average of the equity discount rate and the debt discount rate, with the weights being the proportions of equity and debt in the total assets of the firm. k_o is usually referred to as *the weighted average cost of capital*, or *the over-all capitalisation rate*.

*   *   *

PROOF

From (8.8) we have

$$k_o = \frac{\overline{X}}{V}$$

Substitute $\overline{X} = E + iD$, to obtain

$$k_o = \frac{E}{V} + \frac{iD}{V} \qquad\qquad (8.10)$$

From (8.4) and (8.3) we obtain

$$E = k_e S \quad \text{and} \quad iD = k_d D$$

Substituting these values in (8.10) we find

$$k_o = k_e \frac{S}{V} + k_d \frac{D}{V}$$

QED

*   *   *

If we solve expression (8.9) for k_e we find

$$k_e = k_o + (k_o - k_d)\frac{D}{S} \qquad\qquad (8.11)$$

This relationship states that k_e is higher than k_o by the product $(k_o - k_d)D/S$. Since k_o reflects the business risk of total earnings, the second term is the premium for the additional risk arising from the use of debt for financing the operations of the firm.

The core of the theory of capital structure is the question of what happens to k_e, k_o and k_d as the degree of leverage changes. The standard textbook approach to the theory of capital structure is to state that the optimal leverage is the debt/equity ratio which minimises the over-all capitalisation rate or the weighted average cost of capital. This assertion follows from expression (8.5), $V = \overline{X}/k_o$. Since $\overline{X}$ is independent of the way that the operations of the firm are financed, V is maximised when k_o is minimised. In turn, k_o is a function of both k_e and k_d. The theories which we discuss below differ in their assumptions regarding the effects of increased leverage on k_e and k_d, and hence on k_o.

A. Durand's Valuation Hypotheses

Durand[5] has outlined two approaches to the valuation of the earnings of a firm: the *net income* (NI) approach and the *net operating income* (NOI) approach.

[5] D. Durand, 'The Cost of Debt and Equity Funds for Business: Trends and Problems of Measurement', in *The Management of Corporate Capital*, ed. E. Solomon (Free Press, 1959) pp. 91–116.

These represent diametrically opposite views regarding the effect of leverage on valuation.

(i) *The net income (NI) approach*

This approach postulates that as leverage increases both k_d and k_e remain constant, that is, neither the bondholders (lenders) nor the shareholders consider that increases in debt increase the risk of their earnings. Given that $k_d < k_e$, the substitution of cheap debt for expensive equity (increase in D/V and decrease in S/V) leads to a continuous reduction of the over-all discount rate, k_o, and hence to an increase in the market value of the firm as a whole. The optimal capital structure would be the one at which the total capital consists of debt. In this situation the bondholders are in fact the owners of the firm. The crucial assumption of the NI approach is that neither the bondholders (creditors) nor the shareholders (owners) believe that their respective streams of earnings become more risky as leverage increases.

The relation between k_d, k_e and k_o implied by the NI approach is shown in Figure 8.1. The optimal capital structure is reached when $k_d = k_o$, $\bar{X} = iD$ and $V = D$.

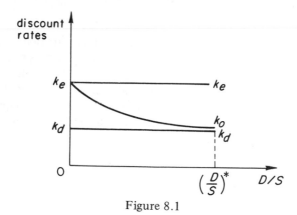

Figure 8.1

(ii) *The net operating income (NOI) approach*

This approach is diametrically opposite to the NI approach. According to this approach, k_d (discount rate of debt) remains constant with increases in leverage. However, the equity discount rate, k_e, rises linearly with increases in debt, because investors become aware of the financial risk of debt and require a higher premium for buying the shares of the firm. The substitution of cheap debt for expensive equity has no effect on the over-all capitalisation rate, k_o, because the favourable effect of the increase in D/V is offset by the increase in k_e. Thus the nominal (or explicit) discount rate of debt is k_d, but its real discount rate is higher. The *cost of debt* has two components: the explicit cost k_d, and the implicit cost resulting from the increase in k_e as leverage rises. The total value of the firm, V, remains unchanged by increases in leverage. The market capitalises (discounts) the value of the firm as a whole, so that the capital structure is a matter of indifference to shareholders. In other words, any capital structure is optimal.

The NOI approach is shown in Figure 8.2.

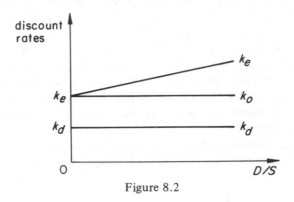

Figure 8.2

Note that Durand does not offer any behavioural explanation of the valuation process. He explicitly states that neither of these approaches is satisfactory.[6]

In the absence of a behavioural background, the NI and the NOI valuation approaches must be considered as definitional relationships rather than complete theories explaining investors' behaviour in capital markets. Subsequently we will see that Modigliani and Miller provided the theoretical framework for these approaches.[7]

B.   The 'Traditionalist' Approach

This approach has various versions. The common characteristic of all of them is that they postulate the existence of an optimal capital structure, a D/S ratio which maximises the total market value of the firm.

We will present two of these versions, one summarised by Modigliani and Miller in their 1958 article, and one presented by Ezra Solomon.[8] In the earlier literature discussions of the leverage effect are generally mixed with other aspects

---

[6] Ibid, p. 115.

[7] Modigliani and Miller, 'The Cost of Capital, Corporate Finance and the Theory of Investment'; also Modigliani and Miller, 'Corporate Income Taxes and the Cost of Capital: A Correction'.

[8] Solomon, *The Theory of Financial Management*; also E. Solomon, 'Leverage and the Cost of Capital', *Journal of Finance*, 1963.

of financial structure. A somewhat vague discussion of the optimal capital structure on traditionalist lines can be found in the writings of Graham and Dodd,[9] and Guthmann and Dougall.[10]

(i) *The Modigliani and Miller summary of the traditionalist view*

The over-all discount (or capitalisation) rate, k_o, declines up to a certain level of indebtedness, and beyond this level k_o starts rising. Since k_o is the weighted average of k_d and k_e it is necessary to examine the way in which these discount rates change with an increase in leverage.

(a) *The relationship between k_d and leverage*

There is a range of debt/equity ratios over which the cost of debt remains constant. When the debt of the firm is low relative to its equity capital, bondholders feel that their income (interest receipts) is secure. Beyond a certain level of indebtedness, however, bondholders feel that their income becomes more risky, and they demand a higher interest rate. Thus beyond a given D/S ratio the debt discount rate, k_d, increases.

(b) *The relationship between k_e and leverage*

There is a range of debt/equity ratios over which the equity discount rate, k_e, remains constant. This is so because when the firm's indebtedness is low shareholders feel that the expected earnings of the firm are adequate to cover the interest payments and secure a satisfactory dividend. Thus at low D/S ratios shareholders do not feel any increase in the risk of their expected stream of earnings and continue, therefore, to discount the stream of prospective earnings of the firm at the initial discount rate, k_e. However, the increase of debt beyond a certain level makes shareholders aware of an increase in their financial risk: their future income $(\overline{X} - iD)$ becomes less secure as debt is added to the financial structure of the firm. Consequently shareholders will require a higher expected return (k_e). Hence at high D/S ratios the equity discount rate, k_e, will rise and the price of shares of the firm will fall.

(c) *The relationship between k_o and leverage*

Since k_o is the weighted average of k_d and k_e, its value will be decreasing over the range of debt/equity ratios where both these discount rates remain constant, as cheap debt substitutes the expensive equity (D/V rises, while S/V falls). The

---

[9] B. Graham and D. L. Dodd, *Security Analysis* (McGraw-Hill, 1940).
[10] H. G. Guthmann and H. E. Dougall, *Corporate Financial Policy*, 3rd edn (Prentice-Hall, 1955).

over-all discount rate k_o will continue to fall over ranges of D/S where k_d starts rising so long as the increase in k_d is more than offset by the increase in D/V, the weight of debt in the capital structure. Over this range k_o is still significantly lower than k_e, despite the fact that k_d is rising. Eventually, however, both k_d and k_e increase as more debt is added to the capital structure, and the over-all discount rate, k_o, rises. Thus the relationship between k_o and D/S is U-shaped in the 'traditional' theory of valuation. According to the traditionalist doctrine, there is an optimal capital structure (optimal D/S ratio) which is reached when the over-all discount (capitalisation) rate is at its minimum level. This is point e in Figure 8.3.

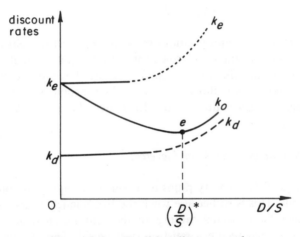

Figure 8.3   Traditionalist approach

(ii) *Solomon's 'revised traditionalist approach' to valuation*

Ezra Solomon[11] hypothesises the existence of three distinct phases as the firm increases its leverage. During the first phase increasing leverage lowers k_o and increases the total market value of the firm. This is due to the following forces: k_e, the rate at which the market discounts (capitalises) net earnings available to shareholders $[S = (\bar{X} - iD)/k_e]$, rises with increasing debt. But the debt discount rate k_d either remains constant or increases very slowly with increased leverage. Thus the over-all k_o falls over this phase because the rise in k_e (and the possible slow rise in k_d) is offset by the increase in D/V and the decline in S/V, i.e. the substitution of 'cheap' debt by 'expensive' equity in the firm's capital structure. The combined effect of increasing leverage on iD, $\bar{X} - iD$, k_d, k_e, D/V and S/V

[11] Solomon, *The Theory of Financial Management.*

is such that the total market value

$$V = \frac{\bar{X} - iD}{k_e} + \frac{iD}{k_d} = \frac{\bar{X}}{k_o}$$ (8.12)

rises. This implies that the over-all discount rate k_o falls in the first phase of increasing debt.

After a certain degree of leverage (which is determined by the capital market's evaluation of the level of business uncertainty involved) is reached, further moderate increases in leverage have little or no effect on total market value. During this phase both k_e and k_d increase (with $k_d < k_e$ always), but S/V falls while D/V rises in the capital structure of the firm, so that the over-all discount rate k_o remains constant, and so does the total market value of the firm, $V = \bar{X}/k_o$.

Beyond this range of 'acceptable leverage' the total market value will decline with leverage, because k_e and k_d rise fast, and the changes in D/V and S/V cannot offset this rise, so that the over-all k_o rises.

Solomon's valuation approach is shown in Figure 8.4.

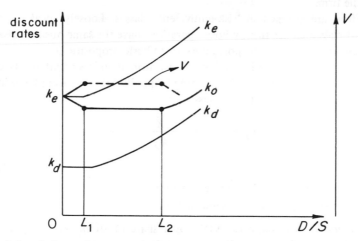

Figure 8.4   Solomon's approach ($L_1 L_2$ is the *range* of optimal capital structures)

C.   The Modigliani–Miller Approach Without Taxes

We said that Modigliani and Miller provided the theoretical framework for the net operating income approach, thus making the latter a theory of valuation with behavioural content, instead of the definitional treatment given to it by Durand.

The basic conclusion of Modigliani and Miller is the same as that of the NOI approach, that is, *in perfect capital markets*, where investors act rationally, the over-all k_o is constant at all degrees of leverage for firms with the same size and the same business risk. Such firms generate identical streams of earnings, with the same degree of business risk, and these streams must have the same total market value, irrespective of differences in leverage. Thus, according to Modigliani and Miller, there is no optimal capital structure for firms with the same business risk (in the absence of corporate and personal taxes). This proposition is diametrically opposite to the traditional view, which postulated the existence of such an optimal capital structure.

In addition to the seven assumptions stated at the beginning of this section, Modigliani and Miller make the following ones:

(1) Individual investors and firms can borrow at the same interest rate, k_d. That is, the supply of borrowed funds for individuals is identical to that for corporations.

(2) Bonds are traded in a perfect capital market, and all bonds have an identical yield, k_d, equal to the market interest rate, i.

(3) Bonds yield streams of returns which are known with certainty. Thus the market interest rate may be regarded as the discount rate of sure income streams.

(4) The market interest rate is constant irrespective of the degree of indebtedness of the firm.

(5) Firms are grouped in 'risk-equivalent' classes. Loosely speaking, a risk-equivalent class includes firms whose operations have the same business risk.

Modigliani and Miller have postulated three basic propositions.

Proposition I. The market value of any firm is independent of its capital structure, and is estimated by discounting (capitalising) its expected earnings, $\bar{X}$, at a rate k_o appropriate to its risk class:

$$V_u = \frac{\bar{X}}{k_o} \quad \text{and} \quad V_L = S_L + D_L = \frac{\bar{X}}{k_o}$$

so that $V_u = V_L$ (8.13)

where V_u = market value of an unlevered firm
V_L = market value of a levered firm

Proposition II. The expected yield of a share of stock, k_e, is equal to the capitalisation rate of a pure equity stream, k_o, plus a premium for the risk arising from the use of debt. This premium is equal to the difference between the over-all discount rate (k_o) and the market interest rate, i, times the debt/equity ratio:

$$k_e = k_o + (k_o - i)D/S$$ (8.14)

This relationship *is assumed to be linear*, in other words k_e increases in a manner to offset exactly the use of cheaper debt as the degree of leverage increases.

Proposition III. Given the firm's production and investment decisions,[12] the firm's financing decisions are a matter of indifference for any of its security

---

[12] Their independence is explained in Appendix 3.1 of Chapter 3.

holders (owners or creditors), because this decision does not affect their wealth situations and opportunities.

Proposition III together with Proposition I imply that production—investment decisions and financing decisions are separable, in the sense that they can be made (taken) independently of one another.

Propositions I and III will be established separately. Proposition II is not an independent proposition; it is derived from Proposition I.

Proof of Proposition I

Proposition I implies that in a perfect capital market investors will assign the same present value to identical expected streams of earnings, irrespective of the capital structure of the firms that produce these earnings. Or, equivalently, rational investors will not be prepared to pay a different total value (V) for two identical firms (in size and business risk) which produce identical expected streams of earnings just because the structure of their capital is different. No matter how the total capital of any firm is divided between equity, S, and debt, D, the total must always sum to its market value, V_L.

To establish Proposition I Modigliani and Miller used an approach akin to *arbitrage*. They proved that if two firms identical in all respects except in their capital structure (the one being levered and the other unlevered) have different market values, individual investors will undertake *arbitrage operations* until the present values of the firms are equalised. In particular, if the levered corporation sells at a premium relative to the unlevered firm (if $V_L > V_u$), a rational investor will change his portfolio: he will sell shares of the 'over-valued' levered firm and buy shares of the 'under-valued' unlevered firm, borrowing on personal account an amount which would give him a *personal leverage* equal to the one which the levered firm 'had created on his behalf'. Conversely, if the market value of the unlevered firm is higher than that of the levered firm (if $V_L < V_u$), the arbitrage operation involves selling the unlevered shares, buying the levered shares, and 'unlevering' them by simultaneously buying a *pro rata* fraction of the firm's debt (bonds). In both cases the 'arbitrage process' will lead to equalisation of the market values of the two firms, since they produce identical earnings ($\bar{X}_L = \bar{X}_u$).

To present the formal proof of Proposition I we will use the following notation:

$V_u = S_u$ = market value of the unlevered firm

$V_L = S_L + D$ = market value of the levered firm

$\bar{X}$ = expected stream of earnings (identical for both firms)

(a) *V_L cannot be larger than V_u*

Consider an investor who holds a fraction β of the outstanding stock of the levered firm. The cost of his portfolio is

$$C_0 = \beta S_L = \beta(V_L - D)$$

and his expected income from this portfolio is β per cent of the levered firm's expected earnings after deduction of the interest payments to bondholders, that is

$$Y_0 = \beta(\overline{X} - iD) = \beta\overline{X} - \beta(iD)$$

Although the investor does not own any of the bonds of the levered firm, he is actually burdened with a *pro rata* corporate debt equal to βD, for which his income is reduced by an interest payment $\beta(iD)$. The debt policy of the (managers of the) firm has created for the investor a leverage equal to $\beta D/\beta S_L$, which is obviously the same as the corporate leverage D/S_L.

If $V_L > V_u$, the investor can switch to a new portfolio which will be cheaper than the original, while it will still yield the same expected income for the investor, and he will have the same degree of leverage. However, this time the leverage will be created by the personal borrowing of the investor ('personal leverage' or 'home-made leverage'). The new portfolio will contain a fraction β of the shares of the unlevered firm, for the acquisition of which the investor borrows on personal account an amount equal to βD. The cost of the new portfolio is

$$C_1 = \beta S_u - \beta D = \beta V_u - \beta D = \beta(V_u - D)$$

given $S_u = V_u$. The expected income from the new portfolio consists of β per cent of the earnings of the unlevered firm. However, the investor will be paying $i(\beta D)$ interest on his personal loan, so that his net income will be

$$Y_1 = \beta\overline{X} - i(\beta D)$$

which is identical to the income of the original portfolio.

However, the new portfolio costs less than the original one if $V_L > V_u$: Comparing C_0 with C_1 we see that the new portfolio is cheaper by an amount

$$C_0 - C_1 = \beta(V_L - D) - \beta(V_u - D) = \beta(V_L - V_u)$$

In summary. If $V_L > V_u$ the investor will sell the shares of the levered firm (thus bidding their price, and hence V_L, down), and he will buy shares of the unlevered firm (thus bidding their price, and hence V_u, up). These 'arbitrage operations' will continue until $V_L = V_u$ (in equilibrium). In switching portfolios the investor creates his own 'personal leverage', which is equal to the 'corporate leverage'.

A numerical example[13] will clarify the above 'arbitrage operations'. Consider a levered and an unlevered firm which have equal earnings (of $50,000) and

---

[13] This example has been worked out with the assistance of Eric Kirzner.

belong to the same risk class, so that investors in the market apply the same capitalisation rate ($k_e = 0.2$) to the income streams of both firms. The levered firm has a debt of $100,000, and the market interest rate (on the debt) is 0.1. The two firms should have the same market value, given that they have equal earnings and equal business risk. However, the fact that investors discount the earnings by the same k_e results in $V_L > V_u$, as shown by the figures in Table 8.1.

Table 8.1

Unlevered firm	Levered firm
$\bar{X} = \$50,000$	$\bar{X} = \$50,000$
$D = 0$	$D = \$100,000$
$i = 0.1$	$i = 0.1$
$iD = 0$	$iD = \$10,000$
$(\bar{X} - iD) = \$50,000$	$(\bar{X} - iD) = \$40,000$
$k_e = 0.2$	$k_e = 0.20$
$S_u = \dfrac{50,000}{0.20} = \$250,000$	$S_L = \dfrac{40,000}{0.20} = \$200,000$
$D/S = 0$	$D/S = 0.50$
$V_u = S_u = \$250,000$	$V_L = S_L + D = \$300,000$

Investors find out that the levered firm is over-valued ($V_L > V_u$). Hence they will sell shares of the levered firm and buy shares of the unlevered firm.

Consider an investor who owns $\beta = 0.01$ (or 1 per cent) of the shares of the levered firm. The cost of his portfolio is

$$C_0 = \beta S_L = 0.01\ (\$200,000) = \$2,000$$

His income from this portfolio is

$$Y_0 = \beta(\bar{X} - iD) = 0.01\ (\$40,000) = \$400$$

and he is 'burdened' with the debt/equity ratio imposed on him by managers ($D/S_L = 0.50$).

By selling his shares of the levered firm, he gets $2,000. To have the same leverage ('home-made', this time), he borrows $1,000. With these proceeds he buys $3,000 worth of shares of the unlevered firm. Thus he owns 0.012 or 1.2 per cent of the unlevered firm ($3,000/250,000 = 0.012$). Hence he will also be receiving 0.012 of the earnings of this firm, that is, an amount of

$$0.012\ (\bar{X}) = \$600$$

The cost of his personal debt is

$$0.10\ (\$1,000) = \$100$$

so that the income of the new portfolio is

$$Y_1 = \$600 - \$100 = \$500$$

It is apparent that with the 'arbitrage action' the investor has the same leverage ($= 0.5$) but a higher income. As he sells shares of the levered firm, their price falls, while the increased purchases of shares of the unlevered firm results in an increase in their price. This will continue until $V_L = V_u$.

(b) V_u *cannot be larger than* V_L

The proof of this statement runs in parallel lines to the arbitrage process described above. We present it in detail in order to illustrate how an individual investor can 'unmake the corporate leverage', i.e. the debt decision of the firm.

Consider an investor who holds a fraction α of the shares of the unlevered firm. The cost of this portfolio is

$$C_0 = \alpha S_u = \alpha V_u$$

and the expected income is

$$Y_0 = \alpha \bar{X}$$

An identical income can also be obtained by buying a fraction α of the shares *and* bonds of the levered firm. The cost of the new portfolio is

$$C_1 = \alpha S_L + \alpha D = \alpha(V_L - D) + \alpha D = \alpha V_L$$

and its expected income is

$$Y_1 = \alpha(\bar{X} - iD) + \alpha(iD) = \alpha \bar{X}$$

which is identical to the income of the original portfolio. This income is also unlevered (like the initial one), since it gives the investor access to α per cent of the levered firm's total earnings, irrespective of its financial structure. By the arbitrage operations the investor 'unmakes' the leverage decided upon by the managers of the firm.

If $V_u > V_L$, the new portfolio is cheaper than the original one by an amount

$$C_0 - C_1 = \alpha V_u - \alpha V_L = \alpha(V_u - V_L)$$

Thus the investor will sell the shares of the unlevered firm and will buy shares of the levered firm, until $V_u = V_L$.

Since V_L can be neither higher nor lower than V_u, it follows that $V_L = V_u$ in equilibrium. This proves the proposition that investors in the market apply the same (over-all) discount rate k_o in estimating the total market value of identical streams of earnings. Thus *the debt policy of the firm is irrelevant to its valuation by investors in the market*. In so far as this fails to be true in the real world, it must be because investors do not act in the ideal manner or circumstances suggested by this theory. In other words, violation of the assumptions of the model may render it invalid in explaining real-world situations. In subsequent paragraphs we will relax some of the assumptions of the model and examine the effects on investors' behaviour.

We conclude that, according to Miller and Modigliani, in perfect capital markets in which investors are rational and can borrow on the same conditions as firms, the over-all discount rate is the same for levered *and* unlevered firms:

$$V_L = \frac{\bar{X}}{k_o} = S_L + D$$

$$V_u = \frac{\bar{X}}{k_o} = S_u$$

Proof of Proposition II

As we have said, Proposition II is not an independent theorem, but is, rather, a relation derived from Proposition I. Proposition II states that there is a *linear* relationship between the equity discount rate k_e and the over-all discount rate k_o:

$$k_e = k_o + (k_o - i) D/S \tag{8.15}$$

The derivation of this relationship is easy. It is based on the following definitions:

(1) k_e is the discount rate of the income accruing to shareholders:

$$S_L = \frac{\bar{X} - iD}{k_e} \quad \text{or} \quad k_e = \frac{\bar{X} - iD}{S_L} \tag{8.16}$$

(2) k_o is the over-all discount rate of all the earnings of the firm:

$$V = \frac{\bar{X}}{k_o} \quad \text{or} \quad k_o = \frac{\bar{X}}{V} = \frac{\bar{X}}{S_L + D} \tag{8.17}$$

From the latter expression we obtain

$$\bar{X} = k_o(S_L + D)$$

Substituting in the expression for k_e we find

$$k_e = \frac{k_o(S_L + D) - iD}{S_L}$$

Rearranging we obtain:[14]

$$k_e = k_o + (k_o - i) \frac{D}{S_L} \tag{8.18}$$

---

[14] Note that this relationship is the same as expression (8.11). However, Modigliani and Miller *postulate that this relationship is linear*, while in its earlier derivation the relationship was general, with no specific assumption regarding its slope.

For this relationship to be linear the slope $(k_o - i)$ must be constant. We saw that k_o is constant, being the discount rate of the total stream of earnings of a given business-risk class. Modigliani and Miller make the assumption that i is constant, that is, the market interest rate does not change with the degree of leverage of the firm. Hence the slope is constant in their model.

It should be apparent that Proposition II is a consequence of Proposition I, which states that k_o is constant at all degrees of leverage. Recall[15] that k_o is by definition the average discount rate, that is, the weighted average of k_e and i, with weights

$$w_1 = \frac{S_L}{V_L}$$

and

$$w_2 = \frac{D}{V_L}$$

Thus we may write

$$k_o = k_e \frac{S_L}{V_L} + i \frac{D}{V_L} = k_e w_1 + i w_2 \qquad (8.19)$$

In the Modigliani–Miller model i remains constant, but k_e rises with debt. Under these conditions, for k_o to remain constant as debt rises, the weights w_1 and w_2 must change in such a way as to offset the rise in k_e. In fact, Modigliani and Miller argue that the gain (advantage) from the increasing use of 'cheap' debt (given $i < k_e$ at all levels of indebtedness) is *exactly offset* by the rise of the cost of equity capital of the levered firm, so that the over-all discount rate remains constant at all degrees of leverage (D/S ratios).[16]

The relationships of k_o, k_e and i with the D/S ratio implied by the Modigliani–Miller theory is shown in Figure 8.5.

The essence of the Modigliani–Miller thesis is that the financing decision of the firm is irrelevant to the valuation of the firm in the absence of taxes. There is no single optimal capital structure. Any debt/equity ratio is optimal since the over-all discount rate is the same at all financial structures (in the absence of taxes and other market imperfections).

The Modigliani–Miller theory of leverage started a long controversy which is still unresolved. The opponents argue that market imperfections are considerable

---

[15] See expression (8.9).

[16] The above-presented proofs of the Modigliani–Miller 'irrelevance' propositions are not complete, in that they do not establish that the advantages accruing to shareholders by the greater use of 'cheap' debt by the firm *are exactly offset* by a drop in the price of their shares, so that their wealth position remains unaffected by the financing decisions of managers. This result is established in Chapter 9, where the *wealth position* of both bondholders and shareholders is examined under different financing and dividend policies of the firm.

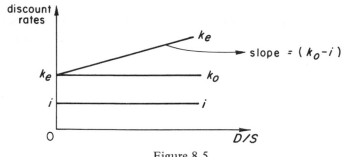

Figure 8.5

so that the arbitrage mechanism does not work freely in the real world. Modigliani and Miller maintain that such market imperfections that exist in the real world do not seriously impair their 'irrelevance' proposition (with the exception of corporate taxes). The main arguments of the controversy about the 'leverage-indifference' hypothesis may be summarised as follows.

Market imperfections

It has been argued that personal leverage is not a perfect substitute for corporate leverage for several reasons.

(1) Firms have limited liability, while individual investors do not. Thus the risk associated with the debt arising from ownership of shares is less than the risk from the same amount of debt borrowed on personal account.

(2) Laws set margin requirements which limit the amount of margin buying that is permitted.[17] For example in the USA margin requirements have been as high as 90 per cent: an individual buying stock on margin must put up at least 90 per cent of their value from his own resources. To this criticism Modigliani and Miller answer by saying that investors need not borrow from the market in order to undertake arbitrage operations: they can sell bonds which they previously held in their portfolios. However, some important investors, such as life-insurance companies, are prohibited from selling their bonds. Others are allowed to have a very small fraction of their funds invested in stocks. In this case they may prefer to buy low-priced risky shares if they have a high yield.

(3) Many institutional investors are actually prohibited from buying stocks on margin, by law, by clauses in their charters, or simply by a 'prudent' policy. Such investors (pension funds, trust accounts, mutual funds, university endowment accounts, and similar funds) have a large volume of investable funds, most of which are not available for the purchase of low-levered shares on margin even when these shares are low-priced (i.e. have a high yield).

(4) Firms, at least those whose shares are traded on the stock exchange, can borrow on more favourable terms than individual investors.

---

[17] 'Margin buying' is the buying of securities with a secured loan from a brokerage firm.

Modigliani and Miller recognise that such institutional restrictions may impair the arbitrage operations. However, they do not agree that such market imperfections affect their theory in any significant way. They think that markets are sufficiently perfect to ensure adequate arbitrage operations, which are the behavioural foundation of their theory.[18]

Even if the arguments concerning the above market imperfections are side-stepped, the Modigliani–Miller irrelevance-of-leverage hypothesis breaks down when corporate taxes are introduced in the analysis.

D.   The Modigliani–Miller Hypothesis With Corporate Taxes

In most Western countries the interest payments on bonds are tax-deductible. The government does in fact subsidise borrowed funds by corporations. This results in higher earnings for shareholders of levered firms, and hence to a higher market value for such firms as compared with the market value of unlevered firms. Thus, when the deductibility of interest payments is taken into account, the market value of a levered firm is *not* independent of its capital structure. Modigliani and Miller proved that the over-all discount rate of levered firms is a decreasing function of the debt/equity ratio.[19]

For simplicity it will be assumed that the corporate tax rate is constant, and that there are no differentials between corporate and personal taxes. (This assumption is relaxed in Chapter 11.)

Let $\bar{X}$ denote the before-tax expected earnings of two firms identical in all respects except for their capital structure, and t_c the corporate tax rate. The after-tax earnings of the shareholders of the unlevered firm are

$$\bar{X}_u = \bar{X}(1 - t_c)$$

The present value of the unlevered firm is found by discounting these earnings at the discount rate k_o appropriate to the business risk of the firm

$$V_u = \frac{\bar{X}(1 - t_c)}{k_o} \tag{8.20}$$

The after-tax total income of a levered firm, $\bar{X}_L$, is partly paid to bondholders in the form of interest payments, iD, and partly to its shareholders in the form of dividends:

$$\bar{X}_L = (\bar{X} - iD)(1 - t_c) + iD \tag{8.21}$$

Rearranging we obtain

$$\bar{X}_L = \bar{X}(1 - t_c) + t_c(iD) \tag{8.22}$$

---

[18] Modigliani and Miller, 'The Cost of Capital, Corporate Finance and the Theory of Investment', pp. 274–6.

[19] Modigliani and Miller, 'Corporate Income Taxes and the Cost of Capital: A Correction'.

Thus the after-tax income of the firm, $\bar{X}_L$, has two components: (a) the interest-payments component, $t_c(iD)$, is a sure stream of earnings (since by assumption the firm earns at all times enough to meet its interest payments), and it is discounted at the market interest rate, i; (b) the dividends component is an uncertain stream of equity earnings, and should be discounted at the discount rate, k_o, appropriate for the particular risk class. Thus

$$V_L = \frac{\bar{X}(1 - t_c)}{k_o} + t_c D \tag{8.23}$$

or

$$V_L = V_u + t_c D \tag{8.24}$$

It follows that the present value of the levered firm, when corporate taxation is taken into account, is higher than that of the unlevered firm by the amount $t_c D$, which is the increase in market value arising from the debt. It is the *tax saving due to the deductibility of interest payments*. Modigliani and Miller argue that the fact that $\bar{X}(1 - t_c)$ is discounted at k_o alone implies that the value of the firm's earnings is *not* affected by the capital structure. The higher V_L of the levered firm is due solely to the tax advantage.

The over-all discount rate of a levered firm, $k_{o,L}$, is no longer a constant if taxation is taken into account, but is a decreasing function of debt. It can be proved that

$$\begin{bmatrix} \text{After-tax} \\ \text{over-all} \\ \text{discount rate} \end{bmatrix} = k_{o,L} = k_o - t_c(k_o - i)\frac{D}{V_L} \tag{8.25}$$

*   *   *

PROOF

By definition

$$V_L = \frac{\bar{X}_L}{k_{o,L}} \quad \text{or} \quad k_{o,L} = \frac{\bar{X}_L}{V_L} \tag{8.26}$$

We have seen from expression (8.22) that

$$X_L = \bar{X}(1 - t_c) + t_c(iD)$$

Solving for $\bar{X}(1 - t_c)$ we obtain

$$\bar{X}(1 - t_c) = \bar{X}_L - t_c(iD) \tag{8.27}$$

Substituting (8.27) in the valuation formula (8.23) we find

$$V_L = \frac{\bar{X}_L - t_c(iD)}{k_o} + t_c D = \frac{\bar{X}_L}{k_o} + t_c\left(\frac{k_o - i}{k_o}\right) D \tag{8.28}$$

Solving for $\bar{X}_L/V_L = k_{o,L}$ we obtain

$$k_{o,L} = \frac{\bar{X}_L}{V_L} = k_o - t_c(k_o - i)\frac{D}{V_L}$$

QED

*   *   *

Thus Modigliani and Miller conclude that in a world of taxable corporate incomes in which interest payments are tax-deductible the over-all discount rate will decline continuously as debt increases.

The difference between the Modigliani–Miller theory and the traditional doctrines is narrowed in a world of taxable corporation income: both theories agree that $k_{o,L}$ will fall up to a certain level of debt. Beyond that 'judicious limit' (which, according to the traditionalists, is set exogenously by capital-market lenders), traditionalists argue that k_o will start rising as debt increases, while Modigliani and Miller maintain that k_o will continue to fall, no matter how far the use of leverage is carried. *Under the Modigliani-Miller model, then, the optimal capital structure would be one in which all capital is debt-financed.* This, of course, would not fool tax inspectors, since in this case the bondholders are in fact the owners of the firm.[20] To avoid such an improbable 'equilibrium', Modigliani and Miller suggest that an *upper limit* to the use of debt is set exogenously by creditors, who would either stop lending funds to a firm beyond what they consider a 'safe' debt/equity ratio, or would demand to be represented on the board of directors of the firm if its debt exceeds a certain level. Furthermore, Modigliani and Miller say that managers would most probably not seek the highest debt/equity ratio permitted by the market for various reasons, such as: (a) safeguarding their freedom of decision-making, which would be restricted if creditors had a representative on the board of directors; (b) safeguarding their job security, which could be endangered if debt increased the risk of insolvency of the firm; and (c) preserving flexibility by maintaining a reserve of untapped borrowing power which would allow the management to finance a profitable investment opportunity which may unexpectedly appear or meet a temporary need for 'emergency' cash. Finally, managers may not exhaust the upper limit of debt allowed by the market, because other forms of financing, notably retained earnings, may in some circumstances be cheaper than debt financing when the tax status of shareholders under personal income tax is taken into account.

The Modigliani–Miller and traditionalist theories of leverage are shown in Figure 8.6.

The after-tax yield on *equity capital*, that is, the discount rate that shareholders apply to estimate the present value of the future stream of earnings

---

[20] See E. Fama and M. Miller, *The Theory of Finance* (Holt, Rinehart & Winston, 1972) p. 173.

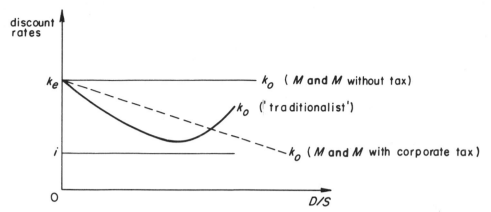

Figure 8.6   The over-all discount rate of a levered firm

available to them, net of tax and interest payments, is

$$
\begin{bmatrix} \text{After-tax} \\ \text{discount} \\ \text{rate of} \\ \text{equity} \\ \text{capital} \end{bmatrix} = k_{e,L} = k_o + (1 - t_c)(k_o - i)\frac{D}{S_L} \tag{8.29}
$$

*   *   *

PROOF

We established, (from expression (8.28), that

$$
V_L = \frac{\bar{X}_L}{k_o} + t_c \left(\frac{k_o - i}{k_o}\right) D
$$

We also know, from expression (8.21), that

$$
\bar{X}_L = (\bar{X} - iD)(1 - t_c) + iD
$$

Substituting (8.21) in (8.28) we obtain

$$
V_L = \frac{(\bar{X} - iD)(1 - t_c) + iD}{k_o} + t_c \left(\frac{k_o - i}{k_o}\right) D
$$

Subtracting D from both sides we find

$$
V_L - D = S_L = \frac{(\bar{X} - iD)(1 - t_c)}{k_o} + \frac{iD}{k_o} - t_c \left(\frac{k_o - i}{k_o}\right) D - D
$$

or

$$
S_L = \frac{(\bar{X} - iD)(1 - t_c)}{k_o} - [(1 - t_c)D] \left(1 - \frac{i}{k_o}\right)
$$

or

$$S_L = \frac{(\overline{X} - iD)(1 - t_c)}{k_o} - (1 - t_c)\left(\frac{k_o - i}{k_o}\right)D$$

Rearranging we obtain

$$k_o = \frac{(\overline{X} - iD)(1 - t_c)}{S_L} - (1 - t_c)(k_o - i)\frac{D}{S_L}$$

But by definition

$$k_{e,L} = \frac{(\overline{X} - iD)(1 - t_c)}{S_L}$$

Therefore

$$k_o = k_{e,L} - (1 - t_c)(k_o - i)\frac{D}{S_L}$$

Solving for $k_{e,L}$ we find

$$k_{e,L} = k_o + (1 - t_c)(k_o - i)\frac{D}{S_L}$$

QED

*   *   *

It should be clear that within the Modigliani–Miller framework the firm's financing decision does affect the price of the securities of the firm. This is reflected in the relationship implied by Proposition II: the higher the degree of leverage, the greater the risk of existing shareholders and hence the greater $k_{e,L}$, the yield they require for keeping the shares of the firm. This means that the shares of highly levered firms sell at a lower price than those of less-levered firms. The fact, however, that the firm can affect the risk of its shares through its financing decisions does not imply that its shareholders are concerned with these decisions. The important result of the Modigliani–Miller model is that *in a perfect capital market the firm's financing decisions do not affect the wealth position of its shareholders, so that there is no reason for them to be interested in these decisions.*[21] A formal proof of this 'wealth theorem' is given in Chapter 9 after the examination of the dividend policy of managers and its effect on the prices of the securities of the firm.

It is the belief of this author that the weakest part of the Modigliani–Miller theory is the reliance on an exogenously determined debt limit, without which their model collapses when corporate taxation is taken into account. Modigliani and Miller state that lenders set credit limits for firms which, however, are not

---

[21] See ibid, p. 186. See also Chapter 9 for a proof of this statement.

'normally' exhausted in the real world, for the reasons earlier discussed. However, Modigliani and Miller do not explain how the creditors define these limits, or the extent to which these limits will be approached by the firm.

II. A MANAGERIAL THEORY OF CAPITAL STRUCTURE

In a recent article this author[22] abandons the goal of stockholder-welfare maximisation of the 'established' theory of finance and adopts the assumptions of the managerial school (Baumol, Galbraith, Marris, Williamson), which postulates that managers pursue the maximisation of their own utility rather than the maximisation of the utility of owner-shareholders. The basis of the model is the Marris–Galbraith model, which assumes a managerial utility function containing two variables: the job security of management as a whole and the rate of growth of the firm. Given the ample evidence that large firms are growth-seekers, the study concentrates on the job-security variable. In particular, the following 'job-security hypothesis' or 'group-behaviour hypothesis' is postulated.

(1) The capital structure of firms is decided so as to safeguard the job security of managers.

(2) Managers feel that their job security is safeguarded if the firm's D/S ratio does not deviate in the long run from the 'typical industry D/S ratio', that is, the average leverage of other firms in the industry which have similar size and other characteristics. Accordingly, managers attempt to adjust the firm's actual D/S ratio to the typical industry leverage. The adjustment is gradual, due to various reasons, such as the availability of internal or external funds, their costs, the attitudes of capital suppliers at any one time, imperfections in the capital markets, and so on.

(3) The use of debt is influenced by the preference of managers for internal finance, defined largely by the growth of earnings and the retention policy of the firm. However, job-security considerations set a limit to the amount of profits that managers can retain. Given that managers are growth-seekers, internal funds are inadequate to cover the financial needs of a fast rate of growth. Hence managers resort to external sources of funds. They have a preference for debt over issue of new stock. Cost considerations of these two sources of funds, as well as the possibility of disturbing the voting control in a way which endangers the managerial job security, make debt a more attractive source of external finance.

(4) The desires of managers regarding the use of debt are tempered by creditors' attitudes. Creditors determine ultimately the debt capacity of the firm, taking into account various factors, such as the firm's size (assets), the firm's future growth potential, the variability of its earnings, and so on. Furthermore, creditors determine the amount of funds which they are willing to offer at various

---

[22] Koutsoyiannis, 'Managerial Job Security and the Capital Structure of Firms'.

(largely externally determined) interest rates, depending on their expectations about the rate of inflation.

From the above considerations it is apparent that in a managerialist framework the determinants of the capital structure of firms are: (i) the 'typical industry debt/equity ratio'; (ii) the past level of capital structure of the firm; (iii) the size (assets) of the firm; (iv) the growth of assets of the firm; (v) the stability of earnings; (vi) the expected rate of inflation; (vii) the rate of growth of earnings; (viii) the retention ratio; (ix) the cost of debt; (x) the cost of new issue of stock; (xi) the corporate tax rate; and (xii) the dispersion of ownership of shares.

The results of an empirical test of the 'job-security' or 'group-behaviour' hypothesis are reported in section V.

III.   THE LEVERAGE DECISION IN PRACTICE

In theory the capital structure should be set at a level consistent with the goal(s) of the firm. Two alternative goals have been discussed in the preceding sections: maximisation of stockholder wealth, and maximisation of managerial job security. Within the framework of stockholder-wealth maximisation the debt/equity ratio should be chosen so as to maximise the market value of the firm to its original owner-shareholders. Given that

$$V = \frac{\bar{X}}{k_o}$$

the market value is maximised when k_o, the over-all discount rate (or the average cost of capital – see Chapter 10) is minimised. As we saw in section II, two conflicting hypotheses have been developed regarding the optimal capital structure (when the goal of managers is stockholder-wealth maximisation). The traditional position is that the k_o curve is U-shaped, implying a unique level of the D/S ratio that maximises the value of the firm. The Modigliani–Miller hypothesis, when corporate taxes are taken into account, implies that the k_o curve is downward-sloping at all levels of indebtedness, so that the optimal capital structure is one which consists of 100 per cent debt. As we will see in section V, empirical studies conducted in this field provide inconclusive evidence regarding the shape of the k_o function. Furthermore, these studies highlighted the enormous difficulties encountered when one attempts to estimate the k_o function (see p. 411). Yet unless this function is accurately estimated it is impossible to define the optimal capital structure, that is, the D/S ratio that minimises k_o (Or, equivalently, maximises the market value of the firm). Thus, even if the goal of managers is stockholder-wealth maximisation, economic theory can provide little assistance to managers in their decision regarding the optimal capital structure.

The managerialist hypothesis, that the capital structure is set at a level that maximises the job security of managers, implies a gradual adjustment of the firm's D/S ratio to the 'typical' ('average') leverage of other similar firms in the industry. The adjustment mechanism highlights the main determinants of the D/S ratio of large corporations. In this way it can assist managers in practice by drawing their attention to the factors which they should take into account when deciding the capital structure of the firm.

A list of the determinants of the capital structure will be compiled and discussed in the next section of this chapter. In the remainder of this section we shall present two methods that are widely used in the real business world as sources of relevant information about the alternative sources of funds:

A. EPS–EBIT analysis
B. Cash-flow analysis

A.   EPS–EBIT Analysis

The basic assumption of this method is that investors are interested only in the size of the earnings per share (EPS), that is, the yield of their investment. (Recall, however, from Chapter 3, that investors' decisions are taken on the basis of both the expected return *and* risk of the securities.)

EPS–EBIT analysis involves the determination of the level of the earnings per share (EPS) at various levels of total earnings before interest and taxes (EBIT $\equiv$ $\bar{X}$) under different methods of financing the operations of the firm.

By definition

$$\text{EPS} = \frac{(\bar{X} - iD)(1 - t_c)}{N} \tag{8.30}$$

where N = number of shares. Rearranging we obtain

$$\text{EPS} = \left(\frac{1 - t_c}{N}\right) \bar{X} - \left(\frac{1 - t_c}{N}\right) iD \tag{8.31}$$

This expression shows the relationship between EPS and EBIT ($\equiv \bar{X}$), given t_c, N, i and D. It is a linear relationship, with intercept

$$- \left(\frac{1 - t_c}{N}\right) iD$$

and slope

$$\left(\frac{1 - t_c}{N}\right)$$

The EPS–EBIT relationship is different under alternative methods of financing, because the slope and intercept depend, as we will presently show, on the adopted financing method.

To illustrate the EPS–EBIT analysis we will examine its application to the evaluation of two alternative financing methods, debt financing and common-stock financing. Other methods of financing may be evaluated on similar lines.

Assume, for simplicity, that the firm has, to begin with, no debt in its capital structure, which consists of N_o shares. The firm wants to raise an additional (given) amount of funds, and is faced with the problem of choosing between using debt financing or issuing an additional number (N_1) of common shares. The criterion will be the size of EPS: the firm will choose the financing method which yields the higher earnings per share. Thus the firm must obtain an estimate of the EPS at different levels of possible total earnings (EBIT) under the two alternative financing methods. Formally this is attained by defining and plotting (on a graph) the EPS–EBIT relationship under each financing method.

(1) With equity financing the EPS–EBIT relationship is derived from definition (8.31) by setting $D = 0$.[23] Thus

$$\text{EPS}_S = \left(\frac{1 - t_c}{N_T}\right) \bar{X} \tag{8.32}$$

where $N_T = N_0 + N_1$. This is a linear relation with zero intercept, and a positive slope, equal to $(1 - t_c)/N_T$.

(2) With debt financing the EPS–EBIT relationship is given by expression (8.31), setting $N = N_o$, that is,

$$\text{EPS}_D = \left(\frac{1 - t_c}{N_o}\right) \bar{X} - \left(\frac{1 - t_c}{N_o}\right) iD \tag{8.33}$$

This is a straight line with a negative intercept and a slope equal to $(1 - t_c)/N_o$. (If the firm had some original debt, the intercept would be larger in absolute value.)

The two lines are plotted in Figure 8.7. Given that they have different slopes (the debt-financing line has a greater slope than the equity-financing line, since $N_o < N_T$), the two lines will intersect at a point which is called the 'point of indifference', because it shows that the firm should be indifferent between the two financing methods, since both have the same EPS. (Mathematically the point of intersection is found by equating (8.32) to (8.33) and solving for $\bar{X}$.)

To the right of the intersection point debt financing yields a higher EPS, while to the left of the intersection common-stock financing yields a higher EPS. Thus the intersection point conveys crucial information to the managers of the firm. The next step in the financing decision involves the assignment of (subjective) probabilities (see Appendix to Chapter 12) to the various levels of $\bar{X}$ (EBIT). Of particular interest are the probabilities of levels of earnings smaller than $\bar{X}^*$ in Figure 8.7. The probabilities involve subjective assessment of general business conditions, as well as the conditions of the particular product and factor markets in which the firm operates (see Chapter 12). It should be clear that the

[23] Note that if the firm has some original debt, the intercept will be different from zero.

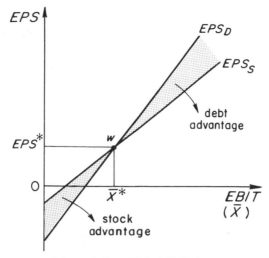

Figure 8.7   EPS—EBIT chart

risk attitudes of managers play an important role in the choice of financing method, since they enter in the assignment of probabilities to the various earnings (EBIT) levels and the final financing decision.

The main weakness of EPS—EBIT analysis lies in its basic assumption, that investors are interested only in the return (EPS) of their investment. It ignores the risk element in investment decisions. Investors choose their portfolios on the basis of both the return and the risk of the various securities (see Appendix 3.1 and Chapter 12). The choice of the financing method which maximises the return does not necessarily mean that it also maximises the share price of current shareholders. Thus EPS—EBIT analysis may result in non-optimal financing decisions. However, the analysis shows some of the determinants of actual (observed) debt/equity ratios, namely:

(a) the absolute amount of earnings, $\bar{X}$;
(b) the height of the corporate tax rate, t_c;
(c) the risk attitude of managers;
(d) the initial capital structure;
(e) the amount of additional fund requirements.

B.   Cash-flow Analysis

This method involves the estimation of total earnings before interest and taxes (EBIT). This in turn requires a forecast of the stream of cash receipts (inflows) and cash payments for the production of the output (cash outflows). The difference is the total earnings (EBIT) from which fixed charges must be met. Forecasts of this sort are called 'cash budgets' and can extend over any number of periods.

Predictions are usually made under a single set of assumptions with respect to general (external) business conditions and particular circumstances expected to prevail in the markets in which the firm operates. However, a cash-flow analysis should include forecasts of cash inflows and cash outflows under different sets of assumptions. For example, a firm might examine the EBIT under the following 'states of business':

(a) severe recession;
(b) mild recession;
(c) normal growth;
(d) very rapid growth;
(e) inflation.

Such forecasts, combined with subjective probabilities for each 'state of business', give probability distributions of earnings for each period. It is these distributions that provide information about probable deviations in actual earnings from their expected values, and hence allow the managers to be prepared for possible downward deviations which may lead to insolvency.

Given the probability distributions of the stream of cash flows, management can determine the amount of fixed charges and debt that the firm can undertake without running a great danger of insolvency. In many cases management defines a 'tolerance limit' for insolvency, that is, a maximum value for the probability of the firm's earnings falling below its fixed charges.[24]

It should be noted that cash-flow analysis is most useful for internal purposes. It 'hedges' management against the risk of insolvency. However, insolvency is only one aspect of the financial risk of shareholders. The other aspect of this risk, namely the danger of having nothing left over for dividends after the fixed charges are met, is not taken into account by cash-flow analysis. Investors are most interested in the latter risk, assuming that the firm will always have enough earnings to cover its fixed charges.

IV. FACTORS DETERMINING THE CAPITAL STRUCTURE

From the discussion in the previous sections we may draw a list of factors which are thought to affect the financing decisions of firms.

(1) *The goal of the firm*

We mentioned that if the goal of managers is the maximisation of stockholder wealth, the optimal capital structure is the one that maximises the market value

---

[24] For a detailed discussion of cash-flow analysis, see G. Donaldson, *Corporate Debt Capacity*, Harvard Business School, 1961. Also G. Donaldson, 'Strategy for Financial Emergencies', *Harvard Business Review*, 1969, pp. 67–79.

of the firm to its original stockholders. If the goal of managers is the maximisation of their job security, the optimal capital structure is the 'typical (average) leverage of other similar firms in the industry'.

(2) *The 'typical' leverage of similar firms in the industry*

According to the managerialist 'job-security hypothesis', managers feel that their job security is threatened if the firm's debt/equity ratio deviates in the long run from the industry average debt/equity ratio. Thus they set the firm's 'target' debt/equity ratio on the basis of the accepted 'typical' leverage of firms similar in size and other characteristics.

(3) *Availability of internal funds: the rate of growth of earnings*

There is ample evidence that managers have a preference for internal funds over external sources of capital. The main determinant of internal funds is the growth of earnings ($g_{\bar{X}}$) of the firm. A high growth rate of earnings enables management to have more funds from retained earnings (even if the retention ratio remains constant), so that less external finance will be required. Thus one might expect a negative relationship between the rate of growth of earnings and the D/S ratio.

Note that the rate of growth of earnings may affect the D/S ratio indirectly in two ways.

(1) A high rate of growth, if financed with debt, will increase the earnings per share by more than if it were financed by common stock (see EPS–EBIT chart: Figure 8.7) due to the tax-deductibility of interest payments. The effect of the growth of earnings on the debt/equity ratio in this event would be positive. This effect, however, may well be expected to be absorbed by the corporate tax rate, which we list below as a separate determinant of the firm's debt/equity ratio.

(2) A high rate of growth of earnings will almost certainly boost the price of the common stock, making equity financing more attractive than debt financing. This effect of $g_{\bar{X}}$ on the debt/equity ratio should be absorbed by the stock price, which we consider as a separate determinant of the capital structure.

(4) *Availability of internal funds: the retention policy of managers*

The amount of internal funds does not depend only on the growth of total earnings but also on the proportion of earnings retained (retention ratio). This in turn depends on the growth potential of the firm and the ability of managers to persuade shareholders that the available investment opportunities are profitable. The retention ratio is expected to be negatively related to the debt/equity ratio, since a high proportion of retained earnings reduces the need for debt financing.

(5) *Degree of concentration of ownership and voting control*

Widely held stocks encourage the issue of new shares when additional funds are required, because the voting control of shareholders is not likely to be changed substantially. If, however, ownership of stocks is concentrated in the hands of a small number of shareholders, management may be reluctant to issue new shares in order to avoid change in the voting control of current shareholders, since such changes may endanger the job security of management as a whole. The relationship between concentration of voting control and the debt/equity ratio is expected to be negative.

(6) *Credit limits (or debt capacity of the firm)*

The attempt of managers to adjust their actual debt/equity ratio to their desired or 'target' level is constrained by the attitudes of creditors. It is generally accepted that lenders in the capital market ultimately define the *debt capacity* of firms, that is, the level of 'safe borrowing' or the amount of debt which firms can undertake without serious danger of financial failure.[25] Creditors form their beliefs about the debt capacity on the basis of such variables as the size of the firm, its potential growth and its business risk.

(a) *The size of the firm.* It is observed that large firms can borrow funds more easily and on better terms than small firms. This may be attributed to creditors' beliefs that larger firms are less likely to become insolvent. In this event 'size' is expected to be positively related to the debt/equity ratio. However, although the size of assets enlarges the debt capacity of firms, large firms may not be willing to avail themselves of the larger availability of loanable funds, preferring to rely on retained earnings. For example, Ford has a debt/equity ratio of 0.08, Gilette 0.21, Reynolds 0.25, Getty 0.08, etc. The reasons for the preference of management for internal financing have been discussed earlier. In fact, since 1945 retained earnings have become the major source of financing of large firms.[26] Under these conditions 'size' and the debt/equity ratio will be negatively related. However, one should expect this influence to be absorbed by the retention ratio, which is an explicit determinant of the firm's capital structure.

(b) *The growth of the assets (size) of the firm.* The growth of assets may be considered as a fairly satisfactory indicator of the future development opportunities of the firm. Furthermore, the growth of assets reflects the total needs for funds of the firm. On both accounts one should expect a positive relation between the growth of assets and the debt/equity ratio, *ceteris paribus*.

[25] W. G. Lewellen, *The Cost of Capital* (Wadsworth, 1969).
[26] *The Economic Report of the President* (Washington, D.C., 1979); Guthmann and Dougall, *Corporate Financial Policy*; J. K. Galbraith, *Economics and the Public Purpose* (Houghton Mifflin, 1973).

(c) *Stability of earnings.* Business risk is measured by the variability of earnings. Creditors are inclined to provide capital to firms whose earnings are stable, since earnings' instability increases the risk of insolvency. For job-security reasons, managers are also affected in their decision to use debt by the stability of the earnings of the firm: stable earnings allow a more liberal use of debt, because the firm can regularly meet the fixed costs of debt. In either case the variability of earnings is expected to be negatively related to the debt/equity ratio.

(d) *Asset structure.* It is sometimes argued that firms with a considerable amount of fixed assets are likely to rely more on debt financing. This is not generally true. We saw in Chapter 3 that the use of capital-intensive techniques increases the variability of earnings, and decreases the flexibility of adjustment of costs when demand is falling. Thus the asset structure affects the capital structure indirectly, via the variability of earnings.

(7) *The cost of debt*

We mentioned earlier that debt has a direct (explicit) cost, consisting of interest payments, and an indirect one (implicit cost), in that it increases the cost of equity capital, $k_{e,L}$.[27] On *a priori* grounds the greater the cost of debt, the less attractive it becomes as a source of finance, *ceteris paribus*.

(8) *The cost of equity financing*

The cost of equity financing is reflected in the price of the shares. An increase (decline) in the stock price creates expectations of 'cheap' ('expensive') equity financing and hence makes debt relatively less (more) attractive. Thus the change in the price of common stock is expected to be negatively related to the debt/equity ratio.

(9) *The corporate tax rate*

As we saw, interest payments are tax-deductible for corporations and this contributes to the attractiveness of debt financing. Thus the corporate tax rate and the debt/equity ratio are expected to be positively related.

(10) *Expectations regarding the rate of inflation*

Inflationary expectations affect both the demand and the supply of loanable funds. Managers may favour debt financing, *ceteris paribus*, because the repayment of debt will be less cumbersome due to the fall in the real purchasing power of money. However, creditors may be unwilling to supply funds in inflationary

---

[27] Recall that $k_{e,L} = k_o + (k_o - i)D/S$.

conditions for the same reason, unless they receive high enough interest rates. However, interest rates are beyond the control of creditors, being defined by government policy. Thus it is more likely that inflationary expectations will have a stronger effect on creditors rather than on borrowers (firms). Under these conditions one should expect a negative relationship between the debt/equity ratio and the rate of inflation.

(11) *Availability of loanable funds*

The supply of debt financing is to a large extent influenced by government policy. The imposition of a 'tight monetary policy' makes debt financing scarce and/or expensive. In such conditions firms are coerced to rely on retained earnings and use more equity financing, despite its higher cost. This factor is closely related to the previous one, since a 'tight monetary policy' is adopted in inflationary periods, and vice versa. Thus the rate of inflation is a fairly good proxy for the availability of loanable funds. Its relation to the debt/equity ratio would be negative.

(12) *General customs in capital markets*

Investors in the market over time form beliefs and customs, some of which are rigid, while others are more flexible. An example of rigid customs is the preference of investors for the securities of banks, insurance companies and public utilities of certain type. Such securities are in general more popular than other securities irrespective of the general expectations prevailing in the market at any one time. An example of flexible attitudes is the change of popularity of certain types of securities. For example, in inflationary periods the investing public prefers stocks to bonds, because of the reduction of the purchasing power of money. Such customs and attitudes affect the capital structure of firms.

V.   EMPIRICAL EVIDENCE ON THE LEVERAGE DECISION

A.   Weston's Study

Weston[28] used multiple regression analysis to test the alternative leverage hypotheses. His estimated function is

$$\hat{k}_o = 5.91 - 0.0265 \frac{D}{V} + 0.0000 A - 0.0822 g$$

$$\text{s.e.} \qquad (0.0079) \quad (0.0001) \quad (0.0024)$$

$$R^2 = 0.53$$

[28] J. F. Weston, 'A Test of Cost of Capital Propositions', *Southern Economic Journal*, 1963, pp. 105–12.

where $k_o = (\bar{X} - iD)/V$

V = market value of debt and stock = $D + S$

A = total assets of the firm (a measure of 'size')

g = compounded rate of growth of earnings per share in the ten years preceding the 1959 date of the study period.

The coefficient of debt is negative (and significant). Based on this finding, Weston concluded that his study provides evidence in support of traditional leverage theory. This conclusion is unwarranted. Weston's results show that k_o decreases with leverage, a finding that is compatible with the Modigliani–Miller hypothesis when corporate taxation is taken into account. Weston does *not* establish a U-shaped k_o function, as implied by traditional theory.

It is not clear why Weston retains in his chosen regression the variable A (size), since it is statistically insignificant and also has the 'wrong' sign. 'Size' can be a proxy for risk, or a proxy for 'ease of marketability' of the securities of the firm. In both interpretations the sign of its coefficient should be negative, while in Weston's study it appears with a positive sign. Weston does not comment on this result.

B. Barges's Study

Barges[29] estimated a quadratic function in order to study the effect of leverage on total market value. In order to avoid the bias involved in using market value as a divisor of debt,[30] Barges employed instead the book value. His sample included sixty-one railroad firms for the year 1956.

His estimated function is

$$\hat{k}_o = 12.39 - 0.244 \left(\frac{D}{V_{book}} \right) + 0.00258 \left(\frac{D}{V_{book}} \right)^2$$

$$R^2 = 0.45$$

This relationship is shown in Figure 8.8.

---

[29] A. Barges, *The Effect of Capital Structure on the Cost of Capital* (Prentice-Hall, 1963).

[30] The dependent variable, k_o, is measured by the ratio

$$\frac{\bar{X} - iD}{V_{market}}$$

If the market value is used as a divisor in the explanatory variables, a positive bias is introduced in the coefficient of leverage. To see this consider two firms identical in all respects (i.e. of same size, same capital structure, etc.) except their location. If the location of firm A is more favourable, the shares of A will have a higher price, that is, $V_A > V_B$. This would result in a lower k_o and a lower D/V for firm A, and a higher k_o and a higher D/V for firm B, and this would give rise to an illusory positive relation between k_o and D/V: since by assumption both firms have the same capital structure, k_o is not related to the debt/equity ratio. This bias would be avoided if the book value of the firm is used in the denominator of debt. The illusory positive relationship between k_o and D/V_{market} is due to the fact that 'V_{market}' reflects the different 'risk' of the two firms (A has a lower risk due to its more favourable location), while V_{book} is the same, *ex hypothesi*.

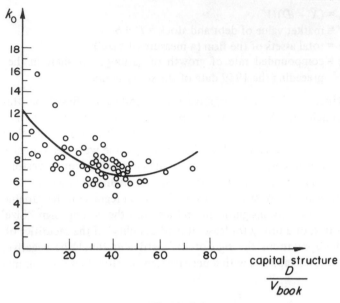

Figure 8.8

Barges's results seem to support the traditionalist approach of a U-shaped k_o function. However: (a) he does not report the standard errors of his coefficients, so we do not know whether his findings are statistically significant; and (b) a casual inspection of Figure 8.8 shows that a linear function could fit the data equally well.

C. Wippern's Study

Wippern[31] attempted to test the Modigliani–Miller leverage hypothesis by formulating his function with the earnings–price ratio as the dependent variable. That is, his empirical specification is cast in terms of Modigliani and Miller's Proposition 2, where the dependent variable is the return on equity capital, k_e. Apart from leverage, Wippern introduced several additional variables in his estimated function, which is of the form

$$k_e = \frac{\text{Earnings}}{\text{Price}} = b_0 + b_1 \, (\text{Leverage}) + b_2(g) + b_3 \left(\frac{Dv}{\overline{X}}\right) + b_4 \, (\log B)$$

$$+ \, b_5 Z_5 + b_6 Z_6 + \ldots + b_{10} Z_{10}$$

[31] R. F. Wippern, 'Financial Structure and the Value of the Firm', *Journal of Finance*, 1966, pp. 615–34.

where:

$$\text{Leverage} = \frac{F}{(X - 2\sigma_X)}$$

F includes interest payments and other fixed charges. The denominator is an estimate of 'normalised minimum expected income value'. Wippern claims that the subtraction of the variance of earnings from their absolute value takes into account inter-industry differences in business risk.

g = growth rate of earnings per share (four-year average).

$\dfrac{Dv}{\overline{X}}$ = dividend payout ratio (four-year average).

B = size variable (book value of net plant).

$Z_5, \ldots, Z_{10}$ = dummy variables (one for each of the six industries used in the sample) to account for systematic inter-industry differences.

On *a priori* grounds Wippern's coefficients would be

$$b_0 = k_o > 0; \quad b_1 > 0; \quad b_2 > 0; \quad b_3 < 0; \quad b_4 < 0$$

Wippern's sample includes fifty firms from six industries: containers, drugs, machinery, oil, paper, rubber. Wippern does not comment on the *a priori* signs of his dummy variables.

Multiple regression analysis was used for the years 1952, 1956, 1961 and 1963, in order to determine the stability of the coefficients among periods of different economic and capital-market conditions. The regression results for the four years showed that the coefficients were fairly stable over time. This finding led Wippern to 'pool together' all the observations in one sample, to obtain the following single set of coefficients:

$\hat{b}_1 = 0.0773,$ coefficient of leverage
     $(t = 3.47)$

$\hat{b}_2 = -0.0825$ coefficient of growth
     $(t = 5.37)$

$\hat{b}_3 = -0.318$ coefficient of the dividend payout
     $(t = 3.77)$

$\hat{b}_4 = -0.0039$ coefficient of size
     $(t = 3.08)$

$\hat{b}_5 = 0.0065$ coefficient of dummy variable for 'oil'
     $(t = 1.47)$

$\hat{b}_6 = 0.0012$ coefficient of dummy variable for 'machinery'
     $(t = 0.32)$

$\hat{b}_7 = -0.0119$ coefficient of dummy variable for 'paper'
     $(t = 3.30)$

$\hat{b}_8 = -0.0176$ coefficient of dummy variable for 'drugs'
$\quad (t = 4.40)$

$\hat{b}_9 = -0.0044$ coefficient of dummy variable for 'rubber'
$\quad (t = 0.98)$

$b_{10} = 0.0021$ coefficient of dummy variable for 'containers'
$\quad (t = 0.46)$

The coefficient of multiple determination (R^2) is 0.589. The estimates of the coefficients are in most cases statistically significant at the 5 per cent level.

The signs of 'size' and 'growth' are consistent with *a priori* expectations.

The negative sign of the dividend payout can be attributed to errors of measurement of expected earnings, *or* can be taken as evidence in support of the hypothesis that investors have a preference for dividends over retentions. Wippern does not commit himself to either of these interpretations, maintaining that the purpose of his study was the testing of the Modigliani–Miller leverage hypothesis alone.

The positive sign of the leverage variable refutes the 'net income' approach. This result, however, is compatible with both the Modigliani–Miller leverage hypothesis and with the 'traditional' view, which postulates that k_e increases beyond a certain level of leverage. To distinguish between these two approaches more information is required. The relationship between k_e and k_o can be expressed in the general form, *ceteris paribus*,

$$k_e = \frac{\bar{X}}{S} = a_0 + a_1 \left(\frac{D}{S} \right)$$

where a_0 = discount rate of an unlevered stream of earnings = k_o

$\qquad a_1$ = coefficient for the debt advantage of levered firms

The Modigliani–Miller approach requires $a_1 = (1 - t_c)(k_o - i)$, while the 'traditional' approach requires $0 < a_1 < (1 - t_c)(k_o - i)$.

Thus the Modigliani–Miller leverage neutrality hypothesis requires that the slope of the k_e function be steeper than the slope of this function implied by the traditionalist approach.

Wippern adjusted his estimates of the leverage coefficients so as to make them applicable to the variable D/S required for the comparisons. Furthermore, he obtained an estimate of the Modigliani–Miller slope by using:

(a) the intercept of his regression (which is an estimate of k_o, provided that the model is correctly specified and measured);
(b) a corporate tax rate of 0.50;
(c) a value of i equal to Moody's Industrial Bond Yield Index.

From his 'adjusted' results Wippern concluded that the slopes of leverage which he estimates are lower than the values which would support the Modigliani–Miller neutrality proposition.

We note that the above conclusion is based on the numerical difference of the slope a_1 of the k_e function. This difference, however, depends on the accuracy of the regression measurements and all the roundabout adjustment procedures and assumptions adopted by Wippern. His claim that his results have the required degree of accuracy for distinguishing between the Modigliani–Miller value of the slope and the value of this slope required by the 'traditional' theory is highly questionable. Wippern's results do not establish the existence of a U-shaped cost-of-capital function. (His specification is not suitable for this purpose.) Concentrating on the positive segment of the cost of equity alone is not very helpful for distinguishing between the two approaches, given the shortcomings of the available data. In order to derive conclusions about the steepness of the slope of the k_e function one needs accurate measures of expectational variables, which are not available.

In conclusion we think that the Wippern study does not provide any conclusive evidence for or against the Modigliani–Miller neutrality theorem.

D.   The Modigliani–Miller 1966 Study

In 1966 Modigliani and Miller[32] published the results of a study in which they attempted (a) to obtain a numerical estimate of the cost of capital, k_o, of the electric utility industry, and (b) to test their leverage-neutrality and dividend-neutrality theorems.

Their specification is a variant of the constant-growth model with a finite time horizon which reduces to the empirical form

$$(V - t_c D) = f\left[\bar{X}(1 - t_c), I^*, \frac{D}{A}, A \right]$$

where $V - t_c D$ = the market value of the firm, net of the sure advantage arising
$\qquad\qquad\qquad$ from the tax-deductibility of debt
$\quad\bar{X}(1 - t_c)$ = after-tax earnings
$\qquad\quad I^*$ = investment opportunities open to the firm, that is, new prospective projects yielding a return higher than the return on existing assets
$\qquad\quad A$ = book value of assets as a measure of 'size'
$\qquad D/A$ = leverage

$$*\qquad\qquad\qquad *\qquad\qquad\qquad *$$

In particular Modigliani and Miller derived the following theoretical finite growth model:

$$V = \left[\frac{X(1 - t_c)}{k_o} + t_c D \right] + \left[(I^*) \frac{k_o^* - k_o'}{k_o'(1 + k_o')} (T) \right]$$

where $k_o' = k_o[(1 - t_c)(D/S)^*]$, with $(D/S)^*$ denoting the 'target leverage' of the firm. The market value of the firm is thus expressed in terms of two components. The first bracketed term is the earnings from existing assets adjusted for the tax saving of debt. The second term is the earnings expected from 'investment

[32] F. Modigliani and M. Miller, 'Some Estimates of the Cost of Capital to the Electric Utility Industry, 1954–57', *American Economic Review*, 1966.

opportunities', I^* (= new assets yielding $k_o^* > k_o$), which will last for T periods. Modigliani and Miller argue that the two components of the expected earnings, $(k_o^* - k_o')/[k_o'(1 + k_o')]$ and T, can be considered the same among the various corporations. That is, all the electric utility corporations have the same k_o and k_o', as well as the same duration of investment opportunities. Thus, Modigliani and Miller assume that these influences will be absorbed by the coefficient of I^* in the regression. The investment opportunities are measured by the expression

$$I_t^* = g_t A_t$$

where g is the simple five-year average growth rate of total assets

$$g_t = \left(\frac{A_t - A_{t-5}}{A_{t-5}}\right)\Big/ 5$$

*   *   *

Modigliani and Miller start with a model which does not include leverage

$$(V - t_c D) = a_0 + a_1 \bar{X}(1 - t_c) + a_2 I_t^* + a_3 A + u$$

where u is the usual random variable, with *a priori* expectations

$$a_0 < 0; \quad a_1 = \frac{1}{k_o} > 0; \quad a_2 > 0; \quad a_3 > 0$$

Their main concern is to obtain a 'good' estimate of the coefficient a_1, which is the inverse of the cost of capital.

The intercept, a_0, is introduced in order to take into account the non-linearity of the relationship between V and $\bar{X}$.

In order to avoid heteroscedasticity Modigliani and Miller divided through their original variables by A (book value of assets):

$$\frac{V - t_c D}{A} = a_0 \frac{1}{A} + a_1 \frac{\bar{X}(1 - t_c)}{A} + a_2 \frac{I^*}{A} + a_3 + \frac{u}{A}$$

They applied OLS to three cross-section samples including US electric utility companies for the years 1954, 1956 and 1957. Although the coefficient of 'size', a_3, was statistically significant in all regressions, they rejected it on the grounds that its value was too high, and that the specification including A as an explanatory variable 'makes little sense from the standpoint of the theory of valuation'.

Furthermore, Modigliani and Miller used a measure for earnings ($\bar{X}$) which is dominated by dividends, and hence casts doubts on the interpretation of the coefficient $\hat{a}_1$, from which they estimate the cost of capital, k_o.

Modigliani and Miller subsequently introduced in their function a leverage variable, D/A, to test whether the use of debt has any (additional) effect on the value of the firm. They found that the coefficient of this variable was statistically insignificant. Thus they concluded that their 'leverage-irrelevance' hypothesis was supported by their empirical findings.

The 1966 study has been heavily criticised on methodological grounds.[33] We will not enter into the various issues in detail. We note, however, that the study has several weaknesses.

(1) The numerical estimates of k_o are very low. This is due to the omission from the function of several important explanatory variables.

(2) The exclusion of 'size' is not justified on *a priori* grounds. 'Size' reduces the risk of the firm and increases the marketability of the stocks. On both accounts, the omission of 'size' and of any risk variable introduces an upward bias to the estimated value of $\hat{a}_1$, that is, a downward bias to the value of k_o (given that $k_o = 1/a_1$).

(3) Similarly, the omission of a dividend variable introduces an upward bias in $\hat{a}_1$ (or, equivalently, a downward bias on k_o), because dividends are positively related to the market value of the firm (V), due to their direct effect on expected earnings (as the 'traditionalist' view maintains), or due to their informational content (as Modigliani and Miller argue).

(4) Another weakness stems from the measure of the expected earnings and of the investment opportunities (see p. 410).

(5) Finally, the insignificance of the leverage variable is compatible not only with the Modigliani–Miller leverage-irrelevance hypothesis, but also with Solomon's 'traditionalist' theory, which postulates that the k_o curve has a flat stretch, that is, a range of debt/equity values over which k_o remains constant.

In summary, the Modigliani–Miller study suffers from omission of important variables, from wrong measurement of the variables, as well as from the way leverage was introduced in the estimated function. The non-linearity implied by the 'traditional' theory cannot be tested with the simple measure (D/A) used by Modigliani and Miller. We may conclude that the 'leverage-irrelevance' hypothesis has not been conclusively tested by Modigliani and Miller. However, the study, and its critique from various researchers, highlights the difficulties which one encounters when attempting to obtain an accurate measure of the cost of capital from an econometric function. Unless the function is correctly specified, the estimate of k_o is bound to be inaccurate.

E.   A Test of the Managerial Theory of Capital Structure

In section II we presented an alternative theory of the capital-structure decision, based on the assumption that managers aim at the maximisation of their own welfare rather than stockholder welfare.[34] We argued that the main concern of

---

[33] The main objections to the Modigliani–Miller approach are well discussed in the following papers: J. Crockett and I. Friend, 'Some Estimates of the Cost of Capital to the Electric Utility Industry: Comment', *American Economic Review*, 1967; M. Gordon, 'Some Estimates of the Cost of Capital to the Electric Utility Industry: Comment', *American Economic Review*, 1967; A. A. Robichek, J. G. McDonald and R. Higgins, 'Some Estimates of the Cost of Capital to the Electric Utility Industry: Comment', *American Economic Review*, 1967.

[34] Koutsoyiannis, 'Managerial Job Security and the Capital Structure of Firms'.

managers is their job security, which is safeguarded if the debt/equity ratio of the firm does not deviate in the long run from the industry average leverage. In other words, the target debt/equity ratio of the firm is set equal to the industry average debt/equity ratio, and managers attempt to adjust gradually their actual debt/equity ratio to the target level. This adjustment process is affected by lenders' attitudes, the availability of internal funds, and the monetary and fiscal policies of the government, which determine the availability and cost of the various sources of funds, and shape managers' and investors' expectations about the future state of the economy.

To test these hypotheses, this author[35] adopted the following empirical specification:

$$(D/E)_{j,t} = b_0 + b_1(D/E)_{I,t-1} + b_2(D/E)_{j,t-1} + b_3(\sigma_x)_j$$
$$+ b_4(SC)_j + b_5(g_x)_j + b_6(RR)_j + b_7(\Delta P/P)_j + b_8(g_A)_j$$
$$+ b_9(A)_j + u_j$$

The variables are defined as follows:

$(D/E)_j$ = debt/equity ratio of the jth firm in the sample

$(D/E)_I$ = average debt/equity ratio of similar firms in the industry

$(\sigma_x)_j$ = standard deviation of the total earnings of the jth firm before interest and tax payments

$(SC)_j$ = shareholders' control, measured by the number of shares per stockholder

$(g_x)_j$ = the rate of growth of earnings of the jth firm

$(RR)_j$ = the retention ratio of the jth firm

$(\Delta P/P)_j$ = percentage price change of the share of the jth firm over the previous period, as a proxy for the expected cost of equity capital

$(g_A)_j$ = growth rate of real capital assets

$(A)_j$ = book value of real assets of the jth firm.

On *a priori* grounds, the coefficients should appear with the following signs:

$$0 < b_1 < 1; \ 0 < b_2 < 1; \ b_3 < 0; \ b_4 < 0;$$
$$b_5 < 0; \ b_6 < 0; \ b_7 < 0; \ b_8 > 0; \ b_9 > 0$$

The above model was estimated by applying OLS to thirty cross-section samples from five US industries: textiles, paper products, electrical equipment and appliances, steel, foods.

The results provide support for the 'managerial job-security hypothesis': there is a partial adjustment of the actual debt/equity ratio of the firm to the 'average' leverage of firms in the industry, subject to externally imposed credit

---

[35] Ibid.

limits by lenders, and to the ease of access of managers to internal funds (retained earnings).

In particular, the results suggest that:

(1) Large firms set a target debt/equity ratio $(D/E)_j$ based on the 'typical' or 'average' leverage of similar firms in the industry. The capital-structure decision of managers is closely related to the leverage policy of their rival firms in the industry, because managers feel 'safe' if they do not deviate in the long run from the norms established in the industry.

(2) The second important determinant of the debt/equity ratio is the firm's 'debt capacity', that is, a debt limit which is set by lenders in the capital market, and which depends on the firm's growth potential.

(3) The availability of internal funds, as determined by the rate of growth of earnings and the dividend-retention policy of management, is more important than the issue of new stock in determining the use of debt.

(4) Contrary to common belief, it seems that neither the variability of earnings nor the size of the firm is a significant explanatory variable of the capital structure of large corporations.

(5) The share-price variable is the least significant of all regressors. This result supports the view that the issue of new stocks is not considered by management as an attractive alternative to debt, and it is compatible with the observed value of new issues of stocks relative to those of bonds during the period covered by the study (1960–74).

The results of this study are of interest because they indicate what are the most important determinants of the capital structure (debt/equity ratio) of the large corporations, which are typical of the modern business world.

9. The Dividend-Retention Decision of the Firm

The dividend policy involves the decision to pay out earnings to shareholders or to retain them for reinvestment in the firm to enhance growth.

The dividend-retention policy affects the cost of capital to the firm (see Chapter 10), which is widely used as a criterion for 'optimal' investment decisions (see Chapter 11). Hence the dividend decision and the growth–investment decision of the firm are closely related. As we shall see in Chapter 10, the firm, in order to finance its investment projects, will first exhaust its internal funds (retained earnings), and will resort to new issues of stock only if these funds are inadequate for attaining the desired rate of growth. The preference of managers for retained earnings is due to their lower cost as compared with the cost of issue of new stock, which may also disturb the voting control and endanger the job security of management as a whole. Furthermore, retained earnings do not require any cash expense, though they have an opportunity cost for the existing (current) shareholders (see Chapter 10). However, excessive retentions may also jeopardise managerial job security, because the dissatisfied shareholders (who receive low cash dividends) may decide to replace the managers of the firm.

Another aspect of dividend policy is the stability of dividend payments over time. A reduction of the dividend payout may affect the price of the stock adversely and create dissatisfaction on behalf of owner-shareholders. It has been observed that increases in the dividend payout lag behind increases in the firm's earnings. This suggests that managers adjust upwards dividend payments only when they are sure that the higher dividend can be maintained in future periods.

It should be apparent from the above considerations that dividend-retention policy involves several intricate issues. In this chapter we will discuss the most important of them.

The organisation of the contents of this chapter is similar to that of Chapter 8. In the first section we present alternative theories of the dividend decision which are based on the assumption that the goal of managers is the maximisation of stockholder wealth. In section II we discuss a managerialist theory of the dividend decision which assumes that the goal of managers is the safeguarding (enhancement) of the job security of the managerial team as a whole. In section III we draw together the various determinants of the dividend decision. Finally, in section IV we summarise the main empirical studies on the determinants of the dividend-retention decision.

I.   THEORIES OF THE DIVIDEND-RETENTION DECISION WHEN THE GOAL OF THE FIRM IS STOCKHOLDER-WEALTH MAXIMISATION

Over the last two decades several theories have been developed on the assumption that the goal of managers is the maximisation of the value of the firm to its original shareholders. These theories debate the question whether the dividend-retention decision affects the price of stocks by influencing the investors' discount rate of the future stream of the firm's earnings.

We may distinguish two schools of thought within the goal of stockholder-wealth maximisation. One school, headed by Modigliani and Miller, argues that the dividend policy of the firm does not affect the price of its stock: investors are indifferent between cash dividends and retained profits in perfect capital markets, *given the investment decision of the firm* (in other words, the investment decision, according to this theory, has been taken prior to the dividend decision). Thus, according to the Modigliani and Miller school, there is no optimal dividend payout which maximises the value of the firm. The second school, headed by Gordon and Lintner, argues that the dividend policy does affect the valuation of the firm. Investors value a dollar of expected dividends more highly than a dollar of expected capital gains from the reinvestment of retained earnings. Investors are not indifferent to the dividend-retention policy of managers. Under these conditions there is an optimal dividend-retention policy which maximises the value of the firm to its original shareholders.

The debate is largely centred upon the assumptions of the Modigliani–Miller model – which are often misunderstood or misinterpreted. We shall begin by presenting this model. We will next discuss alternative theories of the optimal dividend payout.

A.   The Modigliani–Miller 'Dividend-Irrelevancy' Hypothesis

Modigliani and Miller developed their 'irrelevance-of-dividend' hypothesis in two articles.[1] They started with a model of an all-equity firm, which they subsequently extended to a levered firm.

---

[1] F. Modigliani and M. Miller, 'Dividend Policy, Growth and the Valuation of Shares', *Journal of Business*, 1961, pp. 411–33; 'Some Estimates of the Cost of Capital to the Electric Utility Industry', *American Economic Review*, 1966, pp. 334–91.

The assumptions of the Modigliani–Miller dividend model may be summarised as follows.

(1) There is a perfect capital market, in the sense that all traders have the same (costless) information, there are no transactions costs, and no taxes.

(2) Investors are rational, in that they prefer more wealth to less.

(3) All participants in the market are price-takers.

(4) There is *uncertainty* regarding the future stream of earnings of firms. However, investors, having the same information, form *homogeneous expectations*, that is, they maintain the same beliefs regarding the mean and variance of the stream of prospective earnings.

(5) Managers have taken decisions regarding their current and future production and investment plans, and have disclosed this information to the investors.

(6) In order to isolate the dividend effect from the leverage effect, it is assumed that all firms have a given debt/equity ratio. (This assumption is dropped by Modigliani and Miller when they develop their 'generalised model'.)

(7) Firms belong to the same risk class, which is not affected by the investment decision. In other words, the firm expands in the same line(s) of production, but does not diversify.

(8) Finally, it is assumed that the firm *expands* with its investments, but is not a 'growth firm'. This means that investments have the same yield as existing production assets.[2]

The following timing convention has been adopted by Modigliani and Miller:

D = total dividends paid at the beginning of period t to shareholders existing at the start of period $t - 1$

V_t = present value of all the securities of the firm

n_t = number of shares outstanding in period t

m_t = new shares issued in period t

P_t = price per share at the end of period t, quoted without dividend (ex-dividend) at t

k_o = over-all discount (capitalisation) rate

R_t = revenue from the firm's operations in t

L_t = labour and other current production costs in t

$X_t = R_t - L_t$ = expected value of cash flow in period t

I_t = gross investment in period t

$\bar{X}_t - I_t = R_t - L_t - I_t$ = net cash flow in t

The subsequent analysis makes use of the so-called 'basic accounting relationship'

$$[\text{Available funds}]_t = [\text{Uses of funds}]_t$$

---

[2] Modigliani and Miller have developed several growth models in which the yield of new investment (k_o^*) is greater than the yield of existing assets (k_o). These models, however, are not used by the authors in relation to the dividend decision, and thus we shall omit them from this chapter.

The sources of available funds in any one period are the earnings of the firm, $\bar{X}_t$, issue of new stock, $m_t P_t$, and issue of new debt, ΔD_t. Available funds are used for payment of interest, iD_t, investment projects, I_t, and dividend payments, Dv_t. Thus the basic accounting relationship may be written as

$$\bar{X}_t + m_t P_t + \Delta D_t = iD_t + I_t + Dv_t \tag{9.1}$$

(i) *A model with all-equity firms*

In this model it is assumed that the firm has no debt in its capital structure. Given the production–investment decision of the firm, the problem of managers is to decide whether to finance the operations of the firm with retained profits, or an issue of new stock, or a combination of both, so as to maximise the wealth of the current shareholders. Presumably the problem of choice between retained earnings and new stock is of interest only if the dividend-retention decision affects the wealth of existing owner-shareholders, which in any one period consists of the market value of their shares plus the dividends they receive. In symbols, we may write

$$\text{(Wealth)}_{S,t} = Dv_t + n_{t-1} P_t \tag{9.2}$$

It should be noted that, since *ex hypothesi* the firm has no debt, $V_t = S_t = n_t P_t$. If the firm finances its operations with retained earnings only, $n_t = n_{t-1}$, so that $V_t = n_{t-1} P_t$, that is, the old shareholders continue to own the total assets of the firm. If, however, new issue of stock takes place, the value of the firm is shared between old and new shareholders:

$$V_t = (n_{t-1} + m_t) P_t = n_{t-1} P_t + m_t P_t \tag{9.3}$$

The question is: does this dilution of ownership affect the wealth of the original shareholders? Modigliani and Miller argue that it does not. To prove their thesis, they compare the wealth of original stockholders when investment is financed with retained earnings to their wealth when investment is financed with new stock.

(a) *Financing of investment with retained earnings*

Assume that the firm decides to undertake an investment equal to I_1, *and finance it with retained earnings*. This will have two effects on the price of the shares: the reduction in the dividend will lead to a fall in the price of the share; but the expected earnings from the reinvestment of the retained earnings will lead to an equal increase in price ($P_1 > P_0$), that is, there will be *a capital gain which will exactly offset the fall in price* arising from the reduction in current dividends.

To establish this result, Modigliani and Miller argue as follows. Although the stream of cash dividends on a share may stretch on in an indefinitely long time horizon, in any one period the price per share is defined by the expression

$$P_0 = \frac{dv_1 + [P_1 - P_0]}{k_o}$$

(9.4)

This states that the price that an investor pays in period 0 is defined by discounting the dividend to be received at the end of period 1 plus any capital gain from appreciation of the stock.

Rearranging expression (9.4) we obtain

$$P_0 = \frac{dv_1 + P_1}{1 + k_o}$$

(9.5)

This can be extended to the total value of all shares, by multiplying through by n_0:

$$S_0 = V_0 = n_0 P_0 = \frac{Dv_1 + n_0 P_1}{1 + k_o}$$

(9.6)

But $n_0 P_1 = V_1$, since no new stock is issued. Furthermore, from the basic accounting relation we have $Dv_1 = (\bar{X}_1 - I_1)$, given $m_t = 0$ and $D_t = 0$. Substituting in equation (9.6) we find

$$S_0 = V_0 = \frac{\bar{X}_1 - I_1 + V_1}{1 + k_o}$$

(9.7)

In words expression (9.7) states that the market value of shares outstanding at the initial period 0 is completely independent of the dividend to be declared by the directors at the end of the period. The present value depends on three factors: (i) the rate of discount, which is determined exogenously in a perfect capital market; (ii) the firm's production and investment decisions, which are assumed to be taken prior and independently of the dividend to be declared at the end of the period; and (iii) the market value of the shares (and hence on the price per share) at the next period, which *ex hypothesi* does not depend on Dv_1 (recall that P_t is the ex-dividend price).

It can easily be shown that V_1 does not also depend on Dv_2, or any other future dividend:

We may write the present value of the shares outstanding in period 1 as

$$V_1 = \frac{\bar{X}_2 - I_2 + V_2}{1 + k_o} = \frac{\bar{X}_2 - I_2}{1 + k_o} + \frac{V_2}{1 + k_o}$$

(9.8)

Substituting (9.8) in (9.7) we obtain

$$V_0 = \frac{X_1 - I_1}{1 + k_o} + \frac{\bar{X}_2 - I_2}{(1 + k_o)^2} + \frac{V_2}{(1 + k_o)^2}$$

Similarly we may substitute V_2:

$$V_2 = \frac{\bar{X}_3 - I_3^2}{(1 + k_o)} + \frac{V_3}{(1 + k_o)}$$

so that

$$V_0 = \frac{\bar{X}_1 - I_1}{(1 + k_o)} + \frac{\bar{X}_2 - I_2}{(1 + k_o)^2} + \frac{\bar{X}_3 - I_3}{(1 + k_o)^3} + \frac{V_3}{(1 + k_o)^3}$$

We may proceed with the substitution of V_3, V_4, etc., for as many time periods as we choose. Let n be the time horizon of the investors. From the consecutive substitutions we obtain

$$V_0 = \frac{\bar{X}_1 - I_1}{(1 + k_o)} + \frac{\bar{X}_2 - I_2}{(1 + k_o)^2} + \ldots + \frac{\bar{X}_n - I_n}{(1 + k_o)^n} + \frac{V_n}{(1 + k_o)^n}$$

or

$$V_0 = \sum_{t=1}^{n} \frac{\bar{X}_t - I_t}{(1 + k_o)^t} + \frac{V_n}{(1 + k_o)^n}$$

As $n \to \infty$ the last term $(V_n / [1 + k_o]^n)$ can, in general, be expected to approach zero, so that the market valuation expression (for the original shareholders) reduces to the t-period model:

$$V_0 = \sum_{t=1}^{\infty} \frac{\bar{X}_t - I_t}{(1 + k_o)^t} \tag{9.9}$$

Note that in this model $V_0 = S_0$, by assumption, since the firm is unlevered.

(b) *Financing of investment with new stock*

Assume now that the firm finances its investment programme totally or partly by issuing m_1 new shares. This will allow the firm to pay a higher dividend to the old shareholders, since from the basic accounting relationship we have

$$Dv_1 = \bar{X}_1 - I_1 + m_1 P_1 \tag{9.10}$$

However, the market value of the firm will be now shared between the old and new shareholders:

$$V_1 = (n_0 + m_1)P_1 = n_0 P_1 + m_1 P_1$$

Solving for $n_0 P_1$ we find

$$n_0 P_1 = V_1 - m_1 P_1 \tag{9.11}$$

Substituting Dv_1 and $n_0 P_1$ in the basic valuation expression (9.6), we find that the present value of the shares owned by the old shareholders is

$$S_0 = \frac{(\bar{X}_1 - I_1 + m_1 P_1) + (V_1 - m_1 P_1)}{(1 + k_o)} \tag{9.12}$$

or

$$S_0 = \frac{\bar{X}_1 - I_1 + V_1}{(1 + k_o)} \tag{9.13}$$

This is the same result as the one obtained under the assumption of financing investment by retained earnings: expression (9.7). The wealth of old shareholders is the numerator of expression (9.12), from which it is seen that dividends *increase* by $m_1 P_1$, but at the same time the part of the firm's market value belonging to them *is decreased by an equal amount*, so that their total wealth is unaffected by the financing decision of the firm. From this Modigliani and Miller conclude that the dividend policy of the firm is irrelevant (a matter of indifference) to its shareholders, since it does not affect their wealth. Although at first sight paradoxical, this conclusion follows from the assumptions of perfect capital markets and *given investment decisions*. New share financing allows the firm to pay a higher current dividend than when retained-earnings financing is used, but there follows an immediate equal and offsetting reduction in capital gains, so that the old shareholders are no better off with one form of financing than with another.[3]

(ii) *A 'generalised model' with debt and equity financing*

In the previous section we examined the effect of the dividend policy on the *total* market value of a firm which had no debt in its capital structure. In this section the leverage and dividend decisions of the firm are combined in a single model. (It is assumed that the new investment has the same yield as the existing assets of the firm, i.e. $k_o^* = k_o$.)

If the firm uses debt, shareholders and bondholders will be indifferent as to the financing and dividend decisions of the firm only if the *separate* market value of their wealth is unaffected by these decisions.

Given the investment and production decisions of the firm, these will generate an expected stream of earnings in future periods. Thus there is a direct effect of production—investment decisions on the separate market values of the security holders (bondholders and shareholders) of the firm, since their wealth depends on the firm's total earnings. What is disputable is whether the *financing* decisions affect the wealth of security holders. Modigliani and Miller maintain that the firm's financing and dividend decisions do not affect the separate wealth positions of security holders. Their proof runs as follows:

The wealth in period t of *shareholders* existing in period $t - 1$ is

$$W_{S,t} = Dv_t + S_{n,t} = (\bar{X}_t - iD_t) + (V_t - D_t) \qquad (9.14)$$

where Dv_t = dividends paid to common stock outstanding in $t - 1$

$S_{n,t}$ = market value of stock in t, outstanding in $t - 1 = V_t - D_t$

Similarly, the wealth in period t of *bondholders* existing in $t - 1$ is

$$W_{B,t} = iD_t + D_t \qquad (9.15)$$

---

[3] See E. Fama and M. Miller, *The Theory of Finance* (Holt, Rinehart & Winston, 1972) p. 169.

where iD_t = interest payments in t to bondholders existing in $t - 1$
  D_t = market value in t of outstanding debt in $t - 1$

(a) *Financing of investment with retained earnings*

If the firm uses only internal finance from retained earnings in order to finance its investment, the dividends at t are

$$Dv_t = \bar{X}_t - I_t - iD_t$$

This reduction in dividends, Modigliani and Miller imply, will reduce the price of the share. But the reinvestment of the increased retained earnings (at a yield equal to that of the existing assets, k_o) will increase the price of the share (P) by an equal offsetting amount. Thus the over-all effect on P of the change in the dividend payout will be neutral. Under these conditions, and given that there is no issue of new securities (either bonds or stocks), the market value of the firm is

$$V_t = n_t P_t + D_t$$

or, setting $S_{n,t} = n_t P_t$, and solving

$$S_{n,t} = V_t - D_t$$

(Note that $S_{n,t}$ is the value in t of the equity of 'old' shareholders.)
  The wealth of shareholders, with internal financing, is

$$W'_{Sn,t} = (\bar{X}_t - I_t - iD_t) + (V_t - D_t) \tag{9.16}$$

The wealth of bondholders is

$$W'_{B,t} = iD_t + D_t \tag{9.17}$$

(b) *Financing of investment, totally or partly, with new equity*

Assume that new shares are issued, and their value is $m_t P_t$.
  The dividend, under this financing scheme, to the original shareholders is

$$Dv_t = \bar{X}_t - I_t - iD_t + m_t P_t$$

The market value of the firm now consists of the market value of old shares, the market value of new shares and the value of old debt:

$$V_t = (n_t + m_t)P_t + D_t = n_t P_t + m_t P_t + D_t$$

Solving for $n_t P_t$ we find

$$S_{n,t} = n_t P_t = V_t - D_t - m_t P_t$$

Substituting in the wealth expressions (9.14) and (9.15) we find

$$W''_{Sn,t} = (\bar{X}_t - I_t - iD_t + m_tP_t) + (V_t - D_t - m_tP_t) = W'_{Sn,t} \qquad (9.18)$$

$$= \begin{bmatrix} \text{Dividends paid} \\ \text{to original} \\ \text{shareholders} \end{bmatrix} + \begin{bmatrix} \text{Value of shares} \\ \text{of original} \\ \text{shareholders} \end{bmatrix}$$

and

$$W''_{B,t} = iD_t + D_t = W'_{B,t} \qquad (9.19)$$

We observe that the wealth positions of the original shareholders and bond-holders is the same with retained-earnings financing and new-equity financing. This is due to the fact that dividends increase by the amount of the new stock issue (m_tP_t), but at the same time the value of the shares of old shareholders declines by an equal amount: whatever the original shareholders gain from the higher dividend, they lose from a reduction in their capital gains.

(c) *Financing of investment partly with new stock and partly with new bonds*

Under this mixed financing scheme, the dividends of 'old' (original) shareholders is

$$Dv_t = \bar{X}_t - I_t - iD_t + m_tP_t + \Delta D_t$$

The market value of the firm now is

$$V_t = \quad n_tP_t \quad + \quad m_tP_t \quad + \quad D_t \quad + \quad \Delta D_t$$

$$= \begin{bmatrix} \text{Original} \\ \text{equity} \end{bmatrix} + \begin{bmatrix} \text{New} \\ \text{equity} \end{bmatrix} + \begin{bmatrix} \text{Original} \\ \text{debt} \end{bmatrix} + \begin{bmatrix} \text{New} \\ \text{debt} \end{bmatrix}$$

Solving for n_tP_t we obtain

$$S_{n,t} = n_tP_t = V_t - D_t - m_tP_t - \Delta D_t = \begin{bmatrix} \text{Value of shares of} \\ \text{original shareholders} \end{bmatrix}$$

Substituting Dv_t and n_tP_t in the wealth equation (9.14) we obtain

$$W'''_{Sn,t} = [\bar{X}_t - I_t - iD_t + (m_tP_t + \Delta D_t)] + [V_t - D_t - (m_tP_t + \Delta D_t)] = W'_{Sn,t}$$
$$(9.20)$$

$$= \begin{bmatrix} \text{Dividends paid to original} \\ \text{shareholders} \end{bmatrix} + \begin{bmatrix} \text{Value of shares of original} \\ \text{shareholders} \end{bmatrix}$$

The wealth of the original bondholders does not change:[4] it consists of the market value of their bonds, D_t, plus the interest they receive, iD_t:

$$W'''_{B,t} = iD_t + D_t = W'_{B,t}$$

---

[4] It is assumed that bondholders and shareholders protect themselves by a 'me-first' clause when new issues take place.

From this it is seen that new bonds (like new shares) allow the firm to pay higher dividends in the current period than when retained earnings are used. But the new bonds lead to *an immediate equal and offsetting reduction in the old stockholders' share* of V_t, the market value of the firm. The net result is that the wealth of existing (old) shareholders and of existing bondholders is the same under all three methods of financing.

Thus Modigliani and Miller conclude, given the firm's production and investment decisions, which determine the future earnings, $\bar{X}_t$, that its financing decisions are a matter of indifference to its security holders, since their *separate wealth positions* are not affected by these decisions.

It follows that production and investment decisions and financing decisions are separable in perfect capital markets, that is, they can be made independently.

The 'irrelevance-of-dividends' hypothesis has been questioned by several writers on the basis of the observed positive relationship between dividends and share prices. In particular, the opponents of Modigliani and Miller argue that if the irrelevance proposition were true, investors should be indifferent between dividends and retentions. Since several empirical studies show a preference of investors for dividends over retentions, the opponents of Modigliani and Miller conclude that the 'neutrality theorem' is wrong. This interpretation of the Modigliani–Miller irrelevance-of-dividends theorem is incorrect, as we shall see in a subsequent paragraph and in Chapter 10.

B. Market Imperfections and the Modigliani–Miller Model

Several writers argue that the observed preference of shareholders for current dividends can be attributed to market imperfections. Modigliani and Miller maintain that such imperfections tend to be offsetting. We discuss below the effects of some of these imperfections.

(i) *Heterogeneous expectations of investors*

Lintner[5] has established that even with the same amount of information, investors may reach different conclusions regarding the future stream of earnings, because they may assign different probabilities to the prospective outcomes of the firm's operations, depending on their *subjective assessment* of the same facts. If the amount and quality of information also differ for the various investors, we may well expect that the dividend policy of managers affects the portfolio decisions of investors.

Lintner argues that when investors' expectations are not homogeneous (for

---

[5] J. Lintner, 'Dividends, Earnings, Leverage, Stock Prices and the Supply of Capital to Corporations', *Review of Economics and Statistics*, 1962, pp. 243–70.

whatever reason), the Modigliani—Miller irrelevance hypothesis does not hold, because it requires that the new issues of stock be sold at the same price. Divergent expectations imply that the old shareholders think that the value of their stock is at least as high as the prevailing price, while new buyers maintain opposite beliefs, so they would buy a share only if it is sold at a lower price. This means that with divergent investors' expectations the demand curve for stock has a negative slope.

(ii) *Tax effects*

If the assumption of no taxes is relaxed, we have various effects, the most important of which is the effect of the difference between the tax on dividends and the tax on capital gains. In the present personal income tax system in most Western countries, dividends are taxed more heavily than capital gains. Furthermore, capital gains are deferred until the sale of the stocks. The total tax effect depends on the type of investor.

(1) Individuals who belong to the high-income brackets would have a preference for retentions with the expectation of capital gains.

(2) Charitable and educational institutions, foundations, pension trusts and low-income individuals would have a preference for high dividends, since they are exempt from tax on their income from this source.

(3) Casualty insurance companies and taxable corporations are subject to a lower dividend tax than the capital gains tax.

Despite the diverse nature of investors, there is some empirical evidence[6] that there is a negative correlation between dividends and an increase in the tax differential between dividend income and capital gains. There is also evidence[7] of an inverse relationship between dividends and the tax brackets of investors.

This evidence runs contrary both to the Modigliani and Miller neutrality theorem, and to the standard view of many writers who maintain that there is a positive relationship between dividends and stock prices.[8]

Modigliani and Miller discuss briefly the difficulties arising from the relaxation of the assumption of no personal taxes and brokerage fees. However, they do not go into the technicalities of showing how the existence of two different tax rates (t_p on income, and t_g on capital gains, with $t_p > t_g$) and of transactions costs would affect their conclusion about the irrelevance of dividend policy. In

---

[6] J. A. Brittain, *Corporate Dividend Policy* (Brookings Institution, 1966).

[7] E. Elton and M. Gruber, 'Marginal Stockholder Tax Rates and the Clientele Effect', *Review of Economics and Statistics*, 1970, pp. 68–74.

[8] M. Gordon, 'Dividends, Earnings and Share Prices', *Review of Economics and Statistics*, 1959, pp. 99–105; G. Fischer, 'Some Factors Influencing Share Prices', *Economic Journal*, 1961, pp. 121–41; D. Durand, *Bank Stock Prices and Bank Capital Problem* (National Bureau of Economic Research, 1957); D. Graham and G. Dodd, *Security Analysis* (McGraw-Hill, 1951).

this section we will extend their model, incorporating into it personal tax differentials and transactions costs. We will show that with these market imperfections there is an advantage of retentions over cash dividends.

Tax-deferral advantage of retained earnings

Assume that an *unlevered* firm, which generates an expected after-tax income of $\bar{X}(1 - t_c)$, retains all its earnings and reinvests them in projects with a yield k_o, equal to the return on its existing assets. Investors avail from the tax deferral on retentions, by an amount equal to $[\bar{X}(1 - t_c)] t_p$. Assuming no further retentions, the new income stream which will be distributed as dividends in future periods will be

$$\bar{X}(1 - t_c) + \bar{X}(1 - t_c)k_o = \bar{X}(1 - t_c)(1 + k_o)$$

Investors will receive an after-tax income from dividends equal to

$$Dv_t = [\bar{X}(1 - t_c)(1 + k_o)](1 - t_p) \tag{9.21}$$

Without retentions, investors would have to pay immediately taxes on all the earnings, so their after-tax income would be

$$\bar{X}(1 - t_c)(1 - t_p)$$

If they themselves reinvest this income at a yield k_o, their subsequent income in each period will be

$$\bar{X}(1 - t_c) + k_o[\bar{X}(1 - t_c)(1 - t_p)]$$

all of which would be subject to personal tax, so that the after-tax income in this case would be

$$\{\bar{X}(1 - t_c) + k_o[\bar{X}(1 - t_c)(1 - t_p)]\}(1 - t_p) = \bar{X}(1 - t_c)(1 - t_p)[(1 + k_o)(1 - t_p)] \tag{9.22}$$

The advantage of retentions due to the tax deferral is equal to the difference between the two alternative expected streams of earnings:

$$\begin{bmatrix} \text{Deferral} \\ \text{advantage} \end{bmatrix} = [\bar{X}(1 - t_c)(1 + k_o)(1 - t_p)] - [\bar{X}(1 - t_c)(1 - t_p)\{(1 + k_o)(1 - t_p)\}]$$

$$= \begin{bmatrix} \text{Earnings generated by} \\ \text{retentions and re-} \\ \text{investment by firm} \end{bmatrix} - \begin{bmatrix} \text{Earnings generated by} \\ \text{reinvestment by investors} \end{bmatrix}$$

$$= \bar{X}(1 - t_c)(1 - t_p)[(1 + k_o) - \{(1 + k_o)(1 - t_p)\}]$$

$$= \bar{X}(1 - t_c)(1 - t_p)(k_o t_p)$$

This advantage of retentions is positive, given $t_p < 1$. One-dollar retentions (i.e. if $\bar{X}(1 - t_c) = \$1$) benefits investors by an amount equal to $(1 - t_p)(k_o t_p)$ dollars, due to the deferral of personal tax payments.

Capital gains and tax deferral

Assume that the firm retains and reinvests all its earnings. The new total earnings will be, as before,

$$\bar{X}(1 - t_c) + \bar{X}(1 - t_c)k_o = \bar{X}(1 - t_c)(1 + k_o)$$

The earnings increase by $(1 + k_o)$, and so does the value of the shares as a whole. The income that the investors will have, after being taxed for capital gains, is

$$\bar{X}(1 - t_c)(1 + k_o)(1 - t_g) \tag{9.23}$$

This reflects *both* the tax-deferral and the capital-gains effects.

Without retentions investors would receive, after paying their personal tax, an amount equal to

$$\bar{X}(1 - t_c)(1 - t_p)$$

which, if reinvested, would yield a total income

$$k_o \bar{X}(1 - t_c)(1 - t_p)$$

The investors' income position would be

$$\bar{X}(1 - t_c)(1 - t_p) + [k_o \bar{X}(1 - t_c)(1 - t_p)](1 - t_p)$$

that is,

$$\bar{X}(1 - t_c)(1 - t_p)[(1 + k_o)(1 - t_p)] \tag{9.24}$$

Comparing the two income positions, i.e. subtracting (9.24) from (9.23), we find

$$\begin{bmatrix} \text{Deferred tax plus} \\ \text{capital tax advantage} \end{bmatrix} = [\bar{X}(1 - t_c)(1 + k_o)(1 - t_g)] - [\bar{X}(1 - t_c)(1 - t_p) \\ \{(1 + k_o)(1 - t_p)\}]$$

$$= \bar{X}(1 - t_c)[(1 + k_o)(1 - t_g) - (1 - t_p)(1 + k_o - k_o t_p)]$$

$$= \bar{X}(1 - t_c)[(1 + k_o)(1 - t_g) - (1 + k_o)(1 - t_p)$$

$$+ (1 - t_p)k_o t_p]$$

$$= \bar{X}(1 - t_c)[\underbrace{(1 + k_o)(t_p - t_g)}_{\substack{\text{Capital-gains} \\ \text{advantage}}} + \underbrace{(1 - t_p)k_o t_p}_{\substack{\text{Tax-deferral} \\ \text{advantage}}}] \tag{9.25}$$

Given that $t_p > t_g$, the tax-deferral advantage of retentions is reinforced by the capital-gains advantage.

(iii) *Transactions costs and uncertainty of capital gains*

In an imperfect market selling of stocks involves brokerage fees, which may be high in relation to the transaction. If investors have a strong preference for current income, brokerage and other transactions costs will result in a preference for dividends over retained earnings. Furthermore, prices of stocks fluctuate, creating uncertainty regarding capital gains when selling stocks for current-consumption purposes. The uncertainty of fluctuating prices results in a preference for dividends over retentions.

(iv) *Flotations costs*

New issues of stocks have flotation costs. In addition, the demand for stocks is most likely downward-sloping, implying that the new stocks must be sold at a discount. These factors make new equity financing an expensive source of finance and create a preference of investors for retentions (internal finance).

Modigliani and Miller maintain that market imperfections of the kind discussed above tend to be offsetting so that the dividend policy does not affect the valuation of the firm. They attribute the findings of other writers to the use of wrong models, measurement errors and/or confusion of *optimal dividend policy* and *optimal investment decisions.* [9] Even if a significant positive relationship between the dividend payout and share price is established, this is due, they argue, to *the informational content of dividends.* Modigliani and Miller state that corporations are reluctant to cut dividends. Hence managers do not raise dividends unless they anticipate that earnings in the future will be high and stable enough, so as to enable them to maintain the higher dividend payments. Thus an increase in dividends is an indication to investors that the firm's management expects high future earnings. Conversely, a reduction in dividends indicates that management anticipates poor earnings in the future. Thus Modigliani and Miller argue that a change in dividend policy is not important in the sense of showing that investors prefer dividends to retained earnings. The observed fact that stock prices change when the dividend payout changes simply indicates that there is an important information content in dividend announcements. I think that this argument of Modigliani and Miller is not satisfactory, because it renders their neutrality hypothesis into a tautology, that is, a proposition compatible with any observed behaviour of shareholders, and, hence, not testable (see also page 430).

Modigliani and Miller's theory of 'dividend irrelevance' has been attacked by various writers, who argue that the dividend-payout policy of the firm affects the valuation of shares under conditions of uncertainty. We shall examine the most important theories which advocate the existence of an optimal dividend-payout policy.

---

[9] See Fama and Miller, *The Theory of Finance*; and also Chapter 10 of this book.

C.   Myron Gordon's 'Increasing Discount Rates' Hypothesis

Myron Gordon[10] argues that investors are risk-averse and that the uncertainty of an amount of money increases with the period of its receipt in the future. Under these conditions investors may well be expected to discount the elements of the future stream of dividends with increasing discount rates:

$$V_0 = \frac{Dv_0}{(1 + k_1)^1} + \frac{Dv_0}{(1 + k_2)^2} + \frac{Dv_0}{(1 + k_3)^3} + \ldots + \frac{Dv_0}{(1 + k_t)^t} + \ldots \qquad (9.26)$$

where $k_1 < k_2 < k_3 < \ldots < k_t$.

From such behaviour, Gordon concludes that dividend policy influences the value of the firm, because an increase in retentions decreases the current dividend, which is discounted at k_1, and increases future dividends which are discounted at higher discount rates. To illustrate his hypothesis Gordon uses a simple example. He assumes that the firm retains all its earnings in period 1, reinvests the proceeds and distributes the increased earnings as dividends in all future periods. Without any retentions the value of the firm would be given by expression (9.26). With the above assumptions about retentions, the value of the firm (assuming that the investment yield is k, the average of all the k_ts) will be

$$V'_0 = \frac{0}{(1 + k_1)^1} + \frac{Dv_0 + kDv_0}{(1 + k_2)^2} + \ldots + \frac{Dv_0 + kDv_0}{(1 + k_t)^t} \qquad (9.27)$$

The shareholders now give up Dv_0 and receive kDv_0 in perpetuity; but the latter is discounted at rates k_t (where $t = 2, 3, \ldots, \infty$), and it can be shown that kDv_0 so discounted is less than Dv_0. Hence $V'_0 < V_0$, and dividend policy is *not* neutral.

Gordon's argument does not invalidate the Modigliani–Miller irrelevance proposition, so long as the assumption of perfect capital markets holds. In such markets investors can undertake arbitrage transactions and create 'home-made dividends' in the same way as they can create 'home-made leverage', when they think that the firm's capital structure includes a different debt/equity ratio than the one they prefer. In perfect capital markets 'home-made dividends' are perfect substitutes for corporate dividends.[11] However, market imperfections do exist, and hence Gordon's hypothesis may be more relevant (than the Modigliani–Miller model) in explaining real-world situations.

---

[10] Myron Gordon, 'Optimal Investment and Financing Policy', *Journal of Finance*, 1963, pp. 264–72; also M. Gordon, 'The Savings, Investment and Valuation of a Corporation', *Review of Economics and Statistics*, 1962, pp. 37–51.

[11] R. C. Higgins, 'Dividend Policy and Increasing Discount Rates: A Clarification', *Journal of Financial and Quantitative Analysis*, 1972, pp. 1757–62; M. Brennan, 'A Note on Dividend Irrelevance and the Gordon Valuation Model', *Journal of Finance*, 1971, pp. 1115–21.

D. The 'Preference for Current Income' Hypothesis

Some writers have argued that investors pay a higher price for shares when dividends increase, because they have a strong preference for current consumption.

This argument, also, does not invalidate the Modigliani–Miller neutrality theorem if the capital market is perfect. As Walters has observed,[12] whenever the stockholder is dissatisfied with the dividend policy of the firm, he can always 'undo' the corporate decision by buying or selling part of the stock, or by 'lending' or 'borrowing' on the same terms that cash dividends are paid. If dividends are insufficient to satisfy the preference for greater current consumption, the desired proportion of current income can be obtained by selling part of the shares. If dividends (and, hence, current income) is too high, part of the cash can be invested in additional shares.

However, with market imperfections (brokerage fees, etc.) investors may well be expected to have a preference for cash dividends. Under these conditions the dividend policy of the firm may not be neutral.

E. The 'Informational Content of Dividends' Hypothesis

Some empirical studies[13] have shown that the prices of shares in the market change in the same direction with changes in declared dividends. The explanation provided by some of the researchers for this relationship is the 'informational content' of dividends: investors accept current dividends as an indirect measure of the expected future earnings of the firm. Dividends show a greater stability over time than earnings, because managers pursue a 'target dividend payout policy', increasing their 'target payout' only when they believe that future earnings will be high enough to enable them to meet the higher dividend (see section III). Thus substantial information about the future stream of earnings is conveyed to investors by changes in dividends.

Although Walters[14] has questioned the ability of 'announced dividends' to convey more information than the 'announced earnings', since both are random variables, his argument is not convincing, given the observed greater stability of dividends and the fact that managers tend to pursue a target dividend policy.

As we said earlier, Modigliani and Miller accept the 'informational' effect of dividends. They maintain that the real determinant of the value of the firm is its earnings, and dividends are a proxy measure for expected earnings. I think that this part of the Modigliani and Miller argument is weak. If changes in stock prices

---

[12] G. E. Walters, 'Dividend Policy: its Influence on the Valuation of the Enterprise', *Journal of Finance*, 1953, pp. 280–91.

[13] R. Richardson Pettit, 'Dividend Announcements, Security Performance, and Capital Market Efficiency', *Journal of Finance*, 1972, pp. 993–1007; E. Fama, L. Fisher, M. Jensen and R. Roll, 'The Adjustment of Stock Prices to New Information', *International Economic Review*, 1969, pp. 1–26.

[14] G. E. Walters, 'Dividend Policy: its Influence on the Valuation of the Enterprise', *Journal of Finance*, 1953, pp. 280–91.

are found to be positively (and significantly) correlated with changes in dividends, it is impossible to distinguish between the 'informational content' hypothesis and the Modigliani and Miller neutrality theorem: the Modigliani and Miller proposition becomes a tautology. There is clearly some information content in dividend anouncements, but it may or may not be the complete explanation for the stock-price changes that follow increases or decreases in dividends.

F.   The 'Traditionalist' Theory of the Dividend Decision

The traditionalist approach is shown in Figure 9.1. The retention ratio is denoted by b and the dividend payout ratio by $(1 - b)$. To isolate the dividend decision from the leverage and investment decisions, it is assumed that the firm has no debt in its capital structure, and that the investment decision is taken independently of the dividend decision. Investment projects can be financed either from retained earnings or from issue of new stock. Curve A shows the increase in the discount rate that investors would require when new issue takes place, due to the dilution of ownership, flotation costs and underpricing. The greater the issue, the steeper the slope of this curve will be. Curve B shows the preference of investors for dividends. Initially the discount rate declines as the dividend payout increases. Beyond a certain point, however, further increases in the dividend payout are less attractive to investors due to the tax disadvantage of dividend income. Eventually the tax disadvantage causes the preference-for-dividends curve to turn up (the discount rate rises when the dividend payout exceeds point a in Figure 9.1). Curve C shows the combined effect of flotation costs, dilution of ownership, underpricing, preferences for dividends and the tax disadvantage. As the curves are drawn, the dividend preference is sufficiently strong at low payout ratios so as to offset the increasing disadvantages of new stock issues. Thus curve C has a minimum (point Z in Figure 9.1) at which the price of the share is maximised. In this approach the dividend policy of the firm is not neutral. The

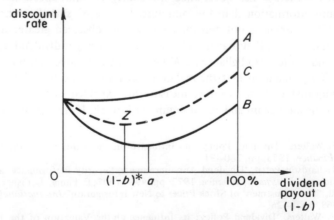

Figure 9.1

optimum dividend payout ratio is $(1 - b)^*$. Note that at all levels of dividend payout it is assumed that there is a net preference of the shareholders as a whole for dividends; but this preference becomes less strong at high levels of dividend payout ratios.

Comparison of the 'traditionalist' approach with the Modigliani–Miller approach

The Modigliani–Miller neutrality hypothesis is illustrated in Figure 9.2. Without transactions costs and without tax differentials there would be two opposite forces in the market. Increased dividends result in increases in the price of stock (lower discount rate); but these increases are *exactly offset* by a decline in the stock price due to the dilution of ownership. Fama and Miller[15] argue that the *'irrelevance-of-dividends' proposition does not require stockholders to be indifferent as between a present dividend and a future dividend or future capital gain.* It states that, once managers have decided the level of investment, an increase in the dividends leads to a corresponding equal and offsetting reduction in the value of the shares, due to the dilution of ownership following the new issue of stock: part of the firm will belong to the new shareholders. Fama and Miller maintain that the traditionalist view of the existence of a unique optimal dividend policy is based on a confusion between an optimal investment decision and an optimal dividend decision.

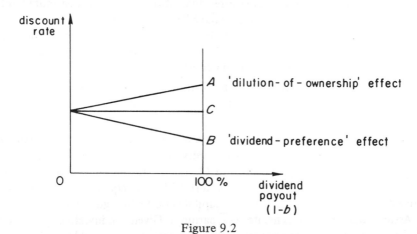

Figure 9.2

There is general agreement that retained profits would not affect the value of shares if the yield from their investment were equal to the yield from alternative investments open to investors. The value of shares would rise if the yield on new investment internally financed is higher than the yield of alternatives open to

[15] See Fama and Miller, *The Theory of Finance*, p. 84.

investors. Similarly, the price of shares would fall if the yield from the reinvestment of retained earnings were lower than what shareholders could earn if they received all earnings in the form of cash dividends and invested them directly as they wanted. Fama and Miller[16] argue that the 'irrelevance proposition' is *not* in conflict with the above view. The conflict is only in appearance, because of the failure to distinguish clearly between an *optimal investment decision* and an *optimal dividend policy*. If an investment financed by retentions has a lower yield than expected, and as a consequence the price of stock falls, the decline is due to the wrong investment decision and not to the wrong finance decision. The fall in price following a poor internally financed investment cannot be attributed to the low dividend payout, unless of course one can establish that the drop in the share price would be smaller if managers had financed the same investment from new stock issues (and less retained earnings).

G.   The 'Residual Theory' of Dividends

The residual theory of dividends provides a simplistic model of the dividend decision. However, it is a useful introduction to the complex issues of the process of the dividend decision in real-world situations.

In perfect capital markets, and given the investment decision of the firm, dividends can be treated as a passive residual: dividends will be distributed only after internal investment opportunities have been exhausted.

(1) Assume zero leverage at this stage, and no taxes. Under these conditions the cost of retained earnings is equal to the cost of new equity capital (see Chapter 11). The dividends are determined by

(a)   the investment opportunities of the firm;
(b)   the cost of retained earnings; and
(c)   internally generated funds, $\bar{X}$.

The investment opportunities are assumed to be presented by the 'marginal efficiency of investment' schedule (MEI curve in Figure 9.3). The construction of this schedule has been explained in Chapter 4. In the same chapter we saw that the optimal level of investment is defined by the equality of the marginal efficiency of investment to the cost of capital (point e in Figure 9.3).

Assume that the firm generates $O\bar{X}$ earnings. Given the investment decision, I^*, the firm will retain and reinvest all its earnings and raise an additional amount of funds equal to $\bar{X}I^*$ by issuing new stock. If the firm's earnings were OI^*, there would be zero dividends and no issue of stock. Only if earnings exceeded OI^* (e.g. $O\bar{X}'$) would the firm pay the 'residual' $I^*\bar{X}'(= O\bar{X}' - OI^*)$ in cash dividends.

(2) If we introduce personal taxes (on income and capital gains), the cost of retained earnings (C_R) would be lower than the cost of new equity (C_E). (See Chapter 11.)

---

[16] See ibid, p. 85.

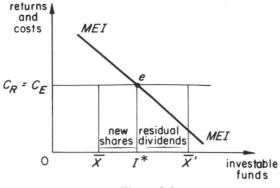

Figure 9.3

Three cases can occur:

(a) In Figure 9.4 the MEI schedule intersects the segment C_R to the left of $\bar{X}$ (the level of total earnings of the firm). The firm will retain OI^* and pay $O\bar{X} - OI^*$ in cash dividends, if its goal is the maximisation of the wealth of its stockholders.

(b) In Figure 9.5 the MEI schedule intersects the segment C_E. The firm will retain (and reinvest) all its earnings and sell new equity of an amount $OI^* - O\bar{X}$.

(c) In Figure 9.6 the MEI schedule intersects the vertical line connecting C_R and C_E. The firm would retain and reinvest all its earnings, paying no dividends and issuing no new stock.

(3) If we assume that the firm is levered, its supply-of-funds curve would consist of two segments (Figure 9.7). The lower segment, C_A, would be the weighted average cost of retained earnings (internal equity) and debt, with weights the target debt/equity ratio L^* and $1 - L^*$ for debt and internal finance

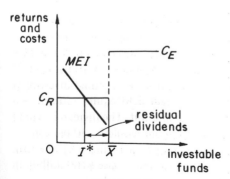

Figure 9.4

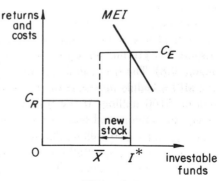

Figure 9.5

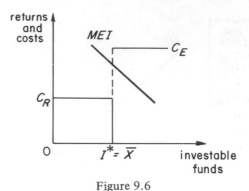

Figure 9.6

Figure 9.7

respectively. The upper segment, C_E, would be the supply of new equity funds (see Chapter 11).

Assume that the firm has a target debt/equity ratio of 50:50. If it generates earnings equal to $\bar{X}$ (in Figure 9.7), the firm can invest up to $2\bar{X}$ with a cost of C_A. Beyond $2\bar{X}$ investment would be financed by new issue of stock at a cost equal to C_E.

So long as the MEI schedule intersects the C_A segment, the firm will distribute some dividends, left over after meeting its debt/equity target ratio. For example, assume $\bar{X} = \$100$m. and $C_A = 0.1$, with a target/equity ratio equal to 50:50 (see Figure 9.8). The firm can invest up to \$200 million at a cost of 10 per cent. If the MEI schedule intersects the C_A segment at point a, the optimal investment will be \$160 million. If the firm is to keep its target debt/equity ratio, it will retain \$80 million and raise new debt of an equal amount. The dividends would be the residual, \$20 million, that is, the dividend payout would be 20 per cent.

If investment opportunities were very large (point b in Figure 9.8), the firm would have zero dividends. It would retain all its earnings, raise \$100 million in new debt, and an additional amount of \$40 million in new stock.

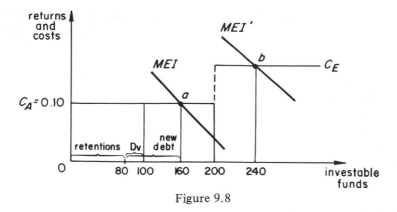

Figure 9.8

In summary. The residual theory of dividends implies that the dividend decision involves the following steps:

(a) Determination of the optimal amount of investment.
(b) Determination of the optimal target debt/equity ratio.
(c) Determination of the amount of equity required to finance the optimal investment, in order to maintain the target debt/equity ratio.
(d) As far as is possible, use of retained earnings to supply the equity needed.
(e) Pay dividends only if earnings are higher than the required equity for financing planned investment projects, while maintaining the target debt/equity ratio. Thus the residual theory of dividends considers dividend policy as a 'residual' or 'passive' decision.

The residual theory of dividends leads to the maximisation of the price of the stock.[17] This can be seen by examining the impact on the price of stocks of deviations from the dividend policy implied by the residual theory. For example, we saw that under the assumptions of a 50:50 target debt/equity ratio, an optimal investment budget of $160 million and earnings of $100 million, the residual theory implies an optimal dividend payout of 20 per cent. Deviations from this payout will result in a reduction of the price of the shares.

(1) Consider first an increase in the dividend payout. For this policy to be implemented, the firm must change some of its other decisions: it can reduce its level of investment below the optimal budget of $160 million, thereby forgoing profitable investment opportunities which would increase its stream of future earnings; or the firm can sell new stock (to replace the reduced retained earnings), thus incurring flotations costs and resorting to underpricing; or the firm can issue new debt, thus deviating from its target debt/equity ratio (optimal capital structure). Any such action is bound to affect adversely the price of the firm's shares.

---

[17] The maximisation of the price of the stock is attained only if the assumptions underlying the theory hold, as we will presently see.

(2) Consider now a reduction in the dividend payout. In order to use the increased retained earnings, the firm can either increase its investment budget beyond the optimal amount (which would involve accepting unprofitable projects), or use the additional retained earnings as a substitute for new debt (which would cause a departure from the target optimal capital structure). Again, these changes in corporate policy would result in a fall of the stock price.

Thus the dividend policy implied by the residual theory will maximise the price of the firm's stock, provided that the assumptions of the theory hold. These assumptions are: (a) a given investment decision; (b) perfect capital markets, which implies that the rate of return investors require on their equity is not affected by the firm's dividend policy.[18]

In the real world capital markets are imperfect. Furthermore, the residual theory of dividends is contradicted by the observed policy of firms of maintaining a stable, target dividend policy. The dividend decision is an 'active policy', not a residual one. As we will see in section III, pursuing a *target dividend policy* is compatible with the managerialist theory of the firm.

A note on the Independence of the Investment and Dividend Decisions

The Modigliani–Miller irrelevance proposition (as well as the residual theory of dividends) requires that investment be an exogenous variable. The dividend policy can be a function of investment. But if investment is also a function of dividend policy, then the irrelevance proposition is no longer valid. Thus the validity of the irrelevance proposition rests ultimately on the determinants of investment.

Statistical investment studies have in general been based on some version of the acceleration principle. An excellent survey of these studies is given by Jorgenson[19] and Fama.[20] There is no evidence that investment depends on dividends. Thus the crucial assumption of Modigliani and Miller, that the production–investment decision and the dividend decision are separable (can be made independently of each other) has not been disproved yet.

II. A MANAGERIAL THEORY OF THE DIVIDEND-RETENTION DECISION: THE 'MANAGERIAL JOB-SECURITY' HYPOTHESIS

In a recent paper this author[21] postulated the hypothesis that managers set the

---

[18] It is interesting to note that Modigliani and Miller's 'irrelevance-of-dividends' hypothesis provides support for the 'residual theory of dividends'.

[19] D. W. Jorgenson, 'Econometric Studies of Investment Behaviour: A Survey', *Journal of Economic Literature*, 1971, pp. 1111–47.

[20] E. Fama, 'The Empirical Relationships Between the Dividend and Investment Decisions of Firms', *American Economic Review*, 1974, pp. 304–18.

[21] A. Koutsoyiannis, *Managerial Job Security and the Dividend Policy of Firms* (Department of Economics Research Series (University of Waterloo, 1981).

firm's target dividend payout at the level accepted as 'typical' by firms similar in size and other characteristics, *ceteris paribus*.

The foundation of this hypothesis is the managerial theory of the firm and the results of recent work on the basic motivation of individual economic units.

The managerial theory of the firm postulates that the goal of managers is the maximisation of their own utility rather than the maximisation of stockholder wealth.[22] The most important argument appearing in the managerial utility function is job security,[23] given that there is no organised market for managers, and managerial mobility between corporations is very low.[24]

Managerial job security is reinforced by growth,[25] which also allows managers to attain other subsidiary goals, such as high salaries, power and status, perquisites, and the resolution of personnel conflict, which is inevitable in large corporations. Thus managers become growth-seekers, searching continuously for profitable investment opportunities.

Recent theoretical work on the basic motivation of economic units has shown that the behaviour of individual economic agents can to a large extent be explained by their desire to be close, in some sense, to certain 'targets' or 'standards' which are gradually shaped over time.[26]

In the case of managers, it seems plausible to argue that deviations from the established code of behaviour in the industry in which the firm operates are undesirable, because they increase the risk of collective loss of managerial employment. A firm cannot indefinitely adopt a lower dividend payout than similar firms in the industry without increasing the risk of an ultimate fall in the price of its shares, a fact that might create shareholder dissatisfaction and set up conditions favouring a takeover raid. In both cases the likelihood of replacement of the managerial team is increased. Adherence to the industry code of behaviour safeguards the job security of managers.

Apart from its theoretical plausibility, the postulated 'job-security hypothesis' is compatible with the observed behaviour of managers. There is strong evidence[27] that managers have a definite preference for retained earnings over alternative sources of finance. The amount of retained earnings has increased substantially in the post 1945 period.[28] At the same time, however, dividend payments have shown a clear upward trend, with increases by far outnumbering dividend cuts.

---

[22] R. Marris, *The Theory of 'Managerial' Capitalism* (Macmillan, 1964); W. Baumol, *Business Behaviour, Value and Growth* (Harcourt, Brace, 1962); O. W. Williamson, *Corporate Control and Business Behaviour* (Prentice-Hall, 1970).

[23] J. K. Galbraith, *Economics and the Public Purpose* (Houghton Mifflin, 1973).

[24] R. Marris, 'A Model of the Managerial Enterprise', *Quarterly Journal of Economics*, vol. 57, pp. 185–209.

[25] Galbraith, *Economics and the Public Purpose*.

[26] H. Leibenstein, *Beyond Economic Man: A New Foundation for Microeconomics* (Harvard University Press, 1976).

[27] G. Grabowski and D. Mueller, 'Managerial and Stockholder Welfare Models of Firm Expenditures', *Review of Economics and Statistics*, 1972, pp. 9–24.

[28] *The Economic Report of the President* (Washington, D.C., US Government Printing Office, 1973).

Most firms have a 'target dividend policy', which shows a clear aversion of managers for dividend cuts.[29] This aversion can be explained by job-security considerations: a cut in the dividend usually has an adverse effect on shareholders' expectations, which results in a fall in the stock price. Shareholder dissatisfaction undermines managerial job security.

In summary. Within the framework of the managerial theory of the firm rational behaviour requires that the dividend policy be set so as to safeguard the job security of the management as a whole. This goal is attained if managers do not deviate, in the long run, from the average dividend payout of similar firms in the industry. Persistent upward deviations, apart from hindering the growth of the firm, may not be sustainable in all time periods, in which case the price of the stock would be adversely affected. On the other hand, persistent downward deviations are likely to induce dissatisfied shareholders to sell their stock, thus disturbing the voting control and hence jeopardising the job security of managers. Taking into account the above considerations, it seems plausible to argue that managers feel most secure in their employment if they keep their dividend payout close to the dividend policies of similar rival firms. Thus managers in any one period attempt to adjust the firm's actual dividend payout to the industry average.

Deviations from the long-run target dividend payout may occur, depending on the profitable investment opportunities open to the firm at any particular time, on the cost of alternative sources of finance, and on general business conditions.

The implementation of the target dividend policy depends on the growth and stability of earnings. It has been observed that managers will not increase the dividend unless they expect that the higher dividend payments can be maintained in the future.

It should be noted that the adjustment of the firm's current dividend payout to the desired (target) level can be attained gradually, due to various reasons, such as the availability of funds, investment opportunities, investors' preferences and attitudes at any one time, general economic and political conditions, and so on.

The results of a test of the managerial theory of the dividend-retention decision are reported in section IV below.

III.   THE DETERMINANTS OF THE DIVIDEND POLICY OF THE FIRM

From the discussion of the previous sections the following set of structural determinants of the dividend decision may be identified.

---

[29] Fischer, 'Some Factors Influencing Share Prices'; also J. C. Van Horne *et al., Financial Management and Policy*, 4th edn (Prentice-Hall, 1977) pp. 310–14.

(1) *The 'typical' dividend payout of the industry*. The managerial theory of the firm implies that the firm's long-run dividend payout is set on the basis of the 'average' or 'typical' payout of the industry. Managers cannot ignore persistently the dividend policy of rival firms without jeopardising their job security.

(2) *The growth of earnings of the firm*. If earnings are growing over time, managers will increase the dividend payout. Increased earnings allow higher dividends *and* higher retained earnings.

(3) *The stability of the earnings of the firm*. For managers to change their dividend policy, the stream of earnings must exhibit stability over time. If earnings are fluctuating widely (even around an upward trend), managers are likely to be reluctant to increase the dividend payout, because of the risk of not being able to pay the increased dividend in all periods.[30] Instability of earnings implies increased risk for stockholders and is likely to affect adversely the price of shares.

(4) *The available investment opportunities*. Theory and empirical evidence strongly support the view that managers are growth-seekers. Furthermore, managers have a definite preference for retained earnings over the other sources of funds. Large firms derive the bulk of their equity capital from retained earnings. One major reason for this development is that retained earnings have no cash cost for the firm (although they have an opportunity cost both for the firm and its shareholders – see Chapter 10). Another reason is the increase of the power of management in large corporations. Managers apparently have been able to persuade owners that retained earnings are used to the best of their interests. These considerations suggest that the greater the investment opportunities available to the firm, the greater the need for funds, and, given the managerial preference for retentions, the greater the tendency to retain a greater proportion of earnings in order to finance investment projects. Hence the dividend payout and investment opportunities are expected to be negatively related.[31] It should be clear that this relationship does not contradict the Modigliani–Miller neutrality proposition. Modigliani and Miller would not disagree with the view that dividends are a function of available investment opportunities. Their 'neutrality theorem' requires that the investment decision be independent of the dividend decision. Fama[32] (and other researchers) has provided evidence that the dividend payout is not an explanatory variable of the investment decision.

---

[30] The instability of earnings in the real world may explain the observed time lag in the upward adjustment of the target dividend payout. Dividends are increased only after the increase in earnings is believed (by managers) to be sustainable in the future. See J. Lintner, 'Distribution of Incomes of Corporations Among Dividends, Retained Earnings, and Taxes', *American Economic Review*, 1956, pp. 97–113; Brittain, *Corporate Dividend Policy*; E. Fama and H. Babiak, 'Dividend Policy: An Empirical Analysis', *Journal of the American Statistical Association*, 1968, pp. 1132–61.

[31] It has actually been observed that firms with high growth potential (Xerox, IBM, Polaroid) have higher retention ratios as compared with firms that show normal growth rates of assets (oil, steel, banking). Industries like tobacco and textiles, which are slow-growth industries, have a higher dividend payout.

[32] Fama, 'The Empirical Relationships Between the Dividend and Investment Decisions of Firms'.

(5) *The expected yield on investment opportunities*. This determines the attitude of shareholders towards an increased retention ratio. If the expected yield on new projects is high, shareholders are likely to accept a lower dividend payout, on the expectation of capital gains which will accrue from the favourable impact of high-yield investments on the price of their shares. Thus the relationship between the dividend payout and the prospective yield on new investment projects is expected to be negative. This relationship, also, does not contradict the Modigliani and Miller neutrality-of-dividend proposition. There is general agreement that a high retention ratio will tend to increase the price of the stock if the retained earnings are invested in projects which have a yield higher than the yield on existing assets. In this event the increase in price would be realised irrespective of the way in which such 'profitable' investment opportunities are financed. What is disputable is the effect of the financing decision *per se*. The traditionalists argue that the price increase would be higher if retentions were lower, while Modigliani and Miller maintain that the financing decision is neutral.

(6) *The availability and cost of alternative sources of funds*. Although retentions are attractive to managers, job-security considerations set a limit on their desire for internally generated funds. Furthermore, there is evidence[33] that internal finance is often inadequate for the investment plans of growth-seeking management. Finally, although the firm has a long-run target dividend policy and a target capital structure, deviations from these targets in the short run take place, depending on the cost of the alternative sources of funds. Retained earnings become more attractive to managers in periods of high costs of external financing. For example, in periods of tight credit the use of debt becomes difficult and expensive, while in periods of expansionary monetary policy low interest rates may make debt a more attractive source of funds, thus facilitating an upward change in the dividend payout. Similarly, in 'bearish' capital markets the issue of new stock becomes expensive due to inevitable underpricing, while if the stock market is 'high' new issues of stock may be sold at a premium, making retentions less necessary. Thus the cost of alternative sources of funds (debt and new equity) are expected to affect the dividend policy of the firm in any one period.

(7) *Shareholders' preferences and the discretion of managers to deviate from shareholder-wealth maximisation*. The managerial theory of the firm assumes that managers have some discretion in setting the goals of the firm so as to maximise their own welfare.[34] We mentioned earlier that managers have a definite preference for retained earnings. Investors in high-income brackets will also favour retentions, due to the higher taxation of dividends as compared with capital gains.[35] Another consideration that weighs in the minds of shareholders,

[33] Over the past twenty years or so there has been a substantial increase in the use of debt for financing the operations of the firm. See *The Economic Report of the President* (Washington, D.C., US Government Printing Office, 1979).

[34] Marris, *The Theory of 'Managerial' Capitalism*; also Galbraith, *Economics and the Public Purpose*.

[35] In the USA dividends are taxed at federal rates of up to 70 per cent, plus additional state taxes, while the tax on capital gains is generally limited to 25 per cent.

and may result in a preference for retentions, is the dilution of ownership coupled with flotations costs and underpricing of shares when funds have to be raised in depressed stock markets. On the other hand, investors dislike the uncertainty arising from the fluctuation of stock prices which follow general economic and political conditions over which they have no control. In these circumstances 'home-made dividends' are less attractive, and investors may acquire a strong preference for cash dividends.[36] Furthermore, for some investors dividends are an important source of income, and institutional investors are keen on cash dividends. Modigliani and Miller argue that in perfect capital markets there will be a 'clientele effect' (investors favouring retentions will be clients/shareholders of firms with low dividend payout, while income-conscious investors will invest in shares with high payout ratios), which on average will be neutral, because any clientele is as good as any other so far as managers are concerned. However, in real-world conditions, where brokerage fees, inconvenience in changing portfolios and fluctuating share prices are important, one would expect a considerable majority of investors to have a preference for dividends over capital gains. Under these conditions, whether managers will be able to retain more profits than shareholders would like depends on how powerful they are. The discretion of managers is inversely related to the dispersion of share-ownership. If shares are widely held, the managers will have a greater discretion, and vice versa.

(8) *Expectations about general business conditions.* In inflationary periods profits tend to increase. Hence managers may decide to increase the dividend payout. Furthermore, in inflationary conditions external financing becomes more attractive, making retentions less important. However, rising prices may create profitable opportunities which could absorb the higher profits and even result in a reduction of the dividend payout. Thus the effects of inflation (general business conditions) on dividends are multiple. The net effect of these opposing influences on the dividend-retention ratio will depend on their strength. Hence the relationship between the dividend payout and the expected rate of inflation is theoretically indeterminate.

(9) *Restrictions imposed by creditors.* When issuing bonds or raising loans, it is common for creditors to set some limits to the amount of earnings that a firm can pay as dividends, in order to ensure that the firm can service the debt. Such restrictions, however, are not important for the large corporations, whose earnings are in general much higher than what creditors consider 'a safe level'.

(10) *Restrictions imposed by law.* In order to prevent stockholders in high-income brackets from using the corporation as a means to avoid the high tax rates of personal income, tax regulations provide for a special surtax on 'improperly accumulated earnings'. However, the burden of proof that retained earnings are excessive is placed on the government authorities, and of course it is very difficult to build such a case against a corporation.

---

[36] H. Bierman Jr and J. E. Hass, *An Introduction to Managerial Finance* (Norton, 1973) pp. 188–90.

IV.   EMPIRICAL EVIDENCE ON THE DETERMINANTS OF THE DIVIDEND-PAYOUT DECISION

A.   The Modigliani—Miller 1966 Study

To test their dividend-neutrality proposition, Modigliani and Miller used the same model and methodology as the one adopted in testing their leverage-neutrality theorem.[37] After rejecting the leverage variable as insignificant, they introduced in their function a dividend variable, measured by the difference

$$\left[\begin{array}{c} \text{Dividend of} \\ \text{firm } j \end{array} \right] - \left[\begin{array}{c} \text{`Average' dividend} \\ \text{of firms in the sample} \end{array} \right]$$

The Modigliani—Miller specification is

$$\left(\frac{V - t_c D}{A} \right) = a_0 + a_1 \frac{\bar{X}(1 - t_c)}{A} + a_2 \frac{I^*}{A} + a_3 \left[dv_j - \begin{array}{c} \text{`Average sample} \\ \text{dividend'} \end{array} \right]$$

This specification assumes that firms follow an 'average dividend policy'. The function was estimated by applying OLS to three cross-section samples of US electric utility companies for the years 1954, 1956 and 1957.

Modigliani and Miller found that the coefficient of the dividend variable was not statistically significant, and concluded that this result provided support to their 'dividend-irrelevance' hypothesis. Their findings are parallel to those which they obtained for leverage: that is, when applying OLS the dividend variable is significant for the year 1954 only, while with the instrumental variables approach the coefficient of dividends is insignificant in all the three years of their study.

Their dividends test has been criticised on the same grounds as their leverage test, plus the following additional ones:

(1) Gordon[38] argued that the instrumental variable for earnings is basically a dividends variable. Therefore, it is not surprising that when an additional dividends regressor is introduced to the model, its coefficient appears as statistically insignificant.

(2) The omission of a leverage variable from the set of regressors, in conjunction with the measure of the dividend variable, introduces a downward bias in the coefficient of the latter and reduces its statistical significance.

Although Modigliani and Miller attempted to defend their estimate of the coefficient of earnings (which is equal to the inverse of the cost of capital, k_o), they openly accept that 'on the matter of the leverage and dividend tests, we would certainly agree with our critics that our results do not close the issue'.[39]

[37] F. Modigliani and M. Miller, 'Some Estimates of the Cost of Capital to the Electric Utility Industry, 1954—57', *American Economic Review*, 1966.

[38] M. Gordon, 'Some Estimates of the Cost of Capital to the Electric Utility Industry: Comment', *American Economic Review*, 1967.

[39] F. Modigliani and M. Miller, 'Some Estimates of the Cost of Capital to the Electric Utility Industry, 1954—57; Reply', *American Economic Review*, 1967, p. 1299.

In principle, however, their specification if basically appropriate for distinguishing between the alternative hypotheses regarding the leverage and dividend effects. But they did not use it appropriately. Furthermore, errors of measurement and wrong specification of their variables cast serious doubts on the validity of their results.

B.   Gordon's Study of the Dividend Effect

Gordon[40] uses the dividend approach to valuation (see Chapter 3). His starting-point is the function

$$P_t = f(Dv_t, g_t)$$

where Dv_t = current dividend

g_t = expected growth in dividend

According to the Shapiro–Gordon[41] constant-growth model, the valuation formula is

$$P_0 = \frac{D_o(1+g)}{k_o - g}$$

where $g = k_o^* b$, with k_o^* = return on investment $(k_o^* > k_o)$, and

b = retention ratio = $(\bar{X} - Dv)/\bar{X}$

Gordon argues that the most important source of growth in dividends is retained earnings. (New debt and issue of new stock at exceptionally favourable prices are relatively unimportant sources of financing new investment.) Furthermore, he argues that although the growth rate can be measured approximately by the expression

$$g = (b)(k_o) = \left(\frac{\bar{X} - Dv}{\bar{X}} \right) \left(\frac{\bar{X}}{A} \right) = \frac{\bar{X} - Dv}{A} = \frac{R}{A}$$

(where $R = \bar{X} - Dv$ = retained earnings),[42] growth prospects are better approximated by R rather than g: 'Investors are interested in growth and not rate of growth, since a high rate of growth, starting with a low initial value, will pay off in the heavily discounted distant future, and it will not be as attractive as a lower rate of growth starting from a higher initial value.'[43]

----

[40] M. J. Gordon, 'Dividends, Earnings and Stock Prices', *Review of Economics and Statistics*, 1959.

[41] M. J. Gordon and Eli Shapiro, 'Capital Equipment Analysis: The Required Rate of Profit', *Management Science*, 1965, pp. 102–10. This model has been presented in Chapter 3.

[42] Note that this measure of g assumes $k_o^* = k_o$, which is inconsistent with the growth model, in which retained earnings are used to finance investments with a yield k_o^* higher than the yield k_o of existing assets.

[43] Gordon, 'Dividends, Earnings and Stock Prices', p. 101.

From these theoretical considerations Gordon derives the empirical form

$$P = a_0 + a_1 Dv_t + a_2 R + u$$

where R = retentions, as a proxy for expected growth in dividends.

According to Gordon, $a_1 = 1/k_o$ = the reciprocal of the rate of return that the market requires on company stock without growth, and $a_2 = 1/k_o'$ = coefficient of what the market is willing to pay for growth. That is, a_2 is the reciprocal of k_o', the return on earnings that will accrue from retentions.

Gordon chose two years (1951, a war year, and 1954, a fairly stable year) and four industries (chemicals, food, steel, machine-tools). He expected a_1 to have a higher value for chemicals (due to its low risk, because of size and stability of earnings), and its value to decline for the other industries in the order they are ranked. ('Food' has stability of earnings; 'steel' has cyclical instability of earnings and hence a higher risk than food and chemicals; 'machine-tools' represent an industry with small-size firms whose earnings are cyclically unstable; thus on both criteria, 'size' and 'stability of earnings', the riskiness increases for food, steel and machine-tools.)

On *a priori* expectations $a_1 > a_2$, because $k_o < k_o'$, where k_o' is the required rate of return on retained earnings. Increases in dividends out of such retentions are uncertain and hence more heavily discounted than cash dividends which are certain.

Gordon does not comment on the constant intercept.

Regarding the values of the parameters between 1951 and 1954, one should expect a_1 to be lower for 1954, while a_2 may also be downward affected in 1954 due to some expectations of recession in that year.

Gordon's results may be summarised as follows.

The estimates of a_1 seem to satisfy mostly the *a priori* expectations set by Gordon: (a) the value of $\hat{a}_1$ is larger for 1954 than 1951; (b) for the year 1954 the value of $\hat{a}_1$ differs among industries as expected ($\hat{a}_1$ is larger for less risky industries); (c) $\hat{a}_1 > \hat{a}_2$ in 1954.

However, Gordon thought that the differences between $\hat{a}_1$ in the various industries, as well as the difference between $\hat{a}_1$ and $\hat{a}_2$ for all industries, were too high. He was also disturbed by the statistical insignificance of the growth-proxy variable for chemicals in 1954.

To improve his results Gordon modified his original model in the following ways. *First*, he divided his variables by the book value of assets in an attempt to capture possible effects of the size of firms on the value of the coefficients of the explanatory variables. Implicit in this approach is that P, Dv and R are non-linearly related. *Second*, apart from current dividends, Dv_t, Gordon introduced in the function $\bar{D}v$, the average dividend of the preceding five years. He did the same for retained earnings. His modified model is

$$\frac{P}{A} = \beta_0 + \beta_1 \frac{\bar{D}v}{A} + \beta_2 \frac{(Dv_t - \bar{D}v)}{A} + \beta_3 \frac{\bar{R}}{A} + \beta_4 \frac{(R_t - \bar{R})}{A} + u$$

The use of $\bar{D}v$ and $(Dv_t - \bar{D}v)$ implies that investors in the market value a stock on the basis of the average dividend during the prior five years *and* the amount by which the current value differs from this average. The same reasoning holds for $\bar{R}$ and $(R_t - \bar{R})$, the proxies for growth of dividends.

On *a priori* grounds:

(a) If $\beta_1 = \beta_2$ (or $\beta_3 = \beta_4$), then investors ignore the average dividend for the prior five years and consider only the current dividend.

(b) $\beta_2 = 0$ implies that the current dividend is ignored, and investors form their expectations on the basis of $\bar{D}v$ alone.

(c) $\beta_1 > \beta_2$ implies that investors adjust to a change in the dividend with a lag, i.e. the elasticity of expectations is less than unity. The opposite is true if $\beta_1 < \beta_2$.

From the results of his revised model Gordon concludes that the estimates $\hat{\beta}_1$ and $\hat{\beta}_2$ are an improvement on his earlier specification, because the coefficient of Dv_t (i.e. β_2) has more acceptable values and spread, and because $\hat{\beta}_2 < \hat{\beta}_1$, confirming the expectation of a time lag in the adjustment of the expectations of investors to changes in Dv_t.

However, Gordon finds the estimates of β_2 and β_3 'disappointing'. In particular, he is disturbed by the fact that $\beta_4 \geqslant \beta_3$, which means that investors are either indifferent to past performance or prefer a share for which retentions have increased to one for which they have fallen.

Gordon's model does not provide a test of either the leverage-neutrality or the dividend-neutrality hypotheses. Retentions are introduced as a proxy for the growth expectations of the firm. In such a model leverage could be tested by introducing an appropriate debt/equity variable. Similarly, the neutrality-of-dividend hypothesis could be tested by including a retention-ratio variable.

As a valuation model, Gordon's specification suffers from mis-specification of the set of explanatory variables (size, leverage, business risk, and retention ratios are not the same for the firms in his sample) as well as from errors of measurement of the included variables. In particular, retentions can hardly be considered a good proxy for growth of dividends.

C.   The Study of Friend and Puckett

This is probably the most confused and confusing study in the field of the 'dividend effect'. The confusion arises from the fact that the writers (in common with most other writers who explored empirically the 'dividend effect') do not understand the implications of their empirical form for investors' behaviour. It is hoped that a detailed discussion of the Friend and Puckett study will clarify several issues which are crucial for a meaningful test of the conflicting dividend hypotheses.

Friend and Puckett[44] maintain the hypothesis that 'for the average firm, irrespective of investor preferences between dividends and capital gains, dividend payout policies are such that at the margin a dollar of retained earnings should be approximately equal in market value to the dollar of dividends forgone'.

This hypothesis, according to Friend and Puckett, would imply, in the model,

$$P_t = a_1 Dv_t + a_2 R_t + u$$

that $a_1 = a_2$.

Other writers using this model have found that a_1 is about four times as high as a_2.[45] Friend and Puckett find this result unacceptable on the basis of 'theoretical considerations'.[46] It seems to us that the 'theoretical considerations' do not imply $a_1 = a_2$, except under some very restrictive conditions. In particular, for an all-equity firm which retains and reinvests earnings at a yield $k_o^* = k_o$, the present value of the firm was seen (in Chapter 3) to be

$$V_0 = \frac{\bar{X}_1}{k_o}$$

We may write this expression in the form $V_0 = (Dv + R)/k_o$, or on a per share basis

$$P_t = \frac{1}{k_o}\,(dv_t) + \frac{1}{k_o}\left(\frac{R}{N}\right)_t$$

Where R/N = retained earnings per share. In this restricted framework the discount rate of dividends is identical to the discount rate of retentions.

However, in the real world firms which remain all-equity financed and expand by reinvesting part of their earnings are rather rare. In growth conditions the model

$$P_t = f(Dv_t, R_t)$$

can provide a framework for testing the alternative dividend hypotheses only if R_t is taken as a proxy for the growth of future streams of dividends (see, for example, the earlier-discussed study of Myron Gordon.)[47] Friend and Puckett, however, do not accept this interpretation of retentions. For them the model

$$P_t = a_0 + a_1 Dv_t + a_2 R_t + u$$

($a_0 = 0$, $a_1 = a_2$) reflects the optimal dividend policy of management aiming at the maximisation of the price of the share to the existing shareholders. They believe that the results of other studies (which show $\hat{a}_1 > \hat{a}_2$) are in error.[48]

[44] I. Friend and M. Puckett, 'Dividends and Stock Prices', *American Economic Review*, 1964, pp. 656–81.

[45] Graham and Dodd, *Security Analysis*; Gordon, 'Dividends, Earnings and Stock Prices'; Durand, *Bank Stock Prices*.

[46] Friend and Puckett, 'Dividends and Stock Prices', p. 657.

[47] Gordon, 'Dividends, Earnings and Stock Prices'.

[48] Friend and Puckett, 'Dividends and Stock Prices', p. 659.

Before proceeding with their own model, we would like to stress that $\hat{a}_1 > \hat{a}_2$ does *not* invalidate the Modigliani–Miller dividend-neutrality theorem. As we saw, this theorem does not require the indifference of investors between current and future dividends or capital gains. It simply states that, in perfect capital markets, if managers have taken their investment decisions independently of dividends to be distributed, any increase in dividends will have to be financed by an equal amount of external finance; the increase in P due to the increase in the dividend payout would be exactly offset by a drop in price due to the dilution of ownership and/or the new debt. Investors' preferences for current dividends can be satisfied, in a perfect capital market, by a process of 'home-made' dividends (see section II). Hence the model

$$P_t = f(Dv_t, R_t)$$

cannot provide a satisfactory framework capable of distinguishing between the alternative dividend hypotheses.

Friend and Puckett state explicitly[49] that $a_1 = a_2$ assumes that the firm has already reached an optimal dividend/retention ratio, and is thus in equilibrium so far as dividend policy is concerned. Implicitly they assume that the optimal dividend-retention ratio is that which maximises the market price of the common shares. The finding $\hat{a}_1 > \hat{a}_2$, they argue, indicates *either* that managers pay too low a dividend over long periods of time, thus diverging from the equilibrium dividend policy (*optimal* dividend policy), or that there are statistical errors in the specified model. They seem to reject the first reason, on the grounds that such behaviour would be irrational for managers, an assumption which is highly questionable given the marginal discretion in large companies. Friend and Puckett believe that the finding that $\hat{a}_1 > \hat{a}_2$ is due to the omission of two variables, 'risk' and 'external finance', and to errors of measurement in the retained-earnings variable. Regarding risk, they argue that firms in an industry differ in size, product differentiation and leverage, that is, they differ in risk. Given that risk is negatively related to price, and to dividends (since managers favour a stable dividend policy), omission of risk variables (e.g. a measure of the variability of earnings for business risk, and a leverage variable for the additional risk using debt) results in an upward bias in the dividend coefficient.

The effect of omission of 'external sources of finance' is not clear in the Friend–Puckett analysis. This is due to their confusion between 'available investment opportunities' and 'methods of financing' these opportunities. According to basic valuation theory (see Chapter 3):

$$P = f\left[\left(\begin{array}{ccc} \text{Earnings} & & \text{Earnings} \\ \text{from existing} & \text{AND} & \text{from investment} \\ \text{assets} & & \text{opportunities} \end{array}\right)\right]$$

---

[49] Ibid, p. 660.

If Modigliani and Miller are correct (i.e. if the capital market is adequately perfect), the way of financing investment opportunities does not have any effect on the valuation of the firm. What matters is the amount of investment opportunities, their expected return $(k_o^* > k_o)$ and their duration. It seems plausible that retentions underestimate the investment opportunities, which are financed by all sources of finance (not only internal but external sources as well). Thus the variable 'external finance' is positively related to price and to retained earnings, and its omission from the function leads to an overestimation of a_2, the coefficient of retentions.

At the same time, one must take into account the fact that internal finance is an alternative to external finance. If managers prefer retentions to external finance, it is apparent that the latter is negatively related to retentions, so that the omission of external finance from the function imparts a downward bias in a_2, given the investment decision.

Thus the effect of the omission of 'external finance' is theoretically indeterminate.

Friend and Puckett argue that the measurement of risk, growth opportunities, and possible sources of finance in the future (and other variables) is very difficult. To take into account the inter-firm differences arising from these factors, they introduce to the function the lagged earnings—price ratio

$$\left(\frac{E_j}{P_j}\right)_{t-1}$$

Given that, by definition, this is the discount rate which the investors applied in $t - 1$ to the earnings available to the shareholders (net of interest and other fixed payments), Friend and Puckett seem to assume implicitly that any inter-firm differences (in pure business risk, leverage, profitability of investment opportunities) that may exist are reflected in the discount rate that investors used in the previous period for each firm's earnings. Thus the coefficient of $(E_j/P_j)_{t-1}$ has no clear *economic* meaning, since it absorbs the effects of all omitted variables. Friend and Puckett do not discuss their *a priori* expectations about the sign of the lagged discount rate, but from their results they seem to accept that a negative coefficient is acceptable. This implies that the lagged discount rate of earnings (to shareholders) is mainly a proxy for *total* risk, so that it cannot be used as a test of the leverage-neutrality hypothesis of Modigliani and Miller.

Friend and Puckett estimated two models:

$$P_j = a_0 + a_1 Dv_j + a_2 R_j + u_j$$

and

$$P_j = \beta_0 + \beta_1 Dv_j + \beta_2 R_j + \beta_3 \left(\frac{E_j}{P_j}\right)_{t-1} + v_j$$

(where u_j and v_j are the usual random variables).

They used cross-section samples for five industries (chemicals, electronics, electric utilities, foods, steel) and for the years 1956 and 1958.

Friend and Puckett fail to see that the introduction of the lagged E/P ratio does not much affect the values of the slopes (a_1 and a_2) of Dv and R, while the constant intercept increases enormously in the second specification. This is puzzling, given that on *a priori* grounds the constant should assume the value of zero.[50] Unfortunately, the writers do not report the standard errors of the intercepts so that we cannot assess their statistical significance. Changes in the intercept imply changes in factors omitted from the function (which are not affecting the slopes substantially in the Friend—Puckett study). Friend and Puckett do not comment on the size of the intercept in their two specifications.

An examination of the results of this study reveals that for 'electronics' and 'electric utilities' $\hat{a}_1 \approx \hat{a}_2$ in the original model. These are growth industries, and R_t may well be thought as a good proxy for the expected growth of future dividends, arising out of profitable investment opportunities. Thus, for these industries at least, the introduction of the lagged E/P ratio does not make any sense, neither in the Friend—Puckett framework nor for testing the conflicting dividend and leverage hypotheses.

The next 'major' change that the authors attempt is the 'correction' of the retention variable, R_t, from errors of measurement, which they attribute to short-run random variations in earnings. They argue that stock prices are related to 'normal' earnings and not reported/accounting earnings of the firm. Reported earnings are subject to a host of short-run economic and accounting errors, and investors, knowing this fact, form their expectations on the basis of 'normal' earnings, which are free from such short-term fluctuations. Friend and Puckett argue that all the error in reported earnings is reflected in retentions, R_t, which are the residual $R_t = \bar{X}_t - Dv_t$. Dividends are assumed to be error-free.

In order to obtain an estimate of 'normal' earnings Friend and Puckett use the 'empirical' expression

$$\frac{\left(\dfrac{E_j}{P_j}\right)_t}{\left(\dfrac{\bar{E}}{\bar{P}}\right)_t} = a_j + b_j t + u_j$$

where $\left(\dfrac{E_j}{P_j}\right)_t$ = discount rate of earnings (of shareholders) of the jth firm, in period t

$\left(\dfrac{\bar{E}}{\bar{P}}\right)_t$ = sample average discount rate of the total earnings (available to shareholders, i.e. after interest and other fixed payments)

[50] See ibid, p. 675.

Having fitted linear regressions of the above form, Friend and Puckett obtain an estimate of 'normal' earnings by the expression

$$E_{j,t}^n = P_{j,t}(\hat{a} + \hat{b}t)\left(\frac{\bar{E}}{\bar{P}}\right)_t$$

Finally, 'normalised' retained earnings are obtained by subtracting Dv_t from E_t^n:

$$R_{j,t}^n = E_{j,t}^n - Dv_{j,t}$$

The Friend–Puckett 'normalisation' procedure seems to us unacceptable on *a priori* grounds. To see this, let us write their trend equation in a slightly different form:

$$\left(\frac{E_j}{P_j}\right)_t = a\left(\frac{\bar{E}}{\bar{P}}\right)_t + (bt)\left(\frac{\bar{E}}{\bar{P}}\right)_t + v_t$$

From this form it is apparent that Friend and Puckett make the implicit assumption that the E/P ratio of each individual firm in the sample is proportional to the sample average $\bar{E}/\bar{P}$ ratio, with the coefficient of proportionality, a, changing autonomously over time.[51] It is not clear why this 'autonomous' change should occur in the real world. Even if it does, one should expect the coefficient b to be negative for large firms, contrary to Friend and Puckett's reported findings. To illustrate: the Friend–Puckett empirical trend-adjustment procedure implies that if, for example, the sample average discount rate increases for the chemical industry as a whole (the average price of stocks of chemicals corporations falls due to recession or other factors), the discount rate of a large firm like Dupont increases relative to the industry average, that is, Dupont appears to the minds of investors as more risky than the 'average' chemicals firm. On *a priori* grounds, one would expect the opposite: if recession conditions lead to a fall in the average price of chemicals, the decline of the price of a 'safe', well-diversified large firm like Dupont should be less than the average fall for the chemicals industry. Thus the positive sign of b for large firms, found by Friend and Puckett, is not readily acceptable.

Apart from the above theoretical reservations of the 'normalisation' procedure, the results obtained when E_{t-1}^n is substituted for E_{t-1} and R_t^n for R_t, are not carefully analysed by Friend and Puckett.

(1) They do not report results for 'electronics' and 'electric utilities' with 'normalised' earnings. As we mentioned earlier, these are growth industries, for which R_t may well be thought of as a good proxy for future increases in dividends arising from profitable investment opportunities. Apparently, the 'normalisation' procedure did not improve the Friend–Puckett results for these two industries.

(2) A comparison of the results suggests that the only important difference

---

[51] See A. Koutsoyiannis, *Theory of Econometrics*, 2nd edn (Macmillan, 1977); also J. Johnston, *Econometric Methods*, 2nd edn (McGraw-Hill, 1972).

that the use of 'normalised' variables makes is a dramatic change in the coefficient of the lagged variable $(E_j^n/P_j)_{t-1}$. The other coefficients are hardly affected (with the exception of the coefficient of R_t^n for the steel industry).

Friend and Puckett fail to comment on these findings. In particular, they fail to explain the huge increase in the absolute value of β_3 (the coefficient of the lagged variable). This can be easily explained if we take into account that the use of E_{t-1}^n in their lagged regressor is dominated by two constants: the sample mean $(\bar{E}/\bar{P})$ and t — which are given (the same) in a cross-section sample of firms in any one period. In particular, the normalised lagged earnings are

$$E_{j,t-1}^n = P_{j,t-1}[\hat{a}_j + \hat{b}_jt]\frac{\bar{E}}{\bar{P}}$$

so that the lagged regressor used in the final Friend—Puckett model is in fact

$$\left(\frac{E_j^n}{P_j}\right)_{t-1} = [\hat{a} + \hat{b}t]\frac{\bar{E}}{\bar{P}}$$

Given that t and $(\bar{E}/\bar{P})$ are the same for all firms in the industry, the lagged regressor differs among firms only so far as $\hat{a}_j$ and $\hat{b}_j$ are different. The absolute values of these coefficients are not reported by Friend and Puckett (except for the $\hat{b}$s of the chemicals industry, which are reported without standard errors). Thus it seems reasonable to infer that the large change in $\hat{\beta}_3$ is to a considerable extent due to the multiplicative factors t and $(\bar{E}/\bar{P})$.

Furthermore, Friend and Puckett fail to give any explanation for the high values of the constant intercept.

It seems to us that the whole study is dominated by the authors' obsession that the gap between $\hat{a}_1$ and $\hat{a}_2$ should not exist. As we pointed out earlier, such an expectation would be correct only if R_t is a perfect proxy for capital gains, since, according to the conventional valuation theory, it is Dv_t and $P_{t+1} - P_t$ which are discounted by the same rate of discount. R_t can at best be a proxy for expected capital gains in the real world, where uncertainty and imperfections in the capital market suggest that $\hat{a}_1$ should indeed be greater than $\hat{a}_2$.[52]

The specification used by Friend and Puckett is inappropriate for testing the Modigliani—Miller 'neutrality-of-dividends' hypothesis, because it does not include any separate retention-policy variable. No one questions the proposition that P will rise with retentions if k_o^*, the rate of return on investment, is very high, or conversely if k_o^* is low. A very profitable investment raises the price of a share regardless of how it is financed. The question at issue is whether the dividend rate (or retention rate) *per se* has an influence on the price of a share. The Friend—Puckett specification is consistent with all the conflicting hypotheses on the dividend-effect issue. Thus an increase in the proportion of earnings paid in dividends will tend to raise the price of the share, but this may be offset by an

---

[52] See Gordon, 'Dividends, Earnings and Stock Prices'.

adverse effect on the growth of earnings resulting from the decrease in retentions (or by an increase in external finance, if the investment decision is given), so that the price P may remain constant. Within the simple framework of Friend and Puckett, the finding that $\hat{a}_1 > \hat{a}_2$ does not refute the Modigliani–Miller dividend-neutrality theorem. Thus the conclusion of Friend and Puckett, that, because $\hat{a}_1 > \hat{a}_2$, 'management might be able to increase stock prices by raising dividends' is unwarranted. Nor does the coefficient β_3 (of the lagged discount rate) help in establishing a negative relationship between P and leverage, since β_3 reflects the effects of all the omitted variables, not only of leverage.

We must conclude that the Friend–Puckett study does not test the conflicting leverage and dividend propositions of the theory of the valuation of the firm.

D.   Brigham's and Gordon's 'Joint-Test' Study

Brigham and Gordon[53] attempted to test jointly the dividend-neutrality and leverage-neutrality theorems of Modigliani and Miller. They used a sample of sixty-nine electric utility companies for the years 1958 and 1962. We will discuss their study in some detail, because, despite its shortcomings, it is the only study that provides a specification capable of distinguishing between the conflicting leverage and dividend hypotheses.

The authors adopt the general growth model (see Chapter 3)

$$P = \frac{dv}{k_e - g}$$

where k_e = equity discount rate (= rate of return required by investors on a share)

g = growth rate = bk^*

b = retention rate

k^* = return on new investment ($k^* > k_e$)

For a levered firm (without taxes) Modigliani and Miller have shown that

$$k_{e,L} = k_o + (k_o - i)\frac{D}{S}$$

Substituting, we obtain

$$P = \frac{dv}{k_o + (k_o - i)\dfrac{D}{S} - g}$$

or

$$\frac{dv}{P} = k_o + (k_o - i)\frac{D}{S} - g$$

[53] E. F. Brigham and Myron J. Gordon, 'Leverage, Dividend Policy and the Cost of Capital', *Journal of Finance*, 1968, pp. 87–103.

Assuming that investors form their expectations within the framework of the constant-growth model, Brigham and Gordon used the above expression to test the two neutrality theorems of Modigliani and Miller. Brigham and Gordon adopted the empirical form

$$\left(\frac{dv}{P}\right)_j = a_0 + a_1(g)_j + a_2 \left(\frac{D}{E}\right)_j + a_3(\sigma_{\overline{X}})_j + a_4(W)_j + a_5(M)_j + u$$

where dv = dividend per share

dv/P = rate of return required by shareholders of a levered firm which retains some of its profits for reinvestment — that is, in this model $dv/P = k_{e,L}$, the equity rate of return of a growth firm which is levered

g = growth rate = bk^*

b = retention ratio = $R/\overline{X}$

k^* = rate of return on new investment = $\overline{X}/E$

D/E = leverage, measured in terms of *book value* of equity, E; the use of book value avoids spurious relations arising from the identity $S = PN$. If P appears in both the left- and the right-hand side of the model, a spurious relation is bound to affect the coefficient estimates

$\sigma_{\overline{X}}$ = variance of total earnings as a measure of risk

M_j = a 'size variable' (measured by the ratio of the assets of the jth firm to the average assets of the firms in the sample). This variable is introduced in order to take into account the reduction in risk with size due to the ease of marketability of shares and the smaller business risk of larger firms

W_j = ratio of the jth firm's sales of electricity to its sales of gas. This variable is included partly as a risk variable and partly as a 'corrective variable of the measure of growth'.[54]

On *a priori* grounds Brigham and Gordon expect

$$a_3 > 0; \quad a_4 < 0; \quad a_5 < 0$$

given that the over-all rate (by which investors discount the dividend stream) will increase with business risk, and will decline with size and degree of diversification.

Brigham and Gordon state that if $a_1 = -1$, then the sample evidence will support the Modigliani–Miller dividend-neutrality theorem. If $0 > a_1 > -1$, then dividend policy will affect the discount rate (and the price of shares); the dividend policy will not be neutral.

---

[54] The authors argue that 'It is generally thought that electric companies are subject to less competitive risks than gas companies. [Furthermore], many gas companies grew at a substantial yet unsustainable rate during the 1950s. Many natural pipelines were completed during this period, giving rise to large, one-time spurts in gas company growth' (ibid).

If $\hat{a}_1 = -1$, then $\hat{a}_0$ will be an unbiased estimate of k_o, the discount rate of an unlevered firm.

If $\hat{a}_2 = (\hat{a}_0 - i)$, then the Modigliani–Miller leverage-neutrality theorem will be supported.

If $\hat{a}_2 < (\hat{a}_0 - i)$, investors prefer corporate to personal leverage, contrary to the Modigliani–Miller leverage theorem.

Brigham and Gordon estimated their model for each year of the 1958–62 period. An examination of their results reveals the following:

(1) The authors do not give the standard error of $\hat{a}_0$, the most important coefficient of their analysis. Recall that $\hat{a}_0$ is an estimate of k_o, the over-all discount rate of an unlevered stream of earnings.

(2) The only significant estimate is the coefficient $\hat{a}_1$ of growth.

(3) The coefficient of leverage is insignificant, and the same holds for the coefficients of all the three 'risk' variables. Despite their insignificance, Brigham and Gordon use the coefficients of the risk variables to 'adjust' $\hat{a}_0$ as follows:

$$\hat{k}_o = \hat{a}_0 + \hat{a}_3\bar{\sigma}_X + a_4\bar{W} + a_5\bar{M}$$

where $\bar{\sigma}_{\bar{X}}$, $\bar{W}$ and $\bar{M}$ are the sample averages of the corresponding variables. This adjustment is required for the *ceteris paribus* clause of what they consider to be the 'correct' specification

$$\frac{Dv}{P} = k_o + a_1(bk^*) + a_2 \left(\frac{D}{E}\right)$$

The coefficient of growth ($g = bk^*$) is considerably lower than the expected value of -1. Brigham and Gordon are not satisfied with this result. Thus they introduce an additional variable, the growth of assets, g_A, in order to take into account possible errors of measurement in g, which, as we saw, they estimated as being equal to bk^*. They argue that, if assets grow, investors may well expect a higher growth in their dividends than the one measured by the product bk^*. In other words, g_A plays an informational role regarding the expected future growth of dividends. Furthermore, bk^* takes into account only the growth arising from retentions, but not growth from external finance. Omission of external finance biases the coefficient of bk^* and possibly the coefficient of leverage. (See the discussion of the study of Friend and Puckett.)

The introduction of g_A somewhat improves the authors' results. However, the inclusion of two growth variables is incompatible with what Brigham and Gordon consider the 'correct' specification for testing the hypothesis that the over-all discount rate is independent of the dividend policy. Thus they adopt the following *arbitrary* measure for growth:

$$g = 0.75\,(bk^*) + 0.25\,(g_A)$$

This implies that if $g_A = bk^*$, then g is set equal to bk^*. If $g_A > bk^*$, one-quarter of the difference is added to bk^* in measuring g.

The results obtained from the new measure of growth are marginally better.

However, the coefficient of the growth variable has still a value considerably larger than -1. From this result Brigham and Gordon conclude that their study provides evidence against the Modigliani and Miller 'dividend-neutrality' hypothesis.

Finally, Brigham and Gordon compare their estimate $\hat{a}_2$ with the difference $\hat{k}_o - i$, where i is the yield on bonds of electric utility companies. They found that $\hat{a}_2$ was much smaller than $\hat{k}_o - i$, and thus they conclude that their study refutes the Modigliani—Miller leverage-neutrality theorem.

These conclusions of Brigham and Gordon may be questioned on several grounds.

(1) Within the empirical form adopted by the authors the finding $\hat{a}_1 < 0$ verifies the generally agreed fact that the over-all discount rate $(= dv/P)$ is inversely related to growth, however financed. Brigham and Gordon's claim, that a value of a_1 larger than -1 refutes the Modigliani—Miller neutrality-of-dividends hypothesis, is not valid. The coefficient a_1 is associated with both the retention policy (as measured by b) and the yield k^*, given that within the constant—growth model $g = bk^*$. The constant-growth model would refute the Modigliani—Miller theory only if k^* were the same for all firms (in which case it would be absorbed by a_1) *and* the coefficient a_1 were insignificant.

(2) The positive sign of the coefficient of leverage is compatible with the Modigliani—Miller leverage theorem, that the over-all discount rate of earnings $(\bar{X})$ is a linear function of leverage. The finding that $\hat{a}_2 < (\hat{k}_o - i)$ may be attributed to various sources of error, such as errors in the variables (g is a completely arbitrary measure of growth; leverage is measured in terms of book values rather than market values, as Modigliani and Miller require), omission of important explanatory variables, and so on.

(3) The constant-growth model adopted by Brigham and Gordon has serious limitations (see Chapter 3). It is hard to accept the basic assumption of this model, that investors apply continuous compounding and that they have infinite time horizons.

(4) Brigham and Gordon make several additional assumptions, and adopt measurement methods of the variables which can be questioned on several grounds.

In summary, we think that the Brigham and Gordon study has serious shortcomings which cast doubt on their conclusions.

From the above survey we may conclude that the existing empirical evidence does not refute *any* of the conflicting leverage and dividends hypotheses. Thus the controversial issues remain still unresolved.

E.   A Test of the Managerial Theory of the Dividend Decision

In a recent paper this author[54] tested the hypothesis that managers set the firm's

[55] Koutsoyiannis, *Managerial Job Security and the Dividend Policy of Firms*.

target dividend payout at the level of the industry average dividend payout, because they feel that this policy safeguards the job security of the managerial team as a whole. The target or desired dividend payout is attained gradually, because various factors restrict managerial discretion.

The empirical specification adopted for the test of the managerial 'job-security hypothesis' is

$$[(DP)_{j,t} - (DP)_{j,t-1}] = b_0 + b_1 [(DP)_{I,t} - (DP)_{j,t-1}] + b_2 (g_{\bar{X}})_{j,t}$$

$$+ b_3 (\sigma_{\bar{X}})_{j,t} + b_4 (I^*)_{j,t} + b_5 (k^*)_{j,t} + b_6 (r)_t$$

$$+ b_7 \left(\frac{\Delta P}{P} \right)_{j,t} + b_8 (SC)_{j,t} + b_9 (GNP_d)_t + u_t$$

where $(DP)_{j,t} - (DP)_{j,t-1}$ = realised (actual) change in the dividend payout ratio of the jth firm in period t

$(DP)_{I,t-1} - (DP)_{j,t-1}$ = desired change in the dividend payout ratio, measured by the deviation of the firm's dividend payout from the most recently observed industry average payout

$g_{\bar{X}}$ = rate of growth of earnings of the jth firm (five-year average)

I^* = investment opportunities of the jth firm (five-year average growth rate of assets)

k^* = expected return on investment opportunities

r = cost of debt-financing

$\Delta P/P$ = expected cost of equity financing, measured by the percentage change of the price of the firm's stock

SC = a measure of dispersion of share-ownership

GNP_d = GNP deflator, as a measure of investors' expectations about general business conditions.

On *a priori* grounds the coefficients should appear with the following signs:

$$0 < b_1 < 1; \ b_2 > 0; \ b_3 < 0; \ b_4 < 0; \ b_5 < 0; \ b_6 < 0; \ b_7 > 0;$$

$$b_8 > 0; \ b_9 \lessgtr 0$$

The specified empirical model was estimated by applying OLS to time-series samples of fifteen large US firms for the 1960–76 period.

The results tentatively suggest that the dividend decision can be explained fairly well by the 'managerial job-security hypothesis'. In particular, it was found that:

(1) The dividend decision of managers is significantly related to the dividend policy of rival firms in the industry. There is a 'partial adjustment mechanism' at work, which supports the hypothesis that firms reach their target dividend payout gradually.

(2) The growth of earnings is an important determinant of the dividend payout. However, contrary to widespread beliefs, the variability of earnings does not seem to have a strong impact on the dividend policy of managers.

(3) Available investment opportunities have a strong effect on the dividend-retention decision. However, the profitability of such investment opportunities does not seem to be an important consideration. This is compatible with *a priori* expectations: for growth-seeking management total investment opportunities are more important than their profitability.

(4) The cost of debt and of new stock issues does not have a significant influence on the dividend decision. This is compatible with the hypothesis of a 'target dividend policy' set on the basis of the industry 'typical' dividend payout. It is also compatible with the hypothesis that managers are growth-seekers rather than cost-minimisers.

(5) In setting the dividend payout, managers are not restricted by considerations of shareholder voting control.

The above findings should be interpreted with great caution, due to data limitations and errors in the measurement of the variables. However, they are interesting enough to stimulate further research in the framework of the 'managerialist' theory of the dividend decision.

10. The Cost of Capital to the Firm

The cost of capital is a critically important topic for several reasons. First, the cost of capital determines the supply of funds to the firm. Second, the cost of capital is widely used by firms for their investment decisions (see Chapters 4 and 11). Third, knowledge of the cost of capital and of how it is influenced by debt and retentions is essential for determining the optimal capital structure and the optimal dividend policy of the firm.[1]

The cost of capital is the weighted average of the individual costs of the various sources of finance (debt, retained earnings, issue of new stock), with the weights being the proportions of each type of finance in the *optimal* long-run capital structure of the firm.

It is apparent from this definition that the determination of the firm's cost of capital requires knowledge of:

(a) the cost of the individual sources of funds; and

(b) the *optimal* weight of each source of funds in the long-run capital structure.

The cost of the individual sources of funds is determined in the stock market, where the prices of the various types of securities (shares, bonds, etc.) are defined by the interaction of investors (lenders-buyers and borrowers-sellers). The cost of a particular type of funds is the rate of return (yield) that investors require for that type of funds.

To understand this, recall (from Chapter 3) that the general valuation expression is

$$V_0 = \sum_{t=1}^{n} \frac{\bar{X}_t}{(1+k)^t} \tag{10.1}$$

[1] The cost of capital is essential for other decisions of the firm, such as leasing, bond-refunding and working-capital policy. The cost of capital is also vitally important in regulated industries, such as the electric, gas, telephone and transportation industries. Regulatory authorities seek to measure a utility's cost of capital, then set prices so that the company will just earn this rate of return. See J. Weston and E. Brigham, *Managerial Finance* (Dryden Press, 1975) p. 594.

where $\bar{X}_t$ = expected earnings from investing in a particular security

k = discount rate or required rate of return (yield) on the investment in the security.

In general, investors in the capital market evaluate each security by discounting the expected stream of earnings from the security by a discount rate appropriate to the riskiness of the security. This discount rate is called the *required rate of return* of the security, because investors will not buy (or hold) the security unless they receive (earn) at least a return equal to this discount rate. Thus, in valuation theory, *the required rate of return on a security, k, is the minimum rate of return necessary to induce investors to buy or hold that security*.

From the firm's standpoint, k is the cost of funds tied in the particular security, because, unless the firm pays a yield on this security equal to k, investors would not buy (or hold) the security, and the firm would be unable to raise funds of the particular type. For example, if k refers to a bond, it is the minimum rate of return that investors expect to earn, in order to buy (or hold) it, while for the firm k is the cost of funds to be raised by bonds (cost of new debt): unless the firm pays k per cent, it will be unable to raise funds by issuing bonds. (This point is further discussed on pp. 469–70.)

In summary, the required rate of return (by investors) on a particular security is the cost of funds (of the particular type) to the firm. The firm's over-all cost of capital is the weighted average cost of the individual sources of funds.

In the first section of this chapter we use the valuation concepts developed in Chapter 3 to explain the mechanics of estimating the cost of the various sources of funds.[2]

In the second section we re-examine the problem of choice of the 'optimal' capital structure of the firm, and we explain the estimation of the weighted average cost of capital of the firm.

In the third section we use the cost of capital to derive the supply-of-funds schedule of the firm.

It should be clear that in this chapter the assumption of certainty (which underlay our analysis of the investment decision in Chapter 4) is abandoned. Under certainty the cost of all sources of funds is the same: it is the risk-free market interest rate. However, under conditions of uncertainty the various sources of funds have a different degree of risk and hence a different cost. The firm's cost of capital is the weighted average cost of the various sources of funds.

---

[2] We stress that the estimation of the cost of capital involves the *mechanics* of finding the cost of the different sources of funds and combining them in order to obtain a numerical value for the average cost of capital of the firm. The *determinants* of the cost of capital are examined in the theory of valuation (which we presented briefly in Chapter 3) and the theory of portfolio selection (which we will develop in Chapter 12).

I.   THE COST OF THE DIFFERENT SOURCES OF FUNDS

In this section we will examine the cost of the three main sources of funds: the cost of debt (issue of new bonds), the cost of equity capital (issue of new stock), and the cost of retained earnings.

There are two equivalent approaches in estimating the cost of the specific sources of finance:

A. Conventionally, the cost of each type of finance is estimated by solving the valuation expression appropriate for each type of funds. Next, these individual costs are assigned some weight according to 'the optimal capital structure' of the firm, and the *average cost of capital* is estimated.

B. In the second approach each individual cost is expressed as a function of k_o, the discount rate (required rate of return) that security owners (investors) apply to estimate the present value of a stream of earnings generated by an *unlevered firm*. Next, k_o is estimated, and it is used to calculate the individual costs of the particular sources of funds. Finally, these costs are weighed according to 'the optimal capital structure' of the firm in order to obtain the weighted average cost of capital.

We shall examine these two approaches in some detail.

A.   The Conventional Method of Estimating the Cost of Capital for Specific Sources of Funds

We said earlier that the cost of a source of funds is the discount rate that equates the present value of the future payments that the firm will have to make to the amount of funds received by the firm (net of underwriting and other costs). Thus the cost of a specific type of financing will be estimated by solving the appropriate valuation expression for the discount rate which investors in the market apply for that particular type of funds. For each of the three main sources of finance we will first derive the appropriate valuation expression (in which k is the required rate of return by investors/suppliers of funds), and next we will be solving this expression for k, to estimate the cost to the firm of these funds.

(i) *The cost of debt* (k_d)

(a) *Perpetual bond*

A perpetual bond is a bond which pays a given *amount* of interest, Y, yearly in perpetuity. The present value of such bond is computed as follows:

$$V_B = \frac{Y}{(1 + k_d)} + \frac{Y}{(1 + k_d)^2} + \ldots + \frac{Y}{(1 + k_d)^\infty}$$

or

$$V_B = Y \sum_{t=1}^{\infty} \frac{1}{(1 + k_d)^t} \tag{10.2}$$

We saw in Chapter 3 that this expression reduces to

$$V_B = \frac{Y}{k_d} \tag{10.3}$$

where Y = annual *amount* of interest (in dollars)

$\qquad k_d$ = required rate of return for the bond issue

Solving for k_d we obtain

$$k_d = \frac{Y}{V_B} \tag{10.4}$$

For example, if the firm issues new bonds and sells them for $100,000, for which it will have to pay total interest (Y) of $7,000 yearly, the before-tax cost of debt is

$$k_d = \frac{\$7,000}{\$100,000} = 7\%$$

However, interest payments are tax-deductible, so that the after-tax cost of debt is

$$k_i = \begin{bmatrix} \text{Cost of} \\ \text{debt after} \\ \text{tax} \end{bmatrix} = k_d(1 - t_c) \tag{10.5}$$

where t_c is the corporate tax rate. In the USA the corporate tax rate is approximately 50 per cent. Thus in our example the cost of (perpetual) debt to the firm is

$$k_d(1 - t_c) = 0.07(1 - 0.50) = 0.035 \text{ or } 3.5\%$$

Because interest charges are tax-deductible, the after-tax cost of debt is substantially less than the before-tax cost.

Note that the cost of debt refers to *new* debt, not to the interest on any old, outstanding debt. In other words, the firm is interested in *the cost of new debt*, or *the marginal cost of debt*. This is the case because the firm considers the cost of debt in relation to its investment decision: the cost of capital is relevant to the decision whether to raise capital to make new investments. Whether the firm borrowed at high or low rates in the past is irrelevant to the investment decision. Past debts and interest payments are important in that they affect the earnings available to stockholders, but they are not relevant for *current* investment decisions (see Chapters 4 and 11).

(b) *Bonds with a finite maturity*

If a firm issues bonds which mature after n periods, the cost of debt is estimated by solving for k_d the expression

$$V_B = \sum_{t=1}^{n} \frac{Y_t}{(1 + k_d)^t} \tag{10.6}$$

and then adjusting k_d for the tax effect. Recall that the solution in this case involves an iterative procedure (see Chapter 3) or the use of special computer programs.

For example, assume that a firm issues three-year maturity bonds which pay $50 interest and have a $1,000 maturity value each (equal to their market (face) value). To find k_d we must solve the equation

$$1,000 = \frac{50}{(1 + k_d)} + \frac{50}{(1 + k_d)^2} + \frac{50}{(1 + k_d)^3} + \frac{1,000}{(1 + k_d)^3}$$

We choose (arbitrarily) an initial discount rate of 0.04 (or 4 per cent). Using Table 2 of Appendix 3.2 of Chapter 3, we find the following present value:

Year	Earnings	PVIF (for 4%)	Present value
1	50	0.962	$ 48.10
2	50	0.925	$ 46.25
3	1,050	0.889	$ 933.45

Total $1,027.80

Since the present value with 4 per cent is 1,027.80 ($> 1,000$), we must try a higher interest rate, say 5 per cent. The results of the iteration are shown below:

Year	Earnings	PVIF (with 5%)	Present value
1	50	0.952	$ 47.60
2	50	0.907	$ 45.35
3	1,050	0.864	$ 907.20

Total $1,000.15

Since the new present value is equal (approximately) to the receipts of the firm from selling the bond ($F_0 = 1,000$), the cost of debt before tax is $k_d = 5$ per cent. The after-tax cost of debt (assuming $t_c = 0.50$) is

$$k_i = k_d(1 - t_c) = 0.50(1 - 0.50) = 0.025 \text{ or } 2.5\%$$

As we saw in Chapter 8, the cost of debt to the firm is affected by the amount of debt that the firm uses in its capital structure (leverage). At low debt/equity (D/S) ratios the cost of debt does not increase, because creditors feel that the earnings (EBIT) of the firm are adequate for payment of the fixed charges of debt. However, the more debt the firm has, the higher the interest requirements; and the higher the interest charges, the greater the probability that earnings will not be sufficient to meet these charges. Creditors will perceive this increasing risk as the debt/equity ratio rises, and they will begin charging a risk premium, above the riskless rate, causing the cost of debt to the firm to rise. Since creditors are risk-averters, they will demand that interest rates be increased to compensate for the increased risk. The relation between the cost of debt and the debt/equity ratio is shown in Figure 10.1.

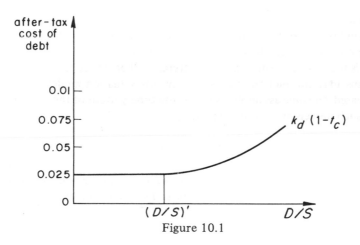

Figure 10.1

This relationship is useful in determining the average cost of capital, since the debt/equity ratio is the weight which will be assigned to the cost of debt (see section II below). It is also useful in the derivation of the supply-of-funds schedule of the firm (see section III below).

(ii) *Cost of new common stock or cost of equity capital* (k_e)

The cost of equity capital is the most difficult to estimate for two main reasons. First, the stream of future earnings is not known as in the case of bonds and preferred stock. (The cost of preferred stock is discussed in Appendix 10.1.)[3] Second, common stock dividends are generally expected to grow. Hence we cannot apply the simple expressions of annuities and perpetuities. However, the general procedure for estimating the cost of equity capital is the same as that for

---

[3] In economic literature the cost of capital to the firm is discussed without taking into account preferred stocks, because they constitute an unimportant source of finance.

any other security: we first derive the appropriate valuation expression, and then we solve it for the discount rate k_e, which (as we saw) is *both* the required rate of return by investors *and* the cost of equity capital to the firm.

In Chapter 3 we developed several valuation models of common stock. We revise them below.

(a) *General valuation model*

We saw in Chapter 3 that the present value of a stock held for n periods is

$$P_0 = \sum_{t=1}^{n} \frac{dv_t}{(1 + k_e)^t} \tag{10.7}$$

This is a general valuation model in the sense that the time pattern of dividends (dv_t) can take any form: dividends (over the n time horizon) can be rising, falling, remain constant, or fluctuating over time. However, the solution of this general model is tedious, especially if n is large. Iterations become complex, and computer programs may not be available. Hence simpler valuation models are commonly used, based on some assumptions about the time pattern of the dividend stream. Three such models are now presented.

(b) *Valuation of stocks with no (zero) growth*

If the stream of expected dividends consists of equal amounts which do not grow over time $(dv_1 = dv_2 = \ldots = dv)$, the general valuation expression reduces to

$$P_0 = \frac{dv}{k_e} \tag{10.8}$$

In this case the cost of capital is the dividend yield

$$k_e = \frac{dv}{P_0} \tag{10.9}$$

(c) *The constant-growth model (or the Shapiro–Gordon model)*

If dividends grow over time at a constant rate g, we saw in Chapter 3 that the valuation expression reduces to

$$P_0 = dv_0 \left(\frac{1 + g}{k_e - g} \right) = \frac{dv_1}{k_e - g} \tag{10.10}$$

Thus the cost of equity capital would be

$$k_e = \frac{dv_1}{P_0} + g = \frac{dv_0(1 + g)}{P_0} + g \tag{10.11}$$

The critical assumptions for the application of this model are: (a) the dividends per share are expected to grow forever at a compound rate of growth g; and (b) this constant-growth rate must be less than the required rate of return ($g < k_e$).

The important factor in estimating k_e in this model is the forecast of the growth rate g. Usually the growth rate over the past five to ten years is assumed to reflect accurately the future rate of growth.[4] If this assumption does not seem plausible, the managers must make every effort to estimate the future rate of growth.

(d) General growth models

If the assumption of constant growth is unrealistic, one should apply other valuation expressions. For example, if for the initial five years the growth is expected to be very high, g_1, while for all subsequent years growth is expected to drop to a lower level, g_2, the appropriate valuation expression is

$$P_0 = \sum_{t=1}^{5} dv_0 \frac{(1 + g_1)^t}{(1 + k_e)^t} + \sum_{t=6}^{\infty} \frac{dv_5(1 + g_2)^{t-5}}{(1 + k_e)^t} \qquad (10.12)$$

It is apparent that the solution for k_e with this model is more complex than the estimation of k_e from the constant-growth model. For this reason the constant-growth model is usually adopted.

If the firm sells the new shares at a price lower than their face value, and incurs flotation costs of f per cent, the general valuation expression becomes

$$P_f = P_0(1 - f) = \sum_{t=1}^{n} \frac{dv_t}{(1 + k'_e)^t} \qquad (10.13)$$

where f is a percentage which takes into account the lower price and the flotation costs. P_f denotes the net receipts, i.e. receipts after the subtraction of flotation costs and underpricing.

In the case of the constant-growth model, k'_e is estimated from the expression

$$k'_e = \frac{dv_1}{P_0(1 - f)} + g \qquad (10.14)$$

For example, if $P_0 = \$100$, and the firm has to sell at a price of $\$90$, and has flotation costs of 2 per cent on the market price P_0 (i.e. flotation costs are

---

[4] The average growth rate should be estimated by the expression of the *geometric* mean

$$g = \sqrt[n]{(g_1)(g_2) \dots (g_n)} \qquad \text{or} \qquad \log(\bar{g}) = \frac{1}{n} \sum_{i=1}^{n} \log(g_i)$$

where n = number of yearly growth rates being averaged.

$2.00), then $P_n = P_0(1 - 0.12)$ or $P_n = 100(0.88) = \$88$. If the expected dv_1 is $5 and $g = 8$ per cent, then the cost of *new* equity capital is

$$k_e' = \frac{\$5}{\$100 \, (1 - 0.12)} + 0.05 = \frac{5}{88} + 0.05$$

or

$$k_e' = 0.057 + 0.05 = 0.107 \text{ or } 10.7\%$$

The cost of new equity is affected by the amount of debt in the capital structure (see Chapter 8). The required rate of return on new equity might be thought to be comprised of three parts

$$k_e' = i + \phi_1 + \phi_2$$

where i = the risk-free interest rate (time value of money)

ϕ_1 = a premium for business risk

ϕ_2 = a premium for financial risk (from the use of debt)

The two types of risk have been discussed in Chapter 3. Recall that the business risk arises from the relative dispersion (variability) of the expected future earnings. The premium for business risk, ϕ_1, is a function of the type of the product of the firm, its diversification, the capital intensity of the method of production, and so on. The premium for financial risk, ϕ_2, depends upon the degree of financial leverage, that is, the amount of debt employed. If the firm has no debt, and its investments consist entirely of government securities, its cost of equity capital will approximate the risk-free rate of interest, i. If the firm invests in assets other than government securities, investors will demand a higher return on their equity, to compensate for the higher business risk. Similarly, if the firm uses debt to finance part of its operations, investors feel the risk of reduced earnings available to them, after payment of interest payments, and ask a premium (ϕ_2) to compensate them for this increased risk.

The above relation is shown in Figure 10.2. This relation is essential in deriving the weighted average cost of capital to the firm and the supply-of-funds schedule (see section III).

(iii) *Cost of retained earnings* (k_R)

A large portion of the firm's operations is usually financed from retained earnings. One might think that such funds have no cost. This is not so. The cost of retained earnings is the opportunity cost of forgone dividends by shareholders. If all earnings were distributed as dividends, the stockholders would have the opportunity to invest these dividends in shares of other firms of the same risk class. Thus the cost of retained earnings is the cost of equity capital, adjusted for: (a) the absence of underpricing and flotation costs; (b) the personal income tax, t_p, that stockholders would pay if they had received the retained earnings in the

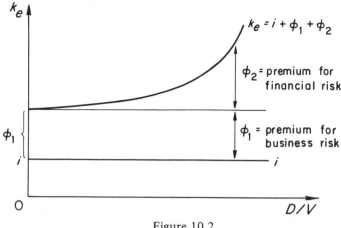

Figure 10.2

form of dividends; and (c) the brokerage fees which stockholders would pay if they were to invest in shares of other firms.

The adjustment for the absence of underpricing and flotation costs is attained by using the current market price P_0 (rather than the 'net receipts', P_f) when solving for k_e the general valuation expression

$$P_0 = \sum_{t=1}^{\infty} \frac{dv_t}{(1 + k_e)^t} \tag{10.15}$$

The k_e obtained from the above expression (or from the constant-growth model) is next adjusted for the weighted average income tax rate for *all* stockholders and the weighted brokerage commission

$$k_R = k_e(1 - t_p)(1 - B) \tag{10.16}$$

where t_p is the weighted average tax rate of *all* shareholders, and B is the weighted average brokerage fees, expressed as a percentage. For example, if the equity cost of capital is 10 per cent, the average tax rate is 40 per cent and B is 3 per cent, the cost of retained earnings is

$$k_R = 0.10 (1 - 0.40) (1 - 0.03) = 5.8\%$$

The computation of the weighted average tax rate is practically impossible, due to lack of data covering the tax brackets of individual shareholders. Some studies[5] suggest that the average tax rate of individual stockholders is in the proximity of 40 per cent. But the weighted average tax rate for the stockholders of a *specific*

---

[5] See Vincent Jolivet, 'The Weighted Average Marginal Tax Rate on Dividends Received by Individuals in the US', *American Economic Review*, 1966, pp. 473–7; also Edwin Elton and Martin Gruber, 'Marginal Stockholder Tax Rates and the Clientele Effect', *Review of Economics and Statistics*, 1970, pp. 68–74.

firm will depend upon the type of its stockholders. Such estimates are extremely difficult.

To bypass this problem some writers[6] have suggested an alternative method for the estimation of the cost of retained earnings: the 'external-yield' method. According to this method, the cost of retained earnings is measured as the opportunity cost *to the firm* (as opposed to individual stockholders) of the retained earnings: the firm should evaluate external investment opportunities (e.g. the acquisition of another firm, or of a division of another company, having the same risk as the acquiring firm), and define the cost of retentions as the highest yield attainable from such external investments.

The 'external-yield' approach has several shortcomings. Estimation of the *firm's* external investment opportunities is not an easy job. Thus most writers use *either* k_e as the cost of retained earnings, *or* k_e adjusted downwards by 40–50 per cent for the tax effect.

In summary, the cost of specific sources of funds in conventional finance theory is found by solving for k the general expression

$$V_0 = \sum_{t=1}^{n} \frac{Y_t}{(1 + k)^t}$$ (10.17)

where V_0 represents the net receipts of the firm.

Applying this procedure, the cost of funds was found to be:

(a) *Cost of debt*

$$k_i = k_d(1 - t_c)$$ (10.18)

where k_d is computed from the expression

$$V_B = \sum_{t=1}^{n} \frac{Y_t}{(1 + k_d)^t}$$ (10.19)

or, for perpetual debt, from the expression

$$k_d = \frac{Y}{V_B}$$ (10.20)

(b) *Cost of new equity: k_e'*

usually estimated by the constant-growth model, which gives

$$k_e' = \frac{dv_1}{P_0(1 - f)} + g = \frac{dv_0(1 + g)}{P_0(1 - f)} + g$$ (10.21)

---

[6] For example, Ezra Solomon, *The Theory of Financial Management* (Columbia University Press, 1963) pp. 53–5.

(c) *Cost of retained earnings:* k_R

$$k_R = k_e(1 - t_p)(1 - B) \tag{10.22}$$

or

$$k_R = \left(\frac{dv_1}{P_0} + g\right)(1 - t_p)(1 - B) \tag{10.23}$$

The above conventional approach does not allow a direct comparison of the costs of the various sources of funds.

B. An Alternative Method for Estimating the Cost of Specific Sources of Funds

(i) *Definitions and relationships*

In this approach the cost of individual sources of funds is expressed as a function of k_o, the discount rate that security owners (investors) apply to estimate the present value of a stream of earnings generated by an *unlevered firm*.

We will first show that the investors' discount rate (k_o) is the unlevered firm's cost of equity capital.

We saw in Chapter 8 that the after-tax expected earnings of an unlevered firm are $\bar{X}(1 - t_c)$, where t_c is the corporate tax rate. The present value of the unlevered firm is

$$V = \frac{\bar{x}(1 - t_c)}{k_o} \tag{10.24}$$

where k_o = investors' *discount rate* for an unlevered stream of earnings. Dividing through by N, the number of outstanding shares, we obtain

$$P = \frac{\bar{x}(1 - t_c)}{k_o} \tag{10.25}$$

where P = price of the share of the unlevered firm
$\bar{x}$ = earnings per share

From expression (10.25), k_o can be interpreted as the *minimum rate of return* required by an investor to induce him to purchase or hold shares of the unlevered firm at the market price P. Thus for the firm k_o is the cost of equity capital, because unless the firm pays a yield on its share equal to k_o, investors would not buy the share (and the firm would be unable to raise equity capital).

Having identified k_o as the cost of equity capital of an unlevered firm, we will develop expressions for the cost of the three main sources of funds in terms of this coefficient. For this we will first derive the internal rate of return (IRR) criterion for investment decisions in a way different from the one developed in Chapter 4.

We saw in Chapter 4 that according to the IRR criterion an investment project should be accepted if its internal rate of return exceeds the cost of funds required to finance it, because in this case the earnings of the firm, and hence the price of its shares, will rise, thus increasing the wealth of current shareholders. Assuming that the goal of managers is the maximisation of this wealth, they should undertake investment projects up to the point where the internal rate of return (marginal efficiency of investment) is equal to the cost of capital.

Put it another way, from the standpoint of the current owners of the firm, an investment is worth undertaking only if it leads to an increase in the market value of their shares (S_L).

Given

$$V_L = S_L + D \tag{10.26}$$

the IRR criterion for investment decisions may formally be expressed as

$$\frac{dS_L}{dI} \geqslant 0 \tag{10.27}$$

(where dI = additional investment), or equivalently

$$\frac{dV_L}{dI} \geqslant 1 \tag{10.28}$$

*   *   *

PROOF

Assume that the additional investment, dI, can be financed either by issue of new stocks or new bonds

$$dI = dS_N + dD_N \tag{10.29}$$

where dS_N = market value of *new* stock
dD_N = market value of *new* debt

For simplicity we assume that the issue of either new stock or bonds does not affect the market value of the already outstanding debt. Thus, by definition, the change in the total value of the firm, following the increase in investment, is equal to the sum of the change in (a) the value of old equity, (b) the value of new equity, and (c) the value of new debt:

$$\frac{dV_L}{dI} = \frac{dS_L}{dI} + \left[\frac{dS_N}{dI} + \frac{dD_N}{dI} \right] = \frac{dS_L}{dI} + 1 \tag{10.30}$$

(given $dS_N + dD_N = dI$, by expression (10.29). In order for

$$\frac{dV_L}{dI} \geqslant 1$$

we must have

$$\frac{dS_L}{dI} \geq 0$$

QED

*　　　　　　*　　　　　　*

The criterion $dS_L/dI \geq 0$ can be expressed in terms of the required rate of return on investment, and in terms of the cost of capital. Recall that the present value of the stream of earnings of a levered firm is

$$V_L = \frac{\bar{X}(1 - t_c)}{k_o} + t_c D \qquad (10.31)$$

Differentiating V_L with respect to I, we obtain

$$\frac{dV_L}{dI} = \frac{d\bar{X}(1 - t_c)}{dI} \times \frac{1}{k_o} + \frac{dD}{dI} \times t_c \qquad (10.32)$$

(Note that dD/dI is the change in debt if new investment is financed with borrowed funds (bonds).)

Equating expression (10.32) to (10.30) and rearranging, we find

$$\frac{dS_L}{dI} = \left[\frac{d\bar{X}(1 - t_c)}{dI} \times \frac{1}{k_o} + \frac{dD}{dI} \times t_c \right] - 1 \qquad (10.33)$$

The condition $dS_L/dI \geq 0$ requires

$$\left[\frac{d\bar{X}(1 - t_c)}{dI} \times \frac{1}{k_o} + \frac{dD}{dI} \times t_c \right] \geq 1 \qquad (10.34)$$

This condition reduces to the requirement

$$\left[\frac{d\bar{X}(1 - t_c)}{dI} \right] \geq k_o \left[1 - \frac{dD}{dI} \times t_c \right] \qquad (10.35)$$

The left-hand side is the change in the after-tax revenue arising from the change in investment, that is, the rate of return on the investment (k_o^*), or IRR. Hence the quantity on the right-hand side is the cost of capital of the firm, since this was *defined* as the minimum rate of return on investment which induces the owner-shareholders to accept this investment, because it increases the market value of their shares. Denoting this quantity by C_A we have:[7]

$$\begin{bmatrix} \text{Cost of} \\ \text{capital} \\ \text{of levered} \\ \text{firm} \end{bmatrix} \equiv C_A = k_o \left[1 - \frac{dD}{dI} \times t_c \right] \qquad (10.36)$$

[7] A formal proof of this expression is given on page 477 below.

Note that this is the cost of capital for a firm which uses debt and equity for financing its investment. Retained earnings will be introduced at a later stage.

From expression (10.36) we can find the individual cost of debt and equity.

(ii) *The cost of pure equity financing of a levered firm* (C_E)

If the firm uses *only new stock* for financing its investment, then $dD/dI = 0$, and the cost of equity capital is found, from expression (10.36), to be equal to the discount rate k_o of an unlevered stream of earnings:

$$C_E = k_o \qquad (10.37)$$

This expression should be modified in order to take into account the flotation costs and underpricing which may be necessary for selling the new issue. If such costs are denoted by a percentage h, the cost of pure equity financing becomes

$$C_E = k_o \left(\frac{1}{1-h} \right) \qquad (10.38)$$

(iii) *The cost of pure debt financing of a levered firm* (C_D)

If the firm uses *only debt* for financing its investment, then $dD/DI = 1$, and from expression (10.36) it is seen that the cost of debt financing is

$$C_D = k_o(1 - t_c) \qquad (10.39)$$

(iv) *The cost of retained earnings* (C_R)

To complete the analysis of the cost of capital, we must examine the cost of retained earnings and incorporate it into the expression of the average cost of funds.

The cost of retained earnings is the return that these earnings should yield (when reinvested by the firm) in order for stockholders to be indifferent between cash dividends and retained earnings.

To simplify the analysis we will assume a one-period time horizon of investors, and we will examine their income and wealth positions under the two alternatives open to them: reinvestment by the firm, or cash dividend subsequently reinvested by themselves.

We saw in Chapter 9 that the dividend which investors will receive at the end of one period is the same in either case. If their wealth is also the same, investors would be indifferent between retained earnings and cash dividends.

(1) If the firm retains all its earnings and reinvests them at a yield C_R, at the end of one period its income will have increased by a factor $(1 + C_R)$:

$$\bar{X}(1 - t_c)(1 + C_R) \qquad (10.40)$$

The price of its shares will also increase by the same factor

$$P(1 + C_R) \tag{10.41}$$

yielding to investors a capital gain equal to PC_R, on which they will have to pay a capital-gains tax of $(PC_R)t_g$. Thus the wealth position of an investor at the end of one period, if the firm retains and reinvests its earnings, is

$$W_1 = P(1 + C_R) - (PC_R)t_g = P[1 + C_R(1 - t_g)] \tag{10.42}$$

(2) If the firm distributes all its earnings as cash dividends, investors will have an after-tax income of

$$\bar{X}(1 - t_c)(1 - t_p) \tag{10.43}$$

which they can reinvest in shares of the same firm (or of other firms in the same risk class) at the current yield k_o. The investors do not expect any rise in the share price (which, thus, remains at the level of $P(1 - t_p)$), so that capital-gains taxes are not relevant. But their wealth will increase as a result of buying more shares. On each share they earn the current yield k_o, so that they will receive an income

$$P(1 - t_p)(1 + k_o) \tag{10.44}$$

Consequently the wealth position of shareholders is

$$W_2 = P(1 - t_p)(1 + k_o) - P(1 - t_p) = P[1 + (1 - t_p)k_o] \tag{10.45}$$

If the investor is to be indifferent between the above two alternatives, his wealth position must be the same. Thus equating (10.42) with (10.45) and solving for C_R we find the required rate of return on retained earnings. That is, the cost of retained earnings is

$$C_R = k_o \left[\frac{(1 - t_p)}{(1 - t_g)} \right] \tag{10.46}$$

If the investor pays a brokerage fee of q per cent on his transactions, the cost of retained earnings is

$$C_R = k_o \left[\frac{(1 - t_p)(1 - q)}{(1 - t_g)} \right] \tag{10.47}$$

Note that the capital-gains tax is paid only if the share is actually sold. If the investor holds the share, we may ignore the capital-gains tax, and the cost of retained earnings becomes

$$C_R = k_o(1 - t_p)(1 - q) \tag{10.48}$$

It should be clear from the above analysis that it is a fallacy to think that retained earnings are free to the firm. If investors are to be better off, retained earnings should be reinvested by managers in projects with a yield at least as high as C_R.[8] The observed (in the real world) increasing use of retained earnings reflects the ease of access of managers to this source of funds rather than the absence of any cost to the shareholders.

The estimation of the cost of retained earnings presents problems, because t_p is the weighted average tax rate for *all* stockholders and q is the weighted brokerage fee for all stockholders. Even if we assume equal brokerage expenses for all investors, the estimation of t_p requires knowledge of the income brackets of investors. Two recent studies in this area provide evidence that the marginal tax rate for shareholders as a whole in the USA is approximately 40 per cent.[9] Under the current taxation laws in the same country, the capital-gains tax is in general one-half of the income tax rate. This suggests that retained earnings have a higher cost for shareholders than debt financing, while new stock issue is probably the most costly source of funds.

In summary. The cost of the three main sources of funds has been expressed as a function of the discount rate, k_o, which investors apply in evaluating the present value of the stream of earnings generated by an *unlevered firm*. Under the present taxation system in most of the developed Western countries, where interest payments by corporations are tax-deductible, and the personal income tax rate is higher than the tax rate on capital gains, the cheapest source of funds is debt, followed by retained earnings, while the most expensive financing method is the issue of new stock. This can be seen by comparing the relevant expressions of the cost of funds, which may be ranked in ascending order as follows:

Cost of debt

$$C_D = k_o(1 - t_c) \tag{10.49}$$

Cost of retained earnings

$$C_R = k_o \left[\frac{(1 - t_p)}{(1 - t_g)} \right] (1 - q) \tag{10.50}$$

(where q = per cent of brokerage fees of stockholders)

Cost of new equity

$$C_E = k_o \left[\frac{1}{(1 - h)} \right] \tag{10.51}$$

(where h = per cent of flotation costs and underpricing of the new shares)

---

[8] It is true that the firm itself need not 'pay' anything for those funds. But investors give up a dividend payment when the firm retains funds and, unless the managers make an investment which generates an equivalent capital gain, investors lose.

[9] Jolivet, 'The Weighted Average Marginal Tax Rate on Dividends Received by Individuals in the USA'; also Elton and Gruber, 'Marginal Stockholder Tax Rates and the Clientele Effect'.

It seems to us that this method of estimating the cost of the particular sources of funds is more meaningful than the conventional approach, which we presented at the beginning of this section, because it allows a direct comparison of the costs involved in using the different sources of funds.

The estimation of the cost of the individual sources of capital requires information on the tax rates t_c, t_p, t_g, and an estimate of the discount rate, k_o, of an unlevered stream of earnings.

Information about the tax rates is available from the tax laws, which, however, require considerable processing in order to obtain a satisfactory value for the parameters t_c, t_p, and t_g.[10]

The estimation of k_o requires an accurate knowledge of the factors which influence the behaviour of investors. In view of the difficulties involved in statistical studies, it has become a widely common practice in financial analysis to use the constant-growth model or some modified version of it. If the firm is levered, the constant-growth expression gives an estimate of the discount rate $k_{e,L}$ which investors are assumed to apply for earnings generated by such a firm:

$$k_{e,L} = \frac{dv_0(1+g)}{P_0} + g \tag{10.52}$$

where dv_0 and P_0 are the last dividend and price quoted, while g is usually estimated from the past rate of growth of dividends or earnings. In many cases estimates of $k_{e,L}$ are obtained for different values of g, in an attempt to define a *range* of the probable error imparted in the estimate of $k_{e,L}$.

The value of k_o is finally obtained by substituting $k_{e,L}$ in the basic relationship:

$$k_{e,L} = k_o + (k_o - k_d)(1 - t_c)\frac{D}{S} \tag{10.53}$$

where D and S are the market values of debt and equity of the firm, and k_d is the firm's cost of debt. This cost is estimated from the valuation expression (10.6):

$$V_B = \sum_{t=1}^{n} \frac{Y_t}{(1 + k_d)^t}$$

The estimate of k_o obtained from the solution of equation (10.53) is next substituted in expressions (10.49), (10.50) and (10.51) to find the cost of debt, the cost of retained earnings and the cost of equity capital.

---

[10] See Jolivet, 'The Weighted Average Marginal Tax Rate on Dividends Received by Individuals in the USA'; and Elton and Gruber, 'Marginal Stockholder Tax Rates and the Clientele Effect'.

The next step in estimating the average cost of capital of the firm is to find appropriate weights for the costs of the individual sources of funds.

*   *   *

In recent years estimates of k_e have been obtained by using the *capital asset pricing model* (CAPM). This model is developed in Chapter 12. We note here that the CAPM involves the following steps:
(1) Estimation for each firm of the regression

$$(R_{j,t} - i_t) = \beta_j(R_{M,t} - i_t) + u_t \tag{10.54}$$

where i_t = the short-term rate of interest on government bonds in period t
$R_{j,t}$ = one-year yield on the stock of the jth firm, i.e.

$$R_{j,t} = \frac{dv_t + (P_{t+1} - P_t)}{P_t} \tag{10.55}$$

$R_{M,t}$ = one-year yield of *all* the stocks traded on the stock exchange. This is often measured by one of the published *stock-yield indexes*, for example the New York Stock Exchange (NYSE) Yield Index.

From the above regression we obtain an estimate of the 'beta coefficient', $\hat{\beta}$, for the jth firm.
(2) Using the $\hat{\beta}$ estimate, the return on equity is next computed by the expression:

$$\hat{R}_j = \hat{k}_{e,j} = \bar{i} + \hat{\beta}_j(\bar{R}_M - \bar{i}) \tag{10.56}$$

where $\bar{i}$ = arithmetic mean of i_t during the sample period
$\bar{R}_M$ = arithmetic mean of the stock market yield on equity during the sample period.

(For a detailed exposition of the capital asset pricing model, see Chapter 12, section III.)

*   *   *

II. OPTIMAL CAPITAL STRUCTURE AND THE WEIGHTED AVERAGE COST OF CAPITAL

A. The Theory of Optimal Capital Structure Revisited

It is essential to understand that although in any one period the firm may use only new stock or new debt or only retained earnings, this does not mean that the individual costs can be used as the basis for accepting or rejecting (in general, evaluating) investment projects. Optimal investment decisions require the use of a weighted average cost of all the sources of finance, with the weights being the proportions of debt and equity in the optimal long-run capital structure of the firm. (See section III of this chapter, and also Chapter 11.)

In Chapter 8 we saw that most writers define the optimal capital structure as the combination of debt and equity in proportions which maximise the value of the firm to its existing shareholders. We saw there that the determination of the 'optimal' weights of debt and equity in a firm's capital structure involves many difficult issues. We will return to this point presently. Meanwhile, *assume* that the firm has somehow determined its optimal capital structure, which it intends to maintain when undertaking new investments. Denoting by L^* the proportion of optimal debt in the firm's capital structure, we may write

$$dD = L^* dI \tag{10.57}$$

or

$$L^* = \frac{dD}{dI} \tag{10.58}$$

where dI denotes new investment, and dD is the additional debt.

It follows that the proportion of optimal equity funds in the firm's capital structure is $1 - L^*$, since, by definition, an investment will be financed either with new debt or with equity capital.

We saw earlier (p. 471) that the firm's cost of capital is given by the expression

$$C_A = k_o \left[1 - \frac{dD}{dI} \times t_c \right] \tag{10.59}$$

It can be easily shown that this cost is the weighted average of the cost of debt and the cost of equity, with weights $w_1 = L^*$ and $w_2 = 1 - L^*$ respectively:

$$C_A = C_D w_1 + C_E w_2 \tag{10.60}$$

$$C_A = C_D L^* + C_E (1 - L^*)$$

or

$$C_A = [k_o(1 - t_c)] L^* + \left[k_o \frac{1}{(1 - h)} \right] (1 - L^*) \tag{10.61}$$

*   *   *

PROOF

Substituting $L^* = dD/dI$ in expression (10.59), we obtain

$$C_A = k_o [1 - L^* \cdot t_c]$$

Adding and subtracting L^* in the bracketed term, we find

$$C_A = k_o(1 - L^* \cdot t_c + L^* - L^*) = k_o [L^*(1 - t_c) + (1 - L^*)]$$

or

$$C_A = [k_o(1 - t_c)]L^* + k_o(1 - L^*)$$

Finally, adjusting for flotation costs and underpricing of new stock issues, we obtain

$$C_A = [k_o(1 - t_c)]L^* + \left[k_o \frac{1}{(1 - h)} \right] (1 - L^*)$$

QED

*   *   *

Expression (10.61), in conjunction with (10.35), establishes that optimal investment decisions (i.e. investment decisions which maximise the value of the firm) require the use of a weighted average cost of capital. (The use of the weighted average cost of capital in investment decisions is discussed in Chapter 11.)

We *assumed* (in the above discussion) that the firm had somehow determined its optimal capital structure. The actual determination of the optimal capital structure, however, involves many theoretical issues, which remain largely unresolved.

We saw in Chapters 8 and 9 that the controversy regarding the existence of an optimal capital structure and an optimal dividend payout has not as yet been resolved. The 'traditionalists' maintain that there exists a debt/equity ratio and a dividend payout that are optimal in the sense that they minimise the over-all discount rate, or, equivalently, maximise the value of the firm to its existing shareholders. Modigliani and Miller maintain that in perfect capital markets there is no optimal capital structure or dividend payout, in the sense that security holders are indifferent to the financing decisions of managers, who are interested only in the stream of earnings generated by the assets of the firm, irrespective of how these earnings have been financed. When imperfections in the capital market are taken into account, the Modigliani–Miller neutrality theorems break down. In their framework the tax-deductibility of interest leads to the absurd conclusion that the optimal capital structure of a firm is one consisting of 100 per cent debt! Since such capital structures are not observed in the real world, Modigliani and Miller modify their conclusion by postulating that firms set a 'target' debt/equity ratio whose determinants, however, they admit are unknown.[11] Their conclusion regarding dividend payout is even more disappointing, since they maintain that their neutrality theorem holds even when market imperfections exist, because these imperfections produce offsetting results. Furthermore, their argument about 'the informational content' of announced dividends renders their hypothesis into an untestable tautology (see Chapter 9).

[11] See F. Modigliani and M. Miller, 'Some Estimates of the Cost of Capital to the Electric Utility Industry', *American Economic Review*, 1966, p. 342 also E. Fama and M. Miller, *The Theory of Finance* (Holt, Rinehart & Winston, 1972).

It is often *assumed* by writers in this field that the firm sets a 'target' debt/equity ratio, which it maintains in the long run, while short-run deviations from the 'target' take place, depending on the external and internal conditions of the firm at any one time. The determinants of this 'target' debt/equity ratio, however, are usually ignored or are vaguely mentioned.[12]

In a recent study[13] this author provided some empirical evidence which supports the hypothesis that the firm sets its 'target' debt/equity ratio at the level of the *average capital structure of similar firms* in the industry in which it operates.

Most of the 'established' textbooks on managerial finance adopt the view that the current capital structure of a firm represents its 'optimal' or 'target' capital structure,[14] though they also point out that the 'weights' should be changed if the firm changes its capital structure.

In view of the above discussion, we conclude that the optimal capital structure is an issue still unresolved. Further research, theoretical as well as empirical, is required before a general theory of optimal capital structure is developed.

B. Determination of the 'Target' Capital Structure in Practice

From the previous discussion it should be apparent that perhaps the greatest difficulty in the estimation of the firm's average cost of capital is the determination of the optimal capital structure, the optimal mix of the various sources of funds. In the preceding paragraph we assumed for simplicity that new investment is financed either with new debt or with new equity. However, in the real world a large part of the investment is financed from retained earnings, which have a cost to shareholders. Hence the weighted average cost of capital is

$$C_A = w_1 C_D + w_2 C_E + w_3 C_R \tag{10.62}$$

and the firm must obtain an estimate, not only of the costs C_D, C_E and C_R, but also of their weights. This implies that the firm must identify precisely its debt capacity and choose an 'optimal' dividend payout. The factors involved are so numerous and complex that the best one can hope for in the present state of the arts is a good approximation. Firms gradually acquire a feeling of their credit capacity, and usually get a direct feedback from their prospective creditors when considering debt financing. Similarly, firms' dividend policy is shaped over time in line with their aspirations and competitive positions.

Valuable insight into the weighting system of the various costs can be obtained by simulation techniques. The financial manager can start from some weights

[12] See, for example, F. Modigliani and M. Miller, 'Corporate Income Taxes and the Cost of Capital', *American Economic Review*, 1963.

[13] A. Koutsoyiannis, 'Managerial Job Security and the Capital Structure of the Firm', *Manchester School*, 1978.

[14] See, for example, J. Van Horne, *Financial Management and Policy*, 4th edn (Prentice-Hall, 1975); also Weston and Brigham, *Managerial Finance*.

which seem to be a 'reasonable' approximation to a 'desirable' or 'target' capital mix and obtain an estimate of C_A. The weights then can be modified and new estimates of the average cost obtained. The sensitivity of C_A to changes in the weights of the different sources of capital can help managers in appraising the 'penalty' which they will have to pay (in terms of a higher cost of capital) whenever they depart from the 'optimal' capital structure.

Table 10.1 includes an illustrative example of the sensitivity of the cost of capital to changes in the weights, w_i. It is *assumed* that the optimal capital structure consists of 40 per cent debt, 50 per cent retained earnings and 10 per cent new equity. It is also assumed that flotation costs amount to 10 per cent, and brokerage fees to 5 per cent for investors as a whole. Finally, we use the available information (from tax legislation and empirical studies) that $t_c = 0.50$, $t_p = 0.40$ and $t_g = (1/2)\, t_p = 0.20$. Under these assumptions the cost of each source of finance, in terms of k_o, is estimated as follows:

$$C_D = k_o(1 - t_c) = k_o(1 - 0.50) = (0.50)k_o$$

$$C_R = k_o \frac{(1 - t_p)}{(1 - t_g)}(1 - F) = k_o \frac{(1 - 0.40)}{(1 - 0.20)}(1 - 0.05) = (0.71)k_o$$

$$C_E = k_o \frac{1}{(1 - B)} = k_o \frac{1}{(1 - 0.10)} = (1.11)k_o$$

Finally, the average cost of capital is computed as follows:

$$C_A = (0.50k_o)w_1 + (0.71k_o)w_2 + (1.11k_o)w_3$$

or

$$C_A = k_o[(0.50 \times 0.40) + (0.71 \times 0.50) + (1.11 \times 0.10)] = 0.666k_o$$

Table 10.1   Sensitivity of the cost of capital to changes in capital structure

Capital structure	C_A Average cost of capital (in terms of k_o)
(1) Assumed 'optimal' structure	
$w_1 = 0.40$, $w_2 = 0.10$, $w_3 = 0.50$	$0.666k_o$
(2) Increased dividends	
$w_1 = 0.40$, $w_2 = 0.20$, $w_3 = 0.40$	$0.706k_o$
(3) Underestimation of debt capacity	
$w_1 = 0.30$, $w_2 = 0.20$, $w_3 = 0.50$	$0.727k_o$
(4) 'Double departure' from optimal mix	
$w_1 = 0.30$, $w_2 = 0.30$, $w_3 = 0.40$	$0.767k_o$

The process is repeated for different weights, and the results are shown in Table 10.1.

From the figures of Table 10.1 it is apparent that the greater the departure from the assumed 'optimal' capital structure, the greater the cost of capital. The increase is not substantial in our particular example. While the numbers chosen in our example are purely illustrative, the order of magnitude is not too unrealistic. Hence we can tentatively infer that the cost of capital is not particularly sensitive to changes in capital structure, at least within the range which may well be expected to be taking place in the real world of the large oligopolistic corporations.

A common fallacy

Before closing the discussion of the estimation of the firm's weighted average cost of capital, we would like to draw the attention of the reader to a common fallacy relating to the optimal capital structure.

We said that the optimal capital structure is defined as the combination of the various sources of funds in proportions which minimise the firm's cost of capital.

Given this definition of the optimal capital structure, and the ranking of the costs of each kind of finance reached in the previous section, one might think that the optimal capital structure is the one with 100 per cent debt. We said, however, in Chapter 8, that the capital market implicitly sets limits to the borrowing ability of the firm, which is thus obliged to resort to retained earnings and new equity, if it needs funds beyond (greater than) its debt capacity. Since retained earnings have a lower cost than new issue of stock, one might say that the firm, after exhausting its debt capacity, should use retained earnings to finance additional profitable investment opportunities, which, if abundant, should absorb all the earnings, reducing cash dividends to zero.[15] This situation, however, is not observed in the real world, where managers pursue a stable dividend policy (see Chapter 9). Hence a firm with adequate profitable investment opportunities will have to resort to all sources of finance.

In summary, the optimal capital structure refers to the long-run mix of the various sources of funds, and should not be determined on short-run considerations of the costs of the individual types of funds.

C. An Illustration of the Estimation of the Cost of Capital in the Real World

In this section we apply the earlier-developed method for the estimation of the cost of capital of the Kellogg Company. The source of information is *Moody's Industrial Manual*.

---

[15] This is the essence of the 'residual theory of dividends', which we discussed in Chapter 9.

Kellogg is the world's largest manufacturer of ready-to-eat breakfast cereals. It accounts for over 40 per cent of the US market. The company is well established in overseas markets and derives about one-quarter of its total revenues from outside North America. In an attempt to counteract intense competition, the company is introducing new items, developing more modern processing techniques and intensifying its market strategy. Although competition is expected to remain strong, the firm's long-term prospects are for continued earnings growth.

Cash dividends have been paid each year since 1922. The W. F. Kellogg Foundation holds approximately 50 per cent of the common stock.

The following data are required for the estimation of the firm's cost of capital.

(i) *Dividends per share ($ per share)*

The rate of growth of dividends over the ten-year period 1961–70 has been approximately 11 per cent per annum (see Table 10.2). It will be assumed that investors in the market will expect this growth of dividends to continue in the future.

Table 10.2   Dividends per share ($ per share)

1961	1962	1963	1964	1965	1966	1967	1968	1969	1970
0.34	0.38	0.43	0.50	0.55	0.50	0.65	0.75	0.80	0.90

(ii) *Kellogg's balance-sheet (31 December 1970)*

From the balance-sheet shown in Table 10.3 we obtain the capital structure shown in Table 10.4. Preferred stocks are omitted, for simplicity.

Table 10.3

Assets (S)		Liabilities (S)	
Cash	5,330,548	Current liabilities	79,006,733
Deposits	36,700,000	Long-term debt	8,438,341
Government securities, etc.	3,267,193	Deferred income tax	11,862,191
Receivables, net	36,198,051	Preferred stock	2,480,800
Inventories	66,271,349	Common stock	18,150,110
Prepayments	11,078,554	Capital surplus*	10,112,521
Net plant and equipment	158,845,695	Retained earnings	217,084,702
Investments	1,215,847		
Patents, etc.	28,228,161		
Total assets	$347,135,398	Total liabilities	$347,135,398

* 'Capital surplus' is an adjustment of the value of equity capital allowed by law.

Table 10.4   Kellogg Company: capital structure (1970)

	$	%
Debt	8,438,341	3.3
Common stock (plus capital surplus)	28,262,631	11.1
Retained earnings	217,084,702	85.6
Total	$253,785,674	100%

(iii) *Interest rate*

Interest charges amounted to $590,660 in 1970. This implies that the interest rate on long-term debt was $r = 0.07$ or 7 per cent.

(iv) *Tax rates*

The following tax rates will be used in the calculation of the various costs of capital:

$$t_c = 0.50; \quad t_p = 0.35; \quad t_g = (1/2)t_p = 0.175$$

Flotation costs are assumed to be 5 per cent, and brokerage costs are assumed zero.

(v) *Price of common share*

From *Moody's Quarterly Handbook* it was found that the price of Kellogg's shares at the end of 1970 was $28.00.

With the above information we may proceed with the estimation of the average cost of capital of the Kellogg Company.

   Step 1. Substituting the relevant figures in the constant-growth expression we find

$$k_{e,L} = \frac{dv_{1970}(1+g)}{P_{1970}} + g = \frac{0.90(1.11)}{28} + 0.11 = 0.03568 + 0.11 = 0.1457$$

Step 2. We next use the expression

$$k_{e,L} = k_o + (k_o - i)(1 - t_c)\frac{D}{S_L}$$

to estimate k_o, the discount rate of an all equity-stream of earnings.

   D is the market value of debt. We assume that the market value is equal to the book value of debt.

S_L is the market value of common stock. It is found by multiplying the price of shares times the number of outstanding shares:

Number of shares = 36,300,220

Market value of shares = S_L = 36,300,220 × $28.00 = 1,016,406,160

Substituting the values of D, S_L, i and t_c we find

$$0.1457 = k_o + (k_o - 0.07)(1 - 0.50) \left(\frac{8,438,341}{1,016,406,160} \right)$$

Solving for k_o we obtain

$$k_o = 0.14539 \approx 14.5\%$$

Step 3. We now have the information required for the estimation of the cost of the individual sources of finance:

$$C_E = k_o \frac{1}{(1-h)} = 0.14539 \left(\frac{1}{0.95} \right) = 0.153$$

$$C_R = k_o \left(\frac{1-t_p}{1-t_g} \right) = 0.14539 \left(\frac{0.650}{0.825} \right) = 0.115$$

$$C_D = k_o(1 - t_c) = 0.14539(0.50) = 0.073$$

Step 4. Using the capital structure (that is, the weights of debt, equity and retained earnings) of the year 1970 we obtain the following average cost of capital of Kellogg:

$$C_A = w_1 C_D + w_2 C_E + w_3 C_R$$

$$C_A = (0.033)(0.073) + (0.111)(0.153) + (0.856)(0.115) = 0.1178 \approx 11.8\%$$

It should be stressed that the estimated average cost of capital ($C_A = 0.118$) should be used for investment decisions only if Kellogg intends to maintain the 1970 capital mix in the future. If the firm intends to change the proportions of debt, equity and retained earnings in its capital structure, the new weights should be used in estimating the cut-off rate of investment. For example, if Kellogg decides not to issue any new stock in the future and maintain the debt proportion at 3.3 per cent, the proportion of retained earnings (in the capital structure) will have to be increased to 0.967. The change in the capital structure results in the following cost of capital:

$$C_A = (0.967)(0.115) + (0.033)(0.073) \approx 0.114 = 11.4\%$$

In general, if the firm's capital structure changes, we must re-estimate its cost of capital, which is used for the appraisal of investment projects.

III.   THE SUPPLY-OF-FUNDS SCHEDULE OF THE FIRM

We said at the beginning of this chapter that the cost of capital is essential for optimal investment decisions. Recall from Chapter 4 that investment decisions require knowledge of the demand schedule for fixed capital goods and of the supply-of-funds schedule of the firm. In Chapter 4 the supply of funds was a straight line, parallel to the horizontal axis, because under certainty all sources of funds have the same cost, which is equal to the market rate of interest.

In Chapter 11 we shall examine the investment decision under uncertainty. The supply-of-funds schedule under uncertainty is different, because under uncertainty the various sources of funds have different costs, depending on their degree of risk. In the previous sections we argued that the various costs must be combined into a weighted average cost of capital (WACC) which is appropriate for investment decisions. In this section we will derive the S_F under uncertainty. We will also explain briefly why the WACC is the appropriate basis for optimal investment decisions.

A.   Derivation of the Supply-of-Funds Schedule

The supply-of-funds schedule relates various amounts of funds to the cost of raising them.

The derivation of the supply-of-funds schedule, S_F, requires knowledge of the individual costs of the various sources of finance, of the optimal capital structure and of the optimal dividend policy of the firm.

Above we derived the costs of the three main types of funds. It was found that:

$$\text{The cost of debt is } C_D = k_o(1 - t_c) \tag{10.63}$$

$$\text{The cost of retentions is} | C_R = k_o \left(\frac{1 - t_p}{1 - t_g} \right)(1 - q) \tag{10.64}$$

$$\text{The cost of new equity is } k_o \left(\frac{1}{1 - h} \right) \tag{10.65}$$

In the following discussion for simplicity we will ignore personal taxes, capital gains tax and the brokerage fees of investors. Thus the cost of retentions will be $C_R = k_o$. This does not alter the analysis, since the ranking of the various sources of funds does not change: debt is the cheapest form of finance, retentions is a more expensive source of finance, and new equity financing is the most expensive of all.

Initially we will assume that each of the sources of funds has a constant cost, irrespective of the amount raised. (This assumption will be relaxed at a later stage.)

Under the above assumptions, the cost of the three main sources of funds is shown in Figure 10.3.

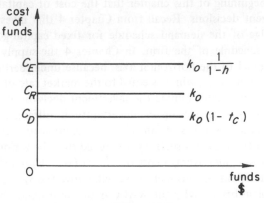

Figure 10.3

In order to obtain the firm's supply-of-funds schedule, the costs of the above sources of funds must be combined in a single figure. This is attained by assigning to these costs weights corresponding to the optimal capital structure of the firm.

We saw, in Chapter 8, that the optimal capital structure is the combination of debt and equity funds that maximises stockholder wealth (according to the traditional and the Modigliani/Miller theory), or the utility of managers (according to the managerial theory of the firm). In the Modigliani and Miller theory, as well as in the 'managerial job-security hypothesis',[16] the proportion of debt in the capital structure takes the form of a target (or limit) which is partly internally (by managers) and partly externally (by creditors) determined. We have denoted this proportion of debt by L^*. Apparently, the optimal proportion of equity is $1 - L^*$. It should be clear that L^* and $1 - L^*$ are the weights which must be used in estimating the firm's supply-of-funds schedule. For investment purposes, these weights must correspond to the proportions with which the firm *intends* to finance its investment. The funds that the firm will raise are *new* or *incremental* capital which will be employed to finance *new* investment projects. In other words, the firm raises additional capital (*at the margin*) to make an additional (*marginal*) investment, and what is required is knowledge of the firm's marginal cost of capital. Consequently the weights must be *marginal weights*, that is, weights which the firm will employ to raise *additional* capital.[17]

In summary, the supply-of-funds schedule is a marginal cost of capital schedule,

---

[16] See Koutsoyiannis, 'Managerial Job Security and the Capital Structure of the Firm'.

[17] Most firms use the weights corresponding to their current capital structure. This is correct only if the firm intends to raise additional (marginal) funds in the same proportions as its present (current) capital structure. If the firm intends to change its capital structure, the new weights must be applied in estimating the supply-of-funds schedule. See Van Horne *et al.*, *Financial Management and Policy*.

which shows the relationship between the weighted average cost of each additional unit of funds (C_A) and the total amount of capital raised during a period, *ceteris paribus.*

Equity capital may be raised either from retained earnings (internal equity) or from issue of new stock (external equity). We saw in Chapter 9 that managers have a preference for retentions, but job-security considerations set a limit to the amount of earnings that management can 'safely' retain.[18] Given the managerial preference and the fact that retentions have a lower cost than new equity, the firm will first exhaust its internal funds, and will resort to new issue of stock only when the retention limit has been reached. Under these conditions, the supply-of-funds schedule will be a step-function with three 'steps'.

(1) If the firm has not exhausted its internal-equity limit, the weighted cost of capital will be

$$C_{A1} = C_R(1 - L^*) + C_D L^* \tag{10.66}$$

or

$$C_{A1} = k_o(1 - L^*) + [k_o(1 - t_c)]L^* \tag{10.67}$$

(2) If the firm uses both sources of equity (retained earnings and new stock), then its cost of capital will be

$$C_{A2} = (w_1 C_R + w_2 C_E)(1 - L^*) + C_D L^* \tag{10.68}$$

where $w_1 + w_2 = 1$. (In this case w_1 and w_2 are the proportions of internal and external equity respectively.)

This cost is higher than C_{A1}. To see this we may write expression (10.68) in the form

$$C_{A2} = \left[k_o\left(w_1 + \frac{w_2}{1 - h} \right) \right] (1 - L^*) + k_o(1 - t_c)L^* \tag{10.69}$$

It can be shown that

$$\left(w_1 + \frac{w_2}{1 - h} \right) > 1 \tag{10.70}$$

so that $C_{A2} > C_{A1}$.

*   *   *

PROOF

Given $w_1 + w_2 = 1$, $0 < w_1 < 1$, $0 < w_2 < 1$. The left-hand side of inequality

---

[18] See A. Koutsoyiannis, *Managerial Job Security and the Dividend Policy of Firms* (University of Waterloo, 1981).

(10.70) gives

$$\frac{w_1(1-h)+w_2}{1-h} = \frac{(w_1+w_2)-w_1h}{1-h} = \frac{1-w_1h}{1-h}$$

Apparently $(1-w_1h)/(1-h) > 1$, given $0 < w_1 < 1$.

QED

*   *   *

(3) If the firm has exhausted its internal funds (retained earnings), equity can be raised only by issue of new stock. In this event the cost of capital is

$$C_{A3} = C_E(1-L^*) + C_R(L^*) \tag{10.71}$$

or

$$C_{A3} = \left[k_o\left(\frac{1}{1-h}\right)\right](1-L^*) + [k_o(1-t_c)]L^* \tag{10.72}$$

Apparently C_{A3} is greater than C_{A2} because

$$\frac{1}{1-h} > \left(w_1 + \frac{w_2}{1+h}\right) \tag{10.73}$$

*   *   *

PROOF

$$w_1 + \frac{w_2}{1-h} = \frac{w_1(1-h)+w_2}{1-h}$$

$$= \frac{(w_1+w_2)-w_1h}{1-h} = \frac{1-w_1h}{1-h} = \frac{1}{1-h} - \frac{w_1h}{1-h}$$

Apparently $1/(1-h) - w_1h/(1-h) < 1/(1-h)$, given that $0 < w_1 < 1$ and $0 < h < 1$.

QED

*   *   *

The supply-of-funds schedule under the above assumptions is shown in Figure 10.4.

The first segment implies financing with debt and retained earnings. The second segment denotes financing with all three sources of funds, while the third segment implies financing with debt and new stock.[19]

---

[19] In a recent paper S. Kardasz ('The Capital-Stock Decision of Subsidiaries', *Economic Enquiry*, vol. XVII, 1979) argues that the supply-of-funds schedule has two linear segments. Kardasz's argument *assumes* that the firm will never be in a situation in which all three sources of funds are used simultaneously. This assumption is not generally true. The position of the firm (on its supply-of-funds schedule) will depend on the available investment opportunities, as we will see in Chapter 11. Thus Kardasz's two-step function is a special case of the three-step function developed in this section.

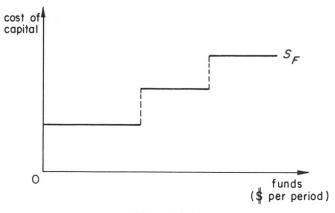

Figure 10.4

If we relax the assumption that the firm can tap the various sources of funds at a constant cost, then S_F will have more segments. If the firm wants to borrow beyond its debt capacity, it will have to pay a higher interest rate. Similarly, if the firm makes a large issue of new stock, the cost of external finance is likely to increase.

In general, we may conclude that in each time period S_F will be a step-function, with each 'higher step' occurring whenever any component cost increases as a result of the volume of capital raised. The beginning of the new 'step' can be calculated by the expression:[20]

$$F = \frac{\left(\begin{array}{c} \text{Total amount of a specific type of funds} \\ \text{used prior to the increase in its cost} \end{array} \right)}{\left(\begin{array}{c} \text{Weight of the specific source of funds} \\ \text{in the firm's capital structure} \end{array} \right)} \qquad (10.74)$$

We will illustrate the derivation of the S_F curve with a numerical example. Assume that

(a) The optimal capital structure of the firm is

$$L^* = 0.23; \ (1 - L^*) = 0.77$$

(b) $k_o = 0.10$
(c) The flotation costs for a new issue of stock is 10 per cent ($h = 0.10$)
(d) The corporate tax rate is 50 per cent ($t_c = 0.50$)
(e) The firm's retained earnings are $40 million
(f) The firm's debt capacity is $15 million. That is, up to $15 million the firm can borrow at a cost of $k_o(1 - t_c) = 0.10(1 - 0.50) = 0.05$ or 5 per cent. Beyond $15 million and up to $22 million the cost of debt increases to 7 per cent. Beyond $22 million the cost of debt increases to 10 per cent.

[20] See Weston and Brigham, *Managerial Finance*.

(g) The firm can issue new stock for $20 million at a cost of

$$C_E = k_o \frac{1}{1-h} = 0.10 \frac{1}{1-0.10} = \frac{0.10}{0.90} = 11 \text{ per cent}$$

Beyond $20 million and up to $40 million the cost of new issues rises to 12 per cent. Beyond $40 million the cost of new stock rises to 14 per cent.

The S_F curve is estimated as follows:

Retained earnings are $40 million. In order to keep its capital structure unchanged, the amount of $40 million must be 77 per cent of the total (additional) funds. That is, the firm can raise a total amount F_1, which is found from the expression

$$40 = 0.77 \, F_1$$

or

$$F_1 = \frac{40}{0.77} = \$51.95 \text{ million}$$

The weighted average cost of F_1 is

$$C_{A1} = k_o(1 - L^*) + k_o(1 - t_c)(L^*)$$

$$C_{A1} = 0.10(0.77) + 0.05(0.23) = 0.0885 \text{ or } 8.85\%$$

Thus the S_F curve will be a straight line up to the amount of $51.95 million. In other words, the firm's cost of capital is 8.85 per cent up to $51.95, which consists of $40 million retentions and $11.95 million debt.

The subsequent 'higher steps' of the S_F curve can be found by applying expression (10.74):

$$\frac{\$15\text{m.}}{0.23} = \$65.22\text{m.}$$

$$\frac{\$22\text{m.}}{0.23} = \$95.65\text{m.}$$

$$\frac{\$40\text{m.}}{0.77} = \$51.95\text{m. (retentions)}$$

$$\frac{\$60\text{m.}}{0.77} = \$77.92\text{m. (retentions} + \$20\text{m. new stock at } 11\%)$$

$$\frac{\$80\text{m.}}{0.77} = \$103.90\text{m. (retentions} + \$20\text{m. new stock at } 11\% + \$20\text{m. new stock at } 12\%)$$

Putting the above amounts in ascending order and calculating the corresponding weighted average cost of capital, we obtain the following information.

(a) **$51.95m.** This amount includes the retained earnings of $40 million and new debt of $11.95 million.

The cost of capital up to $51.95m. was found to be equal to

$$C_{A1} = 0.10(0.77) + 0.05(0.23) = 0.0885 \text{ or } 8.85\%$$

Beyond $51.95m. the firm can still borrow at 5 per cent, but must resort to new stock, which has a cost of

$$C_E = k_o \left(\frac{1}{1-h}\right) = 0.10 \left(\frac{1}{1-0.10}\right) = 0.11 \text{ or } 11\%$$

Thus beyond $51.95m. the cost of capital is

$$C_{A2} = (0.11)(0.77) + (0.05)(0.23) = 0.0962 \text{ or } 9.62\%$$

The next 'step' is $65.22 million. This implies that any amount of funds between $51.95 million and $65.22 million will have a cost of $C_A = 9.62$ per cent.

(b) **$65.22m.** To raise funds beyond $65.22m., the firm has to resort to more expensive debt ($C_D = 7$ per cent), while the cost of equity is $C_E = 11$ per cent.

The cost of capital beyond $65.22m. will be

$$C_{A3} = (0.11)(0.77) + (0.07)(0.23) = 0.1008 \text{ or } 10.08\%$$

Since the next 'step' occurs at $77.92 million, it follows that any amount of funds between $65.22 million and $77.92 million will have a cost of $C_{A3} = 10.08$ per cent.

(c) **$77.92m.** Beyond the amount of $77.92 million, the firm must resort to new additional equity, which costs 12 per cent, while debt still costs 7 per cent.

Thus beyond $77.92 million the cost of capital is

$$C_{A4} = (0.12)(0.77) + (0.07)(0.23) = 0.1085 \text{ or } 10.85\%$$

Since the next 'step' occurs at $95.65m, it follows that any amount of funds between $77.92 million and $95.65 million has a cost of $C_{A3} = 10.85$ per cent.

(d) **$95.65m.** Beyond the amount of $95.65 million the firm has to resort to additional debt, which costs 10 per cent, while equity still costs 12 per cent.

Thus beyond $95.65 million the cost of capital is

$$C_{A5} = (0.12)(0.77) + (0.10)(0.23) = 0.1154 \text{ or } 11.54\%$$

Since the next 'step' occurs at $103.90 million, it follows that any amount of money raised between $95.65 million and $103.90 million will have a cost of 11.54 per cent.

(e) **$103.90m.** Beyond the amount of $103.90 million the firm has to resort to new stock, which has a cost of 14 per cent, while debt still costs 10 per cent.

Thus beyond $103.90m. the cost of capital is

$$C_{A6} = (0.14)(0.77) + (0.10)(0.23) = 0.1308 \text{ or } 13.08\%$$

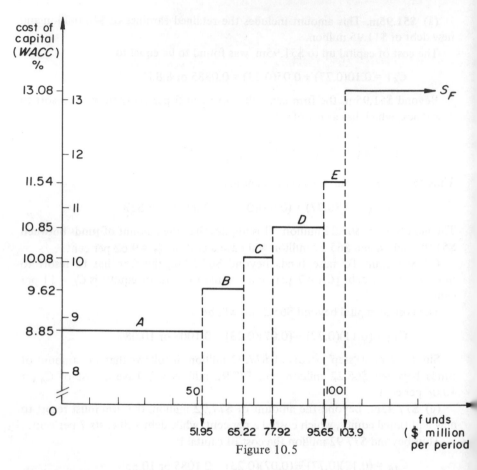

Figure 10.5

The above calculations give rise to the S_F step-function shown in Figure 10.5.

The segments of the S_F function of our example have the following components:

Segment *A* $51.59m. $\begin{cases} \$40.0\text{m. retentions at } 10\% \\ \$11.95\text{m. debt} \qquad \text{at } 5\% \end{cases}$

Segment *B* $13.27m. $\begin{cases} \$10.22\text{m. new stock at } 11\% \\ \$3.05\text{m.} \quad \text{new debt at } 5\% \end{cases}$

Segment *C* $12.70m. $\begin{cases} \$9.78\text{m.} \quad \text{new stock at } 11\% \\ \$2.92\text{m.} \quad \text{new debt at } 7\% \end{cases}$

Segment *D* $17.73m. $\begin{cases} \$13.65\text{m. new stock at } 12\% \\ \$4.08\text{m.} \quad \text{new debt at } 7\% \end{cases}$

Segment *E* $8.25m. $\begin{cases} \$6.35\text{m.} \quad \text{new stock at } 12\% \\ \$1.90\text{m.} \quad \text{new debt at } 10\% \end{cases}$

At all segments the firm is assumed to have a 'target' capital structure consisting of

$$L* = 0.23 \text{ (or 23\%) debt}$$

and

$$(1 - L*) = 0.77 \text{ (or 77\%) equity}$$

Although in the real world the supply-of-funds schedule is likely to be a step-function, of the general form of our example, a smooth upward-sloping S_F curve is often used for analytical purposes. The S_F is horizontal up to the point where retained earnings are exhausted and turns upwards for any larger amount of funds (see Figure 10.6). It is important to remember that all points on this curve denote funds that can be raised at the corresponding weighted average cost of capital, with the weights being the proportions of debt and equity in the firm's target capital structure.

We will use the supply-of-funds curve in Chapter 11, where we examine the traditional theory of the investment decision under uncertainty.

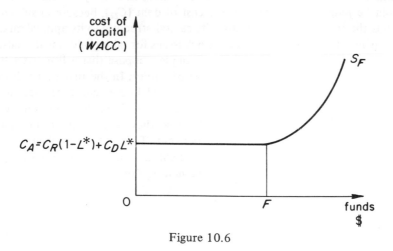

Figure 10.6

B. The Rationale of Using the Weighted Average Cost of Capital (WACC) in Investment Decisions[21]

It is easy to make the fallacy that investment projects financed from one source of funds should be judged on the cost of that particular type of funds. In the short run the firm adopts timing tactics in using its various sources of funds, so

---

[21] The use of the WACC in appraising investment projects is examined in Chapter 11. However, the remarks of this section are essential for understanding the analysis in the next chapter.

as to take advantage of the particular conditions prevailing in the capital market at any one time. For example, in a booming stock market equity financing is likely to be more frequently used, while in periods of low interest rates and easy credit the firm will most probably resort to debt financing. However, in the long run *all* the firm's assets are really financed by a mixture of debt and equity. Investors do not judge a firm on an asset-by-asset basis, but as an entity. They look at all the assets, irrespective of how each one has been financed. These assets generate income streams, which investors evaluate at different discount rates, depending on their business and financial risk. For investors there are levered and unlevered firms, and their earnings are evaluated on the basis of all their assets and all their financing decisions.[22]

For these reasons the firm should decide what is its long-run optimal structure: what proportion of its assets should, *on average*, be financed by debt, retained earnings and new stock issues. These 'optimal' proportions should be used as weights in computing an average cost of funds, which is the appropriate basis for evaluating *every* investment project, in *every* period, even though only one kind of capital may be raised in any particular year.[23] It is wrong to conclude that if a firm intends to issue bonds for an investment in some year, this investment should be judged on the basis of the cost of debt (C_D), because in subsequent periods the firm, in order to restore its capital structure to its optimal mix, will have to resort to retentions or new stock issues for raising additional funds, and these sources have a higher cost. For example, suppose that a firm has a 10 per cent cost of debt and a 15 per cent cost of equity. In the first year it borrows heavily to finance investment projects which yield 11 per cent. In the second year it has projects available which yield 14 per cent, well above the return on previous projects, but it cannot accept them, because they would have to be financed with new equity funds which cost 15 per cent. To avoid this problem the firm should calculate its cost of capital as a weighted average of the various types of funds it uses: debt, retained earnings, and new equity.[24]

[22] See Van Horne *et al.*, *Financial Management and Policy*, ch. 9.
[23] See F. Modigliani and M. Miller, 'Corporate Income Taxes and the Cost of Capital: A Correction', *American Economic Review*, 1963, pp. 433–43.
[24] Weston and Brigham, *Managerial Finance*, p. 595.

APPENDIX: COST OF PREFERRED STOCK (k_p)

A preferred stock is a stock that entitles its owner to a fixed dividend payment. However, this dividend is not a contractual obligation on the part of the firm but can be paid at the discretion of the board of directors. Hence, unlike debt, if the firm does not pay the preferred-stock dividend, it does not become bankrupt. However, the firms that issue preferred stock intend to pay the fixed dividend. Thus the owners of preferred stock have a prior claim on earnings over common-stock owners (but not a prior claim over bondholders). Consequently, for an investor preferred stock is more risky than bonds but less risky than common stock, so that the required rate of return will be higher than the yield of bonds (but lower than the yield of common stock). Most preferred stocks do not have a maturity (are perpetuities), so that their present value is estimated by the expression

$$V_p = \frac{Dv_p}{k_p}$$

where V_p = present value of preferred stock, net of any brokerage fees and other expenses, i.e. V_p represents the *net* receipts from the issue of preferred stock

Dv_p = fixed dividend of preferred stock

k_p = required rate of return of preferred stock

Solving for k_p, we find the cost of preferred stock to the firm:

$$k_p = \frac{Dv_p}{V_p}$$

The cost of preferred stock is not adjusted for taxes, because preferred dividends are paid out of the taxed earnings.

For example, assume that a firm issues new preferred stock, with a face-value of $100 (per share) and a stated dividend of 5 per cent, or $5. For this issue the firm has to pay brokerage fees of $2 per share. The cost of preferred stock to the firm is

$$k_p = \frac{5}{100 - 2} = \frac{5}{98} = 0.051 \text{ or } 5.1\%$$

Because k_p is not adjusted for taxes, the cost of preferred stock is substantially higher than the cost of debt.

If a preferred stock issue can be retired after n periods, the cost of preferred stock is estimated (by iterations or computer) from the general expression

$$V_p = \sum_{t=1}^{n} \frac{Dv_{p,t}}{(1 + k_p)^t}$$

where V_p = the *net receipts* of the firm from the issue of preferred stock. The method of estimation has been explained in Chapter 3.

PART FOUR

The Investment Decision Under Risk and Uncertainty

Introduction

In Chapter 4 we examined the investment decision under certainty. We used discounting in order to take into account the timing of costs and proceeds associated with an investment. Discounting, using an appropriate rate, is a means of adjusting for the timing of earnings, but not for its uncertainty.

Under certainty the acceptance of any investment project cannot alter the business risk of the firm as perceived by investors, who are the suppliers of funds to the firm. The assumption of certainty enabled us to judge the desirability of an investment project on the basis of its prospective earnings alone, which consisted of a stream of proceeds in which each term has a unique value.

However, in the real business world there is a wide range of factors which give rise to risk in fixed investments. Consequently, the length of the economic life and the costs and revenues of any investment proposal is uncertain. The longer the expected life of the investment, the greater its risk, since we have to forecast costs and revenues in more distant periods.

If the acceptance of an investment changes the business risk of the firm, investors are likely to view the firm differently after the adoption of the project. Hence the valuation of the firm may change. In appraising investment proposals management should take into account the impact that their acceptance will have on the firm's risk, as perceived by investors, assuming that the goal of the firm is stockholder-wealth maximisation. In other words, management should assess the likely effects of an investment decision on the price of the share of the firm in the stock market.

In Chapter 11 we present the main models of the 'traditional' theory of the investment decision. In the traditional approach each investment project is judged on the basis of its own total risk and return, in isolation from other existing or prospective investments. In other words, in the traditional theory of the investment decision the worthiness of a given project is assumed to be unaffected by risks of other projects, existing or future ones.

Depending on the amount of information available to the decision-maker, the various models of the traditional theory may be classified in two groups.

(1) *Models of decision-taking under risk*. In these models the decision-maker is assumed to know the probabilities of the possible outcomes of each project.

The most important of these models are (a) the maximisation of expected earnings model, (b) the 'certainty equivalents' model, (c) models using risk-adjusted discount rates, and (d) the weighted average cost of capital model.

(2) *Models of decision-taking under uncertainty*. In these models the decision-maker does not know the probabilities of the various possible outcomes of a project. The most important criteria used for 'optimal' investment decisions under conditions of uncertainty are (a) the *Bayes—Laplace* criterion, (b) the *maximin* criterion, (c) the *minimax* criterion, (d) the *maximax* criterion, (d) the *Hurwicz* criterion, and (e) the *'minimax regret'* criterion. These are commonly used in cost—benefit analysis for the evaluation of projects.

In Chapter 12 we present the modern theory of the investment decision, in which the individual projects are appraised within a portfolio approach. It is argued that an investment project, if accepted, will be part of the portfolio of assets held by the firm. As such, it may affect the risk profile of the firm, and hence the price of its stock. In other words, it is recognised that investment projects are *not* risk-independent.

Within the portfolio approach to the investment decision two schools of thought have developed.

According to one school, any investment project should be judged on the basis of its effect on *the over-all risk of the firm*. This is often called 'the firm-risk approach'. The firm considers sets of investments which consist of combinations (portfolios) of existing investments and proposals for new investment projects. Investments are risk-interdependent, in the sense that earnings from existing assets will be affected by the earnings of new investments. Thus the stream of earnings of the various investments covary. This covariance between existing investments (assets) and proposed new investment projects requires that the interdependence be explicitly considered when appraising the risks of proposed investments. The desirability of any particular investment proposal cannot be considered independently of the risks of other capital investments already in existence or being considered for acceptance. Instead, its risk, and hence its attractiveness, depends in part upon its covariance with existing investments, as well as upon its covariance with other prospective projects. The most important model of the 'firm-risk approach' is the *mean-variance* model, which postulates that managers will choose the investment portfolio that maximises their own utility. This utility is defined by only two parameters: the expected return of the portfolio and its variance (or standard deviation), which is a measure of the portfolio's risk.

According to the second school, an investment proposal should be judged on the basis of its risk-return impact on shareholders' portfolios of stocks rather than on the firm's portfolio of assets. This is often called 'the investor-risk approach'. The investment decision is analysed in the framework of the *capital asset pricing model* (CAPM). In this model the total risk of a security consists of two components: *the systematic risk* and *the unique (non-systematic) risk*. The unique risk is due to particular characteristics of a firm and can be diversified away by the investor, through changes of his portfolio (holdings of stock/securities of various firms). The systematic risk arises from the movements of the prices of all securities in the stock market, and cannot be diversified away by investors. Hence what matters is *not* the total risk of an investment, but its systematic risk. Accordingly, management should ignore the impact that the project has on the firm's total risk (the variability of the firm's earnings). Diversification of assets by the firm is not a thing that matters for shareholders, because, in perfect capital markets, investors can attain diversification by changing their portfolio of securities. The only thing that is important is the project's systematic risk, because investors cannot diversify this risk away. The systematic risk of a project is completely unrelated to the present risk complexion of the firm. Hence the diversification attributes of a project should not be considered in the context of the portfolio of assets of the firm.

The capital asset pricing model was originally developed for investments in securities. Its extension to investments in real (fixed) assets is still in its infancy. The proponents of this model, however, believe that the CAPM 'will be the basis of the next breakthrough' in the theory of the investment decision.[1] A lot of theoretical work is currently being done in this field, and any course on the investment decision which does not cover the capital asset pricing model is considered 'obsolete'. We shall present this model in detail, appraising critically its strengths and weaknesses.

---

[1] See, for example, H. Bierman and J. E. Hass, *An Introduction to Managerial Finance* (Norton, 1973) ch. 14, p. 220.

11. The Traditional Theory of the Investment Decision Under Risk and Uncertainty

I. PRELIMINARY REMARKS

The basic premise of the traditional theory of the investment decision is that each investment proposal should be appraised on the basis of its *total risk* and *expected return*.

In this chapter we discuss the main models of the traditional theory of investment. In section II we examine the kind of information required for the evaluation of risky investment projects. In particular, we discuss measures of the expected profitability and of the risk of investment projects. In section III we present several models of decision-taking under risk. In section IV we discuss briefly the main criteria for optimal investment decisions under conditions of uncertainty.

Although we focus on the investment decision, the concepts and methods of this chapter can be applied to other decisions of the firm under risk and uncertainty.

Before we proceed with our main task, it is important to distinguish between risk and uncertainty, and to discuss the factors which give rise to uncertainty in the real business world.

A. Risk and Uncertainty

On the basis of the state of information available to the decision-maker, models of the firm are classified into *models of certainty*, *models of risk* and *models of uncertainty*.

In a *certainty model* it is assumed that the decision-maker has complete information which enables him to assign a unique outcome (value) to each alternative course of action.

If information is incomplete, we are in a world of noncertainty. Two situations may arise in cases of incomplete information:

(1) *Noncertain situations in which the decision-maker has enough information to calculate and assign probabilities to the possible outcomes of the alternative strategies open to him.* The probabilities of the possible outcomes of the alternative courses of action are known to the economic agent. Under these conditions we have a *decision model under risk.* In other words, models of risk are models in which the decision-maker can assign probabilities to the possible outcomes of alternative strategies: the outcomes of any particular strategy are known up to a probability distribution.

(2) *Noncertain situations in which the probabilities of possible outcomes of the alternative strategies open to the economic agent are unknown.* The decision-maker is unable to calculate the probabilities of the different outcomes of alternative strategies. Under these conditions we have a *decision model under uncertainty.*[1]

B.   Sources of Noncertainty

We may distinguish two types of risk, *business risk* and *financial risk*.

Business risk arises from the uncertainty of the realisation of the expected earnings of the firm. This uncertainty arises from possible changes in the prices of the products and of the factors of production, changes in consumers' tastes, changes in the methods of production, and the reactions (decisions) of competitors. In other words, business risk arises from general 'business conditions' in the economy (general economic and political conditions), specific conditions of supply and demand in the market of products that the firm produces and of the factor inputs which it utilises in its production activity, technological progress, the speed and flexibility with which the firm can reduce its costs when sales decline, and so on.

Financial risk arises from the use of debt for financing the firm's operations. As indebtedness increases, the fixed costs for servicing the debt rise. Since bondholders have a priority claim on earnings, the existence of debt reduces the certainty of the flow of net earnings available to the entrepreneur (after interest payments). Furthermore, the use of debt exposes the entrepreneur to a potential loss of his total equity, if total gross earnings fall below the fixed charges of debt, that is, if the firm becomes insolvent, a situation which may lead to legal bankruptcy.[2]

---

[1] The above classification of problems of non-certainty in (1) decision-making under risk (when probabilities of possible outcomes are known), and (2) decision-making under uncertainty (when probabilities of the possible outcomes are unknown), is attributed to Frank J. Knight, *Risk, Uncertainty and Profit* (Houghton Mifflin, 1921), reprinted by the London School of Economics, *Reprints of Scarce Texts in Economics*, series no. 16, 1933.

[2] See Ezra Solomon, *The Theory of Financial Management* (Columbia University Press, 1963) p. 70.

In this chapter risk and uncertainty cover both types of risk, business and financial. Schematically, the various sources of noncertainty are shown in Figure 11.1.

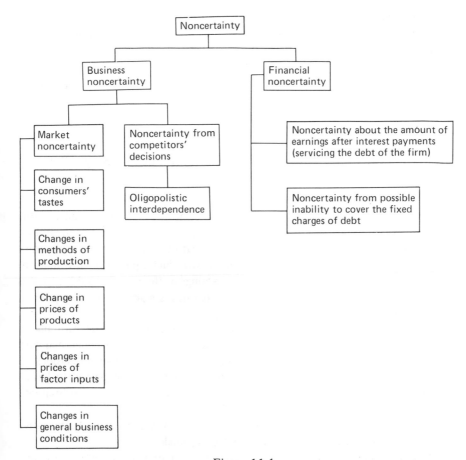

Figure 11.1

Faced with noncertainty, decision-makers cannot assign a unique value to the outcome (profitability) of a particular action/strategy. Each strategy may have several outcomes (depending on the factors discussed earlier), some more likely than others. If the decision-maker can assign probabilities to these outcomes, we have a situation of risk. In this case an 'optimal' decision may be taken based on the probability distribution of the outcomes of each strategy and the risk attitude of the decision-maker. In the next section of this chapter we examine (a) the information which is provided by the probability distributions of the various strategies (projects), and (b) the risk attitude of decision-makers.

II. INFORMATION REQUIRED FOR THE EVALUATION OF RISKY PROPOSALS

The contents of this section are technical. To help the non-mathematically inclined student, we start with simple statistical definitions and concepts. Numerical examples illustrate these concepts. Thus the material is made accessible to all economics students. We believe that the theory of the investment decision is essential to the understanding of the behaviour of growth-seeking managers in the real oligopolistic world. A careful reading of this section will facilitate the understanding of the subsequent analysis of the investment decision.

A. The Probability Distribution of the Earnings of a Single-Period Project

The probability distribution of a project (or strategy) is the set of all possible outcomes (earnings or profits) of the strategy with their respective probabilities. This concept is further discussed later. We note at this point that the probability distribution of a strategy (project) provides two crucial pieces of information: it gives a measure of the average expected earnings of the project; and it provides a measure of its risk. Knowledge of these measures is essential for the appraisal of the project (strategy), as we will presently see.

Here we consider alternative proposals (strategies) open to a decision-maker which have a lifetime of one time period. The decision-maker is concerned with decisions for this particular time period, ignoring the impact of such decisions on future periods. Multi-period projects, i.e. projects which are expected to have a lifetime extending over several time periods, will be examined in a subsequent section of this chapter.

In any decision problem there are at least two (usually several) alternative courses of action (strategies) open to the decision-maker.

With perfect information and certainty each alternative has a unique outcome. From the alternatives the decision-maker chooses the one that maximises his objective function.

When information is incomplete, each alternative course of action (project, strategy) cannot be assigned a unique value. Each alternative has several possible outcomes. It is assumed that the decision-maker can assign *subjective probabilities* to the (uncertain) outcomes of each alternative strategy and form its probability distribution. (The concept of 'subjective probability' is discussed in Appendix 11.1.)

We said that the probability distribution of a project (or strategy) is the set of all possible outcomes (payoffs) of this project with their respective probabilities.

Consider a firm which has to choose between the following three strategies (proposals) in a particular time period:

Strategy *A*   undertake investment in order to change the style of the product
Strategy *B*   reduce the price of the product
Strategy *C*   launch an advertising campaign

We will derive the probability distributions of these strategies and use them in order to obtain a measure of the 'average' profitability and the risk of each alternative strategy.

Assume that all strategies have the same cost, for example $1,000,000. (This assumption will be relaxed at a subsequent stage.) Assume further that each of the above alternative strategies may have three outcomes (levels of profit, or net earnings, or cash flows), depending on whether the future brings inflation, recession or depression. The possible outcomes of the three strategies (profits or net earnings in dollars) are shown in Table 11.1, which is called the *payoff table* of the alternative strategies.

Table 11.1   Payoff table of alternative strategies

General business conditions	Strategies		
	A Change of style	B Price cut	C Advertising
Inflation	$100,000	$50,000	$0
Recession	$50,000	$100,000	$50,000
Depression	-$50,000	-$20,000	$80,000

The interpretation of the payoff table is that if the firm adopts strategy *A* (decides to change the style of its product) and inflation occurs, the firm will realise a profit of $100,000. However, if depression occurs, the change in style will cause a loss of $50,000. Similarly, if the firm adopts strategy *B* (reduces its price) and depression occurs, the firm will suffer a loss of $20,000. And so on.

Finally, assume that the entrepreneur, using any available information and his own judgement and experience, assigns the (subjective) probability 0.60 to the occurrence of inflation, the probability of 0.30 to the occurrence of recession and the probability of 0.10 to the occurrence of depression.

With the above information we can form the probability distribution of the three alternative strategies among which the firm must choose. These probability distributions are shown in Table 11.2.

In statistical theory the information provided by a probability distribution is summarised by two measures: the mean (or expected value), and the variance of the distribution, or its standard deviation.

The *expected value* of a strategy is the weighted average of its possible outcomes under the various states of the economy, the weights being the probabilities

Table 11.2   Probability distributions of alternative strategies

Probability distribution of strategy A		Probability distribution of strategy B		Probability distribution of strategy C	
Possible outcomes (A_i)	Probability $[Pr(A_i)]$	Possible outcomes (B_i)	Probability $[Pr(B_i)]$	Possible outcomes (C_i)	Probability $[Pr(C_i)]$
$100,000	0.60	$50,000	0.60	$0	0.60
$50,000	0.30	$100,000	0.30	$50,000	0.30
−$50,000	0.10	−$20,000	0.10	$80,000	0.10

of the different states of the economy. Formally the expected value of a strategy is the sum of the products of the possible outcomes each multiplied by its probability.[3] If strategy X has n possible outcomes

$$X_1, X_2, \ldots, X_n$$

and associated with each outcome is a probability that the outcome will occur

$$Pr(X_1), Pr(X_2), \ldots, Pr(X_n)$$

then the expected value of this strategy is

$$E(X) = \sum_{i=1}^{n} X_i[Pr(X_i)] \tag{11.1}$$

The expected value can be interpreted as a measure of the 'average payoff' (or average profitability) of the strategy. It is a weighted average of all the possible outcomes, with the weights being the probabilities of occurrence of these outcomes. The expected value is a summary measure of all possible outcomes (profitabilities) of a strategy.

The expected values of the three strategies of our example are

$$E(A) = \sum_{i=1}^{3} A_i[Pr(A_i)] = (\$100{,}000)(0.60) + (\$50{,}000)(0.30)$$
$$+ (-\$50{,}000)(0.10) = \$70{,}000$$

$$E(B) = \sum_{i=1}^{3} B_i[Pr(B_i)] = (\$50{,}000)(0.60) + (\$100{,}000)(0.30)$$
$$+ (-\$20{,}000)(0.10) = \$58{,}000$$

$$E(C) = \sum_{i=1}^{3} C_i[Pr(C_i)] = (\$0)(0.60) + (\$50{,}000)(0.30)$$
$$+ (\$80{,}000)(0.10) = \$23{,}000$$

[3] It is assumed that the variable 'outcome of strategy' is a discrete random variable, that is, a variable which may assume discrete (non-continuous) values.

The *variance* of a strategy is a measure of the variability of the possible outcomes of the strategy around the mean. It is a measure of dispersion: how close do the various outcomes cluster around the mean.

The variance of a strategy X *is defined* as the expected value of the squared deviations of the possible outcomes from their mean (average) value:

$$\text{var}(X) \equiv \sigma_X^2 \equiv E[X_i - E(X)]^2$$

The variance of a strategy is *calculated* from the sum of the products of the squared deviations of the possible outcomes from their expected (mean) value, each multiplied by the probability of occurrence of the respective outcome:

$$\sigma_X^2 = \sum_{i=1}^{n} [X_i - E(X)]^2 Pr(X_i) \tag{11.2}$$

Another related measure often employed as a measure of variability or dispersion of the outcomes of a strategy is the *standard deviation*, which is defined as the square root of the variance:

$$\sigma_X = \sqrt{\sigma_X^2} = \sqrt{\sum_{i=1}^{n} [X_i - E(X)]^2 Pr(X_i)} \tag{11.3}$$

The standard deviation[4] may be interpreted as the weighted average distance of the (uncertain) outcomes from the mean value (average payoff) of the strategy, the weights being the probabilities of the possible outcomes.

The variance or the standard deviation is used as a measure of the risk of a strategy, because risk is associated with the variability of the possible outcomes of a strategy. The greater the variability of the possible outcomes, the more risky the strategy.[5] Thus risk in this chapter is defined as the variability of outcomes and is measured most commonly by the standard deviation.

The variances and standard deviations of the three strategies of our example

---

[4] The rationale for using the standard deviation as a measure of the variability or dispersion of the outcomes of a strategy is that in calculating the variance we had to square the deviations $(X_i - E(X))$, given that

$$\Sigma[X_i - E(X)] Pr(X_i) = \Sigma X_i Pr(X_i) - E(X)[\Sigma Pr(X_i)] = E(X) - E(X) = 0.$$

given that $\Sigma Pr(X_i) = 1$.
Once the calculations of the variance are done, it is plausible to take the square root of the variance, in order to 'correct' for having used the squared deviations in computing its value. In other words, the variance is expressed in squared units, while the standard deviation is expressed in the original units of the variable.

[5] The variance (or the standard deviation) as a measure of risk has several shortcomings. The most serious is that it measures deviations on both sides of the mean. Obviously an entrepreneur is concerned with outcomes having a negative deviation from the expected mean profit of a strategy. Outcomes with values greater than the 'average payoff' are of course desirable. For a discussion of other shortcomings of the variance as a measure of risk, see J. C. Van Horne, *Financial Management and Policy*, 3rd edn (Prentice-Hall, 1975) pp. 29–31. See also the discussion in Appendix 11.2.

are given below:

$$\sigma_A^2 = \Sigma [A_i - E(A)]^2 Pr(A_i) = (100,000 - 70,000)^2 (0.60)$$
$$+ (50,000 - 70,000)^2 (0.30) + (-50,000 - 70,000)^2 (0.10)$$

or

$$\sigma_A^2 = \$2,100,000,000 \quad \text{and} \quad \sigma_A = \$45,800 \text{ (approximately)}$$

$$\sigma_B^2 = \Sigma [B_i - E(B)]^2 Pr(B_i) = (50,000 - 58,000)^2 (0.60)$$
$$+ (100,000 - 58,000)^2 (0.30)$$
$$+ (-20,000 - 58,000)^2 (0.10)$$

or

$$\sigma_B^2 = \$1,176,000,000 \quad \text{and} \quad \sigma_B = \$34,300 \text{ (approximately)}$$

$$\sigma_C^2 = \Sigma [C_i - E(C_i)]^2 Pr(C_i) = (0 - 23,000)^2 (0.60)$$
$$+ (50,000 - 23,000)^2 (0.30)$$
$$+ (80,000 - 23,000)^2 (0.10)$$

or

$$\sigma_C^2 = \$861,000,000 \quad \text{and} \quad \sigma_C = \$20,300 \text{ (approximately)}$$

The probability distributions of the three strategies of our example are graphed in Figures 11.2, 11.3 and 11.4.

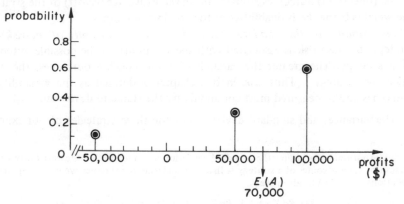

Figure 11.2   Probability distribution of strategy A

The distributions of our example are discrete: the possible outcomes of the strategies (proposals) do not take continuous values. There are only three outcomes for each proposal.

If the outcomes may be assumed to take continuous values, the probability distribution approaches a smooth curve, which may be symmetrical around the mean, $E(X)$, or skewed (see Figures 11.5, 11.6 and 11.7).

In the case of a continuous distribution, it is impossible to obtain estimates of the mean and standard deviation by using expressions (11.1) and (11.3), because

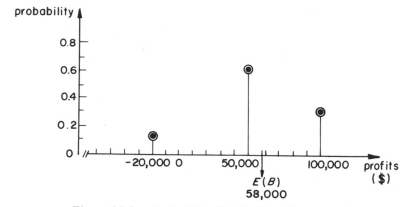

Figure 11.3   Probability distribution of strategy *B*

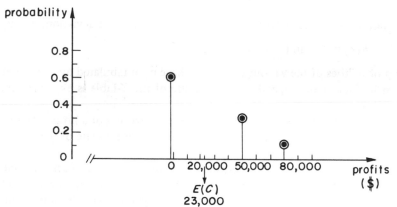

Figure 11.4   Probability distribution of strategy *C*

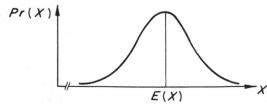

Figure 11.5   Symmetrical distribution

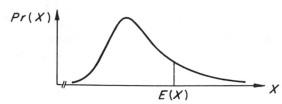

Figure 11.6   Distribution skewed to the right

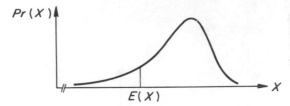

Figure 11.7   Distribution skewed to the left

one cannot know all the possible (infinite) outcomes and their probabilities. A way for obtaining an estimate of the standard deviation is to use the standard normal variable Z and its distribution. From elementary statistics it is known that the variable

$$Z = \frac{X_i - E(X)}{\sigma_X} \tag{11.4}$$

has a normal distribution with zero mean and unit standard deviation, that is

$$E(Z) = 0 \quad \text{and} \quad \sigma_Z = 1$$

The probabilities of the various values of Z have been tabulated by Gauss and are shown in Table 1 of Appendix 11.2 (the use of the Z-table is explained in that appendix).

Assuming that the distribution of the various outcomes of a proposal (project) is normal, we may use expression (11.4) to obtain an estimate of the risk of the project (σ_X), as follows.

(1) We ask management for estimates of *the most likely outcome* and the maximum possible deviation on either side of this outcome. The most likely outcome is considered as the mean of the probability distribution of all the possible outcomes of the proposal. The maximum deviation defines the lowest and highest outcomes of the proposal.

(2) We next ask management to assign a probability to the highest and lowest outcomes. Given this probability, we can find the corresponding value of Z from the Z table (p. 570).

(3) We substitute the value of the mean, the value of Z and either the maximum or the minimum value of the outcomes in expression (11.4) and we solve for σ_X.

As an illustration, consider that management thinks that the most likely outcome of a project is $10,000, with a maximum deviation of ±$4,000. That is, the lowest possible outcome is $6,000 and the highest is $14,000. Assume that management 'feels' that the probability of these extreme outcomes is 5 per cent. From the Z-table (p. 570) we see that if the probability is 5 per cent (on either tail of the distribution), the value of Z is 1.65. Substituting this information in expression (11.4), we find

$$1.65 = \frac{14,000 - 10,000}{\sigma_X}$$

or

$$\sigma_X = \frac{4,000}{1.65} = \$2,424$$

The above approach enables us to obtain the probability information required to determine the mean and the standard deviation of the distribution of all possible outcomes of a *one-period project*. It should be clear that this approach requires that the probability distribution of earnings (payoffs) be normal.

Figure 11.8 shows two symmetrical (normal) distributions of the earnings of two projects, with differing expected values and variances. The distribution of earnings of project *Y* has a smaller mean that the distribution of earnings of project *X*, but the distribution of *X* has a larger variance than the distribution of *Y*.

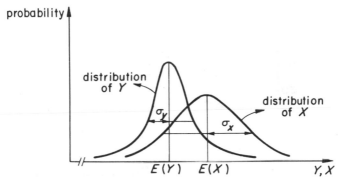

Figure 11.8   Probability distributions with differing expected values and variances

The problem of decision-making under risk amounts to the problem of choosing among such alternative probability distributions describing the possible (uncertain) outcomes of the different courses of action (strategies) open to the decision-maker.

In summary. It is assumed that the decision-maker knows (or can estimate) the possible outcomes (payoffs) of each strategy in different 'states of the environment' ('states of nature', 'general business conditions').

It is further assumed that the decision-maker can compute and assign *subjective probabilities* (see Appendix 11.1) to the various outcomes and form the probability distribution of each alternative strategy.

The expected value and the variance (or standard deviation) are single statistics, summarising an entire distribution of outcomes (payoffs). As such they provide decision-makers with helpful information. The expected value of a strategy is the 'average payoff' or 'average profit' that the decision-maker expects to earn *on average* from the adoption of the particular project. The variance (or standard deviation) is a measure of the riskiness of the project.

With information on the expected value and the variance (or standard deviation), the decision-maker can present the alternative projects with points on a two-dimensional diagram. In Figure 11.9 the expected payoff (average profit) is measured on the vertical axis and the standard deviation (as a measure of risk) is shown on the horizontal axis. Each point on this graph represents the expected-value–risk attributes of a (risky) project. For instance, points A, B and C represent the three strategies (projects) of our earlier example.

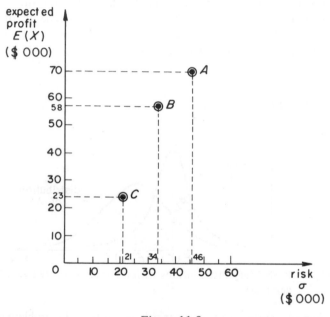

Figure 11.9

B.   The Probability Distribution of the Earnings of a Multi-Period Project

The typical form of a fixed investment project is that it generates earnings over several periods of time in the future. Under uncertainty the terms of the stream of earnings do not have a unique value. In *each time period* the earnings (cash flow) may assume several values (depending on general business conditions and other factors which we discussed earlier), each with some probability. In other words, the earnings in each period are a random variable, and the stream of earnings over the lifetime of the project consists of these random variables. For the evaluation of the project we need the mean (or expected value) *of the stream of uncertain earnings* and its standard deviation.

(i) *The mean of the uncertain stream of earnings*

The estimation of the mean of the uncertain stream of earnings involves the following steps:

Step 1: estimation of the mean of possible earnings *in each time period*. The relevant formula is expression (11.1), that is:[6]

$$\bar{X}_t = E(X_t) = \sum_{i=1}^{m} (X_{tj})Pr(X_{tj}) \qquad j = 1, 2, \ldots, m$$

(where m is the number of possible outcomes in each time period).

It is assumed that decision-makers can assign (subjective) probabilities to the various outcomes in each time period. To some extent these probabilities take into account uncertainty. However, the risk that the earnings will not materialise is measured by the standard deviation of the stream of earnings (see below).

Step 2: discounting of the expected value of possible earnings in each period by the riskless market interest rate, in order to find their present value

$$\frac{\bar{X}_1}{(1 + i)}, \frac{\bar{X}_2}{(1 + i)^2}, \frac{\bar{X}_3}{(1 + i)^3}, \ldots, \frac{\bar{X}_n}{(1 + i)^n}$$

where i = the riskless rate of interest
n = the number of years of the lifetime of the project.

It should be clear that the discounting takes into account the time value of money but not the risk of whether the earnings of the investment will materialise or not. We discount because there are alternative uses for the funds tied up in the project, and investors are unwilling to commit the funds in the project at a zero rate of return.

Step 3: summation of the discounted expected values, to obtain the mean (expected) present value of the stream of earnings. Thus the mean of the probability distribution of *the stream of (uncertain) earnings* is given by the expression

$$\overline{PV} = \sum_{t=1}^{n} \frac{\bar{X}_t}{(1 + i)^t} \tag{11.5}$$

$$* \qquad\qquad * \qquad\qquad *$$

Mathematical derivation of the mean of the distribution of present values of earnings. The present-value variable, in whose distribution we are interested, is

$$Y = \left[\frac{X_{1j}}{(1 + i)} + \frac{X_{2j}}{(1 + i)^2} + \ldots + \frac{X_{nj}}{(1 + i)^n} \right]$$

[6] To simplify the notation, we will use $\bar{X}$ to denote the expected mean value $E(X)$.

Let $k = 1(/1 + i)$. Thus we may write

$$Y = (kX_{1i} + k^2 X_{2i} + \ldots + k^n X_{ni})$$

Taking expected values[7] we obtain

$$E(Y) = kE(X_{1i}) + k^2 E(X_{2i}) + \ldots + k^n E(X_{ni})$$

given that k is a constant. But

$$E(X_{1i}) = \bar{X}_1, E(X_{2i}) = \bar{X}_2, \ldots, E(X_{ni}) = \bar{X}_n$$

Hence

$$E(Y) = k\bar{X}_1 + k^2 \bar{X}_2 + \ldots + k^n \bar{X}_n$$

or

$$\overline{PV} = \sum_{t=1}^{n} k^t \bar{X}_t = \sum_{t=1}^{n} \frac{\bar{X}_t}{(1 + i)^t}$$

QED

*   *   *

To illustrate the application of expression (11.5), we will use it to estimate the mean of the expected returns of two projects, A and B, both of which have a cost of $100.

There are five 'states of nature' (or 'general business conditions'), and the decision-maker has assigned (subjective) probabilities for the occurrence of these 'states' in each period. (The probabilities are different in each period for project A, but, for simplicity, it is assumed that they are the same in all periods for project B.)

The relevant calculations are shown in Tables 11.3 and 11.4. From Table 11.3 we obtain

$$\bar{X}_{A1} = \Sigma(X_{1j}) Pr(X_{1j}) = \$70$$

$$\bar{X}_{A2} = \Sigma(X_{2j}) Pr(X_{2j}) = \$60$$

$$\bar{X}_{A3} = \Sigma(X_{3j}) Pr(X_{3j}) = \$50$$

Thus the expected (mean) present value of the earnings of project A (assuming $i = 0.06$) is

$$\overline{PV}_A = \frac{\$70}{(1 + 0.06)} + \frac{\$60}{(1 + 0.06)^2} + \frac{\$70}{(1 + 0.06)^3} = \$161.40$$

The information for project B is given in Table 11.4. From Table 11.4 we obtain

$$\bar{X}_{B1} = \Sigma(X_{1j}) Pr(X_{1j}) = \$60$$

$$\bar{X}_{B2} = \Sigma(X_{2j}) Pr(X_{2j}) = \$50$$

$$\bar{X}_{B3} = \Sigma(X_{3j}) Pr(X_{3j}) = \$40$$

[7] The basic algebraic rules of expected values are explained in Appendix 12.2 (pp. 635–9).

Table 11.3 Expected earnings of project A

'States of nature' j	Period 1			Period 2			Period 3		
	Possible earnings X_{1j}	Probability $Pr(X_{1j})$	$[(X_{1j})(Pr\,X_{1j})]$	Possible earnings X_{2j}	Probability $Pr(X_{2j})$	$[(X_{2j})(Pr\,X_{2j})]$	Possible earnings X_{3j}	Probability $Pr(X_{3j})$	$[(X_{3j})(Pr\,X_{3j})]$
1	$50	0.10	5	$20	0.10	2	-$40	0.10	-4
2	60	0.20	12	40	0.25	10	30	0.30	9
3	70	0.40	28	60	0.30	18	50	0.30	15
4	80	0.20	16	80	0.25	20	80	0.20	16
5	90	0.10	9	100	0.10	10	140	0.10	14
			70			60			50

Table 11.4 Expected earnings of project B

'States of nature' j	Period 1			Period 2			Period 3		
	Possible earnings X_{1j}	Probability $Pr(X_{1j})$	$[(X_{1j})(Pr\,X_{1j})]$	Possible earnings X_{2j}	Probability $Pr(X_{2j})$	$[(X_{2j})(Pr\,X_{2j})]$	Possible earnings X_{3j}	Probability $Pr(X_{3j})$	$[(X_{3j})(Pr\,X_{3j})]$
1	$40	0.10	4	$30	0.10	3	$20	0.10	2
2	50	0.20	10	40	0.20	8	30	0.20	6
3	60	0.40	24	50	0.40	20	40	0.40	16
4	70	0.20	14	60	0.20	12	50	0.20	10
5	80	0.10	8	70	0.10	7	60	0.10	6
			60			50			40

Thus the expected (mean) present value of the earnings of project B is

$$\overline{PV}_B = \frac{60}{(1 + 0.06)} + \frac{50}{(1 + 0.06)^2} + \frac{40}{(1 + 0.06)^3} = \$134.66$$

We observe that project A has a greater expected profitability, as measured by the mean present value of the stream of earnings.

(ii) *The standard deviation of the stream of uncertain earnings*

We said that risk is defined as the variability of earnings around their mean value. It is measured by the standard deviation of earnings.

The value of the standard deviation (and hence the degree of risk) will differ according to whether the terms of the stream of earnings are independent or correlated from period to period. The greater the correlation (dependence) between the successive terms of the stream of earnings, the greater the standard deviation, and hence the greater the risk of the project.

Case A: Independent Earnings over Time

Suppose the firm is considering an investment project for which the probability distribution of possible earnings in any one period is completely independent of the distribution of earnings in any other period. In other words, the outcome in period t does not depend upon what happened in previous periods and will not affect the earnings of future periods. In this case the standard deviation of the probability distribution of net present value is

$$\sigma = \sqrt{\sum_{t=1}^{n} \frac{\sigma_t^2}{(1 + i)^{2t}}} \tag{11.6}$$

where σ_t is the standard deviation of the probability distribution of possible earnings in period t. The value of σ_t is estimated from expression (11.3):

$$\sigma_t = \sqrt{\Sigma(X_{tj} - \bar{X}_t)^2 \; Pr(X_{tj})}$$

*   *   *

Mathematical derivation of expression (11.6). (The algebraic rules, on which the following derivation is based, are explained in Appendix 12.1.)

By definition

$$\text{var}(Y) = \text{var}(kX_{1j} + k^2 X_{2j} + \ldots + k^n X_{nj})$$

$$= k^2 \, \text{var}(X_{1j}) + (k^2)^2 \, \text{var}(X_{2j} + \ldots + (k^n)^2 \, \text{var}(X_{nj})$$

$$= k^2 \sigma_1^2 + (k^2)^2 \sigma_2^2 + \ldots + (k^n)^2 \sigma_n^2$$

$$= \sum_{t=1}^{n} k^{2t} \sigma_t^2 = \sum_{t=1}^{n} \left(\frac{1}{1+i}\right)^{2t} \sigma_t^2 = \sum_{t=1}^{n} \frac{\sigma_t^2}{(1+i)^{2t}}$$

and

$$\sigma = \sqrt{\sum_{t=1}^{n} \frac{\sigma_t^2}{(1+i)^{2t}}}$$

*   *   *

To illustrate the calculations involved in estimating the risk of projects whose earnings are independent over time, consider our earlier example of the two projects A and B which generate the earnings shown in Tables 11.3 and 11.4. We first have to estimate the standard deviation of earnings in each period and then substitute in expression (11.6).

For project A we have:

$$\sigma_{A1}^2 = \Sigma(X_{1j} - \bar{X}_1)^2 \, Pr(X_{1j})$$

$$= (50 - 70)^2 (0.10) + (60 - 70)^2 (0.20) + (70 - 70)^2 (0.40)$$
$$+ (80 - 70)^2 (0.20) + (90 - 70)^2 (0.10)$$

$$= (400)(0.10) + (100)(0.20) + (0)(0.40) + (100)(0.20) + (400)(0.10)$$

$$= \$120$$

and $\sigma_{A1} = \sqrt{120} = \$10.95$.

Similarly, for period 2, we find

$$\sigma_{A2}^2 = \Sigma(X_{2j} - \bar{X}_2)^2 \, Pr(X_{2j})$$

$$= (20 - 60)^2 (0.10) + (40 - 60)^2 (0.25) + (60 - 60)^2 (0.30)$$
$$+ (80 - 60)^2 (0.25) + (100 - 60)^2 (0.10)$$

$$= (1600)(0.10) + (400)(0.25) + (0)(0.30) + (400)(0.25) + (1600)(0.1($$

$$= \$520$$

and $\sigma_{A2} = \sqrt{520} = \$22.80$.

Finally, for period 3, the standard deviation is

$$\sigma_{A3}^2 = \Sigma(X_{3j} - \bar{X}_3)^2 \, Pr(X_{3j})$$

$$= (-40 - 50)^2(0.10) + (30 - 50)^2(0.30) + (50 - 50)^2(0.30)$$
$$+ (80 - 50)^2(0.20) + (140 - 50)^2(0.10)$$

$$= (8100)(0.10) + (400)(0.30) + (0)(0.30) + (900)(0.20)$$

$$+ (8100)(0.10)$$

$$= \$1920$$

and $\sigma_{A3} = \sqrt{1920} = \$43.82$.

It should be noted that the variability of earnings of project A increases over time. In period 2 the probability distribution is somewhat flatter than in period 1, and in period 3 the probability distribution is even more flat and is also shifted to the left, towards the possibility of lower earnings. Thus the observation of a wider range of outcomes (greater variance) for periods 2 and 3 indicates that greater uncertainty is associated with earnings expected in the more distant future.

Substituting the three variances in expression (11.6), and assuming that the riskless market rate of interest is 0.06, we obtain the standard deviation of the present values of the stream of earnings of project A:

$$\sigma_A = \sqrt{\frac{120}{(1 + 0.06)^2} + \frac{500}{(1 + 0.06)^4} + \frac{1920}{(1 + 0.06)^6}}$$

$$= \sqrt{\frac{120}{1.124} + \frac{520}{1.262} + \frac{1920}{1.419}}$$

$$= \sqrt{106.76 + 412.04 + 1353.07}$$

$$= \sqrt{1871.87} = \$43.26$$

In the same way we calculate the standard deviation of the present values of the stream of earnings of project B. The variance for each period is obtained by applying expression (11.3).

For period 1 we have

$$\sigma_{Bj}^2 = \Sigma(X_{1j} - \bar{X}_i)^2 \, Pr(X_{1j})$$

$$= (40 - 60)^2(0.10) + (50 - 60)^2(0.20) + (60 - 60)^2(0.40)$$
$$+ (70 - 60)^2(0.20) + (80 - 60)^2(0.10)$$

$$= \$120$$

and $\sigma_{B1} = \sqrt{120} = \$10.95$.

For period 2 we have

$$\sigma_{B2}^2 = (30 - 50)^2(0.10) + (40 - 50)^2(0.20) + (50 - 50)^2(0.40)$$
$$+ (60 - 50)^2(0.20) + (70 - 50)^2(0.10)$$
$$= \$120$$

and $\sigma_{B2} = \sqrt{120} = \$10.95$.

For period 3 we have

$$\sigma_{B3}^2 = (20 - 40)^2(0.10) + (30 - 40)^2(0.20) + (40 - 40)^2(0.40)$$
$$+ (50 - 40)^2(0.20) + (60 - 40)^2(0.10)$$
$$= \$120$$

and $\sigma_{B3} = \sqrt{120} = \$10.95$.

Note that although the standard deviation is the same in each of the three periods, the coefficient of variation (which is the ratio of the standard deviation divided by the mean (expected) earnings) is lower for the initial periods and increases over time, because the mean earnings are declining. (The coefficient of variation is explained on pp. 522–4.) Thus the riskiness of project B is also increasing over time.

Substituting the three variances in expression (11.6) we obtain the standard deviation of the present values of the stream of earnings of project B:

$$\sigma_B = \sqrt{\frac{120}{(1 + 0.06)^2} + \frac{120}{(1 + 0.06)^4} + \frac{120}{(1 + 0.06)^6}}$$
$$= \sqrt{106.76 + 95.08 + 84.57}$$
$$= \sqrt{286.4} = \$16.92$$

Knowing the mean present value and the standard deviation, and assuming that the earnings are normally distributed, we can use the standard normal table (p. 570) to construct probability distribution graphs for the two projects. These distributions are shown in Figure 11.10.

The expected (mean) present value of A is seen to be \$161, while that of B is \$134. However, the larger standard deviation and flatter graph of A indicate that A is the riskier project.

The decision-maker must choose between the riskier but more profitable project A and the less risky but also less profitable project B. The criteria for decision will be discussed subsequently.

Case B: Perfect Correlation of Earnings over Time

The assumption of independence of earnings over time is not realistic. For most investment projects the earnings in one period depend partly upon the earnings in previous periods. If an investment project shows little success in the

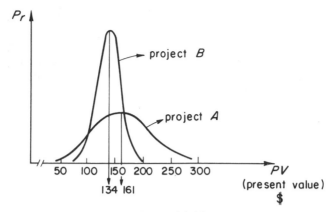

Figure 11.10

early periods, there is a high probability that its profitability (earnings) will also be lower (than originally expected) in subsequent years. To assume that an unfavourable or favourable outcome in the early life of an investment does not affect the subsequent earnings is unrealistic for most investments in the real business world.

An extreme case is to assume that the earnings of a project are perfectly correlated in the different time periods: the earnings in any period are a linear function of the earnings in all other periods. The formula for the standard deviation of a perfectly correlated stream of earnings over time is

$$\sigma = \sum_{t=0}^{n} \frac{\sigma_t}{(1+i)^t} \tag{11.7}$$

As an illustration, consider our earlier example, assuming that the earnings in each one of the three years of the lifetime of the two projects are perfectly correlated. The standard deviation (about the expected (mean) net present value) of project A is

$$\sigma_A = \frac{10.95}{(1+0.06)} + \frac{22.80}{(1+0.06)^2} + \frac{43.82}{(1+0.06)^3} = \$76.41$$

and the standard deviation of the stream of earnings of project B is

$$\sigma_B = \frac{10.95}{(1+0.06)} + \frac{10.95}{(1+0.06)^2} + \frac{10.95}{(1+0.06)^3} = \$29.27$$

We see that these values are considerably higher than in the case of independent cash flows over time. Dependence of the earnings in period t on the level of earnings in previous periods renders the investments more risky, in the sense that it increases their variability (around the mean value).

Case C: Imperfectly Correlated Earnings Over Time

In the real world the stream of earnings of most investment projects are neither independent nor perfectly correlated. Some degree of correlation between the successive terms of the stream of earnings is a more likely situation. In this case the standard deviation will assume a value somewhere between the extreme values of expressions (11.6) and (11.7).

Hillier[8] has developed a model for mixed situations, which, however, suffers from the shortcoming that some terms of the stream of earnings must be assumed to be independent, while the remaining must be assumed to be perfectly correlated.

Van Horne[9] has argued that for partly correlated earnings the use of conditional probability distributions is theoretically the most accurate. However, he concedes that this approach is also the most difficult to apply in practice, due to the amount of information required.

Given the present state of knowledge, this author suggests the following approach. For each project compute the two limiting values of the standard deviation of the stream of earnings, using expressions (11.6) and (11.7). Next choose a value, within that range, depending on whether the management feels that the stream of earnings is moderately or strongly correlated over time. Subjective judgement cannot be avoided in noncertain situations, as we saw earlier. If the decision-maker is assumed to be capable of assigning plausible subjective probabilities to the various outcomes in each time period, he surely can use his judgement for deciding which value of σ is more appropriate in any particular situation.

Given the information on the expected present value (mean) of the stream of earnings from a project and the standard deviation, the decision-maker can draw a two-dimensional diagram on which each project is represented by a point, defined by the project's expected earnings and risk. The two projects of our earlier example (assuming independence of the terms of the stream of earnings over time) are shown in Figure 11.11.

This sort of information is essential for 'optimal' decisions under conditions of risk, as we will presently see.

(iii) *The coefficient of variation as a measure of risk*

The standard deviation is inappropriate for measuring the risk of projects (strategies) which have different costs and different expected profitabilities. Usually a project requiring a higher initial expenditure has a larger expected profitability.

[8] F. S. Hillier, 'The Derivation of Probabilistic Information for the Evaluation of Risky Investments', *Management Science*, vol. 9, 1963, pp. 443–57.
[9] J. C. Van Horne *et al., Financial Management and Policy*, 4th edn (prentice-Hall, 1977) pp. 133–5.

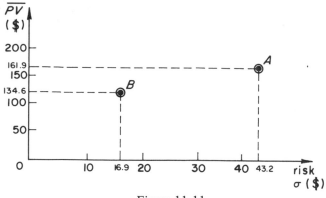

Figure 11.11

If two projects have different costs and expected profitabilities but the same standard deviation, the project with the higher expected profitability is less risky, because the deviations of the various outcomes (around the mean) is *relatively* smaller. For example, consider the probability distributions of two investments, C and D, shown in Figure 11.12. Investment C has an expected value (profitability) of $1,000 and a standard deviation of $300. Investment D has the same standard deviation of $300, but its expected mean profitability is $4,000. It is clear that the *percentage deviation* from the mean of investment C is considerably larger than that from the mean of investment D. In other words, investment C has more risk *per dollar of profit* than investment D. Hence investment C should be assigned a higher degree of risk than investment D. This is attained by using the *coefficient of variation* (*CV*) as a measure of risk for individual projects which are to be compared. The coefficient of variation is the ratio of the standard deviation of a project divided by its expected value:

$$CV_X = \frac{\sigma_X}{E(X)} \qquad (11.8)$$

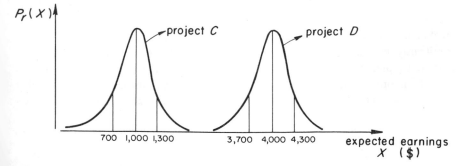

Figure 11.12

The coefficient of variation measures risk as a percentage: it is a measure of risk per unit of expected earnings (profitability).

In our example, the coefficient of variation of the two projects is

$$CV_C = \frac{300}{1,000} = 0.30$$

$$CV_D = \frac{300}{4,000} = 0.075$$

Thus project C is more risky than project D, though both have the same standard deviation.

In this chapter we will be using the coefficient of variation to compare the riskiness of alternative projects whenever the standard deviation might be misleading.

C.   Risk Attitudes of Decision-Makers

Knowledge of the probability distribution of the outcomes of the alternative strategies is not adequate for decision-making under conditions of noncertainty. We must further know the *risk preferences* of the individual decision-maker. Although a strategy has the highest expected profit, it is not certain that the decision-maker will choose it, because this strategy may have a high risk.

The risk preferences of a decision-maker can be inferred from his *utility-of-money function* (or utility-of-wealth function). Such a utility function can be constructed on the lines suggested by von Neumann and Morgestern.[10] In their approach the utility derived from money is measured in arbitrary units, 'utils'. This implies that with the von Neumann–Morgestern approach we obtain an *ordinal utility index* for money income which is valid only for showing the levels of satisfaction of an individual from different amounts of money income. Interpersonal comparisons of satisfaction cannot be made in this approach.

To derive the utility-of-money function of a decision-maker we start by assigning arbitrary amounts of utility (in utils) to two amounts of money representing arbitrarily selected extreme prospects. For example, we assign zero utils to $0, and 100 utils to a profit of $1,000. We next face the individual decision-maker with a hypothetical lottery offering the two (extreme) amounts of money arbitrarily picked, each with a probability of 0.50, and ask him how much he would be prepared to pay for this lottery. Assume that the individual answers that he is prepared to pay $350 for this lottery. We can estimate his total utility for this amount of money ($350) by summing the *expected utility*[11] of the two

---

[10] J. Von Neumann and Oskar Morgestern, *Theory of Games and Economic Behaviour*, rev. edn (Princeton University Press, 1955).

[11] The expected utility of a set of outcomes is defined as

$$E(U_A) = \Sigma U_{Ai}[Pr(U_{Ai})]$$

possible gains, that is,

$$U(\$350) = [U(\$0)\, Pr(\$0)] + [U(\$1{,}000)\, Pr(\$1{,}000)]$$

or

$$U(\$350) = [(0 \text{ utils})\,(0.50)] + [(100 \text{ utils})\,(0.50)] = 50 \text{ utils}$$

We now have three points on the utility-of-money function of the decision-maker:

Income	Total utility
$0	0 utils
$350	50 utils
$1,000	100 utils

Other points on the utility-of-money function may be obtained in a similar way. For example, assume that we ask the individual what amount of money he is prepared to pay for a lottery which would offer a gain of $0 with a probability of 0.20 and a gain of $350 with a probability of 0.80. If he answers that he would pay $220 for this lottery, we can find his total utility for this amount as follows:

$$U(\$220) = [U(\$0)\, Pr(\$0)] + [U(\$350)\, Pr(\$350)]$$

or

$$U(\$220) = (0 \text{ utils})\,(0.20) + (50 \text{ utils})\,(0.80) = 40 \text{ utils}$$

This process of facing the individual decision-maker with repeated hypothetical lotteries, and asking him what he would be prepared to pay for them, would give us several points on his utility-of-money function. If we plot these points on a graph on whose axes we measure total utility and money income, we obtain the individual's utility-of-money function. Let us derive three more points of this curve.

Assume that the decision-maker states that he is prepared to pay $150 for a lottery which would give him the chance of a gain of $0 with a probability of 0.40 and a gain of $350 with a probability of 0.60. From this we can estimate the individual's total utility for the amount of $150:

$$U(\$150) = [U(\$0)\, Pr(\$0)] + [U(\$350)\, Pr(\$350)]$$

or

$$U(\$150) = (0 \text{ utils})\,(0.40) + (50 \text{ utils})\,(0.60) = 30 \text{ utils}$$

Similarly, assume that the decision-maker states that he is prepared to pay $500 for a lottery giving him the chance of a gain of $0 with a probability of 0.30 and a gain of $1,000 with a probability of 0.70. With this information we find

$$U(\$500) = [U(\$0)\, Pr(\$0)] + [U(\$1{,}000)\, Pr(\$1{,}000)]$$

or

$$U(\$500) = (0\ \text{utils}) (0.30) + (100\ \text{utils}) (0.70) = 70\ \text{utils}$$

We now have the following points on the decision-maker's utility-of-money function

Income	Total utility
$0	0 utils
$150	30 utils
$220	40 utils
$350	50 utils
$500	70 utils
$1,000	100 utils

These points are plotted in Figure 11.13.

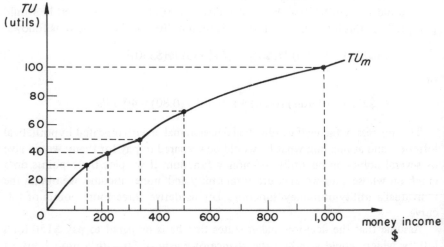

Figure 11.13   Utility-of-money function of a decision maker

The shape of the utility-of-money function reveals the risk attitudes (or risk preferences) of the individual decision-maker, given that the slope of this curve is the marginal utility of money (MU_m).

In general, there are three possible shapes that the utility-of-money function may assume. These shapes are shown in Figure 11.14.

If the utility-of-money function is concave to the money-axis (as in our example), the marginal utility of money declines as income increases. This implies that the individual is *risk-averse* (he is a risk-avoider): a *gain* of an additional unit of money gives him less utility (satisfaction) than a *loss* of one unit of money. This is shown in Figure 11.15. If the initial income of the individual is M, then the utility of an additional dollar (dotted area in Figure 11.15), is

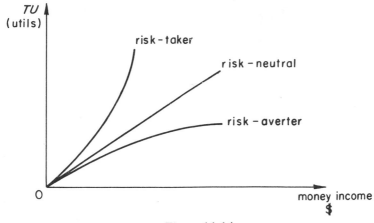

Figure 11.14

smaller than the disutility of a decrease of his income by one dollar (striped area in Figure 11.15). Such an individual would avoid situations (strategies) which include outcomes with possible losses, that is, such an individual would be a risk-averter (risk-avoider). (He would buy a lottery only if it costs less than the expected value of the outcomes.)

If the total utility-of-money curve is convex to the money-axis, the marginal utility of money increases as money income increases (see Figure 11.16). This implies that the individual is a *risk-taker*. An increase of his income by one dollar gives him a greater utility than the disutility from a loss of one dollar. Hence such a decision-maker would choose risky projects with high expected profitabilities.

Finally, if the total utility-of-money function is a straight line, the decision-maker is *risk-neutral* (or indifferent to risk). The MU_m remains constant at all levels of income. An increase of the individual's income by one dollar gives him

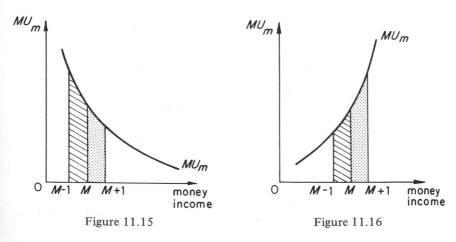

Figure 11.15   Figure 11.16

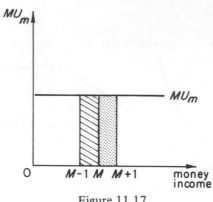

Figure 11.17

the same utility as the disutility from a loss of one dollar (Figure 11.17). Such a decision-maker would not take into account the riskiness of the alternative strategies; he would ignore risk, concentrating on other aspects of the strategy (e.g. its expected profitability, or its impact on the power or the 'image' of the corporation).

Note that in the real world the utility-of-money function may not be a smooth curve. For example, Friedman and Savage[12] have suggested a total utility-of-money curve having the shape shown in Figure 11.18(a). The corresponding marginal utility curve is shown in Figure 11.18(b).

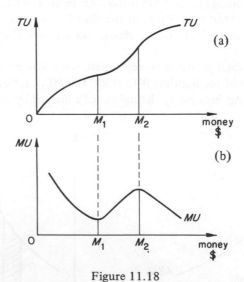

Figure 11.18

---

[12] Milton Friedman and L. J. Savage, 'The Utility Analysis of Choices Involving Risk', *Journal of Political Economy*, 1948, pp. 279–304.

The *TU* curve has three segments: for income levels between \$0 and \$$M_1$ the marginal utility declines; for income levels between \$$M_1$ and \$$M_2$ the *MU* increases; and for income levels greater than \$$M_2$ the *MU* declines again. This implies that the same individual may be risk-averse over some ranges of income and may be a risk-taker over some other levels of income. If he has a low income, he will be risk-averse, but at a higher level of income he may be attracted by risky projects (strategies). However, although such behaviour is possible in the real world, it is generally assumed that individuals are either risk-average or risk-takers at all levels of income.

In this section we have developed several concepts and 'tools'. In the remainder of this chapter we use these concepts and tools to develop various methods for decision-making under risk and uncertainty.

Recall that noncertain situations are usually divided into two groups.

(1) *Situations of risk*, that is, situations in which we have information on the possible outcomes of each strategy and we can estimate the probabilities of these outcomes.

(2) *Situations of uncertainty*, that is, situations in which we have information on the possible outcomes of each alternative strategy, but the probabilities of these outcomes are not known.

For each of these situations of noncertainty we will develop some of the most important methods of taking optimal investment decisions.

III. TRADITIONAL MODELS OF OPTIMAL INVESTMENT DECISIONS UNDER RISK

We have said that in the traditional theory of the investment decision the evaluation of individual projects is based on each project's *total risk* and expected return, without consideration of how the project affects the total risk of the firm, or without taking into account that part of the total risk of the project diversified away by individual investors. (The effect of a project on the risk of the firm as a whole and on the risk of the portfolio of a shareholder is discussed in Chapter 12.)

Within this approach several models have been developed for the evaluation of risky projects. We will examine five of them: (a) the 'maximisation of the expected value of earnings' model; (b) the 'certainty-equivalents' model; (c) the maximisation of the expected value, discounted with 'risk-adjusted discount rates'; (d) the 'maximisation of expected utility' model; and (e) the use of the weighted average cost of capital as a *cut-off* rate (or *hurdle* rate) for investment projects.

In the real world most firms use risk-adjusted discount rates or the weighted average cost of capital for the evaluation of investment projects.

All models assume that the firm has information on the probability distributions of the earnings of the investment projects available to it. The problem is to choose among these available projects the ones that maximise the wealth of existing shareholders.

A.   Maximisation of Expected Earnings

This approach assumes that, among all the alternative strategies open to the decision-maker, he will choose the one with the highest expected mean earnings. In one of our earlier examples (p. 505) the manager of a firm had three alternatives open to him:

A change of product style

$E(A) = \$70 \qquad \sigma_A = \$45.8$

B reduce the price of the product

$E(B) = \$58 \qquad \sigma_B = \$34.3$

C launch an advertising campaign

$E(C) = \$23 \qquad \sigma_C = \$21.3$

On the basis of 'the expected value criterion' the manager would choose strategy A, that is, he would decide to change the style of his product, because this course of action yields the greatest expected earnings (\$70). The fact that A also has the greatest risk is irrelevant in this method.

The basic shortcoming of this method is that it ignores risk. The decision-maker is assumed to be interested only in the expected ('average') profitability of each course of action, irrespective of its riskiness. Although the essence of decision-making under noncertainty is the presence of risk, in this model the risk is ignored.

Alternatively one might argue that this method implicitly assumes that the decision-maker is risk-neutral, since he ignores the risk aspects of the alternatives open to him. However, businessmen are not risk-neutral. In general, if individuals were risk-neutral, there would be no need to distinguish between situations of certainty and noncertainty, since the latter would not make any difference to the decisions of individuals, except for the fact that under certainty strategies would be compared on the basis of their unique outcomes, while under noncertainty strategies would be compared on the basis of their expected values.

B.   The 'Certainty-Equivalents' Model

The 'certainty-equivalents' approach is based on the concept of *utility of money* as developed in section II.

The *certainty equivalent* of a risky project *A* is defined as the amount of cash which would make the decision-maker indifferent between choosing the risky alternative or receiving the amount of cash with certainty. Thus the amount of cash is the certainty equivalent of the risky alternative.

The 'certainty-equivalent' concept is illustrated in Figure 11.19. The curve shows combinations of expected profitabilities (expected values) of the alternative strategies and their risk to which the decision-maker is indifferent. For example, point *Z* represents a course of action (a project, a strategy) with an expected profitability of $20,000 and a risk of $6,000, while point *W* represents another strategy with an expected value of $30,000 and a risk of $9,000. The amount of $10,000 is riskless (with $\sigma = 0$). The decision-maker with this risk–expected-profitability trade-off function is indifferent between receiving the amount of $10,000 in cash (with certainty) and the two risky alternative strategies. The shape of the risk–return trade-off curve implies that the decision-maker is risk-averse. To understand this we have drawn a risk–return trade-off curve in Figure 11.20. From this diagram it is apparent that to 'compensate' the decision-maker for equal increases in the risk, the expected return must increase at an increasing rate ($ab < bc < cd < de < ef$).

The decision-making in the framework of the certainty-equivalents approach involves the following steps.

Step 1. Derivation of the decision-maker's risk–expected-value trade-off function. This, as we saw, is the function expressing the indifference of the decision-maker between receiving an amount of cash with certainty and uncertain amounts of money, each associated with some level of risk. This function describes the risk attitude (the risk preferences) of the decision-maker. In principle, such a trade-off curve can be obtained by behavioural interrogation methods. One such method is outlined below.

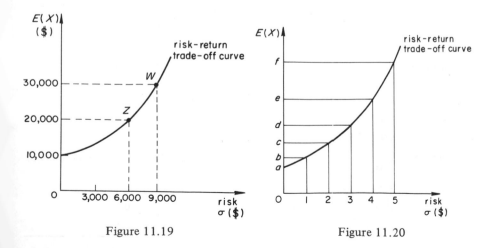

Figure 11.19   Figure 11.20

The decision-maker is asked to choose between an (arbitrarily selected) amount of cash with certainty and a hypothetical free (costless) gamble involving uncertain outcomes, each associated with some probability. This process is repeated, holding the amount of cash constant, but changing each time the hypothetical gamble (its outcomes and their probabilities). Among the (repeated) choices we register only those involving gambles for which the decision-maker expresses indifference between receiving the cash amount of money and taking these gambles. For each one of these gambles we estimate the expected value (mathematical expectation) and the standard deviation, and we plot them on a two-dimensional graph. We thus obtain several points of indifference between the certain payoff (the amount of cash defined in the interrogation procedure) and the uncertain payoffs of the gambles. If we join these points, we obtain the risk—expected-profitability trade-off curve of the decision-maker.

Table 11.5   Gambles with a risk—payoff combination which leaves the decision-maker indifferent

Gamble A   Receive $0 with a probability of 0.40, or $5,000 with a probability of 0.60:

$E(A) = (\$0)\,(0.40) + (\$5,000)\,(0.60) = \$3,000$

$\sigma_A^2 = (0 - 3,000)^2(0.40) + (5,000 - 3,000)^2(0.60) = \$6,000,000$

$\sigma_A = \$2,450$

Gamble B   Lose $5,000 with a probability of 0.30, or win $10,000 with a probability of 0.70:

$E(B) = (-5,000)(0.30) + (\$10,000)\,(0.70) = \$5,500$

$\sigma_B^2 = (-5,000 - 5,500)^2(0.30) + (10,000 - 5,500)^2(0.70) = \$47,250,000$

$\sigma_B = \$6,874$

Gamble C   Lose $7,000 with a probability of 0.20, or win $15,000 with a probability of 0.80:

$E(C) = (-\$7,000)\,(0.20) + (\$15,000)\,(0.80) = \$10,600$

$\sigma_C^2 = (-17,600)^2(0.20) + (4,400)^2(0.80) = \$77,440,000$

$\sigma_C = \$8,800$

Gamble D   Lose $10,000 with a probability of 0.10, or win $25,000 with a probability of 0.90:

$E(D) = (-\$10,000)\,(0.10) + (\$25,000)\,(0.90) = \$21,500$

$\sigma_D^2 = (-31,500)^2(0.10) + (3,500)^2(0.90) = \$110,250,000$

$\sigma_D = \$10,500$

Gamble E   Lose $15,000 with a probability of 0.05, or win $40,000 with a probability of 0.95:

$E(E) = (-\$15,000)\,(0.05) + (\$40,000)\,(0.95) = \$37,250$

$\sigma_E^2 = (-52,250)^2(0.05) + (2,750)^2(0.95) = \$143,687,500$

$\sigma_E = \$11,987$

As an illustration of the above procedure assume that the decision-maker expressed indifference between receiving the cash amount of $1,000 and the gambles shown in Table 11.5. The cash amount of $1,000 is the certainty equivalent of the five gambles, whose risk—payoff combinations are shown in Figure 11.21.

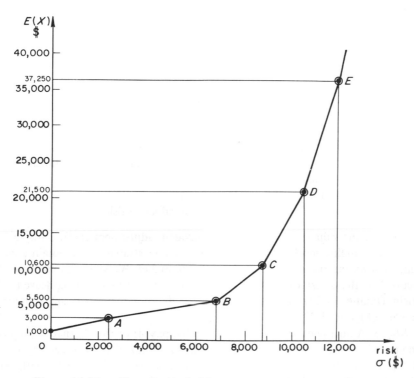

Figure 11.21   Hypothetical risk—expected-value trade-off curve

Step 2. Estimation of the 'certainty-equivalent adjustment coefficients'. From the risk—expected-value trade-off curve we obtain a 'certainty-equivalent adjustment coefficient' for each level of risk. This coefficient, α, for each project is estimated by dividing the certainty equivalent (amount of dollars) by the expected mean profitability of the (risky) project:

$$\alpha_X = \frac{\text{Certainty equivalent}}{E(X)} \qquad (11.9)$$

In our example the certainty-equivalent adjustment coefficients of the five strategies are

$$\alpha_A = \frac{\text{Certainty equivalent}}{E(A)} = \frac{\$1,000}{\$3,000} = 0.33$$

$$\alpha_B = \frac{\text{Certainty equivalent}}{E(B)} = \frac{\$1,000}{\$5,500} = 0.18$$

$$\alpha_C = \frac{\text{Certainty equivalent}}{E(C)} = \frac{\$1,000}{\$10,600} = 0.09$$

$$\alpha_D = \frac{\text{Certainty equivalent}}{E(D)} = \frac{\$1,000}{\$21,500} = 0.05$$

$$\alpha_E = \frac{\text{Certainty equivalent}}{E(E)} = \frac{\$1,000}{\$37,250} = 0.03$$

It should be clear that:

(1) The maximum value of α is unity. It is the adjustment coefficient of the certainty-equivalent amount of cash.
(2) The value of α decreases as risk increases.
(3) The value of α tends to zero at very high values of risk.

Plotting the values of the certainty-equivalent adjustment coefficients against the corresponding level of risk of the alternative strategies, we obtain a curve which shows the risk attitude of the decision-maker. We will call this curve 'the α-curve'. If the decision-maker is a risk-averter this curve will be concave to the origin (Figure 11.22). The 'α-curve' of the decision-maker of our example is shown in Figure 11.23.

Step 3. Adjustment for risk of the expected payoff of the alternative projects. The decision-maker adjusts the expected profitability of each project by multiplying it by the corresponding 'certainty-equivalent adjustment coefficient' which he 'reads' from his 'α-curve'. The adjusted (for risk) values of the strategies are smaller than the original ones, given that $0 < \alpha < 1$.

For example, assume that the decision-maker is considering three strategies

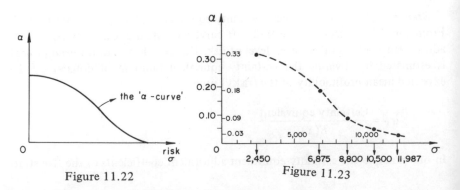

Figure 11.22   Figure 11.23

with the following risk—payoff values:

$$E(W) = \$15,000 \qquad \sigma_W = \$5,000$$

$$E(Y) = \$30,000 \qquad \sigma_Y = \$6,000$$

$$E(Z) = \$45,000 \qquad \sigma_Z = \$8,000$$

From the risk-aversion curve of Figure 11.23 we find the following (approximate) values of the 'certainty-equivalent adjustment factor':

for $\sigma_W = \$5,000 \qquad \alpha_W = 0.25$

for $\sigma_Y = \$6,000 \qquad \alpha_Y = 0.20$

for $\sigma_Z = \$8,000 \qquad \alpha_Z = 0.12$

Thus the risk-adjusted expected profitabilities of the three strategies are

$$E(W)^* = (\alpha_W)\,E(W) = (0.25)\,(15,000) = \$3,750$$

$$E(Y)^* = (\alpha_Y)\,E(Y) = (0.20)\,(30,000) = \$6,000$$

$$E(Z)^* = (\alpha_Z)\,E(Z) = (0.12)\,(45,000) = \$5,400$$

Step 4. Discounting with the riskless interest rate. The above adjustment takes into account the risk of the various projects. In order to take into account the time value of money, the risk-adjusted profitabilities should be discounted by the risk-free market interest rate, i.[13] In this way we obtain the expected mean present value of each project:

$$\overline{PV}_j = \Sigma\,\frac{\alpha_{jt}E(X)_{j,t}}{(1+i)^t}$$

where $\overline{PV}_j$ = present value of the risk-adjusted stream of earnings of the jth project

$E(X)_{j,t}$ = mean of *each term* of the stream of earnings of the jth project

In our example we were considering one-period investment projects which had a single mean value, $E(X)$. Thus, assuming $i = 0.06$, the present values of the expected earnings of each project are

$$\overline{PV}_W = \frac{\alpha_W E(W)}{1+i} = \frac{0.25\,(15,000)}{1.06} = \frac{3,750}{1.06} = \$3,538$$

$$\overline{PV}_Y = \frac{\alpha_Y E(Y)}{1+i} = \frac{0.20\,(30,000)}{1.06} = \frac{6,000}{1.06} = \$5,660$$

$$\overline{PV}_Z = \frac{\alpha_Z E(Z)}{1+i} = \frac{0.12\,(45,000)}{1.06} = \frac{5,400}{1.06} = \$5,094$$

[13] The risk-free rate of interest i can be taken as the yield (to maturity) of government bonds. The yield varies with the maturity of bonds. One should select a maturity comparable with the expected life of the project being considered. See R. W. Johnson, *Capital Budgeting* (Wadsworth Publishing Company, 1970) p. 116.

If investments are multi-period ones, each term in the stream of earnings $E(X)_{j,t}$ should be adjusted by an appropriate $\alpha_{j,t}$ coefficient, depending on the standard deviation $\sigma_{j,t}$ corresponding to that term. (The $\sigma_{j,t}$ are estimated by the methods discussed on pp. 517–22.)

Step 5. Choice among the risky alternatives. The decision-maker chooses the strategy with the highest risk–adjusted profitability. In our example the decision-maker will choose strategy Y, if he uses the certainty-equivalents approach (criterion). (He would choose strategy Z if he were using 'the expected-value criterion').

It should be clear that in the 'certainty-equivalents' approach risk is taken into account by making an adjustment to the numerator of the present-value expression. Thus in this approach risk is kept separate from the time value of money.

C. Risk-Adjusted Discount Rates

An alternative way of taking risk into account is to use risk-adjusted discount rates. In this approach the adjustment for risk is made to the denominator of the present-value expression.

If we let i denote the risk-free rate of interest (the time value of money), δ a risk-adjustment coefficient (or risk premium) and k the risk-adjusted discount rate to be used in determining whether the net present value is positive (and, hence, whether the investment is desirable), then we may write

$$\overline{PV} = \sum_{t=0}^{n} \frac{\bar{X}_t}{(1+k)^t} \tag{11.10}$$

where

$$k = i + \delta \qquad (\delta > 0) \tag{11.11}$$

The size of the risk premium δ depends upon the degree of uncertainty inherent in the project's stream of earnings.

An investment project is accepted if its net present value is positive:

$$\overline{NPV} = \sum_{t=0}^{n} \frac{\bar{X}_t}{(1+k)^t} - C > 0 \tag{11.12}$$

Before we proceed with the discussion of the determination of the value of k appropriate for a particular investment project, it is important to examine the risk pattern implied by expression (11.10). As it stands this expression assumes that the *same* risk-adjusted rate, k, is applied to each year's expected earnings, that is, to each term of the stream of the project's future earnings. This assumption implies a particular risk pattern: risk is assumed to increase at a constant rate over time. To see this we observe that

$$\frac{\bar{X}_t}{(1+k)^t} < \frac{\bar{X}_t}{(1+i)^t} \tag{11.13}$$

since $k > i$. The left-hand side of this inequality is the present value of expected earnings taking into account *both* the time value of money and risk. The right-hand side of the inequality is the present value of expected earnings taking into account *only* the time value of money (but not risk). Hence the ratio of these two present values, which we shall denote by λ, represents the reduction (adjustment) in the present value of expected earnings as a result of risk:

$$\lambda_t = \frac{\bar{X}_t/(1+k)^t}{\bar{X}_t/(1+i)^t} \tag{11.14}$$

In other words, λ_t may be viewed as a *pure* risk-adjustment factor of expected earnings.

We may rewrite expression (11.14) in the form

$$\lambda_t = \left(\frac{1+i}{1+k}\right)^t \tag{11.15}$$

or

$$\lambda_t = \left(\frac{1+i}{1+i+\delta}\right)^t \tag{11.16}$$

It follows from these expressions that using a risk-adjusted discount rate k is equivalent to simple discounting (by using the riskless i) of the expected earnings after they have been adjusted for risk by the factor λ_t, that is,

$$PV = \sum_{t=0}^{n} \frac{\bar{X}_t}{(1+k)^t} = \sum_{t=0}^{n} \frac{\lambda_t \bar{X}_t}{(1+i)^t} \tag{11.17}$$

*   *   *

PROOF

$$\frac{\lambda_t \bar{X}_t}{(1+i)^t} = \left(\frac{1+i}{1+k}\right)^t \times \frac{\bar{X}_t}{(1+i)^t}$$

$$= \frac{(1+i)^t}{(1+k)^t} \times \frac{\bar{X}_t}{(1+i)^t} = \frac{\bar{X}_t}{(1+k)^t}$$

QED

It should be clear that by multiplying $\bar{X}_t$ by λ_t we obtain one type of certainty equivalent. However, λ_t is not necessarily the same as α_t of the 'certainty-equivalents' model.

*   *   *

To illustrate this equivalence, consider a project which has expected earnings of $10,000 in each of three periods. If the chosen risk-adjusted k is 0.20 and the risk-free interest rate is 0.05, then

$$\lambda_t = \left(\frac{1+i}{1+k}\right)^t = \left(\frac{1.05}{1.20}\right)^t = 0.875^t$$

Using λ_t, the $\overline{PV}$ of the project is

$$\overline{PV} = \sum_{t=1}^{3} \frac{\lambda_t \overline{X}_t}{(1+i)^t} = \frac{\lambda_1 \overline{X}_1}{(1+i)^1} + \frac{\lambda_2 \overline{X}_2}{(1+i)^2} + \frac{\lambda_3 \overline{X}_3}{(1+i)^3}$$

where $\lambda_1 = 0.875$
$\qquad \lambda_2 = 0.875^2 = 0.7656 \qquad (1+0.05)^2 = 1.1025$
$\qquad \lambda_3 = 0.875^3 = 0.6699 \qquad (1+0.05)^3 = 1.1576$

That is,

$$\overline{PV} = \frac{0.875(10,000)}{1.05} + \frac{0.7656(10,000)}{1.05^2} + \frac{0.6699(10,000)}{1.05^3}$$

$$= (0.8333)(10,000) + (0.6944)(10,000) + (0.5787)(10,000)$$

$$= 8,333 + 6,944 + 5,787$$

$$= \$21,064$$

Using the risk-adjusted rate of $k = 0.20$, we find

$$\overline{PV} = \sum_{t=1}^{3} \frac{\overline{X}_t}{(1+k)^t}$$

$$= \frac{\overline{X}_1}{1.20} + \frac{\overline{X}_2}{1.20^2} + \frac{\overline{X}_3}{1.20^3}$$

$$= \frac{10,000}{1.20} + \frac{10,000}{1.44} + \frac{10,000}{1.728}$$

$$= (0.8333)(10,000) + (0.6944)(10,000) + (0.5787)(10,000)$$

$$= 8,333 + 6,944 + 5,787$$

$$= \$21,064$$

Thus we have verified that discounting with $k = 0.20$ is equivalent to discounting $\lambda_t \overline{X}_t (= 0.875^t X_t)$ at $i = 0.05$.

Returning to expression (11.15)

$$\lambda_t = \left(\frac{1+i}{1+k}\right)^t$$

we observe that $(1+i)/(1+k) < 1$, since $k > i$, so that λ_t decreases exponentially over time, that is, risk is assumed to compound exponentially through time, if we use a single k for all the $\bar{X}_t$ (the terms of the expected earnings stream) of the project, as is implied by the use of expression (11.10).

Some writers argue that the risk pattern implied by the application of a risk-adjusted discount rate may not be appropriate for all investment projects. In particular, the application of high-risk premiums penalises investments with a long lifetime. To see this we may define a *future-earnings function*, which shows the required future earnings in period t, that gives the same present value when discounted at the risk-adjusted rate k as \$1 discounted at the riskless rate i.

First note that the present value of \$1 discounted at the riskless rate i is

$$P_0 = e^{-it} \tag{11.18}$$

using continuous discounting.

*   *   *

Using discrete discounting we would have

$$P_0 = (1+i)^t$$
$$x_t(1+k)^{-t} = P_0$$
$$x_t(t+k)^{-t} = (1+i)^{-t}$$

and

$$x_t = \frac{(1+i)^{-t}}{(1+k)^{-t}} = \left(\frac{1+k}{1+i}\right)^t$$

*   *   *

By definition

$$x_t e^{-kt} = P_0 \tag{11.19}$$

Hence

$$x_t e^{-kt} = e^{-it}$$

Solving for x_t we obtain the 'future-earnings function'

$$x_t = e^{-it+kt} = e^{(k-i)t} \tag{11.20}$$

or

$$x_t = e^{\delta t}$$

since, by definition, $k = i + \delta$.

By assigning a risk premium to a project, we can find x_t, i.e. the required earnings in period t.

In Figure 11.24 we show the 'future-earnings function' for three different risk premiums.

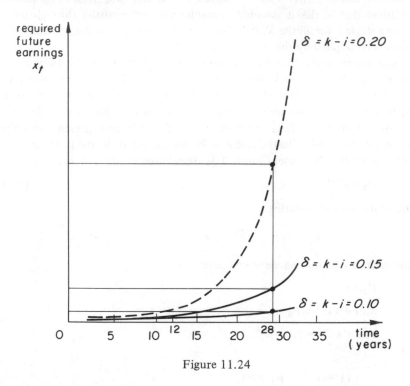

Figure 11.24

It is apparent from Figure 11.24 that increasing the risk premium will not significantly affect the investments which have a short life. (Up to twelve years the required future earnings are not much affected by increasing k.) But the effects of increased k are substantial for investments with a long life. A project with $n = 28$ years must have very high future earnings if $\delta = 0.20$, but only moderate future earnings if $\delta = 0.15$, and low future earnings if $\delta = 0.10$.

We turn now to the problem of the determination of the value of risk premiums and risk-adjusted discount rates. Various methods have been discussed in the financial literature. We will present the most important of these methods.

(i) *Defining risk classes for investments*

Rather than assign a risk-adjusted rate to each project, many firms classify investments on the basis of the risk inherent in their stream of earnings. Three classes are usually distinguished:

(a) low-risk investments
(b) typical-risk investments
(c) high-risk investments

Risk premiums (δs) are then assigned to each investment class, based on intuition, experience and any available information (from consultants, analysts, etc.). For example, management may decide that the following risk premiums are suitable for the firm's investment projects:

(1) $\delta = 0.03$ for low-risk investment projects, such as replacement investments, investments for producing commodities for which there are long-term sales contracts, or investments for meeting increased demand of the existing line of products.

(b) $\delta = 0.10$ for 'typical-risk projects', such as changes in the style or the technical characteristics of existing products.

(c) $\delta = 0.30$ for high-risk projects, such as research and development, new product projects, new technology projects, and so on.

Assuming that the riskless interest rate is $i = 0.06$, the risk-adjusted discount rates would be

$k = 0.06 + 0.03 = 0.09$, or 9% for low-risk projects

$k = 0.06 + 0.10 = 0.16$, or 16% for typical-risk projects

$k = 0.06 + 0.30 = 0.36$, or 36% for high-risk projects

Obviously, this method involves a lot of arbitrary judgement; and intuition is frequently unreliable.

(ii) *Use of the firm's average weighted cost of capital as the risk-adjusted discount rate*

Many writers advocate the use of the firm's weighted average cost of capital as the risk-adjusted discount rate.

Recall that the cost of capital to a firm reflects the capital structure of the firm, the risk of the firm's earnings and the timing of these earnings. Assuming that a firm has a target capital structure, the weights of the various sources of funds will be the 'target weights', i.e. the weights corresponding to the target capital structure. For a given capital structure, the average cost of capital then reflects 'the average risk' of the existing investments and 'the average timing' of the present investments' expected earnings. In other words, given the firm's target capital structure, the firm's average cost of capital combines in one discount rate an allowance for the time value of money and an allowance for risk. Thus, using the firm's average cost of capital as the risk-adjusted discount rate implies that (a) the investment projects have the same 'average risk' as the existing investments, so that the risk complexion of the firm does not change after undertaking the investments, and (b) the timing of the new projects' earnings is the same as the timing of the firm's present earnings. For example, if a transport firm increases its capacity by buying additional trucks identical to those already being used, the firm's weighted average cost of capital is an appropriate discount rate for the expansion investment.

However, if an investment project changes the risk or the timing of the firm's stream of earnings, the weighted average cost of capital is not an appropriate discount rate.

(iii) *Use of the weighted average cost of capital of another firm as the discount rate*

If the proposed investment substantially changes the risk characteristics of the firm, the expected earnings should be discounted at a lower or a higher rate than the firm's cost of capital, depending upon whether the investment is less risky or more risky than the existing group of investments that determine the present risk class of the firm, and hence its present cost of capital. For example, if a food firm decides to diversify in the electronics field, its risk will no doubt increase. The new investment must be discounted at a higher rate than the firm's current cost of capital.

Thus there is a unique cost of capital for every proposed fixed investment: it is the rate of discount that the particular investment must earn in order to leave the market value of the shareholders' equity (the value of the firm) unchanged. If the project is in the same risk class as that of the firm, the current cost of capital is the appropriate discount rate. If the project changes the risk class of the firm, a new different rate must be estimated. Some writers argue that the appropriate rate of discount is the cost of capital of firms already producing the same or similar products to the products that the firm intends to produce with the new investment. This can be estimated from the prices of stocks in the capital market. It is argued that if a firm can estimate its own cost of capital, it can also estimate the cost of capital of other firms already established in the field in which the firm intends to expand with its new investment. (For example, the food firm can estimate the cost of capital of electronics firms.) To the extent that the size or timing of the risk associated with the proposed investment appears to be different from the cost of capital of firms specialising in that field, the firm can adjust the estimated cost of capital.

The difficulties of estimating the cost of capital have been discussed in Chapter 10. The difficulties multiply if a firm wants to estimate the cost of capital of firms operating in another industry. Furthermore, adjustments of that cost of capital are by their nature completely arbitrary.

(iv) *Discount rates found from the risk—return trade-off curve of the decision-maker*

The risk—return trade-off function of the decision-maker may be derived in the same way as the trade-off function of the certainty-equivalents model.

For example, suppose that the risk—return trade-off function of the decision-maker is the curve shown in Figure 11.25. The risk is measured by the coefficient of variation.[14] The decision-maker is indifferent to a riskless investment (e.g. a government bond) with a sure 5 per cent rate of return, a moderately risky project with an expected rate of return of 7 per cent (and a risk of 0.3), and a high-risk project which promises an (expected) return of 23 per cent, with a risk of 1.2. The shape of the risk—return trade-off curve of Figure 11.25 implies that the decision-maker is risk-averse: as risk increases by equal amounts, higher and higher expected returns on the (more-risky) projects are required to compensate for the additional risk.

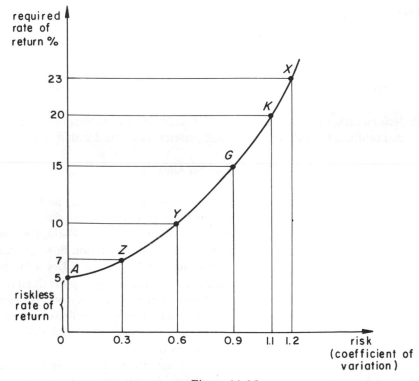

Figure 11.25

The difference between the required rate of return of a project and the riskless rate of interest is *the risk premium*, δ, on the risky project. In the hypothetical example of Figure 11.25 the riskless rate is assumed to be 5 per cent. Thus a 2 per cent risk premium is required for the risky project Z (whose risk is 0.3). Similarly, a 5 per cent risk premium is attached to the risky strategy Y (whose risk is 0.6),

[14] The use of the standard deviation would be confusing, since the expected return is measured as a percentage (see p. 522).

and a risk premium of 18 per cent is required for the risky strategy X (which has a coefficient of variation of 1.2). The decision-maker in our example is indifferent to the risky strategies X, Y and Z, and the riskless investment A.

To illustrate the use of risk-adjusted discount rates, assume that the decision-maker is considering two alternative strategies (each requiring the same cost expenditure). Strategy G has expected earnings of $30,000 with a standard deviation of $27,000 (or a coefficient of variation of 0.9), while project K has an expected value of $31,000, with a standard deviation of $34,100 (or a coefficient of variation of 1.1). From the (hypothetical) risk—return trade-off function we see that the expected earnings of project G should be discounted by 15 per cent, while the expected earnings of project K should be discounted by 20 per cent. Thus the risk-adjusted expected earnings of the two projects are

$$E(G)' = \frac{\$30,000}{1.15} = \$26,087$$

$$E(K)' = \frac{\$31,000}{1.20} = \$25,833$$

The decision-maker will choose project G, because project K, despite its higher expected profit, is too risky, given the risk preferences of the decision-maker.

Concluding remarks on risk-adjusted discount rates

Risk-adjusted discount rates are widely used by firms which classify investments in risk-groups and apply a subjectively defined risk premium to each class.

Risk-adjusted discount rates are popular in the real business world, because managers are accustomed to appraising risks versus rates of return. However, the way risk-adjusted discount rates are determined in practice involves a lot of arbitrariness. Furthermore, a *single* discount rate is usually applied to all the $\bar{X}_t$s (to all the terms of the project's stream of expected earnings). We saw that the use of a single discount rate to each period's earnings assumes implicitly that risk increases at a constant rate over time, and this risk pattern may not be appropriate for all investment projects.

It should be stressed that these shortcomings are avoided if we have the decision-maker's risk—return trade-off function. In this event we can apply a different discount rate to each year's expected earnings, $\bar{X}_t$, depending on the risk of these earnings. However, this is not the way risk-adjusted rates are estimated in practice. Most firms use either arbitrarily defined risk premiums or the current cost of capital of the firm. In both cases the adjustment for risk may be inappropriate.

D. Maximisation of Expected Utility

In this model utilities are assigned to the possible outcomes of each strategy, and each strategy's expected utility is estimated with the expression

$$E(U_X) = \Sigma(U_{Xi}) \, Pr(X_i) \qquad (11.21)$$

where U_{Xi} = utility of the ith outcome of strategy X
$Pr(X_i)$ = probability of the ith outcome of strategy X

Among the alternative strategies the decision-maker chooses the one with the highest expected utility.

The estimation of the expected utility of each alternative course of action requires (a) knowledge of the probability distribution of the possible outcomes of the strategy, and (b) the total utility of money function of the decision-maker. These tools have been developed in section II of this chapter.

To illustrate the utility-maximisation method we will use the utility of money function derived in section II. Assume that a decision-maker considers two strategies A and B. The decision-maker knows the possible outcomes of these strategies and assigns subjective probabilities to their occurrence. This information gives the probability distributions of the two strategies. They are summarised in Table 11.6.

Table 11.6   Subjective probability distributions of the earnings of projects A and B

States of general business conditions	Probability distribution of possible outcomes of project A		Probability distribution of possible outcomes of project B	
	Possible outcome (A_i)	Probability $Pr(A_i)$	Possible outcome (B_i)	Probability $Pr(B_i)$
Inflation	$150	0.60	$0	0.60
Recession	$500	0.30	$1000	0.30
Depression	$350	0.10	$220	0.10

Using the hypothetical total utility of money function of section II we can transform the above distributions of money-outcomes into distributions showing the utilities of the various earnings and their probabilities. This is shown in Table 11.7.

Table 11.7   Utility probability distributions of projects A and B

	Project A			Project B		
Earnings ($)	Utility (utils)	Probability $Pr(A_i)$		Earnings ($)	Utility (utils)	Probability $Pr(B_i)$
$150	30	0.60		$0	0	0.60
$500	70	0.30		$1,000	100	0.30
$350	50	0.10		$220	40	0.10

The expected utilities of the two strategies are

$$E(U_A) = \Sigma(U_{Ai})\, Pr(A_i) = (30)(0.6) + (70)(0.3) + (50)(0.1) = 44 \text{ utils}$$

$$E(U_B) = \Sigma(U_{Bi})\, Pr(B_i) = (0)(0.6) + (100)(0.3) + (40)(0.1) = 34 \text{ utils}$$

According to the principle of maximisation of expected utility, the decision-maker will choose project A, which yields the higher expected utility. If the decision-maker were looking for the highest 'average profitability' (that is, if he were applying the 'expected-value' criterion), he would choose project B, since this project has a higher expected profit:

$$E(A) = \Sigma(A_i)\, Pr(A_i) = (150)(0.6) + (500)(0.3) + (350)(0.1) = \$275$$

$$E(B) = \Sigma(B_i)\, Pr(B_i) = (0)(0.6) + (1{,}000)(0.3) + (220)(0.1) = \$322$$

However, if the risk attitude (risk preferences) of the individual is taken into account, then the individual would choose project A, because of its higher expected utility. The fact that adopting project B has a 60 per cent (0.6) probability of zero profit weighs heavily in the choice of a risk-averter.

The above approach requires knowledge of the utility of money function of the investor and of *the entire probability distribution* of possible outcomes of each strategy. This requirement is difficult to be fulfilled in practice.

A simpler model, the 'mean-variance model', or 'the two-parameter model', has been developed from the work of Markowitz, Sharpe and others. This model requires less information. It will be discussed in Chapter 12.

E.   The Weighted Average Cost of Capital Model

In an earlier part of this chapter (p. 542) we saw that the firm's cost of capital is often used as the risk-adjusted discount rate for investment projects which do not change the risk class of the firm. In this section we show how the firm's weighted average cost of capital is used as a *hurdle rate* or *cut-off rate* for investment projects.

The use of the cost of capital as the hurdle rate for investment decisions requires formally the determination of the firm's marginal efficiency of investment schedule (MEI), and the supply-of-funds schedule (S_F), taking into account risk.

(i) *The MEI schedule under risk*

In Chapter 4 we saw that the marginal efficiency of investment (or the internal rate of return, IRR) is the rate of discount that equates the present value of the stream of future earnings to the cost outlay of the investment.

Under uncertainty the stream of future earnings of a project consists of terms which do not have unique values, but are random variables. Thus for each period we find the expected value of the earnings, $E(X_t)$:

$$E(X_1) = \Sigma(X_{1i}) Pr(X_{1i}) = \bar{X}_1$$

$$E(X_2) = \Sigma(X_{2i}) Pr(X_{2i}) = \bar{X}_2$$

$$\cdot \quad \cdot \quad \cdot$$
$$\cdot \quad \cdot \quad \cdot$$
$$\cdot \quad \cdot \quad \cdot$$

$$E(X_n) = \Sigma(X_{ni}) Pr(X_{ni}) = \bar{X}_n$$

The internal rate of return, r, is estimated from the expression

$$\frac{\bar{X}_1}{(1+r)} + \frac{\bar{X}_2}{(1+r)^2} + \ldots + \frac{\bar{X}_n}{(1+r)^n} - C = 0 \qquad (11.22)$$

or

$$\sum_{t=1}^{n} \frac{\bar{X}_t}{(1+r)^t} - C = 0 \qquad (11.22a)$$

This is the same expression as the one used under certainty (see Chapter 4), with the $\bar{X}_t$ replacing the unique values X_t in the stream of future earnings.

The procedure is repeated for all investment proposals, and projects are ranked in descending order of their IRR. The IRR or MEI schedule is derived by plotting the internal rates of return of the investment opportunities open to the firm against the amount of funds required for these investments.

To illustrate the derivation of the MEI schedule, we will assume that the earnings from the investment projects have the form of an annuity, that is, all the terms in the stream of earnings are equal. This allows us to use Table 4 (of Appendix 3.2 of Chapter 3) to find the IRR of each project.

Suppose that the firm is considering the six investment projects shown in Table 11.8.

Table 11.8

Project	Annual earnings ($\bar{X}$)	Project's life (years)	Initial cost of investment (C)
A	$54,100	5	$200,000
B	$32,850	7	$150,000
C	$41,550	10	$250,000
D	$87,600	6	$350,000
E	$39,550	8	$200,000
F	$105,000	3	$250,000

The internal rate of return of each project can be estimated, using the expression for the present value of an annuity developed in Chapter 3:

$$V_0 = Y \left(\sum_{t=1}^{n} \frac{1}{(1+r)^t} \right)$$ (11.23)

where V_0 = initial cost (for 'buying' the project generating the annuity)
   Y = amount received yearly
   r = internal rate of return

For project A we have

$$200,000 = 54,100 \left(\sum_{t=1}^{5} \frac{1}{(1+r)^t} \right)$$

$$\sum_{t=1}^{5} \left(\frac{1}{(1+r)^t} \right) = \frac{200,000}{54,100} = 3.7$$

From the fifth row of Table 4 (on page 206) we find that the $PVIF_A$ value of 3.7 implies a discount rate equal to 11 per cent (approximately), i.e. $r_A = 0.11$.
   Similarly, for project B

$$150,000 = 32,850 \left(\sum_{t=1}^{7} \frac{1}{(1+r)^t} \right)$$

$$PVIF_A = \sum_{t=1}^{7} \left(\frac{1}{(1+r)^t} \right) = \frac{150,000}{32,850} = 4.57$$

From the seventh row of Table 4 we see that the $PVIF_A$ value of 4.57 implies a discount rate of 12 per cent (approximately), i.e. $r_B = 0.12$.
   For project C we find

$$PVIF_A = \sum_{t=1}^{10} \left(\frac{1}{(1+r)^t} \right) = \frac{250,000}{41,550} = 6.02$$

From the tenth row of Table 4 we find that the $PVIF_A$ value of 6.02 implies $r_C = 0.105$ (or 10.5 per cent) approximately.
   For project D we have

$$PVIF_A = \sum_{t=1}^{6} \left(\frac{1}{(1+r)^t} \right) = \frac{350,000}{87,600} = 4.03$$

From the sixth row of Table 4 we see that the $PVIF_A$ of 4.02 implies $r_D = 0.13$ (or 13 per cent) approximately.

For project E we have

$$PVIF_A = \sum_{t=1}^{8} \left(\frac{1}{(1+r)^t}\right) = \frac{200,000}{39,550} = 5.06$$

From the eighth row of Table 4 we find that the $PVIF_A$ value of 5.06 implies $r_E = 0.115$ (or 11.5 per cent) approximately.

For project F we have

$$PVIF_A = \sum_{t=1}^{3} \left(\frac{1}{(1+r)^t} = \frac{250,000}{105,000} = 2.38\right)$$

From the third row of Table 4 we see that the $PVIF_A$ of 2.38 implies $r_F = 0.125$ (or 12.5 per cent) approximately.

The demand for investment schedule (or MEI schedule) for the above six projects is shown in Figure 11.26.

(ii) *The supply-of-funds schedule, S_F*

The supply-of-funds schedule relates various amounts of funds to the cost of raising them.

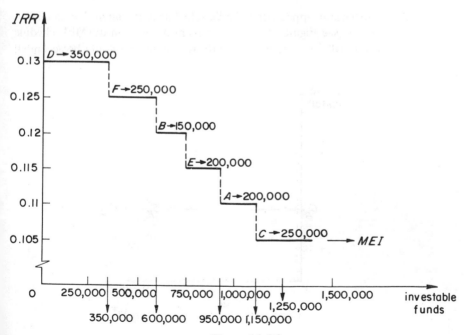

Figure 11.26

Under uncertainty each source of funds has a different cost, because each security has a different degree of risk. We saw in Chapter 10 that the cost of capital is the weighted average of the costs of the various sources of finance:

$$C_A = C_E(1 - L^*) + C_D L^* \tag{11.24}$$

or

$$C_A = \left[k_o \left(w_1 + \frac{w_2}{1 - h} \right) \right] (1 - L^*) + [k_o(1 - t_c)]L^*$$

where k_o = cost of equity of an unlevered firm
   w_1, w_2 = weights of retained earnings and new stock respectively
          $(w_1 + w_2 = 1)$
       h = flotation costs of new stock
       t_c = corporate tax rate
       L^* = optimal (or target) proportion of debt in the firm's capital struc-
          ture
   $1 - L^*$ = optimal equity proportion in the firm's capital structure

In practice, the cost of capital is assumed to have a single value, and this value is used as *the* hurdle rate for investment decisions. In other words, management uses the accept—reject criterion:

Accept a project if its IRR $> C_A$

Formally this behaviour implies that the S_F schedule is a straight line parallel to the horizontal axis (see Figure 11.27). Investment projects on the MEI schedule which have an internal rate of return above the (constant) C_A would be accepted.

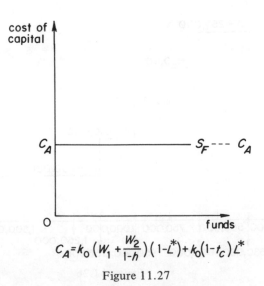

$$C_A = k_o \left(W_1 + \frac{W_2}{1-h} \right) \left(1 - \overset{*}{L} \right) + k_o(1 - t_c) \overset{*}{L}$$

Figure 11.27

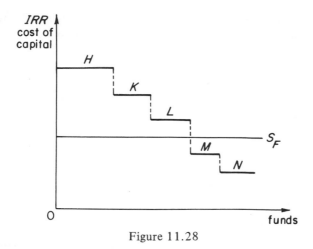

Figure 11.28

In Figure 11.28 investments H, K, L would be accepted, while M and N would be rejected.

This practice may lead to 'wrong' investment decisions. A straight-line S_F curve assumes that the firm (a) will maintain its target capital structure, (b) can borrow any amount of funds at a constant interest rate, and (c) can sell any amount of stock with the same terms as previous issues. Obviously these assumptions are not realistic. If the firm borrows beyond its debt capacity, it will have to pay higher interest rates. Similarly if the firm sells a large amount of stock, it will probably have to sell below the normal price. In both cases the cost of capital will increase. The firm has to estimate its entire S_F curve. In Chapter 10 we saw that in the real world the supply-of-funds schedule is a step-function, like the one shown in Figure 11.29. If the firm needs a large amount of funds, it will

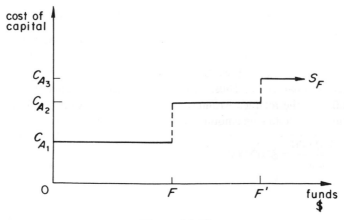

Figure 11.29

have to sell large amounts of bonds and/or stocks, or borrow heavily from banks. This will increase its weighted average cost of capital, due to increases in the cost of debt and/or the cost of equity, even if the firm maintains its target capital structure.

The stepwise shape of the S_F curve denotes the fact that in the real world the cost of capital increases at various levels of funding rather than continuously.

In Chapter 10 we illustrated the estimation of the supply-of-funds schedule with a numerical example. In this section, using the same methodology (of Chapter 10), we will estimate another S_F curve, which is compatible with the MEI schedule of our earlier example. This derivation will make the student more familiar with the technique of finding the various 'steps' of the S_F schedule.

Assume that the cost of the various sources of funds are

$$C_R = k_o = \text{cost of retained earnings} = 0.14 \text{ (or 14\%)}$$

$$C_D = k_o(1 - t_c) = \text{cost of debt} = 0.06 \text{ (or 6\%), assuming a corporate tax}$$
rate of 57 per cent

$$C_E = k_o \frac{1}{1 - h} = \text{cost of new stock} = 0.148 \text{ (or 14.8\%), assuming that}$$
flotation costs, h, are 5.4 per cent

The optimal capital structure of the firm is

$$L^* = \text{proportion of debt} = 0.40$$

$$1 - L^* = \text{proportion of equity} = 0.60$$

The firm has a debt capacity of $400,000, and retentions $420,000.

The firm first exhausts its internal equity, that is, its retained earnings. With debt financing and retained earnings, the average cost of capital is

$$C_{A1} = (0.14)(0.60) + (0.06)(0.40) = 0.108 \quad \text{(or 10.8\%)}$$

With debt financing and new common stock, the average cost of capital is

$$C_{A2} = (0.148)(0.60) + (0.06)(0.40) = 0.113 \quad \text{(or 11.3\%)}$$

Recall, from Chapter 10, that whenever a more expensive source of finance is tapped, there will be a break (a higher 'step') of the S_F curve. In our example the S_F curve will have three 'steps', which may be found with the method developed in Chapter 10. Thus, with the assumed debt capacity of the firm of $400,000, and the retained earnings of $420,000, the 'steps' of the S_F schedule will occur at the following amounts of funds:

$$\frac{420,000}{0.60} = \$700,000$$

and

$$\frac{400,000}{0.40} = \$1,000,000$$

The technique for the derivation of the 'breaks' in the supply-of-funds schedule is simple.

(1) The internal equity (= retained earnings) of $420,000 constitutes 60 per cent of the firm's capital structure. Hence with that amount of equity the firm can have total funds of $700,000,[15] with an average cost of 0.108 or 10.8 per cent. These funds will consist of $420,000 internal equity (retained earnings) and $280,000 new debt.

(2) If the firm wants more funds, the equity will have to be raised by issue of new stock (external equity), since retained earnings have been exhausted. To exhaust its debt capacity, the firm can raise additional debt of $120,000 (since $280,000 of the debt capacity have already been raised). With that amount of new debt the firm can raise total (*additional*) funds of $300,000.[16] Thus the second break in the S_F function occurs at the amount of $1,000,000. Up to $700,000 the average cost of capital is, as we saw, 0.108 (or 10.8 per cent). For the additional $300,000 the average cost of capital rises to 0.113 (or 11.3 per cent).[17] It should be clear that this additional amount of funds consists of $120,000 new debt and $180,000 new stock.

(3) If the firm wants funds beyond the amount of $1,000,000, it must sell more stock and borrow at a higher cost, say $C_D' = 0.072$. (For simplicity we assume that the new stock can be raised at the same cost $C_E = 0.148$). Hence beyond $1,000,000 the S_F schedule has a third 'step', corresponding to the average cost of capital of 11.8 per cent, estimated as follows:

$$C_{A3} = (0.148)(0.60) + (0.072)(0.40) = 0.118$$

The S_F curve of the above example is shown in Figure 11.30.
Combining the MEI schedule of Figure 11.26 with the S_F schedule of Figure 11.30, we find the optimal amount of investment from the point of intersection of these two schedules (Figure 11.31). The firm in our example should accept projects D, F, B and E which have IRRs higher than the cost of capital required

---

[15] This is estimated by the expression

$$\$420,000 = 0.60\, F_1$$

or

$$F_1 = \frac{\$420,000}{0.60} = \$700,000$$

[16] This is estimated from the expression

$$\$120,000 = 0.40\, F_2$$

or

$$F_2 = \frac{\$120,000}{0.40} = \$300,000$$

[17] Recall that with debt and external equity financing the average cost of capital is

$$(0.148)(0.60) + (0.06)(0.40) = 0.113$$

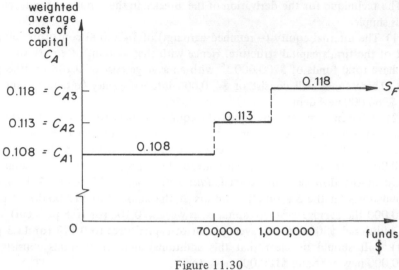

Figure 11.30

to finance them. Projects A and C should be rejected, because they have IRRs lower than the cost of funds (0.118) that would be required to implement them. Thus the optimal amount of investment is $950,000.

The weighted average cost of capital that should be used for comparison with

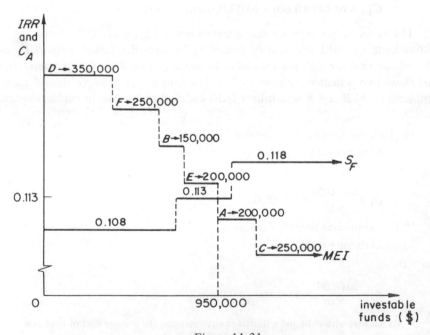

Figure 11.31

the IRR is 0.113, defined by the intersection of the MEI and the S_F curves. This is the cost which would lead to optimal investment decisions.

In summary, the accept—reject criterion is

Accept a project if its IRR $>$ WACC

where WACC $= C_A$ = weighted average cost of capital, defined by the intersection of the MEI and the S_F schedules.

The use of the WACC in investment decisions, either as a risk-adjusted discount rate (as in section III), or as a hurdle (as in this section), is supported by various theorists,[18] and is widely used by firms. Yet it has several shortcomings. First, it combines in one measure time-value considerations and the risk attitudes of the market towards the firm: C_A has both the firm's over-all business and financial risk premiums incorporated. Second, the use of C_A implies that the new investment has the same degree of risk as the firm. Third, the use of the cost of capital assumes that the expected earnings of the new investment have the same timing as the firm's earnings from its existing investments. These assumptions may not hold for all investment proposals.

IV. CRITERIA FOR DECISION-TAKING UNDER UNCERTAINTY

We said that uncertainty refers to situations in which the decision-maker does not know the probabilities of the outcomes of the alternative courses of action open to him.

In this section we shall present briefly five major approaches to decision-making when probabilities are unknown: (a) the *Bayes—Laplace* 'principle of insufficient reason'; (b) the *maximin* criterion; (c) the *minimax* criterion; (d) the *maximax* criterion; (e) the *Hurwicz* criterion; and (f) the *minimax-regret* criterion (or minimax opportunity-loss criterion).

To illustrate the problem of decision-making under uncertainty, consider the following example. A firm has four courses of action open to it: change the style of its product (strategy *A*), change its price (strategy *B*), embark on an advertising campaign (strategy *C*), or introduce a new product to its line of production (strategy *D*). The firm produces goods mainly for export to other countries; hence the results (outcomes) of each alternative strategy depend mostly on whether the value of the dollar will remain constant, increase or decrease in international money markets. Thus each strategy has three possible outcomes, depending on which 'event' will materialise in the future. The firm does *not* know the probabilities of these 'events' (constant dollar, decreasing dollar,

---

[18] F. Modigliani and M. Miller, 'The Cost of Capital, Corporation Finance and the Theory of Investment', *American Economic Review*, 1958, pp. 261–77; also H. Bierman and S. Smidt, *The Capital Budgeting Decision*, 3rd edn (Macmillan, 1975).

increasing dollar), and it does not have any control on them. (Note that in our example the 'events' which will influence the outcomes of the operations of the firm refer to the demand and supply of dollars in international money markets. But in general they may refer to facts unknown to the firm at the time that the decision must be made; they may reflect possible decisions of rival firms; or they may reflect situations brought about by chance. Because of the latter, it is customary to refer to these situations (events) as 'states of nature'. In economics such settings are also referred to as 'general business conditions', or 'rivals' reactions', etc.)

The first step is to construct a payoff table for the possible outcomes of each strategy in each 'state of nature'. The relevant estimates may be done by the firm's marketing department, or by consultants, or by managers on the basis of any pertinent information. The payoff table of our hypothetical example is shown in Table 11.9.

Table 11.9   Hypothetical payoff table of *A, B, C, D* strategies (profit in $ million)

States of nature	Strategy *A*	Strategy *B*	Strategy *C*	Strategy *D*
Constant value of $	$120	$360	−$30	$500
Increasing value of $	−$60	$120	$600	$100
Declining value of $	$240	$480	$300	$120

A.   Dominance and Admissibility of a Project (Strategy)

When the only information about the 'states of nature' is what they might be, it may be possible, nevertheless, to make a choice among the alternative strategies, or at least eliminate some of them, because they are *definitely worse* than others, irrespective of what 'state of nature' will be realised in the future. In our example strategy *A* is definitely worse than *B*, because in any one of the 'states of nature' strategy *B* will bring a greater profit: if the dollar remains constant $120 < $360; if the dollar increases $−60 < $120; if the dollar declines $240 < $600. Thus we say that strategy *A* is *dominated* by strategy *B*, and the choice of *A* is *not admissible*, that is, strategy *A* should not be selected so long as strategy *B* is open to the firm. As a result of this analysis, the decision problem has been somewhat simplified because we have eliminated one strategy as inadmissible. Instead of having to choose among four strategies, we now have to choose only one among the remaining three (*B, C, D*).

In general, one strategy of a decision-maker is said to dominate a second strategy, and the second strategy is said to be inadmissible, if none of the payoffs of the second strategy is preferable to the corresponding payoff of the first, and at least one payoff of the first strategy is preferable to the corresponding payoff of the second. If the columns showing the outcomes of two different strategies are identical, it is impossible to make a logical choice between the two strategies, unless one introduces another criterion (apart from the payoffs), e.g. the possible effects on 'goodwill', or the 'orderly' working of the market, etc.

The process of eliminating non-admissible strategies or discovering strategies with the same payoffs can be of great help, and it is usually the first step in the analysis of a decision-making problem under uncertainty.

B. The Bayes–Laplace Criterion

The Bayes–Laplace criterion states that if there is no information about the probabilities of occurrence of the various events, then one should assign the same probability to each possible 'state of nature' and use these probabilities to estimate the expected value of each alternative action (strategy). The firm would then choose the alternative with the highest expected value. In our example (after eliminating strategy A as non-admissible), the Bayes–Laplace criterion would lead to the choice of strategy B, given that

$$E(B) = \frac{1}{3}(360) + \frac{1}{3}(120) + \frac{1}{3}(480) = \$320$$

$$E(C) = \frac{1}{3}(-30) + \frac{1}{3}(600) + \frac{1}{3}(300) = \$290$$

$$E(D) = \frac{1}{3}(500) + \frac{1}{3}(100) + \frac{1}{3}(120) = \$240$$

The firm would change the price of its product.

The Bayes–Laplace criterion has several shortcomings. The most serious deficiency arises from the fact that the decision-maker does not usually know all the possible outcomes of each strategy. For example, if each of the above strategies has four possible outcomes, but the decision-maker is not aware of this fact, then he should assign a probability of 0.25 to each outcome. Furthermore, since the Bayes–Laplace criterion makes use of the expected-value criterion, it also suffers from the shortcomings of the expected-value approach, which we have discussed previously (see page 530).

The Bayes–Laplace criterion is sometimes called 'the principle of insufficient reason', because it considers all outcomes equally probable.

C.   The Maximin Criterion

In this approach (first suggested by Wald) the decision-maker is assumed to have a pessimistic nature: he always expects the worst outcome to happen. Accordingly, he looks at each column (at the outcomes of each strategy) and finds the minimum payoff. He then selects the strategy with the greatest payoff among these minima. In other words, the goal of the decision-maker is to maximise his minimum payoffs: hence the name of this criterion as the *maximin criterion* – the criterion dictates the choice of the 'maximum payoff' among the 'minima payoffs' of the alternative strategies.

To apply this criterion, we find the worst that can happen from the adoption of each strategy, that is, we find the smallest value of each column of the payoff table. Then we choose the strategy (column) which has the greatest (maximum) of these minima payoffs.

In our example, since we have eliminated the inadmissible strategy A, we look at the three remaining columns of the payoff table (Table 11.9, p. 556):

If the firm adopts B, the worst (minimum payoff is $120.
If the firm adopts C, the minimum payoff is $-\$30$
If the firm adopts D, the minimum payoff is $100.

The largest (maximum) payoff, among these minima, is $120. Thus according to the maximin criterion, the decision-maker adopts strategy B: he chooses to change the price.

Clearly the maximin criterion represents an extremely conservative approach to decision-making. This is the reason why this behaviour is called 'the coward's choice'. To quote Baumol:

> where one's opponent is nature . . . the maximin approach is rather clearly a manifestation of pure cowardice. This is not meant to imply that cowardice is necessarily irrational. On the contrary, there is much to be said for the Falstaffian position of self-preservation. There are persons and situations where the maximin strategy is entirely appropriate, but it's well to recognize the criterion for what it is.[19]

D.   The Minimax Criterion

The maximin criterion is used only when the payoffs are magnitudes such as profits, sales revenue, market share or growth which we want to make as large as we can. If the payoffs are magnitudes such as costs or losses, which we want to make small, we apply the *minimax criterion*. For example, consider the payoff table of two strategies (Table 11.10). Strategy A is duplicating the equipment of

---

[19] W. J. Baumol, *Economic Theory and Operations Analysis* (Prentice-Hall, 1965) p. 552.

Table 11.10   Payoff table of strategies *A* and *B* (costs in $ thousands)

'States of nature'	Strategy *A* Duplicate existing process	Strategy *B* Adopt new process
Inflation	$100	$95
Recession	$90	$100
Depression	$80	$120

a process, strategy *B* is buying equipment of a new process. The payoff matrix (Table 11.10) shows the costs which will be incurred if there is inflation, recession, or depression.

To apply the minimax criterion, we again look for the worst outcome that can occur from the adoption of each strategy. In this case 'the worst' is the largest value in each column of the payoff table. In our example, if the firm adopts action *A*, the worst outcome is a cost of $100 (if inflation develops in the economy). If the firm chooses action *B*, the worst outcome is $120 (if depression occurs, and the firm that buys the new type of machinery will not be able to establish itself and sell a large amount of its commodities, so that the unit costs will be higher than in a period of recession or inflation). The decision-maker will choose the minimum (cost) among these maximum values, that is, he will adopt strategy *A*, he will duplicate the old process.

For all practical purposes the maximin and minimax criteria are equivalent, since minimising maximum losses is the same as maximising minimum profits.

It should be clear that both the maximin and the minimax criteria assume the same pessimistic attitude of the decision-maker: in both situations the decision-maker expects the worst that can happen from each course of action that he may adopt.[20]

E.   The Maximax Criterion

This criterion dictates that one maximises the maximum payoffs corresponding to the alternative strategies. The maximax criterion is used by optimists, who look only at the best possible outcome. To apply the maximax criterion, the decision-maker looks for the best that can happen from the adoption of each strategy, namely, the largest value of each column of the payoff table (provided that the payoffs are profits or other magnitudes which the decision-maker wants to be as large as possible). Then the decision-maker chooses the strategy (column) with the maximum value among the maximum payoffs. In our example of the four alternative strategies (change of style, change of price, advertise, introduce a

---

[20] See A. Koutsoyiannis, *Modern Microeconomics*, 2nd edn (Macmillan, 1979) ch. 19.

new product line), the maximum payoffs of the admissible strategies are:

>Strategy B maximum payoff \$480
>Strategy C maximum payoff \$600
>Strategy D maximum payoff \$500

If the decision-maker is an optimist and uses the maximax criterion, he will choose strategy C (he will launch a major advertising campaign). He disregards the fact that he might also have a loss of \$30 million by choosing C (and the value of the dollar remains constant):

> The maximax criterion, which is a decision rule well suited to the temperament of a plunger, considers only the most glittering prize offered by any strategy and is blind to any other contingencies.[21]

F.   The Hurwicz Criterion

Hurwicz has proposed a criterion which lies somewhere between the pessimistic extreme of the maximin criterion and the optimistic extreme of the maximax criterion. According to the Hurwicz criterion, the decision-maker should use a weighted average of the smallest and largest payoffs of each alternative strategy. The weights will depend on the attitudes of the decision-maker: if he is rather conservative, he will assign a greater weight to the smallest payoff; if he is an optimist, he will assign a greater weight to the highest payoff of each strategy. In our example assume that the decision-maker is a rather conservative person and assigns the weight of 0.75 to the minimum payoff and the weight of 0.25 to the maximum payoff of each strategy. The three admissible strategies would be evaluated as follows:

>Strategy $B = (0.75)(120) + (0.25)(480) = \$210$
>Strategy $C = (0.75)(-30) + (0.25)(600) = \$120.75$
>Strategy $D = (0.75)(100) + (0.25)(500) = \$200$

According to the Hurwicz criterion (and with weights $\alpha = 0.75$ and $(1 - \alpha) = 0.25$) the decision-maker would choose strategy B (he would change the price of his product).

However, if the decision-maker looks 'on the bright side of things', he would assign, say, the weight of 0.20 to the worst (minimum) outcome and the weight of 0.80 to the best (maximum) outcome of each strategy. Thus the three strategies would be evaluated as follows:

>Strategy $B = (0.2)(120) + (0.8)(480) = \$408$
>Strategy $C = (0.2)(-30) + (0.8)(600) = \$450.2$
>Strategy $D = (0.2)(100) + (0.8)(500) = \$420$

---

[21] Baumol, *Economic Theory and Operations Analysis*, p. 552.

The decision-maker will choose strategy C: he will embark on an advertising campaign.

Like the maximin and the minimax criteria, the Hurwicz criterion ignores the less extreme values of the payoffs of each alternative strategy.

G. The Minimax-Regret Criterion

In this approach decisions are taken on a person's fear of not taking the best possible action. In other words, the minimax-regret criterion[22] focuses on the opportunity cost of an incorrect decision on the part of the decision-maker. If the decision he takes turns out to be the wrong one, he suffers some losses (or he has reduced profits) from losing the opportunity of the correct decision, and he has some regret from losing this opportunity. Thus his goal is to minimise the regret from taking the wrong decision.

In applying the minimax-regret criterion the first step is to estimate the losses from adopting a certain action (and missing the opportunity of taking alternative actions). Thus we obtain what is called the *opportunity-loss table* or *regret table*.

If the payoffs are profits or other magnitudes which we want to make as large as possible, the opportunity-loss table is obtained by subtracting each value in a row of the payoff table from the largest value in that row. The rationale of this procedure is easy to understand: the decision-maker examines the outcomes of all strategies *for each 'state of nature'* (that is, he looks at each row of the payoff table). If this 'state of nature' materialises, the correct decision would be the choice of the strategy with the highest payoff (corresponding to this 'state of nature'). If the decision-maker had taken this (correct) decision, he would have the greatest payoff; he would have zero opportunity loss, and hence no regret. If, however, this 'state of nature' turns up and he had chosen any other strategy, he would have taken the wrong decision. He would thus have a loss (and some regret) equal to the difference between the maximum payoff of the relevant row (which corresponds to the correct decision) and the payoff of the other cells of the row. (These cells include the payoffs of the other strategies, which would be the 'wrong' ones if the particular 'state of nature' turns up.) In other words, the loss is equal to the difference between the forgone profit and the actual profit from choosing any other non-optimal (wrong) strategy.

The opportunity-loss table (or regret matrix) of our example (with the three admissible strategies) is shown in Table 11.11.

The interpretation of the opportunity-loss table is as follows:

(1) If the value of the dollar remains actually constant (the first 'state of nature' turns up), the correct decision would be choice of strategy D (start up a new product). If this decision had been taken, there would have been no opportunity loss.

[22] This criterion was proposed by L. J. Savage, *The Foundations of Statistics* (Wiley, 1954).

Table 11.11   Opportunity-loss table of strategies B, C, D ($ million)

States of nature	Strategy B Change price	Strategy C Advertise	Strategy D New product line
Constant value of $	$500 − $360 = $140	$500 − $(−30) = $530	$500 − $500 = $0
Increasing value of $	$600 − $120 = $480	$600 − $600 = $0	$600 − $100 = $500
Declining value of $	$480 − $480 = $0	$480 − $300 = $180	$480 − $120 = $360

If strategy B had been chosen, this would have been a wrong decision, and the firm would have forgone a profit (i.e. would have had an opportunity loss) equal to the 'optimal profit' (profit of the optimal or correct decision) and the actual profit:

$$\left[\begin{array}{l} \text{Opportunity loss} \\ \text{from adopting} \\ \text{(wrongly) strategy } B \end{array} \right] = \$500 - \$360 = \$140$$

Similarly, if strategy C had been chosen, this would have been a wrong decision, and the firm would have had an opportunity loss equal to the 'optimal profit' and the actual profit:

$$\left[\begin{array}{l} \text{Opportunity loss} \\ \text{from adopting} \\ \text{(wrongly) strategy } C \end{array} \right] = \$500 - \$(-30) = \$530$$

The opportunity losses are in fact forgone profits arising from taking decisions which, *ex post*, are found to be the wrong ones, due to the particular 'state of nature' that turned up after the decision had been taken.

(2) If the second 'state of nature' turns up, that is, if the value of the dollar increases, the correct decision is the choice of strategy C (advertise). If the firm had taken this decision, there would have been zero opportunity loss, since the firm would have earned the highest payoff ($600) under this 'state of nature'.

However, if strategy B had been chosen, this would have been (*ex post*) the wrong decision, and the firm would have had an opportunity loss equal to the 'optimal profit' and the actual payoff, i.e.

$$\left[\begin{array}{l} \text{Opportunity loss} \\ \text{from choosing} \\ \text{(wrongly) } B \end{array} \right] = \$600 - \$120 = \$480$$

Also, if strategy D had been chosen (while the value of the dollar increased) this would have been the wrong decision (*ex post*), and the firm would have had an opportunity loss (profit forgone) equal to the difference between the 'optimal payoff' and the actual payoff of strategy D, i.e.

$$\begin{bmatrix} \text{Opportunity loss} \\ \text{from choosing} \\ \text{(wrongly)}\ D \end{bmatrix} = \$600 - \$100 = \$500$$

The third line of the opportunity-loss table may be interpreted in a similar way.

The second step in applying the minimax-regret criterion follows from the philosophy underlying this approach: the decision-maker wants to protect the firm against excessive opportunity losses from taking the wrong decision. In other words, the decision-maker wants to minimise the opportunity losses. To attain this goal the decision-maker applies a *minimax criterion* to the opportunity-loss table. He examines the opportunity losses of each strategy (column) and finds the maximum of these losses (on the pessimistic attitude that the worst will turn up). Then the decision-maker chooses the strategy with the smallest (minimum) of these maximum losses. In our example we have:

(a) maximum opportunity loss of strategy B $480
(b) maximum opportunity loss of strategy C $530
(c) maximum opportunity loss of strategy D $500

According to the minimax-regret criterion, the decision maker will choose strategy B, which has the minimum opportunity loss (among the maximum opportunity losses).

(Note that if the payoffs are costs, losses or other magnitudes that the firm wants to make as small as possible, the opportunity-loss table is obtained by subtracting the smallest value in each row from all the values (cells) in that row.)

Now look at the opportunity-loss matrix (Table 11.12) which is related to the payoff table (Table 11.10) concerning the costs of two alternative processes (methods of production).

Table 11.12   Opportunity-loss table of strategies A and B, related to two production processes

States of nature	Strategy A Duplicate 'old' process	Strategy B Introduce new process
Inflation	$100 − $95 = $5	$95 − $95 − $0
Recession	$90 − $90 = $0	$100 − $90 = $10
Depression	$80 − $80 = $0	$120 − $80 = $40

The interpretation of the opportunity-loss or regret table in this case is as follows:

(1) If we have inflation, the correct decision is strategy B. If the firm had

adopted the wrong (under the inflationary conditions) strategy A, it would have had an opportunity loss of $5, because it would have paid the higher cost ($100) of strategy A.

(2) If recession occurs, the correct decision is strategy A. If the firm had adopted the wrong (under the conditions of recession) strategy B, it would have suffered an opportunity loss of $10, because it would have bought the more expensive (under the recession conditions) machinery of strategy B.

(3) If we have depression, the correct decision is strategy A. If the firm had adopted the wrong strategy B, it would have suffered an opportunity loss of $40, because it would have bought the more expensive machinery of the new process.

Having derived the opportunity-loss matrix, the decision-maker applies to it the minimax criterion, because he wants to minimise his opportunity losses in case of his taking the wrong decision. Recall that the minimax criterion requires firstly the location of the maximum loss of each strategy, and then the choice of the strategy which has the minimum loss (among the maximum losses). In our example the maximum loss of strategy A is $5, and the maximum loss of strategy B is $40. Thus the decision-maker, applying the minimax-regret criterion, will choose strategy A: he will duplicate his 'old' process (method of production).

The minimax-regret criterion focuses on the largest regret value of each column of the opportunity-loss table, and ignores a substantial amount of the information of the other cells of this table. Thus it suffers from the same shortcomings as the maximin, the maximax and the Hurwicz criteria.

APPENDIX 11.1   OBJECTIVE vs SUBJECTIVE PROBABILITIES

In decision-making *subjective* probabilities are more appropriate than *objective* probabilities.

Objective probabilities are *estimated* by observing what fraction of the time similar (repetitive) events have occurred in the past.[23] For example, if at a major airport we look at the arrival times of jets over one year and we observe that out of 12,000 jets 10,320 arrived on time, we *estimate* that the probability that any one flight will arrive on time is 10,320/12,000 = 0.86. Similarly, if by examining the records of university students dropping out in the first year of their studies we find that out of 5,000 freshmen 500 quit their studies before the end of their first year in the university, we *estimate* the probability that any freshman will drop out before the end of his first year as the fraction 500/5,000 = 0.10 (or 10 per cent). This is the 'frequentist approach' of estimating (objective) probabilities: it is based on the frequency with which an outcome occurs when an event is repeated a large number of times.

[23] J. E. Freund and F. J. Williams, *Elementary Business Statistics*, 3rd edn (Prentice-Hall, 1977) p. 97.

The basic characteristics of objective probabilities should be stressed:

(1) Objective probabilities require observations (information) on the number of times an outcome (out of several possible ones) of an event (action, strategy) has actually occurred in the past. This information is not costless in the real world.

(2) Objective probabilities require that the event (action, strategy) is repetitive, that is, it has actually occurred repeatedly in the past.

(3) The greater the number of times that the event (experiment, action, strategy) has been repeated and its outcomes observed and recorded, the more accurate the *estimate* of the objective probability.

(4) Since objective probabilities are based on observed (realised) outcomes, there is no room for disagreement about their values: objective probabilities are the same for all decision-makers. The frequentist approach requires that all reasonable men agree on the values of the probabilities. There is no way of allowing personal differences, experiences and preferences of individual decision-makers to result in a different assessment of the likelihood of uncertain outcomes. A theory of decision-making should *not* rule out the possibility that disagreement about uncertain future situations is possible, even when all persons have the same (objective) information.

(5) A unique (non-repetitive) event cannot be assigned an objective probability. As we will presently see, most business situations are non-repetitive, are unique, given the continuous changes in the socio-economic environment of the firm.

(6) Objective probabilities incorporate *past* information. If the conditions in which an event takes place change, objective probabilities become inaccurate estimates of the likelihood of outcomes in future periods.

The above discussion reveals the main weaknesses of the use of objective probabilities in decision-making by firms in the real world.

First. Most of the decisions which a firm must take are unique, in the sense that the conditions of the economic environment change continuously. It is impossible to obtain past observations of *similar events* to estimate objective probabilities. Few, if any, business situations are clearly repetitive. Actually, most business situations are one of a kind.

Second. Even if objective probabilities were possible to estimate, they are based on *past* conditions, which may well be expected to be different in the future. Thus objective probabilities may be irrelevant for decisions pertaining to future periods.

Third. It is an observed fact that personal differences of economic agents play an important role in decision-making. Individuals who have roughly the same experience and information may assign different probabilities to various outcomes of a strategy.

Fourth. The information requirements for the estimation of subjective probabilities are less than those for the estimation of objective probabilities, as we will presently see.

A subjective probability is a measure of the degree of confidence of a particular individual in the truth of a particular position.[24] Like objective probabilities, subjective probabilities may assume any value between zero and one, and their sum is equal to unity. A probability equal to one implies certainty about the occurrence of a particular outcome. A probability of zero, on the other hand, implies that the particular outcome is impossible to obtain. If an event (strategy, decision) X has n uncertain possible mutually exclusive outcomes ($X_1, X_2, \ldots X_n$), the probability of each outcome must be either zero or positive

$$P(X_i) \geqslant 0 \qquad (i = 1, 2, \ldots, n)$$

and the sum of all probabilities must be equal to one

$$\Sigma P(X_i) = 1$$

since it is certain that one of all n outcomes will occur.

Subjective probabilities are assigned by an individual and show his degree of belief or confidence in the likelihood of occurrence of a particular outcome.[25] In assigning probabilities to the uncertain outcomes of a strategy (event) an individual expresses in quantitative terms his personal assessments of the likelihood of the possible (uncertain) outcomes. Such assessments are based on any available information, as well as on the personal experience, insight and intuition of the individual.

Subjective probabilities are obtained by *behavioural interrogation techniques*. An individual is presented with a series of (probabilistic) alternatives among which he must make actual choices. To illustrate the procedure used to obtain numerical values of subjective probabilities we outline below Savage's *gamble* method.[26]

The decision-maker is presented with a real-world situation, for example an advertising campaign, which has two (uncertain) outcomes: 'effective', or 'ineffective'. We want to obtain the decision-maker's subjective probabilities of these two outcomes.

The decision-maker is faced with the following two gambles, and is asked to choose between them:

(1) *Real-world gamble*. If the advertising campaign turns out to be 'ineffective', you receive $0. If the advertising campaign turns out to be 'effective', you receive $10.

(2) *Hypothetical gamble*. A box contains ten balls, four red and six black. If you draw a red ball you receive $0. If you draw a black ball you receive $10.

The decision-maker is asked to choose between these two gambles. If he chooses the real-world gamble, we infer that he assigns to the outcome 'effective

---

[24] Thomas H. Naylor and John M. Vernon, *Microeconomics and Decision Models of the Firm* (Harcourt, Brace & World, 1969) p. 300.

[25] Ira Horowitz, *Decision Making and the Theory of the Firm* (Holt, Rinehart & Winston, 1970) p. 78.

[26] Savage, *The Foundations of Statistics*.

advertising' a probability higher than 0.60 (which is the probability of a black ball in the hypothetical gamble). If the decision-maker chooses the hypothetical gamble, we infer that he assigns a probability smaller than 0.60 to the uncertain outcome 'effective advertising'. In both cases we do not know the precise value of the probability of the uncertain outcomes. To obtain these values we change the proportions (probabilities) of red and black balls in the hypothetical gamble, and we ask the decision-maker to choose between the new hypothetical gamble and the real-world gamble. The procedure is repeated until the decision-maker expresses indifference between the two gambles. The probabilities of the hypothetical gamble at 'the point of indifference' are the subjective probabilities of the uncertain outcomes of the real-world strategy (situation) with which the decision-maker was faced. For example, assume that when the decision-maker expressed indifference between the two gambles, we had defined the proportion of red and black balls as 0.20 and 0.80 respectively. The fact that the decision-maker expresses indifference between the two gambles implies that he considers the outcome 'effective advertising' equally likely as drawing a black ball. Thus his subjective probabilities for the two uncertain outcomes of the advertising campaign are determined: the decision-maker assigns the subjective probability of 0.80 to the outcome 'effective', and the subjective probability of 0.20 to the outcome 'ineffective'.

Note that instead of two (uncertain) outcomes, we could have defined various degrees of effectiveness to the advertising campaign. For example: 'very successful'; 'successful'; 'not successful'; 'a complete flop'. Accordingly, the hypothetical gamble would involve a box containing balls of four different colours (red, black, white, green) in given proportions. The decision-maker's subjective probabilities for the four (uncertain) outcomes of the advertising strategy would be the proportions of the four differently coloured balls when he would state indifference between the real-world and the hypothetical gamble. If at this 'point of indifference' the proportions of red, black, white and green balls were 0.20, 0.55, 0.20, 0.05 respectively, these proportions would be the subjective probabilities of the four uncertain outcomes of the advertising-campaign strategy.

It should be clear that in the above procedure of choice between alternative gambles, the individual decision-maker evaluates the likelihood of each (uncertain) outcome on the basis of any available information about future business conditions, experience (from past advertising campaigns and competitors' counter-advertising strategies), insight, intuition. Personal characteristics, attitudes and preferences, as well as acquired experience and knowledge from past situations (events, strategies), play an important role in assigning subjective probabilities to uncertain outcomes.

It is assumed that decision-makers are capable of assigning probabilities which are *consistent* and *coherent*.[27] Subjective probabilities are consistent when the

---

[27] B. DeFinetti, 'Foresight: Its Logical Laws, Its Subjective Sources', in E. H. Kyburg and H. E. Smokler (eds), *Studies in Subjective Probability* (Wiley, 1964).

individual assigns the greatest probability to the outcome which he considers (to the best of his judgement) most likely, the next highest probability to the next most likely outcome, and so on. Subjective probabilities are coherent when they preclude a situation in which an unfavourable outcome is bound to occur.

The method of obtaining (estimating) subjective probabilities emphasises the probability of unique (single) events. Such events cannot have an objective probability. Given that in the real world most of the decisions of the firm are one of a kind (unique), it is obvious that the subjectivist approach is preferred. Decisions must be taken in an uncertain environment; hence it is important to have a measure of the decision-maker's degree of confidence (of his beliefs and feelings) about the occurrence of an event.

The procedure of estimating subjective probabilities makes it clear that personal differences among individuals play an important role in decision-making. Individuals who have roughly the same experience and information may assign different probabilities to the uncertain outcomes of an event, depending on their personal characteristics, preferences and attitudes.

Finally, the information required for estimating subjective probabilities is less than for estimating objective probabilities. Subjective probabilities are based on the amount of information that the individual decision-maker actually has at the moment of the estimation of these probabilities. Objective probabilities require information from events which have occurred repeatedly. A number of observations are required before any objective probability can be estimated.

The main shortcoming of the subjective probability approach is that an individual may reach different estimates of probabilities for the same outcomes depending on his position in the firm and on his knowledge of who is going to use his probability estimates. Individuals in an organisation acquire what Cyert and March[28] call a 'position bias' which affects their assessment of the likelihood of uncertain outcomes. For example, sales personnel acquire a 'downward' position bias: they tend to assign low probabilities to high levels of sales. Similarly, production personnel acquire an 'upward' position bias: they tend to assign high probabilities to high levels of costs. Furthermore, information is distorted, consciously or unconsciously, as it passes through the various sections in an organisation. Finally, an individual may give a different probability to an event if his immediate superior will use it, rather than if his ultimate superior will use it. It is entirely possible that an individual is influenced in his assessment of probabilities by knowing where his estimates are going to be used: upon considering the level at which his subjective probabilities will be used, an individual can produce different subjective probabilities for the same events.[29]

Despite such shortcomings, the superiority of the subjective probability

[28] R. M. Cyert and J. G. March, *A Behavioural Theory of the Firm* (Prentice-Hall, 1963).
[29] W. Fellner, 'Distortion of Subjective Probabilities as a Reaction to Uncertainty', *Quarterly Journal of Economics*, vol. LXXV, 1961.

approach in decision-making under risk and uncertainty cannot be seriously questioned.

(1) Subjective probability is the only measure of the noncertainty of single (unique) events. Given that the real business world is characterised by non-repetitive events, the subjectivist approach is preferred. In economics we deal with situations and problems which are mostly unique, given the continuous change in 'general business conditions'. Such problems require decisions which must be taken mostly in the absence of extensive past information of similar situations. For example, the decision to change the price is by its nature a unique situation, in the sense that it will occur under conditions which cannot be identical to past situations of price changes. Such unique situations (events) can be dealt only within the framework of the subjectivist approach.

(2) Given the continuous change in the economic environment, objective probabilities, even if available, can only be suggestive of the likelihood of an outcome, based as they are on historical data. Objective probabilities, estimated from past information, cannot provide the basis of a definitive prediction in a changing environment.

(3) The subjectivist approach allows the decision-maker to use not only any available historical data (incorporated, possibly, in objective probability estimates) but also his personal judgement, experience, tastes and preferences. Different individuals may assign different probabilities to the same events, due to their different characteristics, tastes and preferences.

APPENDIX 11.2   THE STANDARD NORMAL VARIABLE Z AND ITS USE IN MEASURING RISK

The standard normal variable Z has a normal distribution, with zero mean and unit standard deviation. In symbols

$$Z \sim N[E(Z) = 0, \sigma_Z^2 = 1]$$

The probabilities of the various values of Z have been estimated by Gauss. They are shown in Table 11.13. The probabilities are areas under the standard normal curve. The following examples illustrate the use of the 'standard normal table'.

A.   The Use of the Z-Table

The standard normal table (or, briefly, the Z-table), that is, Table 11.13, shows the area (= probability) *to the right of any particular positive value of Z*. Since the distribution of Z is symmetrical (normal), the area to the right of any positive value of Z is equal to the area which lies to the left of the corresponding negative value of Z.

Table 11.13   Areas under the normal curve: the Z-table

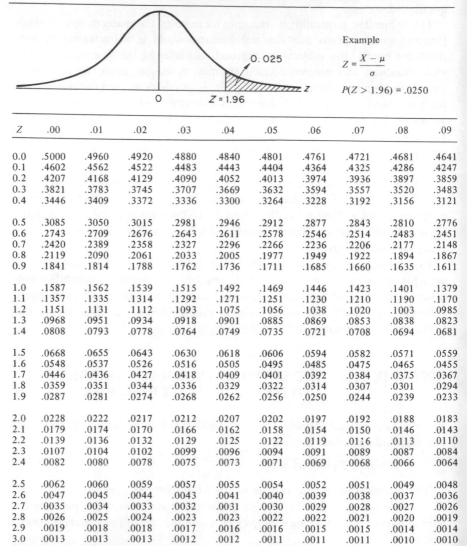

Example

$$Z = \frac{X - \mu}{\sigma}$$

$P(Z > 1.96) = .0250$

Z	.00	.01	.02	.03	.04	.05	.06	.07	.08	.09
0.0	.5000	.4960	.4920	.4880	.4840	.4801	.4761	.4721	.4681	.4641
0.1	.4602	.4562	.4522	.4483	.4443	.4404	.4364	.4325	.4286	.4247
0.2	.4207	.4168	.4129	.4090	.4052	.4013	.3974	.3936	.3897	.3859
0.3	.3821	.3783	.3745	.3707	.3669	.3632	.3594	.3557	.3520	.3483
0.4	.3446	.3409	.3372	.3336	.3300	.3264	.3228	.3192	.3156	.3121
0.5	.3085	.3050	.3015	.2981	.2946	.2912	.2877	.2843	.2810	.2776
0.6	.2743	.2709	.2676	.2643	.2611	.2578	.2546	.2514	.2483	.2451
0.7	.2420	.2389	.2358	.2327	.2296	.2266	.2236	.2206	.2177	.2148
0.8	.2119	.2090	.2061	.2033	.2005	.1977	.1949	.1922	.1894	.1867
0.9	.1841	.1814	.1788	.1762	.1736	.1711	.1685	.1660	.1635	.1611
1.0	.1587	.1562	.1539	.1515	.1492	.1469	.1446	.1423	.1401	.1379
1.1	.1357	.1335	.1314	.1292	.1271	.1251	.1230	.1210	.1190	.1170
1.2	.1151	.1131	.1112	.1093	.1075	.1056	.1038	.1020	.1003	.0985
1.3	.0968	.0951	.0934	.0918	.0901	.0885	.0869	.0853	.0838	.0823
1.4	.0808	.0793	.0778	.0764	.0749	.0735	.0721	.0708	.0694	.0681
1.5	.0668	.0655	.0643	.0630	.0618	.0606	.0594	.0582	.0571	.0559
1.6	.0548	.0537	.0526	.0516	.0505	.0495	.0485	.0475	.0465	.0455
1.7	.0446	.0436	.0427	.0418	.0409	.0401	.0392	.0384	.0375	.0367
1.8	.0359	.0351	.0344	.0336	.0329	.0322	.0314	.0307	.0301	.0294
1.9	.0287	.0281	.0274	.0268	.0262	.0256	.0250	.0244	.0239	.0233
2.0	.0228	.0222	.0217	.0212	.0207	.0202	.0197	.0192	.0188	.0183
2.1	.0179	.0174	.0170	.0166	.0162	.0158	.0154	.0150	.0146	.0143
2.2	.0139	.0136	.0132	.0129	.0125	.0122	.0119	.0116	.0113	.0110
2.3	.0107	.0104	.0102	.0099	.0096	.0094	.0091	.0089	.0087	.0084
2.4	.0082	.0080	.0078	.0075	.0073	.0071	.0069	.0068	.0066	.0064
2.5	.0062	.0060	.0059	.0057	.0055	.0054	.0052	.0051	.0049	.0048
2.6	.0047	.0045	.0044	.0043	.0041	.0040	.0039	.0038	.0037	.0036
2.7	.0035	.0034	.0033	.0032	.0031	.0030	.0029	.0028	.0027	.0026
2.8	.0026	.0025	.0024	.0023	.0023	.0022	.0022	.0021	.0020	.0019
2.9	.0019	.0018	.0018	.0017	.0016	.0016	.0015	.0015	.0014	.0014
3.0	.0013	.0013	.0013	.0012	.0012	.0011	.0011	.0011	.0010	.0010

Example 1. If $Z = 1.96$, the area to the right of this value is found (from the Z-table) to be equal to 0.025. This is interpreted as follows: the probability that Z will have a value greater than 1.96 is 0.025 or 2.5 per cent. In symbols

$$Pr\{Z < 1.96\} = 0.025$$

By symmetry, the probability that Z will assume a value smaller than -1.96 is also 0.025. Thus

$$Pr\{Z < -1.96\} = 0.025$$

These findings are shown in Figure 11.32.

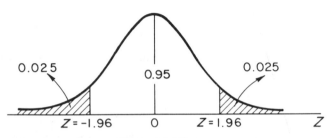

0.025   0.95   0.025

$Z = -1.96$ 0 $Z = 1.96$ Z

Figure 11.32

Example 2. Suppose we want the area (probability) between $Z = 0$ and any positive value Z_i. We subtract the corresponding (to this Z_i) area from 0.50, so that the area between $Z = 0$ and any positive value Z_i is 0.50 minus the tabular value corresponding to Z_i. For instance, the area $0 < Z_i < 2$ is found as follows:

(a) The area to the right of the zero mean is 0.50.
(b) The area to the right of $Z = 2$ is 0.0288.
(c) Therefore, the area between $Z = 0$ and $Z = 2$ is

$$0.5000 - 0.0228 = 0.4772$$

This reads: the probability of Z assuming a value bigger than 0 but smaller than 2 is 47.7 per cent. (See Figure 11.33.)

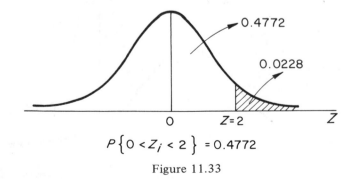

0.4772

0.0228

0    $Z = 2$ Z

$$P\{0 < Z_i < 2\} = 0.4772$$

Figure 11.33

B.   Finding the Probability of Values of any Normal Variable, X, with the use of the Z-Table

Assume that the variable X (e.g. earnings of the firm) has a normal distribution with mean and variance (in thousands of dollars)

$$E(X) = 10 \qquad \sigma_X^2 = 4$$

We want to find the probability that X (earnings in any particular period) will assume a value greater than 12 (thousand dollars).

To find this probability we first 'translate' the X units into Z units, by using the expression

$$Z_i = \frac{X_i - E(X)}{\sigma_X}$$

(This is called 'standardisation of X', because it results in expressing the units of X in units of Z.) Thus

$$Z = \frac{X_1 - E(X)}{\sigma_X} = \frac{12 - 10}{2} = +1$$

We next use the Z-table to find the probability of $Z > +1$. It can be seen (from this table) that

$$Pr\{Z > +1\} = 0.159$$

Hence the probability of $X > 12$ is also 0.159 or 15.9 per cent.

The above procedure is shown in Figure 11.34.

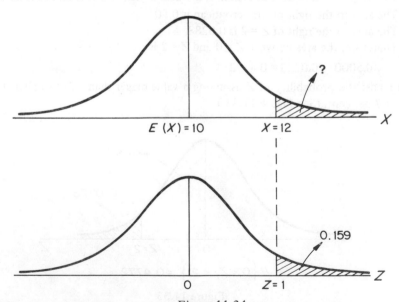

Figure 11.34

C.   Using the Z-Table to Estimate the Risk of a Project

An example will illustrate how the Z-table can be used to estimate the risk of a project of which the management of the firm has some minimal knowledge. Assume that managers have obtained (a) an estimate of the most likely profit (earnings) from a project, (b) an estimate of the maximum upward or downward deviation of earnings (from their most likely value) and (c) an estimate of the probability of such deviation (which depends on general business conditions and/or specific factors relating to the firm or the project under consideration).

If the most likely value of earnings is

$5 million

the maximum deviation is

± 2 million

with a probability of 10 per cent, we have the situation shown in Figure 11.35.

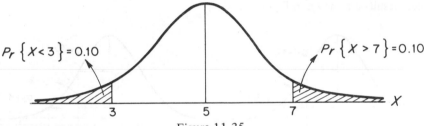

$Pr\{X < 3\} = 0.10$ $Pr\{X > 7\} = 0.10$

Figure 11.35

With this information we can estimate the risk of the project as measured by the standard deviation. The estimate of σ_X is obtained from the solution of the expression

$$Z = \frac{X - E(X)}{\sigma_X}$$

where $X = 7$ (or 3) = maximum (or minimum) deviation of earnings, as maintained by managers

$E(X) = 5$ = most likely value of earnings, as believed by managers

$Z = 1.28$ (or -1.28) – this value is found from the Z-table, and corresponds to the probability of 10 per cent. It is shown in Figure 11.36.

Substituting the management's information in the Z-expression, we obtain

$$1.28 = \frac{7 - 5}{\sigma_X}$$

or

$$\sigma_X = \frac{2}{1.28} = 1.56 \ (\$ \ million)$$

The risk of the project is estimated to be equal to $1.56 million.

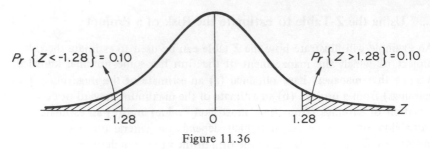

$Pr\left\{Z<-1.28\right\}=0.10$ $Pr\left\{Z>1.28\right\}=0.10$

Figure 11.36

D. Some Basic Results of the Standard Normal Distribution

From the standard normal curve table we see that:

the area between $Z = 0$ and $Z = 1$ is 0.3413
the area between $Z = 0$ and $Z = 1.96$ is 0.475
the area between $Z = 0$ and $Z = 3$ is 0.498

These results are shown in Figure 11.37.

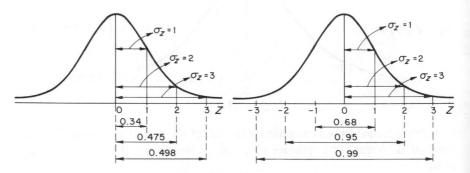

Figure 11.37

Since the Z distribution is symmetrical with unit standard deviation we can state the following very important results (shown in Figure 11.38(b)).

(a) The range 0 ± 1 contains 68 per cent of the values of Z (or the probability of Z taking a value between -1 and $+1$ is 0.68).

(b) The range 0 ± 1.96 contains 95 per cent of the values of Z (or the probability of Z taking a value between -1.96 and $+1.96$ is 0.95).

(c) The range 0 ± 3 contains 99 per cent of the values of Z (or the probability of Z assuming a value between -3 and $+3$ is 0.99).

The above results apply to any normal distribution. This is easily understood if we look back at the transformation formula

$$Z_i = \frac{X_i - E(X)}{\sigma_X}$$

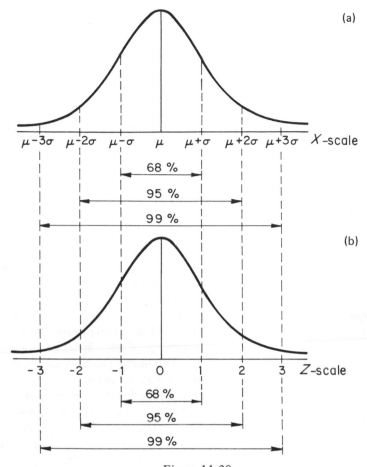

Figure 11.38

and recall that this expression transforms the units of measurement of X into standard Z units (i.e. units of the standard normal variable Z).

From Figure 11.38(a) it is clear that:

(i) The range $\mu \pm \sigma_X$ contains 68 per cent of the values of X (or there is a 68 per cent probability that X will take a value between $\mu \pm \sigma_X$).

(ii) The range $\mu \pm 2\sigma_X$ contains 95 per cent of the values of X (or there is a 95 per cent probability that X will assume a value between $\mu \pm 2\sigma_X$).

(iii) The range $\mu \pm 3\sigma_X$ contains 99 per cent of the values of X (or there is a 99 per cent probability that X will assume a value between $\mu \pm 3\sigma_X$).

12. Modern Theory of the Investment Decision Under Risk

In recent years several models have been developed in which the investment decision of the firm is analysed within the framework of portfolio theory. The basic premise of this theory as applied to the investment decision is that a project, if accepted, will be a new asset in the portfolio of assets held by the firm. Hence investment projects are *not* risk-independent. The stream of earnings of the new project is correlated with the stream of earnings of other investments already in existence or being considered for adoption. This interdependence should be taken explicitly into account when investment proposals are evaluated.

Within the portfolio framework two approaches have been evolved. One postulates that any investment proposal should be evaluated on the basis of its effect on *the over-all risk of the firm*. The other suggests that an investment project should be judged on the basis of its risk—return impact on *shareholders' portfolios of stocks* rather than on the firm's portfolio of assets.

In the first section of this chapter we shall present an introductory exposition of the theory of optimal portfolio selection, paying particular attention to the mean-variance model which has gained popularity in economic literature. In section II we shall examine the application of the mean-variance model to the investment decision of the firm. In this approach the risk of a project is 'firm-oriented', that is, a project is judged on the basis of its risk—return effect on the firm's portfolio of assets. In section III we shall examine the evaluation of investment projects within the framework of the capital asset pricing model (CAPM). In this approach the investment decision of the firm is linked to the portfolio of securities held by investors. That is, the risk of a project is 'investor-oriented'.

I. INTRODUCTION TO THE THEORY OF PORTFOLIO SELECTION UNDER RISK

In Appendix 3.1 of Chapter 3 we examined the selection of a portfolio under certainty. In this section we present the elements of the theory of optimal port-folio selection under risk.

The traditional approach to the problem of choice under risk assumes that rational investors aim at the maximisation of their expected utility.

The maximisation of expected utility model was presented in Chapter 11, in the context of the appraisal of a single investment on the basis of its *total risk and return*. Recall that choice on the basis of the expected utility criterion requires knowledge of the utility of money function of the investor and of the entire probability distribution of possible earnings of each investment.

In this section we extend the expected utility maximisation model to the choice of an *optimal portfolio of investments*. The investor is considering sets of assets. Each such set is a portfolio, having an expected (mean) return and a risk (standard deviation). Among all available portfolios, the investor will want to choose the one that maximises his expected utility.

The expected return of a portfolio may assume different values, each assoc-iated with some probability. Thus for each portfolio we have a probability distribution from which we can find the expected utility of the particular portfolio, given the utility of wealth function of the investor. The process may, in principle, be repeated for each portfolio. Among the available portfolios, then, the investor will choose the one with the highest expected utility.

It is apparent that this approach requires knowledge which is practically impossible to obtain. A simpler model has been developed which requires knowledge of the expected value (mean) and the standard deviation only of the distribution of possible returns of each portfolio (not the entire distribution). This is known as 'the two-parameter' model, or 'the mean-variance' model, because it assumes that decisions under risk are taken on the basis of the above two parameters of the probability distribution of the returns of alternative port-folios of investments.

The development of this model requires knowledge of the mean return and the standard deviation of the various portfolios. We shall first discuss the measure-ment of the expected (mean) return and the risk (standard deviation) of a port-folio. We will then use these concepts to develop the 'mean-variance' model of optimal portfolio selection.

A.   Measurement of the Return and Risk of a Portfolio[1]

The expected return for a portfolio is the weighted average of the expected returns of the securities comprising that portfolio, with the weights being the proportion of funds invested in each security. In symbols

$$E(R_p) = \sum_{j=1}^{n} x_j E(R_j) \tag{12.1}$$

---

[1] This section requires knowledge of some elementary rules of expected values which are summarised in Appendix 12.2.

where $E(R_p)$ = expected value (return) of a portfolio p
$\quad\quad R_j$ = expected value (return) of the jth security in the portfolio
$\quad\quad x_j$ = proportion of funds invested in security j
$\quad\quad n$ = number of securities in the portfolio.

The risk of the portfolio is measured by the standard deviation of the returns of the portfolio, σ_p. The portfolio's standard deviation is given by the expression

$$\sigma_p = \sqrt{\sum_{j=1}^{n} x_j^2 \sigma_j^2 + 2 \sum_{j=1}^{n-1} \sum_{i=j+1}^{n} x_i x_j (\text{cov } R_i R_j)} \tag{12.2}$$

where $\quad\quad \sigma_j^2$ = variance of the returns of the jth security
$\quad\quad\quad x_j$ = proportion of funds invested in the jth security
$\quad\quad\quad x_i$ = proportion of funds invested in the ith security
$\quad \text{cov } R_i R_j$ = covariance of the returns of the ith and jth securities

It can be shown that (proof given in Appendix 12.2):

$$\text{cov }(R_i R_j) = r_{ij} \sigma_i \sigma_j \tag{12.3}$$

where r_{ij} = correlation coefficient between the returns of security i and security j
Thus the standard deviation of a portfolio may be written as

$$\sigma_p = \sqrt{\sum_{j=1}^{n} x_j^2 \sigma_j^2 + \sum_{j=1}^{n-1} \sum_{i=j+1}^{n} x_i x_j (r_{ij} \sigma_i \sigma_j)} \tag{12.4}$$

It is clear from this expression that the risk of a portfolio depends upon (a) the standard deviation of each security, (b) the proportion of funds invested in each security, and (c) the correlation between expected returns of the various securities comprising the portfolio.

The correlation between returns may be positive, negative or zero. In symbols we may write

$$-1 \leqslant r \leqslant 1 \tag{12.5}$$

An $r = +1$ implies that the returns of the two securities change proportionately in the same direction (both returns increase or decrease simultaneously and proportionately). A correlation $r = -1$ implies that the returns of the two securities vary inversely (in opposite directions) in the same proportions. An $r = 0$ shows that the returns of the two securities are independent.

The correlation of returns of two securities can be estimated from the expression

$$r_{ij} = \sum \left(\frac{R_i - \bar{R}_i}{\sigma_i} \right) \left(\frac{R_j - \bar{R}_j}{\sigma_j} \right) P_{ij} \tag{12.6}$$

where P_{ij} = joint probability of R_i and R_j occurring simultaneously.[2]

As an example, consider the standard deviation of a two-asset portfolio:

$$\sigma_p = \sqrt{x_1^2 \sigma_1^2 + x_2^2 \sigma_2^2 + 2x_1 x_2 \ (\mathrm{cov}_{12})} \tag{12.7}$$

or

$$\sigma_p = \sqrt{x_1^2 \sigma_1^2 + x_2^2 \sigma_2^2 + 2x_1 x_2 \ (r_{12} \sigma_1 \sigma_2)} \tag{12.8}$$

(Note that in the two-asset portfolio $x_2 = (1 - x_1)$, since the sum of the weights must be equal to 1.)

From expression (12.8) it is apparent that the sign and the value of the correlation coefficient affects the risk of the portfolio, σ_p. If r has any value less than +1, the risk of the portfolio will be reduced. In other words, if $r = +1$, the investor cannot attain any risk reduction by forming a portfolio of the two securities. But for all other values of r, risk reduction is attained by forming a portfolio of the two securities. As an illustration,[3] consider two securities, A and B, which have the following risk and return:

$$E(A) = 0.05 \text{ (or 5 per cent)} \qquad \sigma_A^2 = 0.02 \text{ (or 2 per cent)}$$

$$E(B) = 0.05 \qquad \qquad \qquad \sigma_B^2 = 0.02$$

Assume that an investor forms a portfolio consisting of 50 per cent of each security, that is,

$$x_A = x_B = 0.50$$

The expected return of the portfolio is found from expression (12.1):

$$E(R_p) = \sum_{j=1}^{2} x_j E(R_j)$$
$$= x_A E(A) + x_B E(B)$$
$$= 0.50 \ (0.05) + 0.50 \ (0.05) = 0.05$$

The return of the portfolio in our example is the same as the return of the individual securities. (This is due to our assumptions of equal returns and equal weights of the two securities.)

The variance of the portfolio is found from expression (12.8):

$$\sigma_p^2 = x_1^2 \sigma_1^2 + x_2^2 \sigma_2^2 + 2x_1 x_2 \ (r_{12})(\sigma_1)(\sigma_2)$$
$$= (0.5)^2 (0.02) + (0.5)^2 (0.02) + 2(0.5)(0.5)(r_{AB})(\sqrt{0.02})(\sqrt{0.02})$$
$$= 0.005 + 0.005 + 0.01 \ (r_{AB})$$
$$= 0.01 + 0.01 \ (r_{AB})$$

---

[2] Joint probabilities are found by using the basic laws of probability. For an elementary exposition of probability laws see A. Koutsoyiannis, *Theory of Econometrics*, 2nd edn (Macmillan, 1977).

[3] This example has been worked out by Eric Kirzner.

(a) If $r_{AB} = +1$, then $\sigma_p^2 = 0.02$. That is, the investor does not attain any reduction in his risk by forming a portfolio of the two securities.

(b) If $r_{AB} = 0.8$, then $\sigma_p^2 = 0.018$. The risk of the portfolio is less than the risk of the individual securities.

(c) If $r_{AB} = 0$, then $\sigma_p^2 = 0.01$. The risk of the portfolio is considerably reduced.

(d) If $r_{AB} = -0.4$, then $\sigma_p^2 = 0.006$.

(e) If $r_{AB} = -1$, then $\sigma_p^2 = 0$.

We observe that the risk of the portfolio decreases as r takes on values less than +1. (This is further discussed on pages 588–92.)

The important fact is that as long as the correlation coefficient between two securities is less than +1 (be it positive or negative), the risk of the portfolio will be less than the weighted average of the two individual standard deviations. By diversification of the portfolio (so that securities are included whose returns are not perfectly positively correlated), the risk of the portfolio is reduced.

However, the objective of portfolio selection is *not* to find a portfolio with minimum risk, but to find a portfolio with the 'optimal' combination of risk (σ_p) and return, $E(R_p)$, the portfolio which maximises the utility of the investor.

B. The Mean–Variance Model of Portfolio Selection

(i) *Assumptions of the model*

(1) It is assumed that *capital markets are efficient*. Efficient capital markets are markets in which the prices of securities reflect all available information: about the economy, about international developments, about financial markets, and about the firms whose shares (securities) are traded in the market. Prices of individual securities adjust very rapidly to new information. Any security has its *intrinsic* value, depending on the expected performance of the firm (expected returns, growth potential, risk, etc.). Prices fluctuate randomly around this value, as investors take into account any available information. Of course, some new events or new information may change the intrinsic value of a stock. Investors perceive rapidly such changes, so that subsequent price changes will be random around the new intrinsic value.[4]

---

[4] Several studies have provided evidence that capital markets are efficient. The various tests are well summarised in the following publications: E. Fama, *Studies in the Theory of Capital Markets* (Praeger, 1972); J. H. Lorie and M. T. Hamilton, *The Stock Market* (Irwin, 1973); A. Seelenfreund, G. C. Parker and J. C. Van Horne, 'Stock Price Behaviour and Trading', *Journal of Financial Quantitative Analysis*, vol. 3, 1968, pp. 263–82. A critical evaluation of the empirical tests (as well as a presentation of evidence about the inefficiency of capital markets) is included in D. Downes and T. R. Dyckman, 'A Critical Look at the Efficient Market Empirical Research Literature as it Relates to Accounting Information', *Accounting Review*, vol. 48, 1973, pp. 300–17.

(2) The goal of the rational investor is to choose the portfolio which maximises his expected utility.

(3) The utility derived from a portfolio depends on its mean (expected return) and its standard deviation. In symbols, the utility function of the investor takes the form:[5]

$$E(U_p) = f[E(R_p), \sigma_p] \qquad (12.9)$$

(4) The decision-maker is risk-averse.

(5) The decision-maker can rank the various portfolios (on the basis of their expected return, $E(R_p)$, and risk, σ_p, with a set of indifference curves.

With these assumptions we can define the 'tools' required for the choice of the 'optimal' portfolio (the one that maximises the utility of the decision-maker). These 'tools' are *the indifference map* of the decision-maker and the *efficient opportunity frontier*, that is, the locus of efficient portfolios among which the decision-maker will choose the one that maximises his utility.

(ii) *The investor's indifference map*

We assume that the decision-maker (investor) knows the expected return and the standard deviation of each portfolio, that he is a risk-averter, and that his utility depends only on the above two statistics (the mean and the standard deviation of the portfolios). Under these assumptions the indifference curves of the decision-maker can be shown on a two-dimensional graph. (The mathematical derivation of the indifference curves in the two-parameter model is given in Appendix 12.1.) On the vertical axis we measure the expected value (mean return) of alternative portfolios and on the horizontal axis we depict the risk of these strategies, measured by the standard deviation (σ_p) of their possible outcomes (payoffs). In figure 12.1 we show a typical indifference curve of a risk-averter.

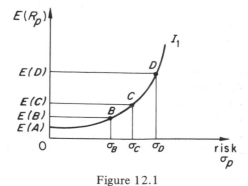

Figure 12.1

[5] For the rationale of the mean-variance model see Appendix 12.1.

An indifference curve is defined as the combinations of expected profit (return) and risk (measured by σ) that yield the same level of expected utility (satisfaction) to the decision-maker. The decision-maker is indifferent between the portfolios (projects, combinations of projects, or securities) A, B, C and D: as we move from portfolio A (which is riskless, since its standard deviation is zero) to B, C and D, the risk increases, but the decision-maker is compensated (for the disutility from the increasing risk) by increased expected profitability (return) of the successive portfolios.

We may draw a set of such indifference curves, and form the indifference map of a risk-avoider. Such a map is shown in Figure 12.2.

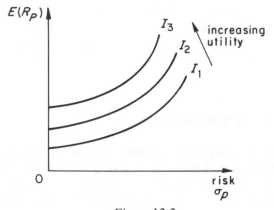

Figure 12.2

The indifference curves (of a risk-averter) have the following properties:

(1) A risk-indifference curve has a positive slope, which denotes the risk-aversion of the decision-maker. In Figure 12.1 we observe that as risk increases (from σ_B to σ_C) the expected profitability must rise (from $E(B)$ to $E(C)$) if the decision-maker is to remain on the same level of satisfaction (utility).

(2) The indifference curves are concave to the vertical axis. This implies (assumes) a diminishing marginal rate of substitution between risk (σ_p) and expected profitability, $E(R_p)$. In Figure 12.1 we see that as risk increases by equal amounts ($\sigma_B\sigma_C = \sigma_C\sigma_D$) the decision-maker requires a greater increase in expected profitability to compensate for the higher risk (the distance from $E(B)$ to $E(C)$ is smaller than the distance between $E(C)$ and $E(D)$).

(3) The risk-indifference curves do not intersect, because if they did the decision-maker would be inconsistent in ranking his preferences. The point of intersection would belong to two different indifference curves, implying two different levels of utility, which is inconsistent.

(4) Finally, the higher to the left an indifference curve, the greater the level of utility: for a given level of risk ($\bar{\sigma}$ in Figure 12.3), the decision-maker enjoys a higher utility the greater the expected profitability. Similarly, for a given level

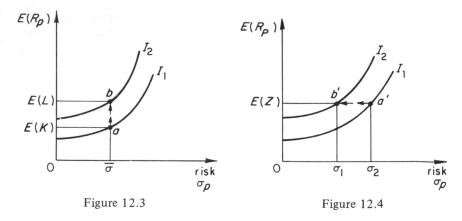

Figure 12.3 Figure 12.4

of expected profitability ($E(Z)$ in Figure 12.4), the decision-maker has a greater utility the smaller the risk ($\sigma_1 < \sigma_2$).[6]

(iii) *The efficient opportunity frontier of two-asset portfolios*

The second 'tool' required for decision-making under risk (within the framework of the maximisation of expected utility criterion) is the derivation of the 'efficient' portfolio choices open to the decision-maker, that is, the derivation of the *efficient opportunity frontier.*

A portfolio is efficient if there is no other portfolio with a higher expected profitability and a lower risk, a higher expected profitability and the same risk, or the same expected profitability but a lower risk. Similarly, a portfolio is inefficient (inferior) if the decision-maker can find another which has (a) the same expected profit with a smaller risk, or (b) a higher expected profit but the same risk, or (c) a higher expected value and a lower risk.[7]

---

[6] The indifference map of a *risk-taker* is shown in Figure 12.5. For a risk-taker risk is 'a good thing', like the expected profitability. Hence his risk-indifference curves have the shape and properties of the usual indifference curves of an individual who is ranking his preferences between combinations of quantities of two 'good' commodities.

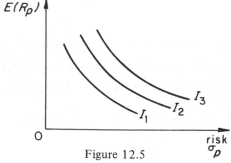

Figure 12.5

[7] This is sometimes called 'the Markowitz mean-variance axiom'. See H. Markowitz, *Portfolio Selection: Efficient Diversification of Investments* (Wiley, 1959) chs 7, 8.

The shape of the efficient opportunity frontier depends on the number of assets in each portfolio, as well as on the assets' expected return and standard deviation, and the correlation between the returns of the assets comprising the portfolio.

We will first examine the efficient frontier of various *two-asset portfolios*. We will then derive the efficient frontier of the *general two-asset portfolio*, that is, a portfolio consisting of two risky assets whose returns are not perfectly correlated. (The various 'special-case models', as well as the 'general two-asset model' will facilitate the understanding of the capital asset pricing model (CAPM), developed in section III.) Finally, we will extend the analysis to *n*-asset portfolios.

(1) *The efficient frontier of two-asset portfolios, with one riskless asset*

Assume that there are only two securities available on the stock market, a riskless one (such as a government bond) which yields a return R, and a share which has risk σ_1 and return R_1. Both securities are infinitely divisible. Note that the return of the riskless security is constant, so that $E(R) = R$ and $\sigma_R = 0$, $\text{cov}(RR_1) = 0$ (see Appendix 12.1).

Although there are only two securities, the assumption that they are infinitely divisible means that the investor can choose an infinite number of portfolios. He can spend all his funds (available for investment) on the riskless security, or on the risky security, or on a combination of both. Suppose he allocates a proportion x of his funds on the riskless security and the remainder $(1 - x)$ on the risky security. The return from this portfolio is

$$R_p = xR + (1 - x) R_1 \tag{12.10}$$

where $0 \leqslant x \leqslant 1$. This return has a distribution with *mean*

$$E(R_p) = xR + (1 - x) E(R_1) \tag{12.11}$$

and *variance*

$$\sigma_p^2 = (1 - x)^2 \sigma_1^2 \tag{12.12}$$

*   *   *

The expected value is found by taking expected values of expression (12.10):

$$E(R_p) = E\{xR + (1 - x)R_1\} = xR + (1 - x) E(R_1)$$

given that R and x are constants. (The rules of expected values are summarised in Appendix 12.2.)

The variance of R_p is found from the rules of expected values which are summarised in Appendix 12.2. Thus

$$\text{var}(R_p) = \sigma_p^2 = \text{var}\{xR + (1 - x) R_1\}$$

$$= \text{var}(xR) + \text{var}\{(1 - x) R_1\} + x(1 - x) 2\text{cov}(RR_1)$$

But var $(xR) = 0$ and cov $(RR_1) = 0$, given x and R are constants; therefore,

$$\sigma_p^2 = \text{var}\left\{(1-x)R_1\right\} = (1-x)^2\sigma_1^2$$

*   *   *

By varying the proportion of funds allocated to the two available securities (x and $1-x$) we may derive the efficient portfolio frontier, which includes the efficient portfolios (as previously defined). This frontier shows the trade-off between return and risk associated with different (efficient) portfolios.

Under our assumptions the efficient frontier is a straight line, defined by the equation

$$E(R_p) = R + \left(\frac{E(R_1) - R}{\sigma_1}\right)\sigma_p \tag{12.13}$$

*   *   *

The derivation of the frontier is easy:

(1) Solve expressions (12.11) and (12.12) for x to obtain:

$$x = \frac{E(R_p) - E(R_1)}{R - E(R_1)} \quad \text{and} \quad x = \frac{\sigma_1 - \sigma_p}{\sigma_1}$$

(2) Equate the above expressions and solve for $E(R_p)$:

$$E(R_p) = R + \left(\frac{E(R_1) - R}{\sigma_1}\right)\sigma_p$$

*   *   *

The efficient frontier is shown by the line RA in Figure 12.6. The intercept of the frontier is the return of the riskless security. It shows the expected return of the portfolio consisting of riskless securities alone ($x = 1$, $1 - x = 0$). The expected return of this portfolio is R and its risk is zero. At the other extreme, point A depicts a portfolio consisting of risky securities alone ($x = 0$, $1 - x = 1$). The expected return and risk of this portfolio are identical to the return and risk of the risky security.

Any point on the frontier shows *a portfolio* formed from a combination of the two securities. For example, at point a (in Figure 12.6) the portfolio includes the riskless security, which absorbs x_1 per cent of the total funds of the investor, and the risky security, which absorbs $1 - x_1$ of these funds. The expected return and risk of this portfolio are $E(R_{p1})$ and σ_{p1}. The closer to A, the higher the risk of the portfolio, and hence the higher the expected return required by the investor to compensate him for the increase in risk.

In general, by varying x between 1 and zero (which is equivalent to changing

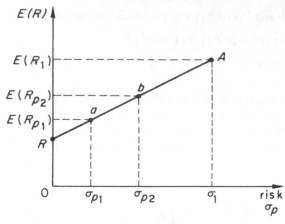

Figure 12.6

the risk, σ_p, between zero and σ_1), we obtain portfolios along the line RA, which represents the efficient opportunity frontier. It should be clear that the frontier consists of efficient portfolios only. The total opportunities open to the investor are defined by the points of the whole area $ORA\sigma_1$. However, any point below the line RA is inefficient, in the sense that the investor can reach a point *on* the frontier, at which the return is higher (with the same risk), or the risk is lower (with the same return), or both the return is higher and the risk is lower, as compared with the point inside the opportunity area and below the line RA.

The slope of the opportunity frontier is $(E(R_1) - R)/\sigma_1$. It shows the increase in return resulting from a unit increase in risk: *it is the price of one unit of risk.*

(2) *The efficient frontier of two-asset portfolios, with cash as the one asset*

In this model we allow for the possibility of holding some of the funds in the form of cash, which is assumed riskless. For simplicity assume that the amount not kept in cash is invested in either the riskless security or the risky one, but *not* in both. Under these assumptions we can easily derive the following:

(a) Point 0 in Figure 12.7 shows that all the funds are kept in cash form. There is no return and no risk in this all-cash portfolio.

(b) Any point on the vertical axis between 0 and R (such as point h in Figure 12.7) denotes a portfolio consisting partly of cash and partly of the riskless security. Such portfolios have zero risk and a return defined by the expression

$$E(R_p) = x(0) + (1 - x) R = (1 - x) R \qquad (12.14)$$

where x is the proportion of funds held in cash. It is apparent that

$$(1 - x) R < R \qquad (12.15)$$

Hence portfolios on the OR line are dominated by (are inferior to) the portfolio R, which has zero risk but a higher return.

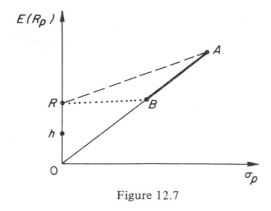

Figure 12.7

(c) Portfolios consisting of cash and the risky security lie on the line OA in Figure 12.7. Such portfolios have a return

$$R_p = (1 - x) R_1$$

whose expected value is

$$E(R_p) = (1 - x) E(R_1) \tag{12.16}$$

and a risk defined by the expression

$$\sigma_p = (1 - x) \sigma_1 \tag{12.17}$$

Portfolios on the segment OB are not efficient because they are dominated by portfolio R, which has a higher return (R), and zero risk. However, portfolios on the segment BA are efficient because by assumption the investor cannot possess simultaneously the riskless security and the risky security A, i.e. portfolios on the line RA are *not* available to him. Thus in this case the efficient opportunity frontier consists of point R and the line BA.

(3) *The efficient frontier of two-asset portfolios, with borrowing*

Another interesting case arises when the investor is allowed to borrow money at the interest rate R and invest it in the risky security. In this case the investor's opportunity frontier is expanded by portfolios which lie on the extension of the line RA, that is, on the segment AZ, in Figure 12.8 (The entire efficient opportunity frontier with borrowing is the line RZ and beyond.)

Up to this point we have examined two-asset portfolios in which one riskless asset was available. In such cases efficient portfolios are combinations of the risky and the riskless securities. So long as a riskless security is available, no efficient portfolio will contain cash. If borrowing is impossible (or undesirable), the efficient investment opportunity set is the line RA. Over this frontier some proportion of the investor's funds are invested in the riskless security, that is, $x > 0$. The most risky portfolio (with no borrowing) is portfolio A, consisting of

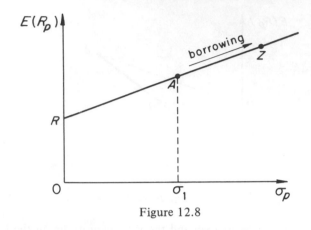

Figure 12.8

risky securities only ($x = 0$). Less risky portfolios (which, however, will have a lower expected return) can be formed by mixing risky and riskless securities. If borrowing is allowed, more risky portfolios than A can be formed, by borrowing at the rate R and then investing both the initial funds and the borrowed money in the risky security, A, obtaining portfolios along the line from A through Z.

(4) *The efficient frontier of portfolios of two risky assets whose returns are perfectly positively correlated*

In this model it is assumed that there are two risky securities, A and B, with the following characteristics:

$$R_1 < R_2$$

$$\sigma_1 < \sigma_2$$

$$r_{12} = +1$$

$$\text{cov}\,(R_1 R_2) = r_{12}\sigma_1\sigma_2 = \sigma_1\sigma_2 \qquad (12.18)$$

The return of any portfolio of these two securities is

$$R_p = xR_1 + (1 - x)\,R_2$$

The expected return of such portfolios is given by the expression

$$E(R_p) = xE(R_1) + (1 - x)\,E(R_2) \qquad (12.19)$$

The variance of these portfolios is derived by using expression (12.7) and the algebraic rules of expected values (see Appendix 12.2). Thus we have

$$\sigma_p^2 = x^2\sigma_1^2 + (1 - x)^2\sigma_2^2 + 2x(1 - x)\,\text{cov}\,(R_1 R_2)$$

$$= x^2\sigma_1^2 + (1 - x)^2\sigma_2^2 + 2x(1 - x)\,(\sigma_1\sigma_2)$$

$$= [x\sigma_1 + (1 - x)\sigma_2]^2 \qquad (12.20)$$

or

$$\sigma_p = x\sigma_1 + (1 - x)\sigma_2 \tag{12.21}$$

The efficient opportunity frontier is a straight line defined by the equation

$$E(R_p) = a + b\sigma_p \tag{12.22}$$

where

$$a = E(R_2) - \sigma_2 b = \text{constant} \tag{12.23}$$

and

$$b = \frac{E(R_1) - E(R_2)}{\sigma_1 - \sigma_2} = \text{constant slope} \tag{12.24}$$

* * *

Mathematical derivation of the efficient opportunity frontier

$$E(R_p) = xE(R_1) + (1 - x)E(R_2) = E(R_2) + x[E(R_1) - E(R_2)]$$

Multiplying the last term of this expression by $(\sigma_1 - \sigma_2)/(\sigma_1 - \sigma_2)$ we obtain

$$E(R_p) = E(R_2) + x(\sigma_1 - \sigma_2) \left(\frac{E(R_1) - E(R_2)}{\sigma_1 - \sigma_2} \right)$$

$$= E(R_2) + x(\sigma_1 - \sigma_2)b$$

Adding and subtracting the term $b\sigma_2$, we obtain

$$E(R_p) = [E(R_2) - b\sigma_2] + xb(\sigma_1 - \sigma_2) + b\sigma_2$$

or

$$E(R_p) = a + b[x\sigma_1 - x\sigma_2 + \sigma_2]$$

$$= a + b[x\sigma_1 + (1 - x)\sigma_2]$$

and

$$E(R_p) = a + b\sigma_p$$

It should be stressed that the line of the efficient frontier does *not* intersect the vertical axis, because σ_p is always positive, as can be seen from expression (12.21). Thus the coefficient a does *not* have the usual meaning of an intercept.

* * *

The efficient opportunity frontier for the perfectly positively correlated securities is the line AB in Figure 12.9. Point A shows a portfolio consisting entirely of the less risky security $(x = 1)$, while point B shows a portfolio consisting entirely of the more risky security $(x = 0)$. Intermediate points show portfolios containing various proportions of the two securities.

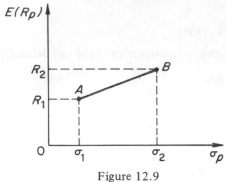

Figure 12.9

The important thing to notice is that the least risky portfolio is the one containing only security A, and it is impossible to reduce this risk by diversification (when the securities are perfectly positively correlated). This is easy to understand. Perfect positive correlation of returns of the two securities means that both move simultaneously in the same direction. Hence it is impossible by acquiring a mix of such securities to reduce the variability of the returns (below the variance of the less risky security).

*   *   *

This conclusion can be verified from an examination of expression (12.21):

$$\sigma_p = x\sigma_1 + (1 - x)\,\sigma_2$$

Since σ_1 is smaller than σ_2, *ex hypothesi*, it follows that σ_p has the lowest possible value σ_1, which is attained if $x = 1$, i.e. when the 'portfolio' includes only security A.

*   *   *

If an investor wants to minimise risk, he will invest only in the less risky security A. (Of course, in this event, he will also have the lowest return, R_1.)

(5) *The efficient frontier of portfolios of two assets whose returns are perfectly inversely correlated*

Again we assume two securities with different returns and risk ($R_1 < R_2$ and $\sigma_1 < \sigma_2$), with $r_{12} = -1$, so that $\text{cov}\,(R_1 R_2) = -\sigma_1\sigma_2$.

The return of the portfolio is $R_p = xR_1 + (1 - x)\,R_2$ with mean

$$E(R_p) = xE(R_1) + (1 - x)E(R_2) \tag{12.25}$$

and variance

$$\sigma_p^2 = [x\sigma_1 - (1-x)\sigma_2]^2 \tag{12.26}$$

The standard deviation of the portfolio is

$$\sigma_p = x\sigma_1 - (1-x)\sigma_2 \tag{12.27}$$

It can be shown (on lines similar to the proof in the preceding paragraph) that in this case the opportunity frontier consists of two linear segments, as depicted in Figure 12.10.

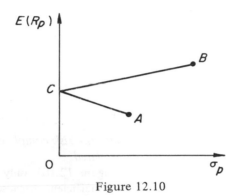

Figure 12.10

In this model risk can be reduced to zero by an appropriate choice of x and $1 - x$, the proportion of funds invested in the two securities. It can be shown that $\sigma_p = 0$ when the proportion of funds invested in the two securities is

$$x = \frac{\sigma_2}{\sigma_1 + \sigma_2} \quad \text{and} \quad (1-x) = \frac{\sigma_1}{\sigma_2 + \sigma_1} \tag{12.28}$$

*   *   *

PROOF

From expression (12.27) we have

$$\sigma_p = x\sigma_1 - (1-x)\sigma_2$$

It is obvious that $\sigma_p = 0$ when

$$x\sigma_1 = (1-x)\sigma_2$$

Solving for x, we find

$$x(\sigma_1 + \sigma_2) = \sigma_2$$

or

$$x = \frac{\sigma_1}{\sigma_1 + \sigma_2}$$

Thus

$$(1 - x) = \frac{\sigma_1}{\sigma_1 + \sigma_2}$$

QED

As an illustration, assume that $\sigma_1 = 0.2$ and $\sigma_2 = 0.3$. In order to reduce σ_p to zero, the investor should allocate his funds as follows:

Spend on security A the proportion $x = \dfrac{0.3}{0.2 + 0.3} = \dfrac{3}{5}$ (of his funds)

Spend on security B the proportion $1 - x = \dfrac{2}{5}$ (of his funds)

His portfolio's risk is

$$\sigma_p = x\sigma_1 - (1 - x)\,\sigma_2 = \frac{3}{5}(0.2) - \frac{2}{5}(0.3) = \frac{1}{5}(0.6 - 0.6) = 0$$

*   *   *

In summary, *diversification can eliminate the risk completely if the returns of the securities are perfectly negatively correlated.*

Although the frontier is ACB (in Figure 12.10), only the segment CB is efficient. Points on the segment CA are inefficient, because they denote portfolios with lower return and/or higher risk as compared with portfolios lying on the CB segment.

(6) *The efficient frontier of the general two-asset model*

In the real world none of the previous extreme cases is observed. Usually the returns of the securities show some correlation (between zero and ± 1). Under these conditions it can be shown that the opportunity frontier is a hyperbola, as shown in Figure 12.11.

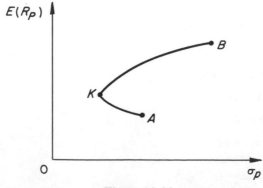

Figure 12.11

Risk can be reduced by diversification but cannot, in general, be eliminated, that is, in this case $(0 < r < |1|)$ there will generally be no portfolio for which $\sigma_p = 0$. The closer the value of the correlation coefficient of the returns of the two assets to $+1$, the more the opportunity locus will approximate the line of Figure 12.9. The closer the value of the correlation coefficient is to -1, the more the opportunity locus will approximate the two-segment line of Figure 12.10. In general, in the intermediate case (of *some* positive or negative correlation of returns of the two assets) the opportunity locus will be a curve such as the one (AKB) of Figure 12.11. The efficient frontier is only the segment KB of this curve.

(iv) *Equilibrium of the investor: choice of the optimal portfolio within the two-asset model*

In Figures 12.12 to 12.14 we show the choice of the optimal portfolio using the first two-asset model in which one security was riskless. The investor reaches equilibrium (maximises his expected utility) when he reaches the highest possible indifference curve.

In general, the optimal portfolio is defined by the point of tangency of the highest indifference curve with the efficient opportunity frontier. In Figure

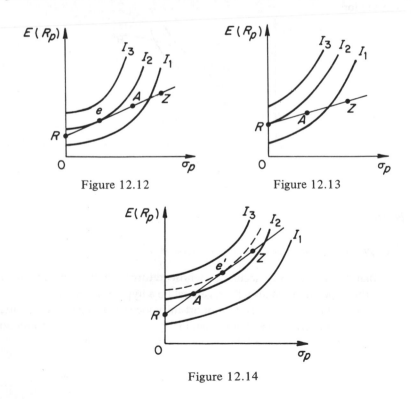

Figure 12.12   Figure 12.13

Figure 12.14

12.12 this portfolio is defined by point e: the optimal portfolio consists of a mix of the riskless and the risky securities since it lies to the left of A, implying $0 < x < 1$. (Recall that x is the proportion of funds invested in the riskless security.)

Figures 12.13 and 12.14 show two possible equilibria, which are known as 'corner solutions'. In both cases the slope of the indifference curve (in equilibrium) is different from the slope of the efficient investment set: the two curves intersect at equilibrium. In Figure 12.13 the investor is so averse to risk[8] that he chooses portfolio R, which includes only the riskless asset. In Figure 12.14 the investor is not strongly averse to risk (as shown by the flat shape of his indifference curves). He invests all his funds in the risky security A. If borrowing were allowed, he could reach a higher indifference curve by borrowing money and investing it at the risky security A; for example, he would be at equilibrium at point e' (where x, the proportion of funds invested in the riskless security, is negative).

The portfolio-selection process is not affected in the case of portfolios including only risky securities. Again, the investor will maximise his utility if he chooses the portfolio defined by the point of tangency of the efficient opportunity frontier with the highest indifference curve (point e^* in Figure 12.15).

The generalisation of the two-asset model to n-asset portfolios is developed in the next section.

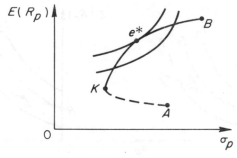

Figure 12.15

(v) *Portfolio selection in the n-asset model*

(1) *The opportunity frontier of n-asset portfolios*

We saw that with two risky securities whose returns are to a certain degree correlated the opportunity locus will in general be a hyperbolic curve.

In the case of three risky assets the opportunity locus is in general represented by a region. We can briefly examine the geometry of this case as an introduction to the formal derivation of the efficient locus in the n-asset case.

---

[8] Recall that the risk-aversion is shown by the slope of the indifference curves.

Assume that there are three assets, *A, B, C*. Portfolios containing any two of these assets will be shown by hyperbolic opportunity loci of the type described earlier. For example, assume that the three assets are represented by the points *A, B* and *C* in Figure 12.16. The locus *AC* represents portfolios composed of some proportions of assets *A* and *C*; the locus *AB* represents portfolios composed of some proportions of assets *A* and *B*; and so on.

Take portfolio *P*, consisting of securities *A* and *B* in the proportions *w* and $1 - w$. Given that these proportions are fixed, portfolio *P* can be considered as *an asset* in its own right. If we want now to add to this 'asset' an amount of security *C*, we can form the opportunity locus *PC*, which contains portfolios of all three securities.

In a similar way we can change *w* and obtain another mix of assets *A* and *B*, for example *P'*, which can next be combined with asset *C*. And so on. We thus obtain a region whose boundary (the 'envelope' curve *AKC* in Figure 12.17) is the frontier of the opportunity locus of three-asset portfolios. The efficient frontier is only the segment *KC* of the frontier.

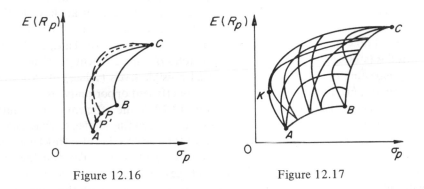

Figure 12.16   Figure 12.17

The above approach is of course illustrative. It is impossible to obtain the efficient locus of portfolios including even a small number of assets with such diagrammatic analysis. A mathematical model for the derivation of the efficient locus has been developed by Markowitz.[9]

Markowitz considers any particular value of expected return and attempts to find, among all portfolios that have this return, the one with the minimum (smallest) risk, as measured by the standard deviation. For example, consider the expected return $E(R)$ in Figure 12.18. All points lying on the line *AHB* denote strategies which have the same expected return, $E(R)$, but different risk (different standard deviations). Points on the segment *HB* (excluding point *H*) show inefficient strategies, because they have the same expected return as strategy *H* but a higher risk. Points on the segment *AH* (excluding *H*) are portfolios better

[9] Markowitz, *Portfolio Selection: Efficient Diversification of Investments*.

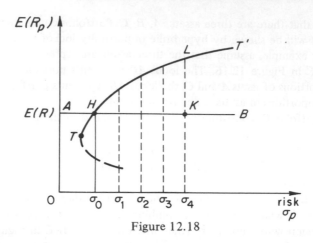

Figure 12.18

than H, because they have the same expected profitability (return) as H but a lower standard deviation (risk). However, such point-strategies are beyond the reach (or beyond the consideration) of the decision-maker either because he does not know of their existence or because they do not exist. Thus, among all portfolios (strategies) on the line AHB, portfolio H is the efficient portfolio.

By repeating the above procedure for all possible levels (values) of expected profitability, $E(R)$, we can trace out the entire efficient opportunity frontier.

In summary. The curve TT' in Figure 12.18 is the efficient opportunity frontier. It is formed from the locus of points representing strategies which have the maximum expected profitability (return) for a given value of σ (risk) *and* the minimum σ (risk) for a given value of expected profitability. Points below the TT' efficient frontier denote inferior strategies, because they have a larger σ (with the same expected value), or a smaller expected value (with the same σ), or both a greater σ and a smaller expected value as compared with other points on the TT' frontier. For example, consider point K. It is inferior to strategy L, because K has the same σ but a smaller expected profitability as compared with L. Strategy K is also inferior to strategy H (both have the same expected return, but K has a higher risk). All strategies on the segment HT' (e.g. point L) are efficient and hence superior to K, because they have both a higher expected value *and* a lower risk as compared with strategy K. Finally, points above the efficient (TT') frontier denote strategies which are superior to those on the frontier, but they are beyond the reach (or the consideration) of the decision-maker, for various reasons.

*   *   *

The above procedure may be formally stated as a minimisation problem subject to certain constraints. The objective function to be minimised in the Markowitz model is

$$\sigma_p^2 = \sum_{j=1}^{n} x_j \sigma_j^2 + \left(\sum \sum_{i \neq j} \right) x_i x_j \, \text{cov} \, (R_i R_j) \tag{12.29}$$

subject to the constraints:

$E(R) = k$ (a constant value of return, different at each 'round' of calculations)

$$\sum_{j=1}^{n} x_j = 1 \quad (n = \text{number of assets in the portfolio})$$

$x_j \geqslant 0$

where x_j = proportion of funds invested in the jth asset. The unknowns are the xs, i.e. the composition of the portfolio. Although the constraints are linear functions of the xs, the objective function is a quadratic equation. Hence simple linear programming is not appropriate. The method of quadratic programming is required to solve this minimisation problem.

The Markowitz model requires knowledge of the expected return (R_j) and the variance (σ_j^2) of each asset in the portfolio, as well as of the covariance of each pair of assets. This implies that, if there are n assets, one must know n returns, n variances and $(n^2 - n)/2$ covariances, that is, altogether

$$2n + \frac{n^2 - n}{2} = \frac{n^2}{2} + 1.5 \, n$$

pieces of information.

Markowitz's model has been of limited practical use, because of its cost for data requirements and computational time. For example, in 1967 a 150-security Markowitz calculation (efficient frontier) required ninety minutes on the IBM 7090 computer, and the cost of its computation was estimated to be $600.

A simpler model for the determination of the efficient portfolio frontier has been developed by W. F. Sharpe, 'A Simplified Model for Portfolio Analysis', *Management Science*, 1963, pp. 277–93. This model will be briefly explained in section III (see p. 611).

*   *   *

(2) *Equilibrium of the investor in the n-asset model*

The 'optimal' n-asset portfolio is the portfolio that maximises the expected utility of the investor (decision-maker). It is determined in the same way as the optimal two-asset portfolio. That is, the optimal n-asset portfolio is defined by the tangency of the efficient opportunity frontier to the highest risk-indifference curve.

The equilibrium of the investor is shown in Figure 12.19. The shaded area in Figure 12.19 represents the opportunity set of all the portfolios available to the

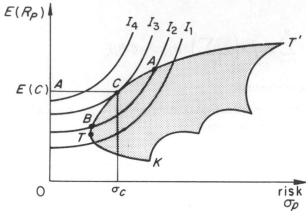

Figure 12.19   Choice of optimal n-asset portfolio under risk: maximisation of
of expected utility

investor, and the segment TT' of the boundary of the set represents the efficient
opportunity frontier in the Markowitz sense.

An investor, faced with only risky assets, who has the particular indifference
map shown in Figure 12.19 will maximise his expected utility by investing in
portfolio C, which has a yield $E(C)$ and standard deviation σ_C. Portfolios such as
A or B are efficient, but lie on a lower indifference curve.

(3) *Implications of the existence of a riskless asset and the possibility of borrowing*

Portfolio C (in Figure 12.19) is the optimal solution to the problem of portfolio
selection only in the case where choice is restricted to risky securities. Let us
now assume that a riskless security exists with a yield R and that the investor
can borrow any amount of funds at the riskless rate R. Under these conditions
the efficient frontier is the straight line RMZ (in Figure 12.20), that is, a line
drawn from R through Z which is tangent to the frontier of the risky portfolios.
Note that of all risky portfolios only M belongs to the *new efficient frontier*. We
saw earlier (expression (12.13)) that the equation of this efficient frontier is

$$E(R_p) = R + \left(\frac{E(R_M) - R}{\sigma_M} \right) \sigma_p \qquad (12.30)$$

Portfolio M dominates all the risky ones, including those on the original efficient
frontier (TT').

The equilibrium of the investor will be defined by the point of tangency of
his highest indifference curve with the new frontier (point P in Figure 12.20).
The closer to R, the greater the proportion of funds invested in the riskless
security. If the tangency occurred at M, the chosen portfolio would consist of
only risky securities (in the proportions implied by M).

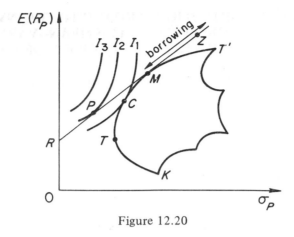

Figure 12.20

If the investor can borrow at the market rate R, he would be at equilibrium at point e (in Figure 12.21), buying portfolio M, spending on it all his own funds plus the borrowed amount.

If the investor cannot borrow (or does not want to borrow) funds at the riskless rate R, then the efficient frontier would consist of two segments: the segment RM of the tangent, and the segment $MM'T'$ of the risky efficient frontier. The optimal portfolio is determined by the point of tangency of the frontier $RMM'T'$ to the highest indifference curve. If the investor has the utility map shown in Figure 12.21, his equilibrium would be portfolio M'. We see that, without borrowing, his expected utility is lower. (M' lies on a lower indifference curve than e. But M' lies on a higher indifference curve than M, if the investor is not very risk-averse.)

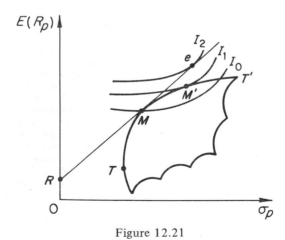

Figure 12.21

II. THE FIRM—PORTFOLIO APPROACH TO THE INVESTMENT DECISION: APPLICATION OF THE MEAN—VARIANCE MODEL TO THE INVESTMENT DECISION OF THE FIRM

In this section we examine the application of the theory of portfolio selection to the appraisal of investment projects.[10]

The portfolio approach to the investment decision assumes that the only thing that is important (to the management) is *the total risk and return of the firm as a whole.* Investment projects are evaluated on the basis of their marginal impact on the total risk and return of the firm. The risk of projects is firm-oriented: the management does *not* consider explicitly (directly) the impact of an investment project on investors' (shareholders') portfolios of securities, but only upon *the portfolio of assets* of the firm.

The firm considers portfolios of assets. These portfolios consist of combinations of existing investments and new projects under consideration. Management estimates the expected return and risk of all available portfolios of fixed assets, and chooses from them the one that maximises its utility.

This procedure of investment decision requires two 'tools': (1) the efficient frontier of portfolios of fixed assets; and (2) a set of indifference curves to represent the utility function of management as a whole, that is, the managerial preferences between return and risk. Let us first examine these tools, and then compare this approach with the traditional theory of single-project evaluation.

A.   The Efficient Frontier of Portfolios of Fixed Assets

An efficient portfolio frontier of fixed assets can in principle be derived on the lines suggested by Markowitz (see pp. 595—7). The first step is the calculation of the expected return and risk of each portfolio (of fixed assets) using expres-

---

[10] The theory of portfolio selection is assumed to apply to investments in fixed capital, as it applies to investments in securities. However, there are some important differences between these two types of investment which should be borne in mind. (1) One difference is the relevant time horizon and transactions costs. Transactions costs associated with purchasing or selling most stocks and bonds are a relatively small fraction of their value. Thus the holder of these assets can make decisions within the framework of a relatively short time horizon. By contrast, the transactions costs for fixed capital investments may be a large fraction of their value, and the relevant time horizon is often the life of the asset. (2) Another important difference is the nature of dependency of the earnings from the investments. The mean earnings of a portfolio of stocks and bonds can be obtained by adding the mean earnings of the securities. But if fixed investments are technically complementary, the sum of the two streams of earnings is greater than the sum of the mean earnings of the two projects. (The earnings from a portfolio consisting of a blast furnace and a rolling mill is often greater than the total amount that could be earned from each of these projects alone.) (3) Some fixed investments may be mutually exclusive, while this is not usually the case with investments in securities. (4) Some investments may be necessary for contingency purposes. Again, such contingency considerations do not arise for investments in stocks and bonds.

sions (12.1) and (12.4). Thus the expected return of a portfolio, p, is

$$E(R_p) = \sum_{j=1}^{n} x_j E(R_j) \tag{12.1}$$

and the risk of the portfolio is

$$\sigma_p = \sqrt{\sum_{j=1}^{n} x_j^2 \sigma_j^2 + \sum_{j=1}^{n-1} \sum_{i=j+1}^{n} x_i x_j (r_{ij} \sigma_i \sigma_j)} \tag{12.4}$$

It is helpful to think that all the existing assets of the firm have an expected return, $E(R_1)$, and a standard deviation, σ_1. Each new project is 'combined' with the existing assets to form a portfolio. Under these conditions the investment decision can be analysed within the framework of the general two-asset portfolio developed in section I. The expected return and risk of a two-asset portfolio is estimated by the following expressions:

$$E(R_p) = xE(R_1) + (1-x) E(R_2) \tag{12.31}$$

$$\sigma_p = \sqrt{x^2 \sigma_1^2 + (1-x)^2 \sigma_2^2 + 2x(1-x) (r_{12} \sigma_1 \sigma_2)} \tag{12.32}$$

where $E(R_1)$ = expected return from *all the existing assets* of the firm

σ_1 = risk of the existing assets, measured by the standard deviation of the earnings from these assets

$E(R_2)$ = expected return of any *new* investment project being considered

σ_2 = risk of the new project, measured by its standard deviation

x = proportion of funds invested in the existing assets

$1 - x$ = proportion of funds to be absorbed by the *new* project

We will illustrate the computational procedure by a numerical example. It is assumed that there are four possible 'states of the economy' (or 'general business conditions'). The return of the existing assets (A), as well as of the contemplated new project (B), depends on which 'state' materialises. The managers believe that the probabilities of the four 'states' are those shown in the second column of Table 12.1. Columns (3) and (4) include the possible returns from existing assets and from the new project, as estimated by management.

Table 12.1   Probability distributions of returns from existing fixed assets (A) and from the new project (B)

(1)	(2)	(3)	(4)
'States of the economy' or 'general business conditions'	Probability of the ith state	Return on all existing fixed assets R_{1i}	Return on new project R_{2i}
State 1 Mild recession	0.20	$R_{11} = 0.03$	$R_{21} = -0.04$
State 2 Severe depression	0.30	$R_{12} = -0.08$	$R_{22} = 0.01$
State 3 Stagnant economy	0.40	$R_{13} = 0.08$	$R_{23} = 0.06$
State 4 Expanding economy (real growth situation)	0.10	$R_{14} = 0.14$	$R_{24} = 0.26$

From the information of Table 12.1, we may compute the expected return from the existing assets, from the new project, as well as from the portfolio of 'all existing assets *and* the new project' (portfolio '*A* and *B*'), assuming that project *B* is a major investment which will absorb 60 per cent of all the funds of the firm (i.e. $x = 0.40$ and $1 - x = 0.60$). Thus

$$E(R_1) = \sum_{i=1}^{4} R_{1i}Pr(R_{1i}) = (0.03)(0.20) + (-0.08)(0.30) + (0.08)(0.40)$$

$$+ (0.14)(0.10) = 0.028$$

$$E(R_2) = \sum_{i=1}^{4} R_{2i}Pr(R_{2i}) = (-0.04)(0.20) + (0.01)(0.20) + (0.06)(0.40)$$

$$+ (0.26)(0.10) = 0.045$$

$$E(R_p) = xE(R_1) + (1-x)E(R_2) = 0.40(0.028) + 0.60(0.045) = 0.0382$$

The risk of the existing assets (σ_1) is estimated from the information of Table 12.2. The risk of the new investment project is estimated from the information of Table 12.3. The risk of the portfolio '*A* and *B*' is estimated from the information of Table 12.4.

The computations shown in the tables can be repeated for all possible portfolios of existing assets and any one of the projects being considered for adoption.

It should be clear from the above discussion that in the firm—portfolio approach each investment project is appraised on the basis of its *marginal risk*, that is, its impact on the risk of the firm's portfolio of existing assets. The 'marginal risk' of an investment depends upon (a) its own risk, and (b) its correlation with existing fixed investments. (If the firm is considering two or more projects *simultaneously*, then the 'marginal risk' of *each* project also depends on its correlation with the other projects, as can be seen from the general expression (12.4).) By itself a new investment project may have a high risk. (In our numerical example $\sigma_2 > \sigma_1$.) However, such a project may be attractive to the firm, if its returns combined with those currently anticipated from existing assets would reduce the over-all risk of the firm. (In our example $\sigma_p < \sigma_1$.)

Each portfolio of fixed assets may be represented by a point on the 'expected return—risk graph' (see Figure 12.22). The firm next traces the efficient frontier of available portfolios, using the Markowitz technique, developed in section I (pp. 595—7).

B. The Managers' Indifference Map

It is *assumed* that the firm's management can express its risk preferences in the form of a set of indifference curves with the usual properties. In other words,

Table 12.2   Risk of existing assets of the firm

(1)	(2)	(3)	(4)	(5)
'States of the economy'	Probability of the ith 'state'	Deviations of the returns from their mean $[R_{1i} - E(R_1)]$	Squared deviations $[R_{1i} - E(R_1)]^2$	Squared deviations multiplied by the probabilities $[R_{1i} - E(R_1)]^2\, Pr(R_{1i})$
State 1	0.20	0.002	0.000004	0.0000008
State 2	0.30	−0.108	0.011664	0.0034992
State 3	0.40	0.052	0.002704	0.0010816
State 4	0.10	0.112	0.012544	0.0012544

$$\Sigma[R_{1i} - E(R_1)]^2\, Pr(R_{1i})$$
$$= 0.005836$$

Risk of all existing assets

$$\sigma_1^2 = \Sigma[R_{1i} - E(R_1)]^2\, Pr(R_{1i}) = 0.005836$$

and

$$\sigma_1 = \sqrt{0.005836} = 0.076394$$

Table 12.3 Risk of the new investment project, B

(1)	(2)	(3)	(4)	(5)
'States of the economy'	Probability of the ith 'state'	Deviations of the returns from their mean $[R_{2i} - E(R_2)]$	Squared deviations $[R_{2i} - E(R_2)]^2$	Squared deviations multiplied by the probabilities $[R_{2i} - E(R_2)]^2 \, Pr(R_{2i})$
State 1	0.20	−0.085	0.007225	0.0014450
State 2	0.30	−0.035	0.001225	0.0003675
State 3	0.40	0.015	0.000225	0.0000900
State 4	0.10	0.215	0.046225	0.0046225

$$\Sigma [R_{2i} - E(R_2)]^2 \, Pr(R_{2i})$$
$$= 0.006525$$

Risk of the new project B

$$\sigma_2^2 = \Sigma [R_{2i} - E(R_2)]^2 \, Pr(R_{2i}) = 0.006525$$

and

$$\sigma_2 = \sqrt{0.006526} = 0.080777$$

Table 12.4 Risk of the portfolio 'A and B'

(1)	(2)	(3)	(4)	(5)	(6) = (5) × (2)
'States of the economy'	Probability of the ith 'state'	Deviations of existing assets $[R_{1i} - E(R_2)]$	Deviations of the new project $[R_{2i} - E(R_2)]$	Product of deviations (3) × (4)	Product of deviations multiplied by probabilities
State 1	0.20	0.002	−0.085	−0.00017	−0.000034
State 2	0.30	−0.108	−0.035	0.00378	0.001134
State 3	0.40	0.052	0.015	0.00078	0.000312
State 4	0.10	0.112	0.215	0.02408	0.002408

Total = 0.00382

$Cov(A \text{ and } B) = \Sigma [R_{1i} - E(R_1)] \, [R_{2i} - E(R_2)] \, Pr(i) = 0.00382$

Correlation coefficient $r_{12} = \dfrac{Cov(A \text{ and } B)}{\sigma_1 \sigma_2} = \dfrac{0.00382}{(0.076394)(0.080777)} = 0.619$

Risk of the portfolio 'A and B':

$$\sigma^2(A \text{ and } B) = x^2 \sigma_1^2 + (1 - x)^2 \sigma_2^2 + 2x(1 - x) \, Cov(A \text{ and } B)$$
$$= (0.40)^2 (0.005836) + (0.60)^2 (0.006525) + 2(0.40)(0.60)(0.00382) = 0.005116$$

Alternatively

$$\sigma^2(A \text{ and } B) = x^2 \sigma_1^2 + (1 - x)^2 \sigma_2^2 + 2x(1 - x)(r_{12}\sigma_1\sigma_2)$$
$$= (0.40)^2 (0.005836) + (0.60)^2 (0.006525) + 2(0.40)(0.60)(0.619)(0.076394)(0.080777) = 0.005116$$

Thus

$$\sigma_p = \sqrt{0.005116} = 0.0715$$

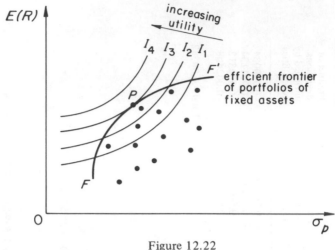

Figure 12.22

the firm—portfolio approach assumes that there exists a collective managerial utility function which gives rise to indifference curves similar to those of an individual investor.[11] A set of such indifference curves is shown in Figure 12.22 above. Each successive (higher) indifference curve represents a higher level of utility.

C.   The Optimal Investment Decision

The optimal investment consists of the choice of the fixed-asset portfolio which maximises the utility of the management as a whole. This is defined by the tangency of the efficient frontier with the highest possible indifference curve. In Figure 12.22 the management will choose the investment portfolio P, because this maximises the collective managerial utility function. The selection of the optimal portfolio determines the new proposals that will be accepted. The projects that are not in the portfolio as it is finally selected would be rejected.

The theoretical foundation of the firm—portfolio approach to the investment decision is not secure, due to the assumption of the existence of a well-defined group utility function. A collective utility function can be derived only under very restricted assumptions.[12] Furthermore, the practical importance of this approach is questionable, given the amount of information that is required.

    However, some writers[13] argue that the framework for evaluating combina-

---

[11] In fact, a group utility function can be derived only under very restricted assumptions. See R. Wilson, 'The Theory of Syndicates', *Econometrica*, vol. 36, 1968, pp. 119–32.

[12] See Wilson, 'The Theory of Syndicates'.

[13] J. C. Van Horne *et al.*, *Financial Management and Policy*, 4th edn (Prentice-Hall, 1977) pp. 184–5.

tions of risky investments implied by the firm–portfolio approach 'is quite useful' even if the managerial utility function is not defined. For example, Van Horne maintains that if the expected return and risk of the various portfolios of investments are estimated and plotted on a two dimensional graph, (such as Figure 12.23), management can eliminate most combinations (portfolios) simply because they are dominated by other portfolios. In Figure 12.23 the firm's management would normally consider only portfolios *A, B, C, D, E* and *F*, because all other portfolios are dominated by (are inferior to) those portfolios. Among those portfolios the managers would choose the one that they 'felt' gave the best combination of expected return and risk to the firm as a whole.

We think that such arguments cannot 'save' the mean-variance model from its basic weaknesses.

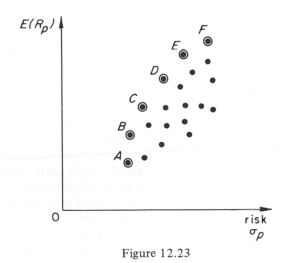

Figure 12.23

D. A Comparison of the Firm–Portfolio Approach with the Traditional Theory of Single-Project Evaluation

It is often argued that the firm–portfolio approach to the investment decision is theoretically superior to the single-project evaluation techniques of the traditional theory of investment. The latter does not provide any direct link between the investment proposals and their impact on the share price (or stockholder-wealth position), while the firm–portfolio approach does provide such a link, by considering explicitly the effect of prospective investments on the risk of the firm as a whole.

This argument implicitly assumes that if the diversification which the firm attains by accepting investment projects reduces the risk of the stream of earnings of the firm, the price of the stock will be increased (because of the reduction in risk).

The advocates of single-project appraisal techniques (and in particular the supporters of the risk-adjusted discount-rate techniques) argue that the diversification effect of investment projects need not concern management, because in efficient (perfect) capital markets investors can attain any desired degree of diversification of their portfolio, and they would do so at a smaller cost.[14] Hence investors would not be prepared to pay to the firm a premium for doing something (i.e. diversify) which they themselves can do more efficiently. The following example illustrates this argument.

Assume that a cosmetics firm considers diversifying, by investing in plant producing foods. Even if the investment in the foods line may have the same (or lower) expected earnings than an investment in expanding the cosmetics production, the risk of foods is less than the risk of cosmetics. Thus the low correlations (possibly even negative correlations) of the earnings from foods with those of cosmetics will reduce the total variance (and hence the risk) of the firm's entire portfolio of investments. As a consequence, the value of the firm will increase. This increase (the proponents of the single-project appraisal approach argue) will be due to the increase in the present value arising from the new investment in foods, and not to the reduced risk of the firm. In other words, the value of the firm will not increase by more than the risk-adjusted net present value of the foods investment viewed in isolation, because investors will not pay (to the firm) more to do something (i.e. diversify in the foods industry) that they can do themselves. Investors can buy stocks of other firms already established in the food industry. They can buy stocks of other firms that have the same net present value and variance of expected returns, even though they may not involve investment in the food industry. The risk of the investment in the food line is independent of the risk of the cosmetics production (existing investments of the firm). It is made independent by efficient (perfect) capital markets, which provide essentially the same opportunities for diversification to risk-averse investors as the firm can provide. Investors can have 'home-made' diversification, by changing their portfolios. In perfect capital markets investors will not pay more to have a firm diversify (through fixed investment) since they can themselves attain the same degree of diversification by changing their portfolios. Diversification in the foods industry is not more valuable (to the shareholder) because it is done by a firm in the cosmetics industry rather than investments by firms in the food industry, whose shares the investor can buy in capital markets if he wishes to diversify his portfolio. Because investors take into account correlations and covariances of the earnings from different shares in their portfolios (see pp. 576–94), management does not have to repeat the process when making investments within the firm.

This does not mean that the value of an investment in the foods line is not affected by the lower risk of its earnings (due to the counter-cyclical pattern of foods earnings as compared with the cyclical pattern of earnings from cosmetics). The capital market recognises the counter-cyclical nature of foods operations

[14] See, for example, R. W. Johnson, *Capital Budgeting* (Wadsworth, 1970).

and has established foods firms in a risk class separate from and lower than the cosmetics firms. Because food production involves a lower risk, investors are prepared to accept a lower yield than they require from investing (buying) in shares of cosmetics firms. The difference in the risk class of foods and cosmetics is reflected in the capitalisation rates assigned by the capital market to their expected dividend streams. And it is this capitalisation rate which is used as the appropriate risk-adjusted discount rate in evaluating investment projects. The cosmetics firm, in appraising a foods investment, should use the capitalisation rate (cost of capital) of firms in the food industry. Since the market has already determined the extra value of a counter-cyclical stream of earnings, and since the cosmetics firm has captured this premium in the lower risk-adjusted discount rate it applies to the expected earnings from the food project, it does not need to determine the correlation of the stream of earnings from the food investment and the stream of earnings from existing fixed investments. Thus the risk-adjusted discount rate is independent of the nature of the existing investments or other new investments being considered by the firm.[15]

Two exceptions to this general principle should be noted:

(1) In some cases a firm may be in such a risky business that there is a significant chance of it going bankrupt. Since an investor cannot diversify his own portfolio to hedge against this possibility, he will be prepared to pay the firm something extra (that is, he will bid up the price of the firm's shares) if the firm can appreciably reduce the risk of bankruptcy through diversification. Similarly, if a risky firm undertakes additional risky investments whose earnings are highly correlated with those from existing assets, investors will value the common stock of the firm at an even lower price, because of the increased probability of bankruptcy. Thus, in cases where an investment significantly reduces or increases the risk of bankruptcy, management is justified in examining the correlation of earnings among new investments and existing assets.

(2) Also, if market imperfections are substantial, 'home-made' diversification may be more costly than 'firm-made' diversification. In some cases 'home-made' diversification may also be impossible for individual investors. For example, some institutional investors are not free to change their portfolios. In these cases management should examine the correlation of the earnings from new investments, as well as the correlation between the earnings from new and existing investments.

These issues will be further discussed at the end of section III (see pp. 622–5).

III. THE STOCKHOLDER–PORTFOLIO APPROACH TO THE INVESTMENT DECISION: THE CAPITAL ASSET PRICING MODEL (CAPM)

The capital asset pricing model is a model of general market equilibrium which

---

[15] See ibid.

has been developed by Sharpe,[16] Lintner,[17] and Mossin.[18] All three models start from Markowitz's normative model, but with their additional assumptions *they provide the framework for analysing the risk of individual securities within a general capital-market equilibrium.*

The basic idea of the capital asset pricing model is that, since investors hold portfolios of securities rather than a single security, it is reasonable to consider the riskiness of each security in terms of its contribution to the risk of the portfolio, and not its own risk if held in isolation. This idea also underlies the portfolio approach developed in the previous section. The importance of the CAPM is that it measures the impact of a security's risk on the total risk of a portfolio in a different way (not in terms of the security's standard deviation and its correlation with the other securities in the portfolio). Risk, in the CAPM, is *investor-oriented*, not firm-oriented. Management, in taking investment decisions, should be concerned with the risk of the portfolio of shareholders rather than the risk of the portfolio of fixed assets held by the firm.

A.   The Assumptions of the CAPM

(1) Investors have homogeneous expectations. That is, all investors view the opportunity set of individual securities in the same way with respect to expected return, standard deviation of each asset, and the correlations of the returns among all the pairs of securities.

(2) Capital markets are perfect, with no transactions or other costs, no taxes and (costless) information available to all traders, who are price-takers. Furthermore, capital markets are efficient, in the sense that the prices of securities reflect all available information, and market prices adjust quickly to new available information. Market participants perceive any recurring price pattern so as to drive price changes around a security's 'intrinsic' value to a random pattern.

(3) Investors have identical time horizons. In the simple version to be presented here the stronger assumption of a one-period time horizon is made.

(4) Investors can borrow and lend funds at the riskless market interest rate *i*.

---

[16] W. F. Sharpe, 'Capital Asset Prices: A Theory of Market Equilibrium Under Conditions of Risk', *Journal of Finance*, 1964, pp. 425–42. Also W. F. Sharpe, *Portfolio Analysis and Capital Markets* (McGraw-Hill, 1970), and W. F. Sharpe, 'Efficient Capital Markets with Risk', Research Paper No. 71, Stanford Graduate School of Business, 1972.

[17] J. Lintner, 'The Valuation of Risky Assets and the Selection of Risky Investments in Stock Portfolios and Capital Budgets', *Review of Economics and Statistics*, 1965, pp. 13–37. Also J. Lintner, 'Security Prices, Risk and Maximal Gains from Diversification', *Journal of Finance*, 1965, pp. 587–616.

[18] Jan Mossin, 'Equilibrium in a Capital Asset Market', *Econometrica*, 1966, pp. 768–83.

B.   The Beta (β) Coefficient of a Security

William Sharpe[19] has postulated that changes in the return of a security depend partly on the specific characteristics of the security and partly on changes of some common factors, which may be termed 'general economic conditions'. These changes, according to Sharpe, can be approximated by the changes of the yield of all securities in the stock market, as measured by a general stock yield index, like 'the Dow–Jones Industrial Average', 'Moody's Index', the New York Stock Exchange (NYSE) index, etc. Thus the total variation in the return of the jth security may be split into two components: *the systematic variation* which is due to changes in the index of 'general business conditions'; and a *unique* (or unsystematic) *variation* which is due to the specific characteristics of the jth security (e.g. the goodwill of the firm, its over-all rating in capital markets, its location, its capital structure, its dividend policy, etc.). We may thus write

$$R_{j,t} = a_j + \beta_j R_{M,t} + \underbrace{\qquad u_{j,t} \qquad} \tag{12.32}$$

$$\underbrace{\phantom{R_{j,t} = a_j + \beta_j R_{M,t}}}$$

$$\begin{array}{cc}\text{Systematic} & \text{Unique (unsystematic)} \\ \text{variation} & \text{variation}\end{array}$$

where $R_{j,t}$ = return of the jth security in period t

$R_{M,t}$ = 'average market yield', that is, the yield of all securities quoted on the stock exchange, measured by an appropriate yield index

$u_{j,t}$ = random term, absorbing the variation in return due to the unique characteristics of the jth firm.

If we denote the risk-free market interest rate by i, we may express the above relation in terms of returns in excess of the risk-free rate, that is,

$$(R_j - i) = a_j + \beta_j(R_M - i) + \qquad u_j \tag{12.34}$$

$$\begin{array}{cc}\text{Systematic} & \text{Unsystematic} \\ \text{variation} & \text{variation}\end{array}$$

The systematic part of expression (12.34) is

$$(R_j - i) = a_j + \beta_j(R_M - i) \tag{12.35}$$

and is called *the characteristic line* of the jth security. In perfect capital markets a_j is zero.[20] Since we have assumed perfect capital markets which are in equilibrium, the characteristic line will have a zero intercept. Thus expression (12.34)

---

[19] W. F. Sharpe, 'A Simplified Model for Portfolio Analysis', *Management Science*, 1963, pp. 277–93.

[20] In using actual market data to estimate the characteristic line, a_j may assume positive or negative values if the market is imperfect, or if the market, though perfect, is in disequilibrium during the sample period.

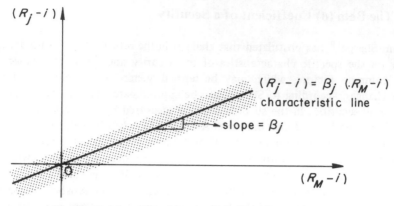

Figure 12.24   The characteristic line of the jth security

reduces to

$$(R_j - i) = \beta_j(R_M - i) + u_j \tag{12.36}$$

The characteristic line of the jth security is shown in Figure 12.24. The dispersion of points around the characteristic line shows the unsystematic variation in the return R_j which is attributable to the unique features of the jth security.

Expression (12.36) may be written in the following slightly different form:

$$R_j = i + \beta_j(R_M - i) + u_j \tag{12.37}$$

The graph of expression (12.37) is shown in Figure 12.25.

The graphs in these two diagrams assume that $\beta > 0$. However, β may also assume negative values.

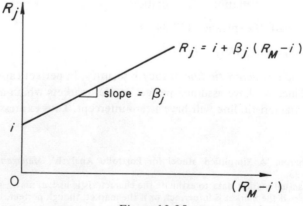

Figure 12.25

In general, the slope of the characteristic line, β (beta), shows how the return of the jth security changes in relation to changes in the 'excess market average yield'. If $\beta = 1$, the returns of the jth security vary proportionately (and in the same direction) with the 'excess market average yield'. If $\beta > 1$, the return of the jth security varies more than proportionately with the 'excess average market yield'. In this case the jth security is called 'aggressive'. If $\beta < 1$, then the stock's return varies less than proportionately with 'the average market yield'. This type of stock is called a 'defensive' investment. If $\beta < 0$, then the stock's return varies inversely with the 'average market yield'. Such stocks may be called 'super-defensive'. (The meaning of the betas is further discussed on pp. 617–22).

For example, if the beta of a particular stock is 1.80 and the market excess return $(R_M - i)$ in a particular period is +2.00 per cent, this would imply an expected excess return for the stock $(R_j - i)$ of +3.60 per cent. In general, the greater the beta for a stock, the greater the variability of its return.

In a subsequent section we will show that the risk of a stock (in the CAPM) is measured by its beta (see p. 618).

C.   The Capital Market Line (CML)

The capital market line is the equation of the efficient frontier of portfolios when a riskless asset is available. Recall that the equation of this line is

$$E(R_p) = R + \left(\frac{E(R_M) - R}{\sigma_M} \right) \sigma_p \qquad (12.38)$$

where M is the only risky portfolio which is included in the efficient frontier (see p. 599). This line is the line RMW in Figure 12.26.

Let us examine more closely portfolio M. Under the assumptions of the CAPM, all investors in equilibrium would hold efficient portfolios, i.e. portfolios on the efficient frontier RMW, which are linear combinations of the risk-free

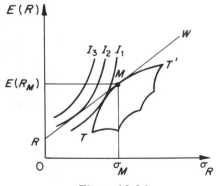

Figure 12.26

security and the risky portfolio M. For the capital market to be in equilibrium, M must be a portfolio which contains every asset exactly in proportion to that asset's fraction of the total value of assets in the market.[21] For example, if security j is x per cent of the total market value of all securities, portfolio M must also include x per cent of the jth security. In effect M is representative of 'the market', and is called '*the market portfolio*'.[22] Conceptually, if the market were out of equilibrium, the prices of assets in M would be instantaneously bid up, and the prices of assets not in M would fall until such time as all assets in the market are held in the 'market proportions'.

It should be stressed that *the capital market line is the risk–return relationship for efficient portfolios only*. We may draw the CML on a risk–return plane for efficient portfolios (on whose axes we measure the return and standard deviation of efficient portfolios), using the subscript p in order to distinguish such efficient portfolios from the general portfolio set. This is done in Figure 12.27, where we have used i to denote the risk-free rate of return. The slope of the CML is $[E(R_M) - i]/\sigma_M$ and is called 'the market price per unit of risk', because it shows the increase in return required to compensate the 'average investor' in the market for a unit increase in risk.

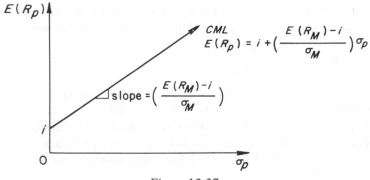

Figure 12.27

The interpretation of the CML is straightforward. The capital market line (and its equation) states that the return of an efficient portfolio (in market equilibrium) is equal to the riskless return plus a *risk premium*, equal to the 'market price of risk' multiplied by the standard deviation of the portfolio. Thus 'the market price of risk' is a *normalised risk premium*.[23] The market price of risk reflects the risk attitudes of all individual investors in the aggregate (or, equivalently, the risk attitudes of the 'average investor' or the 'typical investor').

---

[21] See M. C. Jensen, 'Risk, the Pricing of Capital Assets and the Evaluation of Investment Portfolios', *Journal of Business*, 1969, pp. 167–247.

[22] Ibid.

[23] The risk premium is the difference $[E(R_M) - i]$, and the 'normalisation' consists in its division by the standard deviation of the market portfolio M.

D. The Security Market Line (SML)

The next step is to relate the above market equilibrium to *individual securities*.

Sharpe, Lintner and Mossin have shown that, if the capital market is in equilibrium, the expected return of any individual security[24] will be a linear function of the covariance of its return with that of the market portfolio:

$$E(R_j) = i + \left(\frac{E(R_M) - i}{\sigma_M^2} \right) \text{cov}\,(R_j R_M) \tag{12.39}$$

This is the equation of the *security market line* (SML), which relates the return of a single security to the covariance of its return with that of the market portfolio. *The SML is the most important relationship of the capital asset pricing model, because it defines the risk of any individual security in terms of its contribution to the risk of the market portfolio.* The SML is shown graphically in Figure 12.28.

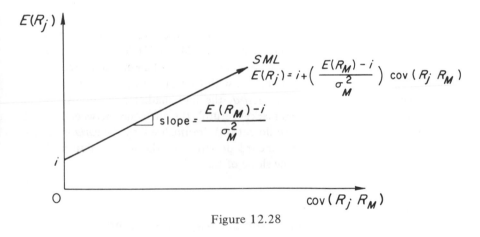

Figure 12.28

The SML states that, in market equilibrium, the return of each individual security is equal to the riskless rate, i, plus a risk premium, which is equal to the 'unit price of the risk of the security', $[E(R_M) - i]/\sigma_M^2$, multiplied by the covariance of the return of the security with that of the market portfolio. The 'unit price of the risk of the security' is the normalised risk premium of the market as a whole. (Note that the 'normalisation' consists of dividing the excess market yield $[E(R_M) - i]$ by the *variance* of the market portfolio.)

* * *

Given that $\text{cov}\,(R_j R_M) = r_{jM}\sigma_j\sigma_M$, the security market line may be expressed

---

[24] Or portfolio, irrespective of whether it is efficient or not.

in terms of the correlation coefficient r_{jM} and the simple standard deviations σ_j and σ_M:

$$E(R_j) = i + \left(\frac{E(R_M) - i}{\sigma_M^2} \right) r_{jM} \sigma_j \sigma_M \qquad (12.40)$$

With this expression we can establish the relationship between the CML and the SML. Recall that the CML is a relationship which holds only for efficient portfolios, while the SML holds for *any* individual security or any portfolio. If the portfolio is efficient, then $r_{jM} = 1$, and the security market line for such a portfolio reduces to the CML:

$$E(R_p) = i + \left(\frac{E(R_M) - i}{\sigma_M} \right) \sigma_p \qquad (12.41)$$

where the subscript p denotes any *efficient* portfolio.

*   *   *

In general, the SML differs from the CML in three respects. *First*, the CML holds for efficient portfolios only, while the SML holds for any security and any portfolio in market equilibrium. *Second*, the risk of an individual security or portfolio is the covariance of its return with that of the market portfolio, and *not* its simple standard deviation. *Third*, the unit market price of risk for an individual security is the 'excess market return' (the difference between the riskless return and the market portfolio return), 'normalised' by the *variance* of the market return, instead of the standard deviation of the market return, which appears in the denominator of the slope of the CML.

E.   The Beta Coefficient and the Security Market Line

The final step in the development of the capital asset pricing model is to express the risk of any individual security in terms of its *beta* coefficient.

We may rewrite the equation of the SML as follows:

$$E(R_j) = i + \left(\frac{\mathrm{cov}\,(R_j R_M)}{\sigma_M^2} \right) [E(R_M) - i] \qquad (12.42)$$

Let us define

$$\beta_j = \frac{\mathrm{cov}\,(R_j R_M)}{\sigma_M^2} \qquad (12.43)$$

so that the SML equation may be written as

$$E(R_j) = i + [E(R_M) - i]\,\beta_j \qquad (12.44)$$

In this way the risk of any security j is measured by its *beta coefficient*, which is a measure of the risk of this security *relative* to the risk of the market portfolio. (Note that i and $E(R_M)$ are constants.)

From expression (12.44) we see that *the risk premium* of any individual security j is

$$\beta_j[E(R_M) - i] \tag{12.45}$$

In other words, the risk premium of any individual security is equal to the excess market yield or market risk premium $[E(R_M) - i]$, weighted by the *relative risk* of this security as measured by its beta coefficient, β_j. Thus, if the CAPM is valid and the capital market is in equilibrium, the expected (one-period) return on *any* particular asset (or portfolio of assets) will be *an exact linear function of the* β_j, as shown in Figure 12.29.[25]

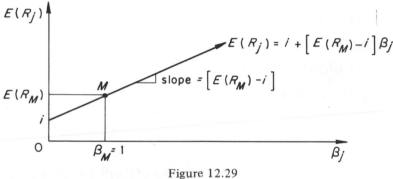

Figure 12.29

Point M represents the expected return of the market portfolio and its risk as measured by its beta coefficient. Since the risk of any security is measured *relative* to the risk of the market portfolio, it is obvious that the beta coefficient of the market portfolio is equal to unity:

$$\beta_M = \frac{\text{cov}(R_M R_M)}{\sigma_M^2} = \frac{\sigma_M^2}{\sigma_M^2} = 1 \tag{12.46}$$

F.   Diversification and the Reduction of the Risk of a Portfolio

We said that the relationship between the expected return of an individual security and its risk (as measured by the beta coefficient) implied by the capital asset pricing model is exact. To understand the implications of this exact relationship, let us re-examine Sharpe's return—risk model.

---

[25] It should be clear that the line in Figure 12.29 is another version of the SML: on the horizontal axis we measure β_j instead of cov $(R_j R_M)$.

Recall that Sharpe postulated the return–risk relationship

$$R_j = i + \beta_j(R_M - i) + \underbrace{\hphantom{}}_{} \quad \underbrace{u_j}_{} \tag{12.47}$$

$$\underbrace{R_j = i + \beta_j(R_M - i)}_{\substack{\text{Systematic}\\\text{variation}}} + \underbrace{u_j}_{\substack{\text{Unsystematic}\\\text{variation}}} \tag{12.47}$$

The random term, u, absorbs the effects of specific features of the jth security, such as the leverage and dividend policies of the jth firm, particular conditions in the firm's product markets and input markets, and so on.[26]

The return R_j has a probability distribution, with mean

$$E(R_j) = i + \beta_j[E(R_M) - i] \tag{12.48}$$

(given that, by assumption, $E(u) = 0$)
and variance

$$\mathrm{var}\,(R_j) = \mathrm{var}\,\{\, i + \beta_j[R_M - i] + u_j \,\} \tag{12.49}$$

Given that i and β_j are constants, we have (see Appendix 12.2):

$$\mathrm{var}\,(R_j) = \beta_j^2\,\mathrm{var}\,(R_M) + \mathrm{var}\,(u_j)$$

or

$$\underbrace{\sigma_j^2}_{\substack{\text{Total}\\\text{risk}}} = \underbrace{\beta_j^2\,\sigma_M^2}_{\substack{\text{Systematic}\\\text{risk}}} + \underbrace{\sigma_{u_j}^2}_{\substack{\text{Unique}\\\text{risk}}} \tag{12.50}$$

Expression (12.50) shows that the total risk of the jth security has two components: *a systematic risk component*, arising from the variance of the 'average market return'; and a *unique risk component*, arising from changes in the particular factors affecting the firm's return.

The systematic risk component ($\beta^2\,\sigma_M^2$) depends on the value of beta and on the variability of the market return. As we have said, the beta coefficient measures the tendency of the return of the jth security to move (change) with the market return R_M. This tendency constitutes a risk, because the market does fluctuate (influenced by general economic and political conditions), and these fluctuations cannot be diversified away by investing in more stocks, because all stocks are affected by general business conditions. Thus $\beta^2\,\sigma_M^2$ is the stock's systematic, or non-diversifiable, or unavoidable risk.

The unique risk component ($\sigma_{u_j}^2$) depends on changes in factors which affect the particular security, but *not* the market. This component of risk is independent of economic, political and other factors that influence securities in a systematic

---

[26] It is assumed that u satisfies the usual assumptions of the random variables incorporated in economic relationships (see Koutsoyiannis, *Theory of Econometrics*). In particular, it is assumed that u has zero mean, constant variance, zero covariance, and is uncorrelated with the market return R_M.

manner. A key assumption of the capital asset pricing model is that this (unsystematic or unique) risk can be eliminated through diversification. Therefore, in the CAPM not all of the risk involved in holding a stock is relevant: part of it can be diversified away, by buying more stocks; the relevant risk is the non-diversifiable (or systematic) risk of the stock, because this risk cannot be diversified away by investing in more stocks, as it depends on such things as changes in the general economic and political conditions (in the country) which affect all stocks. Investors are interested only in the systematic risk component $\beta_j^2 \sigma_M^2$. Since the variance of the market average return (σ_M^2) is exogenously given, the determinant of the risk of each security (in the CAPM framework) is its beta coefficient, β_j. The greater the beta of a security, the greater the risk of that security. A beta equal to unity $(\beta_j = +1)$ implies that the security's return fluctuates proportionately with the market average return. A beta less than unity shows that the security's return fluctuates less than the market return, and, therefore is safer. Securities with $\beta < 1$ are called 'defensive' because they hedge investors against general market fluctuations. A negative beta implies that the price of the stock moves inversely with moves of the stock market. Such a stock may be called 'super-defensive', since it provides a greater protection (to the investor) than simple defensive stocks. A beta greater than unity implies that the yield of the security fluctuates more widely than 'the market'. Securities with $\beta > 1$ are riskier and their yield must be higher. These are called 'aggressive' securities.

To explore the concept of diversification in more depth, we will consider the responsiveness of *a portfolio's* return to changes in the market average return. The return of a portfolio within the CAPM framework is given by the expression

$$R_p = i + \beta_p(R_M - i) + u_p \tag{12.51}$$

where β_p = the beta of the portfolio
u_p = the unique (random, unsystematic) variation in the portfolio's return

The responsiveness of the portfolio's return (R_p) to changes in the market return (R_M) is measured by the beta of the portfolio. The portfolio beta is the weighted average of the betas of the securities comprising the portfolio, with the weights being the proportions of funds invested in the individual securities. In symbols

$$\beta_p = \sum_{j=1}^{n} w_j \beta_j \tag{12.52}$$

where w_j = ratio of the funds invested in the jth security to the total funds (value) of the portfolio
n = number of securities in the portfolio.

Similarly, the random variation u_p is the weighted average of the us of the securities comprising the portfolio:

$$u_p = \sum_{j=1}^{n} w_j u_j \tag{12.53}$$

Substituting (12.53) in (12.51) we obtain

$$R_p = i + \beta_p(R_M - i) + \Sigma w_j u_j \tag{12.54}$$

The risk of the portfolio is the variance of its return:

$$\text{var}(R_p) = \text{var}\,[i + \beta_p(R_M - i) + \Sigma w_j u_j] \tag{12.55}$$

Given that i, β_p and w_j are constants, we have

$$\underbrace{\sigma_p^2}_{\substack{\text{Total} \\ \text{risk}}} = \underbrace{\beta_p^2 \sigma_M^2}_{\substack{\text{Systematic} \\ \text{risk}}} + \underbrace{\Sigma[w_j^2 \sigma_{u_j}^2]}_{\substack{\text{Unique} \\ \text{risk}}} \tag{12.56}$$

*   *   *

PROOF

$\text{var}(R_p) = \text{var}(i) + \text{var}[\beta_p(R_M - i)] + \text{var}(\Sigma w_j u_j)$
(given that the covariances of the three terms are zero)

or $\quad \text{var}(R_p) = \beta_p^2(\sigma_M^2) + \Sigma[\text{var}(w_j u_j)]$

$\qquad\qquad\quad = \beta_p^2 \sigma_M^2 + \Sigma[w_j^2 \sigma_{u_j}^2]$

QED

*   *   *

The term $\beta_p^2 \sigma_M^2$ represents the risk arising from fluctuations in the market average yield. The second term ($\Sigma w_j^2 \sigma_{u_j}^2$) represents the unique risk attributable to the individual securities which are in the portfolio.

The greater the diversification of a portfolio, the less the unique (unsystematic) risk of that portfolio. It has been shown that unsystematic risk is reduced at a decreasing rate towards zero as more randomly selected securities are added to the portfolio. Various studies suggest that fifteen to twenty stocks selected randomly are sufficient to eliminate most of the unique (unsystematic) risk of a portfolio.[27] Thus a substantial reduction in unsystematic risk can be achieved with a relatively moderate amount of diversification.

Conceptually, diversification can be viewed in the way shown in Figure 12.30.[28] As the number of randomly selected securities held in the portfolio is

[27] See J. Evans and S. H. Archer, 'Diversification and the Reduction of Dispersion: An Empirical Analysis', *Journal of Finance*, vol. 23, 1968, pp. 761–7; W. H. Wagner and S. Lau, 'The Effect of Diversification on Risk', *Financial Analysts Journal*, vol. 26, 1971, pp. 48–53; R. C. Klemkosky and J. D. Martin, 'The Effect of Market Risk on Portfolio Diversification', *Journal of Finance*, vol. 30, 1975, pp. 147–54.

[28] F. Modigliani and G. Pogue, 'An Introduction to Risk and Return', *Financial Analysts Journal*, vol. 30, 1974, pp. 74–5.

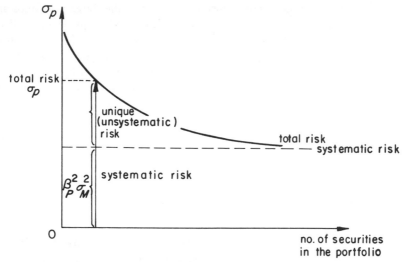

Figure 12.30

increased, the total risk of the portfolio is reduced, due to the reduction in the unsystematic (unique) risk. However, the reduction in σ_p occurs at a decreasing rate. Diversification is said to be efficient when it reduces the total risk of the portfolio to the point where it is equal to the systematic risk (the unsystematic risk having been eliminated).

In summary. For a well-diversified portfolio the unique risk ($\Sigma w_j^2 \sigma_{u_j}^2$) approaches zero. It is implied in the CAPM that the unsystematic risk has been diversified away. The important risk of a stock is its systematic risk, which cannot be diversified away. Hence, within the CAPM, each security (or investment project) should be judged on the basis of its undiversifiable (unavoidable) risk, and *not* on its total risk, since part of it can be diversified away.

The CAPM model and the betas have become popular in recent years.[29] The

---

[29] The beta of a security can be estimated by applying OLS (to time-series data) to the expression

$$(R_j - i) = a_j + \beta_j(R_M - i) + u_j \tag{12.34}$$

The intercept should be zero, if markets are perfect *and* in equilibrium. An intercept different from zero may be attributed to market imperfections and/or market disequilibrium. The beta of a security can also be estimated by the expression

$$\beta_j = \frac{\text{cov}(R_j R_M)}{\sigma_M^2} = \frac{r_{jM}\sigma_j}{\sigma_M}$$

where r_{jM} = correlation between the portfolio return and the 'market return' as depicted by an appropriate *index of yields of stocks* quoted on the stock exchange
σ_j = standard deviation of the yield (return) of the jth stock
σ_M = standard deviation of *the index of yields of stocks*

beta coefficient of mutual funds, pension funds and other large portfolios are presently being calculated by security analysts and used to judge the risk of these portfolios. The CAPM framework is also used to estimate the composition of portfolios with specified degrees of risk. It is too early to judge how well the betas will work as a measure of the risk of portfolios in the long run, but the financial community (investors, firms, security analysts, consulting firms) is actually using them in portfolio selection and security analysis.[30]

We think that the most interesting relationship developed within the capital asset pricing model is the decomposition of the total risk of each individual security into its two components, systematic risk and unique risk:

$$\sigma_j^2 = \underbrace{\beta_j^2 \sigma_M^2}_{\substack{\text{Systematic} \\ \text{risk}}} + \underbrace{\sigma_{u_j}^2}_{\substack{\text{Unique} \\ \text{risk}}} \tag{12.50}$$

The CAPM implies that the unique risk can be diversified away. This follows from the assumptions of the model. If these assumptions do not hold (and in the real world there is little ground to suggest that they do hold), then *the unique risk may be an important factor affecting the valuation of individual securities by investors*. In general, the greater the imperfections of the capital market (transactions costs, taxes, information costs) and the more heterogeneous the expectations of investors, the more important the unique or unsystematic risk of each firm will be in the mind of investors.[31]

G.   Relaxing the Assumptions of the CAPM

In this section we discuss briefly the effect on the risk of securities if the assumptions of the CAPM do not hold.[32]

(1) *Different borrowing and lending rates*

If the borrowing rate is higher than the lending rate, an imperfection is present, and the CML is no longer a simple straight line. The capital market 'line' is found

[30] J. F. Weston and E. F. Brigham, *Managerial Finance*, 5th edn (Dryden Press, 1975) p. 666.

[31] In Chapters 8 and 9 we examined two important factors of the unique risk component of a firm's stock: the leverage and the dividend policies of the firm.

[32] The CAPM has been tested by various writers. The most important of these tests are in the following papers: F. Black, M. Jensen and M. Scholes, 'The Capital-Asset Pricing Model: Some Empirical Tests', in *Studies in the Theory of Capital Markets*, ed. M. Jensen (Prentice-Hall, 1972); M. Blume and I. Friend, 'A New Look at the Capital Asset Pricing Model', *Journal of Finance*, vol. 28, 1973, pp. 19–34; E. Fama and J. MacBeth, 'Risk, Return and Equilibrium: Empirical Tests', *Journal of Political Economy*, vol. 81, 1973, pp. 607–36; P. L. Cheng and R. G. Grauer, 'An Alternative Test of the Capital Asset Pricing Model', *American Economic Review*, 1980.

by drawing two lines tangent to the efficient portfolio frontier (see Figure 12.31). One line is drawn from the lending rate, i_L, and the other from the borrowing rate, i_B. The segment $i_L M_L$ represents combinations of the risk-free asset and the market portfolio M_L. The segment $M_B Z$ (and beyond Z) represents borrowing to invest in the market portfolio M_B. The segment of the capital market 'line' between M_L and M_B is part of the efficient opportunity frontier. Thus the capital market 'line' consists of three segments, two linear segments and a curved segment. It is apparent from Figure 12.31 that the greater the difference between the lending and borrowing rates, the greater the curved segment of the capital market 'line' will be.

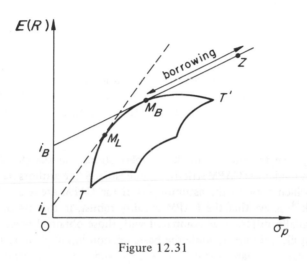

Figure 12.31

(2) *Heterogeneous expectations of investors*

If investors have heterogeneous expectations, each one will have his own capital market line. Thus the over-all capital market line becomes imprecise (fuzzy). However, if heterogeneity of expectations is moderate, the CAPM can be used for an approximate estimation of the return–risk trade-off for individual securities or portfolios. It should be clear, however, that the model loses its precision.[33]

(3) *Transaction costs*

If the transactions costs are substantial, investors may not be willing to attain a fully (efficient) diversified portfolio. This implies that some investors may choose portfolios above or below the efficient frontier or the capital market line, because transaction costs more than offset the advantages of being on the frontier or the

---

[33] J. C. Van Horne, *The Function and Analysis of Capital Market Rates* (Prentice-Hall, 1970) ch. 3.

CML. With transaction costs there may be 'bands' on either side of the efficient frontier or the CML. The CML loses its precise meaning.

(4) Tax differential between dividends and capital gains

As we saw in Chapter 9, tax differences between dividends and capital gains may make high dividend stocks less attractive than stocks which pay low dividends but have a high potential for capital gains. Under these conditions investors in high-income brackets will have a preference for 'capital-gains' stocks. The CML and SML lose their precision as tools for predicting the return—risk trade-off of securities (or portfolios).

(5) Imperfect information

If investors do not have complete (and costless) information, capital markets are not efficient. Lags (and costs) in obtaining information create heterogeneous expectations among investors, and the efficient frontier or the CML become fuzzy.

In summary, the presence of market imperfections and the violation of other assumptions render the CAPM strictly inapplicable. Some authors have developed models in which some of the assumptions of the CAPM are relaxed. Such theoretical work[34] shows that the CAPM is fairly robust, in that its predictions are not substantially different as compared with those obtained when the assumptions are fulfilled. However, while the basic relationship implied by the CML and the SML holds, its meaning is no longer clear and precise. In general, the more serious the imperfections, the greater the unsystematic (unique) risk of the stock. Recall that the capital asset pricing model assumes that this risk can be diversified away. With market imperfections and heterogeneous expectations, the unique risk *cannot* be diversified away.

The basic postulate of the CAPM is that, in equilibrium, the expected return of an individual security is the risk-free rate plus a risk premium which is a linear function of the covariance of the security's return with that of the market:

$$E(R_j) = i + \left[\frac{E(R_M) - i}{\sigma_M^2} \right] \text{cov}(R_j R_M) \qquad (12.39)$$

The greater the cov $(R_j R_M)$, the greater the risk of the security and the greater the return that is required.

Within the CAPM the total risk of a security can be split into systematic and

---

[34] For a review of these studies see M. C. Jensen, 'Capital Markets: Theory and Evidence', in *Studies in the Theory of Capital Markets*, ed. M. C. Jensen (Prentice-Hall, 1972). pp. 373–91. Also J. C. T. Mao, 'Security Pricing in an Imperfect Capital Market', *Journal of Financial and Quantitative Analysis*, vol. 6, 1971, pp. 1105–16.

unsystematic components. Systematic risk is the risk that cannot be diversified away, because it affects all the securities in the stock market. Unsystematic risk is unique to the particular security and can be eliminated in an efficiently diversified portfolio.

*   *   *

The systematic risk is measured by the 'normalised' covariance of the return R_j with the market return, R_M, i.e.

$$\text{Systematic risk} = \frac{\text{cov}\,(R_j R_M)}{\sigma_M}$$

PROOF. From expression (12.50) it is seen that

$$\text{Systematic risk} = \beta_j \sigma_M$$

Given $\beta_j = [\text{cov}\,(R_j M_j)]/\sigma_M^2$ it follows that

$$\text{Systematic risk} = \frac{\text{cov}\,(R_j M_j)}{\sigma_M^2}\,\sigma_M = \frac{\text{cov}\,(R_j M_j)}{\sigma_M}$$

In other words the systematic risk is the covariance of R_j with R_M (= cov $(R_j R_M)$) *relative* to the market standard deviation.

*   *   *

The key assumptions of the CAPM are that perfect capital markets exist and that investors have homogeneous expectations.

H. Using the CAPM to Estimate the Cost of Equity Capital

The CAPM is often used to estimate the cost of equity capital of the firm. In the CAPM the required rate of return on a stock is given by the expression

$$R_j = i + (R_M - i)\,\beta_j + u_j \tag{12.37}$$

Using time-series data, we can apply OLS to the expression

$$(R_{jt} - i_t) = \beta_j (R_{Mt} - i_t) + u_j \tag{12.36}$$

where $R_{jt} = \dfrac{(P_{t+1} - P_t) + Dv_t}{P_t}$ (12.51)

i_t = risk-free rate of interest in period t (e.g. the government bond yield)
R_{Mt} = return for the market index in period t

$$R_{Mt} = \frac{(P_{It+1} - P_{It}) + Dv_{It}}{P_{It}} \tag{12.52}$$

(The subscript I refers to the market index.)

From elementary regression analysis,[35] the estimate $\hat{\beta}$ is obtained from the expression

$$\hat{\beta}_j = \frac{\displaystyle\sum_{t=1}^{T} (R_{Mt} - i_t)(R_{jt} - i_t)}{\Sigma(R_{Mt} - i_t)^2} \tag{12.53}$$

where T is the number of observations in the sample.

Having estimated β_j, the required rate of return can be found from the expression

$$\hat{R}_j = \bar{i} + (\bar{R}_M - i_t)\,\beta_j$$

where $\bar{i}$ = the mean value of i over the time period of the sample

   $\bar{R}_M$ = the mean value of R_M over the time period of the sample.

Once the required rate of return for security j has been estimated, it is used as *the cost of equity capital* in the expression of the weighted average cost of capital of the firm. In fact, we set

$$\hat{R}_j = k_e = \text{cost of equity of the } j\text{th firm} \tag{12.53}$$

It should be stressed that this procedure for estimating the cost of equity capital is valid if the CAPM assumptions hold, i.e. if capital markets are perfect, if investors have homogeneous expectations, *and* if the market is in equilibrium.

This author suggests that the regression be estimated *with* an intercept, which would absorb market imperfections and/or market disequilibrium effects. In this case the appropriate expression for estimating β_j is:[36]

$$\hat{\beta}_j = \frac{\Sigma\,[(R_{Mt} - i_t) - (\overline{R_{Mt} - i_t})]\ [(R_{jt} - i_t) - (\overline{R_{jt} - i_t})]}{\Sigma\,[(R_{jt} - i_t) - (\overline{R_{jt} - i_t})]^2} \tag{12.54}$$

where $(\overline{R_{Mt} - i_t})$ = the sample average value of the differences $(R_{Mt} - i_t)$

   $(\overline{R_{jt} - i_t})$ = the sample average value of the differences $(R_{jt} - i_t)$

I.   The Application of the CAPM to the Investment Decision

The framework of the CAPM has been applied for the evaluation of fixed investment projects.[37]

It should be clear that the capital asset pricing model considers the impact of a fixed investment proposal on *investors' portfolios* of stocks rather than the impact of the proposal on *the firm's portfolio* of fixed assets.

[35] See Koutsoyiannis, *Theory of Econometrics*, ch. 4.
[36] Ibid.
[37] See Mark Rubinstein, 'A Mean-Variance Synthesis of Corporate Financial Theory', *Journal of Finance*, vol. 28, 1973.

Within the CAPM framework an investment proposal is judged on the basis of its systematic risk (and *not* on its total risk), because the unsystematic risk can be diversified away by the individual investors: the firm should not consider the diversification aspects of the project, i.e. management should not worry about how the proposed project affects the stream of the firm's earnings from its existing fixed assets (the firm's present total risk), because individual investors can attain any desired degree of diversification by changing their portfolio of stocks (in perfect capital markets). We will return to this point later. First we outline the procedure of applying the CAPM in taking investment decisions.

Step 1. The firm estimates the required rate of return for the project by using the CAPM expression

$$E(R_Z) = i + \beta_Z [E(R_M) - i] \tag{12.55}$$

(where Z refers to the Z-project).

(a) If the project considered is similar to the existing investments of the firm, then the required rate of return is estimated by using data on the firm's share price and a market yield index, and fitting the regression

$$(R_{Zt} - i_t) = \beta_Z (R_{Mt} - i_t) \tag{12.56}$$

$$\text{where } R_{Zt} = \frac{(P_{Zt} + P_{Zt-1}) + dv_t}{P_{Zt-1}} \tag{12.57}$$

i_t = risk-free rate of interest
R_{Mt} = actual index of market yields (e.g. the New York Stock Exchange or the Toronto Stock Exchange index of yield), given by expression (12.52).

The value of $\hat{\beta}_Z$ is obtained from expression (12.54).

Given $\hat{\beta}_Z$ (from the regression), and given the mean values $\bar{R}_M$ and $\bar{i}$ (from the sample data used in the regression), we can obtain $\hat{R}_Z$. For example, assume that, using data for the 1960–79 period and applying expression (12.54), we obtain

$$\hat{\beta}_Z = 0.4231; \quad \bar{R}_M = 0.0912; \quad \bar{i} = 0.06$$

Then the required rate of return for project Z is

$$\hat{R}_Z = 0.06 + 0.4231 (0.0912 - 0.06) = 0.06 + 0.0132 = 0.0732$$

(b) If the project differs considerably from the existing fixed investments of the firm but is similar to investments of *other firms*, then the management must estimate the beta of those (other) firms, and use the same procedure to obtain the required rate of return of the project under consideration. For example, assume that a tobacco firm is considering the formation of a food subsidiary. As there are several food companies whose stocks are traded in the stock market, the tobacco firm can determine the beta for one of those food companies (or for a group of them) and use it in its calculation of the required rate of return on the contemplated food subsidiary.[38]

Step 2. The management calculates the project's internal rate of return (IRR). Recall that the IRR is the rate of discount which equates the future stream of expected earnings to the cost of acquisition of the investment. The IRR may be estimated from the expression

$$\sum_{t=1}^{n} \frac{A_t}{(1+r)^t} = C_t \tag{12.58}$$

where r = internal rate of return which we developed in Chapter 4.

Step 3. The IRR is compared with the required rate of return, and the project is accepted if the internal rate of return is greater than the required rate $\hat{R}_Z$ (i.e. if $\text{IRR}_Z > \hat{R}_Z$).

The acceptance of projects whose IRR is higher than the required rate of return should result in an increase in the share price of the firm, because investors will bid up the price of the stock until, in equilibrium, the expected returns for all investments of the firm are equal.[39]

Thus, in the CAPM framework, management should undertake investment projects whose internal rate of return is higher than the required rate of return.

If product markets were perfect, such investment opportunities would not exist. In other words, the assumption of perfect capital markets coupled with the assumption of perfect product markets eliminate the possibility of investments whose return is higher than the required return. However, in the real world product markets are imperfect (oligopolistic), and hence investment projects with expected returns higher than the required rate of return are possible.

The main implication of the CAPM is that management should judge the desirability of a project on the basis of its systematic risk alone: diversification by the firm is irrelevant to shareholders,[40] because, in perfect capital markets,

---

[38] Van Horne *et al.* (*Financial Management and Policy*, 4th edn (Prentice-Hall, 1977) p. 177) suggest that the beta for project Z can be estimated by using data on the market yield index, and measuring R_{Zt} with the expression

$$R_{Zt} = \frac{(V_{Zt} - V_{Zt-1}) + A_{Zt}}{V_{Zt-1}}$$

where V_{Zt} = the market value of the Z-project at the end of period t
   A_{Zt} = net cash flow received at the end of period t

Since direct information on the market values V_t and V_{t-1} is not available, Van Horne *et al.* suggest that management uses the prices of similar second-hand investments of various ages. This author thinks that this approach is of little operational (practical) use, since second-hand market data are too difficult to obtain, or do not even exist.

[39] For a proof that if a project's expected return exceeds the required rate (under the above assumptions) share price will increase, see H. Bierman and J. E. Hass, 'Capital Budgeting Under Uncertainty: A Reformulation', *Journal of Finance*, vol. 28, 1973, pp. 119–29.

[40] For a proof of the 'irrelevancy of diversification' decisions by the firm, see L. D. Schall, 'Asset Valuation, Firm Investment, and Firm Diversification', *Journal of Business*, vol. 45, 1972, pp. 11–28.

individual investors can attain the same degree of diversification as the firm, so they would not be prepared to pay a higher price for the share of a company which diversifies. In other words, the CAPM implies that the firm cannot do something for investors through diversification of fixed assets that they cannot achieve themselves (by diversifying their own portfolios of shares). Hence, according to the CAPM, investment projects should be evaluated only on the basis of their systematic risk, *not* on the basis of their total risk, and *not* on the marginal effect on the total risk of the firm as a whole.

In summary, the CAPM implies that an investment project should be judged on the basis of its systematic risk on the portfolio of investors.

However, investors can diversify away the unique (unsystematic) risk only if the assumptions of the CAPM hold. Recall that the critical assumptions of the model are:

(a) Perfect and efficient capital markets, with no transactions costs, in which information can be obtained by investors without delay and without cost.
(b) There are no taxes.
(c) Homogeneous expectations.
(d) The cost of insolvency or bankruptcy of firms is zero. That is, if the firm becomes bankrupt, its assets can be sold at their true economic value without selling costs, legal costs, or delay.

In the real world the above assumptions are not likely to be fulfilled. There are all sorts of market imperfections: the borrowing rate is typically higher than the lending rate; there are transactions costs (brokerage fees and the like); there is a tax differential between dividends and capital gains; information is not costless, and in many cases the lags involved in obtaining information are substantial. With such market imperfections one may well expect that investors' portfolios will not be efficiently diversified. Furthermore, the costs of bankruptcy are substantial, and investors cannot fully protect themselves from the risk of bankruptcy.

Finally, the information required for the estimation of the betas is difficult to obtain, and when the product is new on the market any estimation of the required rate of return with the CAPM is nothing more than a guess. This operational shortcoming of the CAPM renders it of little practical use.

Given the weaknesses of the CAPM, several writers suggest the evaluation of investment projects on the basis of *both* their systematic risk (as estimated from the CAPM) and their total risk to the firm as a whole.[41] If both the CAPM approach and the firm-risk approach for evaluating a project lead to the same (accept) indication, the project should be undertaken and vice versa. A problem

---

[41] In both cases a portfolio approach is implied. In the CAPM a security is judged on the basis of its impact on the risk of the portfolio of the investor. In the total firm-risk approach a project is judged on the basis of its marginal risk to the portfolio of assets of the firm as a whole. It is said that in the CAPM the risk is market-oriented (risk is determined from stock-market behaviour) while in 'the total risk approach' the risk is 'firm-oriented'. See J. C. Van Horne *et al., Financial Management and Policy*, 4th edn (Prentice-Hall, 1977).

arises when one approach suggests the acceptance of the project while the other suggests its rejection. In this case management should assess which approach is more appropriate. If transactions costs are not large, if the possibility of bankruptcy is small, and if the appropriate beta can be estimated satisfactorily, then the solution (acceptance or rejection of the proposal) suggested by the CAPM approach should be adopted. However, if the transactions and information costs in the stock market are substantial, if the possibility of bankruptcy is significant, and if the estimation of the beta is not reliable, then the firm-risk approach should be followed. However, even in this case, one should recognise that a part of the unique risk of the project can be diversified away.

A final remark seems in order. Theorists favour, in their majority, the application of either the CAPM or the firm-risk approach. It should be clear that both methods involve a portfolio framework. The CAPM concentrates on the marginal impact of the systematic risk of an investment project on the risk of investors' portfolios, while the firm-risk approach concentrates on the marginal impact of the investment proposal on the total risk of the portfolio of assets of the firm. The preference of theorists for these approaches lies in the fact that in both methods there is a direct link between the investment proposals and the value of the stock of the firm (see the discussion on pp. 607–9). On the other hand, most firms in practice use the single-project evaluation approach, in which a project is judged on the basis of its total risk, in isolation from other existing investments or other proposed new investments (see Chapter 11). Among the various methods which can be used to evaluate a single project (alone, *not* in the context of a portfolio), the method of risk-adjusted discount rates is the most popular in practice, because managers are familiar with expressing returns on the basis of discount rates. The shortcomings of the single-project approaches have been discussed in Chapter 11. Theoretically the main weakness of these approaches is that there is no direct link between the risk of a project and the price of the stock of the firm in the market. Furthermore, a lot of subjective judgement is often used. Thus it is not sure that this way of reaching investment decisions will be optimal (will maximise the value of the firm to its existing stockholders).

We may conclude that the 'appropriate' method for evaluating investment projects is still an open issue.

APPENDIX 12.1   THE MATHEMATICAL FOUNDATION OF THE MEAN–VARIANCE MODEL

Two theoretical justifications have been suggested for the mean-variance model.

According to one approach, it is assumed that investors *believe* that the probability distributions of returns from shares (or other securities) is normal.

From statistical theory it is known that a normal distribution is completely specified by the values of its mean and variance.[42]

    If the investor maintains such beliefs, then the mean and the variance convey all the information required by him for optimal portfolio selection. The main weakness of this approach is that there is no evidence that investors believe that the returns from prospective investments have a normal distribution. If the distribution of returns is not normal, then the mean and variance are not adequate for its description. Measures of skewness (lopsidedness) and peakedness are necessary to provide additional information to investors. For example, investors are more interested in negative deviations of the returns from the mean (expected) value. Presumably positive deviations are desirable. In this case it would make a lot of difference to the investor to know whether the distribution of returns is lopsided to the right (Figure 12.32) or to the left (Figure 12.33).

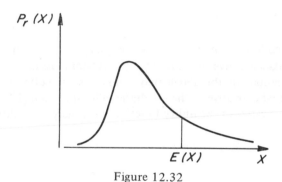

Figure 12.32

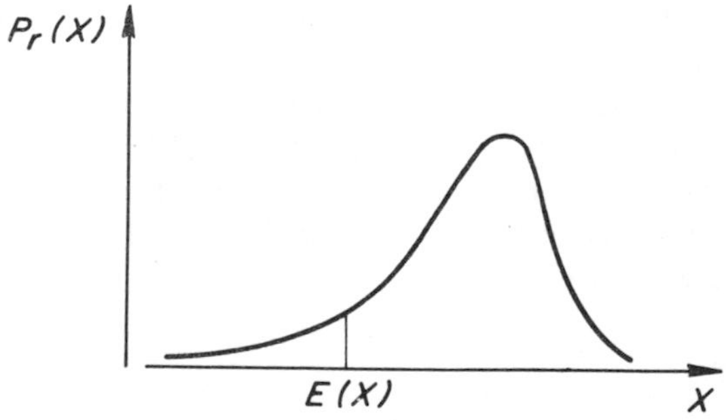

Figure 12.33

---

[42] The equation of a normal distribution is

$$f(x) = \left(\frac{1}{\sigma\sqrt{2\pi}} \right) e^{-[x - E(x)]/\sigma_x}$$

which is defined if $E(x)$ and σ_x are known, given that $\pi = 3.14$ and $e = 2.718$.

Given that the area under the curve is the probability associated with various returns, it is obvious that investors considering two alternative investments with the same mean and variance would prefer the one whose distribution of returns is skewed to the right, if they are risk-averse, because this distribution has a higher degree of protection from negative deviations from the mean, while high positive deviations are possible.

The second theoretical justification of the mean-variance model is based on *the assumption* that investors who aim at the maximisation of their expected utility are risk-averse, and their utility function is quadratic. Let R stand for the return of an investment. Then the quadratic utility function is of the form

$$U_R = aR + bR^2 \qquad\qquad (12.59)$$

where a and b are constants, satisfying the conditions

$$b < 0; \quad -\frac{a}{2b} > R \qquad\qquad (12.60)$$

These two conditions imply that the marginal utility of income (money) is positive but has a negative slope, that is, the investor is *assumed* to be risk-averse.

The implications of the above two conditions are better understood if we consider the first derivative of the quadratic utility function (12.59).

The first derivative of the utility function is the marginal utility of income:

$$\frac{dU}{dR} = a + 2bR = \text{marginal utility of income} \qquad\qquad (12.61)$$

The slope of the marginal utility curve is $2b$.

(a) For this slope to be negative, b must be negative ($b < 0$).

(b) However, the marginal utility of income must be positive, according to the non-satiation axiom. For $a + 2bR > 0$ we must have $R < -a/2b$.

The quadratic-utility approach is theoretically more appealing because (a) it justifies the assumption that the mean return, $E(R)$, and the variance, σ_R^2, are the only information required by investors for optimal portfolio decisions, and (b) it provides a concrete basis for the derivation of the indifference map of investors who are risk-averse.

A.   The Utility of the Investor Depends only on the Mean Return and the Variance of the Earnings Distribution

In this section we will show that with a quadratic utility function the two-parameter approach to portfolio analysis is fully justified. An investor who aims at the maximisation of his expected utility need only know the two parameters,

$E(R)$ and σ_R^2, of the distribution of the various possible outcomes of his investment, because his expected utility depends only on these two values, that is,

$$E(U) = f\{E(R), \sigma_R^2\} \tag{12.62}$$

*   *   *

PROOF

The expected utility is found by taking expected values of the quadratic utility
function (expression 12.59):

$$E(U_R) = E(aR + bR^2) = aE(R) + b[E(R^2)] \tag{12.63}$$

given that a and b are constants.

Adding and subtracting the term $b[E(R)]^2$ we obtain

$$E(U_R) = a[E(R)] + b[E(R)]^2 - b[E(R)]^2 + b[E(R^2)]$$
$$= a[E(R)] + b[E(R)]^2 + b\{E(R^2) - [E(R)]^2\} \tag{12.64}$$

The last term in this expression is the variance of R, because, for any random
variable X, the variance is defined by the expression

$$\sigma_X^2 = E\{X - E(X)\}^2 = E\{X^2 + [E(X)]^2 - 2XE(X)\}$$
$$= E(X^2) + [E(X)]^2 - 2[E(X)]^2$$
$$= E(X^2) - [E(X)]^2 \tag{12.65}$$

Applying this result to the variable R, we obtain

$$\sigma_R^2 = E(R^2) - [E(R)]^2 \tag{12.66}$$

Thus, substituting (12.66) in (12.64), we find

$$E(U_R) = a[E(R)] + b[E(R)]^2 + b\sigma_R^2 \tag{12.67}$$

or

$$E(U_R) = a \text{ [Mean of } R] + b[\text{Mean of } R]^2 + b[\text{Variance of } R]$$

In general, for a risk-averter, we have

$$E(U_R) = f\{E(R), \sigma_R^2\} \tag{12.62}$$

QED

*   *   *

B. The Positive Slope of the Investor's Indifference Curve

We will next show that if the investor is risk-averse and has the quadratic utility function

$$U(R) = aR + bR^2$$

then his risk—return indifference curves will have a positive slope.

$$*\qquad\qquad *\qquad\qquad *$$

PROOF

Recall that an indifference curve is the locus of points along which utility is constant. Thus *the equation of an indifference curve* for a risk-averter, whose preferences can be represented by the above quadratic utility function, is found by setting expression (12.67) equal to a constant, K, which denotes the level of utility of the investor:

$$E(U) = a[E(R)] + b[E(R)]^2 + b\sigma_R^2 = K \text{ (constant)} \tag{12.68}$$

The slope of this curve is the total differential

$$d[E(U)] = \frac{\partial[E(U)]}{\partial[E(R)]} d[E(R)] + \frac{\partial[E(U)]}{\partial[\sigma_R]} d[\sigma_R] = 0 \tag{12.69}$$

The relevant derivatives of expression (12.67) are

$$\frac{\partial[E(U)]}{\partial[E(R)]} = a + 2b[E(R)] = \left\{ \begin{array}{c} \text{Marginal utility of a unit} \\ \text{increase in return} \end{array} \right\} \tag{12.70}$$

and

$$\frac{\partial[E(U)]}{\partial(\sigma_R)} = 2b\sigma_R \tag{12.71}$$

Substituting (12.70) and (12.71) in expression (12.69) we find

$$a + 2b[E(R)]d[E(R)] + (2b\sigma_R)d[\sigma_R] = 0 \tag{12.72}$$

which yields

$$\text{Slope of indifference curve} = \frac{d[E(R)]}{d(\sigma_R)} = -\frac{2b\sigma_R}{a + 2b[E(R)]} \tag{12.73}$$

The denominator $a + 2b[E(R)]$ is the marginal utility of a unit increase in expected return (the marginal utility of (expected) income) and is always positive (on the basis of the non-satiation axiom). Hence the slope of the indifference curve is positive if $b < 0$, the case in which the investor is a risk-averter (as we saw earlier).

QED

$$*\qquad\qquad *\qquad\qquad *$$

Of course we may *assume* that the investor is risk-averse and can rank consistently his preferences. That is, we may *assume* that the indifference curves exist and are convex to the risk-axis. This is what we did when we introduced the investor's indifference map (in section II). The assumption of a quadratic utility function helps justify the positive slope of the indifference curve; and the assumption of risk-aversion allows us to draw convex indifference curves.

The above discussion reveals the weaknesses of the mean-variance model. It is apparent that the assumptions of a normal distribution of expected returns and of a quadratic utility function are restrictive. And the assumption of the existence of smooth convex risk—return curves is an axiom. None of these assumptions is really satisfactory.

The assumption of the existence of a (quadratic) *'group' managerial utility function* is even more tenuous. Group utility functions exist only under very restrictive assumptions.[43]

APPENDIX 12.2   THE ALGEBRA OF EXPECTED VALUES

There are several rules for the algebraic manipulation of expressions involving expected values (which have been used in several of the preceding chapters). The most important of these rules are listed below.

Rule 1. The mathematical expectation of a sum (or a difference) of two random independent variables is the sum (or difference) of their individual expected values.

Let X and Y be two random variables with independent population distributions. We then may write symbolically

$$\boxed{E(X \pm Y) = E(X) \pm E(Y)}$$

PROOF

$$E(X + Y) = \sum_i \sum_j (X_i + Y_j) f(X_i, Y_j) = \sum_i \sum_j X_i f(X_i, Y_j) + \sum_i \sum_j Y_j f(X_i, Y_j)$$

$$= \sum_i X_i \sum_j f(X_i, Y_j) + \sum_j Y_j \sum_i f(X_i, Y_j)$$

But

$$\sum_j f(X_i, Y_j) = f(X_i) = \text{marginal probability of } X_i$$

---

[43] See Wilson, 'The Theory of Syndicates'.

and

$$\sum_i f(X_i, Y_j) = f(Y_j) = \text{marginal probability of } Y_j$$

Therefore

$$E(X + Y) = \sum_i X_i f(X_i) + \sum_j Y_j f(Y_i) = E(X) + E(Y)$$

Rule 2. The expected value of a constant is equal to that constant. Symbolically we may write

$$\boxed{E(k) = k}$$

PROOF

$$E(k) = \sum_i kf(k) = k\Sigma f(k) = k$$

given

$$\Sigma f(k) = \text{sum of probabilities} = 1$$

Rule 3. The expected value of a random variable multiplied by a constant is equal to the constant times the expected value of the variable. Symbolically we may write this rule as follows:

$$\boxed{E(kX_i) = kE(X)}$$

PROOF

$$E(kX_i) = \Sigma(kX_i)f(X_i) = k\Sigma X_i f(X_i) = kE(X)$$

Rule 4. If the variables X and Y are multiplied by any constants a and b, then

$$\boxed{E(aX + bY) = aE(X) + bE(Y)}$$

PROOF

By rule 1, we have

$$E(aX + bY) = E(aX) + E(bY)$$

and by rule 3

$$E(aX + bY) = aE(X) + bE(Y)$$

Rule 5. The variance of the sum of two variables is equal to the sum of the individual variances plus twice their covariance:

$$\text{var}(X + Y) = \text{var}(X) + \text{var}(Y) + 2\,\text{cov}(XY)$$

or

$$\sigma^2_{(X+Y)} = \sigma^2_X + \sigma^2_Y + 2 \text{ cov}(XY)$$

PROOF

$$\text{var}(X + Y) = E[(X + Y) - E(X + Y)]^2$$
$$= E\{[X - E(X)] + [Y - E(Y)]\}^2$$
$$= E[X - E(X)]^2 + E[Y - E(Y)]^2 + 2E\{[X - E(X)][Y - E(Y)]\}$$
$$= \text{var}(X) + \text{var}(Y) + 2 \text{ cov}(XY)$$

Rule 6. The variance of $(aX + bY)$ is given by the expression

$$\text{var}(aX + bY) = a^2 \sigma^2_X + b^2 \sigma^2_Y + 2ab \text{ cov}(XY)$$

PROOF

$$\text{var}(aX + bY) \equiv E[(aX + bY) - E(aX + bY)]^2$$
$$= E[\{aX - E(aX) + bY - E(bY)\}]^2$$
$$= E[\{aX - E(aX)\}^2 + \{bY - E(bY)\}^2 + 2\{aX - E(aX)\}\{bY - E(bY)\}]$$
$$= E[aX - E(aX)]^2 + E[bY - E(bY)]^2 + 2E[aX - E(aX)][bY - E(bY)]$$
$$= \sigma^2_{aX} + \sigma^2_{bY} + 2abE[X - E(X)][Y - E(Y)]$$
$$= a^2 \sigma^2_X + b^2 \sigma^2_Y + 2ab \text{ cov}(XY)$$

Rule 7. The expected value of the product of two *independent variables* is equal to the product of the expected values of the two variables:

$$E(XY) = E(X) E(Y)$$

PROOF

$$E(XY) = \sum_i \sum_j X_i Y_j f(X_i, Y_j)$$

Since X and Y are independent, their joint probability $f(X_i, Y_j)$ is equal to the product of their individual probabilities. Therefore,

$$E(XY) = \sum_i \sum_j X_i Y_j f(X_i) f(Y_j)$$

$$= [\sum_i X_i f(X_i)] [\sum_j Y_j f(Y_j)]$$

$$= E(X)E(Y)$$

Rule 8. If X and Y are two *independent* random variables, their covariance is equal to zero:

$$\boxed{\text{cov}(XY) = 0}$$ (for independent variables)

PROOF

$$\text{cov}(XY) = E\{[X - E(X)][Y - E(Y)]\}$$
$$= E\{XY - YE(X) - XE(Y) + E(X)E(Y)\}$$
$$= E(XY) - E(X)E(Y)$$

By rule 5, for independent variables

$$E(XY) = E(X)E(Y)$$

Therefore

$$\text{cov}(XY) = E(X)E(Y) - E(X)E(Y) = 0$$

Rule 9. The covariance of two random variables which are not independent is

$$\boxed{\text{cov}(XY) = E(XY) - E(X)E(Y)}$$

where

$$E(XY) = \sum_i \sum_j X_i Y_j \, [Pr(X_i Y_j)]$$

and

$$Pr(X_i Y_j) = \text{joint probability of } X_i \text{ and } Y_j$$

Rule 10. The covariance of X and Y can also be found from the expression

$$\boxed{\text{cov}(XY) = r_{XY}\sigma_X\sigma_Y}$$

where r_{XY} = correlation coefficient between X and Y.
This follows from the definition of the (linear) correlation coefficient

$$\boxed{r_{XY} = \frac{\text{cov}(XY)}{\sigma_X\sigma_Y}}$$

Rule 11. If X is a random variable and a and b are constants, then

$$\text{var}(aX + b) = a^2\text{var}(X)$$

PROOF

$$\text{var}(aX + b) = E\{(aX + b) - E(aX + b)\}^2$$
$$= E\{(aX + b) - [aE(X) + b]\}^2$$
$$= E[aX + b - aE(X) - b]^2$$
$$= a^2 E[X - E(X)]^2 = a^2 \text{var}(X)$$

Rule 12. The expected value of the sum of products of two variables is equal to the sum of the expected values of the products. Symbolically

$$\boxed{E\left(\sum_{i=1}^{n} X_i Y_i\right) = \sum_{i=1}^{n} [E(X_i Y_i)]}$$

PROOF

$$E\left(\sum_{i=1}^{n} X_i Y_i\right) = E(X_1 Y_1 + X_2 Y_2 + X_3 Y_3 + \ldots + X_n Y_n)$$
$$= E(X_1 Y_1) + E(X_2 Y_2) + \ldots + E(X_n Y_n)$$
$$= \sum_{i=1}^{n} [E(X_i Y_i)]$$

Concluding Remarks

The last thirty years have seen major changes in the economic environment and in the behaviour of firms.

Oligopoly is the main market structure in the industrialised countries of the Western world. A few hundred giant corporations control, directly or indirectly, the economic activity in these countries.

There is overwhelming evidence that in oligopolistic markets firms avoid price competition, relying increasingly on non-price weapons in their rivalry, such as product diversity and selling activities.

Managers, in their attempts to safeguard their job security or attain other goals, have become relentless growth-seekers. Growth is pursued by expansion of the production capacity of the firm, by vertical integration, by mergers and takeovers and by undertaking direct foreign investment and becoming multinational. The result of such complex growth strategies is the emergence of the few hundred conglomerate enterprises which dominate the economic activity of nations.

Fast technological progress, the rising power of labour unions, increasing government regulation and socio-political developments have all increased business risk and uncertainty.

Monetary and financial developments, as well as tax regulations, have induced firms to adopt complex financing strategies to implement their operating and investment—growth plans.

The developments in microeconomic theory over the last three decades have been impressive. Economic theorists have developed new models and techniques in their attempt to come to terms with the new conditions and behaviour. However, these developments have been compartmentalised in different areas of economics, marketing, business, management science and accounting, due to the narrow specialisation of professional academics.

In this book we have stressed the interdependence of the operating decisions (price, product, sales strategy), the investment—growth decisions and the financing decisions of the firm. All these aspects of competitive behaviour have been presented in a single volume, because the concentration on the price policy alone (as in the neoclassical theory) gives not only a partial picture but also an inadequate one for the analysis of the modern corporation.

In each area there are several models, none of which can claim general acceptance. In all models one can find elements of realism which contribute to our understanding of the decision-making process of firms in the real world. Furthermore, models are being constantly revised, refined, tested and re-evaluated in an attempt to improve their realism and predictive accuracy.

The advances achieved in the various areas of microeconomic theory are considerable. However, the integration of these advances into a unified theory of the firm, in which all decisions are examined simultaneously, has not progressed very far. A lot of theoretical and empirical work is required before a 'general-equilibrium' theory of the firm is developed. An essential step is the recognition that the various decisions of the firm are interlinked.

Select Bibliography

Chapter 1: Product as a Market Weapon

1. Abbott, L., *Quality and Competition*, Columbia University Press, 1955.
2. Ansoff, H. I., 'Toward a Strategic Theory of the Firm', in H. I. Ansoff (ed.), *Business Strategy*, Penguin, 1969.
3. Bernhardt, I. and Mackenzie, K. D., 'Measuring Seller Unconcentration, Segmentation, and Product Differentiation', *Western Economic Journal*, 1968.
4. Brems, H., *Product Equilibrium under Monopolistic Competition*, Harvard University Press, 1951.
5. Chamberlin, E., 'Product Heterogeneity and Public Policy', *American Economic Review*, 1950.
6. Clark, J. M., *Competition as a Dynamic Process*, Brookings Institution, 1961.
7. Fisher, F., Griliches, Z. and Kaysen, K., 'The Costs of Automobile Model Changes since 1949', *American Economic Review*, 1962.
8. Galbraith, J. K., *Economics and the Public Purpose*, Houghton Mifflin, 1973.
9. Heflebower, R. B., 'Toward a Theory of Industrial Markets and Prices', *American Economic Review*, 1956.
10. Heflebower, R. B., 'The Theory and Effects of Non-price Competition', in R. E. Kuenne (ed.), *Monopolistic Competition: Studies in Impact*, Wiley, 1967.
11. Lancaster, K., 'Socially Optimal Product Differentiation', *American Economic Review*, 1975.
12. Leland, H. E., 'Quality Choices and Competition', *American Economic Review*, 1977.
13. Menge, J. A., 'Style Change Costs as a Market Weapon', *Quarterly Journal of Economics*, 1962.
14. Porter, E. M., 'Interbrand Choice, Media Mix and Market Performance', *American Economic Review*, 1976.
15. Scherer, F. M., 'Entry Deterrence in the Ready-to-Eat Breakfast Cereal Industry', *Bell Journal of Economics*, 1978.

16. Spence. M., 'Product Selection, Fixed Costs, and Monopolistic Competition', *Review of Economic Studies*, 1976.
17. Steiner, P. O., 'Program Patterns and Preferences, and the Workability of Competition in Radio Broadcasting', *American Economic Review*, 1953.
18. White, L. J., 'Quality, Competition, and Regulation: Evidence from the Airline Industry', in R. E. Caves and M. Roberts (eds), *Regulating the Product: Quality and Variety*, Harvard University Press, 1975.
19. White, L. J., 'Market Structure and Product Varieties', *American Economic Review*, 1977.
20. Wright, N. R., 'Product Differentiation, Concentration, and Changes in Concentration', *Review of Economics and Statistics*, 1978.

Chapter 2: The Advertising Decision of the Firm

1. Backman, J., *Advertising and Competition*, New York University Press, 1967.
2. Buchanan, N. S., 'Advertising Expenditures', *Journal of Political Economy*, 1942.
3. Comanor, W. S. and Wilson, T. A., 'Advertising, Market Structure and Performance', *Review of Economics and Statistics*, 1967.
4. Comanor, W. S. and Wilson, T. A., *Advertising and Market Power*, Harvard University Press, 1974.
5. Dorfman, R. and Steiner, P. O., 'Optimal Advertising and Optimal Quality', *American Economic Review*, 1954.
6. Doyle, P., 'Economic Aspects of Advertising: A Survey', *Economic Journal*, 1968.
7. Friedland, T. S., 'Advertising and Concentration', *Journal of Industrial Economics*, 1977.
8. Galbraith, J. K., *The Affluent Society*, Houghton Mifflin, 1958.
9. Goldschmid, H., Mann, H. M. and Weston, J. F. (eds), *Industrial Concentration: The New Learning*, Little, Brown, 1974
10. Kaldor, N., 'The Economic Aspects of Advertising', *Review of Economic Studies*, 1950.
11. Lambin, J. J., *Advertising, Competition and Market Conduct in Oligopoly over Time*, North-Holland, 1976.
12. Nelson, P., 'The Economic Consequences of Advertising', *Journal of Business*, 1975.
13. Ornstein, S. I. 'The Advertising–Concentration Controversy', *Southern Economic Journal*, 1976.
14. Schmalensee, R., *The Economics of Advertising*, North-Holland, 1972.
15. Schmalensee, R., 'A Model of Advertising and Product Quality', *Journal of Political Economy*, 1978.
16. Stigler, G. J., 'Economics of Information', *Journal of Political Economy*, 1961.

17. Stigler, G. J., 'Price and Non-Price Competition', *Journal of Political Economy*, 1968.
18. Strickland, A. D. and Weiss, W., 'Advertising, Concentration and Price—Cost Margins', *Journal of Political Economy*, 1976.
19. Taplin, W., 'Advertising Appropriations Policy', *Economica*, 1959.
20. Telser, L. G., 'Advertising and Competition', *Journal of Political Economy*, 1964.
21. Townsend, H., 'Big Business and Competition', in T. M. Rybczynski (ed.), *A New Era of Competition*, Blackwell, 1972.
22. Williamson, O. E., 'Selling Expense as a Barrier to Entry', *Quarterly Journal of Economics*, 1963.
23. Wilson, T. A., 'The Effect of Advertising on Competition: A Survey', *Journal of Economic Literature*, 1979.

Chapter 3: Basic Concepts in Valuation Theory

1. Bauman, W. S., 'Investment Returns and Present Values', *Financial Analysts Journal*, 1969.
2. Baumol, W. J., *Portfolio Theory: The Selection of Asset Combinations*, General Learning Press, 1970.
3. Bower, R. S. and Bower, D. H., 'Risk and the Valuation of Common Stock', *Journal of Political Economy*, 1969.
4. Brigham, E. F., *Financial Management, Theory and Practice*, 2nd edn, Dryden Press, 1979.
5. Fama, E. F., 'Multi-Period Consumption—Investment Decisions', *American Economic Review*, 1970.
6. Gordon, M., *The Investment, Financing, and Valuation of the Corporation*, Irwin, 1962.
7. Haugen, R. A. and Kumar, P., 'The Traditional Approach to Valuing Levered—Growth Stocks', *Journal of Financial and Quantitative Analysis*, 1974.
8. Malkiel, B. G. and Cragg, J. G., 'Expectations and the Structure of Share Prices', *American Economic Review*, 1970.
9. Modigliani, F. and Pogue, G. A., 'An Introduction to Risk and Return', *Financial Analysts Journal*, 1974.
10. Robichek, A. A., 'Risk and the Value of Securities', *Journal of Financial and Quantitative Analysis*, 1969.
11. Van Horne, J. C., *Financial Management and Policy*, 4th edn, Prentice-Hall, 1978.
12. Wendt, P. F., 'Current Growth Stock Valuation Methods', *Financial Analysts Journal*, 1965.

Chapter 4: The Investment Decision of the Firm Under Certainty

1. Bedel, D. P. and Main, J. D., 'Three Problems in Using Ranking Techniques for Capital Budgeting', *Cost and Management*, 1973.
2. Bierman, H. Jr and Smidt, S., *The Capital Budgeting Decision*, 3rd edn, Macmillan, 1971.
3. Fogler, H. R., 'Ranking Techniques and Capital Rationing', *Accounting Review*, 1972.
4. Fogler, H. R., 'Overkill in Capital Budgeting Techniques', *Financial Management*, 1972.
5. Hastie, K. L., 'One Businessman's View of Capital Budgeting', *Financial Management*, 1974.
6. Lewellen, W. G., Lanser, H. P. and McConnell, J. J., 'Payback Substitutes for Discounting Cash Flow', *Financial Management*, 1973.
7. Lorie, J. H. and Savage, L. L., 'Three Problems in Rationing Capital', *Journal of Business*, 1955.
8. Mao, J. C. T., 'The Internal Rate of Return as a Ranking Criterion', *Engineering Economist*, 1966.
9. Myers, S. C., 'Interactions of Corporate Financing and Investment Decisions: Implications for Capital Budgeting', *Journal of Finance*, 1974.
10. Petty, J. W., Scott, D. F. Jr and Bird, M. M., 'The Capital Expenditure Decision-making Process of Large Corporations', *Engineering Economist*, 1975.
11. Sarnat, M. and Levy, H., 'The Relationship of Rules of Thumb to the Internal Rate of Return: A Restatement and Generalization', *Journal of Finance*, 1969.
12. Schnell, J. S. and Nicolosi, R. S., 'Capital Expenditure Feedback: Project Reappraisal', *Engineering Economist*, 1974.
13. Schwab, B. and Lusztig, P., 'A Comparative Analysis of the Net Present Value and the Benefit–Cost Ratios as Measures of the Economic Desirability of Investments', *Journal of Finance*, 1969.
14. Solomon, E., *The Theory of Financial Management*, Columbia University Press, 1963.
15. Teichroew, D., Robichek, A. A. and Montalbano, M., 'An Analysis of Criteria for Investment and Financing Decisions under Certainty', *Management Science*, 1965.
16. Weingartner, H. M., 'Some New Views on the Payback Period and Capital Budgeting Decisions', *Management Science*, 1969.

Chapter: 5 Growth by Merger and Takeover

1. Baruch, L. and Mandelker, G., 'The Microeconomic Consequences of Corporate Mergers', *Journal of Business*, 1972.

2. Conn, R. L., 'The Failing Firm/Industry Doctrines in Conglomerate Mergers', *Journal of Industrial Economics*, 1976.
3. Gorecki, P. M., 'An Inter-Industry Analysis of Diversification in the UK Manufacturing Sector', *Journal of Industrial Economics*, 1975.
4. Gort, M., 'An Economic Disturbance Theory of Mergers', *Quarterly Journal of Economics*, 1969.
5. Hart, P. E. *et al.*, *Mergers and Concentration in British Industry*, Cambridge University Press, 1973.
6. Haugen, R. A. *et al.*, 'An Empirical Test of Synergism in Merger', *Journal of Finance*, 1975.
7. Hindley, B., 'Recent Theory and Evidence on Corporate Mergers', in K. Cowling (ed.), *Market Structure and Corporate Behaviour: Theory and Empirical Analysis*, Gray-Mills, 1972.
8. Hogarty, T. F., 'The Profitability of Corporate Mergers', *Journal of Business*, 1970.
9. Kuehn, A., *Takeovers and the Theory of the Firm*, Macmillan, 1975.
10. Laiken, S. N., 'Merger Myths and Performance Facts', *Canadian Chartered Accountant*, 1973.
11. Levy, H. and Sarnat, M., 'Diversification, Portfolio Analysis and the Uneasy Case for Conglomerate Mergers', *Journal of Finance*, 1970.
12. Lewellen, W. G., 'A Pure Financial Rationale for the Conglomerate Merger', *Journal of Finance*, 1971.
13. Lorie, H. and Helpern, P., 'Conglomerates: The Rhetoric and the Evidence', *Journal of Law and Economics*, 1970.
14. Meeks, G., *Disappointing Marriage: A Study of the Gains from Merger*, Cambridge University Press, 1977.
15. Mueller, D. C., 'A Theory of Conglomerate Mergers', *Quarterly Journal of Economics*, 1969.
16. Mueller, D. C., 'The Effects of Conglomerate Mergers', *Journal of Banking and Finance*, 1977.
17. Singh, A., *Take-overs*, Cambridge University Press, 1971.
18. Singh, A., 'Take-overs, Economic Natural Selection and the Theory of the Firm', *Economic Journal*, 1975.
19. Steiner, P. O., *Mergers: Motives, Effects, Policies*, University of Michigan Press, 1975.
20. Weston, J. F., 'The Nature and Significance of Conglomerate Firms', *St John's Law Review*, 1970.

Chapter 6: Growth by Vertical Integration

1. Arrow, K. J., 'Vertical Integration and Communications', *Bell Journal of Economics*, 1975.
2. Clevenger, T. S. and Campbell, G. R., 'Vertical Integration: A Neglected

Element in Market–Structure–Profit Models', *Journal of Industrial Organization*, 1977.

3. Comanor, W. S., 'Vertical Mergers, Market Power and the Antitrust Laws', *American Economic Review*, 1967.

4. Gordon, M. J. and Halpern, P. J., 'Cost of Capital for a Division of a Firm', *Journal of Finance*, 1974.

5. Gort, M., *Diversification and Integration in American Industry*, Princeton University Press, 1962.

6. Heflebower, R., 'Observations on Decentralization in Large Enterprises', *Journal of Industrial Economics*, 1960.

7. Hirshleifer, J., 'On the Economics of Transfer Pricing', *Journal of Business*, 1956.

8. Hirshleifer, J., 'Economics of the Divisionalized Firm', *Journal of Business*, 1957.

9. Kaserman, D. L., 'Theories of Vertical Integration: Implications for Antitrust Policy', *Antitrust Bulletin*, 1978.

10. Laffer, A. B., 'Vertical Integration by Corporations, 1929–1965', *Review of Economics and Statistics*, 1969.

11. Litzenberger, R. H. and Joy, O. M., 'Decentralized Capital Budgeting Decisions and Shareholder Wealth Maximization', *Journal of Finance*, 1975.

12. McGee, J. G. and Bassett, L., 'Vertical Integration Revisited', *Journal of Law and Economics*, 1976.

13. Mancke, R. B., 'Iron Ore and Steel: A Case Study of the Economic Causes and Consequences of Vertical Integration', *Journal of Industrial Economics*, 1972.

14. Menge, J. A., 'The Backward Art of Interdivisional Pricing', *Journal of Industrial Economics*, 1961.

15. Parsons, D. O. and Ray, E. J., 'The United States Steel Consolidation: The Creation of Market Control', *Journal of Law and Economics*, 1975.

16. Penrose, E., *The Theory of Growth of the Firm*, Blackwell, 1959.

17. Rumelt, R. P., *Strategy, Structure and Economic Performance*, Harvard Business School, 1974.

18. Tucker, I. B. and Wilder, R. P., 'Trends in Vertical Integration in the US Manufacturing Sector', *Journal of Industrial Economics*, 1977.

19. Williamson, O. E., 'The Vertical Integration of Production: Market Failure Considerations', *American Economic Review*, 1971.

Chapter 7: Growth by Foreign Direct Investment

1. Caves, R. E., 'International Corporations: The Industrial Economics of Foreign Investment', *Economica*, 1971.

2. Caves, R. E., 'Causes of Direct Investment: Foreign Firms' Shares in

Canadian and UK Manufacturing Industries', *Review of Economics and Statistics*, 1974.

3. Dunning, J. H. (ed.), *International Investment*, Penguin, 1972.

4. Dunning, J. H. (ed.), *Economic Analysis and the Multinational Enterprise*, Allen & Unwin, 1974.

5. Eastman, H. C. and Stykolt, S., *The Tariff and Competition in Canada*, Macmillan, 1967.

6. Gorecki, P. M., 'The Determinants of Entry by Domestic and Foreign Enterprises in Canadian Manufacturing Industries', *Review of Economics and Statistics*, 1976.

7. Horst, T., 'The Industrial Composition of US Exports and Subsidiary Sales to the Canadian Market', *American Economic Review*, 1972.

8. Hymer, S. and Rowthorn, R., 'Multinational Corporations and International Oligopoly: The Non-American Challenge', in C. P. Kindleberger (ed.), *The International Corporation: A Symposium*, MIT Press, 1970.

9. Karsten, C. F., 'Should Europe Restrict US Investments?', *Harvard Business Review*, 1965.

10. Kindleberger, C. P. (ed.), *The International Corporation*, MIT Press, 1970.

11. Krainer, R. E., 'Resource Endowment and the Structure of Foreign Investment', *Journal of Finance*, 1967.

12. Lall, S., 'Multinationals and Market Structure in an Open Developing Economy: The Case of Malaysia', *Weltwirtshaftliches Archiv*, 1979.

13. Levy, H. and Sarnat, M., 'International Diversification of Investment Portfolios', *American Economic Review*, 1970.

14. Prais, S. J., *The Evolution of Giant Firms in Britain*, Cambridge University Press, 1976.

15. Richardson, J. D., 'On "Going Abroad": The Firm's Initial Foreign Investment Decision', *Quarterly Review of Economics and Business*, 1971.

16. United Nations Department of Economic and Social Affairs, *Multinational Corporations in World Development*, United Nations, 1973.

17. Vernon, R., 'International Investment and International Trade in the Product Cycle', *Quarterly Journal of Economics*, 1965.

18. Vernon, R., *Sovereignty at Bay: The Multinational Spread of US Enterprises*, Basic Books, 1971.

19. Wilkings, M., *The Maturing of Multinational Enterprise: American Business Abroad from 1914 to 1970*, Harvard University Press, 1974.

Chapter 8: The Capital Structure of the Firm

1. Baron, D. P., 'Default Risk and the Modigliani–Miller Theorem: A Synthesis', *American Economic Review*, 1976.

2. Davenport, M., 'Leverage and the Cost of Capital: Some Tests Using British Data', *Economica*, 1971.

3. Durand, D., 'The Cost of Debt and Equity Funds for Business: Trends and Problems of Measurement', in E. Solomon (ed.), *The Management of Corporate Capital*, Free Press, 1959.
4. Ellis, C. D., 'New Framework for Analysing Capital Structure', *Financial Executive*, 1969.
5. Gordon, M., 'Some Estimates of the Cost of Capital to the Electric Utility Industry: Comment', *American Economic Review*, 1967.
6. Handorf, W. G., 'Flexible Debt Financing', *Financial Management*, 1974.
7. Haugen, R. A. and Wichern, D. W., 'The Intricate Relationship between Financial Leverage and the Stability of Stock Prices', *Journal of Finance*, 1975.
8. Koutsoyiannis, A., 'Managerial Job Security and the Capital Structure of Firms', *Manchester School*, 1978.
9. Krouse, C. G., 'Optimal Financing and Capital Structure Programs of the Firm', *Journal of Finance*, 1972.
10. Kumar, P., 'Growth Stocks and Corporate Capital Structure Theory', *Journal of Finance*, 1975.
11. Modigliani, F. and Miller, M., 'The Cost of Capital, Corporate Finance and the Theory of Investment', *American Economic Review*, 1958.
12. Modigliani, F. and Miller, M., 'Corporate Income Taxes and the Cost of Capital: A Correction', *American Economic Review*, 1963.
13. Modigliani, F. and Miller, M., 'Some Estimates of the Cost of Capital to the Electric Utility Industry, 1954–57', *American Economic Review*, 1966.
14. Robichek, A. A., Higgins, R. C. and Kinsman, M. S., 'The Effect of Leverage on the Cost of Equity Capital of Electric Utility Firms', *Journal of Finance*, 1973.
15. Robichek, A. A. and Myers, S. C., *Optimal Financing Decisions*, Prentice-Hall, 1965.
16. Scott, D. F. Jr and Martin, J. D., 'Industry Influence on Financial Structure', *Financial Management*, 1975.
17. Scott, J. H. Jr, 'A Theory of Optimal Capital Structure', *Bell Journal of Economics*, 1976.
18. Solomon, E., 'Leverage and the Cost of Capital', *Journal of Finance*, 1963.
19. Stiglitz, J. E., 'On the Irrelevance of Corporate Financial Policy', *American Economic Review*, 1974.

Chapter 9: The Dividend-retention Decision of the Firm

1. Black, F. and Scholes, M., 'The Effects of Dividend Yield and Dividend Policy on Common Stock Prices and Returns', *Journal of Financial Economics*, 1974.
2. Brennan, M., 'A Note on Dividend Irrelevance and the Gordon Valuation Model', *Journal of Finance*, 1971.

3.   Brigham, E. F. and Gordon, M., 'Leverage, Dividend Policy and the Cost of Capital', *Journal of Finance*, 1968.
4.   Brittain, J. A., *Corporate Dividend Policy*, Brookings Institution, 1966.
5.   Fama, E. F. and Babiak, H., 'Dividend Policy: An Empirical Analysis', *Journal of the American Statistical Association*, 1968.
6.   Friend, I. and Puckett, M. 'Dividends and Stock Prices, *American Economic Review*, 1964.
7.   Gordon, M., 'Dividends, Earnings and Share Prices', *Review of Economics and Statistics*, 1959.
8.   Gordon, M., 'The Savings, Investment and Valuation of a Corporation', *Review of Economics and Statistics*, 1962.
9.   Gordon, M., 'Optimal Investment and Financing Policy', *Journal of Finance*, 1963.
10.   Griffin, P. A., 'Published Earnings, Dividend Announcements and Analysts' Forecasts', *Journal of Finance*, 1976.
11.   Higgins, R. C., 'The Corporate Dividend–Savings Decision', *Journal of Financial and Quantitative Analysis*, 1972.
12.   Kamerschen, D. R. and Pascucci, J. J., 'The Influence of Corporate Control on Dividend Policy', *Journal of Business Administration*, 1971.
13.   Keane, S. M., 'Dividends and the Resolution of Uncertainty', *Journal of Finance and Accounting*, 1974.
14.   Laub, P. M., 'On the Informational Content of Dividends', *Journal of Business*, 1976.
15.   Lintner, J., 'Dividends, Earnings, Leverage, Stock Prices and the Supply of Capital to Corporations', *Review of Economics and Statistics*, 1962.
16.   Modigliani, F. and Miller, M., 'Dividend Policy, Growth and the Valuation of Shares', *Journal of Business*, 1961.
17.   Pettit, R. R., 'Dividend Announcements, Security Performance and Capital Market Efficiency', *Journal of Finance*, 1972.
18.   Stiglitz, J. E., 'On the Irrelevance of Corporate Financial Policy', *American Economic Review*, 1974.
19.   Watts, R., 'The Information Content of Dividends', *Journal of Business*, 1973.
20.   Whittington, G., 'The Profitability of Retained Earnings', *Review of Economics and Statistics*, 1972.

Chapter 10: The Cost of Capital to the Firm

1.   Alberts, W. W. and Archer, S. H., 'Some Evidence on the Effect of Company Size on the Cost of Equity Capital', *Journal of Financial and Quantitative Analysis*, 1973.
2.   Archer, S. H. and Faerber, L. G., 'Firm Size and the Cost of Equity Capital', *Journal of Finance*, 1966.

3. Arditti, F. D., 'The Weighted Average Cost of Capital: Some Questions on its Definition, Interpretation and Use', *Journal of Finance*, 1973.
4. Baumol, W. and Malkiel, B. G., 'The Firm's Optimal Debt–Equity Combination and the Cost of Capital', *Quarterly Journal of Economics*, 1967.
5. Ben-Zion, U. and Shalit, S. S., 'Size, Leverage, and Dividend Record as Determinants of Equity Risk', *Journal of Finance*, 1975.
6. Boness, A. J., 'A Pedagogic Note on the Cost of Capital', *Journal of Finance*, 1964.
7. Brennan, M. J., 'A New Look at the Cost of Capital', *Journal of Finance*, 1973.
8. Brigham, E. F. and Gordon, M. J., 'Leverage, Dividend Policy and the Cost of Capital', *Journal of Finance*, 1968.
9. Jolivet, V. M., 'The Required Rate of Return and Cost of Capital', *Journal of Business Administration*, 1969.
10. Lewellen, W. G., *The Cost of Capital*, Wadsworth, 1969.
11. Linke, C. M. and Kim, M. K., 'More on the Weighted Average Cost of Capital: A Comment and Analysis', *Journal of Financial and Quantitative Analysis*, 1974.
12. Litzenberger, R. H. and Rao, C. U., 'Portfolio Theory and Industry Cost of Capital Estimates', *Journal of Financial and Quantitative Analysis*, 1972.
13. Malkiel, B. G., *The Debt–Equity Combination of the Firm and the Cost of Capital: An Introductory Analysis*, General Learning Press, 1971.
14. Melnyk, Z. L., 'Cost of Capital as a Function of Financial Leverage', *Decision Sciences*, 1970.
15. Nantell, T. J. and Carlson, C. R., 'The Cost of Capital as a Weighted Average', *Journal of Finance*, 1975.
16. Reilly, R. R. and Wecker, W. E., 'On the Weighted Average Cost of Capital', *Journal of Financial and Quantitative Analysis*, 1973.
17. Vickers, D., 'The Cost of Capital and the Structure of the Firm', *Journal of Finance*, 1970.
18. Williams, E. E., 'Cost of Capital Functions and the Firm's Optimal Level of Gearing', *Journal of Business Finance*, 1976.

Chapter 11: The Traditional Theory of the Investment Decision Under Risk and Uncertainty

1. Alderfer, C. and Bierman, H. Jr, 'Choices with Risk: Beyond the Mean and Variance', *Journal of Business*, 1970.
2. Beranek, W., 'The Cost of Capital, Capital Budgeting, and the Maximization of Shareholder Wealth', *Journal of Financial and Quantitative Analysis*, 1975.
3. Chen, H., 'Valuation under Uncertainty', *Journal of Financial and Quantitative Analysis*, 1967.

4. Elton, E. J., 'Valuation of Asset Selection under Alternative Investment Opportunities', *Journal of Finance*, 1976.
5. Elton, E. J. and Gruber, M. J., 'Asset Selection with Changing Capital Structure', *Journal of Financial and Quantitative Analysis*, 1973.
6. Gordon, M. J., *The Investment, Financing and the Valuation of the Corporation*, Irwin, 1962.
7. Hamada, R. S., 'Investment Decisions with a General Equilibrium Mean–Variance Approach', *Quarterly Journal of Economics*, 1971.
8. Hammond, J. S., 'Better Decisions with Preference Theory', *Harvard Business Review*, 1967.
9. Hertz, D. B., 'Risk Analysis in Capital Investment', *Harvard Business Review*, 1964.
10. Hertz, D. B., 'Investment Policies that Pay Off', *Harvard Business Review*, 1968.
11. Johnson, R. W., *Capital Budgeting*, Wadsworth, 1970.
12. Litzenberger, R. H. and Budd, A. P., 'Corporate Investment Criteria and the Valuation of Risk Assets', *Journal of Financial and Quantitative Analysis*, 1970.
13. Mossin, J., 'Security Pricing and Investment Criteria in Competitive Markets', *American Economic Review*, 1969.
14. Robichek, A. and Myers, S. C., *Optimal Financing Decisions*, Prentice-Hall, 1965.
15. Robichek, A. and Myers, S. C., 'Conceptual Problems in the Use of Risk-adjusted Discount Rates', *Journal of Finance*, 1966.
16. Rubinstein, M. E., 'A Mean–Variance Synthesis of Corporate Financial Theory', *Journal of Finance*, 1972.
17. Schall, L. D., 'Firm Financial Structure and Investment', *Journal of Financial and Quantitative Analysis*, 1971.
18. Swalm, R. O., 'Utility Theory: Insights into Risk Taking', *Harvard Business Review*, 1966.
19. Woods, D. H., 'Improving Estimates that Involve Uncertainty', *Harvard Business Review*, 1966.

Chapter 12: Modern Theory of the Investment Decision Under Risk

1. Bierman, H. and Hass, J. E., 'Capital Budgeting under Uncertainty: A Reformulation', *Journal of Finance*, 1973.
2. Blume, M. and Friend, I., 'A New Look at the Capital Asset Pricing Model', *Journal of Finance*, 1973.
3. Greer, S., 'Theory versus Practice in Risk Analysis: An Empirical Study', *Accounting Review*, 1974.
4. Jensen, M. C., 'Risk, the Pricing of Capital Assets and the Evaluation of Investment Portfolios', *Journal of Business*, 1969.

5. Klemkosky, R. C. and Martin, J. D., 'The Effect of Market Risk on Portfolio Diversification', *Journal of Finance*, 1975.
6. Lintner, J., 'The Valuation of Risky Assets and the Selection of Risky Investments in Stock Portfolios and Capital Budgets', *Review of Economics and Statistics*, 1965.
7. Litzenberger, R. H. and Budd, A. P., 'Corporate Investment Criteria and the Valuation of Risky Assets', *Journal of Financial and Quantitative Analysis*, 1970.
8. Modigliani, F. and Pogue, G., 'An Introduction to Risk and Return', *Financial Analysts Journal*, 1974.
9. Mossin, J., 'Equilibrium in a Capital Asset Market', *Econometrica*, 1966.
10. Pettit, R. R. and Westerfield, R., 'Using the Capital Asset Pricing Model to Predict Security Returns', *Journal of Financial and Quantitative Analysis*, 1974.
11. Petty, J. W., Scott, D. F. and Bird, M. M., 'The Capital Expenditure Decision-making Process of Large Corporations', *Engineering Economist*, 1975.
12. Robichek, A. A., 'Interpreting the Results of Risk Analysis', *Journal of Finance*, 1966.
13. Robichek, A. A. and Myers, S. C., 'Valuation of the Firm: Effects of Uncertainty in a Market Context', *Journal of Finance*, 1966.
14. Rubinstein, M., 'A Mean–Variance Synthesis of Corporate Financial Theory', *Journal of Finance*, 1973.
15. Schall, L. D., 'Asset Valuation, Firm Investment, and Firm Diversification', *Journal of Business*, 1972.
16. Sharpe, W. F. 'A Simplified Model of Portfolio Analysis', *Management Science*, 1963.
17. Sharpe, W. F., 'Capital Asset Prices: A Theory of Market Equilibrium Under Conditions of Risk', *Journal of Finance*, 1964.
18. Stapleton, R. C., 'Portfolio Analysis, Stock Valuation, and Capital Budgeting Decision Rules for Risky Projects', *Journal of Finance*, 1971.
19. Weston, J. F., 'Investment Decisions Using the Capital Asset Pricing Model', *Financial Management*, 1973.

Author Index

Subject Index